Journal of Semitic Studies Supplement 35

The Transmission of Targum Jonathan in the West

A Study of Italian and Ashkenazi Manuscripts of the Targum to Samuel

by

Hector M. Patmore

Published by Oxford University Press
on behalf of the University of Manchester
2015

Great Clarendon Street, Oxford OX2 6DP

Oxford University Press is a department of the University of Oxford. It furthers the University's objective of excellence in research, scholarship, and education by publishing worldwide in

Oxford New York

Athens Auckland Bangkok Bogotá Buenos Aires Cape Town Chennai Dar es Salaam Delhi
Florence Hong Kong Istanbul Karachi Kolkata Kuala Lumpur Madrid Melbourne Mexico City
Mumbai Nairobi Paris São Paulo Shanghai Singapore Taipei Tokyo Toronto Warsaw

with associated companies in Berlin Ibadan

Oxford is a registered trade mark of Oxford University Press in the UK
and in certain other countries

Published in the United Kingdom
by Oxford University Press, Oxford

© The University of Manchester, 2015

The moral rights of the author have been asserted
Database right Oxford University Press (maker)

First published 2015

All rights reserved. No part of this publication may be reproduced, stored in a retrieval system, or transmitted, in any form or by any means, without the prior permission in writing of Oxford University Press, or as expressly permitted by law, or under terms agreed with the appropriate reprographics rights organization. Enquiries concerning reproduction outside the scope of the above should be sent to the Rights Department, Journals Division, Oxford University Press, at the address above

You must not circulate this book in any other binding or cover and
you must impose this same condition on any acquirer

A catalogue for this book is available from the British Library

Library of Congress Cataloguing in Publication Data
(Data available)

ISSN 0022-4480
ISBN 978-0-19-876585-1

Cover image: © Bildagentur für Kunst, Kultur und Geschichte, Berlin / Staatsbibliothek zu Berlin – Preußischer Kulturbesitz, Orientabteilung, Ms. Or. fol. 3

Subscription information for the *Journal of Semitic Studies* is available at the journal website:
jss.oxfordjournals.org

Printed in Great Britain by Bell & Bain Ltd, Glasgow

Table of Contents

Key to Symbols and Abbreviations		iv
Manuscipt Sigla		v
Acknowledgements		ix
Introduction		xv
Chapter One	*Status Quaestionis*	1
Chapter Two	Targum in Medieval Italy and Ashkenaz	53
Chapter Three	The Manuscripts	69
Chapter Four	Influence of the Hebrew Text	105
Chapter Five	Agreements with Ancient Versions and Hebrew Manuscripts	149
Chapter Six	Conventional and Contextual Changes	183
Chapter Seven	Exegetical Variants, Clarifications, and the Influence of Liturgical Texts	219
Chapter Eight	Linguistic Features	255
Chapter Nine	Marginal Notes in Codex Reuchlinianus No. 3	261
Chapter Ten	The Targum Text in Liturgical Manuscripts	301
Chapter Eleven	Tosefta Targums	345
Chapter Twelve	Conclusion	355
Chapter Thirteen	Bibliography	365
Chapter Fourteen	Appendices	385
	Appendix 1 Colopha (Chapter Three)	385
	Appendix 2 I705 Marginalia (Chapter Nine)	387
	Appendix 3 Liturgical Sources (Chapter Ten)	399
	Appendix 4 Tosefta Targums (Chapter Eleven)	441
Indices		445

Key to Symbols and Abbreviations

Abbreviated titles of primary sources follows P.H. Alexander et al. (eds), *The SBL Handbook of Style: For Ancient Near Eastern, Biblical, and Early Christian Studies* (Peabody, MA 1999)

t5a^{PM}	*prima manus*
t5a^{correct}	after correction
t705i^{margin}	marginal notes
A	All manuscripts of the Ashkenazi textual family
MW	All manuscripts of the 'Mixed Western' textual family
[…]	Illegible text
Sa[muel]	Unclear characters
Smauel	Original wording
#Samuel#	Corrected wording
Mlt	Multiple manuscripts
¶	Page break
<	Text omitted
Ms.	Manuscript
MT	Masoretic Text
Hebr.	Hebrew
Cent.	Century
Trad.	Tradition
Sg.	Singular
Pl.	Plural
M.	Masculine
F.	Feminine
Ptc	Participle
Pass	Passive

Manuscript Sigla

The sigla used throughout are those of the Standard List of Sigla for Targum Manuscripts produced by Eveline van Staalduine-Sulman in 2011 and revised in January 2014 to accordance with the format agreed at the 2013 meeting of the International Organisation of Targumic Studies (available online at www.targum.nl).

K	Kimhi Commentary according to Soncino 1485 (as recorded by Sperber).
t2i	Urbinati Ebr. 1, Biblioteca Apostolica, Vatican City.
t3i	Barberini Or. 161–164, Biblioteca Apostolica, Vatican City.
t5a	Or. fol. 1–4, Staatsbibliothek, Preußischer Kulturbesitz, Berlin.
t6a	Hébreu 18, Bibliothèque Nationale, Paris.
t7i	B. H. I–VII, Biblioteca Civica Berio, Genoa.
t10r	First Rabbinic Bible (Sperber: b).
t11r	Second Rabbinic Bible (Sperber: g).
t12sc	Antwerp Polyglot (Sperber: o).
t63a	Or fol. 1214 (Kennicott 603; Erfurt 4), Staatsbibliothek, Preußischer Kulturbesitz, Berlin.
t99a	Hébreu 44, Bibliothèque Nationale, Paris.
t133a	Valmadonna 1 (Sassoon 282; Richler 1), Valmadonna Trust Library, London.
t159a	Levy 19 (Kennicott 380), Staats- und Universitaetsbibliothek, Hamburg.
t232i/s	Hébreu 75, Bibliothèque Nationale, Paris.
t700i	Parm. 3187–89, Biblioteca Palatina, Parma.
t701i	Or. 72, Biblioteca Angelica, Rome.
t702s	Montefiore 7 [H 116], Montefiore Endowment (Sperber: c).
t703s	M1–M3, Biblioteca de la Universitaria Salamanca.
t705i	Reuchlinianus No. 3, Badische Hof- und Landesbibliothek Karlsruhe (Sperber: f).
t706s	Opp. Add. 4to, 75, 76, Bodleian Library, Oxford.
t707b	L 229 Jewish Theological Seminary, New York (= Eb 1).
t709b	L 230 Jewish Theological Seminary, New York (= Eb 66).
t710y	Or. 1472, British Library, London (Sperber: m).
t711y	Or. 2210, British Library, London (Sperber: p = base text).
t713a	El. f.6, Thueringer Universitaets- und Landesbibliothek, Jena.
t716y	Or. 2371, British Library, London (Sperber: y).

t718i   Laud Or. 326, Bodleian Library, Oxford.

t720a   Add. 26,879, British Library, London (Sperber: siglum a).

t724b   2, Rav Yosef Kapach Collection, Jerusalem (= Eb 76).

t725a   11 Stiftsbibliothek, Göttweig.

t727y   Or. 1471, British Library, London (Sperber: w).

t734s   Leiria edition (Sperber: d).

t736y   Or. qu. 578/2, Staatsbibliothek, Preußischer Kulturbesitz, Berlin (Sperber: x).

t1126b   MS Ebr. B 133 (including MS Ebr. B 16; Kb 52), Saltykov-Shchedrin State Public Library, St. Petersburg.

t1134y   Sassoon 332, Sassoon Collection, Letchworth (Sperber: j).

t1143y   Or. 2346. British Library, London (Sperber: k).

t1601i   Parm. 3008 (de Rossi 959), Biblioteca Palatina, Parma.

t1614a   Parm. 2894 (de Rossi 1198), Biblioteca Palatina, Parma.

t1618i   Parm. 3132 (de Rossi 61), Biblioteca Palatina, Parma.

t1621i   Vaticani Ebr. 545, Biblioteca Apostolica, Vatican City.

t1631a   Abt. 701, Nr. 759, 5, 6 Landeshauptarchiv Koblenz.

t1639i   Opp. Add. fol. 11 (Neubauer 1057), Bodleian Library, Oxford.

t1647i   Rossiana 437, Biblioteca Apostolica, Vatican City.

t1679i   Sassoon 405, Sassoon Collection, Letchworth.

t2190i   Add. 9403, British Library, London.

t2506b   T-S B 4,36; AS 62, 112, 122, 219, 269, 371, 465, 466, 476, 477, 479, 481, 541, 543–7, 620, 714, 814, 852, 865, 877, 910, 919, Taylor-Schechter Genizah Collection, Cambridge University Library (= Eb 4).

t2520b   4084/1 Bibliothèque Nationale et Universitaire, Strasbourg (= Eb 75).

t2521b   59–67, 70–5, 78–80, 342, 365, 347–48, Judah Levi Nahum Collection (=Eb 91).

t2523b   496, Judah Levi Nahum Collection (= Eb 124).

t2527b   301, 302, 333, 335, Judah Levi Nahum Collection (= Eb 87).

Equivalents to sigla used in A. Sperber (ed.), *The Bible in Aramaic Based on Old Manuscripts and Printed Texts*, Vol. II, *The Former Prophets According to Targum Jonathan* (Leiden 1959).

a	=	t720a		m	=	t710y
b	=	t10r		o	=	t12sc
c	=	t702s		p	=	t711y
d	=	t734s		w	=	t727y
f	=	t705i		x	=	t736y
j	=	t1134y		y	=	t716y
k	=	t1143y				

Equivalents to sigla used in E. Martínez Borobio, (ed.), *Targum Jonatan de los Profetas Primeros en tradición babilónica*, Vol. 2, *I–II Samuel* (Textos y Estudios «Cardenal Cisneros» 38, Madrid 1987).

Eb 1	=	t707b		Eb 87	=	t2527b
Eb 4	=	t2506b		Eb 91	=	t2521b
Eb 66	=	t709b		Eb 124 =		t2523b
Eb 75	=	t2520b		Kb 52	=	t1126b
Eb 76	=	t724b				

Note on Examples Cited from the Targum Manuscripts

Where textual variants in the Targum manuscripts are discussed, for simplicity I have cited the text from a single manuscript. Where other manuscripts agree substantially with this manuscript, they are listed after the equals sign (=). Those manuscripts listed after the equals sign may differ from the cited manuscript in minor and insignificant ways (such as alternative spellings, contracted forms, abbreviations, or their use of *matres lectionis*). Where relevant, a variant reading in a manuscript is given in parenthesis after the manuscript's siglum. Readings that follow the variant *vis à vis* the key point but differ in other respects (e.g. by employing a different preposition elsewhere in the cited unit of text) are preceded by a wavy equals sign (≈), denoting approximately equal.

Note on the Divine Name

The Divine Name is presented with several different forms in Targum manuscripts. For simplicity, I have adopted the form יי throughout. The sense is unaffected.

Translations

Translations of primary and secondary sources are my own, unless otherwise indicated. I have attempted to translated the sources faithfully, but without doing violence to the English language. Occasionally I have given an artificial or stilted translation in order to highlight differences in the underlying Hebrew or Aramaic texts.

Previous Publications

Material from the following articles has been reworked and incorporated into the present volume:

Chapters 4 and 6:
'The Transmission of Targum Jonathan in the West: Initial Results from the Mixed Western Textual Group', *Aramaic Studies* 10 (2012), 23–52.

Chapter 9:
'The Marginal Notes to the Targum Text of Codex Reuchlinianus No. 3', *Aramaic Studies* 10 (2012), 53–85.

Chapter 10:
with J. Tanja, 'Initial Observations Concerning the Text of Targum Samuel Preserved in European Liturgical Manuscripts', in A. Houtman, H-M. Kirn, and E. van Staalduine-Sulman (eds), *A Jewish Targum in a Christian World* (Jewish and Christian Perspectives, Leiden 2014), 63–80.

Acknowledgements

This book is the result of my involvement as a post-doctoral researcher in the project 'A Jewish Targum in a Christian World' based at the Protestant Theological University of the Netherlands, initially in Kampen, later in Amsterdam. As with all works of primary research, this book would never have reached completion without the help and support of family, friends, and colleagues, and it is my privilege to have the opportunity to thank them here publicly.

I must begin with Dineke Houtman, director of the project, to whom I am deeply indebted in so many ways. As a colleague, our discussions, exchanges, and collaborations were enriching, rewarding, and enjoyable. As director of the project, she encouraged me, challenged me, and gave me the necessary space and opportunity to develop as a scholar. I have learnt an awful lot from her and there can be no doubt that without her input this book would not be what it is. I am particularly indebted to Prof. Houtman for her lecture 'Is There a System to the Variant Targumic Readings in Codex Reuchlin?' presented at the fifteenth World Congress of Jewish Studies (Hebrew University of Jerusalem, August 2009), which began a discussion that led to what is now chapter nine of the present volume. Prof. Houtman read multiple drafts of that chapter with great thoroughness and offered many detailed comments, suggestions, and references that significantly enhanced it. Dineke has been not only a valued colleague, but also a very dear friend who, along with husband Daan, helped my wife and me find our feet in the Netherlands and continued to show us warmth and generosity throughout our stay and beyond.

I have been lucky to work with an excellent team who helped make my time in the Netherlands *gezellig* (well, there's no other word for it really!). Johanna Tanja proved an excellent guide to Dutch life and *mœurs* and I think we both benefited from having someone on hand with whom we could drink tea, share our exciting discoveries, and bemoan the various challenges that the project threw up from time to time. Of course we would all have been adrift without Eveline van Staalduine-Sulman, whose experience and expertise was invaluable, and whose own research on Targum Samuel set the direction for the project as a whole. Throughout, our research was certainly sharpened by

Hans-Martin Kirn's characteristic and much valued frankness and by the contributions of our colleagues from De Evangelische Theologische Faculteit te Leuven. Our research assistants, Berthold Bloemendal, André van der Stoel, and Petra Janse-de Boer took much of the strain in preparing and checking transcriptions of the Aramaic texts. Berthold, in particular, worked assiduously on many of the manuscripts that form the basis of the current monograph. Beyond the bounds of the Protestant Theological University of the Netherlands, Gottfried Reeg (Institut für Judaistik, Freie Universität Berlin) and Thomas Kollatz (Salomon Ludwig Steinheim-Instituts) used transcriptions of the manuscripts to create the synopses that made the analysis presented in this book possible: an indispensable contribution.

During the course of the project, I spent a year as a Visiting Research Fellow at the Hebrew University of Jerusalem, a period that enabled me to profit from the extensive resources of The National Library of Israel, the Hebrew University of Jerusalem, and l'École biblique et archéologique française de Jérusalem. I am grateful in particular to Avigdor Shinan, who acted as my academic sponsor, making that stay possible. In the course of that year Uri Melammed (Academy of the Hebrew Language) helped with some of the colopha in my manuscripts and invited me to attend a shabbat service during which I was able to hear the Targum 'live'. Jan Joosten kindly facilitated my séjour at the University of Strasbourg, during which time I added some final touches to this book.

A final stage of the project involved examining many of the manuscripts in the libraries in which they are now held. I am grateful to all the staff of those libraries who ensured that I was able to make the most of what usually turned out to be too short a visit.

Many colleagues read and commented on this work at various stages. Dineke Houtman and Robert Hayward read and commented on the whole; Eveline van Staalduine-Sulman commented on various points in the book at various stages of its development; Steven E. Fassberg, Edward M. Cook, and Stephen A. Kaufman read chapters eight and the comments on linguistic features in chapter ten; Avigdor Shinan commented on an earlier draft of chapter nine; and, Leeor Gottlieb read chapter two and checked my translation of the manuscript colopha, all at the eleventh hour, offering many useful comments and steering me from grave error in several points of detail. I would also like to thank the readers and editors of the Journal of Semitic Studies and Oxford University Press for accepting the work for publication, and Bronwen Campbell, who typeset the whole with great care, attention to detail, and patience.

To all those noted above I owe a profound debt of gratitude. For the failings that doubtless remain, I bear sole responsibility.

Regrettably, serious historical research of this nature does not pay for itself. My position at the Protestant Theological University of the Netherlands and the research costs associated with the project were financed by De Nederlandse Organisatie voor Wetenschappelijk Onderzoek (The Netherlands Organisation for Scientific Research). My year in Jerusalem was made possible by a scholarship from the Israeli Ministry of Foreign Affairs and by the assistance of the Council for British Research in the Levant at the Kenyon Institute, thanks in particular to its then director Jaimie Lovell. I was also able to improve my modern Hebrew during this time with the support of the Rothschild Foundation Europe. My time at the University of Strasbourg was supported in part by La Fondation Académie Hillel under the auspices of La Fondation du Judaïsme Français. I am grateful to all of these organisations, but first and foremost De Nederlandse Organisatie voor Wetenschappelijk Onderzoek, without whose financial support this book would never have been possible.

Our families have, as ever, been wonderfully supportive during our many international moves: travelling to visit us in foreign lands and providing a welcoming home to which we could return. My parents, Janet and Clive, and my wife's parents, Tim and Judith Bartlett, have executed with admirable alacrity the many catering, billeting, taxiing, and baby-sitting duties that fall within the (grand)parental purview. Tim also expunged a few remaining bloopers from my English, sharing the labours with that indefatigable defender of linguistic orthodoxies, Timothy Sykes (aka. Uncle Tim). Our wider families, and especially my brothers, Dougal and Edward, have also fulfilled that most necessary of duties in a project of this nature: taking my mind off it from time to time. Thank you. Both my grandfathers saw the start of this project, but sadly neither lived to see this book reach press. I wish they had.

No one has shared so intimately in the making of this book than my wife, Lydia. During the course of the project, we moved first to the Netherlands, then briefly to Oxford, on to Jerusalem, back to Amersfoort, and wended our way from there to Strasbourg via Beaconsfield and Wokingham before ending up in Cardiff. Under such circumstances her patience and resilience have been quite remarkable. Even when I understood her 'Well, let's think about it' to mean 'Yes! Immediately make plans to relocate to Jerusalem!' she bore it all with (relative) equanimity. During the writing of this book we were also blessed with the birth of our first child, Herbert Samuel, who has filled our lives with joy and wonder. This book is justly dedicated to Lydia in appreciation for all that she has done for us both.

Hector M. Patmore
Llandaff
Pentecost, 2015

In memoriam

Kenneth Reginald Freer 11.10.1922–12.12.2013
Peter Donald Patmore 21.08.1926–17.09.2014

For Lydia

וַתֵּלֶד בֵּן וַתִּקְרָא אֶת־שְׁמוֹ שְׁמוּאֵל כִּי מֵיְהוָה שְׁאִלְתִּיו:

Introduction

If one wishes to know how Jews interpreted the Prophets in the early rabbinic period and what exactly the wording of the Hebrew text was at that time then one must read Targum Jonathan. Its technique may be idiosyncratic, but Targum Jonathan nonetheless translated the Hebrew text with fidelity into a language much more closely related to Hebrew than that of any of the other ancient Versions. Furthermore, as it translated, the Targum made additions and modifications in such a way that what was obscure was made clear and what seemed distant became relevant once again.

The most widely held view of Targum Jonathan's origins is that a progenitor of Targum Jonathan in the form that it is now known was committed to writing in Palestine sometime around the end of the first or start of the second century CE. The text was subsequently modified, expanded, and recast into the local Aramaic dialect in the Babylonian academies, achieving a definitive form by the fourth century. From here the text was subsequently disseminated throughout the Jewish world, among communities widely dispersed across the Middle East, Europe, and North Africa.

That the text reached its definitive form in Babylonia — a point on which there is universal consensus — has been decisive in shaping scholarship on Targum Jonathan over the past two centuries, as will become clear in chapter one. In particular, in recent years members of the so-called 'Escuela targúmica de Barcelona' have produced new critical editions approximating that definitive Babylonian form of the text by using manuscripts preserving authentic Babylonian vocalisation. These 'Babylonian' materials remain the most likely candidates among the available manuscripts to yield the earliest recoverable form of the text, a conclusion confirmed in this study and by earlier stemmatological analysis.[1]

---

1 According to stemmatological research the Babylonian manuscripts are 'the best representatives of the original Targum Samuel'; E. van Staalduine-Sulman, 'An Electronic Edition of Targum Samuel', (Kampen 2009), 25. A note of caution: the vocalisation is secondary. Without doubt it reflects an established reading tradition but the Babylonian system only takes shape in the seventh–ninth centuries and is subsequently adopted by communities

Yet the focus on the Eastern textual traditions (which includes Yemenite as well as the Babylonian textual families) has left the Western textual witnesses largely neglected. This book, it is hoped, will make a small contribution to remedying this state of affairs. But if the Eastern textual tradition is more likely to preserve the earliest recoverable form of Targum Jonathan, why bother with the Western textual tradition at all? There are a number of good reasons for studying the Western textual tradition.

First and foremost, there is currently a widely felt need for new and definitive critical editions of all the books of Targum Jonathan.[2] Any critical edition worth its salt ought to be exhaustive in terms of its use of textual witnesses. If the editor chooses to leave out the readings of a given textual witness or textual tradition, he or she must have good reasons for doing so. Moreover, the priority of the Babylonian materials can only really be confirmed once a comprehensive study of the manuscript from *all textual traditions* has been completed. Only then will a clear (or at least, clearer) picture of Targum Jonathan's transmission history, the relationship between the extant manuscripts and their relative value for text criticism of the Targum text itself emerge. Only once this is achieved will it be possible to evaluate variant readings in an informed way. The results will, of course, have important implications for the use of Targumic variants in text criticism of the Hebrew Bible, a point I will address in more detail in chapters four and five.

A second important reason for examining the Western manuscripts is that they differ significantly among themselves and contain some longer readings that are not found in the Eastern textual tradition. Why? In the West the text's ambiguous status meant that the text was transmitted without the safeguards that ensured consistent reproduction and no moves were made to establish

---

under the moral and juridical influence of the Gaonim from Babylon. J. Ribera Florit 'The Babylonian Masoretic Tradition Reflected in the Mss of the Targum to the Latter Prophets', in E.J. Revell (ed.), *Procedings of the Eigth Congress of the International Organization for Masoretic Studies 1988* (Masoretic Studies 6, Atlanta 1990), 103–8, pp. 104–5. It is probable that manuscripts with genuine Babylonian vocalisation preserve the best consonantal text, but the vocalisation does not guarantee this *ipso facto*.

2   This has been formally expressed by the International Organisation for Targumic Studies, which adopted a resolution at its 2004 meeting to form the International Targum Text Edition Project, a project that aims eventually to produce new critical editions for all the Targums. The relevant documents are available at http://targum.info/IOTS/ittep.html

Introduction

authoritative editions, leaving copyists at liberty to change the text. But why might they have changed the text? What might their motives and intentions have been? And when and from where did these modifications enter into the textual tradition? At a more mundane level, it is also necessary to gauge how accurately the text has been transmitted. Answering these questions will shed light on the role and status of Targum Jonathan within those communities that preserved its text, yielding new insights into the cultural and intellectual world of medieval European Jewish communities.

Such questions are also particularly interesting in respect of the copies of Targum Jonathan produced in Italy and Ashkenaz with which this study is concerned, since the Jewish communities of Italy and Ashkenaz were heirs to so much Palestinian tradition, a point that will reappear throughout the book, notably in chapters nine, ten, and eleven. Do these variant textual traditions preserve material emanating from Palestine? Could any of this material stem from the earliest strata of Targum Jonathan itself prior to its Babylonian redaction?

Finally, a Western text may not be very Western at all. Consider the case of Parm. 2003–4, 2046 of the Biblioteca Palatina in Parma, a manuscript containing Targum Onqelos. The codex was probably written in southern France in the first decades of the fourteenth century, though a note (codex 2004, fol. 283r) locates several ancestors of the naqdan, a certain R. Nathan, in Italy, so the work may have been undertaken there.[3] This same note tells us that the Targum was copied from an exemplar that had been brought from Babylonia and that carried the supra-linear Babylonian vocalisation (מנוקד למעלה בנקוד ארץ אשור). R. Nathan converted the vocalisation into Tiberian signs (נקוד טברני). This example concerns Targum Onqelos of course, and not Targum Jonathan, but it nonetheless nicely highlights an important point (one that will crop up again throughout chapter one): namely that texts travelled. So, in theory at least, a Western manuscript might preserve an authentic Eastern text.

---

3   The full name of the naqdan is given as Rabbi Nathan son of Makhir son of Menahem of Ancona son of Samuel son of Makhir of Oria son of Solomon, who cut off the horn of the jester in Romanza using the Blessed Name, son of Anthos son of Zadok. See B. Richler (ed.), *Hebrew Manuscripts in the Biblioteca Palatina in Parma: Catalogue*, (Jerusalem 2001), No. 74. See further on this phenomenon: P. Kahle, *Masoreten des Ostens: Die ältesten punktierten Handschriften des Alten Testaments und der Targum* (Leipzig 1913), 205. Cf. A. Díez Macho, 'Onqelos Manuscript with Babylonian Transliterated Vocalisation in the Vatican library (Ms. Eb. 448)', *Vetus Testamentum* 8 (1958), 113–33, p. 117.

To this I might add that some Western texts occasionally retain traces of a Babylonian past, for example by their use of *matres lectionis*.[4]

Aims

In short, the value of studying the Western manuscripts of Targum Jonathan is twofold: text-critical and text-historical. Or in other words, how did the text change and why?

The aim of this book is therefore first of all to identify the textual variants in the Western manuscripts of Targum Jonathan. Once identified, the objective is to discern patterns in these variants that might enable us to understand the processes by which the text changed in the course of its European transmission. Could a variant be explained by factors internal to the text (a desire to harmonise details, for example)? Does a variant have a point of reference external to the narrative context, such as a particular historical event? Does it seek to bring the text up to date? Does the variant reflect other known exegetical positions? Do the variants show any distinctive linguistic traits? Is there a pattern of variations that reveal an interpretative trajectory within any given manuscript? What is the relationship between variant readings and the underlying Hebrew text? These, among others, are the sorts of questions that will need to be asked.

By interrogating the variant texts in this way it will be possible to develop a series of categories into which the textual variants might be classified. It is important to stress at the outset that these categories are intended to be heuristic. Some readers may wish to move a variant from one category to another or to suggest a new category altogether (indeed, the author has done both as the project progressed). Such discussion is welcome. Nonetheless, it is hoped that by analysing the variants in this way it will be possible to discern trends and tendencies that might help us understand how and why the text has changed.

---

4   E.g. Ms. Montefiore 7 [H 116] = t702s; J. Ribera Florit 'The Babylonian Tradition of the Targum Jeremiah', in A. Dotan (ed.), *Proceedings of the Ninth Congress of the International Organization for Masoretic Studies 1989* (Masoretic Studies 7, Atlanta 1992), 101–9, p. 102. Cf. E. Martínez Borobio, *Targum Jonatan de los Profetas Primeros en tradición babilónica*, Vol. 2, *I–II Samuel*, (Textos y Estudios 'Cardenal Cisneros' 38, Madrid 1987), 31. Levine points out some apparent traces of former Babylonian punctuation under the Tiberian pointing in the manuscripts employed in his *The Aramaic Version of Jonah* but their vocalisation exhibits many inconsistencies so his observations are difficult to evaluate; É. Levine, *The Aramaic Version of Jonah* (Jerusalem 1975), 23.

Introduction

Scope

I have spoken so far of Targum Jonathan. The current study is limited in scope to the Targum to Samuel. Given that many of the manuscripts contain the whole of Targum Jonathan, it is probable that the conclusions reached in this book will be broadly applicable to the other Prophetic books; only detailed study of the individual books in the relevant manuscripts, however, can confirm such an assumption.

In this study I will examine twelve manuscripts containing the continuous text of Targum Samuel. All twelve (with one exception, which I will discuss in chapter three) were copied by Jewish scribes located in Ashkenaz or in Italy. The choice of manuscripts has been determined by van Staalduine-Sulman's stemmatological analysis of sample verses from all known extant manuscripts containing the continuous text of Targum Jonathan. Briefly, stemmatological analysis assesses how closely or distantly related any two manuscripts may be on the basis of variants in their text. The twelve manuscripts containing the continuous text belong to two distinct textual families. The exact rationale is discussed and the manuscripts described in chapter three. I will also study a further twelve liturgical manuscripts, which are described and analysed separately (chapter ten). My colleague Johanna Tanja has studied the Sephardic manuscripts, completing the picture of the text's European transmission.

We are not concerned in this study with variants in vocalisation. It is possible, of course, that a variant vocalisation might alter the meaning of a word,[5] but in European manuscripts of Targum Jonathan the problems of vocalisation are acute (see chapters three, eight). The vocalisation is not always present (e.g. t718i, t701i) and where present it is generally in a very poor condition. The consonants and vowel pointing may not be the work of the same scribe and may in some cases be derived from a different manuscript (e.g. t7i, t5a).[6] Indeed some European manuscripts — in particular Ashkenazi manuscripts — sometimes combine the reading of two or more manuscripts

---

5 See e.g. J. Ribera Florit, 'Relationship Between Semantics and Vocalisation: Some Examples from Yemenite Manuscripts of Targum Jeremiah', in E. Fernández Tejero and M.T. Ortega Monasterio (eds), *Estudios Masoréticos* (Madrid 1993), 111–17.

6 Cf. also M. Beit-Arié, *The Makings of the Medieval Hebrew Book: Studies in Palaeography and Codicology* (Jerusalem 1993), 162.

into a single text in their consonantal text (so-called 'contamination') resulting in a mixed text both in the consonants and vocalisation (see Conclusion). Furthermore, a few cases are known in which a scribe invented his vocalisation system or transposed vowels from one system (e.g. supra-linear) to their local tradition (e.g. sub-linear).[7] The vocalisation would certainly reward further study; but this lies outside the scope of the present volume.

Finally, the scope of this study is limited by the availability of materials. The number of surviving Western manuscripts containing the continuous text of Targum Samuel is relatively small, a fact that bespeaks the unhappy history of the Jews (and their libraries) in Europe from the late medieval period until our own times. The available raw data must therefore be quite incomplete, though how incomplete is difficult to say. The selection of materials is also dependent on the available cataloguing. I would wager that it is a near certainty that further archival research will turn up new copies of Targum Jonathan. One only needs to think of the history of the famous Neofiti manuscript.

Approach

Transcriptions of all the manuscripts selected for this study were produced on the basis of digital images or microfilms. All the transcriptions were then checked a second time for accuracy. Time and budgetary constraints meant that it was only possible to check manuscripts belonging to the 'Mixed Western' group (see chapter three) against the manuscripts themselves *in situ*. In all other cases, I had to be content with checking the variants a final time against the microfilms or digital images. These transcriptions were then used to create a synopsis of all the texts using the Tübingen System of Text Processing tools (TUSTEP).

In the absence of a single continuous text of the Babylonian text tradition, a

---

[7] See J. Ribera Florit, 'The Babylonian Masoretic', 106; W. Smelik, 'Orality, Manuscript Reproduction, and the Targums', in A. den Hollander, U. Schmid and W. Smelik (eds), *Paratext and Megatext as Channels of Jewish and Christian Traditions: The Textual Markers of Contextualization* (Jewish and Christian Perspectives 6, Leiden 2003), 49–81, p. 77; A. Houtman, 'Planning a New Targum Edition: Look Before you Leap', *Journal for the Aramaic Bible* 2:2 (2000), 213–31, pp. 229–30; E. van Staalduine-Sulman, 'Vowels in the Trees: the Role of Vocalisation in Stemmatology', *Aramaic Studies* 3:2 (2005), 215–40, pp. 216, 227–8, 230, 237.

Introduction

complete Yemenite text (manuscript Or. 1472 of the British Library, London) was selected to provide a base-text against which the European manuscripts could be compared. All the manuscripts belonging to the Yemenite group reflect a stable transmission and are almost textually identical as far as the consonants are concerned to those of the Babylonian tradition. Manuscript Or. 1472 may also have been the ancestor of the largest sub-group within the Yemenite text tradition, making it a good representative choice.[8] This synopsis revealed a significant number of variations from the base text and between the manuscripts. Where significant variants were found, the base text was then correlated with the edition of the Babylonian textual tradition prepared by Martínez Borobio. The Babylonian textual tradition is, like any manually transmitted text, not perfect in every way and sometimes the manuscripts within the Babylonian tradition differ. Nonetheless, at the present time it is the best approximation of the more ancient form of Targum Jonathan.

The vast majority of variants were of little interest (e.g. scribal errors, orthographic variations, etc) and could be eliminated from the analysis. I then attempted to identify patterns in the remaining core of (seemingly) significant variants by checking them against the underlying Hebrew and the ancient Versions, by using various concordance tools,[9] and by searching rabbinic and medieval Jewish literature.[10] No attempt has been made to present all the examples in what follows. Rather, a selection of the more compelling examples from the most interesting categories is offered.

Overview

In the following chapter (chapter one) I will review previous scholarship on the textual development and transmission history of Targum Jonathan in order to develop further the rationale for the current study that I have laid out briefly above, and to embed this study within the broader scholarly discussion. Chapter two offers a very brief account of the role and status of Targum Jonathan in medieval Jewish life in Italy and Ashkenaz in order to give the

---

8 van Staalduine-Sulman, 'An Electronic Edition of Targum Samuel', 30.
9 J.C. de Moor, et al. (eds), *A Bilingual Concordance to the Targum of the Prophets*, 21 Vols (Leiden 1995–2005), and Accordance Bible Software (version 9.6.6, 2012).
10 I have made extensive use of The Responsa Project (Bar-Ilan University) and Cohen (ed.), *Mikra'ot Gedolot 'HaKeter'* series (see bibliography).

reader some insight into the social and historical contexts in which the manuscripts that are the focus of this study were produced. In this chapter I survey briefly other Aramaic texts in circulation, including other Targums, and present what is known of the use of Targum Jonathan in study and in the synagogue liturgy. In chapter three I explain the stemmatological analysis that has defined the scope of the project, describe in detail all the manuscripts examined, and give an account of the quality of their texts and the extent and manner of their correction. The following four chapters present the various trends that the textual variants reflect. In chapter four I demonstrate the extent to which the Hebrew text has influenced the shape of the Targum text in its European transmission. Similarly, in chapter five, I tackle cases of *a priori* agreement with one or more of the ancient Versions (e.g. Septuagint, Vulgate, Peshitta, etc), and consider the significance of variant Hebrew manuscripts for understanding these apparent agreements. Chapter six describes tendencies that I have called 'conventional' and 'contextual' renderings, by which very commonly occurring wording, or wording in the immediate literary context, causes a scribe to modify his text. In chapter seven I discuss the most substantial (and most interesting) variants. I identify and discuss the few truly exegetical expansions that crop up in the manuscripts, the more common tendency to provide various kinds of clarificatory glosses, and finally, I note some cases where a longer form of the text found in liturgical sources appears to have influenced the wording of manuscripts containing the continuous text. In chapter eight I make some brief observations concerning the linguistic characteristics of the European manuscripts. The marginalia of the famous Italian codex, Reuchlinianus No. 3, which have been the subject of much scholarly interest, are analysed in chapter nine. Finally, in chapters ten and eleven I examine two closely connected variant text types: Tosefta Targums found in the manuscripts containing the continuous text of Targum Jonathan; and, Italian and Ashkenazi liturgical manuscripts that contain extracts of Targum Jonathan for certain haftarot readings.

Chapter One

Status Quaestionis

It seems useful to set this study within the broader scholarly context by providing an overview of previous scholarship that has sought to compare manuscripts and printed editions of Targum Jonathan, and make critical judgements concerning their relative value not only text-critically, but also from a cultural-historical point of view. Houtman has already catalogued previous critical editions of the Targum to the Prophets (or projects of text-critical nature),[1] and although some overlap is inevitable, I hope in what follows to be able to add to her overview a description of the theoretical and methodological developments that provided the soil from which these critical editions sprouted.

1. The Awakening of a Text-Critical Consciousness

The critical comparison of manuscripts of the Targum to the Prophets is not a novelty of the modern scientific age. In the first decade of the twelfth century, a certain Zerach bar Yehuda wrote in the margins of the manuscript he was copying variant readings of Targum Jonathan as well as other variant Targum traditions to the Prophets.[2] Although he left no record of the origins of these notes — whether he compiled them himself by consulting multiple manuscripts or simply faithfully copied marginal notes that he found in his *Vorlage* — his work clearly demonstrates that scholars were aware that the then extant copies of Targum Jonathan differed from one another and felt it to be a useful and necessary exercise to bring (some of) these divergent readings together into a single edition. Codex Reuchlinianus No. 3 (= t705i), as the manuscript is now called, is our earliest dated manuscript of the Targum to Samuel.

Though hardly comparable to the elaborate system of marginal notations

---

1 A. Houtman, 'Planning a New Targum Edition', 214–20.
2 See chapter nine.

that Zerach bar Yehuda left us, the presence in some later European manuscripts of 'combined' readings — where a scribe incorporates two variant readings into a single text[3] — nonetheless shows both a recognition that the manuscripts differed and a desire to address this state of diversity. The early printed editions too were conscious of the state of textual pluriformity and attempted to remedy this. Felix Pratensis claimed that his edition of the Rabbinic Bible offered its reader a text restored to its 'true and genuine purity' by the assiduous labours of its editor (though this may be bombast since recent studies suggest he may have relied on a single manuscript).[4]

Interesting as these earlier comparative activities are, they cannot truly be called 'critical'; indeed nothing is known of each scribe's methodology (such as the criteria for variant selection) beyond what can be surmised from the resulting manuscript or edition. The application of scientific methodologies to the study of Jewish literature as a whole, as advocated by the proponents of the *Wissenschaft des Judentums* from the first half of the nineteenth century, was to set the study of Targum Jonathan's textual history on a new footing; a footing from which all modern study has sprung. One of the founding members of the *Verein für Cultur und Wissenschaft der Juden*, and the first to apply this new approach to the text of Targum Jonathan, was Leopold Zunz. In his magnus opus, *Die gottesdienstlichen Vorträge der Juden historisch entwickelt*, published in 1832, Zunz observed — in nothing more than a few lines and some dense footnotes — that the text of Targum Jonathan had not reached our hands unaltered. In his view many additions and variant readings

---

3   Smelik, 'Orality, Manuscript Reproduction, and the Targums', 77; W.F. Smelik, '"Trouble in the Trees!", Variant Selection and Tree Construction Illustrated by the Texts of Targum Judges', *Aramaic Studies* 1:2 (2003), 247–87; reprinted in P. van Reenen, A. den Hollander and M. van Mulken (eds), *Studies in Stemmatology* II (Amsterdam 2004), 167–206, pp. 262–6.

4   Houtman examined the Isaiah Targum of the First Rabbinic Bible against 21 complete manuscripts. She found that where the Rabbinic Bible differed from the corrected text of Codex Solger (Stadtbibliothek, Nürnberg) or its marginal glosses, these variations were always a reading error, misprint, editorial correction, or adaptation towards the Hebrew text. Furthermore, because Codex Solger contained 34 glosses explicitly identified as having been drawn from a different source, Houtman concluded that the Rabbinic Bible could not have used the source against which Codex Solger had been corrected and from which the glosses were drawn, as Smelik had proposed (W.F. Smelik, *The Targum of Judges* [Oudtestamentische Studiën 36, Leiden 1995], 153). Taken together the evidence demonstrated 'a direct and complete dependency of the first Rabbinic Bible on Codex Solger'. A. Houtman, 'Targum Isaiah According to Felix Pratensis', *Journal for the Aramaic Bible* 1 (1999), 191–202, esp. pp. 192–4, 198–9, 202 (citation: 202).

Chapter One. *Status Quaestionis*

did not go back to Jonathan ben Uzziel (whom Zunz took to be the author) but had been introduced by later hands. He points to several sources to substantiate this claim, the most compelling of which are the commentaries of David Kimhi, who occasionally cites differing versions of the Targum with formulae such as 'in one version of Targum Jonathan [it reads]... but in another [it reads]...' or 'Jonathan translated... although in a few versions [it says]...'.[5]

Zunz's study of the Targums was naturally limited by the nature and quality of the texts available to him. He mentions several printed editions in connection with the various Targums he discusses — those of Bomberg (1517), Buxtorf (1618–19), Walton (1654–57), and the Antwerp Polyglot (1568–72), for example — as well as a few manuscripts that he apparently knew only through catalogues.[6] In addition he made extensive use of citations of the Targum in rabbinic and medieval Jewish literature, in particular the biblical commentaries of Kimhi and Rashi and works of lexicography such as Nathan ben Jehiel's *Arukh* and Elia Levita's *Meturgeman*. Zunz knew Targum Jonathan therefore only through European sources. The unintended bias that these textual limitations gave to Zunz's work has had the ironic consequence that some of his conclusions remain sound even though his reasoning can no longer always be thought compelling in light of our greatly advanced knowledge of the Targum's history. For example, while his claim that all hostile references to Rome are secondary no longer seems credible, his assertion that the appearance of *Armilius* in the Targum to Isa. 11:4 is secondary is almost certainly correct since this reading is found only in some European sources (see Sperber ed, *ad loc*).[7]

The situation as far as the availability of editions of the text was concerned was unchanged when Zacharias Frankel examined Targum Jonathan some forty years later. Addressing the question whether or not Targum Jonathan was transmitted in a written form prior to the closure of the Babylonian Talmud in his *Zu dem Targum der Propheten* (1872), Frankel concludes that its origins

---

5 E.g. L. Zunz, *Die gottesdienstlichen Vorträge der Juden historisch entwickelt: Ein Beitrag zur Alterthumskunde und biblischen Kritik, zur Literatur- und Religionsgeschichte* (Hildesheim 1966 [1832]), 66–7. See also Smelik, *Targum of Judges*, 314, 543.

6 Zunz notes the Tosefta Targum to Isaiah found in Ms. Urbinati Ebr. 1 (Biblioteca Apostolica, Vatican = t2i) according to the reproduction in the catalogue of Assemanus and Assemanus, *Bibliothecæ apostolicæ vaticanæ*, 451; Zunz, *Die gottesdienstlichen Vorträge der Juden historisch entwickelt*, 81 note g.

7 Zunz, *Die gottesdienstlichen Vorträge der Juden historisch entwickelt*, 66 note e.

from the hands of respected Babylonian scholars (in his view, R. Joseph, the head of the rabbinic academy in Pumbedita) and its comprehensive nature made such a conclusion likely. Nonetheless he stressed that this could not have been a 'closed' or 'fenced off' text.[8] Rather, the *variae lectiones* and glosses found in the Targum text itself as well as in the commentaries indicated that at a later stage copyists' blunders, marginal notes, and new translations had entered the text. The Tosefta Targums (sometimes identified as such in Kimhi, sometimes integrated into the text) and double-translations also revealed the presence of later additions in Frankel's view, while secondary alteration also accounted for the frequent variations between the four editions that he consulted (i.e. the First Rabbinic Bible, the 1618–19 Basel edition, Walton's Polyglot, and the 1720 Amsterdam edition) and between the continuous text and citations of the Targum in the Talmud, Rashi, and Kimhi.[9]

It was not only in the world of scientific endeavour that the severe limitations of the printed editions then available were felt. A year before the publication of Frankel's *Zu dem Targum der Propheten*, a translation of the Targum to Isaiah produced by Pauli for the *London Society for the Promoting of Christianity amongst the Jews* appeared (1871). In his Preface Pauli accepted the authorship of Jonathan ben Uzziel and therefore believed the Targum to be a pre-Christian work that could reveal what the 'ancient Jewish Church' believed 'before it degenerated through the traditions of the elders'.[10] With remarkable *chutzpah* Pauli found the Targum to concord harmoniously with the Christian Gospel: 'These paraphrases' he writes 'contain the doctrines of Christianity, expressed and enforced in the plainest language'[11] — a view that would have surprised the author(s) of Targum Jonathan as much as it does the modern Targum scholar! He consequently valued it highly as a tool for converting the Jews: 'The unprejudiced Jew by reading this Paraphrase will see, that we Christians believe in no other salvation, than that which their

---

8 'Doch wenn auch diese Targumim schriftlich abgefasst waren, so gab es doch nicht von ihnen einen abgeschlossenen, abgegrenzten Text'. Z. Frankel, *Zu dem Targum der Propheten, Propheten* (Jahresbericht des jüdisch-theologischen Seminars 'Fraenkel'scher Stiftung', Breslau 1872), 20.

9 Frankel, *Zu dem Targum der Propheten*, 10, 19–21, 37–40. See the reaction of A. Geiger, 'Umschau. Das Thargum zu den Propheten', *Jüdische Zeitschrift für Wissenschaft und Leben* 10 (1872), 198–201.

10 C.W.H. Pauli, *The Chaldee Paraphrase on the Prophet Isaiah*, (London 1871), Preface, vi.

11 Pauli, *The Chaldee Paraphrase*, Preface, v.

fathers expected the Messiah should bring', he writes.[12] His sole aim in publishing this edition is thus 'to convince the upright Israelite that the Christian Church interprets the Messianic prophecies in no other sense than the ancient Synagogue did before the coming of Jesus of Nazareth'.[13]

The lack of an accepted edition of the Targum, however, obliged Pauli to make judgements among the available textual witnesses: 'I have followed the text of the Biblia Magna Hebraica (קהילת משה) [i.e. Amsterdam, 1724], the authorised and accepted text of the Synagogue', he writes 'though I prefer the text of the Royal Polyglot [i.e. Antwerp Polyglot], and that of Buxtorff [*sic*], as given in Bishop Walton's Polyglot. Any objection which the Jews would have brought against me, if I had translated from a *Christian* text, must therefore fall to the ground'.[14] Nonetheless Pauli insists that the witnesses need critical comparison: 'I have investigated and compared the best Christian and Jewish editions of this Paraphrase. I give the most important various readings met with in the different copies, with critical and analytical notes'.[15] Despite the acerbic polemic, Pauli's text-critical work shows no real trace of his ideological motivation: he draws freely on citations of the Targum in rabbinic literature, Kimhi, Rashi, the Arukh, and so on, to establish the better reading,[16] and frequently favours the reading of one of the 'Jewish editions'.[17] Indeed the vast majority of his notes concern little more than minor variations between the editions (e.g. misprints, alternative verb forms, singular verses plural nouns, absolute in place of determined state, alternative vocalisations, accidental omissions, etc.).

It is only in his handling of what he considers to be 'interpolations' in the Jewish editions that he again vents his spleen: 'It is a lamentable fact', he writes, 'that the modern rabbies [*sic*] hesitated not to interpolate even those books which are considered by them to be an infallible authority in matters of faith'.[18] These interpolations in fact prove to be rather interesting. Among them one finds the Tosefta Targum to Isa. 10:32, known from multiple sources ('a sadly fabulous

---

12 Pauli, *The Chaldee Paraphrase*, Preface, v–vi.
13 Pauli, *The Chaldee Paraphrase*, Preface, viii.
14 Pauli, *The Chaldee Paraphrase*, Preface, vii.
15 Pauli, *The Chaldee Paraphrase*, Preface, vii.
16 Eg. Pauli, *The Chaldee Paraphrase*, 215 n.1, 222 n.1.
17 Eg. Pauli, *The Chaldee Paraphrase*, 113 n.3.
18 Pauli, *The Chaldee Paraphrase*, Preface, vii n.3.

interpolation'),[19] additions which are otherwise known only from the marginalia of Codex Reuchlinianus No. 3, where they appear under the heading תרגום ירושלמי (i.e. Isa. 49:24–5), an addition to Isa. 17:7 from the Biblia Magna Hebraica not known from other sources (probably originally a corruption),[20] and other smaller pluses, such as the addition of *Armilius* in Isa. 11:4, which I mentioned above.

Both Zunz and Frankel, pioneers in the field, as well as Pauli, were obliged to rely on the then available printed editions despite their evident deficiencies. Unfortunately, the text reproduced in these editions provides a very poor starting point for addressing questions relating to the text as it was in Antiquity. That would be possible only once a version of the text resembling its most antique form had been established on a sound text-critical basis; and for this, access to manuscripts was needed.

The first step towards addressing this need was to appear in the same year as Frankel's ground-breaking study in the form of Paul de Lagarde's edition of the consonantal text of Codex Reuchlinianus No. 3 (Badische Hof- und Landesbibliothek Karlsruhe, Germany) published under the title *Prophetae chaldaice e fide Codicis Reuchliniani*.[21] As well as corrections made by the scribe and his own 'improvements' to the text, de Lagarde recorded in his introduction the extensive marginal notations contained in the manuscript (see chapter nine). De Lagarde used his own edition as the basis for further comparative research, recording, in his introduction to the edition, where the text deviated from the First Rabbinic Bible. He later published a comparison of its text to the Targum for the haftarot for Pesach and Shavuot that he found in Erfurt IV (i.e. Or. fol. 1214, Staatsbibliothek, Preußischer Kulturbesitz, Berlin), a thirteenth century Ashkenazi manuscript containing the Pentateuch with Targum Onqelos, the Megillot, Job, and the Haftarot.[22] De Lagarde offered, however, no analysis of the variations, most of which were simply orthographic.

---

19 Pauli, *The Chaldee Paraphrase*, 38.
20 Pauli translates: 'A man shall not stay himself upon the service of his own making; but his eyes shall hopefully look for the Word, the Holy One of Israel'.
21 P. de Lagarde, *Prophetae chaldaice e fide Codicis Reuchliniani* (Leipzig 1872). A facsimile edition of the complete codex was later published by Sperber: A. Sperber, *The Pre-Masoretic Bible*, Vol. 1, *The Codex Reuchlinianus No. 3 of the Badische Landesbibliothek in Karlsruhe* (Copenhagen 1965).
22 P. de Lagarde, *Symmicta* 2 Vols (Göttingen 1877), Vol. 1, 138–41. Also note his comment on p. 141: 'Unmöglich ist nicht, daß ich kleinigkeiten unangemerkt gelassen habe'!

******

De Lagarde's edition was far from perfect, containing many inaccuracies,[23] but it was nonetheless a breakthrough for the study of the text of Targum Jonathan because for the first time it made widely available the text according to a manuscript that was not only early — to date still our earliest (near) complete manuscript — but also of an extremely high quality. The significance of this development was quickly recognised by Wilhelm Bacher, who embarked on a comparative textual study on the basis of de Lagarde's edition, the results of which he published two years later.

In his 'Kritische Untersuchungen zum Prophetentargum' (1874), Bacher described in general terms the problem facing scholars of rabbinic literature at the end of the nineteenth century, namely that each text was the product of a process of development, not only during its oral transmission, but also after it had received a written form. This was equally applicable to the Targums, which, apart from a few works, such as Samuel David Luzzatto's אוהב גר (1830), which offered some textual variants to Targum Onqelos, had not been worked upon. The principal difficulty in such a work, in Bacher's mind, was gaining access to the necessary manuscripts, which were scattered across numerous libraries. In de Lagarde's edition, the manuscript had come to him, so to speak, so he welcomed the edition warmly.[24]

Although he was particularly interested in the marginal notes of the codex (see below), in the second part of his paper he presented a critical comparison of the main text of Codex Reuchlinianus No. 3 (according to de Lagarde's edition) with the First and Second Rabbinic Bibles (1517, 1525), and with Buxtorf's edition, with the aim of advancing text-criticism of the Targum as

---

23 E.g. Sperber, *The Bible in Aramaic*, IVB, *The Targum and the Hebrew Bible* (Leiden 1973), 18–19; A. Klostermann review of 'P. de Lagarde, *Prophetae Chaldaice e fide codicis reuchliniani* (Leipzig: Teubneri, 1872)', *Theologische Studien und Kritiken* 46:4 (1873), 731–67, esp. pp. 731–54. See also chapter nine. Despite its many imprecisions, de Lagarde's edition served as the basis for several 'critical' editions of the Targum, e.g. M. Adler, 'A Specimen of a Commentary and Collated Text of the Targum to the Prophets: Nahum', *Jewish Quarterly Review* 7:4 (1895), 630–57 (Adler says simply of de Lagarde's edition, 'Not altogether reliable.' p. 631); J.F. Stenning, *The Targum of Isaiah* (Oxford 1949); S. Silbermann, *Das Targum zu Ezechiel nach einer südarabischen Handschrift* (Leipzig 1902).

24 W. Bacher, 'Kritische Untersuchungen zum Prophetentargum nebst einem Anhange über das gegenseitige Verhältniss der pentateuchischen Targumim', *Zeitschriften der Deutschen Morgenländischen Gesellschaft* 28 (1874), 1–72, pp. 1–2.

well as understanding of the history of its development.²⁵

Bacher began by examining the text of Codex Reuchlinianus No. 3 according to de Lagarde's edition on its own terms. He found that the manuscript contained a mixture of peculiarities, mostly of an orthographic nature or relating to the vocalisation, and errors, principally omissions and metathesis, leading him to the conclusion 'that our codex is no paradigm of correctness'. Equally, he found that the three printed editions contained many errors, listing the omissions that he found in all the editions as well as those appearing in only one. The Second Rabbinic Bible and Buxtorf's edition repeat many of the errors of the First Rabbinic Bible, though in both cases he also found unique omissions and additions.²⁶

Bacher then proceeded to a comparative analysis of the witnesses, cataloguing those variant readings within the three printed editions that originated as errors, and for which Codex Reuchlinianus No. 3 preserved the correct reading. In some cases this concerned a variant reading originating in an error appearing in one or both of the Rabbinic Bibles, which had subsequently been 'corrected' in Buxtorf's editions, resulting in a different variant reading. He examined cases of 'double translations' and exegetical traditions, where one or more of the printed versions normally offered a fuller text, though in a few cases Codex Reuchlinianus No. 3 preserved the longer reading. Finally he considered variants that give an alternative explanation of the underlying Hebrew. In most of these cases the text of Codex Reuchlinianus No. 3 proved, in Bacher's view, to be the oldest, although he also found that it had a tendency to accommodate the Targum text to the Hebrew text (a tendency confirmed by my own analysis, see chapter four).²⁷ Some years later Bacher added a further example demonstrating the priority of the reading of Codex Reuchlinianus No. 3 to the list: in a short note published in 1902 Bacher identified one case in which Codex Reuchlinianus No. 3 preserved a verse (Tg. Isa. 54:7) that had, through parablepsis, been omitted in the text tradition reflected in the four editions he had to hand (i.e. Venice 1547, Basel 1618, Amsterdam 1726, and Lemberg 1808).²⁸

---

25 Bacher, 'Kritische Untersuchungen zum Prophetentargum', 2–3, 35–55.
26 Bacher, 'Kritische Untersuchungen zum Prophetentargum', 35–42 (quotation, 37).
27 Bacher, 'Kritische Untersuchungen zum Prophetentargum', 42–52.
28 W. Bacher, 'Isaie, liv, 7.', *Revue des Études Juives* 44 (1902), 283–5, pp. 284–5. According to Bacher, the verse has accidentally been transposed with vs.8 in Codex Reuchlinianus No. 3,

Chapter One. *Status Quaestionis*

Bacher's seminal comparative study provided new insights for the would-be text-critic. Of particular importance was his observation that some readings had in fact resulted from the rectification of errors, so that although the resulting form was apparently 'correct' it was also secondary; in many of these cases the earlier reading was preserved in Codex Reuchlinianus No. 3.[29] However, more broadly, Bacher concluded that the variations between Codex Reuchlinianus No. 3 and the printed editions that he had observed clearly showed that the transmission history of Targum Jonathan had been long and fluid:

> This fact clearly suggests that it took a long time before the text of the Targum achieved a reasonably unchangeable canonical form, and that the copyist or later meturgeman allowed himself to make modifications here and there, either in terms of old changes made in Babylonia, or according to his own insight.[30]

******

Whilst Bacher's interest lay primarily in the field of Rabbinics, Targum Jonathan's transmission history was also a matter of some considerable importance to those within the flourishing school of biblical text-criticism for whom it represented an early and important witness to the Hebrew text. From this school Cornill was the first to embark on comparative studies of the Targum text in order to provide a more reliable basis for the reconstruction of the Targum's Hebrew *Vorlage,* the results of which appeared in his *Das Buch des Propheten Ezechiel* (1886).

Cornill valued the Targum highly not only as a tool for textual criticism of the Hebrew Bible but also as a cultural artefact, considering it to be 'the official Jewish public Bible (*Volksbibel*) of Jesus' time', which explained the text for the benefit of the populace. He placed the origins of Targum in the pre-Christian period — before the Masoretic Text had reached its final fixed form — and the absence of anti-Christian polemic convinced him that the Targum

---

the wording at the start of the two verses being similar (ברגז זעיר/בשעא זעירא). Lambert noted that the same transposition occurred in Ms. Hébreu 1325 (Bibliothèque Nationale, Paris), adding 'la transposition…doit donc être très ancienne'. M. Lambert, 'Note Additionnelle', *Revue des Études Juives* 44 (1902), 285. However, since Ms. Hébreu 1325 is a Yemenite manuscript from the first half of the fifteenth century (see M. Garel, *D'une main forte manuscrits hebreux des collections françaises* [Paris 1991], No. 4), the transposition in the two manuscripts is unlikely to be connected.

29 Bacher, 'Kritische Untersuchungen zum Prophetentargum', 55.
30 Bacher, 'Kritische Untersuchungen zum Prophetentargum', 58.

had been transmitted faithfully. Consequently, he valued the Targum extremely highly for the purposes of text criticism of the Hebrew Bible: 'The Targum is significantly older than the Masoretic Text and therefore the oldest witness for the text of the Old Testament in its native Palestinian soil'.[31]

Yet Cornill also recognised that the Targum's own transmission history needed to be studied carefully if the Targum's *Urtext* was to be recovered. Until the appearance of de Lagarde's edition, Targum research was dependent on one of two recensions: the first represented by the First Rabbinic Bible of 1517 (whence Buxtorf's 1618–19 edition), the second by the Antwerp Polyglot, published 1568–72 (whence the Paris Polyglot, 1645). These two recensions had been collated in the London Polyglot, of which Cornill made use. Cornill therefore welcomed the publication of de Lagarde's edition as heralding in 'a new era for the knowledge and investigation of the Targum'.[32]

Cornill compared the text of Codex Reuchlinianus No. 3 according to de Lagarde's edition (the accuracy of which he overstated, judging it to have been published 'with well-known exemplary accuracy') to that of the First Rabbinic Bible as found in Buxtorf's edition, taking into account the variants of the Antwerp Polyglot as recorded in the London Polyglot (he excluded from his inquiry some extensive sections of Targum from haftarot). He recorded the variants in an extensive critical apparatus, supplemented with occasional critical notes.[33] He subsequently repeated this process for the remaining books of the Latter Prophets.[34]

Based on this critical comparison, he was able to make some general observations about the accuracy and reliability of each of the recensions and their relation one to another for the book of Ezekiel. In general, he found that the majority of variants concerned the interchange of synonyms, Hebraisms, or readings that stood closer to the Masoretic Text in one of the recensions. He found the text of Codex Reuchlinianus No. 3 to stand close to the London Polyglot text, whereas the First Rabbinic Bible more frequently exhibited independent readings. Cornill concluded that while Codex Reuchlinianus No. 3

---

31   Cornill, *Das Buch des Propheten Ezechiel*, 110–11 (quotation, 111), 122–5. See the critique of Dalman, *Grammatik des Jüdisch-Palästinischen Aramäisch*, 15–16.
32   Cornill, *Das Buch des Propheten Ezechiel*, 111–12, 120, (quotation, 112).
33   Cornill, *Das Buch des Propheten Ezechiel*, 112–20.
34   Cornill, 'Das Targum zu den Propheten', *Zeitschrift für die alttestamentliche Wissenschaft* 7 (1887), 177–202.

and the London Polyglot were generally to be preferred, the First Rabbinic Bible contained some peculiarities that were more original. For example, it exhibited a number of small variations from the Masoretic Text that had been revised in Codex Reuchlinianus No. 3 and the London Polyglot.[35]

On the basis of this analysis, Cornill was then able to address the question that really interested him, namely the reconstruction of the Targum's Hebrew *Vorlage*. He found that the presumed Hebrew underlying the Targum agreed in most cases with the Masoretic Text, though not always: he lists numerous instances where the Targum followed the *Qere*, or offered a different vocalisation of the Hebrew text, and so forth.[36] Codex Reuchlinianus No. 3 would go on to serve a long career in the critical apparatuses of editions of the Hebrew Bible: it is, for example, the only Targum manuscript to receive its own siglum in the famous *Biblia Hebraica Stuttgartensia*.

In light of the work of Bacher in particular, by the close of the nineteenth century there could no longer be any doubt that the collation, comparison, and evaluation of the manuscripts of Targum Jonathan was a task that urgently needed to be addressed. However, how this was to be done and upon what methodological basis remained unclear.

2. Recovering The Babylonian Text

If, as seems likely, the text received its final form in the Babylonian academies, then one way forward would be to attempt to recover a text whose form was as near as possible to that which the text had achieved at this final redaction. Although the developing focus on the recovery of the Babylonian form of the Targum was understandably concerned primarily with the Targum to the Torah, the interwoven histories of Targum Jonathan and Onqelos ensured that Targum Jonathan was not neglected. A critical tool in the quest for the recovery of the text's Babylonian form was — and remains — a manuscript's vocalisation. Adalbertus Merx played a crucial role in bringing this tool into the armoury of scholars of Targum Jonathan.

In a visit to London in the Easter of 1881, Merx was granted access to several manuscripts recently acquired by the British Museum that contained

---

35 Cornill, *Das Buch des Propheten Ezechiel*, 120.
36 Cornill, *Das Buch des Propheten Ezechiel*, 110, 121, 126–36.

parts of the Hebrew Bible with Targum, both bearing what Merx considered to be Babylonian vocalisation (the manuscripts concerned were Or. 2211, Or 1467, Or. 1476, now at the British Library). The vocalisation of the Targums in earlier editions (which Merx surveys, pp.143–63) deviated frequently — the result of a mixture of chance and arbitrariness Merx intended to rectify this deficiency by subjecting these newly available manuscripts to a close examination in order to establish whether they could serve as a guideline ('Richtschnur') for the vocalisation of the Targum.[37]

Merx drew from his comparison of the two systems the conclusion that the Tiberian system of vocalisation fixed in graphic form a more recent stage of the pronunciation than the Babylonian system. In his *Chrestomathia Targumica* (1888) he explained the development rather poetically: the Tiberian vowels flowed like streams from their Babylonian source.[38] Merx assumed a date of the middle of the seventh century for the final stabilisation of the Tiberian system, concluding on that basis that the Babylonian system must be somewhat earlier.[39]

In order that other scholars might be able to determine how the manuscripts related to each other and which had taken a later edition of the Targum as their basis, Merx transcribed the text from several manuscripts, presenting them unaltered in a chrestomathy.[40] In 1888 he presented a further anthology with the same aim under the title *Chrestomathia Targumica*, which included several additional manuscripts from the British Museum containing what Merx judged to be the antique Babylonian vocalisation (i.e. Or. 2228, Or. 2363, Or. 1470, Or. 2210), along with a critical apparatus containing the readings of 'the most ancient' manuscripts bearing Tiberian vocalisation (including Codex Reuchlinianus No. 3), and restated his view that the Babylonian version has a

---

37 A. Merx, 'Bemerkungen über die Vocalisation der Targume', in *Verhandlungen des fünften internationalen Orientalisten-Congresses gehalten zu Berlin im September 1881, II, Abhandlungen und Vorträge des fünften internationalen Orientalisten-Congresses gehalten zu Berlin 1881, Section 1, Abhandlungen und Vorträge der semitischen und afrikanischen Section.* (Berlin 1882), 142–88, p. 142.

38 'Vocales in libris tiberiensibus picti ex libris babylonicis haustae sunt, tiberienses sunt rivuli, babylonici fontes', A. Merx, *Chrestomathia Targumica quam collatis libris manu scriptis antiquissimis Tiberiensibus editionibusque impressis celeberrimis ad codices vocalibus Babylonicis instructos* (Porta Linguarum Orientalium 8, Berlin 1888), viii.

39 Merx, 'Bemerkungen über die Vocalisation der Targume', 165–6, 169.

40 Merx, 'Bemerkungen über die Vocalisation der Targume', 170–1.

pre-eminent place in the improvement of the Targum text.[41]

The significance of the phenomenon that Merx's work had so clearly highlighted, namely that the Jews living in the southwestern part of the Arabian peninsula in the area constituting modern day Yemen had inherited and transmitted the Babylonian system of punctuation, was quickly noted, ensuring that Yemenite manuscripts would have a place of primary importance for reconstructing the text of the Targum (both Jonathan and Onqelos).[42]

Shortly after the publication of Merx's works several new editions of Targum Jonathan appeared which took their lead from Merx's observation. Praetorius, acknowledging the faithful nature of the transmission of the text by Yemenite Jews, recognised the need to establish a reliable edition of the Yemenite tradition unaffected by the Tiberian transmission. But, he was overwhelmed by the practical difficulties of this task, namely, the pervasiveness of Tiberian 'contamination'. Instead he fixed on the more modest ambition of presenting the text of the Targum of Joshua according to a well executed manuscript (Or. qu. 578, Staatsbibliothek, Preußischer Kulturbesitz, Berlin), lightly amended, and noting variant readings in haftarot collections that had been made available to him (he does not identify the materials concerned precisely), in de Largarde's edition of Codex Reuchlinianus No. 3, and in the Leiria edition.[43] Praetorius followed this with an edition of Judges (without further theoretical discussion), and in 1902 an edition of Jeremiah by his pupil Ludwig Wolfsohn appeared.[44]

---

41 Merx, *Chrestomathia Targumica*, ix–x.
42 E.g. In his 1906 entry for the *Jewish Encyclopaedia* Bacher wrote: 'the Jews of Yemen received this Targum [Onqelos], like that to the Prophets, with the Babylonian punctuation' citing in support Merx's *Chrestomathia Targumica*; W. Bacher, 'Targum', in C. Adler and I. Singer (eds), *The Jewish Encyclopedia* (New York/London 1903), Vol. 12, 57–63, p. 59. Also Berliner's influential edition of Onqelos; A. Berliner, *Targum Onkelos*, Vol 2 (Berlin 1884), 128–57 (note the citation of Merx on page 131). Cf. Landauer welcomed the work of Merx as a step towards recovering the text with Babylonian punctuation and offered many comparative observations concerning the vocalisation and detailed criticism. S. Landauer, 'Studien zu Merx' *Chrestomathia targumica*', *Zeitschrift für Assyriologie und Vorderasiatische Archäologie* 3:1 (1888), 263–92.
43 F. Praetorius, *Das Targum zu Josua in jemenische Überlieferung* (Berlin 1899), ix cf. v.
44 F. Praetorius, *Das Targum zum Buch der Richter in jemenischer Überlieferung* (Berlin 1899); L. Wolfsohn, *Das Targum zum Propheten Jeremias in jemenischer Überlieferung* (Halle 1902) (covering Jeremiah 1–12). Stenning criticised both of Praetorius' works for being largely dependent on a single manuscript (Or. qu. 578 Staatsbibliothek, Berlin) even though Praetorius himself had claimed to do no more than this; Stenning, *The Targum of Isaiah*, Preface.

Silberman's edition of Ezekiel appeared in the same year. Silberman took the same manuscript as Praetorius as his base, but incorporated more materials for comparison (i.e. de Lagarde's edition of Codex Reuchlinianus No. 3, the First Rabbinic Bible, Buxtorf's edition, and the Antwerp Polyglot according to the 6th edition of the London Polyglot), including citations in Kimhi and Rashi, the comparison of an Erfurt haftarah manuscript to Codex Reuchlinianus No. 3 carried out by de Lagarde,[45] variants that Landauer had found when he compared Codex Solger (Stadtbibliothek, Nürnberg; 1291 CE) with Codex Reuchlinianus No. 3 (unpublished), and finally two haftarah manuscripts that he was able to check himself, though he does not specify which. Silberman's introduction is noteworthy because he states explicitly his view that a text bearing the Babylonian vocalisation would also provide an assurance of a more reliable consonantal text: 'the vowels are to the consonants' he says, 'what the soul is to the body'.[46]

Before the arrival of Sperber's now (in)famous editions, Stenning's 1949 edition of the Targum to Isaiah should also be noted. In Stenning's view the Yemenite manuscripts acquired by the British Museum, short extracts of which Merx had presented in his *Chrestomathia Targumica*, 'clearly represented a more original form of punctuation than the texts provided with sub-linear points'. Following Merx's lead, therefore, Stenning sought 'to provide a critical edition of the Targum of Isaiah based on manuscript authority and in so doing to provide the student of the super-linear vocalisation with reliable material for determining its original form'.[47] The result was an edition based on manuscript Or. 2211 of the British Library (with the errors of transcription corrected), with an apparatus containing variant readings from four other manuscripts (including Codex Reuchlinianus No. 3 according to de Lagarde's edition) and seven haftarah collections. Stenning's edition was welcomed by his contemporaries for having made available new material for the study of the supra-linear pointing — although subsequent discussion of Sperber's edition would show that his choice of manuscript Or. 2211 was far from ideal in this respect — but it also drew criticism for his emendations of his sources, the various inaccuracies in the text, and deficiencies in the apparatus.[48]

---

45 De Lagarde, *Symmicta* I, 138–41.
46 Silbermann, *Das Targum zu Ezechiel*, 5–7 (quotation, 5).
47 Stenning, *The Targum of Isaiah*, Preface.
48 For critique see below, pages 19–22; H.H. Rowley, review of 'J.F. Stenning, *The Targum of*

Chapter One. *Status Quaestionis*

******

There can be no one working in the field of Targum or Hebrew Bible who is not familiar with Alexander Sperber's editions of the Targums, published in four volumes under the heading *The Bible in Aramaic*. In a fifth volume in this collection (volume 4B), entitled *The Targum and the Hebrew Bible*, Sperber provides some autobiographical reminiscences on this enterprise. According to his own recollections, his early interest in the Targum as a witness to the Hebrew text soon led him to the realisation that the Targum had its own style and technique, which could better account for many of its deviations from the Masoretic Text than the assumption of an alternative *Vorlage*. He began his investigations working from the Rabbinic Bibles, but later saw that it was necessary to revise all his material once his attention was drawn to de Lagarde's edition of Codex Reuchlinianus No. 3. This work formed the basis for his doctoral research at the University of Bonn, which he submitted in 1924. Immediately thereafter Sperber embarked on the preparation of an edition of the Targum to the Prophets with the support of the Berlin *Academy for Jewish Research* and made public his intention to publish an edition of the Former Prophets in 1926 in the *Zeitschrift für die Alttestamentliche Wissenschaft* (an announcement that spurred Barnes to compare three Yemenite manuscripts to the editions of de Lagarde and Buxtorf for 'about thirteen chapters' of the Targum to Ezekiel).[49] He adopted de Lagarde's text as a basis for the work of collation (but not for the final edition) because it contained only the consonantal text, allowing Sperber to add vowels as appropriate. He travelled first to Karlsruhe to check the accuracy of de Lagarde's edition, correcting it where necessary, before embarking on the lengthy task of collating manuscripts.[50]

Isaiah', (Oxford: Clarendon Press, 1949)', *Bibliotheca Orientalis* 6:5 (1949), 159–60; W.D. McHardy, review of 'J.F. Stenning, *The Targum of Isaiah* (Oxford: Clarendon Press, 1949)', *The Hibbert Journal* 48 (1950), 190–2. Houtman and Brockington criticised Stenning for the lack of details about the manuscripts concerned; Brockington, review of 'J.F. Stenning, The Targum of Isaiah (Oxford: Clarendon Press, 1949)', *The Journal of Theological Studies* (New Series) 1:1 (1950), 88–9. Houtman, 'Planning a New Targum Edition', 216 n. 16. Cf. also van Zijl, 'Is. XLVIII 7 according to the Targum Br. Mus. Or. Ms 2211', *Vetus Testamentum* 18:4 (1968), 560–1, p. 561.

49 W.E. Barnes, 'The Targum on the Later Prophets', *Journal of Theological Studies* 28 (1927), 283–5. The manuscripts were Or. 1474, Or. 1473, and Or. 2211 (British Library).

50 Sperber, *The Bible in Aramaic*, IVB, 17–19.

His editions of Targum Jonathan to the Former Prophets finally saw the light of day in 1959; the Latter Prophets followed in 1962. The basic text was that of manuscripts Or. 2210 for the Former Prophets and Or. 2211 for the Latter Prophets, both Yemenite manuscripts of the late fifteenth century (1468 and 1475 respectively) belonging to the collections of the British Museum — now in the custody of the British Library. Sperber deviated from the reading of the manuscript in cases of obvious scribal error or *lacunae* — the poorly preserved final leaves of Or. 2211 being supplemented by Or. 1474, also of the British Museum. He recorded in two apparatuses variant readings found in several other manuscripts, haftarot collections, and printed editions.

I will return to Sperber in a moment, but by now it should be clear that the work of Merx decisively shaped the study and publication of Targum Jonathan. But a house is only as strong as the foundations upon which it stands and unfortunately the foundations laid by Merx were problematic. The manuscripts employed by Merx in his 'Bemerkungen über die Vocalisation der Targume', and subsequently in his *Chrestomathia Targumica*, were not genuinely Babylonian in character. Rather, they belonged to a Yemenite tradition that, while maintaining the Babylonian vowel-signs, had been influenced by the Tiberian tradition. What held true for Merx also held true for his successors, including Sperber. Praetorius, Wolfsohn, Silberman, Stenning and Sperber had relied on manuscripts that preserved the Babylonian vowel signs, *but not the Babylonian pronunciation tradition.*[51] Yet by the time Sperber's and Stenning's editions of Targum Jonathan reached the press the need to make such a distinction between Babylonian and Yemenite traditions was already well established thanks to the endeavours of Paul Kahle.

Kahle first published fragments of Targum Jonathan with genuine

---

51 Rather, they belong to the Yemenite-Tiberian (super-linear vowel signs, but Tiberian pronunciation) or the mixed Yemenite (some Tiberian, some Babylonian characteristics) tradition, see A. Díez Macho, *Manuscritos hebreos y arameos de la Biblia: contribución al estudio de las diversas tradiciones del texto del Antiguo Testamento* (Studia Ephemeridis 'Augustinianum' 5, Rome 1971), 24–30. Also M. Martin, 'The Babylonian Tradition and Targum' in R. de Langhe (ed.), *Le Psautier. Ses origines. Ses problèmes littéraires. Son influence: études présentées aux XIIe journées bibliques (29–31 août 1960)* (Leuven 1962), 425–51, pp. 425, 442–3, 446–51; Ribera Florit, 'The Babylonian Tradition of the Targum Jeremiah', 102; M.L. Díez Merino, 'Targum Manuscripts and Critical Editions', in D.R.G. Beattie and M.J. McNamara (eds), *The Aramaic Bible: Targums in their Historical Context* (Journal for the Study of the Old Testament Supplement Series 166, Sheffield 1994), 51–91, pp. 68–70.

Babylonian vocalisation in his *Masoreten des Ostens*, which first appeared in 1913. Although at that point he did not believe it possible to determine with certainty whether or not Targum Onqelos — the Targum with which Kahle was primarily concerned — had been completed in Palestine (he would later argue that it had been composed entirely in Babylon[52]), it was nonetheless certain in Kahle's view that the Targum had received particular attention in the academies of Sura and Nehardea, where its consonantal text had received its final editing ('Endredaktion'), its punctuation, and a masorah. Kahle laid particular stress on Targum Onqelos' masorah as confirming this theory; the lack of a masorah for Targum Jonathan indicated in his view that it had received less attention than Onqelos, though the similarities between the two texts led him to the conclusion that their history was otherwise parallel. By the time the Babylonian academies came to an end the dimensions of both Targums were finalised.[53]

Eastern manuscripts were therefore to be favoured in reconstructing the ancient Babylonian form of the text: 'The Babylonian tradition' Kahle wrote in his *The Cairo Genizah*, the published form of his 1941 Schweich Lectures for the British Academy, 'was handed over, with a few alterations, to the Jews in Yemen'. This tradition had been better preserved in the case of the Targum text than in the Hebrew text, so that some Yemenite manuscripts could be used for the basis of a new critical edition of the Targum.[54] Yet these sources needed to be handled in a more nuanced way than the early enthusiasm engendered by Merx had allowed. The extant Eastern materials needed to be separated into materials preserving genuinely Babylonian characteristics, and those containing the Yemenite tradition, influenced to a greater or lesser extent by the Tiberian tradition. Some of the oldest and most valuable manuscripts (e.g. Or. 1467 and Or. 2363, British Library — again referring to Onqelos) preserved more of the Babylonian characteristics,[55] while the later Yemenite

---

52 P. Kahle, *The Cairo Geniza: the Schweich Lectures of the British Academy 1941* (London 1947), 117.
53 Kahle, *Masoreten des Ostens*, 203. Kahle called Targum Onqelos's masorah 'sehr wichtige Zeugnisse für die orientalische Überlieferung dieses Targums'. Kahle, *Masoreten des Ostens*, 207.
54 Kahle, *Masoreten des Ostens*, 206. Citation: Kahle, *The Cairo Geniza* (1st ed), 127.
55 Kahle, *Masoreten des Ostens*, 206. Kahle judged Merx's edition of these (*Chrestomathia Targumica*) to be quite unreliable.

manuscripts exhibited the influence of the Tiberian system.[56] Kahle placed the beginning of this influence after the decline of the Babylonian academies, perhaps already in the tenth century, although it was probably not free from error even at that early stage.[57]

The Western manuscripts were clearly of a secondary order, Kahle concluded. An independent Tiberian punctuation of the Targum had probably never existed. Rather, Babylonian vocalisation had been set into Tiberian signs when the text had moved to Palestine.[58] Such a process was evident in a number of Western manuscripts of Targum Onqelos.[59] These — like most Western manuscripts — contain many errors reflecting an imperfect understanding of the vocalisation.[60] The Babylonian system is much simpler than the Tiberian, so additional signs were added contributing to the resulting confusion.[61] Kahle knew of no manuscripts of the Targum to the Prophets carrying Tiberian vocalisation that went back to a Babylonian *Vorlage*.

Sperber was familiar with Kahle's work of course, but did not carry through its implications in the production of his editions. In fact, the exact methodological principles upon which Sperber based his editions remain somewhat opaque. In *The Targum and the Hebrew Bible* published in 1973 — long after the editions had probably been completed, as we will see below — Sperber claims that the aim of his edition was 'to present the scholar with the very best text which can be established'. By this Sperber meant a manuscript that was correct in its vocabulary and grammar; unfortunately he found no manuscripts that fulfilled his criteria. Sperber rejected — quite correctly — the alternative possibility of creating an eclectic text and believed — again quite

---

56 Kahle, *Masoreten des Ostens*, 212–41; cf. Martin, 'The Babylonian Tradition and Targum', 442–3. For a clear discussion of the differences between the various systems and its application to Targum Jonathan see J. Ribera Florit, 'The Babylonian Masoretic Tradition', 103–8.
57 Kahle, *Masoreten des Ostens*, 214. Others, for example Martin, placed this decline somewhat earlier, in the eighth century, Martin, 'The Babylonian Tradition and Targum', 436. See further on Kahle, Díez Macho, *Manuscritos hebreos y arameos de la biblia*, 44–60.
58 Kahle, *Masoreten des Ostens*, 204.
59 E.g. de Rossi 12 (aka. Parm. 2003–4 Biblioteca Palatina, Parma; 1311 CE); de Rossi 7 (aka. Parm. 3218 Biblioteca Palatina, Parma; 1475 CE); Or. qu. 680 (aka. 127b Or. qu Staatsbibliothek, Berlin. The basis of the edition of Berliner ed., *Targum Onkelos* [Berlin 1884]); Editio Sabbioneta (1557).
60 Kahle, *Masoreten des Ostens*, 205, 212.
61 Kahle, *The Cairo Geniza*, 128.

rightly — that those manuscripts bearing the Tiberian system of vocalisation were unsuitable because their vocalisation was too inconsistent.[62] Although he acknowledged the significance of the vocalisation of Babylonian fragments, he chose not to employ such fragments (including some that were held in his own institution, the Jewish Theological Seminary in New York, and were known to him) for his editions. He claimed that they were too fragmentary to form the basis of an edition and in any case offered a consonantal text 'in no way better than the average'[63] — the last comment perhaps reflecting a preoccupation with reconstructing the original Targum text for which the vocalisation may only be of limited help.[64]

By process of elimination, therefore, Sperber justified his choice of the complete Yemenite manuscripts of the British Museum. Nonetheless, it remains unclear what sort of a text Sperber believed this manuscript to offer. His language is rather imprecise. Nowhere does he explicitly state that he is presenting a Babylonian text, yet he groups his basic text along with other Yemenite manuscripts appearing in his apparatus under the rubric 'Manuscripts with Babylonian Vocalisation', while referring to them elsewhere as representative of 'the Yemenite vocalisation in its older form'.[65] The ambiguity is such that Kahle accused Sperber of having 'confused Babylonian vowel signs and Babylonian tradition, and published a text furnished with the Babylonian vowels, but which had nothing to do with the Babylonian tradition'.[66] Moreover, Sperber's rejection of the fragments bearing genuinely Babylonian vocalisation is rather feeble. Such fragmentary materials may not have been suitable to serve as a base-text for an edition from a purely practical point of view, but nothing excluded recording their

---

62 Sperber, *The Bible in Aramaic*, IVB, 29–34 (citation: 29).
63 Sperber, *The Bible in Aramaic*, IVB, 30–1, 33–4 (citation: 31).
64 R.P. Gordon, 'Alexander Sperber and the Study of the Targums', in D.R.G. Beattie, M.J. McNamara (eds), *The Aramaic Bible: Targums in their Historical Context* (Journal for the Study of the Old Testament Supplement Series 166, Sheffield 1994), 92–102, p. 98.
65 'Prefatory Remarks' to volumes 2 and 3 of his *The Bible in Aramaic*; Sperber, *The Bible in Aramaic*, IVB, 34. Cf. A. Díez Macho, review of 'Alexander Sperber, *The Bible in Aramaic*, IVB, *The Targum and the Hebrew Bible* (Leiden: Brill, 1973)', *Journal for the Study of Judaism* 6:2 (1975), 217–36, p. 225.
66 P. Kahle, 'Die Aussprache des Hebräischen in Palästina vor der Zeit der Tiberischen Masoreten' *Vetus Testamentum* 10 (1960), 375–85, pp. 383–4. Cf. D. Barthélemy, *Critique textuelle de l'Ancien Testament*, III, *Ézéchiel, Daniel et les 12 Prophètes* (Orbis Biblicus et Orientalis 50/3. Fribourg and Göttingen 1992), ccix.

variant readings in the apparatus.[67]

It seems that Sperber chose not to include these materials for the simple reason that he had more or less completed his editions before he left Europe and Israel to join the Jewish Theological Seminary in New York in 1934, as Sperber himself indicates in several publications: he had already carried out the collation during a stay of two and a half years in England and a summer spent in Rome following the completion of his doctorate in 1924.[68] Díez Macho later recalled that he had seen completed copies of the editions of Targum Onqelos and Jonathan in 1949.[69] The task of beginning the whole project again once a new publisher had been secured after the turmoil of the war must simply have seemed too daunting.[70] After the editions had been published, Sperber would also claim that at some point the entire work of collating the manuscripts and testimonia for the third volume (Latter Prophets) 'had to be done all over again, from scratch, due to circumstances over which I had no control',[71] but he gives no indication of when or what the circumstances were. Perhaps this mysterious episode accounts for the apparent similarities of Sperber's edition of Isaiah to that of Stenning, published in 1949.[72] Sperber's editions — and for that matter much of what he (re)published in his *The Targum and the Hebrew Bible* (volume 4B of *The Bible in Aramaic* series) —

---

67 Díez Macho, review of 'Alexander Sperber, *The Bible in Aramaic*, IVB', 222–3. Cf. D. Winton Thomas, review of 'Alexander Sperber (ed.), *The Bible in Aramaic*, Vol. 1, The Pentateuch According to Targum Onkelos (Leiden: Brill, 1959)', *Journal of Semitic Studies* 5 (1960), 286–8, p. 287.

68 A. Sperber, 'Specimen of a Targum Edition', in S. Lieberman et al. (eds), *Louis Ginsberg Jubilee Volume: on the Occasion of his Seventieth Birthday*, Vol. 1 (New York 1945), 293–303; A. Sperber, 'The Targum Onkelos in its Relation to the Masoretic Hebrew Text', *Proceedings of the American Academy for Jewish Research* 6 (1934/35), 309–51, pp. 310–11. His comment in the prefatory remarks to his edition of Onqelos (*The Bible in Aramaic*, I, *The Pentateuch According to Targum Onkelos*, xvi) imply that the collation was completed before the war.

69 Díez Macho, review of 'Alexander Sperber, *The Bible in Aramaic*, IVB', 217.

70 Kohlhammer of Stuttgart had agreed to publish the editions of Targum Onqelos and Jonathan in the early 1930s; see Sperber, 'The Targum Onkelos in its Relation to the Masoretic Hebrew Text', 311. Cf. L. Díez Merino, 'Targum Manuscripts and Critical Editions', 70–3.

71 Sperber, *The Bible in Aramaic*, IVB, xiii.

72 de Boer accused Sperber of simply reprinting a corrected (on the basis of Rowley's review) version of Stenning's text; P.A.H. de Boer, review of 'M.H. Goshen-Gottstein, *The Book of Isaiah, Sample Edition with Introduction* (Jerusalem: The Hebrew University Bible Project, 1965)', *Vetus Testamentum* 16:2 (1966), 247–52, p. 249. Cf. R.P. Gordon, 'Foreword to the Reprinted Edition', in A. Sperber (ed.), *The Bible in Aramaic*, Vols 1–4 (Leiden 1992).

Chapter One. *Status Quaestionis*

ought therefore to be regarded as *une œuvre de jeunesse*.[73]

It is perhaps unsurprising then that it was precisely Sperber's choice of base text that formed the principal thrust of the criticism of his editions. In an ideal scenario a Babylonian text was to be preferred, but given that such materials were available only in fragments, a Yemenite manuscript preserving Babylonian features could serve as a satisfactory replacement where Babylonian materials were wanting. Sperber had not only neglected those texts with genuine Babylonian vocalisation,[74] but of the manuscripts that Sperber could have adopted as his base text, others are preferable to Or. 2210 and Or. 2211 (British Library). Ribera Florit considered Or. 1474 (British Library) to offer a text that was 'more consistent and with fewer grammatical mistakes' and preserved more of the Babylonian characteristics than Ms. Or. 2211 (Latter Prophets);[75] Barthélemy pointed out that Or. 2211 contains a number of isolated readings;[76] recent stemmatological analysis suggests that a similar conclusion may be drawn for Or. 2010 (Former Prophets).[77] Nonetheless, considered as a work of the late

---

73 Cf. Díez Macho, review of 'Alexander Sperber, *The Bible in Aramaic*, IVB', 217, 224, 228.

74 Martin, 'The Babylonian Tradition and Targum', 425, 442–3, 446–51; Díez Macho, review of 'Alexander Sperber, *The Bible in Aramaic*, IVB', 221; cf. Winton Thomas, review of 'Alexander Sperber (ed.), *The Bible in Aramaic*, I', (on Onqelos), 287.

75 J. Ribera Florit, *Targum Jonatán de los Profetas Posteriores en tradición babilónica: Isaías* (Textos y Estudios 'Cardenal Cisneros' 43, Madrid 1988), 10; Ribera Florit, 'The Babylonian Tradition of the Targum Jeremiah', 108. Furthermore, Or. 2211 contains some forms that were 'mistaken or that, at the very least, are doubtful'; concerning variations in number and gender Or. 1474 more often agreed with the Babylonian fragments than Or. 2211 (but not always), J. Ribera Florit, 'La versión aramaica del Profeta Sofonías', *Estudios Bíblicos* 40 (1982), 127–58, pp. 133–4 (quotation: 133). Cf. Ribera Florit, 'El Targum de Malaquías', *Estudios Biblicos* 48 (1990), 171–97, p. 176; Ribera Florit, 'Targum de Joel', *Miscelanea de Estudios Arabes y Hebraicos, Seccion de Hebreo* 53 (2004), 271–86; Ribera Florit 'La versión aramaica del profeta Ageo', *Anuario de Filología* 4 (1978), 290–1; also Díez Macho, review of 'Alexander Sperber, *The Bible in Aramaic*, IVB', 220–5; E. Martínez Borobio (ed.), *Targum Jonatan de los Profetas Primeros en tradición babilónica*, Vol. 2, *I–II Samuel*, (Textos y Estudios 'Cardenal Cisneros' 38, Madrid 1987), 9. J. Ferrer i Costa, 'El Targum d'Osees en tradició Iemenita', unpublished Ph.D. dissertation (Universitat de Barcelona 1989), 23–4. See also Stenning's discussion of the variations in punctuation in his *The Targum of Isaiah*, xxii–xxvii.

76 Barthélemy, *Critique textuelle de l'Ancien Testament*, III, *Ezechiel, Daniel, et les 12 Prophètes*, ccix. Cf. A. Houtman, 'Wat is er met de lijdende knecht gebeurd? De lezing van Jesaja 52:13–53:12 volgens Targoem Jonathan', *Nederlands Theologisch Tijdschrift* 59:3 (2005), 235–51, p. 240. Barthélemy's observation (among other things) makes van Zijl's conclusions in his 'Is. XLVIII 7 according to the Targum Br. Mus. Or. Ms 2211' questionable.

77 E. van Staalduine-Sulman, 'An Electronic Edition of Targum Samuel', 27–30. But cf. Smelik's conclusion, see note 145.

1920s, Sperber's choices seem less problematic.[78]

In addition to these fundamental errors, Sperber's editions contain numerous errors,[79] although this ought not to be overstated: based on van Zijl's two lists of errata[80] and his own study of the Minor Prophets, Gordon concluded that these errors were mostly confined to the vocalisation or confusion between *waw* and *yod*, concluding that 'the incidence of *significant* consonantal errors is quite small, and no greater than in many another work of comparable dimensions'. Since the vocalisation is not of the authentic Babylonian tradition the significance of inaccuracies in recording the vocalisation is in any case limited.[81] We must also keep in mind that in terms of their consonantal text, the Yemenite and Babylonian manuscripts rarely differ from one another.[82]

The reaction to Sperber's work made clear that the labours of Kahle had set the study of the text of Targum Jonathan (and Onqelos) on a new trajectory: the Babylonian tradition could no longer be set aside. The gauntlet that Kahle had thrown down was taken up by one of his pupils, Díez Macho, who in turn inspired the work of further generations of Targum scholars, forming what is now sometimes referred to as 'La Escuela targúmica de Barcelona'.[83]

---

78 Díez Macho, review of 'Alexander Sperber, *The Bible in Aramaic*, IVB', 221.
79 E.g. Martínez Borobio found that Sperber had failed to transcribe all of the signs appearing in manuscript Or. 2210; E. Martínez Borobio (ed.), *Targum Jonatan de los Profetas Primeros en tradición babilónica*, Vol. 1, *Josué – Jueces*, (Textos y Estudios 'Cardenal Cisneros' 46, Madrid 1989), 12. Barthélemy found it necessary to recheck the witnesses cited by Sperber; Barthélemy, *Critique textuelle de l'Ancien Testament*, III, *Ezechiel, Daniel et les 12 Prophètes*, ccix.
80 J. van Zijl, 'Errata in Sperber's Edition of Targum Isaiah', *Annual of the Swedish Theological Institute in Jerusalem* 4 (1965), 189–91; van Zijl, 'A Second List of Errata in Sperber's Edition of Targum Isaiah', *Annual of the Swedish Theological Institute in Jerusalem* 7 (1968–9), 132–4.
81 van Zijl, 'Errata in Sperber's Edition of the Targum Isaiah'; van Zijl, 'A Second List of Errata in Sperber's Edition of Targum Isaiah'; R.P. Gordon, 'Sperber's Edition of the Targum to the Prophets: a Critique', *Jewish Quarterly Review (New Series)* 64 (1973–4), 314–21, pp. 318–19 (citation: 318). Cf. Gordon, 'Alexander Sperber and the Study of the Targums', 102; S. Segert, review of 'Alexander Sperber (ed.), *The Bible in Aramaic, Vol. 1, The Pentateuch according to Targum Onkelos* (Leiden: Brill, 1959); Alexander Sperber (ed.), *The Bible in Aramaic, Vol. 2, The Former Prophets according to Targum Jonathan* (Leiden: Brill, 1959)', *Archiv Orientální* 28:4 (1960), 701–4, pp. 702–4.
82 van Staalduine-Sulman, 'An Electronic Edition of Targum Samuel', 17, 22, 24–5, 27–8, 46–7.
83 See J. Ribera Florit, 'Las investigaciones Targúmicas en España a partir de la obra de A. Díez Macho (1984–2001)', *Miscelanea de Estudios Arabes y Hebraicos, Seccion de Hebreo* 50 (2001), 849–58, pp. 850–1, 853–5, 858. Díez Merino, 'Los discipulos de la escuela targúmica de la Universidad de Barcelona'; L. Díez Merino, 'Los fundadores de la escuela targúmica de la Universidad de Barcelona', *Henoch* 12 (1990), 77–97. On the work of Díez Macho in

Chapter One. *Status Quaestionis*

Díez Macho followed the earlier viewpoint of Kahle concerning the origins of Targum Jonathan: its language, like that of Targum Onqelos, was of Palestinian origin, but showed a clear Babylonian linguistic stamp, especially in the vocalisation. The scientific desideratum was therefore to prepare an edition of a text (or texts) based on manuscripts of a genuinely Babylonian character — that is, preserving the super-linear vowels *and the pronunciation tradition* — Sperber's edition having fallen short of this goal.[84] It was not to be thought, however, that 'Babylonian' manuscripts necessarily came from Sura or Nehardea, or even from Babylonia. Rather, that they had been copied by Jewish communities under the moral and juridical influence of the Gaonim from Babylon — there were 'Babylonian' synagogues in Palestine, Syria, and Egypt, for example — a tradition that itself varied depending on the academy, location, and epoch. The indigenous traditions of the Jews of Yemen were also strongly influenced by the Babylonian tradition, and only much later the Tiberian tradition, so Yemenite manuscripts could often be valuable witnesses to the Babylonian tradition.[85]

Before work could begin on a critical edition, then, suitable manuscripts needed to be identified and studied. To this end over a period of two decades Díez Macho examined the Targum fragments of the Jewish Theological Seminary in New York,[86] where an extensive collection of valuable codex remnants from south Arabian manuscripts was held, and the collections of various libraries in Europe, whose holdings of materials from the Cairo Genizah provided a rich new seam of texts of genuine Babylonian character, at

---

particular, see Díez Merino, 'El Profesor Alejandro Díez Macho y los estudios aramaico-targúmicos (12-V-1916 a 6-X-1984)' *Estudios Bíblicos* 43 (1985), 5–56.

84 A. Díez Macho, *El Targum: introducción a las traducciones aramaicas de la Biblia* (Barcelona 1972), 72–3, 109–12; A. Díez Macho, 'Importants manuscrits hébreux et araméens aux États Unis', International Organization of Old Testament Scholars, *Volume du Congrès, Strasbourg 1956* (Supplements to Vetus Testamentum 4, Leiden 1957), 39. Díez Macho discusses the various refinements to the classification of Babylonian materials proposed by Kahle and Yevin in his *Manuscritos hebreos y arameos de la Biblia*, 44–5, 50–60.

85 Díez Macho, 'Importants manuscrits hébreux et araméens aux États Unis', 33–4. Cf. Ribera Florit 'The Babylonian Masoretic Tradition Reflected in the Mss of the Targum to the Latter Prophets', 104–7.

86 According to Goshen-Gottstein, Díez Macho overlooked very little, although his attention on the Genizah fragments meant that he missed some Tosefta Targums (in the Prophets: Isa. 10:32; Judges 5) found in the Yemenite codices; M. Goshen-Gottstein, 'Biblical Manuscripts in the United States', *Textus* 2 (1962), 28–59, p. 50.

least for the Targum.[87] This last point is important because in many cases it was only the Targum text that preserved its Babylonian character. As the Babylonian schools declined in the tenth century the Tiberian system gradually took over, but because Aramaic had ceased for the large part to be a language of composition it had 'crystallised', and was therefore less susceptible than the Hebrew text (since Hebrew continued to be used, and therefore developed) to the pervasive influence of the Tiberian system. This proved to be the case, for example, for many of the manuscripts held at the Jewish Theological Seminary in New York, which had been written in a Yemenite hand between the twelfth and fourteenth centuries.[88]

Díez Macho described and classified the materials he examined according to their vocalisation. In addition to those manuscripts of a genuinely Babylonian character, Díez Macho divided the remaining Yemenite manuscripts into two categories: Yemenite-Tiberian (i.e. super-linear vowel signs, but Tiberian pronunciation), and mixed Yemenite (some Tiberian, some Babylonian characteristics). The majority of Yemenite manuscripts belong to these last two groups.[89]

Of the numerous fragments he studied, he singled out manuscripts 229 and 240 of the Jewish Theological Seminary in New York as appropriate to serve as a base text for new critical editions.[90] According to his analysis, manuscript 229, which contains the Hebrew text and Targum of Judges 16:17 to 2 Kgs

---

87 Díez Macho, *Manuscritos hebreos y arameos de la Biblia*, 41–8; Díez Macho, 'Importants manuscrits hébreux et araméens aux États Unis', 35.

88 A. Díez Macho, 'Nuevos manuscritos bíblicos babilónicos', *Estudios Bíblicos* 16 (1957), 235–77, pp. 245–53, 264. Cf. A. Díez Macho, 'Importante hallazgo bíblico', *Estudios Bíblicos* 13 (1954), 207–10; Kahle, *The Cairo Genizah* [1959], 64; Ribera Florit 'The Babylonian Masoretic Tradition Reflected in the Mss of the Targum to the Latter Prophets', 105–7; J. Ribera Florit, 'La puntuación babilónica del Targum de Jeremías en relación con la del texto hebreo', *Sefarad* 52 (1992), 201–8, pp. 206–7; Ribera Florit, 'Fragmento babilónico hebreoarameo del profeta Jeremías', 259. Equally, in manuscripts carrying the complicated punctuation (BK) the Targumic glosses tended to reflect the Tiberian punctuation less than those sections of the text that follow the Hebrew text, Ribera Florit, 'La versión aramaica del profeta Nahum', *Anuario de Filología* 6 (1981), 291–322, p. 297. Martínez Borobio, *Targum Jonatan de los Profetas Primeros en tradición babilónica*, Vol. 2, *I–II Samuel*, 9, 13.

89 Díez Macho, *Manuscritos hebreos y arameos de la Biblia*, 24–9.

90 Díez Macho, *El Targum*, 72–3, 109–12; Díez Macho, 'Importants manuscrits hébreux et araméens aux États Unis', 35–8, 40–2, 43, 40; Díez Macho, *Targum to the Former Prophets: Codex New York 229 from the Library of the Jewish Theological Seminary of America* [in Hebrew] (Jerusalem 1974), 31–3.

5:24 (though some pages are missing[91]), had probably been copied in the twelfth century from a Babylonian *Vorlage* by a Yemenite scribe; although the influence of Yemenite vocalisation was occasionally evident, the *prima manus* preserves the simple Babylonian vocalisation for the majority of the text.[92] The same held true for manuscript 240 (Isa. 35:9–38:11; 40:20–7; 42:21; 43:3–12), which also dates from the twelfth century, and which also preserved the classical Babylonian vocalisation in the *prima manus*.[93] Where these manuscripts were wanting, the missing text could be supplied by a number of other manuscripts of Targum Jonathan preserving the Babylonian vocalisation identified by Díez Macho and published in numerous articles and collections.[94]

It was the academic 'descendants' of Díez Macho, and in particular his student Josep Ribera Florit, who were now finally able to realise Kahle's hope of an edition of the Targum according to manuscripts of the genuine Babylonian type[95] — as far as this proved possible — on the basis of the foundations that Díez Macho had laid.[96] Ribera Florit's doctoral thesis,

---

91 Díez Macho published a facsimile of the manuscript, Díez Macho, *Targum to the Former Prophets: Codex New York 229* (the contents are listed on page 8).

92 Díez Macho concludes: '*Toda edición crítica de Jonatán ben 'Uzziel habrá de tomar a este Ms. como base* [his italics]'. A. Díez Macho, 'Un manuscrito yemeni de la Biblia babilonica: el Ms. 299 (Emc.105) del Seminario Teologico Judio de Nueva York', *Sefarad* 17 (1957), 237–79, pp. 237–8, 278–9 (quotation: 238). Cf. Díez Macho, *Targum to the Former Prophets: Codex New York 229*, 31–3. See further Díez Macho, 'Nuevos manuscritos bíblicos babilónicos', 241.

93 See Díez Macho, *Manuscritos hebreos y arameos de la Biblia*, 175, 253–68; Díez Macho, 'Manuscritos babilónicos de la Biblia procedentes del Yemen II (Textos Arameos)', *Augustinianum* 9 (1969), 427–545, pp. 429–30, 439–42, in which he notes that the vocalisation frequently agrees with that of Or. 1474 (British Library), he also notes here in a critical apparatus where the text deviates from Stenning's edition; and, A. Díez Macho, 'A New Fragment of Isaiah with Babylonian Pointing', *Textus* 1 (1960), 132–43, pp. 132–3.

94 In addition to those publications already mentioned the following concern Targum to the Prophets: A. Díez Macho, 'Nuevos manuscritos importantes, biblicos o liturgicos, en Hebreo o Arameo', *Sefarad* 16 (1956), 3–22, §23, §38, §39, §40, §42, §43 (cf. §47; §50; §60; §61); A. Díez Macho, 'Valiosos manuscritos bíblicos en la biblioteca nacional y universitaria de Estrasburgo', *Estudios Biblicos* 16 (1957), 83–8, §5, §6, §8; Díez Macho, 'Nuevos manuscritos bíblicos babilónicos'; Díez Macho with J.A.G. Larraya, 'El Ms. 4084 ff. I–II de la biblioteca nacional y universitaria de Estrasburgo : un largo fragmento del Targum de Jonathan ben ' Uzziel en texto babilonico'; A. Díez Macho with J.A.G. Larraya, 'El Ms. 4083 f. 9 de la biblioteca nacional y universitaria de Estrasburgo: fragmento de Amós 1.8–3.7, en Hebreo y Targum babilónicos', *Estudios Biblicos* 19 (1960), 75–90, 361–8, pp. 91–2; Díez Macho, *Manuscritos hebreos y arameos de la Biblia*, 159–91.

95 Kahle, *The Cairo Geniza*, 127. Cf. Kahle, *Masoreten des Ostens*, 214.

96 See Ribera Florit, 'Las investigaciones Targúmicas en España a partir de la obra de A. Díez Macho (1984–2001)', 53–5.

published in a revised form in which he reproduced those manuscripts containing the Targum to the Latter Prophets in its Babylonian tradition with a description and a comparative table showing some morphological differences between the Yemenite and Babylonian systems,[97] provided the basis for several editions of the Latter Prophets. In many cases the Babylonian materials were highly fragmentary (Malachi, Zephaniah, Haggai, Jeremiah, Ezekiel, Isaiah) or completely wanting (Joel, Obadiah). In these cases Ribera Florit filled the gaps (in some cases he gave a synoptic presentation) with the Yemenite manuscripts Or. 1474 and Or. 1473 of the British Library,[98] which though influenced by the Tiberian tradition preserved more of the Babylonian features than the text employed by Sperber (Or. 2111, British Library).[99]

---

[97] J. Ribera Florit, *Biblia babilonica: Profetas Posteriores (Targum)* (Salamanca 1977), following earlier publications of some materials: J. Ribera Florit, 'Fragmento babilónico hebreo-arameo del profeta Jeremías (Ms. 238b del JThS – ENA St. 20; Jer 31, 22a–32, 1h)', *Anuario de Filología* 2 (1976), 253–70 (transcription and translation of fragment); Ribera Florit, 'Fragmento babilonico-yemeni sobre los Profetas', in L. Álvarez Verdes and E.J. Alonso Hernández (eds), *Homenaje a Juan Prado: miscelánea de estudios bíblicos y hebraicos* (Madrid 1975) (description of a fragment not included in Yevin's catalogue that Kahle's family had given to Díez Macho. The fragment contained Ezek. 45:17–24 in the Aramaic, vs. 18–25 in the Hebrew. The vocalisation of the Aramaic was fundamentally Babylonian, being of the mid-Babylonian type — a development of the pure Babylonian type that had not been affected by Tiberian influence).

[98] J. Ribera Florit, 'El Targum de Abdías', in A. Hilhorst, E. Puech and E. Tigchelaar (eds), *Flores Florentino: Dead Sea Scrolls and other Early Jewish Studies in Honour of Florentino Garcia Martinez* (Supplements to the Journal for the Study of Judaism 122, Leiden 2007), 713–27; Ribera Florit, 'El Targum de Malaquias'; Ribera Florit, 'La versión aramaica del profeta Sofonías'; Ribera Florit 'La versión aramaica del profeta Ageo'; Ribera Florit, 'La versión aramaica del profeta Nahum'; Ribera Florit, *Targum Jonatán de los Profetas Posteriores en tradición babilónica: Ezequiel* (Textos y Estudios 'Cardenal Cisneros' 62, Madrid 1997); Ribera Florit, *Targum Jonatán de los Profetas Posteriores en tradición babilónica: Isaías*; Ribera Florit, *Targum Jonatán de los Profetas Posteriores en tradición babilónica: Jeremías* (Textos y Estudios 'Cardenal Cisneros' 52, Madrid 1992); Ribera Florit, 'Targum de Joel'. A further description of the fragments of Jeremiah with Babylonian punctuation (divided into simple, middle, and complicated systems), is given in Ribera Florit 'The Babylonian Tradition of the Targum Jeremiah', 103–5. The need for an edition of Habakuk is noted by Ribera Florit in his 'El Targum de Habacuc', *Anuari de Filologia* E, 11 (2002–3), 319–32, but no edition is given (instead the article discusses techniques and exegesis), 319–20, 331. Translations with critical introductions: Ribera Florit, *Traducción del Targum de Jeremías* (Biblioteca Midrásica 12, Estella 1992); Ribera Florit, *El Targum de Isaías: versión crítica, introducción y notas* (Biblioteca Midrásica 6, Valencia 1988); Ribera Florit, *Targum de Ezequiel: introducción, traducción crítica y notas* (Biblioteca midrásica 27, Estella 2004).

[99] Ribera Florit, 'El Targum de Abdías', 714–16; Ribera Florit, 'El Targum de Malaquias', 176; Ribera Florit 'La versión aramaica del profeta Ageo', 290–1; Ribera Florit, 'La versión aramaica

Martínez Borobio provided editions of the Former Prophets (1–2 Samuel, Joshua, Judges, 1–2 Kings), using manuscript 229 of the Jewish Theological Seminary in New York (see above, page 24) where he could, and relying 'for want of anything better' on manuscript 230 of the Jewish Theological Seminary (= Eb66 / t709b), the text of which had been 'strongly Tiberianised', to provide a continuous text. Occasionally he was forced to draw on another manuscript of the late Babylonian (i.e. Yemenite) type, namely manuscript 2 (Collection Rav Yosef Kapach, Jerusalem = Eb76 / t724b), which he judged to be of 'inferior quality', or, when the situation became truly desperate, on Or. 1471 (British Library), which has completely lost its Babylonian characteristics, and a manuscript of a similar type, namely Or. 1472 (British Library).[100]

In a 1989 doctoral thesis directed by Ribera Florit, Ferrer Costa presented a critical text of the Targum to Hosea. On account of the fragmentary nature of the Babylonian materials, he followed the method established by Díez Macho (and followed by Ribera Florit) of adopting a Yemenite manuscript of good quality (namely Or. 1474, British Library) as a base text and comparing the four available Babylonian fragments.[101] Ferrer Costa's edition went beyond those of Ribera Florit and Martínez Borobio, however, by including variants from five Western manuscripts and three early printed editions representing Ashkenazi (including Italian) and Sephardi textual traditions,[102] as well as an additional Yemenite manuscript (i.e. Or. 2211, British Library). Although the Babylonian fragments were too small for such analysis, the consonantal variants, mostly from manuscript T-S AS 62,193, 367 (Cairo Genizah Collection, Cambridge; Eb 16), are listed. The two Yemenite manuscripts revealed a certain kinship. The

---

del profeta Nahum' (a comparison between the Tiberian-Yemenite manuscripts and the Babylonian fragments is given, pp. 295–8); Ribera Florit, 'The Babylonian Tradition of the Targum Jeremiah', 102 (describes the vocalic quality of mss. Or. 2211, Or. 1474, and Or. 1473, British Library).

100 Martínez Borobio, *Targum Jonatan de los Profetas Primeros en tradición babilónica*, Vol. 1, *Josué - Jueces* (citation 11–12); Martínez Borobio, *Targum Jonatan de los Profetas Primeros en tradición babilónica*, Vol. 2, *I–II Samuel* (citation 11; description of manuscripts 11–18); Martínez Borobio, *Targum Jonatan de los Profetas Primeros en tradición babilónica*, Vol. 3, I–II *Reyes*.

101 Cairo Genizah Collection, Cambridge, T-S 2.7 (Eb 54), T-S AS 62,193,367 (Eb 16); T-S 15.1 (Kb 7); Firkowitsch Collection, Leningrad, I,132 (Kb 54,82a–84a).

102 I.e. Codex Reuchlinianus No. 3, Urbinati Ebr. 1 (Biblioteca Apostolica, Vatican), Montefiore 7 (Montefiore Endowment), Villa-Amil 4 (Biblioteca Complutense, Madrid), Ms M-3 (Biblioteca de la Universitaria, Salamanca), First and Second Rabbinic Bibles, Antwerp Polyglot.

base text contained a good number of unique readings. The two Alfonso de Zamora manuscripts transmitted substantially the same text (showing only copyist errors and some variations in the use of matres lectionis), while the remaining Western manuscripts showed no real kinship either among themselves or in respect of the other groups. The two Rabbinic Bibles were almost identical. The Antwerp Polyglot is dependent on the Alfonso de Zamora textual tradition (variants being merely typographical errors or mistakes by the corrector).[103]

Ferrer Costa's study represents an important development, in that it is the first attempt to separate the various witnesses into textual groups on the basis of textual variants. The number of textual witnesses consulted is, however, limited so the results remain preliminary. Unfortunately the impact of this important work has been limited because it was never published (and is, moreover, written in Catalan).[104]

3. Comprehensive Collation of Manuscripts

Let us now return briefly to Sperber. As we have seen, the criticism that Sperber's editions offered a poor representation of the Babylonian textual tradition reflected a trend in the study of the text of Targum Jonathan that can be traced back to Merx. Yet criticism of Sperber's editions also crystallised a second trend that can equally be traced back to the nineteenth century and which would become decisive for the direction of study in the decades that followed, namely the desire for a comprehensive coverage and comparison of the extant textual witnesses.

Sperber himself thought it desirable to include manuscripts representative of every textual tradition,[105] and to this end his editions incorporated at different points in the texts variant readings from Yemenite (Or. 1474, 1473, Or. 2371, British Library, London; Or. qu. 578, Staatsbibliothek, Preußischer Kulturbesitz, Berlin), Sephardi (Montefiore 7 [H116] then of the Montefiore Library, Jew's College, London), and Italian/Ashkenazi (Add. 26879, British Library, London; Codex Reuchlinianus No. 3 manuscripts, printed editions

---

103 Ferrer Costa, 'El Targum d'Osees en tradició Iemenita', 22–59.
104 He published a translation (in Catalan) with introductory notes on the basis of his critical edition in which he expressed his intention to publish the critical edition soon; Ferrer Costa, 'El Targum d'Osees. Traducció crítica catalana del text arameu'.
105 Sperber, *The Bible in Aramaic*, IVB, 143

Chapter One. *Status Quaestionis*

belonging to the Sephardi (Antwerp Polyglot; Leiria edition) and broadly Ashkenazi (First and Second Rabbinic Bibles) traditions, Yemenite haftarot (Sassoon 332, Letchworth; Or. 2364, Or. 1470 British Library, London), as well as citations of Targum in medieval Jewish literature.

Sperber's coverage was, however, far from exhaustive. In a particularly acerbic assault — in which he insisted that Sperber's editions did not even deserve the title '*critical*' — Dominique Barthélemy complained that the limited range of manuscripts employed by Sperber and his failure to offer any Tiberian vocalisation rendered it impossible to achieve a precise representation of the complexity of the textual situation.[106] The committee of the Hebrew Old Testament text project under Barthélemy's direction attempted to remedy the situation, but in the end the magnitude of the task meant that only two manuscripts (Or. Fol. 1–4, Staatsbibliothek, Preußischer Kulturbesitz, Berlin; Urbinati Ebr. 1, Biblioteca Apostolica, Vatican) as well as two editions of questionable value (Walton's Polyglot; *Mikraot Gedolot* ed. J.Levensohn and J.M.Mendelsohn, Warsaw 1860–6) could be added to those collated by Sperber, supplemented on occasion by other sources.[107] From among these witness, the committee attempted to reach its own conclusions concerning the Targum's original reading — indeed in certain cases differing Targum readings are evaluated in the critical notes[108] — but the quantity of data meant that only limited comparative work was possible and, in any case, the value of the Targum for text critical work on the Hebrew text proved to be limited since it generally supports the standard Masoretic Text.[109]

Barthélemy was not of course in the business of making a new edition of the Targums, yet the limited quantity of new material he was able to bring to the table serves as a reminder of exactly how herculean for a single scholar Sperber's undertaking had been. Even accepting that Sperber's coverage of the

---

106 Barthélemy, *Critique textuelle de l'Ancien Testament*, III, *Ézéchiel, Daniel et les 12 Prophètes*, ccix.

107 E.g. For the text of Isaiah he also consulted Ms. Hébreu 1325 (Bibliothèque Nationale, Paris) and Stenning's edition; for Jeremiah he consulted Ms. Heb. d.26 (Bodleian Library, Oxford; from Yeivin, *Genizah Bible fragments with Babylonian massorah and vocalisation*); Barthélemy, *Critique textuelle de l'Ancien Testament*, II, *Isaïe, Jérémie, Lamentations*, 65, 840.

108 E.g. D. Barthélemy, *Critique textuelle de l'Ancien Testament*, II, *Isaïe, Jérémie, Lamentations*, 829; Barthélemy, *Critique textuelle de l'Ancien Testament*, III, *Ézéchiel, Daniel et les 12 Prophètes*, 287, 638, 642, and elsewhere.

109 Barthélemy, *Critique textuelle de l'Ancien Testament*, III, *Ézéchiel, Daniel et les 12 Prophètes*, ccix.

extant materials was not exhaustive, that the logic behind his inclusion or omission of secondary materials is not clear, and that he often failed to report or misreported variants in the secondary sources,[110] we must nonetheless recognise that Sperber made available readings from multiple Western sources in a format that made (albeit limited) comparative study of Targum Jonathan's textual witnesses possible for the first time. More importantly his work made readily apparent to the wider scholarly audience how diverse the extant textual witnesses of Targum Jonathan were and how badly needed a truly exhaustive scientific edition still was — and indeed still is.

To date, no edition has appeared that provides a complete picture of the textual situation, so, as Gordon noted, 'if some cannot do with Sperber, few of us can do without him'.[111] Nonetheless, others have brought more raw textual data into the scholarly domain. Levine published an edition of the Targum to Jonah in 1975, which took manuscript Urbinati Ebr. 1 (Vatican) as its base text — a choice that is difficult to regard as anything other than arbitrary[112] — and recorded 'for control purposes' variant readings from sources 'representing the various European and North African stemmata'.[113] More recently Ribera Florit has also stressed the need to compare the Eastern and Western text traditions and to evaluate the textual variants.[114] To this end he included multiple Western sources in an apparatus to his editions of

---

110 See Gordon, 'Sperber's Edition of the Targum to the Prophets: a Critique', 319–20; Díez Merino, 'Targum Manuscripts and Critical Editions', 72–3; A. Houtman, 'Textual Tradition of Targum Jonathan to Isaiah', in J. Targarona Borrás (ed.), *Jewish Studies at the Turn of the Twentieth Century: Proceedings of the 6th EAJS congress, Toledo, July 1998*, Vol. 2 (Leiden 1999), 145–53, p. 146.

111 Gordon, 'Alexander Sperber and the Study of the Targums', 92. For example, although able to work from his own edition of the text, Ribera Florit still supplemented this with the variants from Sperber in *Traducción del Targum de Jeremías*.

112 Levine acknowledges that 'the ultimate scientific *desideratum*' is an edition based on text(s) with Babylonian vocalisation. He therefore rejects Sperber's edition because it is based on a manuscript with 'contaminated *Yemenite* vocalisation'. But he also acknowledges that this goal is unattainable in the case of Jonah because only a single fragment covering Jon. 3:5–4:11 remains (which he records in an appendix). Levine ostensibly chooses Urbinati Ebr. 1 (Biblioteca Apostolica, Vatican) because it is 'one of the most competently written, and it contains a complete text'. This is hardly the solution to the problem he identifies. É. Levine, *The Aramaic Version of Jonah*, (Jerusalem 1975), 22–5.

113 Levine, *The Aramaic Version of Jonah*, 23. But not all of the manuscripts are easy to identify on the basis of his references.

114 Ribera Florit, 'Targum de Joel', 274.

Zephaniah, Nahum, and Joel.[115]

The desire to offer a more comprehensive coverage of the extant textual witnesses had not been alien to earlier editions either of course. Silberman's 1902 edition of a Yemenite text, for example, incorporated variant readings from multiple sources, as I mentioned above (page 14). A few years prior, in 1895, Adler had presented an initial attempt at a new edition (publishing a specimen of the text of Nahum) intended as a means of addressing the shortcomings of the previous printed editions — though he was cautious not to call it a 'critical edition', preferring instead 'collated text'.[116] Adler presented the text of Walton's Polyglot — an unworthy choice — with a critical apparatus containing variant readings from five manuscripts and several printed editions accompanied by occasional critical notes.[117] Adler punctuated the text himself, following Levy,[118] noting that the texts varied considerably in terms of their punctuation and were therefore unreliable.[119] Adler gives no reason for his choice of manuscript.

******

These editions provided Targum scholars with raw data, which in turn needed to be analysed in order to map the text's transmission on a chronological and geographical matrix, against which one might judge the value of each source from both a text-critical as well as a cultural-historal perspective. Sperber himself was the first to be able to attempt such an analysis on the basis of his

---

115 Zephaniah and Nahum: First and Second Rabbinic Bible, Montefiore 7 [H 116] (Montefiore Endowment), Codex Reuchlinianus No. 3, Antwerp Polyglot, Ms. Or. 2211 (British Library, London). Ribera Florit, 'La versión aramaica del profeta Nahum;' Ribera Florit 'La versión aramaica del profeta Sofonías.' Joel: Urbinati Ebr. 1 (Biblioteca Apostolica, Vatican), Codex Solger (Stadtbibliothek, Nürnberg), and 'Alfonso de Zamora manuscripts' (he does not specify which, presumably Ms. M1-M3, Biblioteca de la Universitaria, Salamanca; Ms. 7542, Biblioteca Nacional, Madrid). Ribera Florit, 'Targum de Joel.'

116 Adler, 'A Specimen of a Commentary and Collated Text of the Targum to the Prophets. Nahum', 630.

117 The manuscripts concerned were: Add. 26879, Or. 2211, and Or. 1474 (British Library, London), Montefiore 7 [H 116] (then of the Montefiore Library, Jew's College); and Opp. Add. 76 (Bodleian Library, Oxford). In addition to these five manuscripts Adler recorded variants found in de Lagarde's edition of Codex Reuchlinianus No. 3, the First Rabbinic Bible, the Antwerp Polyglot, and a 1866 printing of the *Mikraoth Gedoloth*.

118 J. Levy, *Chaldäisches Wörterbuch über die Targumim und einen grossen Theil des Rabbinischen Schriftthums* (Leipzig 1867–8).

119 Adler, 'A Specimen of a Commentary and Collated Text of the Targum to the Prophets. Nahum', 630–1.

own collation of the textual witnesses. In the final volume of his series of editions, *The Bible in Aramaic*, volume 4B, Sperber offers some observations concerning the transmission of the Targum, based on his collation of numerous texts (much of which is mere repetition of material he had published nearly half a century earlier or material drawn from his 1924 doctoral thesis[120]). He observed two phenomena that had affected the shape of the Targum text in the process of transmission: correction and the incorporation of marginal material.

Later copyists (or editors) had attempted to 'improve' the text, Sperber argued, by correcting it, thereby disfiguring the original characteristics of the Targum. Such 'improvements' normally attempted to reflect more closely the underlying Hebrew, for example by employing the corresponding Hebrew word in an Aramaised form, ensuring that a Hebrew word is always translated by the same Aramaic equivalent (sometimes to the detriment of the sense), or even imitation of the consecutive *waw* (implying a less than perfect grasp of the function of *waw consecutivum* in Hebrew).[121] This phenomenon was the result of two factors: 'the gradual decline of the understanding of the grammatical and lexicographical characteristics of the Aramaic language', which began when Aramaic ceased to be a language spoken by the Jews, on the one hand, and the 'gradually increasing respect for and veneration of the exact wording of the Hebrew Bible' on the other.[122] By the time of Codex Reuchlinianus No. 3 these 'corrections' were already firmly embedded in the text and the younger the text the more obvious these changes were. Sperber even claimed that manuscripts with the super-linear vocalisation 'which in general represent the Targum in a more genuine form, are victims of this trend, too'.[123] This last point may be strictly true, but it may be more accurate to say that this occurs only in isolated cases in the Eastern tradition, whereas it is widespread in Western manuscripts.

---

120 A. Sperber, 'Zur Sprache des Prophetentargums', *Zeitschrift für die Alttestamentliche Wissenschaft* 45 (1927), 267–87; Sperber 'Zur Textgestalt des Prophetentargums', *Zeitschrift für die Alttestamentliche Wissenschaft* 44 (1926), 175–6. Cf. Díez Macho, review of 'Alexander Sperber, *The Bible in Aramaic*, IVB', 219.

121 Sperber, *The Bible in Aramaic*, IVB, 19, 27. This phenomenon is seen in several of the examples given in chapter three of Sperber's *The Bible in Aramaic*, IVB. Note that Sperber makes use of 21 manuscript sources for purposes of comparison here, many of which are not included in his editions (14 in the Former Prophet; 9 in Latter Prophets).

122 Sperber, *The Bible in Aramaic*, IVB, 23–4. A point already made in his 1926 article, 'Zur Textgestalt des Prophetentargums', 175.

123 Sperber, *The Bible in Aramaic*, IVB, 25, 28–9.

In addition to 'correction' of the text, Sperber gave a few examples of cases in which material that had originally stood in the margins — and still did in some of the witnesses — or that had been marked as an addition by the heading 'tosefta' had subsequently been incorporated into the running text without indication.[124]

A third phenomenon observed by Sperber in the process of comparing the materials he collated was that of 'doublets', where some textual witnesses have two (or more) words to represent a single word in the Hebrew text, while other textual witnesses have only one. Sperber understood this phenomenon as reflecting the work of two schools of translators, one who defined their task as providing a 'literal translation', from which they deviated only for the sake of clarity or to demonstrate the validity of rabbinic interpretation, while the second handled the text in a more 'Midrash-like' fashion.[125] This explanation reflects a rather naïve and ahistorical handling of the materials and is as a result more complicated than is necessary. These cases can be explained much more simply in one of two ways: one possibility is that a copyist combined the reading of two manuscripts;[126] a second possibility is that the original reading of the Targum had two words where the Hebrew text had only one: in one of the two manuscripts that Sperber compared, one of these two words has been omitted (either to reflect more closely the Hebrew text or simply in error).

In his introduction to his edition of the Targum to Jonah, which I mentioned above (page 30), Levine offers some generalities concerning the textual variants in the manuscripts he collated. 'Targum manuscripts differ one from another in text, orthography and matters of syntax and morphology', he writes. 'The textual variants include independent readings, fuller readings and order (inversion and transposition). Grammatical variants involve orthography (particularly defective versus vocalic rendition, indication of the tetragrammaton and abbreviations), phonetics (vocalisation particularly), morphology (including verb forms, nouns, prepositions, adverbs and conjunctions), and variant syntax. Scribal errors include omissions (primarily homeoteleuta) and grammatical errors (involving gender, number, prepositions and suffixes)'. These differences did not, however, obscure the manuscripts'

---

124 Sperber, *The Bible in Aramaic*, IVB, 4–5.
125 Sperber, *The Bible in Aramaic*, IVB, 3 (examples: 191–2).
126 Smelik, 'Orality, Manuscript Reproduction, and the Targums', 77; Smelik, 'Trouble in the Trees!', 262–6.

basic homogeneity: 'the various manuscripts' he concludes, 'all contain the same essential text in different recensions'.[127]

A student of Díez Macho, Luis Díez Merino, attempted in an article of 1993 to characterise Targum Jonathan's transmission history more broadly. He argued that the Targum to the Prophets has been transmitted in three separate versions: one Babylonian (i.e. the 'official' Targum), one Palestinian, preserved in some Genizah fragments, and one fragmentary (i.e. the marginalia of Codex Reuchlinianus No. 3). The Babylonian version, he claimed, has been transmitted in three different traditions: Babylonian, Yemenite, and Tiberian.[128] But, as Ribera Florit pointed out, such a characterisation of Targum Jonathan's history is rather jumbled. There are not three versions, but two: one complete and essentially Eastern, one fragmentary and essentially Palestinian; nor are there three Masoretic traditions, but two: one essentially Babylonian and one Tiberian. The tradition that Díez Merino had called Yemenite can not truly be regarded as a tradition. Rather, its consonantal tradition is to be identified with the Eastern tradition while its Masoretic tradition belongs fundamentally to the Tiberian Masoretic tradition, with remnants of the Babylonian (a *mixtum compositum*). Equally there are cases in which Babylonian vocalisation has been transposed into Tiberian signs.[129]

A year later Díez Merino published a further article ('Targum Manuscripts and Critical Editions') addressing the question of how comprehensive coverage of the extant textual witnesses should be realised within a new critical edition. He argued that each textual tradition needed to be presented separately, with its *stemma codicum* showing 'a panoramic sketch of the copies stemming from an original', and with all the witnesses of the family quoted in the critical apparatus.[130] In principle, this is wise counsel, but again Díez Merino's language is imprecise so that it is difficult to envisage how he intended this to be realised in a methodologically sound way.

First, he insists on the need to distinguish the consonantal text traditions

---

127 Levine, *The Aramaic Version of Jonah*, 22–4.
128 Díez Merino, 'La triple recensión del Targum a los Profetas (babilónica, yemení y palestina) con sus tres tradiciones (babilónica, yemení y tiberiense)', in H. Merklein, K. Müller and G. Stemberger (eds), *Bibel in jüdischer und christlicher Tradition: Festschrift für Johann Maier zum 60 Geburtstag* (Bonner biblische Beiträge 88, Frankfurt am Main 1993), 275–98.
129 J. Ribera Florit, 'Punctualizciones sobre las diversas recensiones y tradiciones del Targum de los Profetas', *Anuari de Filologia*, E, *Estudis hebreus i arameus* 15 (1993), 149–53, pp. 152–3.
130 Díez Merino, 'Targum Manuscripts and Critical Editions', 51, 91.

from 'the linguistic form in which they are transmitted' (i.e. their vocalisation).[131] He then goes on to argue for a division of the materials of Targum Jonathan into five traditions, each of which must be handled separately according to the schema mentioned above: Babylonian, Yemenite, Babylonian-Tiberian (in which the Babylonian vocalisation had been transposed into Tiberian vowel signs), Sephardic and Tiberian.[132] This is perplexing: in dividing the materials in this way Díez Merino mixes arbitrarily the two traditions (i.e. consonants and vocalisation) that he insisted we must distinguish ('if we do not distinguish them, we will be confused'[133]). 'Babylonian-Tiberian' is to be distinguished from the 'Tiberian' because of the character of its vocalisation, while the Sephardic tradition is to be distinguished from the Tiberian (presumably) because of distinctive variants in the consonantal text.

Díez Merino was undoubtedly correct to claim that the Sephardic tradition 'has its own identity'[134] (see below), but his use of such categories is nonetheless problematic. In discussing how the 'Tiberian' tradition might best be presented he suggests three possibilities: 1) Select a chief manuscript for each of the three parts of the Bible (he suggests Codex Reuchlinianus No. 3 for Targum Jonathan); 2) Select the most important manuscript for each book and then collate this with manuscripts 'that can offer the most likely variants within the same tradition'; and finally, 3) look for a good manuscript of the entire Aramaic Bible and afterwards collate this with the most important families in a 'stemma codicum'. He suggests three possibilities: manuscript Urbinati Ebr. 1 (Biblioteca Apostolica, Vatican), the Second Rabbinic Bible, or one of Alphonso de Zamora's (Sephardi!) manuscripts.[135] Do Alphonso de Zamora's manuscripts belong then to the Tiberian or the Sephardi tradition or both? Díez Merino muddles his own categories of textual traditions.

Equally, we need to set a question mark next to his assertion that the Sephardi text tradition is 'very old and correct' (not least because he gives no indication as to how old 'very old' is), since his research only shows that those

---

131 Although his argument is hard to follow because he also includes genuine Palestinian Targums under the category 'Western tradition', along with Western manuscripts of Targum Jonathan (he mentions Urbinati Ebr. 1); Díez Merino, 'Targum Manuscripts and Critical Editions', 62–8.
132 Díez Merino, 'Targum Manuscripts and Critical Editions', esp. 76–7, 91.
133 Díez Merino, 'Targum Manuscripts and Critical Editions', 62.
134 Díez Merino, 'Targum Manuscripts and Critical Editions', 77.
135 Díez Merino, 'Targum Manuscripts and Critical Editions', 75–6.

manuscripts produced in the early sixteenth century on the orders of Cardinal Cisneros were probably faithful replicas of the manuscripts they copied (their *Vorlagen*), a fact that bespeaks only a single stage in the transmission process (and then the very latest stage of manual transmission) rather than the tradition as a whole.[136]

******

Fulfilling the need to achieve a more comprehensive coverage of the extant materials and to establish the relationship between all the available materials by placing them onto a family tree using scientific methodologies — the necessity of which was foreseen by Merx over a century ago[137] — has been one of the principal achievements of the 'Kampen School'.

For the past two decades scholars based at the Protestant Theological University of the Netherlands, located in Kampen, have sought in various research projects and publications to give a more complete picture of the textual situation, which in turn might allow a complete transmission history of Targum Jonathan to be reconstructed.

The first results saw the light of day with the publication, in 1995, of Smelik's doctoral thesis under the title *The Targum of Judges*. Based on a survey of catalogues Smelik identified 24 substantially complete manuscripts

---

136 This claim is based on the identification of one of the exemplars used for the reproduction of Targum Onqelos; L. Díez Merino, 'Fidelity and Editorial Work in the Complutensian Targum Tradition', in J.A. Emerton (ed.), *Congress Volume - Leuven 1989* (Supplements to Vetus Testamentum 43, Leiden 1991), 360–82, p. 382. Cf. Smelik, *The Targum of Judges*, 642, who concluded that the character of the variants in the Sephardi tradition pointed to a 'relatively late' text. N.B. The Targum of the Prophets was not included in the Complutensian Polyglot, but Cardinal Cisneros ordered translations from Aramaic into Latin of all the Old Testament books to be made; Díez Merino, 'Fidelity and Editorial work in the Complutensian Targum Tradition', 363. See further, Díez Merino, 'La Biblia aramea de Alfonso de Zamora', *Cuadernos bíblicos* 7 (1981), 63–98, p. 95 (on Zamora's life pp. 63–70, works pp. 70–98); Díez Merino, 'La Biblia aramea completa de la Universidad de Salamanca', *Helmantica* (2001), 173–227; Díez Merino, 'Targum del profeta Zacarías en la tradición sefardí', *Aula Orientalis* 17–18 (1999–2000), 269–85 (reproduces text of M-2, Biblioteca de la Universitaria, Salamanca, collating where legible Villa-Amil 4, Biblioteca Complutense Madrid, both by Zamora); Díez Merino, 'Los manuscritos targúmicos españoles', in R. Aguirre and F. García López (eds), *Escritos de Biblia y oriente: miscelánea conmemorativa del 25.o aniversario del Instituto Español Bíblico y Arqueológico (Casa de Santiago) de Jerusalén* (Bibliotheca Salmanticensis. Estudios 38, Salamanca 1981), 359–86, (a list of manuscripts and printed editions from Spain. Mostly repeating material published elsewhere).

137 Merx, 'Bemerkungen über die Vocalisation der Targume', 170.

of the Targum to Judges, five of which were Yemenite, the remainder of Western provenance, in addition to more than one hundred fragments and haftarot collections. Since Martínez Borobio had presented the Eastern textual tradition, Smelik focussed on collating Western texts. Some manuscripts could be only partially collated or had to be excluded from analysis either for practical reasons or due to the poor quality of the transmission.[138] As well as discussing many of their variant readings in the body of his commentary, Smelik incorporated these additional sources into a 'provisional' *stemma codicum*. By evaluating the textual divergencies and agreements between the manuscripts he aimed 'to achieve a clear picture of the textual development of T[argum] Jon[athan] Judges through its material witnesses and the position of the manuscripts along the actual line(s) of development'.[139]

He began this process by eliminating those variants that were inconsistently dealt with in most manuscripts, often simply reflecting the whim of individual scribes. This included orthographic variants, preferences for די or ד- or final א or ה, the interchange of שׂ and ס, and the use of *matres lectionis,* which he found were sometimes omitted simply to fit the available space on a line.[140] Except in cases where it presupposed a correction of the consonantal text (e.g., לָהּ when ליה should have been written), the vocalisation was of questionable value for establishing the relationships between manuscripts and was therefore also to be excluded from the analysis. There were two reasons for this: first, the vocalisation and consonants did not necessarily derive from the same hand and may in some cases be derived from distinct *Vorlagen*; and secondly, the neglect of Targumic Aramaic among European Jews meant that the Western Targum manuscripts contained many inconsistencies and errors.[141]

Smelik then employed six criteria against which the agreements and deviations between the manuscripts could be measured and the relationship

---

138 Mss B.H. III Biblioteca Civica Berio, Genoa (poorly legible microfilm); Ms Hébreu 75, Bibliothèque Nationale, Paris (microfilm obtained too late); Ms Or. fol. 1210, 1211 Staatsbibliothek, Berlin (under restoration); Ms A.46 Sachsische Landesbibliothek, Dresden (unreadable due to damage); Kennicott 471, Biblioteca Apostolica, Vatican (lost). Due to poor quality of transmission: Ms parm 3187, 3188, 3189, Biblioteca Palatine, Parma.
139 Smelik, *The Targum of Judges*, 113–30 (citation: 130).
140 Smelik, *The Targum of Judges*, 130–1. Cf. the phenomenon noted in t701i whereby the last word of one page is repeated at the start of the next page sometimes with a variant spelling, see page 94.
141 Smelik, *The Targum of Judges*, 131–2.

between the manuscripts could be established: (1) Pluses; (2) Minuses; (3) Substitutions; (4) Modifications; (5) Errors; (6) Tosefta Targums. He identified a number of readings common to the majority of the Western manuscripts and deviating from the Eastern text in almost all its textual witnesses, so that the Western textual tradition can be distinguished as a whole from the Eastern.[142] Smelik found, however, that the Western textual tradition was much less consistent than the Eastern. 'The Western Text' he concluded 'accommodated more freedom to change the text (i.e. substitution, supplementation and subsequent reduction of pluses) than the Eastern Text'.[143] Such accommodation of the text included revisions either towards (a sometimes variant) Hebrew text or on the basis of exegetical traditions, and the tendency to 'parallelisation' (i.e. associative and complementary translation techniques) and to harmonise readings.[144] The Eastern textual tradition was marked, by contrast, by a high degree of internal consistency, with the Yemenite manuscripts showing only occasional traces of the influence of the Hebrew text or improvements or harmonisation within the text of Targum Jonathan.[145]

Within the Western tradition itself Smelik was able to identify several distinct textual groupings. The first consisted of four manuscripts all of Sephardi provenance, exhibiting a high degree of commonality (Smelik uses the term 'very homogeneous'), thereby confirming the existence of a distinct Sephardic tradition. Some of the distinct readings of Sephardi tradition clearly represent grammatical improvements or adjustments towards the Hebrew text, suggesting that the tradition is late relative to the other traditions.[146]

Although the Ashkenazi manuscripts proved to be 'not very homogeneous', Smelik was nonetheless able to distinguish two sub-groups, adding the cautionary note that 'at least one of these groups is far from self-evident, and both of them share many readings with the Sephardi textual tradition'. The first

---

142 Smelik, *The Targum of Judges*, 132–3.
143 Smelik, *The Targum of Judges*, 187.
144 Smelik, *The Targum of Judges*, 643.
145 Interestingly his analysis placed the consonantal text of Or. 2210 (British Library) closer to the Babylonian fragments than the remaining Yemenite manuscripts, suggesting on this basis that its text might be older; Smelik, *The Targum of Judges*, 642.
146 Smelik, *The Targum of Judges*, 134, 642–3. The manuscripts are: Ms 1, Bibliotheca Antigua de la Universitaria, Salamanca (Alcalá de Henares, Spain; 1532 CE); Ms 7542, Biblioteca Nacional, Madrid (Spain, 1533 CE); Opp Add 4° 75, Bodleian Library, Oxford (Soria or Tudela, Spain; *c.* 1300 CE); 'Kennicott 5', Bodleian Library, Oxford (Segovia, Spain; 1487 CE).

of these sub-groups consisted of five manuscripts. It showed agreement with the Sephardi group in some readings and inconsistencies within the group in terms of the Tosefta Targums.[147] Of the second Ashkenazi group Smelik says, 'though it is convenient to treat the remaining M[anuscripts]... as a separate group, they do not constitute a family in the true sense of the word'. Their homogeneity as a group consisted principally in a negative characteristic (i.e. not agreeing with readings distinct to another group), rather than a positive one (i.e. shared variant readings). Occasionally all four witnesses diverge. Analysis of the group was further problematised by the fact that two of the manuscripts (11 Stiftsbibliothek, Göttweig = t725a; Or. 72, Biblioteca Angelica, Rome = t701i) were unreliable as textual witnesses. Smelik therefore admitted the possibility that the manuscripts belonging to this group constitute 'no group at all, but simply share readings common to the hypothetical Old Western Text, or an early subdivision of that text-type'. One manuscript in particular (11 Stiftsbibliothek Göttweig= t725a) contained many 'cross-readings' (i.e. it sometimes agrees with the Sephardi group, sometimes with the first Ashkenazi group) and often attested unique readings.[148]

Smelik qualified his grouping of the text (i.e. 'stemma') with the adjective 'provisional', since the material itself made the task far from certain. The relatively small number of manuscripts made it difficult to establish statistical probability; the poor state of the text's transmission resulted in a great deal of 'noise' in the form of numerous errors; and finally, 'developments in any one direction could be reversed at a later stage, for example when obvious errors were corrected later by a trained scribe, such as accidental Hebraisms'.[149] Nonetheless, his analysis results in plausible

---

147 Smelik, *The Targum of Judges*, 142. Or. Fol. 1–4, Staatsbibliothek, Preußischer Kulturbesitz, Berlin (Ashkenaz; fourteenth century); Codex Solger, Stadtbibliothek, Nürnberg (Ashkenazi; 1291); El. f.6, Thüringer Universitäts- und Landesbibliothek, Jena (Ashkenaz; thirteenth/fourteenth century); Hébreu 18, Bibliothèque Nationale, Paris (Ashkenaz; fourteenth–fifteenth century). Ms B.H. III, Genoa (Ashkenazi, 1467) was included in the group only tentatively because Smelik was only able to collate the first five chapters, though even then the quality of the microfilm made collation difficult. See Smelik, *The Targum of Judges*, 126–7.

148 Smelik, *The Targum of Judges*, 142–3, 147 (citation: 147). The manuscripts are: Ms 11, Stiftsbibliothek, Göttweig (Ashkenaz; fourteenth century); Urbinati Ebr. 1, Biblioteca Apostolica Vatican (Ashkenaz; *c.* 1294 CE); Laud. Or. 326, Bodleian Library, Oxford (Ashkenazi; twelfth century); Or. 72, Biblioteca Angelica, Rome (Frascati, Italy; 1326 CE).

149 Smelik, *The Targum of Judges*, 130.

groupings. The broad division between manuscripts of Sephardi and Ashkenazi provenance reflects the geographical realities of late medieval European Jewry, suggesting the general validity of the results, even noting the presence of some readings that crop up in manuscripts belonging to more than one group ('cross-readings').[150]

In 2002 a second doctoral thesis emerged from the Kampen School, this time from the hand of Eveline van Staalduine-Sulman, which took the two books of Samuel as its subject matter. Van Staalduine-Sulman conducted a survey of catalogues and was able to identify 25 substantially complete manuscripts of the Targum of Samuel, of which Sperber had used only seven. From among these 25, van Staalduine-Sulman made a selection of manuscripts based on two criteria: first that the manuscript did not contain a large number of errors, and secondly, that the manuscript was not closely related to one of the manuscripts used by Sperber.[151] The result was that six complete manuscripts were selected.[152] Van Staalduine-Sulman collated in full some selected chapters from these manuscripts and scanned the remainder for exegetical variants.[153] In addition, she consulted some additional fragments and haftarot collections that had not been included in the editions of Sperber, Martínez Borobio, or in Kasher's edition of Tosefta Targums, with the result that she found a few minor exegetical variants not registered in those editions.[154] Van Staalduine-Sulman dealt with a number of the textual variants found in these manuscripts in the body of the commentary; she noted briefly three types of 'copyist's interference' that recurred throughout the manuscripts, namely the 'correction' of the Targum text (sometimes towards the Hebrew text), conflated readings (where two readings are combined), and the

---

150 Smelik, *The Targum of Judges*, 149–50.
151 van Staalduine-Sulman, *The Targum of Samuel*, 50 n. 11.
152 Or. Fol. 1–4, Staatsbibliothek, Preußischer Kulturbesitz, Berlin (Ashkenaz; fourteenth century); B.H. III–IV, Biblioteca Civica Berio, Genoa (Ashkenaz; 1466/67 CE); Parma 3187, Biblioteca Palatina, Parma (Ashkenaz; thirteenth/fourteenth century); El. f.6, Thüringer Universitäts- und Landesbibliothek, Jena (Ashkenaz; thirteenth/fourteenth century); 'Kennicott 5', Bodleian Library, Oxford (Segovia, Spain; 1487 CE); Or. 72, Biblioteca Angelica, Rome (Frascati, Italy; 1326 CE).
153 The selection of chapters consisted of all the haftarot both of the annual and triennial cycle, special haftarot, and five further passages as a check. In sum, the following chapters were collated entirely: 1 Samuel 1–2, 4–6, 9, 11–12, 15–17, 20–1, 2 Sam. 5:11–7:29; 21–23:8, 24.
154 See, van Staalduine-Sulman, *The Targum of Samuel*, 49–51, 53–8.

introduction of Tosefta Targums.[155] An extensive analysis of the mutual relationship between the manuscripts and an assessment of their value for reconstructing ancient forms of the text, however, lay outside the scope of van Staalduine-Sulman's already extensive monograph.

To these two should be added the revised form of my own doctoral thesis, which studies the interpretation of Ezek. 28:11–19 in rabbinic and patristic sources, in the principal ancient Versions, and in the Targum. The production of a truly critical text lay outside the scope of that study, but I was nonetheless able to consult 23 manuscripts on microfilm or digital image, plus the single fragment that was of relevance from the Cambridge Cairo Genizah collection. I used the stemmata produced by Houtman and van Staalduine-Sulman to give an indicative grouping of the manuscripts. This was far from ideal, since these studies were based on other books of Targum Jonathan (i.e. Samuel, Isaiah), but it seemed preferable to a grouping based simply on each manuscript's provenance, which may be unreliable.[156] Excluding errors and insignificant variants, I proposed some minor emendations to the text based on the remaining variants, prioritising readings from Eastern manuscripts, then the Italian and Sephardi groups, and finally the Ashkenazi group.[157] As textual studies of Targum Jonathan develop and a comprehensive critical edition is eventually produced, these results may need to be revised.

The direction that the creation of stemmata for the Targum text would eventually need to take was initially signalled by Houtman, who in 1999 published an important paper in which she presented the results of her own analysis of the Targum of Isaiah that made use of established models employed in stemmatological research in other disciplines. Given the quantity of data, there was a clear need to create a reliable stemma 'without having to scrutinise all the textual material first'. One practical solution was to begin with the continuous text tradition, using all the available manuscripts, the first two Rabbinic Bibles, and the Babylonian traditions (according to Ribera Florit's edition, combining the fragments into a 'virtual' manuscript for practical reasons), and to base the analysis on a sampling of the text. The criteria for the

---

155 van Staalduine-Sulman, *The Targum of Samuel*, 129–31.
156 Houtman, 'Textual Tradition of Targum Jonathan to Isaiah', 152. But see my comments on p. 362.
157 H.M. Patmore, *Adam, Satan, and the King of Tyre: The Interpretation of Ezekiel 28:11–19 in Late Antiquity* (Jewish and Christian Perspectives 20, Leiden 2012). 87–101.

selection of sample units were that they should be representative of the whole manuscript and should avoid theologically controversial pericopes and the beginning or end of textual units, which are more likely to have become the subject of later rewriting.[158]

Houtman subjected these sample units to the established stemmatological analysis known as the 'three-step method'.[159] Using this method the manuscripts are first clustered into subfamilies based purely on quantitative grounds (step 1); manuscripts that may have been intermediary in the process of transmission are then identified (step 2), which establishes a chain of relationships between the witnesses; and, finally, the direction of the relationship is determined by identifying the 'root' of the genealogical tree on qualitative grounds (step 3). In short, the first two steps calculated the affinity between the witnesses, while the value of the variants is established in the final stage.[160]

By the application of this method to the text of Isaiah, Houtman separated the manuscripts into four groups: an Eastern tradition, a Sephardi tradition, a tradition connected to the Rabbinic Bibles, and an Ashkenazi tradition. The manuscripts belonging to the Eastern tradition were all remarkably close to one another, with the distinction between Yemenite and Babylonian traditions only to be seen in the vocalisation. Or. 2211 (British Library) stood extremely close to the Babylonian Fragments, vindicating Sperber's choice of this manuscript as his base text (see above, pages 16, 21). By contrast, the Western tradition is much more heterogeneous, with the Ashkenazi manuscripts forming a distict grouping more on account of their differences from manuscripts in other groups than by their mutual likeness. The remaining two groups showed a greater degree of cohesion. The Sephardi cluster contained only Sephardi manuscripts, so made sense on external grounds too. The printed editions and Codex Solger (Stadtbibliothek, Nürnberg) formed a distinct cluster, which belonged to the Western tradition, but did not show 'a clear kinship to either the Ashkenazi or the Sephardi tradition', to the extent that Houtman regarded it as a separate group.[161] At this stage in her research, Houtman understood the

---

158 Houtman, 'Textual tradition of Targum Jonathan to Isaiah', 146–7 (citation: 146).
159 Orthographic variants, abbreviations, and vocalisation were not taken into account; Houtman, 'Textual Tradition of Targum Jonathan to Isaiah', 148–50.
160 Houtman, 'Textual Tradition of Targum Jonathan to Isaiah', 148–9.
161 Houtman, 'Textual tradition of Targum Jonathan to Isaiah,' 149–52 (citation: 151). The groups

data to point to Codex Solger and the First Rabbinic Bible being 'indirectly related through a common ancestor', though subsequent study led her to modify this view to conclude that the relationship was one of 'direct and complete dependency of the First Rabbinic Bible on Codex Solger'.[162] Her study of the differences between the First and Second Rabbinic Bible indicated that the editor of the Second Rabbinic Bible, Jacob ben Hayyim, had employed more Sephardi manuscripts than his predecessor, Felix Pratensis.[163]

Several of the manuscripts did not fit into any of the groups. Manuscript Hébreu 96 (Bibliothèque Nationale, Paris), although written in Spain in a Sephardi semi-cursive script with sub-linear vocalisation, stood closer to the Yemenite than to the Sephardi text tradition. Houtman suggested that this may be an eclectic text, based on different exemplars, an assumption that was corroborated by the occurrence of variant readings introduced by the formulae תרגום ירושלמי and תרגום אחר. The Ashkenazi manuscript Or. fol. 2 (Staatsbibliothek, Preußischer Kulturbesitz, Berlin) did not conform to any group, perhaps because of the high quantity of errors it contained. Parma 3188 (Biblioteca Patatina, Parma) and Add. 26879 (British Library, London) were both carelessly written and contained many errors.[164]

******

These groundbreaking studies made readily apparent just how important the selection and weighting of variants would be for the reliability of any given stemma. Furthermore they highlighted some of the idiosyncrasies of the

---

are as follows: Group 1 (Eastern tradition): Cluster A — Babylonian Fragments; Or. 2211 (British Library, London); Hébreu 1325 (Bibliothèque Nationale, Paris); Cluster B — Gaster 673 (John Rylands Library, Manchester); Or. 1474 (British Library, London); Lutzki 239 (Jewish Theological Seminary, New York); Cluster C — Qafih 5 (Yosef Qafih collection). Group 2 ('broadly Sephardi tradition'): Cluster A — Codex Solger (Stadtbibliothek, Nürnberg), First Rabbinic Bible; Second Rabbinic Bible; Cluster B — Montefiore 7 [H 116] (Montefiore Endowment); Kaufmann A13 (Hungarian Academy of Science, Budapest); Hébreu 75 (Bibliothèque Nationale, Paris); Opp. Add 4° 76 (Bodleian Library, Oxford); Villa Amil 4 (Biblioteca Complutense, Madrid). Group 3 (Ashkenazi tradition): Hébreu 18 (Bibliothèque Nationale, Paris); Codex Reuchlinianus No. 3; El. f.6 (Universitätsbibliothek, Jena); Urbinati Ebr. 1 (Biblioteca Apostolica, Vatican); Ms 11 (Stiftsbibliothek, Göttweig); B.H. V (Biblioteca Civica Berio, Genoa).

162 Houtman, 'Targum Isaiah according to Felix Pratensis', 202; 'Textual Tradition of Targum Jonathan to Isaiah', 151.
163 Houtman, 'Textual Tradition of Targum Jonathan to Isaiah', 151.
164 Houtman, 'Textual Tradition of Targum Jonathan to Isaiah', 152.

Targum text, which future stemmatological analysis would need to take into account. This problem was addressed by Smelik, Houtman and van Staalduine-Sulman, in a number of subsequent articles.

In a study presented in 2000 to *l'Association internationale Bible et informatique* conference ('How to Grow a Tree', published 2002), Smelik sought to refine further the categories employed in the qualitative stage of the production of a stemma, by examining the value for establishing genealogical relationships between textual witnesses (both manuscripts and editions) of shifts in orthography, shared errors, the use of abbreviated forms, and the separation or contraction of particles. He examined these features in two closely related manuscripts, namely M1-M3 (Biblioteca de la Universitaria, Salamanca) and Ms. 7542 (Biblioteca Nacional, Madrid), which were copied in 1532 and 1533 respectively by a single scribe, Alfonso de Zamora, and in the First and Second Rabbinic Bibles. His analysis demonstrated that in most cases variants belonging to these categories are due to the copyists, or, in the case of errors and their correction in particular, could have been arrived at independently at different points in the transmission. Yet while vocalisation, the separation and contraction of particles, and abbreviations are of no value at all in the process of forming a stemma since they merely reflect scribal convention and sometimes typographical considerations, variations in orthography and common errors can sometimes support a relationship established on the basis of other criteria though they cannot serve to establish a genealogical relationship. For example, Smelik notes an odd variant reading in the First Rabbinic Bible that results from the filling out of an abbreviation in Codex Solger (Stadtbibliothek, Nürnberg); this confirms the relationship between the two texts, in spite of their differing.[165]

Several further types of variant readings were dealt with in two further studies that aimed to sift out the 'purely random' variants from those that genuinely disclosed patterns and tendencies.[166] In his 'Orality, manuscript reproduction, and the Targums' (2003) Smelik identifies a number of

---

165 W. Smelik, 'How to Grow a Tree: Computerised Stemmatology and Variant Selection in Targum Studies', in J. Cook (ed.), *Bible and Computer: the Stellenbosch AIBI-6 Conference: Proceedings of the Association Internationale Bible et Informatique, 'From alpha to byte'*, University of Stellenbosch, 17–21 July, 2000 (Leiden 2002), 502–15 (note 514 n54). Cf. Smelik, 'Trouble in the Trees!', 255–6.
166 Smelik, 'Trouble in the Trees!', 251.

'corrections' introduced, often haphazardly, by the scribes, including the harmonisation of perceived discrepancies between the Aramaic and the Hebrew text either deliberately or subconsciously; the accidental introduction of the wording of the Hebrew (occasionally following non-standard manuscripts of the Hebrew text), marginal notations, the integration of alternative readings from other copies (i.e. 'conflations'), or traditional variants known by heart (i.e. memorised passages).[167] Changes to grammatical properties (such as gender, number, status and morphology), the omission or addition of the copulative or relative particle, and variations in the preposition, were also found to be in most cases either Hebraism or idiomatic; as such they likewise belong to this category of variants that were 'susceptible to multiple introduction' and therefore valueless in the stemmatological procedure.[168]

Having eliminated the 'noise', Smelik turned his attention in a second paper ('Trouble in the Trees!'), published in the same year, to describing those variants that would produce a more reliable family tree. He identified four such categories: pluses, minuses, substitutions, and semantic shifts (i.e. replacing one lexeme with a synonym or very near-synonym). Yet even within these categories he found a significant number of cases in which 'multiple introduction' could not be ruled out. Minuses and pluses frequently proved to be errors, sometimes through an attempted correction towards the Hebrew, as the result of standardised language (i.e. 'stereotyped phrasing', e.g. the addition of בית), or by the combination of the reading of two manuscripts resulting in an erroneous double translation (i.e. contamination).[169] 'Stereotyped phrasing' also caused verbs, nouns, and adjectives to be substituted, as did Hebrew variant readings and dialectic changes, which meant that the original term had become redundant.[170] Other substitutions and semantic shifts consisted of theological or exegetical changes inspired by non-textual considerations and were consequently

---

167 Smelik, 'Orality, Manuscript Reproduction, and the Targums', 76–80 (of these 'the Hebrew text underlying the Aramaic translation is a primary source for contamination of the Aramaic manuscripts', 78).
168 Smelik, 'Trouble in the Trees!', 256, 260, 266–8.
169 Smelik, 'Trouble in the Trees!', 263–6.
170 Smelik, 'Trouble in the Trees!', 260–1. I question the pertinence of this last point since Aramaic was no longer a living language one might say that all the Targum's language is in some sense 'redundant'.

unlikely to have arisen independently.[171]

Finally, Smelik put his proposed categories to the test using stemmatological models developed by Evert Wattel of the Free University in Amsterdam. Two tools were employed: similarity graphs, which show the relationships between the texts on the basis of each category of variant, and 'shock waves', which detect non-linear influences between the groups of textual witnesses, such as when a scribe switches from copying one exemplar to another at some point in his text (resulting in a *textus mixtus*).[172] In short, application of these mathematical models confirmed Smelik's hypothesis: the four categories, i.e. pluses, minuses, substitutions, and semantic shifts, once cases that might be an error or might reflect non-linear influences had been eliminated, produced the most reliable family tree.[173] Furthermore, one of the important outcomes of the 'shock wave' analysis was that it suggested that contamination was widespread among the Western textual witnesses. The contamination was not 'successive', where a scribe switches exemplar at some point in the text, but 'simultaneous and incidental', where a copyist consults a second exemplar either throughout the process of copying or sporadically. This is clear in the case of conflations, but Smelik suggested that a large number of the 'contaminations' were in fact the result of different scribes making the same 'corrections' to their texts independently under the influence of the Hebrew text, and so could be used in the process only with caution.[174]

In 2004 Houtman considered the value of Tosefta Targums (one of the six criteria used by Smelik in his 'provisional' stemma, see page 37) for establishing the 'kinship' relationship between manuscripts. To this end she compared the presence of Tosefta Targums in the text and in the margins (excluding the unique readings of Codex Reuchlinianus No. 3) to the stemma 'based on an unbiased sample of the witnesses', which her earlier study of the text of Targum Isaiah had produced ('Textual Tradition of Targum Jonathan to Isaiah'). This study revealed that, although *grosso modo* the distribution of Tosefta Targums reflected the established stemmatological groupings, there

---

171 Smelik, 'Trouble in the Trees!', 261–2. He refers to a set of semantic shifts in his *The Targum of Judges* 594–6, which relate to the interchange of the titles כהנא and כומרא (the Western texts are shown to offer the later reading).
172 Smelik, 'Trouble in the Trees!', 269.
173 Smelik, 'Trouble in the Trees!', 276–9, 283–4.
174 Smelik, 'Trouble in the Trees!', 279–81.

Chapter One. *Status Quaestionis*

were some notable exceptions that would skew the stemma if (as Smelik had done) they had been incorporated into the initial stage of stemma formation.[175]

In 2005 van Staalduine-Sulman published a study triggered by Smelik's pessimistic assessment of the value of vocalisation in the process of producing a stemma, which he had described as 'fraught with difficulties'.[176] Taking a sample survey of verses from only those manuscripts containing the continuous text, she constructed three separate stemmata (using the 'three-step method' already adopted by Houtman, see pages 41–2), one using the consonantal text, one the vowels, and one the pronunciation tradition that lay behind the vowels, which she was then able to compare.[177] The results of this analysis showed that 'pure vocalisation does not give reliable data, but pronunciation patterns do', since 'pronunciation patterns appear to be divided along the same lines as the consonantal patterns'. This held true even in cases where it seemed likely that the consonantal text and the vocalisation did not originate from the same hand, suggesting the presence of strong local traditions. The pronunciation could not, however, be used to establish relationships between manuscripts, but it could be of utility in refining a stemma produced on the basis of the consonants alone, in particular by confirming individual relationships between witnesses.[178]

In 2009 van Staalduine-Sulman made available online the results of a full stemmatological analysis of the consonantal text of Samuel.[179] Applying the criteria described in her earlier paper to 1 Samuel 1–3, she produced a stemma of 63 textual witnesses, including complete or substantially complete manuscripts, larger fragments, printed editions, and four Yemenite haftarot collections, selected at random in the hope of reaching well-founded conclusions about liturgical texts. Despite the presence of much contamination,

---

175 A. Houtman, 'Different Kinds of Tradition in Targum Jonathan to Isaiah', in P. van Reenen et al. (eds), *Studies in Stemmatology II* (Amsterdam and Philadelphia 2004), 269–83, pp. 276–9 (citation: 275).
176 van Staalduine-Sulman, 'Vowels in the Trees', (citation: 216).
177 The stemma of the consonantal text was established using substitutions, semantic shifts, pluses and minuses, and variant word-order. Tosefta Targums were excluded (contra Smelik, see page 38), following Houtman's analysis. In order to establish relationships between manuscripts, one must have at least two variant readings, both witnessed in at least two manuscripts. E. van Staalduine-Sulman, 'Vowels in the Trees', 218–23.
178 van Staalduine-Sulman, 'Vowels in the Trees', 238–9 (citation: 238). van Staalduine-Sulman, 'An Electronic Edition of Targum Samuel', 227–40.
179 van Staalduine-Sulman, 'An Electronic Edition of Targum Samuel'.

her results showed three principal textual groupings: one Eastern, one Western, and one connected to the Rabbinic Bibles.

The text of the Eastern tradition was 'bare', that is to say it contained fewer pluses in comparison to the other groups. The group was composed of three subgroups. There was little to distinguish between the Babylonian and Yemenite sub-groups and both exhibited strong internal coherence.[180] The third sub-group, which van Staalduine-Sulman named 'Italian,' contained a somewhat richer tradition and is odd, both in terms of its composition and in relation to the other sub-groups, because it contains manuscripts of diverse provenances (some Ashkenazi, some Italian, one Sephardi) and lacks strong internal coherence.[181]

The Western group contained a much richer textual tradition, which could be further divided into Sephardic and Ashkenazi traditions, though neither of these groups exhibited strong internal coherence except in individual cases.[182] The final group contained the First and Second Rabbinic Bibles, the London Polyglot, which was based on the Sixth Rabbinic Bible (Basel, 1618–19), and one manuscript, Codex Solger (Stadtbibliothek, Nürnberg), which had served as the *Vorlage* for the First Rabbinic Bible (see page 43). As one might expect, the group was marked by strong internal coherence.[183]

Based on these results van Staalduine-Sulman was able to draw some general conclusions concerning the text's transmission. First, she noted that the Babylonian and Yemenite sub-groups exhibited the correct historical order, that is: the older the manuscript the closer its kinship with the other branches in the stemma. By contrast, the Sephardi sub-group and the group connected to the Rabbinic Bible appeared to show the reverse order, the result of simultaneous contamination, while the Ashkenazi and 'Italian' sub-groups showed no historical order, a reflection of the lack of coherence within these groups. This result suggested that 'it is historically very likely that the proto-Eastern roots are indeed the origin of the entire stemma. The fact that all Babylonian manuscripts, which also represent the oldest vocalisation system, are older than the Yemenite manuscripts, favours them

---

180 van Staalduine-Sulman, 'An Electronic Edition of Targum Samuel', 26–30.
181 van Staalduine-Sulman, 'An Electronic Edition of Targum Samuel', 30–2. See further chapter three.
182 van Staalduine-Sulman, 'An Electronic Edition of Targum Samuel', 33–8.
183 van Staalduine-Sulman, 'An Electronic Edition of Targum Samuel', 38–41.

as the best representatives of the original Targum Samuel'.[184]

******

The past decade has witnessed the appearance of a few publications relating to Targum Jonathan's transmission history outside the Kampen School.

Chilton undertook a comparison of manuscript Hébreu 75 (Bibliothèque Nationale, Paris) to the Rabbinic Bibles and to Codex Reuchlinianus No. 3, which he published in 2002. He concluded that 'in terms of textual affiliation, the manuscript seems to mediate between the type of the Codex Reuchlinianus [No. 3] and the type of the Rabbinic Bibles'.[185] According to Chilton, the text of this manuscript also contained 'additional renderings (some of them unique), which in [Codex] Reuchlinianus [No. 3] would be marginal, [but] are here incorporated within the text'.[186] He noted that the manuscript tends to reflect more closely the Masoretic Text than Or. 2211 (British Library, London), which he takes as his base text, although this tendency is inconsistent; a comparable tendency is also present in the Rabbinic Bibles and their antecedents.[187] In addition, he notes the text's oddities in spelling, some of the text's unique readings, and what he called 'substantive agreement with [Codex] Reuchlinianus [No. 3]',[188] though the agreements were subsequently found to lack any real significance (Sperber's base text, i.e. Or. 2211, simply contained an isolated reading).[189]

The most recent book-length comparative study of Targum manuscripts is that of Ahuva Ho, which considers the Targum to Zephaniah (2009). Unfortunately Ho's handling of the manuscripts is rather confused and her reasoning is frequently quite unconvincing, so that the conclusions reached can only be accepted with caution.

Without showing any awareness of previous stemmatological research on the

---

184 van Staalduine-Sulman, 'An Electronic Edition of Targum Samuel', 24–5.
185 B. Chilton, 'HEBR. 75 in the Bibliothèque Nationale', in Paul V.M. Flesher (ed.), *Targum and Scripture: Studies in Aramaic Translations and Interpretation in Memory of Ernest G. Clarke* (Studies in the Aramaic Interpretation of Scripture 2, Leiden 2002), 141–8, 141.
186 Chilton, 'HEBR. 75 in the Bibliothèque Nationale', 141.
187 Chilton, 'HEBR. 75 in the Bibliothèque Nationale', 144.
188 Chilton, 'HEBR. 75 in the Bibliothèque Nationale', 144–7.
189 Houtman review of 'Paul V.M. Flesher (ed.), *Targum and Scripture in Aramaic Translations and Interpretation in Memory of Ernest G. Clarke* (Studies in the Aramaic Interpretation of Scripture 2, Leiden 2002)', *Journal for the Study of Judaism in the Persian, Hellenistic and Roman Period*, 35:1 (2004), 77–9, p. 78.

text of Targum Jonathan, Ho embarks on an analysis of 21 manuscripts, some of which she appears to have known only through Sperber's edition, though she does not specify which ones.[190] These manuscripts are grouped together under the rubrics Palestinian, Ashkenazi, Babylonian-Yemenite and Sephardi, but the logic of such a grouping is completely unclear, and factors of no relevance whatsoever to the textual tradition *per se*, such as the divisions of the Hebrew text or the *mis-en-page*, are used in places to substantiate these groupings.[191] There are six manuscripts belonging to the Sephardi group, including 'one from Italy'[192]; this is presumably manuscript Hébreu 96 (Bibliothèque Nationale, Paris), which is listed as having an Italian scribe in the National Library of Israel catalogue, though Ho does not specify. The grouping of genuinely Babylonian manuscripts with the Yemenite manuscripts would seem to disregard the important distinction between the two groups, established long ago. Codex Reuchlinianus No. 3 is accorded its own category, 'Palestinian', apparently on account of its punctuation[193] (but surely by the same logic, manuscripts bearing Tiberian vocalisation must also be categorised as Palestinian?). Ho says of the manuscript that 'its significance lies in its ancient Palestinian version of the Prophets in both Hebrew and Aramaic',[194] although she also describes the manuscript as Ashkenazi. She concludes that the punctuation and apparently also the presence of תרגום ירושלמי readings in the margins, 'point to a manuscript that originated in Palestine well before 1105 when it was copied in Europe'.[195] It is difficult to know what to make of this. Ho is presumably referring to the text contained in the manuscript itself; indeed, a failure to distinguish adequately between a textual tradition and its particular manifestation in an individual manuscript is a problem that pervades her entire book.

Aside from the obvious objection that an analysis that seeks to determine the textual affinity between manuscripts cannot begin by an arbitrary grouping of the material, her method for establishing the interrelation between texts is

---

190 A. Ho, *The Targum of Zephaniah: Manuscripts and Commentary* (Studies in the Aramaic Interpretation of Scripture 7, Leiden 2009), 34.
191 Ho, *The Targum of Zephaniah*, 425.
192 Ho, *The Targum of Zephaniah*, 36.
193 Ho, *The Targum of Zephaniah*, 35. Among the numerous minor errors that appear in this volume, I noted on page 70 that an edition of the Aramaic text of Codex Reuchlinianus No. 3 is attributed to Paul Kahle. This should read Paul *de Lagarde* (cf. 30).
194 Ho, *The Targum of Zephaniah*, 38.
195 Ho, *The Targum of Zephaniah*, 40.

quite unclear. In a section entitled 'stemmatic research', Ho examines each manuscript 'to discern its uniqueness within its group, compared to other groups'(!) using four criteria: omissions, pluses, substitutions, and metathesis, which will also allow the detection of what Ho calls 'cross-transmission', a term that remains unexplained.[196] These criteria are not inherently problematic, but Ho's analysis and the conclusions she draws from their application certainly are.

Manuscript Or. 2211 (British Library, London) is taken as the base text against which the other manuscripts are compared. Even if we set aside the objection that it is well known that this manuscript contains many singular readings (see page 21), Ho frequently treats that text of manuscript Or. 2211 as though it preserves without error or deviation the form the text assumed at the Babylonian redaction. Where all the textual witnesses share a unique variant when compared to manuscript Or. 2211, this indicates in Ho's view 'the transmission of Palestinian textual traditions in two opposite directions: Europe in the west and Babylonia in the east, probably before 1105 [the possible date of Codex Reuchlinianus No. 3], then on to Yemen. The survival of Palestinian traditions in Yemen attests to an early textual transmission'.[197] Rather than assuming, as Ho does, that where Western, Babylonian, and Yemenite manuscripts agree against manuscript Or. 2211, this can be attributed to the perpetuation of a Palestinian form of the text that pre-dates the Babylonian redaction,[198] one might more simply and more plausibly postulate that a later deviation has arisen in manuscript Or. 2211 or its predecessors, either accidentally or deliberately (a proposition that, confusingly, Ho herself admits on a few other occasions).[199]

To give a concrete example, in her analysis of the Palestinian group (containing only one manuscript, Codex Reuchlinianus No. 3) she identifies ten omissions, when compared to manuscript Or. 2211. Of these, in seven cases all other Yemenite manuscripts and most — or in three cases all — other witnesses share the same omissions, which concern the copula, a preposition, or the definite object marker in six of the seven cases. Ho derives from this observation the conclusions that the omissions 'reflect the Palestinian version

---

196 Ho, *The Targum of Zephaniah*, 69.
197 Ho, *The Targum of Zephaniah*, 76 cf. 72–184.
198 E.g. Ho, *The Targum of Zephaniah*, 82, 83, 97, 110, 425, and frequently.
199 Ho, *The Targum of Zephaniah*, 90, 135.

that survived the Babylonian redaction, omissions carried into the Yemenite textual tradition in their first migration from Palestine'.[200] Such a conclusion is preposterous. In fact, these seven omissions tell us something about manuscript Or. 2211 (i.e. that it contains a unique plus at these points), rather than anything about the text of Codex Reuchlinianus No. 3.

Such faulty reasoning is evident throughout the book and has an impact equally on the integrity of the stemmatic groupings, where Ho is often inattentive to the presence of shared readings in other textual traditions. For example, of the thirteen readings that Ho identifies as shared by all Ashkenazi manuscripts, all but two (one relating to orthography, one to vocalisation) also appear in other textual traditions, so that their value for demonstrating the cohesion of the Ashkenazi group is substantially diminished.[201] Her use throughout of consonantal variants and variants in the vocalisation without distinction,[202] and frequent use of the omission or addition of the copula,[203] raise further questions about the credibility of her results.[204]

While the work lacks the necessary scientific basis to sustain its own conclusions, in so far as they do not contradict the results of sounder scholarship, we might accept some of Ho's general conclusions, namely, that the Yemenite manuscripts stand closest to the genuine Babylonian fragments,[205] and that the Ashkenazi and Sephardi manuscripts exhibit less consistency and a higher frequency of errors. One might also accept as plausible Ho's view that the comprehension of Targumic Aramaic was weaker in the Ashkenazi and Sephardic zone than in Yemen: Where the Yemenite manuscripts diverge they often use genuine Aramaic alternatives, whereas the Western manuscripts more frequently perpetuate erroneous forms.[206] None of these conclusions is, however, new.

---

200 Ho, *The Targum of Zephaniah*, 72.
201 Ho, *The Targum of Zephaniah*, 126.
202 Smelik, 'Trouble in the Trees!', 172; van Staalduine-Sulman, 'Vowels in the Trees'.
203 van Staalduine-Sulman, 'An Electronic Edition of Targum Samuel' 16; Smelik, 'Trouble in the Trees!', 189. Cf. Houtman, 'Different Kinds of Tradition', 272.
204 In particular compare her own comments: Ho, *The Targum of Zephaniah*, 426.
205 Though some of the examples upon which she bases this conclusion share the variant reading with manuscripts noted in Sperber's critical apparatus that are not of Yemenite or Babylonian provenance (e.g. Zeph. 1.6, 10; 2.15), so once again one must proceed with caution.
206 Ho, *The Targum of Zephaniah*, 100, 133, 166–7.

Chapter Two

Targum in Medieval Italy and Ashkenaz

Whatever the origins of the Targum, by the middle of the Talmudic period the reading of the Targum had become an integral part of the liturgy, with the use of Aramaic, a language familiar to the audience, intended to make the sometimes perplexing biblical Hebrew more accessible.[1] But for the Jews of medieval Europe, who produced the manuscripts with which this book is concerned, Aramaic played no practical role in their daily lives. Yet the continued importance of the Targum among European Jews is attested by the number of extant manuscripts and its inclusion in the Rabbinic Bibles. This raises the question why did European Jews continued — at no little expense and effort[2] — to produce copies of the Targum? What role did the text of Targum Jonathan have among the Jewish communities of Italy and Ashkenaz in the period from which our manuscripts date (twelfth and fifteenth centuries)? And, to what extent was its Aramaic used and understood?

A definitive answer to these questions would require the entire corpus of medieval Jewish literature to be carefully sifted — a task that lies far beyond what is possible in this study. Here I can offer only some brief and preliminary comments. In short, during the period with which this study is concerned the Targum continued to play a role in the life of Italian and Ashkenazi Jewry in three ways:[3]

(a) it was cited widely by medieval commentators on the Bible and rabbinic literature;

(b) it was used in private preparation of the prescribed biblical sections of the liturgical calendar; and,

(c) it was maintained by some Jewish communities as part of the public recitation in the Synagogue, where it was also cited in sermons.

---

1 S.C. Reif, *Judaism and Hebrew Prayer: New Perspectives on Jewish Liturgical History* (Cambridge 1993), 130.
2 Books in large format, for example, had considerable market value, 'the equivalent of a flock of sheep'; C. Sirat, *Hebrew Manuscripts of the Middle Ages* (ed. and trans. N. de Lange, Cambridge 2002), 45–6, 53 (citation).
3 As outlined already by É. Levine, 'The Targums', in M. Sæbø (ed.), *Hebrew Bible/Old Testament, The History of its Interpretation*, Vol. I, *From the Beginnings to the Middle Ages (Until 1300)*, Part 1, *Antiquity* (Göttingen 1996), 323–31, p. 330.

The Transmission of Targum Jonathan in the West

1. Other Aramaic Texts in Circulation

Before I address texts of the Targum directly, it is worth recalling that although Aramaic was never the *lingua franca* of European Jews, it was far from entirely neglected during the period in which our manuscripts were copied. The bilingual (Hebrew/Aramaic) make-up of much rabbinic literature guaranteed the continued use of Aramaic in the context of study and halachic discourse. Aside from the Targums, texts that were partly or completely composed in various dialects of Aramaic continued to be copied and used by European Jews during the medieval period: the Babylonian and Palestinian Talmudim and some of the popular Midrashim (e.g. Genesis Rabbah, Leviticus Rabbah, Pesiqta de Rab Kahana), for example, circulated widely in medieval Europe and demanded of their readers a more than superficial knowledge of Aramaic.

Included among the Aramaic elements within these texts are numerous citations of the Targum to the Prophets, differing on occasion from the standard text of Targum Jonathan.[4] The Targum is cited, for example, in the Talmudim, Midrash Rabbah, Midrash Samuel, Midrash Tanhuma, Midrash Psalms, Pesikta de Rav Kahana, and Pesikta Rabbati, all of which are known from medieval European manuscript sources.

Of the Aramaic literature in circulation in this period, less well known perhaps are works such as the Scroll of Antiochus. This work, which describes the wars of the Hasmoneans and the origins of the festival of Hanukkah, was composed in a Western Aramaic dialect, though probably revised in Babylonia, in a language that imitates ancient sources, in particular Targum Onqelos.[5] Although the Scroll of Antiochus is much more widely attested in Sephardi sources from the period, it was also known in Italy and the Ashkenazi zone;[6]

---

4 For a recent study of this phenomenon (including a review of previous scholarship on the subject) and its implications for understanding the development of Targum Jonathan see A. Houtman and H. Sysling, *Alternative Targum Traditions: The Use of Variant Readings for the Study in Origin and History of Targum Jonathan* (Studies in the Aramaic Interpretation of Scripture 9, Leiden 2009), 137–234.

5 H.L. Strack and G. Stemberger, *Introduction to the Talmud and Midrash*² (trans. and ed. M. Bockmuehl, Edinburgh 1996), 331.

6 For example, at the end of various biblical manuscripts, e.g. Harley 1861, British Library London, Ashkenazi, thirteenth–fourteenth cent. (Torah, Haftarot, Megillot, Job); Parm. 2009–2010, Biblioteca Palatina Parma, Italian, fourteenth cent. (Torah + Writings); Hebr. 45 Staats- und Universitaetsbibliothek Hamburg, Italian, 1487 (Prophets + Writings).

the Italian scholar Isaiah di Trani even knew of the custom of reading the scroll in the synagogue on Hanukkah.[7]

Equally, there is some evidence that Aramaic continued as a language of composition among European Jews, for example, in the composition of short liturgical poems (*piyyutim*), which I will discuss below, and the Zohar, a work that, despite its attribution to the second century rabbi Simeon bar Yohai, was probably (mostly) composed by the Sephardi Moses de Leon in the thirteenth century in an artificial Aramaic drawn primarily from Targum Onqelos and the Bavli that was intended to give the work an air of antiquity.[8]

2. Other Targums in Use

Although this study is concerned with the use of Targum Jonathan, it is worth noting that Targum Jonathan belonged to a much wider pool of Targumic literature in use among European Jews between the twelfth and the fifteenth centuries. As one might expect, Targum Onqelos circulated widely. Indeed, history has bequeathed us hundreds of Italian and Ashkenazi manuscripts containing the Torah accompanied by Targum Onqelos.[9] Yet interest in the Targums among Italian and Ashkenazi Jews was by no means confined to the 'canonical' Targums, Jonathan and Onqelos. Far from it: the region incorporating Italy and Ashkenaz was evidently a melting pot for variant Targum traditions.

Italy preserved a strong tradition of Targumic learning that bears traces of Italian Jewry's strong connections with Palestinian centres.[10] Targum Neofiti, for example, is known to us only through a single manuscript of Italian provenance,

---

7   R. Isaiah de Trani, פסקי הרי"ד, Vol. 2, 548 (on Sukkah 44b).
8   P.V.M. Flesher, 'The History of Aramaic in Judaism', in J. Neusner, A.J. Avery-Peck and W.S. Green (eds), *The Encyclopedia of Judaism*, Vol. 1 (Leiden 2003), 85–96, pp. 91–2. On the important question of composition in Aramaic in contexts in which Aramaic was not a spoken language, see L. Gottlieb, 'Composition of Targums after the Decline of Aramaic as a Spoken Language', *Aramaic Studies* 12 (2014).
9   A quick search in the National Library of Israel's manuscript catalogue produced over 400 entries from the fifteenth century and earlier.
10 A. Milano, *Storia degli ebrei in Italia* (Torino 1963), for references in the relevant period, see 62, 65, 87. One is reminded, in this regard, that our only complete manuscript of the Jerusalem Talmud (Or. 4720 Universiteitsbibliotheek, Leiden) was copied in Italy in 1289.

copied in the first decades of the sixteenth century.[11] In addition to its main text, which is Palestinian in character, this manuscript also contains a number of interesting marginal notes exhibiting apparent variant readings of a Palestinian Targum[12] belonging to the same textual family as some Ashkenazi manuscripts of the Fragment Targums,[13] as well as citations of Targum Jonathan with a differing text showing Palestinian elements.[14] The sole manuscript of Targum Pseudo-Jonathan, which contains some essentially Palestinian material (along with much else),[15] now known to us[16] is also the work of sixteenth century Italian (or Ashkenazi) Jewry.[17] The compendium of Targum extracts found in Codex Reuchlinianus No. 3 is also evidence of the rich variety of Targum traditions connected to the Prophets that were circulating in Italy by the twelfth century (see chapter nine).

---

11 Codex Neofiti was written in Italy in an Italian hand, pre 1517; see B. Richler, (ed.) with M. Beit-Arié in collaboration with N. Pasternak, *Hebrew Manuscripts in the Vatican Library: Catalogue* (Studi e Testi 438, Vatican City 2008), 528.

12 A. Díez Macho, *Neophyti 1: Targum Palestinense Ms de la Biblioteca Vaticana, I, Génesis*, (Madrid and Barcelona 1968), 42–8; E.G. Clarke, 'The Neofiti I Marginal Glosses and the Fragmentary Targum Witnesses to Gen. VI–IX', *Vetus Testamentum* 22 (1972), 257–65, and further references there.

13 A. Díez Macho, 'Un Nuevo Manuscrito del Targum Fragmentario', 547–51.

14 E.g. Deut. 32:1 cites Tg. Isa. 51:6; 65:17; Gen. 40:23 cites Tg. Jer. 17:5, 7 (also cited in Frag. Tg.^{P}); see J. Ribera Florit, 'Elementos Comunes del Targum a los Profetas y del Targum Palestinense', in N. Fernández Marcos, F. Trebolle Barrera and F. Fernández Vallina (eds), *Simposio bíblico Español (Salamanca 1982)* (Madrid 1984), 477–93, p. 479; M. McNamara, *The New Testament and the Palestinian Targum to the Pentateuch* (Analecta Biblica 27, Rome 1966), 213 n. 67.

15 For a brief overview see M. Maher, *Targum Pseudo-Jonathan: Genesis. Translated, with Introduction and Notes* (The Aramaic Bible 1B, Collegeville, MN 1992), 1–11.

16 De Rossi (*c.* 1511–77) records seeing two manuscripts, one belonging to the Foa family of Reggio, which was ascribed to Jonathan ben Uzziel; the other belonging to Samuel Cases of Mantua, which bore the title Targum Yerushalmi. The former served as the basis of the *editio princeps* (1590–1) but is now lost, the latter is British Library manuscript Add. 27031. A. de Rossi, *The Light of the Eyes*, (trans. Joanna Weinberg; New Haven 2001), 183–4 (see notes 12, 13). According to de Rossi this explains why the late-thirteeth century Italian Kabbalist and halachic authority Menahem Recanate (or Recanati) quotes a Palestinian Targum under these two names. The citations of Recanate were collated by M. Ginsburger (siglum ״ס) in his *Das Fragmententhargum: Thargum jeruschalmi zum Pentateuch* (Berlin 1899), 91–122 (on the basis of earlier works, see p. xiv).

17 Italian hand according to É. Levine, 'British Museum Aramaic Additional Ms 27031', *Manuscripta* 16:1 (1972), 3–13, p. 3; German according to G. Margoliouth, *Catalogue of the Hebrew and Samaritan manuscripts in the British Museum* Part 1 (London 1899), §99. The censor's mark is dated 1593 (or 1598).

Chapter Two. Targum in Medieval Italy and Ashkenaz

That history has bequeathed us only Italian manuscripts of Targums Neofiti and Pseudo-Jonathan bespeaks the relative good fortune enjoyed by Italian Jews and their manuscripts in the past five centuries rather than any lack of interest in Targumic traditions on the part of Ashkenazi Jews. In fact, quite the contrary is true: Targum Pseudo-Jonathan was certainly widely known in Ashkenaz (as we will see below); the so-called Fragment Targums, which contain selections of Palestinian Targums to the Pentateuch, are known from six manuscripts of which three are Ashkenazi[18] (the Fragment Targums are also cited widely by medieval authors[19]); and the extant manuscripts of the Targum of Chronicles are all German.[20]

Some traditions are preserved in manuscripts from both regions. The Targums to the Five Scrolls (Megillot) as well as Psalms, Job, and Proverbs are known from medieval manuscripts of both Italian and Ashkenazi provenance,[21] as are the Tosefta Targums to the Prophets (see chapters ten and eleven).

3. Study of Targum Jonathan

Since Zunz published his groundbreaking *Die gottesdienstlichen Vorträge der Juden historisch entwickelt* in 1832 it has been widely recognised among

---

18 Ebr. 440, Biblioteca Apostolica, Vatican (German, thirteenth century); Codex Solger, Stadtbibliothek, Nürnberg (1291 CE); Universität B. H. fol. 1 Universitätsbibliothek, Leipzig (thirteenth century); see M.L. Klein, *The Fragment-Targums of the Pentateuch: According to their Extant Sources* (Analecta Biblica 76, Rome 1980), 26–33.

19 Ginsburger, *Das Fragmententhargum*, 91–122; C. Heller, 'A Critical Essay on the Palestinian Targum to the Pentateuch', [in Hebrew] *Haibri* (New York 1921) esp. 9–20; M.M. Kasher, *Torah Shelema*, Vol 24, *Aramaic Versions of the Bible* [in Hebrew] (Jerusalem 1974), 15–21.

20 Urbinati Ebr. 1, Biblioteca Apostolica, Vatican (1294 CE, Germany); Or. fol. 1210–11 Berlin, Staatsbibliothek Preußischer Kulturbesitz (1343 CE, Erfurt?); Ee. 5.9 University Library, Cambridge (1347 CE; that the scribe was German is clear from his marginal notes, see Schiller-Szinessy, *Catalogue of the Hebrew Manuscripts Preserved in the University Library, Cambridge*, (Cambridge 1876), Vol. 1, 36). The Targum of Chronicles was obviously known only in confined circles, however, since Elias Levita (1468/69–1549), who was born in Germany (Neustadt) but passed his scholarly life in northern Italy, stated that no Targum of Chronicles existed, see R. Le Déaut and J. Robert, *Targum des Chronique, (Cod. Vat. Urb. Ebr. 1)*, Vol. 1, *Introduction et traduction* (Analecta Biblica 51, Rome 1971), 10. On Kimhi see A. Sperber, *The Bible in Aramaic*, IVA, *The Targum and the Hebrew Bible* (Leiden 1968), 69–70.

21 Among the manuscripts in this study, e.g. Urbinati Ebr. 1, Biblioteca Apostolica, Vatican (1294 CE German), Or. 72 Biblioteca Angelica, Rome (1323 CE, Italian). For details of the extant manuscripts of the individual Targums see the relevant volumes in series *The Aramaic Bible* (M. McNamara, K. Cathcart, M. Maher, eds).

scholars that the medieval European commentators frequently cited Targums. Occasionally they cited a text of the Targum to the Prophets that differed in significant ways from the standard text of Targum Jonathan, and in some cases these variant readings displayed Palestinian characteristics.[22] Although his explanation of this phenomenon — that the citations were remnants of a once complete Palestinian Targum — is no longer thought credible by the majority of Targum scholars, Zunz's study highlighted nearly two centuries ago the extent to which a Targum (or Targums) to the Prophets was used by the principal medieval authors from Italy and Ashkenaz.

Indeed, among those works composed in Italy and Ashkenaz in the period with which we are concerned, a version of the Targum to the Prophets is cited in (among others):[23] Menahem ben Solomon's *Sekhel Tov* (1139 CE, Italy) and *Even Bohan* (1143 CE, Italy),[24] Nathan ben Yehiel's *Arukh* (1101 CE, Rome),[25] the *Yalkut Shimoni* (thirteenth century, Germany), Menahem ben Elakim's *Arukh Goren* (fourteenth century, Germany), and Hezekiah ben Manoah's

---

22 Zunz, *Die gottesdienstlichen Vorträge der Juden historisch entwickelt*, 70–1, 80–2. Cf. also M. Goshen-Gottstein's introduction in his *Fragments of Lost Targumim* 2 Vols [in Hebrew] (Bar-Ilan Institute for the History of Jewish Bible Research: Sources and Studies 1:3; Ramat-Gan 1983, 1989).

23 Houtman and Sysling compiled a list of such citations gleaned from earlier literature; Houtman and Sysling, *Alternative Targum Traditions*, appendices 1 and 2. The list is not exhaustive (containing predominantly quotations that vary from the standard text of Targum Jonathan rather than every citation of Targum Jonathan).

24 Bacher writes of Menahem ben Solomon's remarks concerning the Targum to the Prophets in *Even Bohen* that they 'exhibit an intimate acquaintance with, and a profound study of the same. He has some good remarks on the hermeneutical method of Jonathan, whom he invariably names as the author of the Targum to the Prophets; in many instances he explains words of the Targum and the reasons why the passage was thus translated; he compares passages, notes conformity and discrepancies in the Targum of the Prophets; he occasionally criticises the author, but much more often refers to him as his authority, by which he strengthens exegetical views of his own'. According to Bacher the citation in *Even Bohen* show traces of Palestinian Targum. W. Bacher, 'Notes on the Critique of the Text of the Targum of the Prophets', *Jewish Quarterly Review* 11 (1899), 651–5 (citation: 652).

25 For a description of the work and its impact, and a biography of Nathan ben Jehiel see I.M. Ta-Shma, *Talmudic Commentary in Europe and North Africa: Literary History, I, 1000–1200* [in Hebrew] (Jerusalem 1999), 217–21. Griño discusses the citations of Targum in the Aruk; R. Griño, 'El Meturgeman de Elias Levita y el 'Aruk de Natan Ben Yehiel como fuentes de la lexicografia targumica', *Biblica* 60 (1979), 110–17. On its relation to Palestinian Targums to the Pentateuch see S. Speier, 'The Relationship between the "Arukh" and "Targum Neofiti I"', [in Hebrew] *Leshonenu* 31:1 (1966), 23–32; 31:3 (1967), 189–98; 34–3 (1970), 172–9 and C.D. Ginsburger, *Pseudo-Jonathan: Thargum Jonathan ben Usiël zum Pentateuch nach der Londoner Handschrift Brit. Mus. add. 27031* (Berlin 1903), ix–x.

Chapter Two. Targum in Medieval Italy and Ashkenaz

Perush ha-Torah (thirteenth century, French), the Tosafot on the Babylonian Talmud and the super-commentaries on Rashi's Biblical commentaries (both phenomena originating among Rashi's pupils),[26] Samson ben Abraham of Sens' *Commentary on the Mishnah* (late twelfth–early thirteenth century, France), Solomon ben Samson's *Siddur Haside Ashkenaz* (eleventh century, Worms, Germany), and the Mahzor Vitry composed by Simhah ben Samuel (died before 1105 CE, Vitry, France). The breadth of genres in which the Targum appears is striking, extending from commentaries on biblical and rabbinic literature, and works concerned with matters of philology and lexicography to haggadic, liturgical and devotional compositions. Targumic traditions relating to the Prophets were evidently widely integrated into rabbinic learning (as well as elementary instruction) across Italy and Ashkenaz by the end of the eleventh century.[27]

In addition to the literary works mentioned above, the *rishonim* of Ashkenaz and Italy draw on the Targums to resolve the many practical and halachic matters with which they were addressed. Both Targum Onqelos and Jonathan are consulted, for example, to establish whether the phrase לעלם ולעלמי עלמיא in the *qaddish* should be spelled with or without the conjunctive *waw* (Tg. Isa. 6:3; Tg. Onq. Exod. 15:18).[28] Perhaps more surprisingly, Targum Pseudo-Jonathan is cited as authoritative on a halachic matter relating to a bill of divorce (*get*).[29] The uniquely rich exegesis of Targum Pseudo-Jonathan also proved itself to be a fruitful resource: its elaborate rendering of Deut. 22:5, for example, which adds to the biblical prohibition against a man wearing women's clothing a prohibition against a man shaving his bodily hair, serves to settle a question concerning the use of scissors

---

26 For example, Shemaiah of Troyes (eleventh century), a pupil of Rashi, cites the reading of 'Targum Yerushalmi' to Ezekiel in a note bearing his name that is incorporated into Rashi's *Commentary to Ezekiel* (27:17). He writes: אני שמעיה מצאתי במקרא תרגום ירושלמי "בחיטי מנית ופנג" דחושלא וקילויא.

27 On the role of Targum in Jewish education in Ashkenaz and Italy see further Houtman, 'The Role of the Targum in Jewish Education in Medieval Europe', in A. Houtman, H-M. Kirn and E. van Staalduine-Sulman (eds), *A Jewish Targum in a Christian World* (Jewish and Christian Perspectives 27, Leiden 2014), 81–98, pp. 86–91.

28 R. Jacob b. Moses Moellin (Germany; 1360?–1427 CE), *New Responsa of Rabbi Yaacov Molin – Maharil*, ed. Y. Satz [in Hebrew] (Jerusalem 1977), §27.

29 I.e. whether it is correct to spell the month Iyyar with one or two yods; R. Jacob b. Moses Moellin, *Responsa of Rabbi Yaacov Molin - Maharil*, ed. Yitzchok Satz [in Hebrew] (Jerusalem 1979), § 189 (cf. Tg. Ps.-J. Exod. 16.1; Num. 1:1, 18; 9:11; 10:11).

(rather than a razor) to cut a beard.[30]

To the list of authors cited above one must add Rabbi Solomon ben Isaac, *alias* Rashi (1040–1105 CE), from Troyes in northern France, arguably the most influential commentator on Bible and Talmud of the period. Rashi makes frequent use of the Targums; Grossman has even described them as being 'among Rashi's most important sources'.[31] Rashi considered the Targum to belong to the Oral Law,[32] whose explanatory translation mitigated the possibility of dispute over the correct interpretation of obscure passages,[33] and provided access to the text for the benefit of women and the ignorant (עמי הארץ).[34] It was, he explains, the vernacular among the Babylonians, who relied on Targum Onqelos to understand the Law. According to Rashi they were not so particular about Targum Jonathan however;[35] a view Rashi apparently shared since he states in his commentary to the Babylonian Talmud (Megillah 24a) that he believes it unimportant if the meturgeman erred when translating the Prophets

---

30 By the twelfth–thirteenth century French scholar, R. Jacob of Marvège (France), Jacob of Marvège, שאלות ותשובות מן השמיים, §36. The Italian scholar Isaiah ben Mall di Trani (the Elder) cites a text close to Tg. Ps.-J. Num. 6:11 as affirming the view that the sin of a Nazirite defiles his Naziriteship (*Teshuvot HaRid: the Responsa of Rabbi Isaiah the Elder* [in Hebrew], ed. A.J. Wertheimer (Jerusalem 1967), §8).

31 A. Grossman, 'The School of Literal Jewish Exegesis in Northern France', in M. Sæbo (ed.), *Hebrew Bible/Old Testament: The History of its Interpretation*, Vol. 1, Part 2, *The Middle Ages* (Göttingen 2000), 338. The frequency with which Rashi cites Targum is in contrast to his grandson and pupil Samuel ben Meir, *alias* Rashbam (*c.*1080–5–*c.*1174 CE), who makes extremely limited use of Targum, citing it rarely (see E.Z. Melamed, *Bible Commentators*, Vol 1, [in Hebrew] [Jerusalem 1978], 481–2), reflecting his focus on *peshat* (see M. Berger, 'Rabbi Samuel Ben Meir's Attitude Toward Midrash', in H. Blumberg et al. [eds], *"Open Thou Mine Eyes..." Essays on Aggadah and Judaica Presented to Rabbi William G. Braude on his Eightieth Birthday and Dedicated to his Memory* [Hoboken, NJ 1992], 21–40) rather than implying his ignorance of the sources.

32 Rashi, *Commentary on tractate Qiddushin* 49a. See E. Viezel, 'Targum Onkelos in Rashi's Exegetical Consciousness', *The Review of Rabbinic Judaism* 15 (2012), 1–19. Cf. S.D. Fraade, 'Rabbinic Views on the Practice of Targum, and Multilingualism in the Jewish Galilee of the Third–Sixth Centuries', in L.I. Levine, *The Galilee in Late Antiquity* (New York and Jerusalem 1992) 262–4; Fraade, 'Scripture, Targum, and Talmud as Instruction: a Complex Textual Story from the *Sifra*', in J. Magness and S. Gitin (eds), *Hesed ve-emet: Studies in Honor of Ernest S. Frerichs* (Brown Judaic Studies 320, Atlanta, GA).

33 Rashi, *Commentary on tractate Megillah* 3a.

34 A view without a strong foundation in the classical rabbinic literature, Fraade, 'Rabbinic Views on the Practice of Targum', 258 n. 10. Cf. the comments in *Sefer huqqei ha-Torah* (statute seven), cited in Houtman, 'The Role of the Targum in Jewish Education in Medieval Europe', 87, also her comments on 88.

35 Rashi, *Commentary on tractate Megillah* 21b.

Chapter Two. Targum in Medieval Italy and Ashkenaz

since halachic instruction was not derived from it.[36]

Rashi cites Targum Onqelos and Jonathan extensively throughout his commentaries, usually with an introductory phrase (e.g., כדמתרגם יונתן בן עוזיאל, כתרגומו, ויונתן תרגם, כתרגומו פירושו). As one might perhaps expect, he makes more extensive use of them in the Torah and in sections serving as haftarot than elsewhere in the Prophets.[37] There are many instances in which Rashi simply cites the Targum without providing any further comment — evidently assuming a familiarity with the Targum on the part of his audience. More frequently, however, the Targum plays a more fundamental role in the development of his exegesis: he uses the Targum to determine the correct sense where a Hebrew word has more than one possible meaning; to clarify the meaning of uncommon words, or poetic, parabolic, or prophetic language; and to fill out what is merely implied in the Hebrew text (מקרא קצר).[38] His citations are not always of the Targum to the verse under discussion: Onqelos is cited to explain passages in the Prophets and *vice versa*,[39] and both appear in his commentaries on the Babylonian Talmud. On occasion Rashi provides a translation in Hebrew of the explanation offered by the Targum, sometimes without giving the Aramaic; on other occasions he simply gives its gist, or derives his exegesis from the Targum, either without acknowledging his source or with an introductory formula to indicate that his explanation is based on the Targum. Where he feels it to be necessary, Rashi even explains the meaning of the Targum.[40]

Rashi's acquaintance with the Targum and his esteem for its insights were evidently profound, though far from out of the ordinary when one compares the works of the likes of Nathan ben Yehiel or Menahem ben Solomon. Interestingly, unlike other writers of the period, Rashi apparently knew neither of Targum Pseudo-Jonathan,[41] nor the Targums to the Writings,[42] although he

---

36 Commenting on ובנביא שלשה פסוקים he writes: אם ירצה ולא איכפת לן אם יטעה דלא נפקא מיניה הוראה 'If he so wishes, it is not a concern for us if he errs, because no [*halachic*] instruction will follow from it.' See Smelik, 'Orality, Manuscript Reproduction, and the Targums', 54–5.
37 Melamed, *Bible Commentators*, Vol 1, 380
38 For examples see Melamed, *Bible Commentators*, Vol 1, 380–3.
39 E.g. Rashi, *Commentary on Samuel*, 2 Sam. 13:9 (citing Tg. Onq. Lev. 2:5).
40 For examples see Melamed, *Bible Commentators*, Vol 1, 387–8, 392.
41 A conclusion reached long ago by A. Berliner (*Beiträge zur Geschichte der Raschi-Commentare* [Berlin 1903], 28–30). Bromberg challenged Berliner's conclusion ('האם ראה רש"י תרגום יונתן בן עוזיאל.') but his proposal was swiftly rebutted by A. Kasher, 'האם ראה רש"י תרגום יונתן בן עוזיאל', *Sinai* 58–1–2 (Year 30: 1965), 90–3, D. Rieder, 'האם ראה רש"י את תרגום יונתן בן עוזיאל.'

The Transmission of Targum Jonathan in the West

did know the second Targum of Esther, which he calls Targum Yerushalmi.[43] They had evidently not yet penetrated the academic circles of northern France.[44]

Rashi's use of Targum also highlights a difficulty in using the citations of medieval authors in the study of the Targum. In a number of cases the Targum to the Prophets cited by Rashi differs from the text now known to us. Evidently the manuscripts from which Rashi worked were sometimes deficient — indeed Rashi occasionally corrects the text of the Targum.[45] Rashi certainly knew of some textual variants in Targum Jonathan, either by consulting multiple copies of the Targum or from marginal annotations.[46] But, caution is required in saying too much on the basis of his citations: sometimes he seems to be citing from the Targum but is actually citing from a talmudic source;[47] and more fundamentally, the text of Rashi's commentaries (including his citations of Targum) differs between manuscripts.[48]

'האם ראה רש״י את תרגום יונתן, Halevy .M and 93–4 ,(1965 :30 Year) 1–2:58 30 *Sinai* ,עחיאל'.
'האם ראה רש״י, Weil of comments the also See .191 ,(1966 :31 Year) 60:3–4 *Sinai* ,בן עחיאל'.
'עוד לשאלה האם, Madan and 96 ,(1966 :30 Year) 1–2:59 30 *Sinai* ,את תרגום יונתן בן עחיאל'.
'ראה רש״י את תרגום יונתן בן עחיאל, Sinai 60:1–2 (Year 31: 1966), 95 Cf. Melamed, *Bible Commentators*, Vol. 1, 378–9, 395 and 482 (on Rashbam's use of a תרגום ירושלמי to the Torah).

42 Rashi, *Commentary on tractate Megillah* 21b. The citation of Targum in his commentary to Lamentations 4:1 refers to the translation equivalent (עמא for כהה) employed in Tg. Onq. Lev. 13:6, 56 (cf. Tg. Jon. Ezek. 21:12) not to Targum Lamentations (as P.S. Alexander, *The Targum of Lamentations: Translated, with a Critical Introduction, Apparatus, and Notes* [The Aramaic Bible 17B. Collegeville, MI 2008], 62, 64). Rashbam by contrast cited from a Targum to Job and Proverbs; Melamed, *Bible Commentators*, Vol 1, 482.

43 Rashi, *Commentary on Deuteronomy*, 3:4 (cf. his commentary to 1 Kgs 10:19).

44 The Tosafists, however, contradict Rashi's statement concerning a Targum to the Writings (Tosafot *Megillah* 3), perhaps indicating the date of its arrival in northern France.

45 For examples see Melamed, *Bible Commentators*, Vol 1, 394. Cf. E. Deutsch, *Literary Remains of the late Emanuel Deutsch, with a Brief Memoir* (London 1874), 365.

46 E.g. Rashi, *Commentary to Zephaniah* 2:2. See here A. Ho, *The Targum of Zephaniah: Manuscripts and Commentary* (Studies in the Aramaic Interpretation of Scripture 7, Leiden 2009), 174–6.

47 For examples see Melamed, *Bible Commentators*, Vol 1, 394–5.

48 For an example in the Prophets see Speier, '"תרגום יונתן ופירוש רש״י לישעיה יד, לא: "ואין בודד במועדו', *Tarbiz* 34:2 (1965), 194–5. Also C.B. Diamond, 'The Dependence of Rashi and Kimhi on Targum in their Commentaries on Amos', unpublished MA thesis (Hebrew Union College 1963).

Chapter Two. Targum in Medieval Italy and Ashkenaz

4. Targum in the Liturgy in Italy and Ashkenaz

Certainly by the end of the period with which this study is concerned (i.e. twelfth–fifteenth century) the custom of accompanying the weekly scripture reading with Targum was not observed in Italy or Ashkenaz, as can be inferred from the lack of manuscript evidence and from various contemporary secondary sources.[49] For example, in the opinion of the German sage R. Gershom ben Judah Me'or Ha-Golah (c. 960–1028 CE), recorded by Simhah b. Samuel in the Mahzor Vitry, those who did not read the Targum of the Torah (which he refers to as תרגום דרבנן) were not fulfilling their obligation (citing b.Megillah 3a).[50] On the other side of the argument, R. Zedekiah b. Abraham Anav cites as current the opinion that their vernacular language (הלעז שלנו), i.e. Italian, stands in the place of the Targum, on the grounds that Aramaic was the vernacular of their ancestors.[51] The Targum, it was clear, was not used, because it was not understood.[52]

The reading of Targum during the liturgy does, however, appear to have been customary in the case of some of the festivals. The Torah readings for the Seventh Day of Passover (Exod. 13:17–15:26) and the First Day of Shavuot (Exodus 19–20) were accompanied by a recitation of a Targum to these verses;

---

49 In Spain, the custom died out in the tenth century according to A. Díez Macho, 'Nueva fuente para el Targum Palestino del día séptimo de Pascua y primero de Pentecostés', *Salmanticensis* 28 (1981) 235–57, p. 234. Samuel the Nagid (993–1055/56 CE) records that the custom had ceased; I. Elbogen, *Jewish Liturgy: a Comprehensive History* (trans. R.P. Scheindlin; Philadelphia 1993 [1913 German ed.; 1972 Hebrew ed.]), 154. By the time of Judah ben Barzillai (late eleventh–early twelfth century) the Targum was treated merely as a commentary; Smelik, 'Orality, Manuscript Reproduction, and the Targums', 73.

50 S. Hurwitz (ed.), מחזור ויטרי לרבינו שמחה (Jerusalem 1963), 98. There are similarities to the responsum of Natronai Gaon, who wrote 'Those who do not translate but say, "We do not need to translate using the translation of our masters. Instead we translate into our own language, into the language of the public", do not fulfil their obligation...' (Seder Rav Amram Gaon, שחרית של שבת). Cf. Isaac ben Moses of Vienna (c.1200–70), ספר אור זרוע (Zhitomir 1862), §1.11. See further Houtman, 'The Role of the Targum in Jewish Education in Medieval Europe', 89–91, 94.

51 Shibbolei ha-Leket (שבלי הלקט) 29a §78. See P. Sh. Lehnardt, 'The Role of Targum Samuel in European Jewish Liturgy', in A. Houtman, H-M. Kirn, and E. van Staalduine-Sulman (eds), *A Jewish Targum in a Christian World* (Jewish and Christian Perspectives 27, Leiden 2014), 32–62, p. 46 n. 20. Similarly the Tosafists defended their custom of not reading the Targum on the basis of b.Megillah 23b, cf. Houtman, 'The Role of the Targum in Jewish Education in Medieval Europe', 87, 90–1.

52 Elbogen, *Jewish Liturgy*, 151–4.

the text, which differs from one manuscript to another, is a conflation of Targum Onqelos, Palestinian Targum, and later additions to the text.[53] The number of festival prayer books (mahzorim) attesting to this custom is legion.[54] A few other Torah readings are sparsely represented among the extant manuscripts, for example, the Torah reading for Simhat Torah.[55] The same scattered picture holds true for the Targum to the haftarot, as we will see in chapter ten. As Lehnardt has pointed out, one might account for this in one of two ways: either (1) the custom of reading the Targum throughout the liturgical year was once widespread in Europe but was in the process of dying out during the period with which this study is concerned, or (2) this situation reflects a partial implementation of the requirement imposed by Babylonian halachah, the influence of which on Jewish communities in Christian Europe grew during the tenth and eleventh centuries. Lehnardt argues that the latter is more likely.[56]

The practice of composing Aramaic liturgical poems (*piyyutim*) to serve as introductions (*reshuyot*) to the reading of the Targum to the Torah during the seventh day of Passover and the first day of Shavuot, which is widely attested in medieval Ashkenazi (particularly French) sources, indicates that the Torah

---

[53] S.A. Kaufman and Y. Maori, 'The Targumim to Exodus 20: Reconstructing the Palestinian Targum', *Textus* 16 (1991), 13–78, pp. 16–23; Díez Macho, 'Nueva fuente para el Targum Palestino del día séptimo de Pascua y primero de Pentecostés' (with text according to a thirteenth century French mahzor); Díez Macho, 'The Recently Discovered Palestinian Targum: its Antiquity and Relationship with the Other Targums', in *Congress Volume, Oxford, 1959* (Supplements to Vetus Testamentum 7, Leiden 1960), 222–45, pp. 237–9. A number of mahzorim are discussed in U. Gleßmer, *Einleitung in die Targume zum Pentateuch* (Texte und Studien zum Antiken Judentum 48, Tübingen 1995) see 154–64. For the text in Mahzor Vitry see Hurwitz, מחזור ויטרי לרבינו שמחה, 305–6. Cf. also L. Díez Merino, 'Mahzor Vitry and the Palestinian Targum to the Prophets', in U. Hoxen, H. Trautner-Kromann and K.L. Goldschmidt Salamon (eds), *Jewish Studies in a New Europe: Proceedings of the Fifth Congress of Jewish Studies in Copenhagen 1994* (Copenhagen 1998), 199–211.

[54] Kaufman and Maori examined six mahzorim in their 'The Targumim to Exodus 20: Reconstructing the Palestinian Targum'. To give just a few additional examples of Italian mahzorim following the Roman rite: Ms. parm. 1898–9, Biblioteca Palatina, Parma (late fifteenth century); Ms. parm. 2221, Biblioteca Palatina, Parma (fourteenth century); Ms. parm. 2403, Biblioteca Palatina, Parma (early fourteenth century); Ms. parm. 2577, Biblioteca Palatina, Parma (mid-fourteenth century); Ms. parm. 2884, Biblioteca Palatina, Parma (fourteenth century); Ms. Ross. 436, Biblioteca Apostolica, Vatican (c.1400 CE); Ms. Ross. 437, Biblioteca Apostolica, Vatican (Lucca, 1447 CE).

[55] E.g. Ms. Vat. ebr. 545, Biblioteca Apostolica, Vatican, (Ortona, 1419/20 CE; mahzor, Roman rite); Ms. parm. 2069, Biblioteca Palatina, Parma (1453 CE; siddur, Roman rite); Ms. parm. 3135, Biblioteca Palatina, Parma (Imola, 1458 CE; mahzor, Roman rite).

[56] Lehnardt, 'The Role of Targum Samuel in European Jewish Liturgy', 44–7.

Chapter Two. Targum in Medieval Italy and Ashkenaz

portion served a liturgical function in the Middle Ages.[57] Perhaps the most well known of these is the *Akdamut* composed in Worms in the eleventh century by R. Meir ben Isaac Nehorai as an introduction to the reading of the Targum to the Torah for the first day of Shavuot. The text of the *Akdamut* itself apparently draws on Targum Onqelos and Jonathan.[58] Some examples of *reshuyot* intended to introduce the Targum reading for the festival haftarot are also known from Italian and Ashkenazi sources, implying a liturgical use of the Targum of the haftarot in these areas (though the *reshuyot* may have been retained after the custom of reading the haftarah Targum had died out).[59]

The presence of the Targum readings in mahzorim does not guarantee *ipso facto* that the texts were read publicly in the context of the synagogue liturgy since some mahzorim were composed for personal rather than communal use.[60] The instructions that precede the Targum of 2 Samuel 22 (haftarah for the seventh day of Passover) in the Italian and French mahzorim studied in chapter ten, clearly imply a public recitation of the text.[61] The Ashkenazi sources are more reticent in this regard and the remaining Ashkenazi sources examined in chapter ten, though clearly reflecting earlier liturgical patterns, are unlikely to have actually been read during the synagogue service.

---

57 Ginsburger published several examples for the seder for the 7th day of Pesach, which had been composed by medieval Ashkenazi liturgical poets; M. Ginsburger, 'Aramäische Introduktionen zum Thargumvortrag an Festtagen', *Zeitschrift der Deutschen Morgenländischen Gesellschaft* 44 (1900), 113–24. Cf. Ginsburger, 'Les Introductions Araméennes a la Lecture du Targoum', *Revue des Études Juives* 73 (1921), 14–26, 186–94. On the custom for *Shavuot* see R. Meir b. Baruch of Rothenburg (c. 1215–93 CE), שאלות ותשובות מהר"ם מרוטנבורג (Sudilkov 1835), Part 4 No. 59. See further Lehnardt, 'The Role of Targum Samuel in European Jewish Liturgy', 46–51.

58 J. Hoffman, '*Akdamut*: History, Folklore, and Meaning', *Jewish Quarterly Review* 99:2 (2009), 161–83, pp. 169–70; 175 n. 35, n. 37; 176 n. 45; 177 n. 50; 179 n. 59. Cf. W. Bacher 'Alte aramäische Poesien zum Vortrage des Haphtara-Targum', *Monatsschrift für die Geschichte und Wissenschaft des Judenthums* 22:5 (1873), 220–8, p. 226.

59 See Bacher 'Alte aramäische Poesien zum Vortrage des Haphtara-Targum', for a discussion of those *reshuyyot* copied in Codex Reuchlinianus No. 3 (Some of which he considered to be Ashkenazi compositions). Also Fleischer, 'Prayer and Piyyut in the Worms Mahzor', 42–4. See examples in Hurwitz (ed.), מחזור ויטרי לרבינו שמחה, 171–3. For examples from Oriental sources see, M.L. Klein, 'Introductory Poems (*R'shuyot*) to the Targum of the *Haftarah* in Praise of Jonathan Ben Uzziel', in S.F. Chyet and D.H. Ellenson (eds), *Bits of Honey: Essays for Samson H. Levey* (Atlanta, GA 1993), 43–56.

60 B. Narkiss, 'Mahzor', in M. Berenbaum and F. Skolnik (eds), *Encyclopaedia Judaica²*, Vol. XIII (Detroit 2007), 363–6, pp. 364–5.

61 Cf. also Lehnardt, 'The Role of Targum Samuel in European Jewish Liturgy', 51–8.

The Transmission of Targum Jonathan in the West

As archaic as the retention of an Aramaic Targum in the liturgy may seem, it is worth remembering that Targum was not the only Aramaic element of the liturgy. Despite the emergence of Hebrew as the chosen medium of prayer in the late-geonic period, some Aramaic elements were retained in prayers but 'only when it had so long been associated with a particular prayer that it appeared to be an act of revolution to alter it'.[62] The *Kaddish*, a doxology giving praise to the name of the Lord, is phrased (largely) in Aramaic; in some recensions of the *Kaddish*, particularly those preserved in Ashkenazi sources, the phraseology is clearly dependent on usage in the Targums.[63] Likewise, the *Kedushah de-Sidra*, a prayer originating in the ancient custom of studying prophetic texts after Morning prayer, incorporates the Targum of Isaiah 6:3.

Conclusions

To summarise, the context in which our manuscripts of the Targum to Samuel were written was one in which Aramaic remained an important language, though knowledge of the language was largely passive, a fact that accounts for the poor state of some of our texts (as we will see in the following chapters) as well as those known to Rashi, as I noted above. Its original liturgical role was largely neglected, confined to some of the major festivals in Italian and some French rites. The principal role of Targum Jonathan was in study. Targum Jonathan circulated among a *mélange* of other Targumic traditions, both to the Pentateuch and the Prophets, so there was obviously significant interest in the Targums in general in the centres of Jewish learning in both Italy and Ashkenaz, particularly as a tool for the study and explication of the Hebrew text. As Philip Alexander put it, the Targums 'were valued as convenient repositories of traditional exegesis'.[64]

---

62 Reif, *Judaism and Hebrew Prayer*, 130 (citation), 137, 145.
63 A. Lehnardt, *Qaddish: Untersuchungen zur Entstehung und Rezeption eines rabbinischen Gebetes* (Texts and Studies in Ancient Judaism 87, Tübingen 2002), 45–62; Lehnardt, '"Therefore they ordained to say it in Aramaic" Some Remarks on Language and Style of the Kaddish', in J. Targarona Borrás and Á. Sáenz-Badillos (eds), *Jewish Studies at the Turn of the Twentieth Century: Proceedings of the 6th EAJS congress, Toledo, July 1998*, Vol. 1, *Biblical, Rabbinical, and Medieval Studies* (Leiden 1999), 303–10.
64 P.S. Alexander, 'Jewish Aramaic Translations of Hebrew Scriptures', in M.J. Mulder (ed.) *Mikra: Text, Translation, Reading and Interpretation of the Hebrew Bible in Ancient Judaism and Early Christianity* (Peabody, MA 2004 [1988]), 217–53, p. 241.

Chapter Two. Targum in Medieval Italy and Ashkenaz

This last point is nicely illustrated by the *mise en page* of two of our manuscripts, namely ms. Or. 72 Biblioteca Angelica, Rome (Italian, 1326 CE; siglum: t701i) and ms. Add. 26,879 British Library, London (Ashkenazi, thirteenth century; siglum: t720a), which place the Hebrew text in the centre of the page surrounded by various commentaries and the Targum. In these manuscripts Targum Jonathan is set on a par with Rashi, Kimhi, *etc.*, whereas in the majority of our manuscripts the Aramaic and Hebrew text alternate, normally verse by verse, indicating that the Targum was intrinsically bound to the Hebrew original and was to be read in tandem with it.[65] In two of our manuscripts, namely ms. Laud Or. 326 Bodleian Library, Oxford (Ashkenazi, twelfth century? Siglum: t718i) and ms. Hébreu 75 Bibliothèque Nationale, Paris (Sephardi? Or Italian? fourteenth– fifteenth century; siglum: t232i/s), the Hebrew text is absent, only Hebrew lemmata are given at the start of each verse of the Targum. These manuscripts were intended to be used (probably by a single reader or student, see the description of the manuscripts in chapter three) in conjunction with the Hebrew text, as the presence of Hebrew lemmata implies, but such a *mise en page* breaks the close association with the Hebrew text so readily apparent in the other manuscripts.[66]

Targum Jonathan was far from a mere crystallised relic. The value with which it was regarded is marked, among other things, by its preservation on parchment, even though paper production began in Italy as early as 1210, and its inclusion in 'Giant Bibles' (e.g. ms. Urbinati Ebr. 1, Biblioteca Apostolica, Vatican; siglum t2i; ms. Barberini Or. 161–164 Biblioteca Apostolica, Vatican; siglum t3i), which were very expensive and often dedicated to synagogues or to study circles.[67]

---

65 Smelik, 'Orality, Manuscript Reproduction, and the Targums', 72.
66 On the relationship between format and function in medieval Targum manuscripts see further Houtman, 'The Role of the Targum in Jewish Education in Medieval Europe', 93–5; and E. van Staalduine-Sulman, 'A Variety of Targum Texts', in A. Houtman, H-M. Kirn, and E. van Staalduine-Sulman (eds), *A Jewish Targum in a Christian World* (Jewish and Christian Perspectives 27, Leiden 2014), 9–31.
67 C. Sirat, *Hebrew Manuscripts of the Middle Ages*, 45–6, 108. As there were no Jewish scriptoria the majority of medieval Hebrew books were copied for private use by the user himself; see M. Beit-Arié, 'The Script and Book Craft in the Hebrew Medieval Codex', in P. van Boxel and S. Arndt (eds), *Crossing Borders: Hebrew Manuscripts as a Meeting-place of Cultures* (Oxford 2009), 21–34, p. 23; Beit-Arié, *Hebrew Codicology: Tentative Typology of Technical Practices Employed in Hebrew Dated Medieval Manuscripts* (Jerusalem 1981 [1976]), 11.

Chapter Three

The Manuscripts

1. Selection of Manuscripts

The selection of manuscripts containing the continuous text of Targum Jonathan to the book of Samuel, which I examine in this study, has been determined by the *stemma codicum* produced by van Staalduine-Sulman. This stemma analysed all the known complete or substantially complete manuscripts and editions of Targum Samuel, as well as some fragments and haftarot collections. Van Staalduine-Sulman created the stemma by applying established stemmatological models to a sample survey of sixty-five verses drawn from throughout the two books of Samuel (including some haftarah readings).[1] The result was a stemma based solely on similarities and differences in the text, rather than external factors, such as the script, codicology, provenance, etc.

The stemmatological analysis identified six major text families: Babylonian, Yemenite, Ashkenazi, Sephardic, a group containing Codex Solger (Stadtbibliothek, Nürnberg) and the Rabbinic Bibles, and a group that van Staalduine-Sulman named 'the Italian Tradition'.[2] These textual families broadly correspond to distinct geographical and cultural zones (e.g. all Yemenite manuscripts belong to one text family, those belonging to the Sephardic group can be plausibly connected to Sephardic Jewry, etc.), but this is not always the case.

For purely pragmatic reasons van Staalduine-Sulman gave the last group the designation 'Italian', although this was not intended to describe the manuscripts' provenance.[3] Within the 'Italian' group, however, only two of the manuscripts

---

[1] van Staalduine-Sulman 'An Electronic Edition of Targum Samuel', 13–21.
[2] van Staalduine-Sulman, 'An Electronic Edition of Targum Samuel', 22–47.
[3] She writes: 'Because one family contains several manuscripts that are now preserved in Italy ([t2i, t3i, t7i, t700i, t701i]) and two manuscripts are written in Italian script and are of Italian provenance ([t701i, t705i]), I decided to call it the Italian family'; van Staalduine-Sulman, 'An Electronic Edition of Targum Samuel', 30.

are of Italian provenance (t705i, t701i[4]), one is Sephardic (t232i/s), and the remainder are Ashkenazi as we will see below, so the designation 'Mixed Western' would be preferable and is adopted in what follows.

One possible explanation of this phenomenon is that the high degree of contact between Jews across regional borders and the frequently itinerant nature of medieval European Jewish existence resulted in a high degree of cross-fertilisation between textual traditions.[5] From a historical perspective, one might also plausibly postulate a geographical connection to either Italy or part of the Ashkenazi zone (Germany?), since the connections — including the exchange of scholars and materials — between Italian and German Jewry in particular, are known to have been strong.[6]

Manuscript t232i/s, however, does not appear to fit this picture. Its script and codicology point clearly towards Sepharad. One possibility is that the scribe was an immigrant. Indeed, study of almost all the extant dated medieval Hebrew manuscripts revealed that about one-fifth of them were written by immigrant scribes,[7] and numerous examples are known of Sephardi scribes completing manuscripts in locations in Italy in the period prior to the general expulsion (1492).[8] The manuscript's date (fourteenth–fifteenth century) would

---

4   Interestingly Smelik's analysis of Targum Judges in this manuscript placed it in the Ashkenazi textual tradition, with particular affinities to Ms. Laud. Or. 326; Smelik, *The Targum of Judges*, 126.
5   See also my 'The Transmission of Targum Jonathan in the West: Initial Results from the Mixed Western Textual Group', *Aramaic Studies* 10 (2012), 23–52, pp. 23–9, 51.
6   See for example A. Grossman, *The Early Sages of Ashkenaz: Their Lives, Leadership and Works (900–1096)* [in Hebrew] (Jerusalem 1981), 19–21, 35–8, 79–80, etc.; I.M. Ta-Shma, *Creativity and Tradition: Studies in Medieval Rabbinic Scholarship, Literature and Thought* (Harvard, MA 2006), 70–9; M. Beit-Arié, *Hebrew Manuscripts of East and West: Towards a Comparative Codicology. The Panizzi Lectures 1992* (London 1993), 63.
7   Beit-Arié, *Hebrew Manuscripts of East and West*, 7–8.
8   M. Beit-Arié and E. Engel, *Specimens of Medieval Hebrew Scripts*, Vol. II, *Sefardic Script* (Jerusalem 2002), give several examples of manuscripts copied in Italy by Sephardi scribes: Parm 2750 (Biblioteca Palantina, Parma; Salerno, S. Italy, 1266), p. 70; Hébr. 637 (Bibliothèque Nationale, Paris; Geraci Siculo, Sicily, or Gerace Superiore, S.Italy, 1371), p. 86; Can Or. 81 (Bodleian Library, Oxford; Piscia, Central Italy, 1396), p. 92; Cod. Hebr. 77 (Bayerische Staatsbibliothek, Munich; Bologna, north-central Italy, 1397), p. 93; Parm. 2179 (Biblioteca Palantina, Parma; Piacenza, north Italy, 1444), p. 107; Add. 19943 (British Library, London; Ferrara, north- central Italy, 1447), p. 109; Ms 2514 (Jewish Theological Seminary, New York; Naples, S. Italy, 1457), p. 114; Opp Add 4° 177 (Bodleian Library, Oxford; Mantua, S. Italy, 1470), p. 123; Parm. 3053 (Biblioteca Palantina, Parma; Bari, S. Italy, 1473), p. 126; Cod. Hebr. 302 (Bayerische Staatsbibliothek, Munich; Reggio di Calabria, S. Italy, 1484), p. 134; Harl. 5719 (British Library, London; Mantua, N. Italy, 1488), p. 134; Med. Ms. Heb. 5 (Countway Library of Medicine, Boston; Naple, S. Italy, 1490), p. 137; Cod.

Chapter Three. The Manuscripts

certainly favour a migratory context. Yet, immigrant scribes normally adopted local codicological practices,[9] and this is not the case with t232i/s. Similarly, analysis of other biblical books contained in this manuscript do not support an Ashkenazi or Italian milieu: Houtman's analysis of Targum Isaiah locates its text in a Sephardic group, while Smelik's analysis of Targum Judges located its text in an 'oriental' group, consisting solely of this manuscript.[10] Indeed, t232i/s shares some variant readings exclusively with texts of the Sephardic group.[11] I will return to this puzzle in the conclusion.

In this study I analyse two of these textual families: the Mixed Western group, and the Ashkenazi group. Unlike the Mixed Western group, the Ashkenazi group is composed exclusively of manuscripts of Ashkenazi provenance. Of these two groups the Mixed Western group is particularly interesting because, although the manuscripts are all the product of Western Jewry, the stemmatological model shows that the text is close to the Eastern textual tradition.[12]

Not all the manuscripts analysed by van Staalduine-Sulman are included in the current study. Two were excluded from the Mixed Western group, namely Ms. Parm. 3187–89 (Bibliotheca Palatina, Parma) and Ms. Add. 9403 (British Library, London). The former is exceptional within the Mixed Western group: its text may have been influenced by a Sephardic tradition. In any case, it contains very many errors and singular readings. Ms. Add. 9403, which is in any case fragmentary, is closely related to Parm. 3187–89, if not directly dependent upon it.[13]

From the Ashkenazi group Ms. Or. fol. 1210–1211, Staatsbibliothek, Berlin, was excluded. This manuscript, written in a clear Franco-German script and completed in 1343 CE, most likely in Erfurt or its vicinity, and noted for its marvellous masorah written in decorative micrography, has been said to

---

Hebr. 244 (Bayerische Staatsbibliothek, Munich; Parvia, N. Italy, 1438), p. 194; Sloane 3265 (British Library, London; Naples, S. Italy, 1480), p. 204.

9 Beit-Arié, *Hebrew Manuscripts of East and West*, 7–8.
10 Houtman, 'Textual Tradition of Targum Jonathan to Isaiah', 149; Smelik, 'Trouble in the Trees!' 287.
11 See my 'The Transmission of Targum Jonathan in the West', 50.
12 van Staalduine-Sulman, 'An Electronic Edition of Targum Samuel', 22–3. I wish to thank van Staalduine-Sulman for providing me with the raw data that Dr Wattel's research on the texts produced.
13 van Staalduine-Sulman, 'An Electronic Edition of Targum Samuel', 32, 46.

represent 'the technical and artistic Ashkenazic medieval bookmaking in its perfection'.[14] The manuscript was not included for practical reasons: the available microfilms contain only selected pages and I was unable to obtain new images because the manuscript was under restoration. Thankfully the stemmatological analysis suggests we are not missing too much. The Targum text is extremely close to that of manuscript t713a (see below); it may even have served as the *Vorlage*. If so, then the scribe has corrected some of the errors in t713a (and introduced some of his own!), based on other Ashkenazi manuscripts.[15]

Thus, the following manuscripts containing the continuous text of Targum Samuel have been used.[16] Each manuscript's siglum precedes the manuscript's shelfmark and location.[17] The manuscript descriptions are ordered according to the sigla.

2. Description of the Manuscripts

2.a. The Mixed Western Group

t2i : Ms. Urbinati Ebr. 1, Biblioteca Apostolica, Vatican City

This codex, the largest in the collection of the Vatican library, contains the Hebrew Bible with Targum (Samuel 298^r–365^r), with each verse of the Hebrew text followed immediately by the Targum, or in the case of Esther by the Targum and Targum Sheni. The production of 'giant Bibles' was a style of book-making that originated in Christian monasteries in the middle of the eleventh century in Rome and was subsequently adopted by Jewish communities in Ashkenaz and Italy.[18]

That it contains the complete Hebrew Bible and is in a good state of

---

14 O. Hahn, et al., 'The Erfurt Hebrew Giant Bible and the Experimental XRF Analysis of Ink and Plummet Composition', *Gazette du livre médiéval* 51 (2007), 16–29', 16.

15 van Staalduine-Sulman, 'An Electronic Edition of Targum Samuel', 34.

16 In addition to the secondary works cited below, use has been made of the database prepared by the Targum Institute of the Protestant Theological University of the Netherlands (available via: www.targum.nl) and the additional bibliography there, and the database of the Institute of Microfilmed Hebrew Manuscripts, National Library, Israel (available via: www.jnul.huji.ac.il).

17 A full list of sigla is given in the front matter of the book.

18 D.J.D. Kroeze and E. van Staalduine-Sulman, 'A Giant Among Bibles: "Erfurt 1" or Cod. Or. fol. 1210–1211 at the Staatsbibliothek zu Berlin', *Aramaic Studies* 4 (2006), 193–205, esp. p. 198.

Chapter Three. The Manuscripts

preservation has resulted in it attracting much scholarly attention.[19] The Hebrew text and Targum are laid out in three columns and both carry Tiberian punctuation.

The vocalisation exhibits many inconsistencies[20] and peculiarities. According to Levine (on the Targum to Jonah) it preserves traces of Babylonian features.[21] Díez Macho considered the vocalisation to preserve in part the Ben Naphtali system.[22] One of the most distinctive features observed in the process of transcribing the text of the books of Samuel is the use of *hatef qamets* under a consonant which is followed by vocalic *waw* (for *shureq*), which remains unvocalised (e.g. בְּקֻודְשָׁיָא 1 Sam 1:1; כֻלְבֵּיהּ 1 Sam 13:21, בּוּכְרָא 1 Sam 17:13, רֻוגְזָא 1 Sam 17:28, etc.). The manuscript also contains several words that have been left without vowel points. Only a few of these cases relate to errors,[23] the majority do not,[24] and in any case some are very common words, the vocalisation of which even a naqdan with limited comprehension of the Aramaic could easily have reconstructed. The obvious explanation that the omission of vocalisation signals a correction by the naqdan does not seem applicable. In several examples other manuscripts offer a variant reading of the words concerned.[25] Taken together, the peculiarities of the vowels and the sporadic omission of vocalisation points to the naqdan having used a different manuscript from that used for the consonantal text, a phenomenon that we know of from other manuscripts.[26]

---

19 For a summary of the use of this manuscript in editions and previous research see L. Díez Merino, 'Targum al Cantar de los Cantares' (texto arameo del Códice Urbinati 1 y su traducción)', *Anuario de Filología* 7 (1981), 237–84, pp. 238–44.

20 Ribera Florit, 'The Babylonian Tradition of the Targum Jeremiah', 109.

21 Levine, *The Aramaic Version of Jonah*, 23–4.

22 A. Díez Macho, 'A New List of the So-Called 'Ben Naftali' Manuscripts, Preceded by an Inquiry into the True Character of these Manuscripts', in G. Rolles Driver, D. Winton Thomas and W. Duff McHardy (eds), *Hebrew and Semitic Studies: Presented to Godfrey Rolles Driver, in Celebration of his Seventieth Birthday 20 August 1962* (London 1963), 16–52.

23 E.g. הלא כמא דאתפרע 1 Sam. 6:6; וכען אם וכען אשכחית 1 Sam. 20:29; דהוה יתיב דוד בקרוי 2 Sam. 27:11.

24 E.g. כבר 1 Sam. 2:1; ותתנהון 1 Sam. 12:14; משריותך 1 Sam. 15:17; כען 1 Sam. 28:22; ברוון 2 Sam. 6:5; ובחניה 2 Sam. 12:3; בתנך 2 Sam. 12:8; אחוהא 2 Sam. 13:10; בני מלכא קטילו 2 Sam. 13:32; אשרי 2 Sam. 18:14; גבר 2 Sam. 19:9; מיליתא 2 Sam. 20:15; לית 2 Sam. 22:5; לקבלה initial *lamed* vocalised 2 Sam. 23:5; גברא second occurrence 2 Sam. 24:9.

25 E.g. 1 Sam. 12:14; 2 Sam. 6:5; 2 Sam. 12:3, 8; 2 Sam. 13:32; 2 Sam 19:9; 2 Sam. 24:9 also לאנצאת (for לאנצאה?) in 1 Sam. 13:21.

26 Smelik, 'How to Grow a Tree', 512–13.

The Transmission of Targum Jonathan in the West

A Tosefta Targum is found to Isa. 10:32–3, and further Aramaic additions appear to Isa. 66:1, 2, 23. The Palestinian Targum to Isa. 66:1 is a recension of that found in Codex Reuchlinianus No. 3 under the heading 'Targum Yerushalmi', though its text is inferior.[27] The Aramaic work, the Dream of Mordecai, is included after Esther and another hand has added Rashi's commentary in the margins of the Pentateuch.

The codicology and palaeography of this manuscript points to an Ashkenazi origin: The quires are quaternion (eight leaves), the common method of composition in Ashkenaz, and a system rarely found in Italy,[28] and the script is an Ashkenazi square script[29] (German?[30]). The use of the masorah to form decorative designs of plants and animals is also a typical feature of the Ashkenazi zone,[31] and the presence of Targum Chronicles is consistent with an Ashkenazi provenance.[32] The recent catalogue of Hebrew Manuscripts in the Vatican Library edited by Richler suggests Germany as the place of provenance.[33]

Colophon (f. 979v):

> I, Isaac son of Rabbi Simeon the Levite, provided the masorah for half of the book dedicated to R. Eleazar son of Samuel, may God grant him, his sons and the sons of his

---

27 P. Grelot, 'Deux Toseftas targoumiques inédites sur Isaïe LXVI', *Revue Biblique* 79 (1972), 511–43, pp. 514–27.
28 Beit-Arié, *Hebrew Codicology*, 43–5.
29 Richler, *Hebrew Manuscripts in the Vatican Library*, 599.
30 L. Mortara Ottolenghi, 'La decorazione del codice biblico ebraico della biblioteca «Berio» di Genova', *Miscellanea di Storia Ligure* 4 (1966), 68–84, p. 80; C.A. Fontela, 'El Targum al Cantar de los Cantares (Edicion Critica)', unpublished Ph.D. dissertation (la Universidad Complutense de Madrid 1987), 61; P.S. Knobel, 'Targum Qoheleth: A Linguistic and Exegetical Inquiry', Inquiry', unpublished Ph.D. dissertation (Yale University 1976), 11.
31 Sirat, *Hebrew Manuscripts of the Middle Ages*, 50; for a comparison of the decoration of Ms. Urbinati Ebr. 1 to that of Mss. B.H. I–VII, Genoa see Mortara Ottolenghi, 'La decorazione del codice biblico ebraico della biblioteca «Berio» di Genova', 81–2.
32 Targum Chronicles is known from only two additional manuscripts (a fourth manuscript was destroyed in the bombing of Dresden in 1945), both Ashkenazi, i.e. Or. fol. 1210–1211 Staatsbibliothek (Preußischer Kulturbesitz), Berlin (Ashkenazi, 1343); Cambridge University Library Ee. 5.9 (Ashkenazi, 1347). However, Targum Chronicles appears to have been little known in the period prior to printing, see Le Déaut and Robert, *Targum des Chroniques*, 10; J.S. McIvor, *The Targum of Chronicles. Translated, with Introduction, Apparatus, and Notes* (The Aramaic Bible 19, Edinburgh 1994), 14.
33 Richler, *Hebrew Manuscripts in the Vatican Library*, 599. Le Déaut and Robert, *Targum des Chroniques*, 15, propose Rhineland, with a question mark, where there was a tradition of editing manuscripts of a great size.

sons to study it until the end of all the generations, Amen.[34] I finished in the year 5055, on the 15th of Kislev.

According to the colophon half of the masorah was completed on 5055, that is November-December 1294 CE.[35] The masorah seems to have been added by two scribes (the hand changes at f.536v),[36] one of whom was also responsible for adding the colophon,[37] confirming this assertion. Whether or not he also copied the main text is a matter of dispute.[38]

t3i : Ms. Barberini Or. 161–164, Biblioteca Apostolica, Vatican City

The codex, another 'giant Bible', in four volumes contains the Hebrew Bible with Targum, with each verse of the Hebrew text followed immediately by the Targum. The text is laid out in three columns and the Hebrew text and Targum both carry Tiberian punctuation. The books of Samuel are found in the second of the four volumes (i.e. Or. 162; folios 39^v– 87^v). Four lines have been left blank on folio 45^r, where the text of Targum 1 Sam. 8:22 is missing. The Hebrew text is present, so it seems likely that the Targum to this verse was missing in the scribe's *Vorlage*. A Tosefta Targum to Gen. 44:18 appears in the margin (37v), while the Tosefta Targums to Josh. 6:1, Isa. 10:32–3, Obad. 1 and Hab. 3:1, are integrated in the text without indication. The script is an Ashkenazi square script, though folios 1–22 (Gen. 1–28:4) have been completed by another hand. The characters *beth* and *kaph*, *mem* and *samek*, fluctuate in shape so that in some cases they are impossible to distinguish.

The colophon (Barb. Or. 164, 164^v) reads as follows:

> I, Jechiel the scribe, wrote this book, being translated, from the first of Kislev in the year '56 to the first of Adar in the year '57 for R. Jacob son of Isaac.

---

34 The words from אמן סלה are in a smaller script.
35 Not 1295 as Assemanus and Assemanus, *Bibliothecæ apostolicæ vaticanæ*, 411 (followed by others). On the correct date according to the Christian calendar see, Díez Merino, 'Targum al Cantar de los Cantares', 238; Le Déaut and Robert, *Targum des Chroniques*, 15 n. 27.
36 Richler, *Hebrew Manuscripts in the Vatican Library*, 599; R. Weiss, *The Aramaic Targum of Job* [in Hebrew] (Tel-Aviv 1979), 49–50 inc. 50 n. 58; T. Metzger and M. Metzger, *Jewish Life in the Middle Ages: Illuminated Hebrew Manuscripts of the Thirteenth to the Sixteenth Centuries* (New York 1982), 310 no. 240.
37 The lettering is the same according to Weiss, *The Aramaic Targum of Job*, 49 n. 57.
38 Weiss, *The Aramaic Targum of Job*, 50; Fontela, 'El Targum al Cantar de los Cantares (Edicion Critica)', 62.

That is between 10th of November 1295 and 26th of January 1297 CE. There then follows, in a smaller hand, a blessing:

> May the Rock grant him and his seed after him to study it! As is written: 'May this book of the Law not depart from your mouth! Study it day and night in order that you might take care to do according to all that is written in it, because then you will make your ways prosper and you will have success.' (Josh. 1:8)[39] As is written: 'Moses charged us with the law, as a possession for the assembly of Jacob.' (Deut. 33:4) As is written: 'So you who held fast to the LORD your God are all alive today.' (Deut. 4:4). 'Have strength and courage because you shall cause [the people] to inherit it' (Josh. 1:6)

The scriptural citations are all vocalised.

t7i : Mss. B.H. I–VII, Biblioteca Civica Berio, Genoa, Italy

This manuscript, a 'giant Bible', contains the Pentateuch, Prophets, and Writings with the Targum alternating with the Hebrew verse (Samuel, vol. 3, 251^r–286^v; vol.4, 287^r–336^r). Rashi is added in the outer margin. The Dream of Mordechai in Aramaic follows Esther (748^v–749^v). The text contains Tosefta Targums (e.g. to Judg. 5:3, 5:5, 5:8; Zech. 2:14–4:7). The text is laid out in three columns, with the Hebrew and Aramaic text alternating. The Hebrew and Targum have Tiberian punctuation. The parashiyyot of the annual cycle are indicated in the Pentateuch and there are indications for the haftarot in the margins.

The manuscript is Ashkenazi. The quires are typically quaternion (eight leaves), a typically Ashkenazi feature,[40] the hand is an Ashkenazi square script,[41] and the decoration reflects that milieu:[42] The opening word of each Bible book is decorated and surrounded by a frame of micrographic masorah, including floral and animal motives, a typical Ashkenazi feature.[43] The name of the scribe (Meir) is also typical of France and

---

39 Cf. the colophon of Codex Reuchlinianus No. 3, below.
40 Beit-Arié, *Hebrew Codicology*, 43–4.
41 'franco-tedesco' (i.e. French/German) according to V.A. Martelli and L. Mortara Ottolenghi, *Manoscritti biblici ebraici decorati: provenienti da Biblioteche italiane pubbliche e private* (Milan 1966), 74; A. Luzzatto, 'La Bibbia ebraica della biblioteca 'Berio' di Genova', *Miscellanea di Storia Ligure* 4 (1966), 41–65, p. 41.
42 Mortara Ottolenghi, 'La decorazione del codice biblico ebraico della biblioteca «Berio» di Genova', 73–4, 80–1, cf. 84.
43 Sirat, *Hebrew Manuscripts of the Middle Ages*, 50. The decoration is described by Martelli and Mortara Ottolenghi, *Manoscritti biblici ebraici decorati*, 75–6.

Chapter Three. The Manuscripts

Germany, though the vicissitudes of Jewish life in central-Western Europe in the period mean that Provence or even Italy cannot be excluded as the place of composition.[44]

The vocalisation and consonants are obviously taken from different manuscripts. The *hatef qamets* is used in a similar way to that which I noted in t2i (e.g. 1 Sam. 18.11), for both *holem* and *shureq*. Vocalic consonants (*waw/yod*) are often deleted and the vowel is written under the preceding letter (i.e. for *hireq, holem, qibbuts*), though this is inconsistent.

Several words are left unvocalised in the manuscript. The vertical strokes with which the scribe normally marks a deletion are absent. In some cases the form is incorrect (1 Sam. 24:19; 1 Sam. 25:22), and in some cases the word probably ought to be deleted (e.g. 1 Sam. 25:9). Since the *Vorlage* of the consonants and vocalisation were different it may be that the word was missing (or the vocalisation illegible) in the vocaliser's *Vorlage* or that the vocaliser was not sure which form was correct.

A colophon at the end of Deuteronomy (198^r) reads in large letters as follows[45]:

> Finished and completed: the five fifths of the Law, praise be to God, who gives light to all the world. Let us be strong and resolute. Meir. May his Rock guard him!

The text continues in smaller characters:

> Finished and completed: the book of Deuteronomy, praise be to God who is a hero above all heroes and king above all kings and princes, and powerful above all those with power. I finished it on Sunday of the parasha 'You shall have no other God'[46], the year of 'Your eyes will see the king in his beauty directly' (≈ Isa. 33:15, 17). May he send us a redeemer to redeem all Israel joined together in the year 'God will cause us to laugh' (≈ Gen. 21:6)[47] with glory and splendour. He will redeem us from among the hostile nations; He will return us to our land happy and exalted; He will lift us up on the wings of eagles, He who illuminates the land and its inhabitants and illuminates all luminaries.

---

44 Luzzatto, 'La Bibbia ebraica della biblioteca 'Berio' di Genova', 54.

45 The colopha are barely legible on the microfilm. I follow the transcription of Luzzatto, 'La Bibbia ebraica della biblioteca 'Berio' di Genova', 50–9 (plates 3, 5).

46 I.e. Parasha יתרו (Exod. 18:1–20:26), see Luzzatto, 'La Bibbia ebraica della biblioteca 'Berio' di Genova', 52 n. 29.

47 The scribe indicates the date using chronograms by citing Isa. 33:17, then gives a paraphrase of Gen. 21:6. The first two words of Isa 33:17 and the first word Gen. 21:6 give the value 198 = 1438 CE. See Luzzatto, 'La Bibbia ebraica della biblioteca 'Berio' di Genova', 52 n. 30, n. 31, 53.

The Transmission of Targum Jonathan in the West

Before reverting to the large ornamental charqcter for the closing benediction:

> May the writer come to no harm! Amen, Amen.

The text again reverts to the smaller lettering, in order to add the following advice:

> A man should always write his name upon his book, lest someone else comes along from the market and takes it. Thus I have written my name and that of my father in here in order to show to people my right. I am he, Meir ... and you must know. May He who gives light to Israel protect and sustain me.[48]

The scribe also adds his name, Meir, at various other points in the codex.[49] A page in a different hand added in the first volume of the codex at a later stage provides a sort of index for the whole. The scribe includes several notes among the various lists, including at the end of the list of the Prophetic Books:

> The words of the Prophets and the Twelve are finished, praise be to God, the God of the spirits of all flesh.
>
> These are the Writings and the Five Scrolls in order, which I wrote. These are the signs in the year of goodness and of blessing.

A special sign stands above the four letters ב ר כ ה of the final word, indicating that the scribe is using a chronogram. The value of the four letters is 227, corresponding to 1467 CE.

1232i/s : Ms. Hébreu 75, Bibliothèque Nationale, Paris, France

This manuscript appears to be of Sephardi provenance, so its presence in a textual group otherwise consisting of Italian and Ashkenazi manuscripts requires further discussion (see page 358).

The manuscript itself contains Targum Onqelos, Targum Jonathan (Samuel 124ʳ–155ᵛ), Megillat Antiochus in Aramaic, and Testament Naphtali. Palestinian Targums are added to the Torah (to Gen. 38:25–6, f.10ʳ; Gen. 44:18 f.13ᵛ; Num. 32:3 f.75ᵛ) and clearly indicated; multiple Tosefta Targums to the Prophets are also present (e.g. Josh. 5:1; 5:3; 5:8; 5:14; 5:16; 5:26; 1 Sam. 17:8; Isa. 6:1; Zech. 2:14–4:1), which are integrated into the text without

---

[48] As with the scribe's use of מאיר throughout the codex, the last stanza is a pun on his name. It could read, 'He who is Israel's, Meir'.

[49] Luzzatto, 'La Bibbia ebraica della biblioteca 'Berio' di Genova', 54.

further indication. Oddly, a *Ketiv-Qere* is marked in the Aramaic at several points (e.g. 1 Sam. 22.18; 2 Sam. 8.3; 2 Sam. 13:37; 2 Sam. 18:12; 2 Sam. 23:9). The ordering of the Latter Prophets (i.e. Isaiah, Jeremiah, Ezekiel), which matches that of the Vulgate, is explained by the Sephardic copyist — Sephardic manuscripts tended to use the 'Christian' order.[50] The text of Targum Jonathan is immediately followed by an Aramaic blessing (299ᵛ): בריך רחמנא דיהב חילא לעבדיה בר אמתיה אמן 'May the Merciful One, who gives strength to his servant, the son of his maidservant, be blessed! Amen!'

The Targum is presented in a single column, with the exception of poetic sections in hemistiches (e.g. 2 Sam. 22:1–51; 153ʳ–154ᵛ) and lists in columns (e.g. 1 Sam 30:27–31; 141ʳ; three columns). According to Sirat, such a *mis en page* suggests that the work was intended for a single reader or student.[51] Each verse is introduced by Hebrew lemmata. The hand is a Sephardi semi-cursive script; Chilton cites examples of similar scripts copied in Italy.[52] The text has full Tiberian vocalisation and accentuation, which is a later addition and frequently errs. Frequent confusions in the vocalisation suggest that the punctuator was not the scribe of the main text. The normal composition of the quires is four sheets (eight leaves), conforming to Sephardi convention (though not exclusively Sephardi).[53]

The manuscript's date is impossible to establish on the basis of the colophon.[54] The manuscript in fact contains three colophons in a semi-cursive Sephardi script different from that of the main text, one at the end of Targum Onqelos (98ᵛ), at the end of Targum Jonathan (300ʳ), and at the end of Megillath Antiochus (302ʳ). They contain three clearly legible but impossible dates. The colophon following Targum Jonathan reads as follows:

> Among all wise things that Onqelos composed this is the book about which he himself said, 'This is the foundation of the world (and there is wisdom in studying in it all the wise things that are in the world) and a building (all the lands), and a column (seven pairs).'[55] It was completed in time at the end of ... from 3577, in the days of...

---

50 van Staalduine-Sulman, 'An Electronic Edition of Targum Samuel', 50.
51 Sirat, *Hebrew Manuscripts of the Middle Ages*, 46.
52 Chilton, 'HEBR. 75 in the Bibliothèque Nationale', 143.
53 Beit-Arié, *Hebrew Codicology*, 48–9.
54 On the reliability of colophons see Sirat, *Hebrew Manuscripts of the Middle Ages*, 208–11.
55 Cf. Gen. 7:2, 3.

The Transmission of Targum Jonathan in the West

Some further words at one time stood below this colophon, but these are now illegible (erased?). A word seems to have originally followed באחרית, which has since been rubbed out. The date given here, 3577, would equate to 183 BCE. The manuscript, in fact, dates from the thirteenth–fifteenth century.

t701i : Ms. Or. 72, Biblioteca Angelica, Rome, Italy

This manuscript was produced in Italy. The manuscript contains the Former Prophets and Writings, accompanied by the Targum and several commentaries (Samuel 40^v–80^r). At the end of the codex (folios 296–343) are various other works, principally grammars. The Hebrew text stands in the centre of the page, surrounded by various commentaries, including those of Italian scholars such as Isaiah di Trani and Benjamin ben Jehuda of Rome; the Targum stands in the inner column. No Tosefta Targums are noted. The Hebrew text appears to be an Italian square script,[56] while the Targum is in a different semi-cursive Italian script and is unvocalised. The quires are composed of five sheets (ten leaves), a composition typical of Italy.[57]

The codex was produced in at least two stages, as is indicated by the numeration of quires, which begins again with the Writings, and by the presence of two colophons (123^v, 340^v) giving differing dates and locations. The colophon at the end of the Former Prophets reads as follows:

> The commentary on [the books of] Kings was completed by Menachem Zemach son of R. Abraham Jacob, son of R. Benjamin, of blessed memory, son of R. Jehiel, for R. David son of Joseph son of Kimhi, of blessed memory, and I completed it on Monday the 14th of Kislev in the year '87, in Frascati, the town on the river Marana. Peace.

The date (i.e. 5087) equates to the 10th of November 1326 CE. The remainder of the codex had already been completed in 1323.[58] The elaborate style of decoration and the use of giant ornate letters at the beginning of book are consistent with such a dating.[59] The colophon relates to the commentaries and Targum only, which were copied by Menachem Zemach (and possibly others since the handwriting changes in places) who signed his name in various formulae, e.g. in the colophon to

---

56 C. Bernheimer, *Paleografia ebraica* (Firenze 1924), 386.
57 Beit-Arié, *Hebrew Codicology*, 44–5.
58 According to the colophon following David Kimhi's Grammar (f.326), see A. di Capua, 'Catalogo dei codici ebraici della bibliotheca Angelica', in *Cataloghi dei codici orientali di alcune biblioteche d'Italia* (Firenze 1878), 85–103, p. 88 (no. 27).
59 Martelli and Mortara Ottolenghi, *Manoscritti biblici ebraici decorati*, 50.

Chapter Three. The Manuscripts

Benjamin's commentary on Chronicles on (286ʳ). The Hebrew text must predate 1326 CE and was copied by an unknown scribe.

t705i : Codex Reuchlinianus No. 3, Badische Hof- und Landesbibliothek Karlsruhe, Germany

Codex Reuchlinianus No. 3 is our oldest genuinely Italian manuscript. The manuscript has occasionally been identified as being of German provenance,[60] and although there is some correlation between Franco-German and Italian codicology, which is natural given the historical links between the Jewish communities in these areas,[61] a number of features point towards a place of provenance in Italy.[62] The composition of its quires, which use five sheets, is typical of Italian manuscript production, the normal custom in Ashkenaz being to use only 4.[63] The script and the graphic fillers are similar to those of Ms. Urbinati Ebr. 2 (Biblioteca Apostolica, Vatican), a manuscript written *c.*1100 CE in Italy in an Italian square script.[64] The system of dating in the colophon, which calculates the number of years since the destruction of the Temple (לחורבן בית הבחירה) in the West is also characteristic only of Italy.[65] The various owners' messages in the manuscript, though later, add circumstantial evidence in support of an Italian provenance.[66] Reuchlin himself purchased the

---

60 E.g. W. von Abel and R. Leicht, *Verzeichnis der Hebraica in der Bibliothek Johannes Reuchlins* (Pforzheimer Reuchlinschriften 9, Ostfildern 2005), 97; citing K. Schilling (ed.), *Monumenta Judaica: 2000 Jahre Geschichte und Kultur der Juden am Rhein, I, Katalog: Eine Ausstellung in Kölnischen Stadtmuseum 15. Oktober 1963–15 März 1964* (Köln 1963), §B219.

61 Beit-Arié, *Hebrew Codicology*, 16.

62 Study of the manuscript by members of the l'Institut de Recherche et d'Histoire des Textes (CNRS, Paris) and the Israel Academy of Sciences and Humanities (Jerusalem), under the auspices of the Committee of Hebrew Palaeography, reached the conclusion that the manuscript could be considered 'avec plus ou moins de certitude, être d'origine italienne'. C. Sirat, et al., *Codices hebraicis litteris exarati quo tempore scripti fuerint exhibentes*, III, *de 1085 à 1140* (Monumenta Palaeographica Medii Aevi: Series Hebraica, Turnhout 2002), 9, see also 11, 50–1. For a full description of the manuscript along with sample plates, see 50ff.

63 See Beit-Arié, *Hebrew Codicology*, 44–5; and 45 n. 78, on the similarity between Ashkenazi and Italian manuscripts, 16. Contra Delitzsch, *Liber Jeremiae* (ed. S. Baer; Leipzig 1890), 6, cited in W. Brambach, *Die Handschriften der Badischen Landesbibliothek in Karlsruhe*, II, *Orientalische Handschriften: Neudruck mit bibliographischen Nachträgen* (Wiesbaden 1970 [1892]), 6–7.

64 See Richler (ed.), *Hebrew Manuscripts in the Vatican Library: Catalogue*, 600.

65 Sirat, *Hebrew Manuscripts of the Middle Ages*, 219. For בית הבחירה = Jerusalem Temple, cf. b.Sanh.20ᵇ.

66 The first named owner is Avigdor, son of Daniel, who obtained the book in 1368. The two notes (folios 1ʳ and 384ʳ) are transcribed by Baer, who identifies the purchasers as belonging

manuscript in Rome in 1498 for 11 gold Rhenish guilders (385^v).

The manuscript is written in what is probably an Italian square script,[67] and contains the Prophets with Targum Jonathan, the Hebrew and Aramaic appearing on alternating verses laid out in two columns. The text exhibits unusual vocalisation, apparently reflecting an uncommon pattern of pronunciation,[68] which has been the subject of much scholarly discussion.[69] The vocalisation may not be the work of the main scribe.[70]

With the exception of Josh. 10:12–32 (between folios 11/12) and 1 Sam. 12:21–16:23 (between folios 66/67), the books are complete (Samuel 54^v–113^v). The folios containing 1 Sam. 12:21–16:23 have been cut out; in one place (1 Sam. 12.25) a marginal note is still readable on the remainder of a page. The missing pages have been restored on paper at a later date.

At the back of the codex one finds five Aramaic hymns to Jonathan ben Uzziel (383^r–383^v) and a list of haftarot for the year and for the festivals by two other hands (384^v–385^r). The haftarot are indicated in the margins.

---

to the Mansi or Piatelli families from Rome; cited in Brambach, *Die Handschriften der Badischen Landesbibliothek in Karlsruhe*, II, 7–9.

67 Prijs, 'Über Ben Naftali-Bibelhandschriften und ihre paläographischen Besonderheiten', *Zeitschrift für die Alttestamentliche Wissenschaft* 69 (1957), 171–84, p. 172; although sometimes considered to be Ashkenazi, the two scripts being difficult to distinguish, e.g. von Abel and Leicht, *Verzeichnis der Hebraica in der Bibliothek Johannes Reuchlins*, 97.

68 van Staalduine-Sulman, 'Vowels in the Trees', 237.

69 Sperber, *The Pre-Masoretic Bible*, I, *The Codex Reuchlinianus*, xiii–l esp. xxv–xxxiii; S. Morag, 'The Vocalisation of Codex Reuchlinianus: Is the "Pre-Masoretic" Bible Pre-Masoretic?', *Journal of Semitic Studies* 4:3 (July 1959), 216–37. See also Meyer's review of A. Sperber, *Corpus Codicum Hebraicorum Medii Aevi*, II, *The Pre-Masoretic Bible. Codex Reuchlinianus, No. 3 of the Badische Landesbibliothek in Karlsruhe (formerly Durlach No. 55), with a General Introduction: Masoretic Hebrew*, by A. Sperber (Copenhagen 1956) – *Codices Palatini*, I, *The Parma Pentateuch (Ms. Parma No. 1849, formerly de Rossi No. 2)*, Vol. 1–3, by A. Sperber. Ebenda: 1959 – *A Grammar of Masoretic Hebrew, a General Introduction to the Pre-Masoretic Bible*, by A. Sperber (Copenhagen 1959). *Vetus Testamentum* 11 (1961), 474–86, esp. pp. 482–6. See further, Prijs, 'Über Ben Naftali-Bibelhandschriften und ihre paläographischen Besonderheiten'; C.D. Ginsburg, 'The Dageshed Alephs in the Karlsruhe-MS., being an Explanation of a Difficult Massorah', in *Verhandlungen des Fünften Internationalen Orientalisten-Congresses* II:1 (Berlin 1882), 136–41; Merx, 'Bemerkungen über die Vocalisation der Targume', 181–8; P. Kahle, *Masoreten des Westens*, II, *Das palästinische Pentateuchtargum, die palästinische Punktation, der Bibeltext des Ben Naftali* (Text und Untersuchungen zur vormasoretischen Grammatik des Hebräischen 4; Beiträge zur Wissenschaft vom Alten und Neuen Testament 50, Stuttgart 1930), 51, 55.

70 van Staalduine-Sulman, 'Vowels in the Trees', 227; van Staalduine-Sulman, 'An Electronic Edition of Targum Samuel', 19.

Chapter Three. The Manuscripts

The colophon (382^v), reads as follows:

> This book of the Prophets (including) the Targum and the (Hebrew) text was completed by Zerach bar Yehuda the younger, the scribe, in the year 4866 since the creation and 1038 since the destruction of the Temple, may it be rebuilt soon in our time! May (the Lord) grant us to study them (i.e. the Prophets) and to teach without plague or affliction. So may the writing be fulfilled in me! 'May this book of the Law not depart from your mouth! Study it day and night in order that you might take care to do according to all that is written in it, because then you will make your ways prosper and you will have success.' (Josh. 1:8)

The two dates given in the colophon do not appear to agree. Reckoned from the date of creation, the manuscript was completed in the year 1105/1106 CE; but if one calculates from the destruction of the temple the date would be 1107/1108 CE.[71] According to Sirat *et al* Zerach bar Yehuda wrote the manuscript for his personal use.[72]

The manuscript contains a great many marginal notes pertaining to the Targum text, of differing lengths and type. These have been dealt with below (in chapter nine).

t718i : Ms. Laud Or. 326, Bodleian Library, Oxford, England

This manuscript contains Targum Jonathan to the Former Prophets (Samuel 24^v–47^r), preceded by various readings of different schools for the Writings (e.g. various readings of Ben Naphtali and Ben Asher compared to each other, different lists of *Ketiv-Qere*, etc.). There is a Tosefta Targum to 1 Sam. 17:8, which is integrated into the text without indication (30^v). The Targum is laid out in three columns and each verse is introduced by the first word of the Hebrew verse to which it corresponds (i.e. lemmata). There is no punctuation. The main text has been completed by several scribes, and the hands, all of which are Ashkenazi,[73] can be easily distinguished. The normal composition of the quires is four sheets (eight leaves), which would also point towards an Ashkenazi place of origin.[74] There is no colophon, but the name Samuel is

---

71 See von Abel and Leicht, *Verzeichnis der Hebraica in der Bibliothek Johannes Reuchlins*, 100 n. 16.
72 Sirat, et al., *Codices hebraicis*, III, *de 1085 à 1140*, 50.
73 R.A. May (ed.), compiled under the direction of M. Beit-Arié, *Catalogue of the Hebrew Manuscripts in the Bodleian Library: Supplement of Addenda and Corrigenda to Vol. I* (A. Neubauer's Catalogue) (Oxford 1994).
74 Beit-Arié, *Hebrew Codicology*, 43–4.

pointed out several times (e.g. on 24v, 25r, 30r etc. and is presumably the name of the scribe (NB. 1–2 Samuel 24v–47r).[75] The manuscript may be as early as the twelfth century.[76] Several pages of the manuscript have been cut, probably for use in bindings (e.g. fols 8, 16, 41).

2.b. The Ashkenazi Group

t5a : Ms. Or. fol. 1–4, Staatsbibliothek (Preußischer Kulturbesitz), Berlin, Germany

This fourteenth century manuscript (the punctuation is later, 1455 CE), written in Ashkenazi square scripts contains the Pentateuch, Former and Latter Prophets, and the Writings all accompanied with Targum (Samuel vol. 2, i.e. Or. fol. 3, 60r–133r).[77] The Aramaic composition, the Dream of Mordechai, is included after Esther. Two folios are missing from volume 3 (Or. fol. 2), which contains the Latter Prophets (i.e. Amos 3:7ff), and the section containing 1 Sam. 14:26–47 (vol 2, fol. 208) is from another manuscript, though the *mise en page* is the same and the hand is also an Ashkenazi square script. In the margins are alternative readings to the Targum indicated by 'ס'א (i.e. ספר אחר) in all the volumes. Tosefta Targums are integrated in the text without indication at several points (e.g. Isa. 10:32–3; Hab. 2:11; 3:1–2; Zech. 2:14–16, 3:1–4.7).[78]

The text is laid out in three columns, with the Targum alternating with the Hebrew verse, except in poetic sections (e.g. 2 Samuel 22). Within the books of the Prophets most of the haftarot are indicated. The quires are normally composed of four sheets (eight leaves), the common practice in Ashkenaz.[79] The opening word of each Bible book is highlighted and decorated and surrounded by a frame of micrographic masorah decorated with floral and

---

75 As Neubauer, *Catalogue of the Hebrew Manuscripts in the Bodleian Library,* no. 179. In one case the name 'Israel' is also decorated (fol. 25), probably in error since it is the last word of the line and the name Samuel stands as the last word of the line immediately preceding it and is also decorated.

76 According to May (ed.), *Catalogue of the Hebrew Manuscripts in the Bodleian Library,* no. 179; Smelik, *The Targum of Judges,* 124, dates it to the fourteenth century, citing Neubauer's catalogue. However, Neubauer's catalogue does not give the date.

77 Werner, *Jüdische Handschriften Restaurieren. Bewahren. Präsentieren. Vol. 1, Jüdische Kultur im Spiegel der Berliner Sammlung* (Berlin 2002), Vol 1 §4; M. Steinschneider, *Die Handschriften-Verzeichnisse der Königlichen Bibliothek zu Berlin,* Vol. 2 (Berlin 1878), §1.

78 See R. Kasher, *Targumic Toseftot to the Prophets* [in Hebrew] (Sources for the Study of Jewish Culture 2, Jerusalem 1996), §§ 107b, 142a, 144a.

79 Beit-Arié, *Hebrew Codicology,* 43.

animal motifs, covering half the page, a typical feature of Ashkenazi manuscripts.[80] There is a short colophon at the end of Chronicles:

> Let us be strong and resolute. May the scribe, Baruch bar Abraham, come to no harm! Amen. Selah.[81]

t6a : Ms. Hébreu 18, Bibliothèque Nationale, Paris, France

According to Sed-Rajna, the large format of the manuscript (535–6 x 363–6 mm) reflects a trend towards the end of the thirteenth century in North East France or across the border in Germany to produce giant Bibles.[82] The manuscript could be slightly later (i.e. fourteenth century). Sed-Rajna identifies the script as Franco-Ashkenazi, Zotenberg as German.[83] As one might expect, most of the quires are quarternions. Although no colophon from the *prima manus* is recorded, the corrector of volume 2 (Hébreu 18), a certain Menahem b. Perets Trabot, working in Governolo in the province of Mantua, Italy, added a colophon after the text (fol. 671), stating that his work was completed by 1512 CE.

The manuscript is divided across two volumes, the first containing the Pentateuch and the Writings (vol. 1, Hébreu 17), the second, the Prophets (vol. 2, Hébreu 18); the Hebrew is accompanied by Targum throughout (Samuel fol. 89–197). The Aramaic Dream of Mordechai is included after Esther. Tosefta Targums have been incorporated into the running text without indication (e.g. Judg. 5:5; 1 Sam. 17:8 and Zech. 4:2, 3, 7),[84] and some alternative readings to the Prophets are indicated in the margins by ס"א or בס"א (i.e. ספר אחר) and ג"א (i.e. גרסה אחרת), sometimes with two or three readings to a single point in the text.[85]

The text is *mise en page* in three columns, except the poetic sections, which

---

80 Sirat, *Hebrew Manuscripts of the Middle Ages*, 50. See Werner, *Jüdische Handschriften*, Vol 1 §4 for illustration.
81 Cf. the catchword on f.170 Vol 3 (Or. fol. 2): אברהם is decorated with a lion on a shield.
82 Sed-Rajna, *Les manuscrits hébreux enluminés des bibliothèques de France* §73. Garel, *D'une main forte*, §117 opts for Germany (dating the manuscript to c.1300), following Zotenberg, *Manuscrits orientaux* §17 et 18.
83 G. Sed-Rajna, *Les manuscrits hébreux enluminés des bibliothèques de France* (Corpus of Illuminated Manuscripts 7, Oriental Series 3, Leuven 1994), §73; H. Zotenberg, *Manuscrits orientaux. Catalogues des manuscrits hébreux et samaritains de la bibliothèque Impériale* (Paris 1866), §17 et 18.
84 See Kasher, *Targumic Toseftot to the Prophets*, §§ 24d, 53b, 144a. See also chapter eleven.
85 See Smelik, *The Targum of Judges*, 1995.

are in hemistiches (e.g. 2 Samuel 22); the Targum alternates with the Hebrew verse. The initial letters of each biblical book are written in grand size. The haftarot are indicated in the Prophets, and a second hand, probably the corrector, gives a list of the parashiyyot and haftarot (fol. 671).

t713a : Ms. El. f.6, Thüringer Universitäts- und Landesbibliothek, Jena

This Ashkenazi manuscript contains the Prophets with Targum Jonathan (Samuel 69^r–147^r) alternating with the Hebrew verses. The text is laid out in three columns and is written in a German square script of the thirteenth or fourteenth century.[86] Two leaves covering Hos. 4:8–7:5 have been cut out and the last leaf of the folio is missing (i.e. Mal. 3:22–4). Some Tosefta Targums have been integrated into the text without indication (e.g. Judg. 5:3, 5; 1 Sam. 17:8).[87] The quires are normally composed of four sheets (eight leaves), the common practice in Ashkenaz.[88] The first word of Joshua has been decorated, and that of the books of Judges, Jeremiah and the Twelve have a highlighted opening word. A space has been left for a highlighted opening word for Samuel, Kings, Ezekiel and Isaiah but the opening word has not been completed.

t720a : Ms. Add. 26879, British Library, London, England

Manuscript Add. 26,879 was probably written in the thirteenth century; a partially erased deed of transaction (f. 2^r) records that the manuscript was sold in 1359 CE, fixing its *terminus ante quem*.[89] The fine handwriting is Ashkenazi (Franco-German[90]), the Hebrew text and Targum written in square script (the Targum in a smaller font), Rashi's commentary in a semi-cursive Ashkenazi script. The quires are typically composed of twelve leaves (i.e. six sheets), sometimes eight. Composition of quires in four sheets (i.e. quaternion) is the norm in Ashkenaz, and composition with six sheets is rare.[91]

The manuscript contains the Hebrew text of the Prophets accompanied by

---

86 Róth, *Hebräische Handschriften*, Vol. 2, ed. H. Striedl with L. Tetzner (Verzeichnis der Orientalischen Handschriften in Deutschland VI, 2, Wiesbaden 1965), §213.
87 See chapter eleven.
88 Beit-Arié, *Hebrew Codicology*, 43.
89 Margoliouth, *Catalogue of the Hebrew and Samaritan Manuscripts in the British Museum*, Part 1, §187. Levine erroneously lists the manuscript as dating from the seventeenth cent. Levine, *The Aramaic Version of Jonah*, 23.
90 Margoliouth, *Catalogue of the Hebrew and Samaritan Manuscripts in the British Museum*, Part 1, §187.
91 Beit-Arié, *Hebrew Codicology*, 43–4, 46.

Targum and the commentary of Rashi (Samuel 50ʳ–108ʳ). Some pages are missing, including all but a few words of Jeremiah (also 1 Kgs 8:8–16:25; Isa. 53:12–66:24; Hos. 1:1–9:16; 12:4–14:10; Joel 1:1–2:11). The Hebrew text stands in the centre of the page, with the Targum in the inner margin[92] (with occasional Hebrew lemmata) and Rashi's commentary written in geometric forms — usually circles — in the outer column. The haftarot are frequently indicated, either in the margin or by a blank line in the Targum, in which the name of the shabbat is sometimes written. The manuscript contains numerous Tosefta Targums to the Prophets (e.g. Judg. 5:1, 5, 8, 11, 15, 26; 1 Sam. 17:8; Isa. 10:32; Zech. 2:14–4:7; Hab. 3:1, 2, 11), which are integrated into the text without further indication.[93]

t725a : Ms. 11, Stiftsbibliothek Göttweig, Germany

A fourteenth century manuscript in a German square script containing the Prophets with Targum Jonathan (Samuel 64r–141r).[94] Rashi's commentary has been added in the margin to Josh. 1:1–4:17. Elsewhere in the margins one finds alternative readings to the Targum marked 'ס'א (i.e. ספר אחר) in the same hand.[95] A few Tosefta Targums have been incorporated into the running text without indication (e.g. 1 Sam. 17:8; Obad. 1:1).[96]

The Targum alternates with the Hebrew verse and the text is presented in three columns, except in poetic sections (e.g. 2 Samuel 22). Each biblical book begins with a highlighted opening word with the exception of Isaiah, with depictions of all manner of flora and fauna (some fantastical) in micrographic masorah. The composition of the quires is the typical Ashkenazi format, namely four sheets (eight leaves), with few exceptions.[97]

---

92 A feature of Ashkenazi manuscripts from the fourteenth century; see E. Attia, 'Targum Layout in Ashkenazic Hebrew Manuscripts: Preliminary Methodological Observations', in A. Houtman, H-M. Kirn and E. van Staalduine-Sulman (eds), *A Jewish Targum in a Christian World* (Jewish and Christian Perspectives 27, Leiden 2014), 99–122, pp. 110–12; Houtman, 'The Role of the Targum in Jewish Education in Medieval Europe', 88–90, 94.

93 See Kasher, *Targumic Toseftot to the Prophets* §§21, 24d, 25b, 26b, 27a, 29, 53b, 107b, 144a. See also chapter eleven.

94 A.Z. Schwarz, *Die hebräischen Handschriften in Österreich* (außerhalb der Nationalbibliothek in Wien), Vol I, Bibel — Kabbala (Leipzig 1931), Vol 1 §2.

95 Schwarz, *Die hebräischen Handschriften in Österreich*, Vol 1 §2.

96 See Kasher, *Targumic Toseftot to the Prophets* §§53b, 136. See also chapter eleven. There are no Tosefta Targums to Judges according to Smelik, *The Targum of Judges*, 121.

97 Beit-Arié, *Hebrew Codicology*, 43.

The Transmission of Targum Jonathan in the West

3. The Quality of the Transmission (Scribal Errors and Corrections)

An evaluation of the errors present in each of our manuscripts is necessary for two reasons: first, in order to judge the likelihood that textual variants, in particular omissions, are simply errors; and, secondly, in order to evaluate the competence of the scribe, and therefore the probability that the scribe of the manuscript was responsible for deliberate textual emendation.

It is not necessary to sift all the scribal errors. The following observations give just a few examples, mostly from 1 Samuel 1–10, which I used as a sample text. Errors, such as the confusion of graphically similar letters (e.g. ד/ר, ב/כ, ו/י, ז/נ/ו), in particular certain prefixes (e.g. -ל and -ב; -מ and -ב) in common expressions (e.g. 1 Sam. 20:27 ביומא דבתרוהי t710y, t232i/s, t701i, t705i, t2i, t3i; מיומא דבתרוהי t7i, t718i), or the omission or addition of the copula, are common in all our manuscripts, so are ignored in what follows. Likewise, the interchange of homophonous letters (e.g. ס/שׂ).[98]

3.a. The Mixed Western Group

t2i Ms. Urbinati Ebr. 1

t2i exhibits very few accidental omissions, either by parablepsis[99] or by simple carelessness (i.e. random omissions).[100] There are no cases of dittography, Hebraism, or graphic confusions between letters in 1 Samuel 1–10, and metathesis is rare.[101]

The manuscript contains only a few corrections, which could be the work of a second hand.[102] The punctuator indicates several errors by leaving a word unvocalised.[103] In one case he vocalises the top lefthand arm of the *mem* of the word עולימא as if it were a *yod* to create the plural (i.e. 1 Sam. 21:3). The single case in which a deletion is indicated by vertical strokes above the letters (2 Sam. 24:12 חדא ##*תלת* יוי אמר) and the deletion of an occurrence of the divine name

---

98 Smelik gives a nice example of this from Ms. Or. 72 (i.e. t701i): last word of f.39v is למיסגי, but its repetition as a catch-word on f. 40r is למישׂגי! Smelik, *The Targum of Judges*, 131.
99 E.g. 1 Sam. 4:8 אלין אבון for אלין אנון; 1 Sam. 4:9 לגברין פלשתאי instead of לגברין גיברין פלשתאי.
100 E.g. 1 Sam. 2:10 omits שמיא מן; 1 Sam. 9:7 omits אנהנא.
101 E.g. 1 Sam. 12:17 בישתכון סגיאה for סגיאה בישתכוי; 1 Sam. 21:6 לא דכן הוא אף ואף לקודשא for לקודשא ואף דכן; 2 Sam. 3:22 איתיאו עמהון for עמהון איתיאו; 2 Sam. 13:6 לחיתתא for חליטתא.
102 Cf. É. Levine, *The Aramaic Version of Ruth* (Analecta Biblica 58, Rome 1973), 14.
103 E.g. 1 Sam. 20:29 אשכחית ##*וכען* אם *וכען*; 1 Sam. 27:11 בקרוי ##*דוד* *יתיב*.

by enclosing the word in a little box(!) (i.e. 1 Sam. 16:8 ##*יוי קדם יוי) may therefore be the work of the *prima manus*. A single case of word-omission is remedied by the placement of the missing word in the margin, with a placement marker in the text (i.e. 1 Sam. 7:9 ואסקיה #חדא#** דחלבא); a missing letter from a word is added above the word in minuscule lettering (i.e. 2 Sam. 17:29 ומככין*#ומשככין#).

Although this study does not examine the vocalisation of the various manuscripts, the peculiarities of t2i's vocalisation have been widely noted for several of the biblical books. Specifically, the current vocalisation exhibits many inconsistencies and has evidently been copied from a different manuscript from the manuscript used for the consonantal text, so that the two frequently do not agree (e.g. in matters of *matres lectionis*).[104]

t3i Ms. Barberini Or. 161–164

The scribe of t3i was notably less diligent in his work than the scribe of t2i, to which the manuscript is closely related.[105] Although there are no lengthy omissions such as one finds in t701i, small omissions resulting from parablepsis[106] and random omissions[107] appear slightly more frequently than in t2i, as do cases of dittography,[108] metathesis,[109] and Hebraisms.[110]

The sheer quantity of cases of graphic confusion between letters in t3i is

---

104 Levine, *The Aramaic Version of Jonah*, 26, 35 n.57 (Levine repeats his observations almost verbatim in his *The Aramaic Version of Lamentations* (New York 1976), 20–2; *The Aramaic Version of Qohelet* (New York 1978), 84–6; and, 'Codex Urbinates Ebr. 1; A "Targum" Text', *Biblische Zeitschrift* 24 [1980], 95–100); Le Déaut and Robert, *Targum des Chroniques*, 15–16, 19 (and further comments, 20–1); Smelik, *The Targum of Judges*, 122 n. 35, 123; Díez Merino, 'Targum al Cantar de los Cantares', 244–5; Fontela, 'El Targum al Cantar de los Cantares (Edicion Critica)', 61; E. White, 'A Critical Edition of the Targum of Psalms', unpublished Ph.D. dissertation (McGill University 1988), 41; Weiss, *The Aramaic Targum of Job*, 49.
105 van Staalduine-Sulman, 'An Electronic Edition of Targum Samuel', 32.
106 E.g. 1 Sam. 1:6 omits מן קדם יוי by skipping to מנה; 1 Sam. 2:2 omits דעתיד by skipping to דייסק; 1 Sam. 4.20 skips from לא to ולא omitting אתיבת ולא; 1 Sam. 17.7 omits four words between two occurrences of דמורניתיה; 1 Sam. 20.42 omits three words between two occurrences of דיוי; etc.
107 E.g. 1 Sam. 2.31 omits אבוך; 1 Sam. 9:14 omits לבית.
108 E.g. 1 Sam. 2:8 עם צדיקיא עם רברבי עלמא (for: עם צדיקיא רברבי עלמא), though it is not impossible that this is a deliberate amendment; 1 Sam. 12:3 וית מן אנסית ומיד מן אנסית ומיד מן קבילית; etc.
109 E.g. 1 Sam. 5:9 והות מחתא דיוי בקרתא שגושי רב לחדא for והות מחתא דיוי לחדא שגוש רב לחדא; 1 Sam. 5:10 עיקרונא for עיקרונאי; 1 Sam. 22:19 וחמר ואימר for ואימר וחמר; 2 Sam. 5:6 בארעיותך for באעדיותך (also graphic confusion between *dalet* and *resh*).
110 E.g. 1 Sam. 1:16 לא תכלים for לא תתן תכלים (MT = אל תתן); 1 Sam. 3:6 ברי for בני (also 1 Sam. 14:50); 2 Sam. 23:37 צלק דמבני עמון for צלק דמן עמון (or צלק העמוני).

staggering.[111] Interestingly the resulting form is often a possible lexeme that, nonetheless, makes no sense in the context, occasionally with comical results.[112] This observation implies that the scribe did not understand the text he was copying.

The manuscript has been vocalised and at a later stage corrected. Many erroneous forms have thereby been given vowel points. Superfluous words or letters (all vocalised) are struck through;[113] some incorrect letters have been redrawn,[114] or the correct form written immediately above the letter concerned.[115] Replacement text (vocalised) is written in the margin and the text to be replaced (also vocalised) is marked with dots above each letter[116] or by supra-linear vertical strokes at each end of the lexeme concerned.[117] Omissions are added in the margin; a placement marker appears in the main text.[118]

t7i Mss. B.H. I–VII

There are only a few, mostly single words, accidental omissions in t7i, most of which do not result from parablepsis.[119] Metathesis and graphic confusion between letters are equally infrequent.[120] Other errors are more common (e.g. dittography,[121] Hebraism[122]).

---

111 E.g. 1 Sam. 1:13 נייך for נייה; 1 Sam. 2:1 בדיואל for בר יואל; 1 Sam. 2:31 תרע for דרע; 1 Sam. 10:18 ידכון for יתכון; 1 Sam. 13:21 ברזל for פרזל (error? cf. Tg. Onq. Deut. 8:9 variants); 2 Sam. 5:2 את for אף; 2 Sam. 6:21 לפקד׳ ידי for לפקדא יתי.

112 E.g. 2 Sam. 6:2 דשכנתי׳ שריא עיל מן כלביא עלוהי 'whose Presence dwells upon the *dogs*(!)' for כרוביא!

113 E.g. 1 Sam. 1:17 לשלם #איזילו#*איזילו*ואמר; 1 Sam. 8:5 מלכא #ממנא#*ממלנא* ;כען 1 Sam. 8:14 ייסב *חד*## ויתן.

114 E.g. 1 Sam. 25:21 ואתיב#*ואעיב*; 1 Sam. 29:8 אשכחתא#*אשכה תא* (the *taw* has been redrawn to fill in the space).

115 E.g. 1 Sam. 9:5 אבא#*אבה*.

116 E.g. 1 Sam. 7:10 ויהמם וינגפו לפני ישראל#*ושגישנון ואיתברו קדם ישר*׳.

117 E.g. 1 Sam. 11:12 מן לשאול#*אל שמואל*׳ עמא.

118 E.g. 1 Sam. 2:2 אלהא #**אלא**; דתקיף 1 Sam. 13:7 בתרוהי #**אתכבשו**; 1 Sam. 14:43 שאול עמא וכל #***; 1 Sam. 31:11 ית *גלעד*** יבש יתבי; **אל יונתן**# חוי. All vocalised with the exception of 1 Sam. 2:2.

119 E.g. 1 Sam. 1:11 omits קדמך (גלי); 1 Sam. 2:5 omits עתידא; 1 Sam. 2:19 omits אמיה ליה עבדא זעיר ומעיל (a whole line in the *Vorlage*?); 1 Sam. 2:20 omits ואמר; 1 Sam. 5:2 omits דיוי; 1 Sam. 10:5 omits נחתין; 1 Sam. 13:16 the entire verse is omitted, perhaps because the beginning words and final word of the verse are identical in the Hebrew and the Aramaic; 1 Sam. 19:4 skips from ארי to וארי omitting four words.

120 E.g. 1 Sam. 1:16 אקמותי for אקביותי; 1 Sam. 6:4 לכולהון for לכולכון; 1 Sam. 12:14 ותפלחון for תפלחון.

121 E.g. 1 Sam. 2:6 דיוי גבורתא אלין כל יוי for דיוי גבורתא אלין כל (the word יוי begins the following verse); 1 Sam. 2:15 יתסקון לא עד אף (the repeated phrase starts a new line); 1 Sam. 2:30 הל׳ בר שבט בנימין אנא מזעירי; 1 Sam. 9:21 אמר וכען עלמא עד קדמי for אמר וכען עלמא עד קדמי וכען עד עלמא

Chapter Three. The Manuscripts

Corrected errors in t7i are relatively few in number. Omissions, including some amounting to several words, have been restored by the corrector; the missing text (vocalised) is written in the margin, a placement marker stands in the text.[123] Replacements for incorrect words also stand in the margin; a dot marks the erroneous form.[124] Occasionally micro-lettering is used to correct one or two letters.[125] Letters or words swapped by metathesis are marked with a *beth* and an *aleph* respectively to indicate that they ought to be read in reverse order. An intriguing feature of this manuscript is that the corrector very frequently restores (in micro-lettering) the 'missing' letters from words that have been abbreviated (usually to preserve the left hand column edge), including some extremely common words,[126] perhaps with the intention of aiding the reader.

t232i/s Ms. Hébreu 75

Accidental omissions are numerous in t232i/s. These are mostly random omissions (usually single words),[127] cases of omission by parablepsis being less frequent.[128] Many of the manuscript's cases of dittography have been corrected.[129] Cases of uncorrected metathesis abound,[130] but Hebraisms,[131] and

---

הלא בר שבט בנימין אנא מזעירי שיבטיא דישראל for שיבטיא בנימן דישר׳ (repeated under influence of preceding phrase).

122 E.g. 1 Sam. 4:11 ותרין בני עלי for ושני בני עלי; 1 Sam. 5:3 אשדודים for אנשי אשדוד or אשדודאי; 1 Sam. 13.3 ית איסטרטיג for ית נציב איסטרטיג (MT: את נציב); 1 Sam. 18:21 לו for ליה.

123 E.g. 1 Sam. 3:4 #אנא#** הא; 1 Sam. 7:6 #ומליאו מייא#**; 1 Sam. 7:8 #לשמואל#**; 1 Sam. 14:4 #ודוד וגברוהי מסטר טורא מכא והוה#**; 1 Sam. 23:26 #מיכא ושינא דכיפא מעיברא#**; 1 Sam. 25:13 #וזריזו גבר ית חרביה#**.

124 E.g. 1 Sam. 22:18 #לדוד#*.

125 E.g. 1 Sam. 7:13 #בפלשתאי#*פלשתאי; והוה מחתא דיוי 1 Sam. 23:10 #לקעילה#*לקרתא*.

126 E.g. 1 Sam. 17:49, 57 #פלשתאה#*פלש׳*; 1 Sam. 17:57 #ואיתיה#*ואיתי*; 1 Sam. 18:1 #דיהונתן#*דיהונ׳*.

127 E.g. 1 Sam. 1:1 omits בטורא; 1 Sam. 1:18 omits ואמרת; 1 Sam. 2:12 omits רשיעין; 1 Sam. 2:26 omits קדם יוי; 1 Sam. 3:17 omits כען; 1 Sam. 6:4 omits חדא; 1 Sam. 6:20 omits דיוי; 1 Sam. 8:9 omits ארי; and frequently.

128 E.g. 1 Sam. 2:21 reads רביא שמואל משמיש קדם יוי for רביא שמש קדם יוי; 1 Sam. 5:8 omits five words between two occurrence of אלהא דישראל; 1 Sam. 5:9 omits 6 words between occurrences of לעקרון; etc.

129 Corrected cases: e.g. 1 Sam. 10:10 ואתו לתמן for ואתו תמן לתמן; 1 Sam. 13:3 פלישתאי די בגיבעתא ושמעו פלישתאי for פלישתאי די בגיבעתא ושמעו פלישתאי די בגיבעתא ושמעו פלישתאי; Uncorrected cases: e.g. 1 Sam. 14:6 מעצור למיפרק בסגיאי או בזעירי for מעצור בזעיר למיפרק בסגיאי או בזעירי; 1 Sam. 14:38 הלכא כל ריש עמא for הלכא כל ריש עמא; 1 Sam. 17:7 ונטיל תריסא נטיל for ונטיל תריסא אזיל.

130 E.g. 1 Sam. 1:13 נדיין for ניידן; 1 Sam. 1:24 מכילתא חדא דקימחא for מכילתא חדא דקמיחא; 1 Sam. 3.17 כדין יעביד לך יוי for כדין יעביד יוי לך; 1 Sam. 4:7 מאמתלי for מאתמלי; 1 Sam. 20:2

graphic confusion between letters are less widespread.[132] t232i/s is particularly prone to errors resulting from the physical layout of the material, such as repeating the last word of one line at the beginning of a new line[133] or skipping over words when a new line begins.[134] Likewise, the scribe sometimes copies the Hebrew text midway through copying the Aramaic verse (subsequently deleted), suggesting that he worked from an interlinear text.[135]

Although a staggering amount of errors remain in the text, the corrector has been far from idle. No more than a few verses at a time go by without a correction appearing, the overwhelming majority of which relate to accidental omissions and additions of whole words. The deletion of numerous superfluous words (mostly dittography) is indicated by the addition of two vertical strokes above the (unvocalised) word;[136] omissions are written (vocalised) in the margin, a placement marker stands above the line in the text. Sometimes the marginal correction introduces an error.[137] Although this study does not examine the vocalisation of the various manuscripts, it is worth noting that the vocalisation of t232i/s is recurrently faulty, either replicating the vocalisation of the Hebrew[138] or guessing at vowels based on the consonants.[139]

t701i Ms. Or. 72

The scribe of t701i (or his *Vorlage*) repeatedly omits long sections of texts due to parablepsis. For example, at 1 Sam. 5:3–4, the scribe's eye skips between

---

פיתגמא רבא או פיתגמא זעירא for פיתגמא זעירא או פיתגמא רבא; etc.

131 E.g. 1 Sam. 14:45 את for ית; some possible cases: 1 Sam. 4:2 ארבעת (= MT), for ארבעא or ארבעה; 1 Sam. 5:4 כפת ותרתין, for ותרתין פסת (MT = כפות); 1 Sam. 20:22 שלחך for שיזבך (MT = שלחך).

132 E.g. 1 Sam. 17:5 גלפין 'engravings, settings' for גלבין 'scales' (error?); 2 Sam. 1:19 אמרין for איכדין.

133 E.g. 1 Sam. 1:13 וקלה is repeated (left unvocalised to indicate the mistake).

134 E.g. 1 Sam. 2:2 omits לית from דתקיף לית יימרון (the word יימרון ends a line). Later corrected. 1 Sam. 4:19 omits בעלה as he starts a new line (i.e. וכערת | ודאיתקטיל).

135 E.g. 1 Sam. 25:11 שירותי ##לגוזזי *טבחתי*; וית 1 Sam. 25:24 קדם רגלוהי ##*על רגלין* פלת.

136 E.g. 1 Sam. 1:15 ##*קדם*; נפשי* 1 Sam. 1:23 ##*רביא*; דתיחסלין 1 Sam. 1:24 ##*חד*; דחמר 1 Sam. 1:27 מן קדמוהי ##*קדמוהי*; etc.

137 E.g. 1 Sam. 2:5–6 גבורתא דיוי# גבורתא דיוי כל אילין ותחרוב תצדי משריתהא יסופון עממיא סגי #**, i.e. dittography.

138 E.g. 1 Sam. 1:8 לָךְ (= Hebr. t232i/s even appears to mark the *zaq.qatan, i.e.*, above the letter); 1 Sam. 2:1 אָפְתַּה; 1 Sam. 1:6 פְתַח.

139 E.g. 1 Sam. 1:12 דתפסיק: consonantal form could be *pael* (תְּפַסִּיק) or *aphel* (תַּפְסִיק); the vocalisation of t232i/s reads דְתָפְסִיק, an impossible form.

Chapter Three. The Manuscripts

two occurrences of קדם ארונא דיוי, thereby omitting no less than twenty intervening words. If one assumes a column width in the *Vorlage* of t701i of approximately 25 characters, then a number of the manuscript's omissions by parablepsis would correspond to the omission of one or more complete lines.[140] Many shorter omissions by parablepsis are also found.[141] Although parablepsis is relatively widespread, t701i makes relatively few random omissions.[142] Cases of dittography are common,[143] but metathesis,[144] Hebraisms,[145] and graphic confusions between letters are relatively infrequent.[146] Some cases of grammatical discord are found.[147]

The text has been corrected frequently.[148] Some cases obviously stem from the *prima manus*, who has begun to write a word incorrectly, realised his error before completing the word, and so begun again.[149] In these cases the aborted form is marked by supra-linear dots. The scribe (or his *Vorlage*) had some difficulties with pronominal suffixes: the final ה is sometimes lacking from the third person male suffix, but added to the first person singular suffix in other instances; likewise the male and female third person singular suffix are often interchanged.[150]

---

140 E.g. 1 Sam. 9:18–19 skips between occurrences of חזוא, omitting 7 words (*c.* 28 characters; 1 line?); 1 Sam. 10:11–12 skips between occurrences of האף שאול, omitting 13 words (*c.* 50 characters; 2 lines?); 1 Sam. 20:30 skips from לבר ישי (*sic*) to דבר ישי, omitting 9 words (*c.* 34 characters; 1 line?); 1 Sam. 25:31 skips between occurrences of לריבוני, omitting 11 words (*c.* 47 characters; 2 lines?); 1 Sam. 28:19 skips between occurrences of בידא דפלישתאי, omitting 12 words (*c.* 48 characters; 2 lines?); etc.

141 E.g. 1 Sam. 1:27 omits דבעיתי from קדמוהי מן בעותי ית לי יוי ויהב under influence of preceding word; 1 Sam. 12:15, four words omitted between two occurrences of במימרא דיוי; 1 Sam. 25:13, scribe's eye skips from חריזו to וחריז, omitting four words; etc.

142 E.g. 1 Sam. 9:2 omits שאול; 1 Sam. 9:25 omits עם; 1 Sam. 10:11 omits וחזו.

143 E.g. 1 Sam. 3:10 ואמר שמואל מליל ארי שמע עבדך for ואמר שמוי ארי מליל ארי שמע עבדך; 1 Sam. 3:13 דינין דיני על ישי'; 1 Sam. 8.1 וחזו אינש אינש אשדוי; 1 Sam. 5:7 אנא מן מן אינש; 1 Sam. 10:16 ועל עיסק עיסק; and frequently.

144 E.g. 1 Sam. 4:2 וסדרו קרבא פלשתאי for וסדרו פלשתי' קרבא; 1 Sam. 13:3 תקע פלישי' ושמעו ושאול for ושמעו פלשתאי ושאול תקע.

145 E.g. 1 Sam. 1:14 אמתי for מתי; 1 Sam. 11:5 והא שאול אחר בתר תוריא for והא שאול אתא בתר תוריא (MT = והנה שאול בא אחרי הבקר).

146 E.g. 1 Sam. 2:30 דינך for דיני; 1 Sam. 3:8 וסבר for ודבר; 1 Sam. 4:3 ויהי בינבא for ויהך בינבא. A more extreme case: 2 Sam. 1:25 איתקטילתא for איתון טלתא?

147 E.g 1 Sam. 30:8 הדין משריתא perhaps under influence of MT?

148 Martelli and Mortara Ottolenghi, *Manoscritti biblici ebraici decorati*, 48.

149 E.g. 1 Sam. 1:7 שנה בשנה ##*ב* (begins with second word in error); 1 Sam. 2:6 שליט *בלמ*## בעלמא; 1 Sam. 2:29 קדשי ##*קוש**.

150 See Smelik, *The Targum of Judges*, 126.

There is no particular indication that the remaining corrections stem from a later hand.[151] In the majority of cases the correction adds a single letter that has been omitted in error: the missing letter is written above its intended position in the word.[152] In a couple of places a ית has been neglected; this is later supplied in the margin, with a dot marking its placement in the line.[153] Other forms of deletion are marked by dots[154] or vertical strokes[155] above the offending letter(s), or by a diagonal stroke crossing right through the letter.[156] The scribe occasionally repeats the last words of one page at the start of the next page and sometimes these two readings do not agree.[157]

t705i Codex Reuchlinianus No. 3

t705i has been executed with a great deal of diligence. There are no instances of parablepsis in 1 Samuel 1–10. There are a few small random omissions (i.e. omissions that cannot be explained by parablepsis).[158] Other forms of scribal error are uncommon (i.e. dittography,[159] metathesis[160]), and there are only one or two clear cases of Hebraism,[161] and graphic confusion between letters.[162]

The *prima manus* left a few errors which have been subsequently corrected. In several cases a word has been omitted or repeated as the scribe started a new line or column: missing words are restored, written at the end or beginning of the line.[163] One case was noted in which a word that was originally missing has

---

151 See Smelik, *The Targum of Judges*, 126.
152 E.g. 1 Sam. 2:28 #והבית*#ויה*ית#; 1 Sam. 2:30 #לדימקרין#*לדי*מיקרין; 1 Sam. 5:6 #ואדינון*#וא*צדינון; 1 Sam. 7:3 #ועשתרתא*#וע*שתתא; 1 Sam. 9:1 #דבית#*בית*#; 1 Sam. 9:4 #מברא*#מתברא*#; 1 Sam. 9:16 #אר*#ארי*#; 1 Sam. 10:25 #בספרא#*בסי*פרא*.
153 E.g. 1 Sam. 6:13 #ית*** עיניהון #וזקפו; 1 Sam. 9:8 #ית** אורחנא לנא.
154 E.g. 1 Sam. 2:17 גבריא ##*ית* בזו.
155 E.g. 1 Sam. 2:2 #סגיד#*סג*י*.
156 E.g. 1 Sam. 8:2 אביה #תינינה*#התיניניה* ושום.
157 E.g. 1 Sam. 10:21 ¶ויתאחד¶ ואיתאחד; 1 Sam. 17:13 ¶תלתה¶ תלתא; 1 Sam. 17:48 ואזל¶ואזיל¶.
158 E.g. 1 Sam. 2:5 omits ותחרוב תצדי; 1 Sam. 3:7 omits פיתגם; 1 Sam. 9:13 omits לבית.
159 One possible case: 1 Sam. 1:20 וקראת ית שמיה שמואל ארי אמרת ארי מן קדם יוי שאלתיה; remaining witnesses read without second ארי.
160 E.g. 1 Sam. 2:1 וצליאת חנה ברוח נבואה ואמרת for וצליאת חנה ואמרת ברוח נבואה. 1 Sam. 6:9 (NB. לבית שמש הוא מן קדמוהי עבידת לנא ית בישתא for לבית שמש הוא מן קדמוהי ית עבידת לנא בישתא remainder read איתעבידת in place of עבידת, possibly the origin of the error); 1 Sam. 12:3 מיניה for מניה; 2 Sam. 5:5 תלת ותלתין for תלתין ותלת; 1 Sam. 27:1 מדעם לי for לי מדעם; עיני מניה for עיני.
161 E.g. 1 Sam. 3:4 יהה for יוי; 1 Sam. 6:6 מצרים for מצראי.
162 E.g. 1 Sam. 9:4 שעט for שבט; 1 Sam. 10:25 ממוסא for נומסא.
163 E.g. 1 Sam. 1:10 #היא#***; 1 Sam. 2:30 ישמשון #אבנך#** ובית; 1 Sam. 7:7 ישראל# #*** ושמעו פלישתאי על.

been restored and the corresponding word was also missing in the Hebrew and has also been restored there.[164] The letters of deleted words are marked with dots;[165] in at least one case the word is deleted after it has been vocalised.[166] Other accidental omissions are written above the line in their intended position,[167] or in the case of longer omissions, in the margin with a placement marker above the line in the text.[168] Vowel letters (ו, י) were added to some words, probably when the vocalisation was added.[169]

t718i Ms. Laud Or. 326

t718i has been copied carelessly. One finds very many accidental omissions in the manuscript, sometimes of notable length. Lengthy omissions due to parablepsis are widespread.[170] Many such examples would correspond to an assumed line length of *c.* 16/17 characters in t718i's *Vorlage*. Some long random omissions are found,[171] but generally random omissions are short.[172] Dittography is common.[173] In a number of cases the scribe begins a new verse with the first words of the verse that immediately precedes or follows, before continuing with the verse in hand.[174] Occasionally lengthy sections are written

---

164 2 Sam. 16:5 #דוד#** מלכא ואתא.
165 E.g. 1 Sam. 4:10 ריגלי ##גבר* גבר.
166 2 Sam. 24:1 ישראל ##דבית*.
167 E.g. 1 Sam. 1:6 #לאקניותה#לאקיותה*; *; 1 Sam. 1:9 #כהנא#כהן*; 1 Sam. 2:30 קושטא #ייו#** אמר; 1 Sam. 3:19 פיתגמוהי #ממכל** בטיל ולא; 1 Sam. 10:3 #בביתאל#ביתאל*.
168 E.g. 1 Sam. 8:16 חמריכון #*** ורית שפיריא.
169 E.g. 1 Sam. 2:2 #מינך#מנך*; 1 Sam. 3:9 #ותימר*ותמר#*.
170 E.g. 1 Sam. 4:4–5 omits eight words between two occurrences of ארון קיימא דיוי; 1 Sam. 4:21–2 omits 11 words between occurrences of גלא יקרא מישראל; 1 Sam. 10:20–1 omits five words between occurrences of דבית בנימן; etc. Complete verses are occasionally omitted because first word(s) are identical with the foregoing or following verse (e.g. 1 Sam. 14:42; 2 Sam. 7:28).
171 E.g. 1 Sam. 5:3–4 omits והא דגון רמי על אפוהי על ארעא קדם ארונא דיוי.
172 E.g. 1 Sam. 2:10 omits מן שמיא; 1 Sam. 3:11 omits בישראל; 1 Sam. 6:3 omits (תנוח) לא; 1 Sam. 7:6 omits ית בני ישראל; 1 Sam. 8:6 omits מלכא; 1 Sam. 8:9 omits בהון; 1 Sam. 8:18 omits ההוא מן; and frequently.
173 E.g. 1 Sam. 2:36 לאישתפלא לאי ליה, remaining לאישתפלא ליה (i.e. the scribe notices his error before completing the word; no attempt has been made to delete the incorrect insertion); 1 Sam. 3:16 אנא הא ואמר ואמר; 1 Sam. 7:6 ההוא ביומא וצמו ביומא וצמו; 1 Sam. 14:4 שינא דכיפא מעיברא מיכא ושינא דכיפא מעיברא מיכא for שינא דכיפא מעיברא מיכא ושינא דכיפא מיכא מעיברא (also metathesis); etc.
174 E.g. 1 Sam. 2:31 begins דישראל אלהא יוי אמר בכין, the first words of the preceding verse; 1 Sam. 5:3 begins ואקדימו בצפרא for ואקדימו, the following verse begins ואקדימו בצפרא; 1 Sam. 23:25 begins ואזל שאול וגברוהי for ואזל שאול מסטר טורא מיכא וגברוהי, the following verse begins ואזל שאול מסטר טורא מיכא.

twice.[175] Cases of metathesis are widespread.[176] Since the manuscript contains only the Aramaic text it is perhaps unsurprising that no Hebraisms were noted.[177] Graphic confusion between letters is common.[178] t718i also exhibits a tendency to elide words.[179]

The text of t718i is corrected in numerous places; in many cases this must be the work of the *prima manus*. He is frequently obliged to add missed letters, adding these above the intended position in the word.[180] Where he has written the wrong letter, he often reshapes the character or overwrites it with the correct letter.[181] Extraneous letters are crossed out;[182] occasionally a replacement letter is then written above.[183] Superfluous words are marked with a vertical stroke above the first and last letter.[184] The insertion of a space is indicated by a dot above and an arrow beneath the relevant point in the text.[185] Some missing words are supplied in the margin (with a placement marker in the text), apparently by a second hand. These are single words, apparently corrections derived from the context (for example a missing negation) rather than a sign that the text has been corrected against a less faulty manuscript.

---

175 E.g. 1 Sam. 14:1 והוה יומא ואמר יונתן בר שאול לעולימא נטיל זיניה ונעביר לאיסטרטיג פלישתאי למגזת מכמס והוה יומא ואמר יונתן בר שאול לעולימא נטיל זיניה ונעביר לאיסטרטיג פלישתאי דיכי דמעיברא ולאבוהי לא חוי.

176 E.g. 1 Sam. 2:1 קדם יוי גלן, for גלן קדם יוי; 1 Sam. 2:8 שמואל ברי for ברי שמואל; עובדי בני אנשא for עובדי בני אנשא; 1 Sam. 2:30 וכען אמר יוי קושטא for אמר יוי וכען קושטא; 1 Sam. 3:10 בזמן כזמן for כזמן בזמן; 1 Sam. 5:3 אינש אשדוד ביומא דבתרוהי for ביומא דבתרוהי אינש אשדוד; 1 Sam. 14:4 שינא דכיפא מעיברא מיכא ושינא דכיפא מיכא מעיברא for שינא מעיברא דכיפא מיכא ושינא מיכא דכיפא מעיברא שינא (also dittography); etc.

177 E.g. 1 Sam. 10:11 לבר קיש for לבן קיש; 1 Sam. 22:8 בני for ברי.

178 E.g. 1 Sam. 1:13 רויא for רביא; 1 Sam. 2:36 יהי לאישתפא for ייתי לאשתפלא; 1 Sam. 3:20 מתמן 'from there' for מהימן 'trusting'; 1 Sam. 7:6 לבהון for לבכון; 2 Sam. 15:19 חברין for עברין.

179 E.g. 1 Sam. 12:6 ודאסיקית, for ודאסיק ית; 1 Sam. 12:11 ושלחית for ושלח יוי ית; 1 Sam. 15:2 דכמן ליה for דכמגיליה.

180 E.g. 1 Sam. 1:3 *לזעירא*[מי]#*זעירא*; *למסגד*#*מיסגד*; 1 Sam. 3:1 *ביומא*#*ביומיא*; 1 Sam. 5:9 אינשי ישראל מן *טורא*#*ב[ט]ורא*; 1 Sam. 5:12 *לא*#*דלא*; 1 Sam. 9:4 *טורא*#*ב[ט]ורא*; 1 Sam. 7:11 *מצפיא*#*מצפיא* ורדפו.

181 E.g. 1 Sam. 1:16 *יוי*#*בת* רישעא; 1 Sam. 2:5 קדם *ורומא*#*ורומי*; 1 Sam. 2:14 *מדבחא*#*דלדבחא*; 1 Sam. 2:16 *דסיסקון*#*דסיסקון*; 1 Sam. 3:5 *תוב*#*יתוב* קרייתי (reshaped into foot of *taw*!); 1 Sam. 6:7 *ועיבידו*#*ע*.

182 E.g. 1 Sam. 1:11 *יומוהי*#*יומי*; 1 Sam. 2:2 *אילא*#*אילא*; 1 Sam. 6:15 *אסיקו*#*ואסיקו*.

183 E.g. 1 Sam. 2:5 *עתידא*#*עתידא*; 1 Sam. 6:19 *עקרא*#*יתירא*; 1 Sam. 7:12 *סעדא*#*סגדא*; 1 Sam. 6:19 *שבעא*#*שבען*.

184 E.g. 1 Sam. 2:1 *עכבריכ*##*דמחבלין*; 1 Sam. 4:16 ##*ניבלין* *ניבלין*##*מאן*; 1 Sam. 6:5 ית ארעא ##*וקבילו*; 1 Sam. 7:7 ##*בישתא*#*יבישתא* ית רבתא הדא; 1 Sam. 6:9 קדם יוי 1 Sam. 7:9 *אלהנא*## על ישראל.

185 E.g. 1 Sam. 2:1 *בריואל*#*בר יואל* ואף הימן.

Chapter Three. The Manuscripts

3.b. The Ashkenazi Group

t5a Ms. Or. fol. 1–4

The text of t5a is affected by manual scribal errors only very lightly. The scribe was more prone to skip a single word at random,[186] than any other type of error, though such omissions are still relatively infrequent. Occasional cases of dittography,[187] metathesis,[188] Hebraism,[189] elision[190] and confusions of grammatical number or gender are found.[191]

Many of these occurrences, however, have subsequently been corrected,[192] so that the final form of the text is relatively clean. There are a few scattered corrections of the consonants and many affecting vocalisation that may indicate that the text has been corrected against a second manuscript(s), which belonged to a different textual tradition from that from which the consonants have been copied. This has certainly happened in t6a; the cases in t5a are much less certain, but it is possible.[193] If the text has been corrected in this way, then the correction has been desultory; judging from the variants the second manuscript(s) could easily have been another Ashkenazi manuscript.[194]

A second hand, seemingly the naqdan, has made a great many minor corrections in the manuscript (including to the Hebrew text). Omissions are restored in the margin,[195] a circle marks the placement in the verse. Corrected forms are also written in the margin, the erroneous form in the main text being

---

186 E.g. 1 Sam. 1:28 קדם for קדם יוי; 1 Sam. 2:1 על ניבלין for על ידי ניבלין; 1 Sam. 15:17 omits שבטא.

187 E.g. 1 Sam. 2:23 דרבנין עמא דיוי (other manuscripts without דיוי); taken over from following verse. Left unvocalised by naqdan); 1 Sam. 4:16 מן סידרא דקרבא ואנא מן סידרא for מן סידרא ואנא מן סידרא דקרבא.

188 E.g. 1 Sam. 2:15 *prima manus* בה, corrected to הב.

189 E.g. 2 Sam. 9:3 נכה רגלים instead of לקי בתרתין רגלוהי. Possibly also 1 Sam. 13:17 שועל instead of דרומא.

190 E.g. 1 Sam. 2:2 *prima manus* וניסגי corrected (supralinear) to וניס סגי.

191 E.g. 1 Sam. 1:24 עימה 'with him', for עימה 'with her'. 1 Sam. 4:20 *prima manus* נשיא דקיימין (i.e. lack of agreement in gender between noun and participle). Corrected.

192 See examples in preceding footnotes.

193 A possibility advanced already by Smelik, *The Targum of Judges*, 122 and van Staalduine Sulman, *The Targum of Samuel*, 54.

194 E.g. 1 Sam. 20:28 t5a[PM] ואתיב יהונת' ית שאול אבוהי (= t720a, t725a, t718i), t5a[correct] < אבוהי (= t710y, t6a, t713a, t2i, t3i, t7i, t232i/s, t701i, t705i. Or correction of conventional rendering?); 2 Sam. 8:2 t5a[PM] תרין חבלין (= t3i, t7i, t232i/s, t701i, t705i, t718i), t5a[correct] תרין עדבין (= t710y, t713a, t720a, t725a, t2i); 2 Sam. 19:38 t5a[PM] ועביד ליה ית דתקין בעינך (= t710y, t6a, t713a, t720a, t3i, t232i/s, t705i, t718i), t5a[correct] ועביד ליה כמא דתקין בעינך (= t725a, t2i, t7i, t701i).

195 E.g. 1 Sam. 2:14 לתמן #אלדבחא** דאתן כל ישראל לכל עבדין כדין.

The Transmission of Targum Jonathan in the West

left unvocalised or being struck through.[196] Missing individual letters are tagged to the start or end of a line when possible, squeezed between the existing letters, or added supra-linear.[197] Superfluous letters are crossed through.[198] Incorrect letters are struck through and their replacement written above or below the original letters,[199] or reshaped where possible.[200] The deletion of whole words is indicated by supra-linear dots and occasionally unvocalised words[201] (though it is not clear whether every unvocalised form should be read as deleted).

t6a Ms. Hébreu 18

The *prima manus* of t6a has been even more careful than t5a. There are very few omissions;[202] cases of dittography, transposition, and Hebraisms are all infrequent.[203] In a few cases it is clear that the scribe introduced an error under the influence of nearby wording.[204] Like all the manuscripts in the Ashkenazi group, parts of speech are not always correctly accorded.[205]

Correction of these minor errors is less extensive than t5a, but the evidence that the manuscript has been corrected against a different textual tradition is much more definitive than it is for t5a.[206] The corrected form of the text more often stands closer to the Babylonian textual tradition than the text of the *prima manus*,[207] but the correction seems to have been carried out somewhat

---

196 E.g. 1 Sam. 2:15 לגברא דדבח *בה*#הב#*בישרא 1 Sam. 2:15 עד לא *יקרבון*#יתסקון (unvocalised); 1 Sam. 2:15 (struck through).

197 E.g. 1 Sam. 1:11 מללא רברבן אם מיגלא גלי קדמך *סיגוף*#בסיגוף# אמתך (start of line); 1 Sam. 2:3 ייפקון #ולא#*לא* (between letters); 1 Sam. 1:12 מדסגיאת*#מדאסגיאת# לצלאה; 1 Sam. 2:2 והוה* #וניס סגי#*וניסגי* (supra-linear).

198 E.g. 1 Sam. 1:5 #איתמנע#*איתימנע*; 1 Sam. 1:9 #דאישתיא#*דאישתיאו*; 1 Sam. 1:24 בתורין #תלת#תלתין*.

199 E.g. 1 Sam. 1:1 #צוף#*אסף* בר (above); 1 Sam. 1:13 לחוד #בליבה#*בליבא* מצליא* (below).

200 E.g. *yod* extended into waw 1 Sam. 1:6 #לאקנייתה#*לאקנייתה*.

201 E.g. 1 Sam. 1:23 ואמר *יהוה*## לה (dots); 1 Sam. 2:5 כין ירושלים ##*חורין*# כין למיהוי בני חורין (unvocalised).

202 E.g. 1 Sam. 1:14 omits עלי.

203 E.g. 1 Sam. 9:7 מקבל ואם instead of ואם מקבל; 1 Sam. 4:11 *prima manus* מתו (= MT) instead of אתקטלו (or deliberate revision to MT?). Subsequently corrected.

204 E.g. 1 Sam. 23:25 למעון for למבעי (copied from later in verse דמעון); 1 Sam. 3:7 אולפן for פיתגם based on wording of earlier in verse.

205 E.g. 1 Sam. 4:20 דקיימין נשיא; 1 Sam. 14:45 פורקנא רבא הדא; 1 Sam. 30:8 משריתא הדין (perhaps under influence of MT?).

206 A fact already noted by van Staalduine-Sulman, 'An Electronic Edition of Targum Samuel', 34.

207 E.g 2 Sam. 15:26 t6a[PM] כמא דרעוא (= all Ashkenazi and Mixed Western texts), t6a[correct] כמא דתקן

Chapter Three. The Manuscripts

sporadically so it is difficult to identify the source. Many of the examples cited in the following chapters from either the *prima manus* or corrected form of t6a evince this tendency (for practical reasons, I usually record only variants, not agreements; so in many cases, for example, where the corrected form of t6a agrees with the Babylonian tradition, this reading is not noted separately).

Corrections of whole words, whether they be a replacement for the wording in the main text[208] or the restoration of an omission,[209] are normally written in the margin with a supra-linear symbol marking the insertion point in the text. Missing letters are written supra-linear at the insertion point,[210] as are replacement letters, the redundant letter(s) being crossed through.[211]

t713a Ms. El. f.6

The text preserved in manuscript t713a is in a poor state.[212] Random omissions[213] and omissions by parablepsis[214] are very common, as are cases of dittography.[215] Transpositions[216] and Hebraisms[217] are less frequent, though still apparent in significant numbers. One finds discord in grammatical number or gender.[218]

Although a great number of omissions remain in the text, very many have

---

(= t710y); 1 Sam. 1:18 t6a[PM] קדמך (= t713a, t720a), t6a[correct] בעינך (= t710y, t5a, t725a, all Mixed Western); 1 Sam. 30:12 t6a[PM] פלח (= t5a, t713a, t720a, t7i[PM], t701i), t6a corrected פילס (= t710y, t725a, t2i, t3i, t232i/s, t705i, t718i); 1 Sam. 30:17 t6a[PM] גמליא (= t713a, t720a, t2i, t7i, t705i[margin]), t6a[correct] ינקיא (= t710y, t725a[correct], t3i, t232i/s, t701i, t705i, t718i), and very many other cases.

208 E.g 1 Sam. 1:18 #בעינך*קדמך #רחמין אמתך תשכח; 1 Sam. 2:1 פומי #אתפתח*איתי*; 1 Sam. 2:19 #למעד מעד*#לזמן מזמן* ליה ומסקא.

209 E.g. 1 Sam. 1:11 אינשאף בני #בגו**#בר; 1 Sam. 1:5 #ולד**#מינה איתמנע.

210 E.g. 1 Sam. 1:15 #עיקת*#עקת*; 1 Sam. 1:15 #אישתי*#אישתתי*; 1 Sam. 17:46 *ואיקלינך*#ואיקטלינך.

211 E.g. 1 Sam. 1:13 #בליבא*#בליבה*; 1 Sam. 1:18 #לאורחא*#לאורחה*. Also crossed through when there is no replacement, e.g. 1 Sam. 1:24 #ובמכילתא*#ומכילתא*.

212 As noted already by van Staalduine-Sulman, *The Targum of Samuel*, 56.

213 E.g. 1 Sam. 1:1 < בטור; 1 Sam. 9:27 < דין כיומא; 1 Sam. 10:26 < עמא מן קצת; 1 Sam. 13:3 < בשופרא תקע ושאול; 1 Sam. 15:17 < שבטא, and so on.

214 E.g. 1 Sam. 1:8 < אכלת לא ולמה (corrected in margin); 1 Sam. 1:26 < נפשך חיי ריבוני; 1 Sam. 17:49 omits four words between עינה; 1 Sam. 28:14 < ארעא על, and so on.

215 E.g. 1 Sam. 9:6 וכען וכען (corrected); 1 Sam. 10:19 קצתון דין יומא קצתון (corrected).

216 E.g. 1 Sam. 2:1 לי יוי דיהב for לי יוי דיהב; 1 Sam. 22:8 קים ברי גזר for ברי קים גזר.

217 E.g. 1 Sam. 4:6 פלשתים for פלישתאי; 1 Sam. 4:8 and 1 Sam. 6:6 מצרים for מצראי; 1 Sam. 15:35 התאבל for אתאבל.

218 E.g. 1 Sam. 10:4 גריצין (i.e. feminine noun; correct plural is גריצן); 1 Sam. 14:45 הדין רבתא פורקנא.

been corrected,[219] usually in the margin with a marker indicating the insertion point.[220] Where possible, omitted words or letters are restored in micrography at the end or beginning of a line.[221] Missing letters are sometimes added supralinear.[222]

t720a Ms. Add. 26879

t720a and t713a are textually very similar and, as a result, share many of the same errors. Despite the quality and elegance of the manuscript, the Targum text of t720a is in a slightly worse state than that of t713a, since the scribe adds to the errors that he inherited from his *Vorlage*. One notes this effect particularly as far as omissions are concerned: both random omissions[223] and those caused by parablepsis.[224] An omission would, of course, be harder to spot and correct, if one's competence were limited. Many cases of transpositions,[225] Hebraisms,[226] and discord in grammatical number or gender[227] are inherited from the *Vorlage*. The scribe's failure to correct such deficiencies again indicates an inadequate comprehension of the text. The scribe further degrades the quality of the text by introducing new copyist's errors,[228] such as dittographies.[229]

Nonetheless, there are a few minor corrections. The *prima manus* is probably responsible for the few occasions at which an erroneous letter is overwritten, or a missing letter squeezed between the original consonants or

---

219 As noted already by van Staalduine-Sulman, *The Targum of Samuel*, 56.
220 E.g. 1 Sam. 1:5 #ויוי#** קד ומן; 1 Sam. 1:8 #ולמה לא אכלת#**; 1 Sam. 1:11 #ויעול דוכרני קדמך#** ולא תרחק ית אמתך#.
221 E.g. 1 Sam. 1:6 #ויוי*#תור#*איתמנע מן קד/ מנה ולד; 1 Sam. 1:25 #תוראית *תור#*ונכסו ית.
222 E.g. 1 Sam. 2:23 האילין#כפיתגמיא*#כפיתגמא* תעבדון למה.
223 t720a has the same random omission as t713a at, e.g., 1 Sam. 9.27; 1 Sam. 10:26; 1 Sam. 15:17. Examples not shared with t713a: 1 Sam. 2:21 < קדם יוי; 1 Sam. 2:31 < דרע; 1 Sam. 3:3 < בית; 1 Sam. 4:9 < כמא דאשתעבדו לכון ותהון לגברין גיברין; and so on.
224 E.g. probably inherited from *Vorlage* (i.e. = t713a): 1 Sam. 17:49 omits four words between עינוהי; 1 Sam. 2:30 omits איקר ודמסרין על שמי. Product of scribe of t720a: 1 Sam. 7:7 omits 3 words between two instances of ישראל.
225 E.g. Inherited from *Vorlage*: 1 Sam. 22:8 גזר ברי קיים for גזר קיים ברי.
226 E.g. Inherited from *Vorlage*: 1 Sam. 4:8 and 1 Sam. 6:6 מצרים for מצראי; 1 Sam. 15:35 התאבל for אתאבל. Product of scribe of t720a: 1 Sam. 4:21 כבד for יקרא.
227 E.g. 1 Sam. 1:24 עימיה 'with him', for עימה 'with her' (see t5a); 1 Sam. 10:4 גריצן (= t713a); 1 Sam. 30:8 משריתא הדין (see t6a).
228 E.g. 1 Sam. 5:7 אלקנא for אלהא; transposition in 2 Sam. 5:3 קדם יוי בחברון for בחברון קדם יוי.
229 E.g. 1 Sam. 5:12 די לא מיתו די לא מיתו; 1 Sam. 10:10 אתו לתמן לתמן (in both cases the second occurrence is left unvocalised, indicating a correction); 1 Sam. 8:18 ולא יקביל יוי יתכון צלותכון (remainder omit יתכון; cf. termination of following word).

written supra-linear.[230] The *prima manus* also seems to have 'completed' a few of the abbreviated forms, having first marked the final letter with a supra-linear vertical stroke signalling an abbreviation.[231] The intention is presumably to aid the reader. Perhaps the abbreviated forms stood in his *Vorlage*. At a secondary stage omissions have occasionally been restored in the margin.[232]

t725a Ms. 11 Göttweig

The text preserved in manuscript t725a is in a very bad way indeed. Every type of error is well represented. Large chunks of text (as well as many small ones) are omitted by parablepsis.[233] Dittography,[234] random omissions,[235] transpositions,[236] Hebraisms,[237] and grammatical discord[238] are all to be found in abundance. Most of the errors are not known from other manuscripts, increasing the likelihood that they originated with the scribe who copied the manuscript. If this were the case then he was clearly far from diligent in his work and his competence in Aramaic obviously questionable.[239] Even if his *Vorlage* were faulty, his failure to spot and correct so many errors, in particular those that render the text meaningless or grammatically incoherent (i.e. that can be easily spotted without comparing the text to a good copy), implies a lack of competence.

Many errors, including some of the long omissions by parablepsis, remain after the vocalisation has been added, perhaps implying that the naqdan worked from the same (or a similar) faulty *Vorlage*. Nonetheless, the corrector

---

230 E.g. overwritten: 1 Sam. 2:21 #שמואל*#שמול*; 1 Sam. 2:23 #דאנא#*דאנע*; written between: 1 Sam. 8:20 #אנחנא*#אנחא*; supra-linear: 1 Sam. 10:14, 16 #אח אבוהי#*לאחבוהי*.

231 E.g. 1 Sam. 4:19 #מעדיא*#מעדי*; אתת פנחס; 1 Sam. 11:8 #ישראל*#ישר׳*; בני.

232 E.g. 1 Sam. 8:7 #מלכא*** מלמיהוי # עליהון; 1 Sam. 14:3 בר פינחס #דאיכבוד #** אחוהי.

233 E.g. 1 Sam. 5:10 omits 7 words between instances of ארונא; 1 Sam. 7:7 omits 3 words between instances of ישראל (as t720a); 1 Sam. 13:6 omits 3 words between occurrences of ארי; 1 Sam. 20:29 omits 9 words between two cases of אחי.

234 E.g. 1 Sam. 15:22 למימרא דיוי הא קבלא למימריה for למימרא דיוי הא קבלא למימרא דיוי.

235 E.g. 1 Sam. 1:28 דיהי משמש for די משמש; 1 Sam. 2:5 < פומהון; 1 Sam. 4:18 < אורח; 1 Sam. 14:39 < דפרק ית ישראל.

236 E.g. 1 Sam. 12:4 אנסתנא ולא עשקת for עשקתנא ולא אנסתנא; 1 Sam. 24:5 כנף די לשא׳ for כנף מעילא דלשאול for כנף מעילא די לשאול and 1 Sam. 24:6 כנפא דלשאול די לשאול.

237 E.g. 1 Sam. 1:23 בנה for ברה; 1 Sam. 4:6 פלישתאי for פלשתים; 1 Sam. 5:3 אנשי אשדודים for אנשי אשדוד; 1 Sam. 6:6 מצראי for מצרים.

238 E.g. 1 Sam. 2:35 מלכו קיימין for מלכו קיימא.

239 A point already noted by Smelik, *The Targum of Judges*, 122; also Ho, *The Targum of Zephaniah*, 61.

has dealt with some of the smaller omissions, adding omitted words in the margin, with a supralinear circular stroke marking the placement in the line.[240] Similarly the naqdan has managed to squeeze some individual letters into the space between existing letters.[241] Cases involving a change in the number of a verb are quite common.[242] Abbreviated forms have been 'completed' on a few occasions (the original ending of the word being marked by a short vertical stroke).[243] Incorrect letters have been scribbled out, then the correct letter written above,[244] or reshaped.[245] On multiple occasions the *hireq yod* appears to have been scribbled out.[246] Deletions are marked by two short vertical strokes to the top of the letters,[247] by being struck through with a horizontal line,[248] or by the incorrect word being left unvocalised.[249]

3.c. 'Combined' Readings

A further phenomenon affecting our manuscripts is the creation of 'combined' readings (also termed 'conflations').[250] Such cases arise when a manuscript combines the reading of two or more *Vorlagen* into a single text.

To give just a few examples:

	t710y	Variant	Combined reading
1 Sam 17:7	שית מאה תקלי ברזלא	שית מאה סילעין דברזלא	שית מאה סלעין תקלין דברזלא
	six hundred **shekels** of iron	six hundred **sela** of iron t705i	six hundred **sela shekels** of iron t2i

---

240 E.g. 1 Sam. 2:13 גבר #כל**#**** עמא; 1 Sam. 4:8 אנן #אלין******#האילין*****אילין; 1 Sam. 4:13 דשאול****** ואמר קיש לשאול# בריה 1 Sam. 9:3 ארונא****** דיויו#וית 1 Sam. 6:15; וגברא****** אתא#לחואה.

241 E.g. 1 Sam. 3:1 האינון #ביומיא*****ביומא***** כסי; 1 Sam. 3:18 האלין #פתגמיא*****פתגמא***** כל; 1 Sam. 4:8 רברבין *****אילין#*****האילין.

242 E.g. 1 Sam. 4:6 ארי ידעוא***** וידעו*****יהודאי; 1 Sam. 4:7 פלשתאי ודחילו#*****ודחיל*****; 1 Sam. 5:3 אנש ואקדימו#*****ואקדימ; 1 Sam. 6:11 ית ארונא *****ושויאו*****ושויא etc.

243 E.g. 1 Sam. 2:1 פומי #אפתח#*****אפת *****דישר; 1 Sam. 7.3 וישיזב #בלחודוהי****** בלחודי.

244 E.g. 1 Sam. 2:2 איתנביאת #דאתור#*****דאסור *****מלכא.

245 E.g. 1 Sam. 9:1 בר צרור *****אביאל#לי*****אבי[ח] בר קיש.

246 E.g. 1 Sam. 1:22 ויתחזי #ואיתננה*****ואיתנינה רביא; 1 Sam. 1:26 הכא #עמך*****עימך***** דאיתעתדת; etc.

247 E.g. 1 Sam. 2:1 דיקום ##*****למ***** דעתיד שמואל by the *prima manus*?

248 E.g. 1 Sam. 3:8 שמואל ##*****עוד***** וקם; 1 Sam. 3:8 ואזל ##*****עוד***** מיקרי.

249 E.g. 1 Sam. 9:9 ארי חזוא ##*****חזוי***** עד.

250 Bacher, 'Kritische Untersuchungen zum Prophetentargum', 46–7; Smelik, 'Orality, Manuscript Reproduction, and the Targums', 76–80; van Staalduine-Sulman, *The Targum of Samuel*, 130.

Chapter Three. The Manuscripts

1 Sam 22:22	בכל נפש בית אבוך …upon every **soul** of your father's house.	בכל אנש בית אבוך …upon every **man** of your father's house. t2i = t725a	בכל נפש אנש בית אבוך …upon every **soul of a man** of your father's house. t720a = t713a
1 Sam 27:7	יומין וארבעה ירחין a **year (lit. days)** and four months	עידן בעידן וארבעה ירחין a **year (lit. time by time)** and four months t705i = t6a^{correct}, t713a, t720a, t725a	יומין עידן בעידן וארבעא ירחין a **year (lit. days)**, a **year (lit. time by time)**, and four months t5a
2 Sam 8:2	two **lots** (עדבין) to die and a full **lot** (עדבא) to live…	two **portions** (חבלין) to die and a full **portion** (חבלא) to live… All MW	two **portions** (עדבין) to die and a full **portion lot** (חבלא עדבא) to live… t6a = t713a
2 Sam 15:3	פתגמך תקנין ויאין your words are **right** and proper	פתגמך טבין ויאן your words are **good** and proper t2i	פתגמך טבין תקנין ויאן your words are **good right** and proper t5a
2 Sam 18:16	זער יואב ית עמא Joab **lessened** the people	מנע יואב ית עמא Joab **held back** the people t2i = t713a, t720a	זעיר מנע יואב ית עמא Joab **lessened, held back**, the people t3i
2 Sam 23:11	Shammah son of Agee the **inhabitant of the mountains** (טוראה).	Shammah son of Agee **who is from Harar** (דמן הרר) t232i/s = t701i, t5a^{correct}, t713a	Shammah son of Agee, **who is from Harar, the inhabitant of the mountains** (דמן יהרר טוראה) t2i = t725a (≈ t6a^{correct})

The resulting form is, as the reader will see, usually inelegant and ungrammatical. It is as though the desire to preserve an alternative reading has overridden the desire to produce a coherent text. One finds examples of this phenomenon scattered throughout the Ashkenazi and Mixed Western manuscripts, some undoubtedly inherited from *Vorlagen*, though examples are more prevalent in manuscripts t713a, t6a, t5a, and t2i than most.

Conclusions

Of our manuscripts, t705i, t2i, and t7i have been executed with reasonable care, so we can assume a degree of comprehension of the text on the part of the scribes. By contrast, the scribe of t3i appears to have been relatively careful in his work, yet a number of features in the manuscript suggest that his comprehension of the Aramaic was limited. The workmanship in t701i, t718i, and t232i/s is sloppy, and even where the text has been corrected (i.e. t701i, t232i/s) very many faults remain. It is possible to infer that these manuscripts were produced in contexts where the Targum text was little valued and perhaps poorly understood. Of the manuscripts belonging to the Ashkenazi group, manuscripts t5a and t6a — both impressive examples of craftsmanship that were evidently produced at great expense — preserve a text of reasonable quality. The text preserved in the remaining three manuscripts, by contrast, is in a rather sorry state. t5a and t6a are also of particular interest because they appear to have been corrected against a different textual tradition.

Chapter Four

Influence of the Hebrew Text

It is perhaps only natural that the Hebrew text has exerted the strongest influence over the Targum text as it was copied and re-copied through the centuries. After all, the most common *mise en page* among our manuscripts is interlinear, with a single verse of the Hebrew text being followed immediately by a single verse of Targum. The Hebrew text would still have been fresh in the copyists mind when he came to write the Targum and sometimes, it seems, the propensity to amend an obvious deviation was overwhelming. Indeed, that copyists harmonised the Targum with the Hebrew text has long been recognised: Chilton described such harmonisation as 'the besetting sin of scribes of the Targum'.[1] Yet, the revision has been neither systematic or comprehensive: even after the revisions the Targum remains the Targum, complete with exegetical elaborations *vis à vis* the Hebrew text.

1. Pluses

The most obvious and convincing examples of this phenomenon involve the addition of one or more words by the copyist, where these are missing in the manuscripts of the Babylonian textual tradition. For example:

---

1 B. Chilton, *The Isaiah Targum: Introduction, Translation, Apparatus and Notes* (The Aramaic Bible 11, Edinburgh 1987), xxix. The phenomenon was already noted by Sperber, *The Bible in Aramaic*, IVB, 19. In the process of collating texts for his editions, Sperber noticed that the text of the First Rabbinic Bible had been revised towards the Hebrew of its *Vorlage*. Also Bacher, 'Kritische Untersuchungen zum Prophetentargum', 53–4; Smelik, 'Trouble in the Trees!', 267 cf. 261 ('the parent text casted [sic] a long shadow over its translations'); Smelik, *Targum of Judges*, 642–3. Of the examples discussed below van Staalduine-Sulman noted that the following were 'in conformity with the Hebrew text' or otherwise indicated that they represented a correction towards the Hebrew: 1 Sam 5:4; 6:1, 8, 18; 9:5, 7; 10:7; 11:3, 11; 12:11, 18, 25; 13:12; 14:7; 19:9; 20:4, 16; 25:13, 23, 29; 27:1; 2 Sam 1:2, 10; 2:16; 3:1; 4:2, 10; 5:10; 6:1, 4, 6; 10:3; 11:15; 12:19; 13:11, 16; 15:15; 17:13; 20:2; 21:5, 19; 22:44; 23:20; 24:7; van Staalduine-Sulman, *The Targum of Samuel*, *ad loc* in her commentary and 130.

The Transmission of Targum Jonathan in the West

1 Sam. 15:32

Babylonian Tradition

Agag said, Please my lord (בבעו רבוני),
death is bitter (מריר מותא).

≈ LXX: Εἰ οὕτως πικρὸς ὁ θάνατος
= Peshitta: ܐܝܟܢܐ ܡܪܝܪ ܗܘ ܡܘܬܐ

Tg. Variants

Agag said, Please my lord, **take away** the
bitterness of death (אעדי מריר מותא).
t720a = MT:
= MT: אכן סר מר המות

The original form of the Targum as preserved in the Babylonian textual tradition may in fact represent the Hebrew סר in the reading רבוני 'my lord' (i.e. via Hebrew שׂר).[2] Manuscript t720a nonetheless represents its verbal value.

Some further examples are as follows:

1 Sam. 30:25

Babylonian Tradition

...and he set it for a decree of judgement for Israel
(ושויה לגזירת דין לישראל)

Tg. Variants

...and he set it **for a covenant** and for a decree of judgement for Israel
(ושויה לקיים ולגזירת דין בישראל)
t713a = t720a (omits copula: לגזירת)
= MT: וישמה לחק ולמשפט לישראל
(mlt mss בישראל)
Cf. Tg. Onq. Exod. 15.25; Tg. Josh. 24.25

2 Sam. 3:8

Babylonian Tradition

Am I not the head? (הלא רישא אנא)

Tg. Variants

Am I not a **dog's** head? (הלא רישא דכלבא אנא)
t7i = t701i, t5a^{correct}, t6a, t720a, t725a (כלב; error)
(Sperber: t716y, t10r, t734s, t12sc)

= MT: הראש כלב אנכי

The Hebrew כלב is, in fact, rendered figuratively by גבר הדיוט in the Babylonian text of Targum Jonathan, a point apparently missed in the Western manuscripts.[3]

2 Sam. 15:23

Babylonian Tradition

...all the people were crossing on the desert road (על אפי אורח מדברא)

Tg. Variants

...all the people were crossing the desert on a road
(על אפי אורח ית מדברא)
t232i/s = t6a, t713a

---

2   D. Barthélemy, *Critique textuelle de l'Ancien Testament*, I, *Josué, Juges, Ruth, Samuel, Rois, Chroniques, Esdras, Néhémie, Esther* (Orbis Biblicus et Orientalis 50/1, Fribourg and Göttingen 1982), 188.

3   Bacher, 'Kritische Untersuchungen zum Prophetentargum', 46.

Chapter Four. Influence of the Hebrew Text

= mlt Hebr. mss על פני דרך המדבר

= Peshitta: ܟܠ ܐܦܝ ܐܘܪܚܐ ܕܡܕܒܪܐ

= MT: על פני דרך את המדבר

2 Sam. 17:3

Babylonian Tradition	Tg. Variants
I will bring all the people back to you. All of them will return (יתובון כולהון)...	I will bring all the people back to you. **When** all of them return (כד יתובון כולהון)... t2i = t7i, t6a, t725a (Sperber: t734s, Kimḥi) = MT: כשוב הכל

The reading of the Septuagint is probably conjecture based on a difficult Hebrew text: 'I will bring all the people back to you, *as a bride turns towards her husband* (ὃν τρόπον ἐπιστρέφει ἡ νύμφη πρὸς τὸν ἄνδρα αὐτῆς)...'[4]

2 Sam. 17:13

Babylonian Tradition	Tg. Variants
...then we will throw it into the river until no stone remains there (תמן אבנא).	...until not **even** a stone remains there (תמן אף אבנא). t6a (Sperber: t12sc) = MT: שם גם צרור

2 Sam. 23:20

Babylonian Tradition	Tg. Variants
...son of a man fearing sins, who had deeds (דליה עובדין)...	...who had a **great many** (סגי) deeds... t713a = t720a, t718i (סגיאות) = MT: רב פעלים

The intended sense of the resulting text remains far from clear. t705i remedies the obscurity by adding a gloss: 'good deeds (עובדין טבין)' (also t727y. Cf. Peshitta).[5]

In two cases the translation of the Targum is non-literal, so that the relationship to the Hebrew text is not direct. Nonetheless, certain European manuscripts have attempted to represent elements in the Hebrew text more literally. For example:

1 Sam. 25:29

Babylonian Tradition	Tg. Variants
...and to seek to kill you (ולמבעי למקטלך)	...and to seek **your soul** to kill you (ולמיבעי ית נפשך למיקטלך) t705i = MT: ולבקש את נפשך

---

4 Barthélemy, *Critique textuelle de l'Ancien Testament*, I, 278–80.
5 See van Staalduine-Sulman, *The Targum of Samuel*, 689 n. 1525.

The Transmission of Targum Jonathan in the West

'To seek to kill' (בעי + קטל) is the normal means of expressing the idiomatic Hebrew 'to seek someone's soul' (נפש + בקש) (e.g. Tg. 1 Sam. 20:1; 22:23; 23:15; 25:29; Tg. 2 Sam. 4:8; 16:11). The revision here clearly replicates elements in the Hebrew. It is noteworthy that the expression is not revised in the same way in t705i when it occurs elsewhere in Targum Samuel.

2 Sam. 21:19

Babylonian Tradition	**Tg. Variants**
David, son of Jesse, weaver of the curtain of the Temple, killed Goliath…	David, son of Jesse, weaver of the curtain of the Temple, **who was from Bethlehem** (דמבית לחם), killed Goliath…
	t705i = t7i, t5a[correct], t6a, t713a, t720a (Sperber: t716y, t10r, Kimhi)
	= MT: ויך אלחנן בן יערי ארגים בית הלחמי

The Targum identifies Elhanan as David in line with midrashic tradition.[6] The addition here apparently deals with the reference to בית הלחמי, which is otherwise neglected (the reference to the Temple being derived from ארגים).

2 Sam. 16:8

Babylonian Tradition	**Tg. Variants**
The Lord has brought back upon you all the sins (חובי) of the house of Saul.	The Lord has brought back upon you all the **blood of** the sins (דמי חובי) of the house of Saul.
	t713a = t720a
	= MT: כל דמי בית שאול

In the following cases the addition appears to replicate the wording of the underlying Hebrew and the likelihood is that this is what has occurred. Nonetheless, in these cases we cannot exclude altogether the possibility that the addition is intended to aid sense, rather than replicate the structure of the Hebrew.

1 Sam. 2:27

Babylonian Tradition	**Tg. Variants**
Thus says the Lord, 'I was revealed (אתגלאה אתגליתי) to the house of your father…'	'…**Behold!** I was revealed (האיתגלאה אתגליתי) to the house of your father…'
= LXX: Ἀποκαλυφθεὶς ἀπεκαλύφθην	t720a = t713a
= Peshitta: ܐܬܓܠܝܘ ܐܬܓܠܝܬ	= MT: הנגלה נגליתי

---

6   See van Staalduine-Sulman, *The Targum of Samuel*, 630.

Chapter Four. Influence of the Hebrew Text

The adverb -הֲ may have an exclamatory nuance in the Hebrew here (i.e. 'Certainly I have revealed myself …!').[7]

2 Sam. 12:19

Babylonian Tradition	Tg. Variants
David said to his servants, The boy is dead (מית רביא).	David said to his servants, **Is** the boy dead? (Or: 'Surely the boy is dead!' המית רביא). t5a = t713a, t720a (Sperber: t716y, t734s, t12sc)
= 2 Hebrew mss מת הילד = Peshitta: ܡܝܬ ܠܗ ܛܠܝܐ	= MT: המת הילד

The Hebrew manuscripts lacking the interrogative preposition are Oxford, Bodleian Library Ms Kennicott 5 (Sephardi, 1487 = Kennicott 85) and Copenhagen, The Royal Library Cod. Hebr. 6 (Sephardi, fourteenth/fifteenth cent. = Kennicott 176).

1 Sam. 1:11

Babylonian Tradition	Tg. Variants
…the affliction of your maidservant is revealed (מיגלא גלי) before you…	…**if** the affliction of your maidservant be indeed revealed (אם מגלא גלי) before you… t2i = t3i, t7i, t232i/s, t705i, t718i, A (Sperber: t702s, t734s, t12sc, t10r)
	= MT: אם ראה תראה

1 Sam. 9:7

Babylonian Tradition	Tg. Variants
…but what shall we take to the prophet of the Lord, even we have run out of provisions (אף אנחנא זודין עטרו ממננא) …	…but what shall we take to the prophet of the Lord **because** even we (ארי אף אנחנא) have run out of provisions… t6a (≈ t713a, t720a ארי אף אנחנא)
= Vulgate: *quid feremus ad virum panis defecit in sitarciis nostris*	= MT: כי הלחם אזל מכלינו

A less clear-cut case that may belong to this category is found in 2 Sam. 19:36:

2 Sam. 19:36

Babylonian Tradition	Tg. Variants
Will I again hear the sound of the lyre (בקל כנרין) and hymns (ותשבחן)?	Will I again listen to the sound **of those praising** with lyre (בקל משבחן בכינרין) and with hymns (ובתושבחן)? t720a = t713a
	Cf. MT: אם אשמע עוד בקול שרים ושרות

---

7 P. Joüon and T. Muraoka, *A Grammar of Biblical Hebrew* (Subsidia Biblica 27, Rome 2006), §161b.

The two participles in the Hebrew שרים ושרות, are translated with two different nouns in the Babylonian textual tradition of the Targum. While the association between the Aramaic verbal root שבח 'to praise' and derived nouns (e.g. תושבחה 'praise, hymn') with the Hebrew root שיר is frequent (Judg. 5:12; 2 Sam. 22:1; Isa. 26:1; 30:29; 42:10 etc. Cf. verb Judg. 5:3; 1 Sam. 18:6; Isa. 5:1; 42:10 etc), the Aramaic כנרא 'lyre' is not connected to this Hebrew root in Targum Jonathan outside this verse. The addition in manuscripts t713a and t720a seeks not only to capture the force of the Hebrew's participles, but also to provide a semantically more fitting translation of the Hebrew.

2. Alternative Translation Equivalent

In the following examples, one or more of the European manuscripts provides an alternative lexeme to that found in the Babylonian tradition that more closely resembles the underlying Hebrew. In all cases, however, the Babylonian textual tradition also has an Aramaic lexeme that commonly translates the underlying Hebrew lexeme, so that both the original reading of the Babylonian text and the variant reading of the European manuscripts might be considered 'correct' within the context of Targum Jonathan's translation technique. Yet the rendering of the Babylonian textual tradition is either overtly exegetical or translates the Hebrew *ad sensum*. The variants in the European manuscripts provide a translation *ad verbum*. It is, of course, not always easy to distinguish lexemes belonging to this category from the simple random interchange of common vocabulary (described in chapter six).

In most cases, however, the influence of the Hebrew text reveals itself in a much simpler way, by the swapping of the original Aramaic lexeme for an Aramaic lexeme cognate with the underlying Hebrew. For example:

1 Sam. 14:7

Hebrew	Babylonian Tradition	Tg. Variants
See, I am with you **as one mind!** (כלבבך)	See, I am with you **according to your will!** (כרעותך) (cf. Vulgate: *ero tecum ubicumque volueris*)	See, I am with you **as one mind!** (כלבבך)
		t713a = t232i/s, t720a

Chapter Four. Influence of the Hebrew Text

1 Sam. 19:9

Hebrew	Babylonian Tradition	Tg. Variants
and an evil spirit of the Lord **was** (ותהי) on Saul...	and an evil spirit from before the Lord **rested** (ושרת) upon Saul...	and an evil spirit from before the Lord **was** (והות) upon Saul...
		t6a[PM] = t713a, t720a (both transpose בישא after קדם יוי). (Sperber: t734s)

Both Aramaic terms are common translation equivalents in Targum Jonathan.

1 Sam. 20:4

Hebrew	Babylonian Tradition	Tg. Variants
Whatever your soul **says** (תאמר)...	t2506b: Whatever your soul **desires** (רעיא)... *or* t707b: Whatever be the will (רעוא) of your soul...	Whatever your soul **says** (תימר)...
		t705i

The reading of the Babylonian text tradition is reflected in the Septuagint (Τί ἐπιθυμεῖ ἡ ψυχή σου), and may derive from an alternative *Vorlage* (probably נפשך תאוה cf. e.g. Deut. 12:20; 14:26; 18:6; 1 Sam. 2:16; 2 Sam 3:21; 1 Kgs 11:37).[8]

1 Sam. 28:15

Hebrew	Babylonian Tradition	Tg. Variants
...Why have you **enraged** me (הרגזתי) to come up?	Samuel said to Saul, Why have you **troubled** me (ואזעתני) to come up?	...Why have you **enraged** me (ארגזתני) to come up?
		t5a

The Aramaic root זוע 'to move, shake, trouble' is used frequently in Targum Jonathan for the synonymous Hebrew רגז (e.g. in Tg. Samuel: 1 Sam. 14:15; 2 Sam. 7:10; 22:8). The use of its Aramaic cognate in t5a replicates the sense of the Hebrew much more closely, however.

2 Sam. 2:16

Hebrew	Babylonian Tradition	Tg. Variants
...and they **fell** (ויפלו) together.	...and they were **killed** (ואתקטילו) together.	...and they **fell** (ונפלו) together.
		t705i (Sperber: t10r, t716y) cf. t5a[PM] ואיתקטילו ונפלו כחדא

---

[8] Bacher, 'Kritische Untersuchungen zum Prophetentargum', 52.

A comparable case is found in 2 Sam. 11:17 (Babylonian tradition: ואתקטל 'and he was killed...'; t720a ונפל 'and he fell' = MT: ויפל).

2 Sam. 2:26

Hebrew	Babylonian Tradition	Tg. Variants
Will the sword [lit.] **consume** (תאכל חרב) for ever?	Will the sword **kill** (תקטיל חרבא) for ever?	Will the sword [lit.] **consume** (תיכול חרבא) for ever?
		t725a (Sperber: Arukh)

The Hebrew אכל (lit. 'to eat') is frequently understood in its figurative sense by Targum Jonathan and translated as such with the Aramaic קטל 'to kill.' On several occasions this translates the same idiom encountered here in which a sword is said to 'eat' or 'consume' (root אכל; e.g. Tg. 2 Sam. 11:25; 18:8; Tg. Jer. 2:30; 46:10, 14; Tg. Nah. 2:14).

2 Sam. 11:15

Hebrew	Babylonian Tradition	Tg. Variants
and he wrote in the **document** (בספר)...	and he wrote in the **letter** (באיגרתא)...	and he wrote in the **document** (בספרא)...
		t720a

The Aramaic noun אגרתא 'letter' is used frequently for the Hebrew ספר in Targum Jonathan (e.g. 1 Kgs 21:8, 9, 11; 2 Kgs 5:5, 6, 7; 10:1; 19:14, etc.), including in the preceding verse (2 Sam. 11:14) where it is retained by t720a.

In other cases one or more of the European manuscripts changes the existing Aramaic lexeme for one that, though not cognate, more closely replicates the semantic range or signification of the Hebrew in cases where the Babylonian tradition renders the Hebrew text according to Targumic exegesis. For example:

1 Sam. 6:1

Hebrew	Babylonian Tradition	Tg. Variants
in the **field** (בשדה) of the Philistines	in the **towns** (בקרוי) of the Philistines	in the **field** (בחקל) of the Philistines
		t2i = t6a^{PM} (בחקליה), t713a, t720a, t725a

The reading of the Masoretic Text is supported by the Septuagint and probably also stood in the *Vorlage* of Targum Jonathan since the Aramaic קרוא 'town' is used a handful of times to translate the Hebrew שדה 'field' (i.e. Tg. 1 Sam. 27:7, 11; Tg. 2 Kgs 2:26; Tg. Obad. 19). This translation is, however, clearly exegetical in nature and a number of European manuscripts revert to the

Chapter Four. Influence of the Hebrew Text

literal rendering, חלק 'field'. Indeed, similar changes occur in European manuscripts in the two other occurrences of Aramaic קרוא 'town' for Hebrew שדה 'field': In 1 Sam. 27.7 manuscript t725a reads בחקלא פלשתא' (sic) in place of בקרוי פלשתאי; and in 1 Sam. 27:11 t713a replaces בקרוי פלשתאי with בחקל פלשתאי.

1 Sam. 9:7

Hebrew	Babylonian Tradition	Tg. Variants
…what shall we bring to the **man** (לאיש)?	…what shall we bring to the **prophet** (לנביא)?	…what shall we bring to the **man** (לגברא)?
		t2i (Sperber: Kimhi)

Both Aramaic terms (גבר, נביא) are common translation equivalents for the Hebrew איש 'man' throughout Targum Jonathan, though גבר is more frequent as one might expect (e.g. נביא: 1 Sam. 2:27; 9:6, 8, 10; etc. גבר 1 Sam. 2:13, 25; 4:10; 6:19; 8:22; 10:11, 25 etc.). The use of לגברא in t2i in place of לנביא may be an attempt to reflect a variation in the Hebrew. The first occurrence of לנביא in the Babylonian text renders the underlying Hebrew that reads simply איש; the underlying Hebrew of the second occurrence is איש האלהים, rendered נביא דיוי in the Babylonian tradition. t2i replicates the distinction in the Hebrew by employing גבר for the first example, and נבייא דיוי in the second.

1 Sam. 10:7

Hebrew	Babylonian Tradition	Tg. Variants
…**do** (עשה) for yourself whatever you find appropriate (תמצא ידך) …	…**establish** (אתקין) for yourself the instruments of government…	…**make** (עביד) for yourself the instruments of government…
		t2i (Sperber: t10r)

Both verbs are common translation equivalents for Hebrew עשה. A comparable example is found in 1 Sam. 28:17, where the Eastern manuscript evidence is mixed (t710y: וקיים יוי ליה; t707b, t5a: ועבד יוי ליה; MT: ויעש יהוה לו).

1 Sam. 13:2

Hebrew	Babylonian Tradition	Tg. Variants
…the rest of the people he sent away each man to his own **tent** (לאהליו).	…the rest of the people he sent away each man to his own **town** (לקרווהי).	…the rest of the people he sent away each man to his own **tent** (למשכניה).
		t720a

The Aramaic קרוא 'town' is used elsewhere for the Hebrew אהל 'tent' (e.g.

The Transmission of Targum Jonathan in the West

Tg. 1 Sam. 4:10; Tg. 2 Sam. 18:17).[9]

1 Sam. 16:21

Hebrew	Babylonian Tradition	Tg. Variants
...and he **stood** (ויעמד) before him.	...and he **served** (ושמיש) before him.	...and he **stood** (וקם) before him.
		t2i

1 Sam. 20:31

Hebrew	Babylonian Tradition	Tg. Variants
...bring him to me because he is [literally:] a son of death (בן מות).	...bring him to me because he is a **man** deserving death (גבר חייב קטול).	...bring him to me because he is a **son** deserving death (בר חייב קטול).
		t705i = t6a^{PM}, t713a, t720a

The Hebrew בן is translated on several occasions with גברא 'man' (e.g. Tg. 1 Sam. 2:12; 10:27; 14:52; 18:17; 25:17; Tg. 2 Sam. 2:7; 3:34; 13:28; 17:10), twice in the book of Samuel for the formula בן מות (i.e. Tg. 1 Sam. 26:16 [in plural]; Tg. 2 Sam. 12:5). In both these cases the European manuscripts contain variants. In 2 Sam. 12:5 manuscript t713a offers the same variant (בר for גבר). In Targum 1 Sam. 26:16, where the Hebrew idiom is plural (בני מות), there are multiple variants: the Babylonian textual tradition reads גברי חייבי קטול; t6a, t2i, t701i (+ t7i and t705i with orthographic variants[10]) add בני before this expression (i.e. בני גברי חייבי קטול); t725a casts the 'men' into the singular (i.e. גברא חייב קטול) and t232i/s has a singular 'son' (i.e. בר גברי חייבי קטול).

1 Sam. 30:20

Hebrew	Babylonian Tradition	Tg. Variants
Then David **took** (ויקח) all the sheep...	Then David **captured** (ושבא) all the sheep...	Then David **took** (ונסיב) all the sheep...
		t2i = t725a

Targum Jonathan employs the Aramaic שבי 'to take captive' with reasonable frequency to translate the Hebrew לקח 'to take' (e.g. Tg. 1 Sam. 4:11, 17, 19, 21, 22; 5:1; 27:9; 30:16, 18),[11] but here the two European manuscripts prefer to reflect the underlying Hebrew more directly. Indeed the frequency with which Aramaic שבי renders Hebrew לקח in Targum Jonathan

---

9 Cf. LXX εἰς τὸ σκήνωμα αὐτοῦ '...to his quarters'.

10 t7i: חובי; t705i ברי.

11 Bacher, 'Kritische Untersuchungen zum Prophetentargum', 52–3.

may well account for the example in the preceding verse (1 Sam. 30.19) where t6a^{PM}, t713a, t720a, t725a, t2i, and t3i read 'everything that they captured (דשבו) for themselves...', where the Babylonian tradition has 'everything that they took (דנסיבו) for themselves' (see chapter six).

2 Sam. 5:10

Hebrew	Babylonian Tradition	Tg. Variants
...and the Lord, the God of Hosts, was **with** him (עמו).	...and the Memra of the Lord, the God of Hosts, was **aiding** him (Lit: at his aid; בסעדיה).	...and the Memra of the Lord, the God of Hosts, was **with** him (עימיה). t720a

The idiom 'was aiding him' (literally: 'at his aid') is classic Targumic exegesis (e.g. 1 Sam. 3:19; 10:7; 16:18; 17:37; 18:12, 14, 28; 20:13; 2 Sam. 7:3, 9; 14:17). Here it may be intended to avoid the possible anthropomorphic implication of the Hebrew text (i.e. that God was physically present with him). In this case t720a prefers a more literal rendering.

In all of these cases both the reading offered by the Babylonian textual tradition and the variants belonging to the European manuscripts are common translation equivalents found elsewhere in the corpus of Targum Jonathan. However, in all of the cases above, the variants in the European manuscripts more closely reflect the Hebrew, either by employing a cognate lexeme (i.e. Tg. 1 Sam. 14:7; 19:9; 20:4; 28:15; Tg. 2 Sam. 2:16, 26; 11:15), or, as one finds in the remaining cases, by offering a lexeme that more closely reflects the semantic range of the underlying Hebrew.

3. Cases Involving Proper Names

The Targum aims to offer a translation of the Hebrew text that enables the audience to understand the text (at least in the way that the Targumist wished it to be understood!). To this end, personal or place names are sometimes translated according to their perceived etymology.[12] In some such cases one or more European manuscript(s) expunged the Targumic exegesis in favour of preserving the name as the Hebrew text has it.

A good example of this is found in 1 Sam. 12:11:

---

12 E.g. 1 Sam. 1.1 הרמתים צופים becomes רמתא מתלמידי נבייא.

The Transmission of Targum Jonathan in the West

1 Sam. 12:11

Hebrew	Babylonian Tradition	Tg. Variants
the Lord sent **Jerubbaal** and **Bedan** (את ירבעל ואת בדן)	the Lord sent **Gideon** and **Samson** (ית גדעון וית שמשון)	the Lord sent **Jerubbaal** and **Bedan** (ית ירובעל וית בדן). t701i (Sperber: t12sc 'Jerubbaal') the Lord sent **Gideon** and **Bedan** (ית גדעון וית בדן). t705i

The Babylonian text tradition, which despite the diversity of the ancient Versions had a *Vorlage* identical to the Masoretic Text at this point in the text,[13] gives an exegetical rendering of the two names in the Hebrew text: Jerubbaal is the nickname given to Gideon (cf. Judg. 6:32). The name Bedan is otherwise unknown in the Hebrew Bible, but since he is here referred to along with other Judges (Jephtah, Samuel, and Jerubbaal = Gideon), rabbinic tradition has identified Bedan with Samson (e.g. b.Roš Haš 25a), Samson being of the tribe of Dan (i.e. בדן → בן דן). Manuscripts t701i and t705i replace this exegetical explanation with the wording of the Hebrew (cf. page 272).

Further examples:

2 Sam. 23:11

Hebrew	Babylonian Tradition	Tg. Variants
Shammah, the son of Agee the Hararite (הררי).	Shama son of Aga, who was **from the mountainous region** (טוראה)... Cf. t705i דמן טורא	Shama son of Aga, who was **from Harar** (דמן הרר)... t232i/s = t701i, t5a, t713a (Sperber: t10r, t702s, t12sc, t716y, Kimhi combine both readings)

The Septuagint too takes הררי as a gentilic noun (i.e. ὁ Ἀρουχαῖος). Manuscripts t725a, t2i and the corrected form of t6a offer a combined reading here (e.g. t6a[correct] טורא הרר דמן; see pages 102–3). Manuscripts t232i/s and t701i repeat this revision at 2 Sam. 23:33, the only other occurrence of the Hebrew הררי 'Hararite' in the Prophets (elsewhere only 1 Chron. 11:34, 35, where Tg. has מן הרר).[14]

---

13 See Barthélemy, *Critique textuelle de l'Ancien Testament*, I, 173–4.

14 The reading of t10r is one of the 'Hebraisirende Aenderungen' noted by Bacher, 'Kritische Untersuchungen zum Prophetentargum', 53.

Chapter Four. Influence of the Hebrew Text

2 Sam. 24:7

Hebrew	Babylonian Tradition	Tg. Variants
They came (ויבאו) to the **fortress of Tyre** (מבצר צר).	They entered (ועלו) a **fortified town** (לקירוין כריכן)...	They came (ואתו) to **Mivtsar Tsor** (למבצר צר)... t2i = t7i, t701i, t705i, t725a (Sperber: t12sc; t702s, t734s combine both readings)

The Babylonian tradition translates the Hebrew according to its sense.[15] Some of the European manuscripts, however, have taken the Hebrew as a place name (on the interchange of את and עלו see page 196), as the Septuagint has done (Μάψαρ Τύρου[16]).

In one case, the reading of the Babylonian tradition appears to agree with variant Hebrew manuscripts.

2 Sam. 12:27

Hebrew	Babylonian Tradition	Tg. Variants
...I have even conquered the **city of waters** (את עיר המים).	I have even conquered the **royal city** [lit. town of the kingdom] (קרית מלכותא). = 2 Hebr. mss עיר המלוכה	I have even conquered the **city of water** (קריתא דמיא). t713a = t7i (קרית דמיא), t6a (קרית מיא), t720a

Yet this apparent agreement must be regarded with scepticism, since both the variant Hebrew manuscripts[17] and the Targum may have harmonised the reading of verse twenty seven with that of verse twenty six (probably deliberately in the Targum, accidentally in the two Hebrew manuscripts), where we are told that Joab captured the royal city (Hebr. עיר המלוכה; Aram. קרית מלכותא).

An interesting case of the contrasting tendency is found in 1 Sam. 6:18:

---

15 Cf. Kimhi's explanation: מבצר שהיה בצור גבוה, perhaps guided by Targum.
16 With multiple spelling variants in LXX manuscripts, see A. England Brooke, N. McLean and H. St.J. Thackeray (eds), *The Old Testament in Greek: According to the Text of Codex Vaticanus, Supplemented from other Uncial Manuscripts, with a Critical Apparatus Containing the Variants of the Chief Ancient Authorities for the Text of the Septuagint, Vol. 2, Part 1, I and II Samuel* (Cambridge 1927), ad loc.
17 Hebrew of t725a; Hebrew of t705i.

The Transmission of Targum Jonathan in the West

1 Sam. 6:18

Hebrew	Babylonian Tradition	Tg. Variants
...and until **Abel the great** (ועד אבל הגדולה) upon which they had set down the Ark of the Lord...	...and until the **Great Stone** (ועד אבנא רבתא) upon which they had set down the Ark of the Lord...	...and until the **valley in which was the Great Stone** (ועד מישר דביה אבנא רבתא) upon which they had set down the Ark of the Lord...
		t720a

The Masoretic Text is almost certainly a corruption, albeit an ancient one.[18] The alternative reading, אבן 'stone', is not only a better fit with the verbal construction (...הניחו עליה 'upon [which] they caused to rest [the Ark]') and the narrative context (see 1 Sam. 6:15), it is also well supported by the Septuagint (λίθου τοῦ μεγάλου[19]) followed by the Old Latin (*ad lapidem magnum valde*[20]). It is therefore probably the reading of the Hebrew text from which the Targum was translated.[21]

The majority of Hebrew textual witnesses, however, read אבל (a few manuscripts have אבן;[22] unfortunately the text is missing among the Qumran fragments). In the Masoretic Text of 1 Sam. 6:18 this is vocalised אָבֵל, a place name 'Abel' (cf. 2 Sam. 20:14). It appears as a compound place name in 1 Kgs 4:12; 19:16; Judg. 7:22 (אבל מחולה), and Judg. 11:33 (אבל כרמים). Targum Jonathan translates all these occurrences with the Aramaic מישרא 'plain, valley', evidently deriving this translation from the Hebrew אוּבָל 'river, stream' — a lexeme known in Classical Hebrew only from the book of Daniel — thereby giving an etymological explanation of the reading of the Masoretic Text as it stands. In an unvocalised text such a reading of the Hebrew would of course be possible (assuming the defective spelling אָבָל). Manuscript t720a attempts to reconcile the discordance between the Targum and the Hebrew text as it now stands. In other words, manuscript t720a seeks to represent the form אבל in the Aramaic. This is achieved by adopting a common etymological explanation for this name.

---

18 Cf. Vulgate: *ad Abel magnum*. See Barthélemy, *Critique textuelle de l'Ancien Testament*, I, 154.
19 Note the absence of the definite article, which is supplied in several manuscripts, see Brooke, McLean and Thackeray (eds), *The Old Testament in Greek*, ad loc.
20 According to Brooke, McLean and Thackeray (eds), *The Old Testament in Greek*, ad loc.
21 Contra van Staalduine-Sulman, *The Targum of Samuel*, 251, who assumes that it is the Targumist who emends the Hebrew in order to harmonise with 1 Sam. 6:14.
22 Rashi and Isaiah di Trani in the Commentaries on Samuel, *ad loc*, explain that the lamed has replaced the nun, citing another example from Neh. 13:7.

Chapter Four. Influence of the Hebrew Text

4. Alternative Prepositions

There are numerous examples where a variant preposition is found in one or more European manuscripts that more closely resembles the Hebrew text as found in Codex Leningradensis. The following are just a few examples:

1 Sam. 9:21

Hebrew	Babylonian Tradition	Tg. Variants
Why have you spoken **to** me (אֵלַי)...	Why have you spoken **with** me (עִימִי)...	Why have you spoken **to** me (לוֹתִי)... t713a = t720a (Sperber: t12sc לִי)

1 Sam. 12:10

Hebrew	Babylonian Tradition	Tg. Variants
...now save us from the hand of our enemies and we will serve **you** (וְנַעַבְדֶךָ)!	...now save us from the hand of our enemies and we will serve **before you** (ונפלח קדמך)!	...now save us from the hand of our enemies and we will serve **you** (ונפלחנך)! t2i

1 Sam. 14:12

Hebrew	Babylonian Tradition	Tg. Variants
Come up **to** us (אֵלֵינוּ)!	Come up [literally:] **upon** us (עלנא)!	Come up **to** us (לותנא)! t2i = t6a

2 Sam. 15:6

Hebrew	Babylonian Tradition	Tg. Variants
...all Israel who came for a judgement **to** the king (לְמִשְׁפָּט אֶל הַמֶּלֶךְ).	...to all Israel who were coming to bring a legal case **before** the king (למדן קדם מלכא).	...to all Israel who were coming for a judgement **to** the king (לדינא לות מלכא). t3i (cf. t705i: למדן לות מלכא) (Sperber: t716y, t10r)

The definite object marker is affected in the same way. For example:

1 Sam. 15:24

Hebrew	Babylonian Tradition	Tg. Variants
because I was afraid **of** (יָרֵאתִי אֶת) the people...	because I was afraid **from** (דחילית מן) the people...	because I was afraid **of** (דחילית ית) the people... t2i = t713a, t720a

The verb דחל 'to fear' frequently indicates its object with מן (e.g. Tg. 1 Sam. 2:12; 3:15; 7:7; 12:14 etc.).

The following example provides a more complex case, where the omission

The Transmission of Targum Jonathan in the West

of vocabulary not found in the Hebrew also occurs:

1 Sam. 12:18

Hebrew	Babylonian Tradition	Tg. Variants
...and all the people were exceedingly afraid of the Lord and of Samuel (את יהוה ואת שמואל).	...and all the people were exceedingly afraid **from before** the Lord and **from the words of** Samuel (מן ק׳ יוי ומפתגמי שמואל)	...and all the people were exceedingly afraid of the Lord and Samuel (ית יוי וית שמואל).
		t705i

The formula מן and מן קדם are the equivalent of the definite object marker (את e.g. Tg. 1 Sam. 2:12; 3:17; 12:14, 24; Tg. 2 Sam. 6:9; 12:16.). The word פתגמא is Targumic addition (cf. e.g. Tg. 1 Sam. 3:20; 19:3, 4; 20:10, 12; etc.).

As I cautioned above, it is often difficult to separate cases of accommodation the Hebrew text from cases of random interchange of common vocabulary. This problem is particularly acute when prepositions are involved, since prepositions are extremely susceptible to being swapped at random (see pages 215–16), so the resulting agreement with the Hebrew text may be entirely coincidental.

5. Replacing Rare or Unique Translation Equivalents with Common Ones

In some cases the interchange of wording may represent an attempt to 'correct' the Targumic text by introducing the expected translation equivalent, that is to say, the more commonly occurring translation equivalent, where the original text preserved in the Babylonian tradition has an unusual (and therefore unexpected) one. In these cases the Hebrew text has clearly exerted an influence over the copyist: the copyist recognised that the choice of vocabulary is not the habitual choice for the underlying wording of the Hebrew. In a few cases the translation equivalent proposed by the Babylonian textual tradition is otherwise unattested or rarely employed in Targum Jonathan and does not directly reflect the sense of the Hebrew. The variant reading in our European manuscripts attempts to 'correct' the original reading of the Babylonian tradition, by providing the expected translation equivalent.

Chapter Four. Influence of the Hebrew Text

1 Sam. 14:49

Hebrew	Babylonian Tradition	Tg. Variants
...the name of the **firstborn** (הבכירה) was Merab...	...the name of the **eldest** (שום רבתא) was Merab...'	...the name of the **firstborn** (שום בוכריתא) was Merab...
		t725a

The Hebrew בכיר occurs only here in the Prophets; where it occurs in the Pentateuch it is rendered with the Aramaic רב in Targum Onqelos (Tg. Onq. Gen. 19:31, 33–4, 37; 29:26). It is not impossible, however, that the Babylonian textual tradition reflects a variant Hebrew *Vorlage* here: a handful of manuscripts of the Septuagint read τῆς πρεσβυτέρας and the Peshitta ܩܫܝܫܬܐ.

1 Sam. 25:23

Hebrew	Babylonian Tradition	Tg. Variants
Abigail saw David and she hurried and **got down** (ותרד) from the ass.	Abigail saw David and she hurried and **dismounted** (ואתרכינת) from upon the ass.	...she hurried and **got down** (ונחתת) from upon the ass.
		t705i = t5a

This is the only occurrence of the root רכן for Hebrew ירד in Targum Jonathan.

1 Sam. 25:37

Hebrew	Babylonian Tradition	Tg. Variants
It came to pass in the morning when the wine had **gone out** (בצאת היין) from Nabal.	It came to pass in the morning when the wine had **weakened** (כד פג) from Nabal.	...when the wine had **gone out** (כד נפק) from Nabal.
		t6a

The root employed in the Babylonian text, פוג 'to vanish, evaporate, be faint or weak', is rare and occurs only here in Targum Jonathan for the Hebrew root יצא. t6a prefers the more direct rendering נפק.

1 Sam. 26:7

Hebrew	Babylonian Tradition	Tg. Variants
Abner and the people were **lying** around him (שכבים סביבתו)	Abner and the people were **camping** around him (שרן סחרנוהי).	Abner and the people were **lying** around him (שכבין סחרנוהי).
		t705i

The root שרי translates the Hebrew שכב only here and in the Targum to Hos. 2:20 (then in *aphel*). The cognate שכב however is employed extremely frequently throughout Targum Jonathan (thirty times in Targum Samuel alone e.g. 1 Sam. 2:22; 3:5, 9; 26:5; etc.).

The Transmission of Targum Jonathan in the West

2 Sam. 3:1

Hebrew	Babylonian Tradition	Tg. Variants
The war between the house of Saul and the house of David was **long** (המלחמה ארכה)...	There was a **fierce** war (קרבא תקיף) between the house of Saul and the house of David...	There was a **long** war (קרבא אריכא) between the house of Saul and the house of David... t720a

The choice of the Aramaic cognate אריך in manuscript t720a clearly results in a text that is closer to the Hebrew, whereas the reading of the Babylonian tradition adheres to typically Targumic idiom (e.g. 1 Sam. 14:52; 2 Sam. 2:17; 11:15).[23] The Aramaic תקיף 'strong', is nowhere else used to translate the Hebrew ארך 'long' in Targum Jonathan.

2 Sam. 10:3

Hebrew	Babylonian Tradition	Tg. Variants
Is it not in order to investigate the city (a few mss: the land) and to spy it out and to **overthrow** it (ולהפכה) (that) David sent his servants to you?	Is it not in order to investigate the land and to spy it out and to **investigate** it (ולמבדקה) (that) David sent his servants to you?	...to spy it out and to **overthrow** it (ולמהפכה)... t705i

This is the sole case of Aramaic בדק 'to inspect, search out' translating Hebrew הפך (here: 'to overthrow, overturn') in Targum Jonathan.[24] Since the Hebrew הפך is used in a range of contexts, several Aramaic equivalents are employed (frequently חזר, for example). The cognate Aramaic הפך 'to turn, overturn' is employed elsewhere (e.g. Tg. Judg. 7:3; Tg. 2 Kgs 5:26).

The following case probably also belongs to this category, but the textual witnesses present a mixed picture.

1 Sam. 25:25

Hebrew	Original reading?	Babylonian Tradition = 'Variant'?
...this man of **wickedness**/man of Belial (איש הבליעל).	...this **foolish/insane** man (גברא שטיא). A, t2i, t3i, t7i, t232i/s, t701i, t718i (Sperber:	...this **wicked** man (גברא רשיעא). t705i = t724b (Sperber: t710y, t711y i.e. base text)

---

23 But cf. Old Latin (according to Brooke, McLean and Thackeray (eds), *The Old Testament in Greek, ad loc.*): *pugna magna*.

24 The Targumist may have understood the root הפך to have the sense 'examine carefully', as in the saying of Ben Bag Bag הפך בה והפך בה דכלה בה m.'Abot 5.22; van Staalduine-Sulman, *The Targum of Samuel*, 542.

122

t716y, t727y, t10r, t702s,
t734s, t12sc)

The adjectival participle שטי 'insane, foolish' is used only here to render בליעל (either a proper name, 'Belial', or a common noun, 'wickedness, worthlessness'), but it is clearly a word play on Nabal's name (i.e. Hebr. נָבָל adj. 'foolish').[25] בליעל is typically translated with רשיע 'wicked' (i.e. Tg. 1 Sam. 2:12; 25:17, 25; 30:22; Tg. 2 Sam. 16:7; 20:1; 23:6; Tg. Nah. 2:1). In this case Martínez Borobio's base text (t724b), as well as manuscript t710y and Sperber's base text (t711y), all share the reading of t705i. It may be the original reading, yet it is harder to imagine the reading 'wicked' being changed into 'foolish' than *vice versa*, so the reading of t724b, t711y, and t705i may all be corrections, offering the 'expected' translation equivalent.

In the following cases the original reading of the Targum, though not unique, is sufficiently rare that we can suspect the process of correction to be at work. The resulting form can also be said to represent the underlying Hebrew 'more literally'.

2 Sam. 20:8

Hebrew	Babylonian Tradition	Tg. Variants
…and it fell out as he went out (יצא ותפל).	…and he was taking strides as he went (אזיל ופסע).	…and he was taking strides as he went out (נפק ופסע).
		t232i/s

The Aramaic נפק 'to go out' is the common equivalent for the Hebrew יצא, whereas אזל 'to go' translates this verb only three times in Targum Jonathan, all in Targum Samuel (2 Sam. 16.5[x2]; 20.8).

1 Sam. 24:12

Hebrew	Babylonian Tradition	Tg. Variants
See that there is no **evil** in my hand (אין בידי רעה)!	See that there is no **sin** in my hand (לית בידי חוב)!	See that there is no **evil** in my hand (לית בידי ביש)!
		t725a

The Aramaic בישא 'evil' for Hebrew רעה 'evil, wickedness' is frequent (e.g. Tg. 1 Sam. 6:9; 10:19; 12:17, 19, 20; 20:7, 9, 13; 23:9; 24:10, 18; 25:17, 21, 26, 28, 39; and frequently). The Aramaic חוב 'sin', however, rarely corresponds to Hebrew רעה in Targum Jonathan (only: 1 Sam. 26:18 and Jer. 12:4;[26]

---

25 van Staalduine-Sulman, *The Targum of Samuel*, 442 n. 1902.
26 Cf. Tg. variants to 1 Sam. 12:17; Jer. 11:17; Hos. 10:15.

The Transmission of Targum Jonathan in the West

compare also the variant verb in 1 Sam. 24:12, see page 199).

1 Sam. 6:8

Hebrew	Babylonian Tradition	Tg. Variants
and you will place (ונתתם) it on the cart…	and you will **bring** it **down** (ותחתון) on the cart…	and you will **place** (ותתנון) it on the cart…
		t2i = A + MW (Sperber: t702s, t734s, t12sc, t10r)

The root נחת is used again for Hebrew נתן only at Targum Jer. 5:24.

1 Sam. 25:13

Hebrew	Babylonian Tradition	Tg. Variants
two hundred remained [literally:] upon the vessels (ישבו על הכלים).	two hundred remained **to guard** the vessels (אשתארו למטר מניא).	two hundred remained [literally:] upon the vessels (אישתארו על מניא).
		t705i

The text preserved by the Babylonian tradition offers a characteristically Targumic explanatory gloss, which t705i removes in favour of a more literal rendering of the Hebrew. The use of the Aramaic root נטר for the Hebrew preposition על occurs again in Targum Jonathan only at 1 Sam. 30:24.

1 Sam. 25:39

Hebrew	Babylonian Tradition	Tg. Variants
David sent and **spoke** about Abigail (וידבר באביגיל)…	David sent and **asked** about Abigail (ושאיל באביגיל)…	David sent and **spoke** about Abigail (ומליל באביגיל)…
		t2i = t713a

The verb שאל 'to ask, inquire', though arguably more fitting in the context, is used only once again in Targum Jonathan for the root דבר (Tg. Judg. 14:7; Tg. Jer. 12:1). The marginal note in t705i to this point in the text also seems to reflect this phenomenon, in addition to introducing an explanatory gloss (ל׳ א׳ ושדר דוד ומליל על עיסק אביגיל, see page 273).

1 Sam. 30:24

Hebrew	Babylonian Tradition	Tg. Variants
like the portion of those who sit [i.e. **remain**] upon the things (הישב על הכלים)…	like the portion of those who **remain to guard** the things (דאשתאר למטר מניא)…	like the portion of those who sit [i.e. **remain**] to guard the things (דיתיב למטר מניא)…
		t2i = t720a, t725a

Contextually the sense is barely altered in the three European manuscripts; nonetheless the Aramaic יתב, the basic meaning of which is 'to sit', replicates

Chapter Four. Influence of the Hebrew Text

precisely the semantic range of the Hebrew ישב (the two being connected etymologically). The Aramaic שאר for Hebrew ישב occurs only once again (in 1 Sam. 25:13, see discussion on page 124), where it is retained by all the European manuscripts studied.

2 Sam. 15:15

Hebrew	Babylonian Tradition	Tg. Variants
according to all that my master the king may **choose** (יבחר)...	according to all that my master the king may **say** (דיימר)...	according to all that my master the king may **desire** (דיתרעי)... t705i = t232i/s, t713a, t720a

The Hebrew root בחר is translated frequently with the Aramaic רעא (in Tg. Sam.: 1 Sam. 2:28; 8:18; 10:24; 12:13; 20:30; 2 Sam. 6:21; 16:18 cf. 1 Sam. 16:8, 9, 10), but only here in Targum Jonathan with the root אמר 'to say'.[27]

2 Sam. 17:21

Hebrew	Babylonian Tradition	Tg. Variants
they said to David, Get up and cross the **water** (המים) with haste...	they said to David, Get up and cross the **Jordan** (ירדנא) with haste...	...and cross the **water** (מיא) with haste... t2i = t725a

In Targum Jonathan it is only in the preceding verse (1 Sam. 1:20) that the Hebrew מים 'water' is translated 'Jordan', in typically Targumic fashion. In the preceding verse all European manuscripts retain the word 'Jordan', though t725a adds beforehand מי, i.e. 'the waters of the Jordan.'

5.a. Babylonian Tradition Supported by Hebrew Manuscripts or Ancient Versions

As I noted on a few occasions in the preceding sections (i.e. variants to 2 Sam. 12:19; 12:27; 15:23 above), there are a few cases in which one or more Hebrew manuscript(s) and/or the ancient Versions support the reading of the Babylonian tradition whereas one or more European manuscript(s) reflect the Hebrew text of Codex Leningradensis (i.e. the mainstream Masoretic Text).

---

27 Cf. One cursive manuscript of the Septuagint reads αινειτε (see Brooke, McLean and Thackeray eds, *The Old Testament in Greek, ad loc*).

The Transmission of Targum Jonathan in the West

1 Sam. 4:17

Hebrew	Babylonian Tradition	Tg. Variants
Israel fled before the Philistines (לפני פלשתים)	Israel **fled** from before the Philistines (מן קדם פלישתאי)	Israel fled before the Philistines (קדם פלשתאי)
	= Hebrew mss + citation מפני LXX: ἐκ προσώπου ἀλλοφύλων Peshitta: ܡܢ ܩܕܡ ܦܠܫܬܝܐ	t2i = t3i, t7i, t701i, t718i, t5a, t725a (Sperber: t734s, t10r)

Although the Aramaic מן קדם 'from before' can be found in a few places for the Hebrew לפני 'before' (e.g. Tg. 1 Kgs 8:59; 9:3; Tg. Isa. 17:13; Tg. Hab. 3:5), it usually translates מפני or מלפני (e.g. Tg. Josh. 23:5, 13; Tg. 1 Sam. 8:18; 18:12; 21:7 etc.), so the Babylonian textual tradition may well reflect an alternative *Vorlage* that shared the reading of the medieval Hebrew manuscripts,[28] and citations in rabbinic literature.[29]

1 Sam. 17:44

Hebrew	Babylonian Tradition	Tg. Variants
Come to me and I will give your flesh to the birds of the air and the beasts of the **field** (לבהמת השדה)!	Come to me and I will give your flesh to the birds of the air and the beasts of the **land** (ולבעירא דארעא)!	Come to me and I will give your flesh to the birds of the air and the beasts of the **field** (ולבעירא דחקלא)!
	= mlt mss (הארץ) LXX: τοῖς κτήνεσιν τῆς γῆς Vulg: *bestiis terrae*	t2i = t7i, t705i, t713a, t720a, t725a[correct] (Sperber: t734s, t12sc, t711y i.e. base text)

---

28 I.e. Oxford, Bodleian Library Ms Poc. 347–8 (Sephardi, fifteenth cent. = Kennicott 3); Oxford, Bodleian Library Ms Hunt. 11–12 (Ashkenazi/'charactere Germanico' [Kennicott, 342] beginning thirteenth cent. = Kennicott 4); Oxford, Bodleian Library Ms Tanner 173 (Ashkenazi, thirteenth cent. = Kennicott 30); Oxford, Bodleian Library Ms Kennicott 5 (Sephardi, 1487 = Kennicott 85); Cambridge, University Library Mm. 5.27 (Sephardi, fourteenth cent. = Kennicott 89); Cambridge, St. John's College A 2 (Ashkenazi/Italian? twelfth cent. = Kennicott 96); London, British Library Loan 1 (Sephardi, fifteenth cent. = Kennicott 128); Copenhagen, The Royal Library Cod. Hebr. 1 (Sephardi, 1251 = Kennicott 173); Kennicott 224 (see note 84 on page 181); Parma, Biblioteca Palatina Cod. Parm. 2874 (Sephardi, 1335 according to Kennicott = Kennicott 250); Parma, Biblioteca Palatina Cod. Parm. 2808 (Ashkenazi, thirteenth cent. = de Rossi 2); Parma, Biblioteca Palatina Cod. Parm. 1832 (Sephardi, fifteenth = de Rossi 4); Parma, Biblioteca Palatina Cod. Parm. 3106 (Ashkenazi, thirteenth cent. = de Rossi 226); Parma, Biblioteca Palatina Cod. Parm. 1996–1997 (Sephardi, 1468 = de Rossi 413); Parma, Biblioteca Palatina Cod. Parm. 2520 (Sephardi, fifteenth cent. = de Rossi 688); Parma, Biblioteca Palatina Cod. Parm. 2174 (Sephardi, fourteenth cent. = de Rossi 701); London, British Library Or. 2201 (Sephardi, 1300 = Ginsburg 14); London, British Library Add. 15252 (Sephardi fourteenth/fifteenth cent. = Ginsburg 34); London, British Library Kings 1 (= Sephardi, 1384 = Ginsburg 36); London, British Library Or. 2626–2628 (Sephardi, 1483 = Ginsburg 52); London British Library Or. 2348 (Yemenite, 1469 = Ginsburg 40).

29 y.Soṭah 8.10; Sifre Deut 198.9; Midr. Tanḥ. to Deut. 20.9; Deut. Rab. 5.11.

Chapter Four. Influence of the Hebrew Text

The reading הארץ is found in twenty two manuscripts (plus the *prima manus* of a further eighteen, including the Hebrew text of t725a) in the collections of Kennicott and de Rossi. The Aramaic ארעא is used elsewhere in Targum Jonathan to translate Hebrew שדה 'field' (e.g. Tg. Judg. 5:18; 20:6; Tg. Ezek. 31:4), so even given the evidence of the Versions, it is not a watertight certainty that the Babylonian text tradition reflects a different Hebrew text. In any case, the European manuscripts clearly reflect an adjustment to a text reading השדה.[30] It is interesting to note that the *prima manus* of t725a reads ולבעירא דארעא, with the Babylonian tradition.

To these examples the following cases should be added:

2 Sam. 22:44

Hebrew	Babylonian Tradition	Tg. Variants
You will [literally:] **keep** me (תשמרני) at the head of people (לראש גוים)...	You will **appoint** me (תמנינני) head of nations...	You **kept** me (נטרתני) head of the nations...
		t720a

In this case the reading of the Babylonian textual tradition appears to reflect the Hebrew תשימני, which is the reading found in Ps. 18:44 at this point. It is possible that the Babylonian tradition reflects an alternative *Vorlage* of the Hebrew text.[31] Nonetheless, t720a has clearly revised his text towards a Hebrew text sharing the reading of Codex Leningradensis (i.e. תשמרני or possibly ותשמרתי, hence the perfect).

It is tempting to suggest that the agreement between the Babylonian tradition and the ancient Versions demonstrates the priority of the reading in the Babylonian tradition, but we cannot be so decisive. The agreement may represent a genuine Targumic translation (1 Sam. 17:44) or the influence of common Targumic idiom (1 Sam. 4:17), pure coincidence (1 Sam. 3:16;

---

30 van Staalduine-Sulman, following Sperber's base text, takes the reading 'field' to be the original, suggesting that the emendation to 'land' might be 'an attempt to restore the usual parallelism of heaven and earth.' van Staalduine-Sulman, *The Targum of Samuel*, 383.

31 An alternative Vorlage is supported *prima facie* by LXX 'Lucianic' (i.e. mss: boc₂e₂ according to sigla of Brooke, McLean, Thackeray edition; see Brock, *The Recensions of the Septuagint Version of 1 Samuel* [Torino 1996], 18): ἔθου; citation in Sop. 8.1 and Hebr. Ms Parma, Biblioteca Palatina Cod. Parm. 2168 (Ashkenazi, thirteenth cent. = de Rossi 614): תשימני. Although I suspect accommodation to or influence of the wording of Ps 18.44 in these sources. Cf. also Peshitta ܘܢܣܝܡܢܝ. NB. The Aramaic מנא 'to appoint' is used in the ספר אחר reading to 2 Kgs 25:18, where the underlying Hebrew is שמרי הסף.

25:36), or an attempt to resolve a difficulty in the Hebrew (2 Sam. 14:21). Nonetheless, when one considers the evidence cumulatively, it seems likely that the European manuscripts have attempted to accommodate their Aramaic texts to a Hebrew text containing the reading that we find in Codex Leningradensis, and if this is the case then the reading of the Babylonian tradition is indeed the original.

In the following cases the Eastern manuscript evidence is mixed:

1 Sam. 3:16

Hebrew	Eastern Mss.	Tg. Variants
Eli called Samuel (ויקרא עלי את שמואל) and said, 'Samuel, my son!'	Eli called **to** Samuel (וקרא עלי לשמואל) and said, 'Samuel, my son!' t710y (Sperber: t711y i.e. base text, t720a, t10r, t12sc) = Hebr. mss: ויקרא עלי אל שמואל = LXX εἶπεν Ἡλὶ πρὸς Σαμουήλ	Eli called Samuel (וקרא עלי ית שמואל) and said, 'Samuel, my son!' t2521b = t3i, t7i, t232i/s, t705i, t718i, t5a (Sperber: t727y, t716y, t734s

In this case the Babylonian text according to Martínez Borobio's edition (i.e. t2521b) reads ית שמואל. The reading of t710y, a manuscript Yemenite in character, is however supported by the Septuagint and is found in twenty five of the manuscripts consulted by Kennicott and twenty four of those examined by de Rossi, so there is a reasonable chance that this reading has some antiquity. The interchange of prepositions and definite object markers is however relatively fluid in the transmission history of the Targum (see pages 215–16).

1 Sam. 25:36

Hebrew	Eastern Mss.	Tg. Variants
she did not tell him anything small **and** big (קטן וגדול) until the morning light.	she did not tell him anything small **or** big (פתגם זעיר או רב) until the morning dawned. t710y A few Hebr mss קטן או גדול LXX: ῥῆμα μικρὸν ἢ μέγα Vulgate: *verbum pusillum aut grande*	she did not tell him anything small **and** big (זעיר ורב) until the morning dawned. t707b = t2i, t3i, t7i, t232i/s, t701i, t718i, t5a, t6a, t713a, t720a, t725a (Sperber: t10r, t702s, t734s, t12sc, t727y, t716y, t711y i.e. base text)

Likewise, in this case the support of the Septuagint (the medieval Hebrew manuscripts[32] are of little or no significance) leads us to wonder if t710y is not

---

32 I.e. Oxford, Bodleian Library Ms Hunt. 11–12 (Ashkenazi/'charactere Germanico' [Kennicott,

Chapter Four. Influence of the Hebrew Text

the original reading of the Targum, though we cannot exclude the possibility that its text has been harmonised with the occurrence of the same expression in 1 Sam. 22:15.

5.b. More Complex Cases

1 Sam. 26:10

Hebrew	Babylonian Tradition	Variant
יהוה יגפנו או יומו יבוא ומת או במלחמה ירד ונספה	מן קד׳ יוי יתימחי או יומיה ימטי וימות או בקרבא ייחות ויתקטיל	מן קדם יוי ימותיניה או יומיה ייתי וימות או בקרבא יחות ויסוף
the Lord will **strike** him, or his day will come and he will die, or he will go down in battle and **perish**.	from before the Lord he will be **struck** or his day will come and he will die or in battle he will go down and **be killed**	from before the Lord he will **kill** him or his day will come and he will die or in battle he will go down and he will **perish**
		t5a

Although some of the vocabulary is commonly interchanged (see discussion on page 197) the multiple occurrences here strongly suggest a deliberate attempt to replicate the Hebrew text. It is possible the entire phrase was missing from t5a's *Vorlage* (or a predecessor) and has been reconstructed using conventional equivalents (for the Aram. סוף for Hebr. ספה cf. Tg. Jer. 12:4).

6. Adjustments of Person or Number

We have already noted above numerous examples in which the Babylonian tradition of Targum Jonathan offers a text that differs from the Hebrew of Codex Leningradensis, but one that is supported by one or more of the ancient Versions, suggesting that the reading of the Babylonian tradition is the original one. To these examples, I wish to add some further examples that concern variants in number or person. First, in the verb:

1 Sam. 17:31

Babylonian Tradition	Variant
…and they recounted [them] before Saul and **they** brought him (ודברוהי).	…and they recounted [them] before Saul and **he** brought him (ודבריה).

342] beginning thirteenth cent. = Kennicott 4); Cambridge, St. John's College A 2 (Ashkenazi/Italian? twelfth cent. = Kennicott 96); Parma, Biblioteca Palatina Cod. Parm. 3293 (Ashkenazi, 1351 = de Rossi 305); Parma, Biblioteca Palatina Cod. Parm. 3187–3189 (Ashkenazi, fourteenth cent. = de Rossi 737).

The Transmission of Targum Jonathan in the West

	t2i = t6a, t713a, t720a
= Hebr. Ms. ויקחוהו	= MT: ויקחהו Cf. 2 Mss ויקחו

LXX (recension of Origen): εἰσήγαγον αὐτὸν
LXX 2 mss: παρέστησαν αὐτὸν;
LXX mlt mss: παρέλαβον αὐτὸν καὶ εἰσήγαγον πρὸς Σαούλ.

The Hebrew manuscripts concerned are: ויקחוהו Copenhagen, The Royal Library Cod. Hebr. 17 (1346 = Kennicott 174); ויקחו Oxford, Bodleian Library Ms Digby Or. 32–33 (Italian/Ashkenazi, fourteenth cent. = Kennicott 1); Milano, Biblioteca Ambrosiana 13 (Spanish hand, fourteenth cent.[33] = Kennicott 195).

2 Sam. 3:22

Babylonian Tradition	Variant
...the servants of David and Joab came (plural אתו) from the camp...	...the servants of David and Joab came (singular אתא) from the camp...
	t701i (Sperber: t10r)
= 2 Hebrew mss באו (+ Sebir)	= MT: בא
LXX παρεγίνοντο	
Peshitta: ܐܬܘ	
Vulgate: *venerunt*	

The Hebrew manuscripts concerned are the Hebrew text of t705i (= Kennicott 154), and Copenhagen, The Royal Library Cod. Hebr. 17 (1346 = Kennicott 174).

1 Sam. 17:39

Babylonian Tradition	Variant
לית אנא יכיל למיזל	לא איכול למיזל
I **am** not able to go... (present)	I **will** not be able to go...(future)
= LXX Οὐ μὴ δύνωμαι πορευθῆναι	t701i
= Vulgate: *non possum sic incedere*	= MT: לא אוכל ללכת I **will** not be able to go... (future)

Three further examples relating to nouns or pronominal suffixes are found:

1 Sam. 5:10

Babylonian Tradition	Variant
They have brought the Ark of the God of Israel around (אסחרו) **to us** (לותנא) to kill us and **our** people (עמנא)!	They have brought the Ark of the God of Israel around (איסתחרו) **to me** (לותי) to kill us and **our** people (עמנא)!

---

33 Bernheimer, *Codices hebraici bybliothecae Ambrosianae* (Florence 1933), §13 (details not available in the catalogue of the Israeli National Library).

Chapter Four. Influence of the Hebrew Text

	t725a (Sperber: t711y i.e. base text, t734s)
	...to **us** (לותנא) to kill us and **my** people (עמי)!
	t5a
= LXX πρὸς ἡμᾶς	≈ MT: הסבו **אלי**...להמיתני ואת עמי?
= Vulgate: *ad nos*	

The following case involves a simple change in persons in some of the textual witnesses but haplography in others.

1 Sam. 6:4

Babylonian Tradition	Variant
... one plague put upon all of **you** (מחתא חדא שויא לכלכון)...	one plague put upon all of **them** (לכולהון)...
	t7i
= Hebr. mss מגפה אחת לכלכם	= MT: מגפה אחת לכלם
= Vulgate: *omnibus vobis*	

Manuscript t7i represents a simple revision towards a text identical to Codex Leningradensis. Manuscripts t725a and t2i, however, offer yet another reading: 'one plague for you (לכון)'. This evidently reflects a Hebrew text in which haplography has occurred between the two occurrences of the letter *kaph* (לכלכם → לכם). This contracted form is reflected in the Septuagint (ὑμῖν) and Peshitta (ܠܟܘܢ).

In the following cases the Eastern manuscript evidence is not uniform but, given the evidence of the Versions, there is a reasonable chance that manuscript t710y preserves the original reading:

1 Sam. 9:8

t710y	Variants
See there is one silver coin in my hand and **we** will give [it] (ונתין) to the prophet of the Lord...	...and **I** will give [it] (ואתין) to the prophet of the Lord...
t710y (Sperber: t716y, t727y, t720a, t10r)	t707b
	= t2i, t3i, t7i, t232i/s, t701i, t705i, t718i, t6a, t725a (Sperber: t711y i.e. base text, t734s, t12sc)
= LXX (1 manuscript): δώσωμεν	= MT: ונתתי
Peshitta: ܢܬܠ	
Vulgate: *demus*	

The Septuagint manuscript concerned is the cursive manuscript Ferrara, Bibl. Com., Gr. 188 i.

The Transmission of Targum Jonathan in the West

1 Sam. 10:11

t710y	Variants
...and the people said (plural ואמרו), each man to his friend, 'What has happened to the son of Kish?'	...and the people said (singular ואמר), each man to his friend, 'What has happened to the son of Kish?'
t710y (Sperber: t716y, t727y, t10r)	t707b
	= t2i, t3i, t232i/s, t701i, t705i, t718i, t6a, t725a (Sperber: t10r, t734s, t12sc, t711y i.e. base text)
= 2 Hebrew mss ויאמרו העם LXX mlt mss (Codex Alexandrinus εἶπαν / mlt mss εἶπον) Peshitta mss ܘܐܡܪܝܢ ܥܡܐ Vulgate: *dixerunt ad invicem*	= MT: ויאמר העם

The Hebrew manuscripts concerned are the Hebrew text of t705i and Vatican Urb. Ebr. 2 (Italian, *c.* 1100 = Kennicott 225). It is equally possible in this case that t710y has conformed the number of the verb to the preceding verb (i.e. ויחז). The same question must be asked of the versional evidence. A much more doubtful case is the following:

2 Sam. 5:24

t710y	Variants
...when you hear the sound of the cry in the **top** (singular בריש) of the trees...	...in the **tops** (plural ברישי) of the trees...
t710y (Sperber: t702s, t705i)	t709b
	= t2i, t3i, t7i, t232i/s, t701i, t718i, A (Sperber: t10r, t734s, t12sc, t727y, t716y, t711y i.e. base text)
= Peshitta: ܒܪܝܫ	= MT: בראשי הבכאים
= Vulgate: *in cacumine pirorum*	

The Yemenite manuscripts are all heavily influenced by the Tiberian tradition and the versional evidence is not strong. Nonetheless, it is possible that t710y preserves the original reading.

None of the cases presented in this section can be taken on its own as definitive proof that the Babylonian tradition (or, in some cases, one or more of the Yemenite manuscripts) preserves the original reading of the Targum, which reflected an alternative Hebrew *Vorlage* (as the versional evidence suggests): in all the cases just given the Hebrew text itself presents an oddity or an unexpected feature (hence the *sebir* marginal note to 2 Sam. 3:22) that any translator may have been tempted to correct. That being said, taken

Chapter Four. Influence of the Hebrew Text

together with the other examples adduced elsewhere (see also chapter five) it is at least plausible to suggest the Babylonian tradition here preserves the original reading, whereas the textual variant in one or more of the European manuscripts has been accommodated towards the Masoretic Text.

If this conclusion is correct, then in a couple of remaining cases where there is no supporting evidence in the Versions it can nonetheless plausibly be assumed that the Babylonian tradition preserves the original reading, while the variant in one or more of the European manuscripts is an attempt to accommodate the text to a Hebrew text following the reading of Codex Leningradensis. For example:

1 Sam. 15:6

Hebrew	Babylonian Tradition	Tg. Variants
לכו סרו רדו	איזיל זור איתפרש	איזילו זורו איתפרשו
Go! Turn aside! Go down! (plural)	Go! Turn aside! Separate yourself! (singular)	Go! Turn aside! Separate yourselves! (plural)
	Cf. LXX ἄπελθε καὶ ἔκκλινον	t720a = t713a

2 Sam. 1:10

Hebrew	Babylonian Tradition	Tg. Variants
אשר על זרעו	דעל דרעוהי	דעל דרעיה
that were upon his **arm**…(singular)	that were upon his **arms**…(plural)	that were upon his **arm**…(singular)
		t705i = t7i, t6a, t713a (Sperber: t716y, t10r, t12sc, Rashi)

7. Ketiv—Qere

In a few cases the Babylonian tradition follows the reading of the *Qere* (according to the masorah compiled by Gérard Weil from multiple manuscripts and published in the *Biblia Hebraica Stuttgartensia*), while one or more European manuscript(s) follows the *Ketiv*.

	Babylonian Tradition	Qere	Tg. Variants	Ketiv
1 Sam. 2:16	לא (= t705i margin פליג)	לא	ליה t705i = t701i (Sperber: t727y, t711y i.e. base text)	לו
1 Sam. 27:8	וגיזראי	הגזרי	וגריזאי t725a	הגרזי

| 2 Sam 12:9 | קדמי | בעיני | קדמוהי
t2i = t3i, t6a,
t713a, t720a
(Sperber: t716y,
t702s, t734s) | בעינו |

In one further case the Eastern manuscript evidence is mixed:

	Babylonian Tradition	Qere	Tg. Variants	Ketiv
2 Sam. 14:22	דעבדך t710y (Sperber: t727y, t711y i.e. base text, t720a, t702s, t12sc)	עבדך	דעבדיה t707b = t701i, t705i, t718i (Sperber: t716y, t10r, t734s)	עבדו

Although the *Qere* notations are found only in medieval manuscripts, the practice of *Ketiv—Qere* probably originated as a reading tradition that accompanied the text, rather than a written tradition, and is relatively early, being mentioned in rabbinic literature (e.g. b.'Erub 26a).[34] It is therefore historically possible that the Targum originally followed the *Qere*. Equally, since by its nature the Targum seeks not only to translate but also to make clear the meaning of the Hebrew text, it is not impossible that the Targum introduced a reading along the lines of the *Qere* to resolve an oddity in the Hebrew text (in each of these cases the *Qere* reading is preferable — 1 Sam. 27:8 excepting). On the other hand, it is clear that the European manuscripts reflect an accommodation of the Aramaic text to a Hebrew text preserving the same orthography as the main text of Codex Leningradensis.

However, one example is found where the reverse correspondence prevails *prima facie,* namely where Babylonian tradition follows the *Ketiv* and a number of European manuscripts the *Qere*:

---

34 E. Tov, *Textual Criticism of the Hebrew Bible*[3], 2 Vols (Minneapolis, MN 2011), Vol 2, 54–9.

Chapter Four. Influence of the Hebrew Text

	Babylonian Tradition	**Ketiv**	**Tg. Variants**	**Qere**
2 Sam. 18:12	ולא	ולא	ולו t2i = t232i/s^{correct}, t705i, t5a (Sperber: t716y, t727y, t10r, t702s, t734s, t12sc) ואלו t6a = t3i, t713a, t720a (Sperber: t711y i.e. base text).	ולו

This case, however, may not relate to the system of *Ketiv—Qere* at all, but to variant readings in Hebrew manuscripts, since multiple manuscripts[35] follow the *Qere* reading in their main text.

8. Minuses

There are also many examples in which words or short phrases that do not occur in the underlying Hebrew text but are present in the Babylonian tradition (and other witnesses) are also absent in one or more of the manuscripts belonging to the Mixed Western and Ashkenazi groups. It goes without saying that in these cases the possibility that the word(s) has been omitted accidentally cannot be overlooked.

1 Sam. 4:3

Babylonian tradition	ניסב **כען** לנא משילו
	Let us **now** take [the Ark of the covenant of the Lord] for ourselves from Shiloh…
Variant	ניסב לנא משילו

---

35 Oxford, Bodleian Library Ms Poc. 347–8 (Sephardi, fifteenth cent. = Kennicott 3); Oxford, Bodleian Library Ms Hunt. 11–12 (Ashkenazi/'charactere Germanico' [Kennicott 342], begin thirteenth cent. = Kennicott 4); Oxford, Bodleian Library Kennicott 6 (Sephardi, fourteenth–fifteenth cent. = Kennicott 86); Cambridge, Gonville & Caius College Library 404/625 (Ashkenazi, thirteenth/fourteenth cent. = Kennicott 93); London, British Library Harley 5722 (Sephardi, 1428–9 = Kennicott 112); Parma, Biblioteca Palatina Cod. Parm. 2874 (according to Kennicott: Sephardi cursive, 1305 = Kennicott 246; the manuscript is no longer extant, see Richler, *Hebrew Manuscripts in the Biblioteca Palatina in Parma*, §484); Parma, Biblioteca Palatina Cod. Parm. 2874 (Kennicott, 434 'Germanice, scriptus forte fuit seculo 13 exeunte'. = Kennicott 249); Parma, Biblioteca Palatina Cod. Parm. 2874 (Sephardi, 1335 according to Kennicott = Kennicott 250); Parma, Biblioteca Palatina Cod. Parm. 2874 (Sardinia, 1310 according to Kennicott = Kennicott 251); Zurich, Zentralbibliothek Or. 158 (1494 = Kennicott 253).

The Transmission of Targum Jonathan in the West

	Let us take [the Ark of the covenant of the Lord] for ourselves from Shiloh...
	t705i
Hebrew	נקחה אלינו משלה
	Let us take [the Ark] for ourselves from Shiloh...

1 Sam. 5:4

Babylonian tradition	ותרתין פסת ידוהי קציצן **מחתן** על סקופתא
	...and his two cut off hands **fallen** upon the threshold.
Variant	ותרין פסת ידוהי קציצן על איסקופתא
	...and his two hands cut off upon the threshold.
	t705i = t2i
Hebrew	ושתי כפות ידיו כרתות אל המפתן
	...and his two hands cut off upon the threshold.

The Armenian and Ethiopic versions offer a reading closer to that of the Babylonian tradition.[36]

1 Sam. 6:18

Babylonian tradition	**הא היא** בחקל יהושע
	...**see! It is** in the field of Joshua...
Variant	בחקל יהושע
	...in the field of Joshua...
	t3i
Hebrew	בשדה יהושע
	...in the field of Joshua...

1 Sam. 9:5

Babylonian tradition	מן **עיסק** אתניא
	...from the **business** of the asses...
Variant	מן אתניא
	...from the asses...
	t2i
Hebrew	מן האתנות
	...from the asses...

1 Sam. 12:25

Babylonian tradition	If you indeed do evil **deeds** (אבאשא תבאשון **עובדיכון**), not only you but also your king will be destroyed!
Variant	If you indeed do evil (אבאשא תבאשון), not only you but also your king will be destroyed!
	t2i = t232i/s, t725a (Sperber: t727y, t716y)

---

36 According to Brooke, McLean and Thackeray (eds), *The Old Testament in Greek*, ad loc.

Hebrew	ואם הרע תרעו גם אתה גם מלככם תספו
	If you indeed do evil, not only you but also your king will be destroyed!

The Septuagint may reflect a nominal form (i.e. ἐὰν κακίᾳ κακοποιήσητε).[37]

1 Sam. 13:13

Babylonian tradition	תפקידת **מימרא** דיוי
	...the commandment of **the Memra of** the Lord...
Variant	תפקידתא דיוי
	...the commandment of the Lord...
	t718i
Hebrew	מצות יהוה
	....the commandment of the Lord...

1 Sam. 14:13

Babylonian tradition	ונפלו **מטענין** קדם יונתן
	So they fell **stabbed** before Jonathan...
Variant	ונפלו קדם יונתן
	So they fell before Jonathan...
	t3i
Hebrew	ויפלו לפני יונתן
	So they fell before Jonathan...

1 Sam. 15:16

Babylonian tradition	Samuel said to Saul, Wait and I will tell to you that which **was said from before** the Lord (דאיתמלל מן קדם יוי) with me in the night...
Variant	Samuel said to Saul, Wait and I will tell to you that which the Lord said (די מליל יוי) with me in the night...
	t2i
Hebrew	ויאמר שמואל אל שאול הרף ואגידה לך את אשר דבר יהוה אלי הלילה
	Samuel said to Saul, Hold on and I will tell to you that which the Lord said to me in the night...

The laboured expression in the Babylonian textual tradition is a typical means of avoiding anthropomorphic descriptions of God in Targum Jonathan. Manuscript t2i provides a more direct representation of the Hebrew.

1 Sam. 17:29

Babylonian tradition	t707b: הלא פתגם הוא **אמרית**
	t707b: Is it not [just] a word [that] **I spoke**?
	t2506b: הלא פתגמא הוא **דאמרית**
	t2506b: Is it not [just] a word that **I spoke**?

---

37 Several cursive manuscripts read κακοποιοῦντες κακοποιήσητε, Brooke, McLean and Thackeray (eds), *The Old Testament in Greek, ad loc.*

Variant	Was it not [just] a word? t705i (Sperber: t711y i.e. base text)	הלא פיתגם הוא
Hebrew	Was it not [just] a word?	הלוא דבר הוא

Van Staalduine-Sulman assumes the longer form of the Babylonian tradition to be an 'addition', supplied because of the otherwise 'terse style' of the end of the verse.[38] It is much more likely that the Babylonian tradition preserves the original text here.

1 Sam 20:16

Babylonian tradition	So Jonathan made a **covenant** with the house of David.	וגזר יהונתן **קים** עם בית דויד
Variant	So Jonathan covenanted with the house of David. t7i (Sperber: t716y, t727y)	וגזר יהונ׳ עם בי׳ דו׳
Hebrew	So Jonathan covenanted with the house of David.	ויכרת יהונתן עם בית דוד

1 Sam. 23:11

Babylonian tradition	**Is it likely** that Saul will come down?	**הסביר** למיחת שאול
Variant	Will Saul come down? t725a = t2i	היחות שאול
Hebrew	Will Saul come down?	הירד שאול

1 Sam. 28:3

Babylonian tradition	They buried him in the hill country **and they mourned over him, each man** in his own city	וקברוהי ברמתא **וספדו עלוהי אנש** בקרתיה
Variant	They buried him in the hill country in his city t232i/s	וקברוהי ברמתא בקרתיה
Hebrew	They buried him in Ramah and in his city	ויקברהו ברמה ובעירו

The addition וספדו עלוהי אנש may originally have been taken over from earlier in the verse (i.e. וספדו עלוהי כל ישראל). Indeed, according to Martínez Borobio's edition the text is erased in manuscript t707b, though it is retained in

---

38 van Staalduine-Sulman, *The Targum of Samuel*, 361 n. 1259.

Chapter Four. Influence of the Hebrew Text

t710y and the other Yemenite manuscripts consulted by Sperber.

1 Sam. 29:3

Babylonian tradition	…but I have not found anything **evil** (מידעם **ביש**) in him…
Variant	…but I have not found anything (מדעם) in him… t2i = t705i (Sperber: t727y)
Hebrew	ולא מצאתי בו מאומה
	…but I have not found anything in him…

2 Sam. 1:2

Babylonian tradition	ועפרא **רמי** ברישיה
	…and dust **thrown** on his head.
Variant	ועפרא על רישיה
	…and dust upon his head. t705i
Hebrew	ואדמה על ראשו
	…and earth upon his head.

The reading of t705i conforms to the Hebrew text, but deviates from the conventional idiom of Targum Jonathan (cf. Tg. 1 Sam. 4:12; Tg. 2 Sam. 15:32).[39]

2 Sam. 4:2

Babylonian tradition	The two men were the chiefs of sections of **two** armies (רישי **תרתין** משרין)…
Variant	The two men were the chiefs of sections of armies (רישי משריין)… t2i = t5a (Sperber: t716y, t10r)
Hebrew	ושני אנשים שרי גדודים
	The two men were the chiefs of troops

This example is one of the 'hebraisirende Aenderungen' note by Bacher.[40]

2 Sam. 4:2

Babylonian tradition	הוו **עם** בר שאול
	…they were **with** Saul's son.
Variant	הוו בר שאול
	…they were a son of Saul [sic]. t705i
Hebrew	היו בן שאול
	…they were a son of Saul [sic].

---

39 van Staalduine-Sulman, *The Targum of Samuel*, 477 n. 3.
40 Bacher, 'Kritische Untersuchungen zum Prophetentargum', 53.

The Transmission of Targum Jonathan in the West

By offering a text closer to the Hebrew, t705i in fact perpetuates an apparent error in the Hebrew text here, which is resolved by the remaining manuscripts as well as in the two marginal notes in t705i (see page 280).

2 Sam. 4:10

Babylonian tradition	...and he was like one bringing [good] news in his **own** eyes (כמבסר בעיני **נפשיה**)...
Variant	...and he was like one bringing [good] news in his eyes (כמבשר בעינוהי)...
	t2i = t232i/s^{PM}, t713a, t720a, t725a
Hebrew	והוא היה כמבשר בעיניו
	...and he was like one bringing [good] news in his eyes...

Exactly the same change (i.e. omission of נפש) occurs in manuscripts t725a and t2i when the idiom 'in one's own eyes' occurs again in 2 Sam. 6:22 (i.e. Babylonian tradition: 'I will be low in my own eyes' ואיהי מכיך בעיני נפשי). Aside from these two cases this idiom is to be found on two other occasions in Targum Jonathan (i.e. Tg. 1 Sam. 15:17; Tg. Isa. 5:21 cf. Tg. Onq. Num. 13:33), stressing the reflexive nature of the action.

2 Sam. 6:1

Babylonian tradition	David **continued** to gather (ואוסיף עוד דויד **למכנש**) all the chosen ones of Israel...
Variant	David gathered together(?) again (ואוסיף עוד דויד) all the chosen ones of Israel...
	t705i = t2i, t720a, t725a
Hebrew	ויסף עוד דוד את כל בחור בישראל
	David gathered together(?) again every chosen one in Israel...

The sense of the Hebrew here is unclear: either an infinitive is missing or the verb יסף conveys the sense 'to join together' (cf. e.g IQS 8.19). The Babylonian tradition smooths out the difficulty, whereas t720a, t725a, t2i, t705i cause the same difficulty in the Aramaic (the sense 'to be gathered together' is attested in Syriac in *'ettaphal*).

2 Sam. 6:4

Babylonian tradition	ונטלוהי מבית אבינדב דבגבעתא **אתן** עם ארונא דייי
	They carried it from the house of Abinadav which was on the hill, **coming** with the Ark of the Lord

Chapter Four. Influence of the Hebrew Text

Variant	ונטלוה׳ מבית אבינדב די בגבעת׳ עם ארונא דיוי
	They carried it from the house of Abinadav which was on the hill, with the Ark of the Lord.
	t2i = t7i, t5a, t713a, t720a (Sperber: t734s, t716y, t727y)
Hebrew	וישאהו מבית אבינדב אשר בגבעה עם ארון האלהים
	They carried it from the house of Abinadav which was on the hill, with the Ark of God.

2 Sam. 8:6

Babylonian tradition	בכל אתר דהליך
	...in every **place** that he went.
Variant	בכל דהליך
	...everywhere that he went.
	t7i (But cf. 2 Sam. 8:14 where t7i reads בכל אתר דהליך for בכל אשר הלך MT)
Hebrew	בכל אשר הלך
	...everywhere that he went.

2 Sam. 13:11

Babylonian tradition	She drew near **before him but he did not want** to eat (לקדמוהי **ולא** אבא למיכל) and he overpowered her...
Variant	She drew near to him [in order for him] to eat (ליה למיכל) but he overpowered her...
	t2i = t3i, t7i, t701i, t718i, t232i/s (לותיה), t6a, t720a, t725a (Sperber: t716y, t727y, t10r, t702s, t734s, t12sc)
Hebrew	ותגש אליו לאכל ויחזק בה
	She drew near him [in order for him] to eat and he overpowered her...

The phrase 'and he did not want...' is a Targumic gloss occasioned by the lack of subject in the Hebrew (the implication of the Hebrew is that it is Tamar who will be eating!).

2 Sam. 13:16

Babylonian tradition	...concerning the matter of this great evil: after what you have done with me **you are commanding** to send me away (את אמר לשלחותני)...
Variant	...after what you have done with me to send me away (לשלחותי)...
	t2i = t232i/s, t5a, t720a, t725a
Hebrew	הרעה הגדולה הזאת מאחרת אשר עשית עמי לשלחני
	...this evil is greater than the other that you have done with me to send me...

The omitted phrase ('you are commanding') represents an attempt by the Targumist to establish the correct relationship between the elements in the Hebrew text.

The Transmission of Targum Jonathan in the West

2 Sam. 15:20

Babylonian tradition ואתיב ית אחך עמך **ואעביד עמהון** טיבו וקשוט

…and repay your brothers with you **and I will do with them** goodness and truth!

Variant ואתיב ית אחך עמך טיבו וקשוט

…and repay your brothers with you goodness and truth!
t2i

Hebrew והשב את אחיך עמך חסד ואמת

…and repay your brothers with you mercy and truth!

2 Sam. 18:11

Babylonian tradition ומדין לא מחיתהי תמן **ורמיתהי** לארעא

Why did you not strike him there **and throw him** to the ground?

Variant ומה דין לא מחיתהי תמן לארעא

Why did you not strike him there to the ground?
t232i/s

Hebrew ומדוע לא הכיתו שם ארצה

Why did you not strike him there to the ground?

2 Sam. 18:20

Babylonian tradition לא גבר **כשר** לבסרא ית יומא הדין

You are not a man **fit** to deliver news this day…

Variant לא גבר בסרא ית יומא הדין

You are not a man of news this day…
t2i = t725a

Hebrew לא איש בשרה אתה היום הזה

You are not a man of news this day…

The laconic style of the Hebrew here apparently fails to provide a reason for Joab's refusal to let Ahima'az the son of Zadok take the message. This accounts for the original Targumic gloss preserved in the Babylonian textual tradition.

2 Sam. 20:2

Babylonian tradition All the men of Israel went up from after David **to go** after Sheva (**למיזל** בתר שבע) the son of Bichri…

Variant All the men of Israel went up from after David after Sheva (שבע בתר) the son of Bichri…
t705i = t2i, t7i, t232i/s, t713a (שב added as marginal correction), t720a, t725a (Sperber: t734s)

Hebrew ויעל כל איש ישראל באחרי דוד אחרי שבע בן בכרי

All the men of Israel went up from after David after Sheva the son of Bichri…

142

Chapter Four. Influence of the Hebrew Text

The verb is implied but not given in the Hebrew text. For the sake of clarity the Targum has supplied it.[41]

2 Sam. 20:11

Babylonian tradition	...and whoever is for David, **let him go** after (ייזיל בתר) Joab.
Variant	...and whoever is for David, after (בתר) Joab.
	t2i = t3i, t713a, t720a[PM] (Sperber: t734s, t12sc)
Hebrew	ומי אשר לדוד אחרי יואב
	...and whoever is for David, after Joab.

The laconic style of the Hebrew demands the addition of a verb. This is provided in the original reading of the Babylonian textual tradition (cf. Old Latin: *si quis est cum David eat cum Ioab*).[42]

2 Sam. 21:8

Babylonian tradition	and the five sons of **Merab whom** Michal, the daughter of Saul, **raised** (מירב דרביאת מיכל), which she bore to Adriel...
Variant	and the five sons of Michal (מיכל), the daughter of Saul, which she bore to Adriel...
	t2i = t3i, t6a, t725a
Hebrew	ואת חמשת בני מיכל בת שאול אשר ילדה לעדריאל
	and the five sons of Michal the daughter of Saul, which she bore to Adriel...

The phrase 'from Merab whom [Michal] raised' is an explanatory gloss in the Targum, which harmonises the text with 1 Sam. 18:19, where it is said that Merab (and not Michal) was given to Adriel.[43] The harmonisation has also been made in two Hebrew manuscripts and multiple manuscripts of the Septuagint.[44] Because the phrase is not in the (standard) Hebrew text, t6a, t725a, t2i, and t3i remove it.

8.a. Babylonian Tradition Supported by the Ancient Versions

In a few cases in which one or more European manuscript(s) contains a minus *vis à vis* the Babylonian text tradition, the reading of the Babylonian text tradition is supported by one or more variant Hebrew manuscript or one or more of the ancient Versions. For example:

---

41 van Stalduine-Sulman, *The Targum of Samuel*, 607 n. 987.
42 van Stalduine-Sulman, *The Targum of Samuel*, 609 n.1007.
43 See further van Stalduine-Sulman, *The Targum of Samuel*, 618.
44 See Brooke, McLean and Thackeray (eds), *The Old Testament in Greek, ad loc.*

The Transmission of Targum Jonathan in the West

1 Sam. 14:18

Babylonian tradition	...because the Ark of the Lord was in that day **with** the sons of Israel (t2506b: עם בני ישראל; t707b: ועם)
Variant	...because the Ark of the Lord was in that day **and** the sons of Israel (*sic.* ובני ישראל). t2i = t725a
Hebrew	כי היה ארון האלהים ביום ההוא ובני ישראל
	...because the Ark of the Lord was in that day **and** the sons of Israel (*sic*).
Versions	Hebr. Ms: בני עם ישראל (cf. Kimhi, *Commentary on Samuel, ad loc*)
	Vulgate: *cum filiis Israhel*
	Peshitta: ܥܡ ܒܢܝ ܐܝܣܪܐܝܠ
	Cf. LXX: ἐν τῇ ἡμέρᾳ ἐκείνῃ ἐνώπιον Ισραηλ; Old Latin (according to Palimpsestus Vindobonensis): *in illa die ante populum Israel*.

The variant Hebrew manuscript is Or. Fol. 1–4 Berlin, Staatsbibliothek, Preußischer Kulturbesitz (i.e. t5a; Ashkenazi, fourteenth cent.).

2 Sam. 6:6

Babylonian tradition	...and Uzza stretched forth **his hand** (ידיה) to the Ark of the Lord (בארונא דיוי)...
Variant	...and Uzza stretched forth to the Ark of the Lord (בארונא דיוי)... t720a = t7i (omits 'Uzza'. Error?)
Hebrew	וישלח עזא אל ארון האלהים
	...and Uzza stretched forth to the Ark of the Lord...
Versions	Hebrew Ms, Citation, 4Q51: את ידו
	LXX: τὴν χεῖρα αὐτοῦ
	Vulgate: (*extendit*) *manum* (*Oza*)
	Peshitta: ܐܝܕܗ

The variant Hebrew manuscript concerned is London, British Library Or. 2364 (Yemeni, fifteenth cent. = Ginsburg 51); the rabbinic citation, b.Soṭah 35[a].

The following example is concerned merely with agreement in number.

1 Sam. 11:11

Babylonian tradition	...they struck the sons of Amon until the day grew hot and **there were** some who remained (והוו דאישתארו) but they were scattered...
Variant	...and **it was that** [some] remained (והוה דאשתארו) but they were scattered... t2i = t705i (Sperber: t734s)
Hebrew	ויהי הנשארים ויפצו
	...and it was that there were some remaining but they were scattered...
Versions	LXX ἐγενήθησαν (but variants in manuscripts).

Chapter Four. Influence of the Hebrew Text

Although I argue in this book in favour of the priority of the Babylonian text tradition of Targum Jonathan, the value of the above agreements must be subjected to the same degree of scepticism that we apply to agreements between variants in European Targum manuscripts and the ancient Versions (see chapter five). Agreements in number can easily be incidental (compare the example in 1 Sam. 17:31, given in §6 above, in which the plural accords with the preceding verb, ויגדו 'and they recounted'). The Hebrew of 1 Sam. 14:18 is evidently difficult, so it is possible that all the ancient Versions (including the Targum) represent attempts to remedy the confusion. The example from 2 Sam. 6:6 is however well supported by ancient authorities, including the Hebrew text of Samuel from Qumran, so it is a near certainty that the Babylonian tradition of Targum Jonathan preserves the original reading of the Targum in this case and that this corresponds to a genuine alternative Hebrew *Vorlage*. The change in manuscripts t720a and t7i is, therefore, certainly a secondary adjustment of the text towards a Hebrew text where the wording was missing (as it is in Codex Leningradensis). Even where considerable doubt remains, however, such as in cases of adjustments in number, the default position should be to ascribe priority to the Babylonian tradition with the burden of proof resting on the Western manuscripts.

Conclusions

It is clear that the text of Targum Samuel has been frequently accommodated to the Hebrew text during its transmission. The text has been altered to bring it into closer conformity to the underlying Hebrew, either by replacing words with alternatives that more closely reflect the Hebrew, by omitting words that do not correspond to the Hebrew, or by adding words to represent features in the Hebrew that are represented only abstractly in the Babylonian text tradition.

This phenomenon is by no means confined to Western manuscripts however. Consider the following case:

1 Sam. 11:11

MT	ויכו את עמון עד חם היום
	…and they smote the Ammonites until the day became hot…
t710y	…and they smote the Ammonites (ומחו ית עמון) until the day became hot…
	(Sperber: t716y, t727y, t12sc)

The Transmission of Targum Jonathan in the West

Babylonian tradition	…and they smote the **sons of** Ammon (ומחו ית **בני** עמון) until the day became hot…
	= t5a, t6a, t713a, t720a, t2i, t705i (Sperber: t711y i.e. base text, t10r, t734s)
Hebrew mss[45]	ויכו את בני עמון
	…and they smote **the sons** of Ammon
Versions	LXX: ἔτυπτον τοὺς υἱοὺς Αμμων
	Peshitta: ܘܡܚܘ ܠܒܢܝ ܥܡܘܢ
	Old Latin: *et percussit filios ammon*

The Old Latin reading is that of Palimpsests Vindobonensis (Beuron no. 115).[46] The versional evidence and attestation in t707b make it almost certain that 'the sons of Ammon' is the original reading of the Targum. t710y, a manuscript of the Yemenite family that nonetheless stands close to the Babylonian tradition in its consonantal text, has apparently lost the wording 'the sons of' under the influence of the prevailing Hebrew text.

The process of adaptation towards the Hebrew text has been far from systematic. No manuscript shows consistency. The process has been applied only sporadically and haphazardly. This point is neatly illustrated by the expression 'within all the border of Israel'. In the following examples European manuscripts (note t713a) produce a text closer to the underlying Hebrew:

1 Sam. 11:3

Babylonian tradition	בכל תחום **ארעא** דישראל
	…within all the border **of the land** of Israel.
Variant	בכל תחום ישר'
	…within all the border of Israel.
	t713a = t720a (Sperber: t10r)
Hebrew	בכל גבול ישראל
	…within all the border of Israel.

1 Sam. 27:1

Babylonian tradition	בכל תחום **ארעא** דישראל
	…within all the border **of the land** of Israel.

---

45 Hebr. Mss: Oxford, Bodleian Library Ms Hunt. 11–12 (Ashkenazi/'charactere Germanico' [Kennicott 342], begin thirteenth cent. = Kennicott 4); Hebrew of t713a (= Kennicott 182).

46 African, fifth cent. according Fischer, 'Palimpsestus Vindobonensis, II, Manuscript 115 of the Books of Kingdoms, 1 Rg 1,14–4 Rg 17,19', 326, 348; see N. Fernández Marcos and J. Ramón Busto Saiz (eds), *El texto antioqueno de la Biblia griega, I, 1–2 Samuel* (Textos y Estudios 'Cardenal Cisneros' 50, Madrid 1989), l–liv.

Chapter Four. Influence of the Hebrew Text

Variant		בכל תחום ישראל
	...within all the border of Israel.	
	t713a = t232i/s (Sperber: t12sc)	
Hebrew		בכל גבול ישראל
	...within all the border of Israel.	

2 Sam. 21:5

Babylonian tradition		בכל תחום **ארעא** דישראל
	...within all the border **of the land** of Israel.	
Variant		בכל תחום ישראל
	...within all the border of Israel.	
	t705i = t232i/s	
Hebrew		בכל גבל ישראל
	...within all the border of Israel.	

Yet, the frequency with which the longer form of the phrase (i.e. 'the border of *the land* of Israel') occurs causes three European manuscripts (again, note t713a) to add ארעא 'land' when the expressions crops up in 1 Sam. 11:7 though there is no warrant for this in the Hebrew:

1 Sam. 11:7

Babylonian tradition		בכל תחום ישראל
	...within all the border of Israel.	
Variant		בכל תחו' **ארעא** דישראל
	...within all the border **of the land** of Israel.	
	t2i = t713a, t6a (Sperber: t716y, t727y)	
Hebrew		בכל גבול ישראל
	...within all the border of Israel.	

The adjustment to the text is inconsistent, even within a single manuscript (e.g. t713a) and this implies that the revision has been far from a conscious effort to tidy up the text or produce an Aramaic text more faithful to the Hebrew.

Moreover, no clear or consistent pattern of agreement between the manuscripts in either the Ashkenazi or the Mixed Western group is discernible. That said, there are some manuscripts in which the tendency to accommodate to the Hebrew text is more readily apparent than others: in particular t720a, t713a, t6a from the Ashkenazi group; t705i and t2i from the Mixed Western group.[47] Of course these manuscripts are all related to one another (some closely, some distantly), so we should expect that some readings have simply

---

47 van Staalduine-Sulman noted already the stronger tendency in t720a and t705i; van Staalduine-Sulman, *The Targum of Samuel*, 130.

been adopted from their respective *Vorlagen*. Given the poor state of the text in t720a and t713a, for example, we must suspect that many of the cases found in those manuscripts have been taken over from their respective *Vorlagen*, rather than being the innovation of the scribes themselves.

Where there is agreement across textual groupings, in some cases this is most likely a regional variation (e.g. Tg. 1 Sam. 6:1, page 112); in other cases the agreement is more difficult to explain (e.g. t705i, t10r, and t716y share the variant reading at Tg. 2 Sam. 2:16, page 111). Coincidence clearly plays a role in agreements across text groupings where the variation concerns a preposition or the adjustment of person or number.

The instances of unique readings — readings found in only one manuscript — are high. Concerning the use of alternative lexemes, about half the examples cited above are unique. Although it is intrinsically more likely that a unique variant is the innovation of the scribe of the manuscript in which the variant is attested, this cannot be taken for granted, since the content of manuscripts that have been lost, destroyed, or remain to be found or correctly identified, remains unknown and we cannot know what has been taken over from the *Vorlage*.

The prevalence of unique readings among the instances of minuses (about two thirds) is understandable since this type of revision is the easiest to achieve, requiring the least aptitude in Targumic conventions or Aramaic. Accidental omission is also quite possible in the case of minuses, the scribe simply forgetting to add the word in the Aramaic because it is missing in the Hebrew (and so the Hebrew does not act like a prompt).

Manuscripts t701i and t718i contain almost no genuine examples of this revisionary tendency. Both contain a high number of scribal errors, suggesting that the text was poorly understood. A lack of proficiency would certainly account for the absence of revisionary tendencies, since a degree of comprehension and competence in Targumic Aramaic is implied by the deliberate adjustment of the text.

The cumulative evidence implies a deliberate intervention in the text, but it is almost impossible to say whether any given instance was deliberate, a subconscious slip, or accident. Our witnesses probably reflect a mixture of these.

Chapter Five

Agreements with Ancient Versions and Hebrew Manuscripts

Within the European Targum manuscripts a number of variant readings are to be found that agree, at least superficially, with one or more of the principal ancient Versions and/or with variant readings found in Hebrew manuscripts,[1] and/or citations in rabbinic and medieval Jewish literature. We are therefore confronted with the possibility that these medieval manuscripts occasionally preserve some genuinely ancient alternative readings of the Targum, which might reflect an alternative Hebrew *Vorlage*. Before we can consider this possibility, however, we must consider the possibility that the agreement between the Targum and one or more of the ancient Versions may be the result of the direct influence of one on another, rather than evidence that both reflect a common alternative Hebrew *Vorlage*.

The Targums and the Peshitta share a common language, albeit in distinct dialects, and in many places the reading of the Peshitta departs from the Hebrew text in ways that are reminiscent of Targumic technique or, on occasion, resemble the reading of one of the extant Targums. Consequently, the possibility that some form of literary relationship exists between the Peshitta and our Targum (whether direct or indirect) occupied the minds of earlier generations of scholars, primarily in respect of the Pentateuch and to a lesser extent the Prophets.[2] In the case of the books of Samuel, such a thesis was

---

1 Established on the basis of C.D. Ginsburg, *The Earlier Prophets. Diligently Revised According to the Massorah and the Early Editions with the Various Readings from mss. and the Ancient Versions* (London 1926 [1894]); B. Kennicott, *Vetus Testamentum hebraicum cum variis lectionibus*, Vol. 1 (Oxford 1776); J.B. de Rossi, *Variae lectiones veteris testamenti ex immensa Mss. editorumq. codicum congerie haustae et ad samar. textum, ad vetustiss. versiones, ad accuratiores sacrae criticae fontes ac leges examinatae*, Vols 1–2 (Parma 1785), Vol. 2; de Rossi, *Scholia critica in V. T. libros sue supplementa ad varias sacri textus lectiones* (Parma 1798), 38–42 and the critical apparatus of BHS , which incorporates Cairo Genizah manuscripts. Details of the manuscripts' current holding library, date, and palaeography are taken from the National Library of Israel's database. Where the database holds no records other catalogues have been consulted (references given *ad loc*). It has not been possible to trace the manuscripts in every case; some have probably been lost or destroyed, particularly those held in Germany and the Netherlands before the Second World War.

2 For a summary of previous research see P.B. Dirksen, 'The Old Testament Peshitta', in M.J.

advanced in the early part of the twentieth century by Peters. Following the principles and conclusions laid out in his earlier work, *Peschittha und Targumim des Pentateuchs* (1935), Peters argued that Peshitta Samuel was derived from a written Targum, the agreements between Peshitta Samuel and Targum Samuel being sufficient to demonstrate that they shared a common ancestor ('Stammvater'). Both texts had undergone a historical development and this suggested, in Peters' opinion, that in some cases the Peshitta preserved the reading of its underlying Targum ('zugrunde liegenden Targum'), where the reading of the Targum in its current form was the result of revision towards the Hebrew text.[3]

Peters' work on Samuel was an attempt to rebuff de Boer, who had considered Peters' proposal for the Pentateuch as a possible means of accounting for similarities between the two texts in the books of Samuel. De Boer had reached the conclusion that Peters' proposal could not be supported by unequivocal textual evidence. In de Boer's view the overwhelming majority of cases of agreements could be more simply explained by other factors, such as their translation technique.[4] De Boer's more cautious approach to the data is reflected in much subsequent work on the question of the relationship between Peshitta and Targum in the books of the Prophets. In recent years studies have been completed on the books of Joshua, Judges, Kings, Isaiah, the Minor Prophets, and of particular interest for the present study, Samuel.[5] From these

---

Mulder (ed.) *Mikra: Text, Translation, Reading and Interpretation of the Hebrew Bible in Ancient Judaism and Early Christianity* (Peabody, MA 2004 [1988]), 255–97, pp. 264–85 (on the Prophets: 285–90); Dirksen, 'Targum and Peshitta : Some Basic Questions', in P.V.M. Flesher (ed.), *Targum Studies*, Vol. 2, *Targum and Peshitta* (South Florida Studies in the History of Judaism 165, Atlanta, GA 1998), 3–13; M.P. Weitzman, *The Syriac Version of the Old Testament: an Introduction* (University of Cambridge Oriental Publications 56, Cambridge 1999), 84–129 (on the Prophets: 107–9).

3 C. Peters, 'Zur Herkunft der Pešitta des ersten Samuel-Buches', *Biblica* 22 (1941), 25–34, esp. 32–4.
4 P.A.H. de Boer, *Research into the Text of 1 Samuel I–XVI: a Contribution to the Study of the Books of Samuel* (Amsterdam 1938), 40–3. Cf. Dirksen, 'The Old Testament Peshitta', 287.
5 Smelik, *The Targum of Judges*, 234–90; P.S.F. van Keulen, 'Points of Agreement Between the Targum and Peshitta Versions of Kings Against the MT: a Sounding', in P.S.F. van Keulen and W.Th. van Peursen (eds), *Corpus Linguistics and Textual History: a Computer-assisted Interdisciplinary Approach to the Peshitta* (Studia Semitica Neerlandica 48, Assen 2006), 205–35; A. van der Kooij, *Die Alten Textzeugen des Jesajabuches: Ein Beitrag zur Textgeschichte des Alten Testaments* (Orbis Biblicus et Orientalis 35, Freiburg and Göttingen 1981), 259–70, pp. 289–90; A. Gelston, 'The Twelve Prophets: Peshitta and Targum', in P.V.M. Flesher (ed.), *Targum Studies*, Vol 2, *Targum and Peshitta* (South Florida Studies in the History of Judaism 165, Atlanta, GA 1998), 119–39; C.E, Morrison, *The Character of the Syriac Version of the*

Chapter Five. Agreements with Ancient Versions and Hebrew Manuscripts

researches a scholarly consensus has emerged that holds that the points of agreement between the Targums and the Peshitta do not support a theory of literary dependence.[6] By applying what van Keulen has called a 'minimalistic approach',[7] that is to say by excluding cases where coincidental agreement is plausible — such as those caused by scribal error, similarities in translation techniques, the common demands of the source language, a common variant (Hebrew) *Vorlage*,[8] accommodations to the context, and so forth — very few cases remain, and those that do remain can generally be explained adequately by the influence of Jewish exegetical traditions on the Peshitta. A theory of literary dependence also struggles to account for the substantial number of cases of conspicuous *dis*agreement between the Peshitta and the Targum, particularly in instances in which the underlying Hebrew is difficult so that one might reasonably have expected the Syriac translator to have sought help in the Targum.[9] Nonetheless, some have not wanted to rule out entirely the possibility that the translator of the Peshitta occasionally consulted a written Targum.[10]

First Book of Samuel (Monographs of the Peshitta Institute Leiden 11, Leiden 2001), 98–145. Cf. also Weitzman, *The Syriac Version of the Old Testament*, 107–9; M.P. Weitzman, 'Peshitta, Septuagint and Targum', in René Lavenant (ed.), *VI Symposium Syriacum 1992: University of Cambridge, Faculty of Divinity 30 August – 2 September 1992* (Orientalia Christiana Analecta 247, Rome 1994), 51–84, pp. 79–80.

6   The article of J.C. de Moor and F. Sepmeijer ('The Peshitta and the Targum of Joshua', in P.B. Dirksen and A. van der Kooij (eds), *The Peshitta as a Translation: Papers Read at the II Peshitta Symposium held at Leiden 19–21 August 1993* [Monographs of the Peshitta Institute Leiden 8, Leiden 1995], 129–76) is the exception. They offered a more optimistic reading of the data. Their conclusion, that the translator made use of the Targum but wanted to show he was not following it slavishly (176), though imaginative, is not convincing; see Weitzman, *The Syriac Version of the Old Testament*, 109. Cf. also the seemingly contrary conclusion in M.C.A. Korpel, J.C. de Moor and F. Sepmeijer, 'Consistency with Regard to Tenses: Targum and Peshitta in Two Samples from Deutero-Isaiah', in Association Internationale Bible et Informatique (AIBI); la Faculté des Lettres de l'Université de Provence, *Bible et informatique: traduction et transmission: actes du cinquième colloque international, Aix-en-Provence, 1–4 September 1997* (Travaux de Linguistique Quantitative 65, Paris 1998), 195–220, pp. 217–18 (note also their unjustified criticism of van der Kooij, 217 n. 66).

7   van Keulen, 'Points of Agreement Between the Targum and Peshitta Versions of Kings Against the MT: A Sounding', 209.

8   The Peshitta is translated directly from a Hebrew *Vorlage*; (in Samuel) Morrison, *The Character of the Syriac Version of the Frst Book of Samuel*, 3; cf. van der Kooij, *Die Alten Textzeugen des Jesajabuches*, 270.

9   In 1 Samuel: see, Morrison, *The Character of the Syriac Version of the First Book of Samuel*, 142–4.

10 E.g. Smelik, *The Targum of Judges*, 289, van der Kooij, *Die Alten Textzeugen des Jesajabuches*, 270, 290. Cf. R.P. Gordon, *Studies in the Targum to the Twelve Prophets: from Nahum to Malachi* (Supplements to Vetus Testamentum 51, Leiden 1994), 129; L.G. Running,

Although the possibility of a direct literary relationship between the Targum and the Septuagint seems intrinsically less likely, such a theory has had its proponents. That the Septuagint and the Targum occasionally resemble one another in matters of substance (i.e. excluding common errors and such like) has been frequently noted. This resemblance is generally understood to be the result of similar exegetical positions or techniques, particularly in dealing with textual or theological difficulties in the Hebrew,[11] and as such does not establish a literary relationship between the two,[12] as a handful of scholars have proposed.[13] Equally, Delekat's theory that the Septuagint is translated from an

---

'A Study of the Relationship of the Syriac Version to the Massoretic Hebrew, Targum Jonathan, and Septuagint Texts in Jeremiah 18', in A. Kort and S. Morschauser (eds), *Biblical and Related Studies Presented to Samuel Iwry* (Winona Lake, IN 1985), 227–35.

11 M. Meiser, 'Samuelseptuaginta und Targum Jonathan als Zeugen frühjüdischer Geistigkeit', in M. Karrer and W. Kraus, with M. Meiser (eds), *Die Septuaginta: Texte, Kontexte, Lebenswelten*, Wissenschaftliche Untersuchungen zum Neuen Testament 219 (Tübingen 2008), 323–35 esp. pp. 325–6. Cf. J. Ribera Florit, 'Relación entre el Targum y las Versiones antiquas antiquas: los Targumes de Jeremías y Ezequiel comparados con LXX, Peshitta y Vulgata', *Estudios Biblicos* 52 (1994), 317–28; R. Le Déaut, 'La Septante, un Targum?', in R. Kuntzmann and J. Schlosser (eds), *Études sur le Judaïsme hellénistique: congrès de Strasbourg (1983)* (Paris 1984), 147–95; M. Harl et al., *La Bible d'Alexandrie*, 23.4–9, *Les Douze Prophètes* (Paris 1999), 34, 94, 249, 330; G. Dorival, *La Bible d'Alexandrie*, 4, *Les Nombres* (Paris 1994), 73.

12 L.H. Brockington, 'Septuagint and Targum', *Zeitschrift für die alttestamentliche Wissenschaft* 66 (1954), 80–6 (on Isaiah); Le Déaut, 'La Septante, un Targum?', 164–5; C. Dogniez, 'Some Similarities Between the Septuagint and the Targum of Zechariah', in H. Ausloos et al. (eds), *Translating a Translation: The LXX and its Modern Translations in the Context of Early Judaism* (Leuven 2008), 89–102, p. 102; N. Fernández Marcos, 'Der Barberini-Text von Hab 3 – eine neue Untersuchung', in Heinz-Josef Fabry and Dieter Böhler (eds), *Im Brennpunkt: Die Septuaginta*, Vol. 3, *Studien zur Theologie, Anthropologie, Ekklesiologie, Eschatologie und Liturgie der Griechischen Bibel*, Beiträge zur Wissenschaft vom Alten und Neuen Testament 174 (Stuttgart 2007), 151–80, pp. 157–9.

13 Bons, Joosten, and Kessler have recently (2002) cautiously revived the question on the basis of instances of near identical interpretation in Tg. and LXX: 'Quelques-uns de ces exemples posent la question de savoir si les targumistes n'ont pas subi, d'une manière ou d'une autre, une influence du texte de la LXX (voir notamment Os 6, 11 et 11, 12)'. E. Bons, J. Joosten and S. Kessler (eds), *La Bible d'Alexandrie*, Vol. 23:1, *Les Douze Prophètes; Osée* (Paris 2002), 51. Cf. further Z. Frankel, *Ueber den Einfluss der palästinischen Exegese auf die alexandrinische Hermeneutik* (Leipzig 1851), esp. 202–3, 229–30; P. Churgin, 'The Targum and the Septuagint', *The American Journal of Semitic Languages and Literatures* 50:1 (1933), 41–65, esp. 56, 61–2. Brown's theory that Greek loan words in Tg. Onq. provide 'decisive evidence' for its (and by extension Tg. Jon.'s) direct literary dependence on LXX (197) lacks any credibility, not least because the ten(!) loan words that he claims establish his thesis (esp. 206–10) are widely attested across Aramaic dialects including in sources pre-dating the Septuagint; J.P. Brown, 'The Septuagint as a Source of the Greek Loan-words in the Targums', *Biblia* 70:2 (1989), 194–216.

Chapter Five. Agreements with Ancient Versions and Hebrew Manuscripts

Aramaic *Vorlage* is no longer thought credible.[14] It is worth recalling, before we proceed, that the Lucianic recension of the Septuagint and Peshitta may be related.[15]

Finally, the Vulgate. Jerome knew Aramaic, was by his own admission strongly influenced by Jewish exegesis, and may have known a written Targum tradition, at least towards the end of his life,[16] so the possibility that the Vulgate has been directly influenced by readings in the Targums is not intrinsically incredible. While theoretically possible, however, concrete evidence that Jerome consulted a written Targum as he prepared the Vulgate is nonetheless still lacking.[17] This is a question that would certainly reward further research.

To my knowledge, this question has not been addressed in relation to the Old Latin, which preserves evidence of the Latin Bible prior to Jerome and offers a secondary witness to the Septuagint,[18] though any connection with

---

14 L. Delekat, 'Ein Septuagintatargum', *Vetus Testamentum* 8 (1958), 225–52; see van der Kooij, *Die Alten Textzeugen des Jesajabuches*, 29–30.

15 E.g. Weitzman, *The Syriac Version of the Old Testament*, 83.

16 C.T.R. Hayward, *Saint Jerome's Hebrew Questions on Genesis: Translated with Introduction and Commentary* (Oxford Early Christian Studies, Oxford 1995), 15–23 esp. 21–3; Hayward, 'Saint Jerome and the Aramaic Targumim', *Journal of Semitic Studies* 32:1 (1987), 105–23, p. 121; Hayward, 'Jewish Traditions in Jerome's Commentary on Jeremiah and the Targum of Jeremiah', *Proceedings of the Irish Biblical Association* 9 (1985), 100–14, pp. 113–14; B. Kedar, 'The Latin Translations', in M.J. Mulder (ed.) *Mikra: Text, Translation, Reading and Interpretation of the Hebrew Bible in Ancient Judaism and Early Christianity* (Peabody, MA 2004 [1988]), 299–338, p. 317.

17 Although Stummer was inclined to the view that the rabbinic authorities (Gewährsmänner) from whom Jerome sought advice on textual matters had consulted written Targums and passed their readings on to Jerome, he did not overstate the evidence; F. Stummer, 'Beiträge zu dem Problem "Hieronymus und die Targumim"', *Biblica* 18 (1937), 174–81 esp. 174–5, 180–1. Klein and Smelik adopt similar models, S. Klein, 'Targumische Elemente in der Deutung biblischer Ortsnamen bei Hieronymus', *Monatsschrift für Geschichte und Wissenschaft des Judentums* 83:1 (1939), 132–41, p. 132; Smelik, *The Targum of Judges*, 291–315 (esp. 313–15); Hayward, 'Jewish Traditions in Jerome's Commentary on Jeremiah and the Targum of Jeremiah', 108–9.

18 The Old Latin is established in this chapter on the basis of Fernández Marcos and Busto Saiz, *El Texto Antioqueno de la Biblia Griega El Texto Antioqueno de la Biblia Griega*, I, *1–2 Samuel*. Fernández Marcos and Busto Saiz consulted the most important witnesses to the Old Latin, making use of more recent editions than had been available to the editors of BHS (see Fernández Marcos and Busto Saiz (eds), *El Texto Antioqueno de la Biblia Griega*, I, *1–2 Samuel*, xlv–lxxi). In addition the following were checked: the works of Lucifer of Cagliari; B. Fischer, 'Palimpsestus Vindobonensis, II, Manuscript 115 of the Books of Kingdoms, 1 Rg 1,14–4 Rg 17,19' in his *Beiträge zur Geschichte der lateinischen Bibeltexte* (Vetus Latina: Die Reste der altlateinischen Bibel 12, Freiburg 1986), 315–81 (text: 334–65); C. Morano

The Transmission of Targum Jonathan in the West

the Targum seems quite unlikely.

Analysis

What then of the possibility that medieval European Targum manuscripts occasionally preserve some genuinely ancient alternative readings of the Targum? Although the discussion must be further nuanced, in essence two possibilities exist to account for the apparent agreement between medieval European Targum manuscripts and the ancient Versions and/or Hebrew manuscripts: 1) the agreement is pure coincidence, the two sources having arrived independently at the same alternative reading by accident or deliberate adjustment to the text; or, 2) the European Targum manuscript reflects a variant Hebrew text, either through revision of the Targum text towards a Hebrew text differing from the Masoretic Text, or by preserving a genuinely ancient alternative.

1. Variants Supported By Ancient Versions + Hebrew Manuscripts

Those agreements bearing the most significance for this study are those where the alternative reading is supported not only by one or more of the ancient Versions but also by extant Hebrew manuscripts.

1.a. Pluses

1 Sam. 14:44

MT	thus God will do	כה יעשה אלהים
Babylonian tradition	thus the Lord will do	t707b: כדין יעביד יוי
t2i = t3i, t7i, t701i, t718i, t5a[PM], t6a, t713a, t720a, t725a	thus the Lord will do **for me** (Sperber: t702s, t734s, t12sc, t10r)	כדין יעביד **לי** יוי
Hebrew mss (more than 60) Versions	thus God will do **for me** LXX: τάδε ποιήσαι μοι ὁ θεὸς Peshitta: ܗܟܢܐ ܢܥܒܕ ܠܝ ܐܠܗܐ Vulgate: haec faciat **mihi** Deus	כה יעשה **לי** אלהים

Rodríguez, *Glosas marginales de* Vetus Latina *en las Biblias Vulgatas españolas: 1–2 Samuel* (Textos y Estudios 'Cardenal Cisneros' de la Biblia Políglota Matritense 48, Madrid 1989).

Chapter Five. Agreements with Ancient Versions and Hebrew Manuscripts

1 Sam. 27:11

MT	כל הימים אשר ישב בשדה פלשתים
	all the days that he was dwelling in the field (i.e. territory) of the Philistines.
Babylonian tradition	כל יומיא דיתיב בקירוי פלישתאי
	all the days that he was dwelling in the cities of the Philistines.
t2i	כל יומיא דהוה יתיב **דוד** בקרוי פלשתאי
	all the days that **David** was dwelling in the cities of the Philistines.
Hebrew mss[19]	כל הימים אשר ישב **דוד** בשדה פלשתים
	all the days that **David** was dwelling in the field (i.e. territory) of the Philistines.
Versions	LXX: πάσας τὰς ἡμέρας, ἃς ἐκάθητο **Δαυείδ** ἐν ἀγρῷ
	Peshitta: ܟܠܗܘܢ ܝܘܡܬܐ ܕܝܬܒ ܒܩܘܪܝܐ ܕܦܠܫܬܝܐ

In manuscript t2i the word 'David' has been left unvocalised in both Hebrew and Aramaic text (a correction? See pages 73 and 88).

2 Sam. 11:7

MT	ויבא אוריה אליו
	And Uriah came to him
Babylonian tradition	ואתא אוריה לותיה
	And Uriah came to him
t2i = t3i, t725a	(t232i/s לותיה דדוד) ואתא אוריה לות **דוד**
	And Uriah came to **David**
Hebrew mss[20]	ויבא אוריה אל **דוד**
	And Uriah came to **David**

---

19 Hebr. Mss: Cambridge, University Library Mm. 5.27 (Sephardi, fourteenth cent. = Kennicott 89); Milano, Biblioteca Ambrosiana B 56 Inf. (Ashkenazi, thirteenth cent. = Kennicott 187); London, British Library Add. 21161 (Ashkenazi, twelfth cent. = Kennicott 201); Parma, Biblioteca Palatina Cod. Parm. 2874 (Kennicott, 434 'Germanice, scriptus forte fuit seculo 13 exeunte.' = Kennicott 249); Parma, Biblioteca Palatina Cod. Parm. 2874 (Sephardi, 1335 according to Kennicott = Kennicott 250); Parma, Biblioteca Palatina Cod. Parm. 3091 (Ashkenazi, 1296 = de Rossi 380); Parma, Biblioteca Palatina Cod. Parm. 3286–3287 (Ashkenazi, thirteenth/fourteenth cent. = de Rossi 440); Parma, Biblioteca Palatina Cod. Parm. 2854 (Ashkenazi, thirteenth cent. = de Rossi 663).

20 Hebr. Mss: Kennicott 70 (no further information. Kennicott dates to fifteenth cent. = Coxe, *Catalogus codicum mss.*, Collegii Corporis Christi §8?); London, British Library Harley 5774–5775 (Sephardi, 1396 = Kennicott 113); Copenhagen, The Royal Library Cod. Hebr. 1 (Sephardi, 1251 = Kennicott 173); Milano, Biblioteca Ambrosiana B 56 Inf. (Ashkenazi, thirteenth cent. = Kennicott 187); Hamburg, Staats- und Universitaetsbibliothek Cod. Hebr. 9 (Ashkenazi, thirteenth cent. = Kennicott 614); Parma, Biblioteca Palatina Cod. Parm. 2874 (according to Kennicott: Sephardi cursive, 1305 = Kennicott 246; Ms no longer extant, see Richler, *Hebrew Manuscripts in the Biblioteca Palatina in Parma* §484); Kennicott 224 (see note 81 below).

The Transmission of Targum Jonathan in the West

Versions   Vulgate: *et venit Urias ad David*
                Old Latin: *et venit Urias ad Davit*
                Peshitta: ܘܐܬܐ ܐܘܪܝܐ ܠܘܬ ܕܘܝܕ

t3i has probably taken over the reading from its *Vorlage*, which may have been t2i.[21] The reading of the Old Latin is according to Palimpsest Vindobonensis.[22]

2 Sam. 23:16

MT   ולא אבה לשתותם
    ...but he did not want to drink it [i.e. the water]

Babylonian tradition   ולא אבא למשתיהון
    ...but he did not want to drink it

t705i = t701i   ולא אבה **דוד** למשתהון
    ...but **David** did not want to drink it

Hebrew mss[23]   ולא אבה **דוד** לשתותם
    ...but **David** did not want to drink it

Versions[24]   LXX mss ('Lucianic'): καὶ οὐκ ἐβούλετο **Δαυιδ** πιεῖν αὐτό

When the same phrase (ולא אבה לשתותם) occurs in the following verse (2 Sam. 23:17) manuscript t2i specifies the subject by adding the name 'David', a reading not supported by the ancient Versions but found in one Hebrew manuscript.[25]

The cases sited above specifically involve the explicit identification of a subject or object by means of an addition in cases where the identity remains obscure in the Hebrew text. This is a revisionary tendency strongly discernible throughout the Western Targum manuscripts (see pages 241–4).

Other examples point equally to the influence of idiomatic phraseology. For example:

---

21 van Stalduine-Sulman, 'An Electronic Edition of Targum Samuel', 32.
22 See note 18.
23 Hebr. Mss: London, British Library, Harley 5774–5775 (Sephardi, 1396 = Kennicott 113); Vatican, Urbinati Ebr. 1 (Ashkenazi, 1294 = Kennicott 228); Parma, Biblioteca Palatina Cod. Parm. 3106 (Ashkenazi, thirteenth cent. = de Rossi 226); Parma, Biblioteca Palatina Cod. Parm. 2514, 2515 (Italian, 1425. = de Rossi 319 margin); Parma, Biblioteca Palatina Cod. Parm. 2175 (Sephardi, 14th cent. = de Rossi 679 margin).
24 LXX mss: boc$_2$e$_2$ (according to the sigla of the Brooke, McLean and Thackeray edition), which form a single grouping and belong to the so-called 'Lucianic' recensions; see Brock, *The Recensions of the Septuagint Version of I Samuel*, 18.
25 I.e. Paris, Bibliothèque Nationale, Heb.1–3 (Ashkenazi, 1286 = Kennicott 158).

Chapter Five. Agreements with Ancient Versions and Hebrew Manuscripts

1 Sam. 9:1

MT	ויהי איש מבן ימין ושמו קיש
	There was a man from Benjamin and his name was Kish…
Babylonian tradition	There was a man from the tribe (והוה גברא משיבטא) of the house of Benjamin and his name was Kish…
t705i = t718i, t6a^{PM}, t713a, t720a	There was a **certain** man from the tribe (והוה גברא **חד** משיבטא) of the house of Benjamin and his name was Kish…
Hebrew mss[26]	ויהי איש **אחד**
	There was a **certain** man
Versions	Peshitta: ܘܗܘܐ ܓܒܪܐ ܚܕ

The variant Hebrew manuscripts, variant Targum manuscripts, and Peshitta, may all have been influenced by similar usage elsewhere (e.g. 1 Sam. 1:1; 11:7; 2 Sam. 18:10)

1 Sam. 20:28

MT	ויען יהונתן את שאול
	Jonathan answered Saul…
Babylonian tradition	Jonathan answered Saul (שאול)…
t718i = t5a^{PM}, t720a, t725a	Jonathan answered Saul **his father** (שאול **אבוהי**)…
	(Sperber: t734s)
Hebrew mss[27]	שאול **אביו**
	…Saul **his father**…
Versions	Peshitta: ܠܫܐܘܠ ܐܒܘܗܝ

Both the Targum and the variant Hebrew readings may have been influenced independently by identical usage elsewhere (e.g. 1 Sam. 20:32 cf. 1 Sam. 19:4). In t5a the plus 'his father' has been erased in both the Hebrew and the Aramaic.

---

26 Hebr. Mss: Oxford, Bodleian Library Ms Digby Or. 32–33 (Italian/Ashkenazi, fourteenth cent. = Kennicott 1); Oxford, Bodleian Library Ms Tanner 173 (Ashkenazi, thirteenth cent. = Kennicott 30).

27 Hebr. Mss: Oxford, Bodleian Library Ms Marshall Or. 3 (Ashkenazi, thirteenth cent. = Kennicott 23); Kennicott 70 (no further information; start fifteenth cent. according to Kennicott); London, British Library Harley 5709 (Ashkenazi, thirteenth–fourteenth cent. = Kennicott 109); Hebrew of t5a (= Kennicott 150); St. Paul im Lavanttal, Benediktinerinnezstift 84.1 (Ashkenazi, 1277 = Kennicott 151); Milano, Biblioteca Ambrosiana E 52 Inf (Ashkenazi, thirteenth/ fourteenth cent. = Kennicott 196); Kennicott 294 (twelfth cent. according to Kennicott. Identity uncertain: probably §413 in Steinschneider, *Die hebræischen Handschriften der K. Hof- und Staatsbibliothek in Muenchen*, i.e. Sephardi, fourteenth/fifteenth cent.).

The Transmission of Targum Jonathan in the West

1 Sam. 25:37

MT	ותגד לו אשתו את הדברים האלה
	...then his wife told him these words...
Babylonian tradition	...then his wife told him these words (ית פיתגמיא האילין)...
t720a = t713a	...then his wife told him **all** these words (ית **כל** פיתגמיא האלין)...
Hebrew mss[28]	**כל** הדברים האלה
	...**all** these words
Versions	LXX mlt mss: πάντα τὰ ῥήματα ταῦτα

The expression 'all the words' is common (e.g. 1 Sam. 3:17–19; 8:10, 21; 19:7; 25:9, 12; etc. Cf. chapter six §1).

2 Sam. 7:4

MT	ויהי דבר יהוה אל נתן לאמר
	the word of the Lord came to Nathan saying...
Babylonian tradition	והוה פתגם נבואה מן ק' יוי עם נתן למימר
	a word of prophecy from before the Lord was with Nathan saying...
t232i/s	והוה פיתגם נבואה מן קדם יוי עם נתן **נבייא** למימר
	a word of prophecy from before the Lord was with Nathan **the prophet** saying...
Hebrew mss + Citations[29]	נתן **הנביא**
	...Nathan **the prophet**...
Versions	LXX mss ('Lucianic')[30]: Ναθὰν τὸν προφήτην (= Ethiopic)
	Peshitta: ܢܬܢ ܢܒܝܐ

The plus may be connected to t232i/s's tendency to introduce common conventional readings (cf. e.g. Tg. 2 Sam. 7:2; 12:25; Tg. 2 Kgs 1:8, 10, 22, 23, 32, 34, 38, 44, 45, etc.); equally it may simply be harmonisation with 2 Sam. 7:2.

The introduction of the interrogative pronoun to make explicit the presence of a question, where this is clearly implied by the context, fits within a general

---

28 Hebr. Mss: Cambridge, St. John's College A 2 (Ashkenazi/Italian? twelfth cent. = Kennicott 96); Hebrew of t705i (= Kennicott 154).

29 Citations: Midr. Ps 62.4. Hebr. Mss: Cambridge, St. John's College A 2 (Ashkenazi/Italian? twelfth cent. = Kennicott 96); Paris, Bibliothèque Nationale, Heb. 1–3 (Ashkenazi, 1286 = Kennicott 158), Kennicott 428 (no further information; start fourteenth cent. according to Kennicott); Parma, Biblioteca Palatina Cod. Parm. 3187–3189 (Ashkenazi, fourteenth cent. = de Rossi 737); Parma, Biblioteca Palatina Cod. Parm. 3106 (Ashkenazi, thirteenth cent. = de Rossi 226).

30 LXX mss: boc_2e_2 i.e. 'Lucianic' recensions, see note 24 above.

Chapter Five. Agreements with Ancient Versions and Hebrew Manuscripts

trend in the Ashkenazi and Italian manuscripts to offer minor clarifying glosses (see chapter seven §2):

1 Sam. 30:8

MT	וישאל דוד ביהוה לאמר ארדף אחרי הגדוד הזה האשגנו
	David inquired of the Lord, saying, 'I will pursue after this troop. Should I overtake it?'
Babylonian tradition	David inquired of the Memra of the Lord, saying, 'I will pursue (ארדוף) after this troop. Should I overtake it?'
t7i = t5a, t6a, t713a	David inquired of the Memra of the Lord, saying, '**Should I pursue** (הארדוף) after this troop. Should I overtake it?'
Hebrew mss + Citations	הארדף
	'**Should** I pursue ...?'
Versions	LXX: **Εἰ** καταδιώξω ὀπίσω τοῦ συστρέμματος
	Old Latin: **Si** persequar post praedones istos

The interrogative particle, which is lacking in the Hebrew (including the Hebrew of t7i, t713a, t6a), is found in the Septuagint and some Old Latin manuscripts,[31] as well as in Hebrew manuscripts[32] and some rabbinic sources of a textually and historically complex nature.[33] It is clear from the context that this is a question rather than a statement (וישאל דוד ביהוה לאמר Cf. question formulae in 1 Sam 14:37; 23:11).[34]

2 Sam. 18:29

MT	ויאמר המלך שלום לנער לאבשלום
	The king said, 'Peace to the young man, to Absalom?'
Babylonian tradition	The king said, 'Peace (שלם) to the young man, to Absalom?'
t2i = t7i, t705i	The king said, **Is it well** (השלם) with the young man, Absalom?

---

31 Specifically, the marginal glosses in Spanish Vulgate Bibles; see Morano Rodríguez, *Glosas marginales de Vetus Latina en las Biblias Vulgatas españolas: 1–2 Samuel*, ad loc.

32 I.e. Oxford, Bodleian Library Ms Tanner 173 (Ashkenazi, fourteenth fourteenth cent. = Kennicott 30); Firenze, Biblioteca Medicea Laurenziana Plut.I.30 (rabbinic square/'charactere Germanico' [Kennicott, 408], 1295 = Kennicott 168).

33 Pesiq. Rab. 8 (ד״א ה׳ אורי); Midr. Pss 18:31(vrs); 79.1(vrs). See Strack and Stemberger, *Introduction to the Talmud and Midrash*, 296–302, 322–3.

34 D. Kimhi, *Commentary on Samuel* – according to the edition of M. Cohen (ed.), *Mikra'ot Gedolot 'Haketer* (Ramat-Gan 1993), ad loc (cf. Joseph Caspi, *Commentary on Samuel*, ad loc) explains that there is a means of posing questions without using the interrogative particle (-ה), giving other examples (i.e. Gen. 3:1; 27:24).

The Transmission of Targum Jonathan in the West

Hebrew mss (+ Sebir)[35]	**Is it well**…	השלום
Versions	Cf. Vulgate: *estne pax puero Absalom*	

The introduction of the interrogative may be a harmonisation with 2 Sam.18:32.[36]

The introduction of demonstrative adjectives and relative pronouns is a phenomenon that one encounters relatively frequently throughout the Ashkenazi and Italian Targum manuscripts.

1 Sam. 3:18

MT	Samuel told him all the words and he did not conceal [anything] from him.	ויגד לו שמואל את כל הדברים ולא כחד ממנו
Babylonian tradition	Samuel told him all the words (פיתגמיא) and he did not conceal [anything] from him.	
t725a	Samuel told him all **these** words (פתגמיא **האלין**) and he did not conceal [anything] from him.	
Hebrew mss + citation[37]	…all **these** words…	כל הדברים **האלה**

---

35 Hebr. Mss: Oxford, Bodleian Library Ms Tanner 173 (Ashkenazi, thirteenth cent. = Kennicott 30); Cambridge, St. John's College A 2 (Ashkenazi/Italian? twelfth cent. = Kennicott 96); Hebrew of t705i (= Kennicott 154); Paris Bibliotheque Nationale, Heb. 1–3 (Ashkenazi, 1286 = Kennicott 158); Milano, Biblioteca Ambrosiana B 56 Inf. (Ashkenazi script, thirteenth cent. = Kennicott 187); London, British Library Add. 21161 (Ashkenazi, twelfth cent. = Kennicott 201); Kennicott 224 (see note 81 below); Parma, Biblioteca Palatina Cod. Parm. 2874 (Kennicott, 434 'Germanice, scriptus forte fuit seculo 13 exeunte.' = Kennicott 249); Parma, Biblioteca Palatina Cod. Parm. 2874 (Sephardi, 1335 according to Kennicott = Kennicott 250); Parma, Biblioteca Palatina Cod. Parm. 2874 (Sardinia, 1310 according to Kennicott = Kennicott 251); Paris, Bibliothèque Nationale, Heb. 9 (rabbinic square/'Germanice scriptae' [Kennicott, 472], 1304 = Kennicott 355); London, British Library Add. 14760 (Ashkenazi, pre-1292 = Ginsburg 21); London, British Library Add. 9398 (Ashkenazi, thirteenth cent. = Ginsburg 27); Parma, Biblioteca Palatina Cod. Parm. 2808 (Ashkenazi, thirteenth cent. = de Rossi 2); Parma, Biblioteca Palatina Cod. Parm. 3105 (Ashkenazi, twelfth–thirteenth cent. = de Rossi 211); Parma, Biblioteca Palatina Cod. Parm. 3286–3287 (Ashkenazi, thirteenth/fourteenth cent. = de Rossi 440); Parma, Biblioteca Palatina Cod. Parm. 2854 (Ashkenazi, 13th thirteenth cent. = de Rossi 663). According to de Rossi the ה is subsequently deleted in Kennicott 249, 250, 251.

36 As van Stalduine-Sulman, *The Targum of Samuel*, 598 n. 913.

37 The reading of variant Hebrew manuscripts and a citation is given in the apparatus criticus of BHS, but I have not been able to identify the sources in which this variant is to be found, i.e. there is no record of this variant in Kennicott, de Rossi, Ginsburg, Aptowitzer, nor the Responsa Project database.

Chapter Five. Agreements with Ancient Versions and Hebrew Manuscripts

Versions	LXX ms[38]: πάντας τοὺς λόγους **τούτους**

The masorah note (יג חס האלה) highlights the relative rarity of this construction (Cf. Gen. 24:66; Exod. 4:30; Lev. 8:36; Deut. 1:18; Jer. 26:2, 12; 30:2; 36:2, 13, 20, 28), the more common formulation taking the demonstrative adjective.

1 Sam. 7:1

MT	ויבאו אתו אל בית אבינדב בגבעה
	…and they brought it [i.e. the Ark] to the house of Abinadav in the hill country…
Babylonian tradition	…and they brought it [i.e. the Ark] to the house of Abinadav in the hill country (לבית אבינדב בגבעתא)…
t2i = t3i, t7i, t232i/s, t705i, t701i, t6a, t713a, t720a, t725a	…and they brought it [i.e. the Ark] to the house of Abinadav **which is** in the hill country (לבית אבינדב **די** בגבעתא)… (Sperber: t10r, t12sc)
Hebrew mss (more than 30)	**אשר** בגבעה
	…**which is** in the hill country…
Versions	Peshitta: ܕܒܓܒܥܬܐ
	Cf. LXX: τὸν ἐν τῷ βουνῷ

1 Sam. 28:20

MT	לא אכל לחם כל היום וכל הלילה
	…he did not eat bread all day or all night
Babylonian tradition	…he did not eat bread all day or all night (כל יממא וכל ליליא)
t3i	…he did not eat bread all **that** day or all the night
	(כל יומא וכל **ההוא** ליליא)
Hebrew mss[39]	לא אכל לחם כל היום **ההוא** וכל הלילה
	…he did not eat bread all **that** day or all the night

---

[38] LXX ms: Rome, Chigi, R. vi. 38 (Brooke, McLean, Thackeray = b'; Rahlfs = 19), part of the 'Lucianic' group.

[39] Hebr. Mss: Cambridge, Gonville & Caius College Library 404/625 (Ashkenazi, thirteenth/fourteenth cent. = Kennicott 93); Copenhagen, The Royal Library Cod. Hebr. 1 (Sephardi, 1251 = Kennicott 173); marginal addition Firenze, Biblioteca Medicea Laurenziana Plut.I.45 (rabbinic square, fifteenth/sixteenth cent. = Kennicott 162); Copenhagen, The Royal Library Cod. Hebr. 6 (Sephardi, fourteenth/fifteenth cent. = Kennicott 176); Parma, Biblioteca Palatina Cod. Parm. 2874 (according to Kennicott: Sephardi cursive, 1305 = Kennicott 246; Ms no longer extant, see Richler, *Hebrew Manuscripts in the Biblioteca Palatina in Parma* §484); Parma, Biblioteca Palatina Cod. Parm. 2174 (Sephardi, fourteenth cent. = de Rossi 701); Parma, Biblioteca Palatina Cod. Parm. 3290 (Ashkenazi, thirteenth/fourteenth cent. = de Rossi 716); Parma, Biblioteca Palatina Cod. Parm. 3073 (Sephardi, fourteenth cent. = de Rossi 789); Parma, Biblioteca Palatina Cod. Parm. 2155 (Italian, thirteenth cent. = de Rossi 13); Parma, Biblioteca Palatina Cod. Parm. 3293 (Ashkenazi, 1351 = de Rossi 305).

The Transmission of Targum Jonathan in the West

Versions   Vulgate: *non comederat panem tota die illa*.
Peshitta: ܕܠܐ ܐܟܠ ܠܚܡܐ ܟܠܗ ܝܘܡܐ ܗܘ ܘܟܠܗ ܠܠܝܐ.
Cf. LXX: οὐ γὰρ ἔφαγεν ἄρτον ὅλην τὴν ἡμέραν καὶ ὅλην τὴν νύκτα ἐκείνην

The testimony of the ancient Versions is varied here.

All the cases given above result from revisionary tendencies observable elsewhere in the Ashkenazi and Italian Targum manuscipts, so the agreement with the Versions is coincidental. There remains, however, a few agreements that do not reflect such revisionary tendencies. For example:

1 Sam. 26:1

MT	הלוא דוד מסתתר בגבעת החכילה על פני הישימן
	Is not David hiding in the hill country of Hachilah, towards Jeshimon?
Babylonian tradition	Is not David hiding in the hill country (מיטמר בגיבעת) of Hachilah, which is towards Jeshimon?
t725a[pm]	Is not David hiding **with us** in the hill country (מטמר **עמנא** בגבעת) of Hachilah, which is towards Jeshimon?
Hebrew mss[40]	מסתתר **עמנו**
	... hiding **with us**...
Versions	LXX: σκεπάζεται **μεθ' ἡμῶν** ('Lucianic': κρύπτεται παρ' ἡμῖν)

The addition 'with us' has subsequently been deleted by the naqdan in t725a.

2 Sam. 13:30

MT	הכה אבשלום את כל בני המלך ולא נותר מהם אחד
	...Absalom smote all the sons of the king and there did not remain from them one.
Babylonian tradition	...and there did not remain from them one (מינהון חד).
t2i = t713a, t720a, t725a	...and there did not remain from them **so much as** one (מנהון **עד** חד).
Hebrew mss[41]	מהם **עד** אחד
	...from them **so much as** one...

---

40 Hebr. Mss: Cambridge, Gonville & Caius College Library 404/625 (Ashkenazi, thirteenth/fourteenth cent. = Kennicott 93); Cambridge, St. John's College A 2 (Ashkenazi/Italian? twelfth cent. = Kennicott 96); Hebrew of t5a (= Kennicott 150); Parma, Biblioteca Palatina Cod. Parm. 2808 (Ashkenazi, thirteenth cent. = de Rossi 2).

41 Hebr. Mss: Oxford, Bodleian Library Ms Tanner 173 (Ashkenazi, thirteenth cent. = Kennicott 30); Hebrew of t713a (= Kennicott 182).

Chapter Five. Agreements with Ancient Versions and Hebrew Manuscripts

Versions	LXX: οὐ κατελείφθη ἐξ αὐτῶν **οὐδὲ εἷς**
	LXX 'Lucianic': οὐχ ὑπολέλειπται ἐν αὐτοῖς **ἕως ἑνός**
	Vulgate: *non remansit ex eis **saltem** unus* (Cf. Old Latin: *et non est ex illis relictus nec unus*).

The Old Latin is that of Palimpsest Vindobonensis.

2 Sam. 13:31

MT	וכל עבדיו נצבים קרעי בגדים
	…and all his servants were standing [with] rent garments.
Babylonian tradition	…and all his servants were standing while rending their garments (מעתדין כד מבזעין לבושיהון).
t720a	…and all his servants were standing **by him** while rending their garments (קיימין **עילווהי** כד מבזעין לבושיהון).
Hebrew ms.[42]	נצבים **עליו**
	…were standing **by him**…
Versions	LXX: οἱ περιεστῶτες **αὐτῷ** διέρρηξαν τὰ ἱμάτια αὐτῶν
	(Cf. Armenian = *Stabant circum*)
	Cf. Vulgate: *qui adsistebant ei sciderunt vestimenta sua*.

1.b. Alternative Vocabulary

As with the cases involving pluses given above, many cases involving the interchange of vocabulary can be explained by processes internal to the Targum. For example, the following variant results from the (accidental?) influence of frequently occurring vocabulary:

2 Sam. 5:6

MT	וילך המלך ואנשיו ירושלם
	The king and his men went to Jerusalem…
Babylonian tradition	**The king** and his men went (ואזל מלכא) to Jerusalem…
t701i = t718i	**David** and his men went (ואזל דוד) to Jerusalem…
Hebrew mss[43]	וילך **דוד**
	David (and his men) went…
Versions	LXX: καὶ ἀπῆλθεν **Δαυείδ**
	Cf. Peshitta: ܘܐܙܠ ܕܘܝܕ

Both the Targum and the variant Hebrew readings may be influenced (independently) by identical usage elsewhere (e.g. וילך דוד 1 Sam. 22:1, 3, 5; 23:5; 26:25; 30:9; 2 Sam. 5:10; 6:2, 12; 16:13; 21:12).

---

42 Hebr. Ms: Oxford, Bodleian Library Ms Tanner 173 (Ashkenazi, thirteenth cent. = Kennicott 30).

43 Hebr. Mss: Oxford, Bodleian Library Kennicott 10 (Ashkenazi, thirteenth cent. = Kennicott 84); Copenhagen, The Royal Library Cod. Hebr. 17. (1346 = Kennicott 174).

The Transmission of Targum Jonathan in the West

Similarly, the following examples evidently attempt to 'correct' the text.

2 Sam. 14:4

MT	ותאמר האשה התקעית אל המלך
	The woman of Tekoah **said** to the king…
Babylonian tradition	The woman, who was from Tekoah, **said** (ואמרת אתתא) to the king…
t705i = t5a, t713a, t720a (≈ t725a ואתא)	The woman, who was from Tekoah, **came** (ואתת איתתא) to the king…
	(Sperber: t727y, Kimhi)
Hebrew mss (more than 20)	ותבא האשה
	The woman… **came**…
Versions	LXX: καὶ εἰσῆλθεν ἡ γυνὴ ἡ Θεκωεῖτις
	Peshitta: ܘܥܠܬ ܐܢܬܬܐ
	≈ Vulgate: *itaque cum **ingressa** fuisset mulier*

There are good grounds for believing that the Septuagint reflects the original reading here. As it stands, the Hebrew text as we find it in Codex Leningradensis records the woman speaking twice to the king. One might translate the complete verse as follows: 'The woman of Tekoah spoke (ותאמר) to the king, then fell to the ground upon her face and worshipped and said (ותאמר) "Help, O king!"' The reading of the Septuagint and the Western manuscripts of the Targum offers a preferable narrative sequence (cf. e.g. 2 Sam. 9:6).[44]

Nonetheless a few cases remain where there is no clear reason for the change in the Targum:

2 Sam. 5:1

MT	ויאמרו לאמר הננו עצמך ובשרך אנחנו
	…and they spoke saying, 'See we are your bone and your flesh!'
Babylonian tradition	…and they spoke saying (ואמרו למימר), 'See we are your relative and your flesh!'
t705i	…and they spoke **to him** (ואמרו ליה), 'See we are your relative and your flesh!'
	(Sperber: t702s)

---

44 As van Staalduine-Sulman, *The Targum of Samuel*, 566 n. 639.

Chapter Five. Agreements with Ancient Versions and Hebrew Manuscripts

Hebrew mss[45]	2 mss. ויאמרו לו לאמר they spoke **to him saying**
	Mlt mss. ויאמרו **לו** they spoke **to him**
	Ms. ויאמר **אליו** they spoke **to him**
	4Q51 omits לאמר
Versions	LXX: εἶπαν **αὐτῷ** Ἰδοὺ ὀστᾶ σου...
	≈ Peshitta: ܘܐܡܪܘ ܠܗ ܗܐ ܓܪܡܝܟ ܘܒܣܪܟ

There is a tautology in the Hebrew of Codex Leningradensis, which is resolved in the variant Hebrew manuscripts and in Targum manuscript t705i. Interestingly we note that manuscripts t701i and t2i combine the two readings, i.e. ואמרו ליה למימר הא אנחנא קריבך.

2 Sam. 17:12

MT	ולא נותר בו ובכל האנשים אשר אתו גם אחד
	...and there will not remain even one in it or among the people that are with him.
Babylonian tradition	...and there will not remain even one (אף חד) in it or among the people that are with him.
t705i = t701i	...and there will not remain **so much as** one (**עד** חד) in it or among the people that are with him.
	עד אחד
	...**so much as** one...
Hebrew mss[46]	
Versions	Cf. LXX: καί γε ἕνα
	Cf. Vulgate: *ne unum quidem*

Compare the example from 2 Sam. 13:30 above.

---

[45] I.e. לו לאמר Kennicott 224 (see note 81 below); Parma, Biblioteca Palatina Cod. Parm. 2874 (Sephardi, 1335 according to Kennicott = Kennicott 250); Parma, Biblioteca Palatina Cod. Parm. 3290 (Ashkenazi, thirteenth/fourteenth cent. = de Rossi 716); Parma, Biblioteca Palatina Cod. Parm. 3286–3287 (Ashkenazi, thirteenth/fourteenth cent. = de Rossi 440); Parma, Biblioteca Palatina Cod. Parm. 3200 (Ashkenazi, thirteenth cent. = de Rossi 545); Parma, Biblioteca Palatina Cod. Parm. 3091 (Ashkenazi, 1296 = de Rossi 380); Parma, Biblioteca Palatina Cod. Parm. 2854 (Ashkenazi, thirteenth cent. = de Rossi 663). — לו: Oxford, Bodleian Library Kennicott 6 (Sephardi, 14 fourteenth/fifteenth cent. = Kennicott 86); Parma, Biblioteca Palatina Cod. Parm. 3244 (Sephardi, thirteenth cent. = de Rossi 191). — אליו: Hebrew of t705i (= Kennicott 154); Nürnberg, Stadtbibliothek Solg. Ms. 1–7.fol. (Ashkenazi, 1291 = Kennicott 198). The masorah accompanying the Hebrew text of t705i has לאמר marked פליג.

[46] Hebr. Mss: Oxford, Bodleian Library Ms Kennicott 5 (Sephardi, 1487 = Kennicott 85); Hebrew of t705i (= Kennicott 154).

The Transmission of Targum Jonathan in the West

1.c. Variations in Person or Number (inc. Pronominal suffix)

There is frequent agreement in person or number between variant Targum manuscripts and the ancient Versions and Hebrew textual witnesses. These are of little significance since they are mostly cases of minor improvements or clarifications, which could easily have arisen independently.

1 Sam. 9:11

MT	...and **they** said to them, 'Is the seer here?'	ויאמרו להן היש בזה הראה
Babylonian tradition	...and **they** said (ואמרו) to them, 'Is the seer here?'	
t705i = t2i	...and **he** said (ואמר) to them, 'Is the seer here?'	
Hebrew mss + Citations[47]	...and **he** said...	ויאמר
Versions	Peshitta: ܘܐܡܪ ܠܗܘܢ ܐܢܬܘܢ	

1 Sam. 10:14

MT	...and **he** said, 'To search for the donkeys.'	ויאמר לבקש את האתנות
Babylonian tradition	...and **he** said, 'To search for (ואמר למבעי) the donkeys.'	
t705i	...and **they** said, 'To search for (ואמרו למיבעי) the donkeys.'	
Hebrew ms.[48]	...and **they** said, 'To search for...'	ויאמרו לבקש
Versions	LXX: καὶ εἶπαν ('Lucianic' : εἶπον)	
	Vulgate: *responderunt*	
	Peshitta[mss]: ܘܐܡܪܘ	

1 Sam. 26:23

MT	...because the Lord has given you today into/by a hand...	אשר נתנך יהוה היום ביד
Babylonian tradition	...because the Lord has handed you over this day into/by a hand (דמסרך יוי יומא דין ביד)...	
A + MW	...because the Lord has handed you over this day into **my** hand (דמסרך יוי יומא דין בידי)...	
	(Sperber: t702s, t734s, t12sc, t10r)	
Hebrew mss (more than 40)	...because the Lord has given you today into **my** hand...	אשר נתנך יהוה היום בידי

---

47 Hebr. Ms: Oxford, Bodleian Library Ms Digby Or. 32–33 (Italian/Ashkenazi, fourteenth cent. = Kennicott 1). Citation: Midr. Psa. 7.

48 Hebr. Ms: Copenhagen, The Royal Library, Cod. Hebr. 17. (1346 = Kennicott 174).

Chapter Five. Agreements with Ancient Versions and Hebrew Manuscripts

Versions   LXX: ὡς παρέδωκέν σε κύριος σήμερον εἰς χεῖράς **μου**
                   Peshitta: ܕܐܫܠܡܟ ܡܪܝܐ ܝܘܡܢܐ ܒܐܝܕܝ
                   Vulgate: *tradidit enim te Dominus hodie in manu* **mea**
                   Old Latin: *sicut tradidit te hodie in manibus* **meis**

The Old Latin reading is from Lucifer of Cagliari.[49]

2 Sam. 7:23

MT   ולעשות לכם הגדולה ונראאות
                         ...doing for **you** the great deed and awesome deeds...

Babylonian tradition   ...doing for **you** (ולמעבד לכון) great deeds and mighty deeds...

t705i = t713a, t720a   ...doing for **them** (ולמעבד להון) great deeds and mighty deeds...

Hebrew mss[50]   לעשות להם
                         ...doing for **them**...

Versions   Vulgate: *faceretque* **eis**
                   Cf. Peshitta: ܘܠܡܥܒܕ ܠܗܘܢ

The Hebrew is problematic here, but the reading להם is doubtless secondary; the key phrase (לעשות לכם) is missing from the synoptic passage in Chronicles (1 Chron. 17:21).[51]

2 Sam. 22:44

MT   ותפלטני מריבי עמי
                         You will deliver me from the divisions of **my people**
                         (cf. Ps. 18:44: עם)

Babylonian tradition   You will deliver me from division of **the people**
                                (ותשיזבנני מפלוגת עמא)

t705i = t2i, t6a^{PM}, t713a,   You will deliver me from division of **the peoples**
t720a, t725a   (ותשזבינני מפלוגת עממיא)

---

49 Lucifer of Cagliari, *De Athanasio*: G.F. Diercks (ed.), *Luciferi calaritani opera quae supersunt* (Corpus Christianorum Series Latina 8. Turnhout 1978), I, xv, l.68.

50 Hebr. Mss: Hebrew of t713a (= Kennicott 182); Parma, Biblioteca Palatina Cod. Parm. 3104 (Ashkenazi, 1335 = de Rossi 20); Parma, Biblioteca Palatina Cod. Parm. 3109 (Sephardi/Eastern, eleventh–thirteenth = de Rossi 21); Parma, Biblioteca Palatina Cod. Parm. 2174 (Sephardi, fourteenth cent. = de Rossi 701).

51 See H.J. Stoebe, *Das zweite Buch Samuelis* (Kommentar zum Alten Testament 8:2, Gütersloh 1994), 233.

The Transmission of Targum Jonathan in the West

Hebrew mss	ותפלטני מריבי עמים
(+ Sebir)[52]	You will deliver me from the divisions of **peoples**
Versions	LXX: καὶ ῥύσῃ με ἐκ μάχης **λαῶν**

Several liturgical texts of 2 Samuel 22 also use the plural here, but indefinite (i.e. עממין; see page 330).[53] The variant Western manuscripts may well be harmonising with reference to the people in the plural in the surrounding verses (e.g. 2 Sam. 22:41, 45, 46 etc.).

In the following case there is no consensus between the textual witnesses to the Babylonian tradition:

1 Sam. 19:9

MT		ודוד מנגן ביד
	...and David was playing [it] **by hand**.	
t2506b	...and David was playing [it] **by hand** (ביד).	
t724b = t7i	...and David was playing [it] **with his hand** (בידיה).	
Hebrew mss[54]		ודוד מנגן בידו
	...and David was playing [it] **with his hand**	
Versions	Vulgate: *porro David psallebat in manu **sua***	
	≈ LXX: καὶ Δαυεὶδ ἔψαλλεν ταῖς χερσὶν **αὐτοῦ**	
	≈ Old Latin: *et ecce David citharizabat in manibus **suis** / et ecce psallebat in manibus **suis***	

If the reading of t2506b is the original (perhaps unlikely given the versional evidence) one could equally consider the reading of t724b and t7i independent improvements or corrections, rather than a revision *per se* (cf. 1 Sam. 18:10).[55]

---

52 Hebr. Mss: Hebrew of t5a (= Kennicott 150); London, British Library Add. 14760 (Ashkenazi, pre-1292 = Ginsburg 21); London, British Library Or. 4227 (Ashkenazi, fourteenth cent. = Ginsburg 24); Parma, Biblioteca Palatina Cod. Parm. 3109 (Sephardi/Eastern, eleventh–thirteenth = de Rossi 21); Parma, Biblioteca Palatina Cod. Parm. 1885 (Ashkenazi, 1473 = de Rossi 594); Parma, Biblioteca Palatina Cod. Parm. 2174 (Sephardi, fourteenth cent. = de Rossi 701).

53 The Babylonian text tradition of the Targum reflects what may have been the original reading of the Hebrew text i.e. עם, Barthélemy, *Critique textuelle de l'Ancien Testament*, I, 308.

54 Hebr. Mss: Hebrew of t5a (= Kennicott 150); Kennicott 224 (see note 81 below); London, British Library Add. 15252 (Sephardi, fourteenth/fifteenth cent. = Ginsburg 34).

55 The Old Latin readings are taken from marginal notes in Spanish Vulgate Bibles, see Fernández Marcos and Busto Saiz (eds), *El texto antioqueno de la Biblia griega*, I, *1–2 Samuel*, xlvii–l (i.e. *et ecce David citharizabat in manibus suis*) and Lucifer of Cagliari, *De Athanasio*, I, xiii, 1.60 (i.e. *et ecce psallebat in manibus suis*). Fernández Marcos and Busto Saiz were understandably selective in their use of this author (see Fernández Marcos and Busto Saiz, *El texto antioqueno de la Biblia griega*, I, *1–2 Samuel*, lxi). They did not include this reference, presumably considering it an allusion rather than a citation. On the difficulty of

Chapter Five. Agreements with Ancient Versions and Hebrew Manuscripts

1.d. Minuses

Like the preceding category, where Ashkenazi and Italian Targum manuscripts and the ancient Versions and Hebrew manuscripts share a common 'minus', this is to be attributed to coincidence.

	MT	Babylonian Tradition	Variant	Versions
1 Sam. 4:6	קול התרועה הגדולה	קל יבבא רבא	t3i, t718i omits רבא	Hebr. mss, Peshitta omit הגדולה
1 Sam. 12:12	ותאמרו לי	ואמרתון לי	t718i omits לי	Peshitta, LXX omit לי
2 Sam. 4:7	ויסירו את ראשו	ופסקו ית רישיה	t2i, t725a omit section	Peshitta, Vulgate omit section.
2 Sam. 7:19	ותקטן עוד זאת בעיניך	וזערת עוד דא קדמך	t2i omits עוד	LXX, Old Latin mss, Peshitta omit עוד.
2 Sam. 7:19	גם אל בית עבדך	t710y: ומלילתא אף על בית עבדך (t709b omits בית)	t725a, t2i omit אף	Hebr. mss, Peshitta, LXX omit גם.

Some cases of minuses are beyond doubt pure coincidence. In 2 Sam. 18:3, for example, manuscript t3i omits the section corresponding to the Hebrew ואם ימתו חצינו לא ישימו אלינו לב ('and if the half of us die, they will not worry about us'). The same section is omitted in two Hebrew manuscripts,[56] multiple Septuagint manuscripts (plus the Ethiopic version),[57] and the Peshitta, yet it is evident that the omission is the result of *homeoteleuton* between the two occurrences of לא ישימו אלינו לב 'they will not worry about us'. Although we cannot adjudicate on the remaining cases with such certainty, coincidence seems the most likely explanation to account for these agreements.

---

distinguishing citation from allusion in Lucifer of Cagliari's work see Diercks (ed.), *Luciferi calaritani opera quae supersunt*, cxi; for textual affinity of citations see cv–cxiii. For a short biography of Lucifer of Cagliari see C. Moreschini and E.Norelli, *Early Christian Greek and Latin Literature: a Literary History*, II, *From the Council of Nicea to the Beginning of the Medieval Period* (trans. M.J.O'Connell, Peabody, MA 2005 [1996]), II: 250–2 and Diercks, *Luciferi calaritani opera quae supersunt*, vii–xxxvii.

56 I.e. Oxford, Bodleian Library Ms Tanner 173 (Ashkenazi, thirteenth cent. = Kennicott 30); Parma, Biblioteca Palatina Cod. Parm. 2874 (Kennicott, 434 'Germanice, scriptus forte fuit seculo 13 exeunte.' = Kennicott 249).

57 See Brooke, McLean, Thackeray edition *ad loc*.

The Transmission of Targum Jonathan in the West

1.e. Analysis

It is unlikely in the extreme that Western Targum manuscripts preserve ancient readings of the Targum derived from an alternative *Vorlage* similar to that which lies behind the Septuagint, Vulgate, Peshitta, etc. On the contrary, the evidence presented above suggests that the agreement is the result of late revisions of the Targum text. First, in those cases where the alternative wording found in the Western manuscripts follows the pattern of a revisionary tendency discernible in the Western manuscripts we must assume that the change is the result of internal revision of the Targum and that agreement with the ancient Versions is coincidental. Where the alternative reading does not reflect the revisionary tendencies of the Western manuscripts we can assume that the text has been revised towards a Hebrew text that differed from Codex Leningradensis. I have shown in the preceding chapter that the text of Targum Samuel was accommodated to the Hebrew text during its Western transmission; furthermore we know from the collections of Kennicott and de Rossi that Hebrew manuscripts produced in European (predominantly Ashkenazi) communities from the twelfth to the fourteenth centuries contain many variant readings with which the Western Targum manuscripts occasionally agree.[58] Consequently it is plausible to suggest that in the West the Targum text has been revised towards locally available Hebrew manuscripts, the text of which occasionally differed from that of Codex Leningradensis, with the result that these differences are now also reflected in the Western text of Targum Samuel.

The majority of those cases involving pluses or alternative vocabulary can be connected to other revisionary tendencies evident in the Ashkenazi and Italian manuscripts (see chapters 6–7). Specifically, we find the specification of the subject or object (i.e. 1 Sam. 14:44; 27:11; 2 Sam. 11:7; 23.16); the introduction of idiomatic phraseology (i.e. 1 Sam. 9:1; 11:11; 20:28; 25:37; 2 Sam. 5:6); making explicit the implied sense (i.e. 1 Sam. 30:2; 2 Sam. 18:29); minor corrections (i.e. 1 Sam. 25:15; 2 Sam. 14:4); and the introduction of a demonstrative adjective or the relative pronoun (1 Sam. 3:18; 7:1; 28:20). It is not impossible, of course, that in some — or even all — of these cases the text

---

58 Our knowledge of variant Hebrew manuscripts is still heavily indebted to the labours of Kennicott and de Rossi who consulted almost exclusively twelfth–fourteenth century European manuscripts. Kennicott, *Vetus Testamentum hebraicum cum variis lectionibus*, Vol. 1; de Rossi, *Variae lectiones veteris testamenti*, Vol. 2; de Rossi, *Scholia critica in V. T.*, 38–42.

Chapter Five. Agreements with Ancient Versions and Hebrew Manuscripts

has been accommodated to a variant Hebrew text. Where the effect of typical revisionary tendency is in doubt, we can plausibly account for the agreement with the second hypothesis, namely that the text has been accommodated to a variant Hebrew text. This seems likely in a few cases of pluses (i.e. 1 Sam 26:1; 2 Sam. 13:30, 31) and variant vocabulary (i.e. 2 Sam. 5:1; 17:12). There is therefore no case for assuming that genuinely ancient alternative readings of the Hebrew have been preserved. At best the Western Targum manuscripts are secondary witnesses to variants in medieval Hebrew manuscripts.

In the case of the example from 1 Sam. 26:23 the variant reading is found in all the manuscripts belonging to the pure Ashkenazi and the Mixed Western group and is also reflected in the witnesses to what Sperber called 'the Tiberian trend' (i.e. European manuscripts and printed editions),[59] so the variant reading may have arisen at an early stage in the text's Western transmission on the basis of a variant Hebrew text(s) in transmission in that region.

2. Variants Supported by Hebrew Manuscripts but not the Ancient Versions

The second of the two hypotheses proposed above, namely that the Targum text has been revised towards Hebrew manuscripts differing from Codex Leningradensis, is further strengthened by the presence of variant readings supported by medieval witnesses to the Hebrew text but not by the principal ancient Versions. Again it is possible that the agreement is coincidental, i.e. resulting from revisionary tendencies clearly detectable within the Western Targum manuscripts or by accident.

2.a. Pluses

One finds cases of the introduction of idiomatic phraseology, for example:

2 Sam. 17:11
MT   כחול אשר על הים
                    ...like the sand which is **by the sea**...
Babylonian tradition   ...like the sand which is **by the sea** (כחלא דעל ימא)...

---

[59] A. Sperber. (ed.), *The Bible in Aramaic Based on Old Manuscripts and Printed Texts, Vol. II, The Former Prophets According to Targum Jonathan* (Leiden 1959), vi.

The Transmission of Targum Jonathan in the West

t7i = t232i/s, t6a^{correct}, t713a ...like the sand which is **on the seashore** (כחלא דעל **כיף** ימא)
(Sperber: t727y, t12sc)

Hebrew mss[60]   כחול אשר על **שפת** הים
...like the sand which is **on the seashore**

This idiom is common within the Targum (cf.; Tg. Josh. 11:4; 15:5; 18:19; Tg. Judg. 7:12; Tg. 1 Sam. 13:5; Tg. 1 Kgs 5:9; 9:26; Tg. Onq. Gen. 22:17; Tg. Onq. Exod. 14:30).

1 Sam. 6:9
MT   אם דרך גבולו יעלה בית שמש הוא עשה לנו את הרעה הגדולה הזאת
If it goes in the direction of its border, (towards) Beth Shemesh, then it is he who has done this great evil to us...

Babylonian tradition   ...then from before him this great evil has been done to us
(אתעבידת לנא בשתא רבתא הדא)...

t2i = t725a   ...then from before him **all** this great evil has been done to us
(אתעבידת לנא ית **כל** בישתא רבתא הדא)...

Hebrew mss[61]   את **כל** הרעה
...**all** (this) great evil...

---

60 Hebr. Mss: Oxford, Bodleian Library Ms Hunt. 11–12 (Ashkenazi/'charactere Germanico' [Kennicott, 342] beginning thirteenth cent. = Kennicott 4); Cambridge, Gonville & Caius College Library 404/625 (Ashkenazi, thirteenth/fourteenth cent. = Kennicott 93); Cambridge, St. John's College A 2 (Ashkenazi/Italian? twelfth cent. = Kennicott 96); Hebrew of t5a (= Kennicott 150); Parma, Biblioteca Palatina Cod. Parm. 2874 (Sephardi, 1335 according to Kennicott = Kennicott 250); Parma, Biblioteca Palatina Cod. Parm. 2874 (according to Kennicott: Sephardi cursive, 1305 = Kennicott 246 *margin*; see Richler, *Hebrew Manuscripts in the Biblioteca Palatina in Parma* §484); Parma, Biblioteca Palatina Cod. Parm. 3212–3213 (Italian, thirteenth cent. = de Rossi 1); Parma, Biblioteca Palatina Cod. Parm. 3106 (Ashkenazi, thirteenth cent. = de Rossi 226); Parma, Biblioteca Palatina Cod. Parm. 2938 (Sephardi, fourteenth cent. = de Rossi 341); Parma, Biblioteca Palatina Cod. Parm. 2939–2941 (Ashkenazi, fourteenth cent. = de Rossi 554); Parma, Biblioteca Palatina Cod. Parm. 3290 (Ashkenazi, thirteenth–fourteenth cent. = de Rossi 716); Parma, Biblioteca Palatina Cod. Parm. 3200 (Ashkenazi, thirteenth cent. = de Rossi 545); Parma, Biblioteca Palatina Cod. Parm. 3184–3186 (Ashkenazi, thirteenth cent. = de Rossi 596).

61 Hebr. Mss: Cambridge, Gonville & Caius College Library 404/625 (Ashkenazi, thirteenth/fourteenth cent. = Kennicott 93); London, British Library Arundel Or. 16 (Ashkenazi, thirteenth cent. = Kennicott 130/Ginsburg 5); Milano, Biblioteca Ambrosiana B 56 Inf. (Ashkenazi, thirteenth cent. = Kennicott 187); Zurich, Zentralbibliothek Or. 158 (1494 = Kennicott 253); London, British Library Or. 4227 (Ashkenazi, fourteenth cent. = Ginsburg 24); London, British Library Or. 2091 (Ashkenazi, thirteenth cent. = Ginsburg 26); Parma, Biblioteca Palatina Cod. Parm. 3104 (Ashkenazi, 1335 = de Rossi 20); Parma, Biblioteca Palatina Cod. Parm. 1833 (Sephardi, thirteenth/fourteenth cent. = de Rossi 579); Parma, Biblioteca Palatina Cod. Parm. 2854 (Ashkenazi, thirteenth cent. = de Rossi 663); Parma, Biblioteca Palatina Cod. Parm. 3105 (Ashkenazi, twelfth/thirteenth cent. = de Rossi 211).

Chapter Five. Agreements with Ancient Versions and Hebrew Manuscripts

The idiom 'all evil' (בישה + כל) is common (e.g. Tg. Judg. 9:57; Tg. 1 Sam. 10:19; 12:20; Tg. 2 Sam. 19:8; Tg. 1 Kgs 2:44; 9:9; 16:7; Tg. 2 Kgs 22:20; Tg. Jer. 1:16; 16:10; 19:15; 22:22; 32:23, 32, 42; 33:5; 35:17; 36:3, 31; 41:11; 44:2; 51:24, 60; Tg. Ezek. 16:23; 20:43; Tg. Hos. 7:2; 9:15).

Equally, one finds cases where the wording has been influenced by the presence of similar phraseology in the nearby literary context. For example:

1 Sam. 20:30

MT	ויחר אף שאול ביהונתן
	Then Saul grew angry with Jonathan…
Babylonian tradition	Then Saul's wrath grew fierce against Jonathan (ותקיף רגזא דשאול ביהונתן)…
t2i = t3i	Then Saul's wrath grew fierce against Jonathan **his son** (ותקיף רוגזא דשאול ביהונתן **בריה**)…
Hebrew mss (more than 20)	ביהונתן **בנו**
	…against Jonathan **his son**…
Versions	Cf. LXX: καὶ ἐθυμώθη ὀργῇ Σαουλ ἐπὶ Ιωναθαν σφόδρα (= ביהונתן מאד?)

The wording 'Jonathan his son' is taken over from 1 Sam. 20:27.

2 Sam. 5:3

MT	וימשחו את דוד למלך על ישראל
	…and they anointed David as king over Israel.
Babylonian tradition	…and they anointed David (ומשחו ית דוד) as king over Israel.
t705i = t720a, t5a[PM]	…and **there** they anointed David (ומשחו **תמן** ית דוד) as king over Israel. (Sperber: t702s)
Hebrew mss[62]	וימשחו **שם** את דוד
	…and **there** they anointed David…

The variant wording in the Western Targum and Hebrew manuscripts is taken from 2 Sam. 2:4.[63]

2 Sam. 6:8

MT	ויקרא למקום ההוא פרץ עזה עד היום הזה
	…one calls that place Uzzah's Breach until this day.

---

62 Hebr. Mss: Cambridge, University Library Mm. 5.27 (Sephardi, fourteenth cent. = Kennicott 89); Paris, Bibliothèque Nationale, Heb. 29 (1494 = Kennicott 210); Kennicott 224 (see note 81 below).

63 As van Staalduine-Sulman, *The Targum of Samuel*, 507 n. 209.

The Transmission of Targum Jonathan in the West

Babylonian tradition	...one calls that place (וקרא לאתרא ההוא) 'the place in which Uzzah died' until this day.
t713a	...one calls **the name of** that place (וקרא **שמא** דאתרא ההוא) 'the place in which Uzzah died' until this day.
Hebrew mss[64]	ויקרא **שם** המקום ההוא ...one calls **the name of** that place

The idiom 'one calls the name of that place' is found in 2 Sam. 5:20.

2.b. Alternative Vocabulary

A similar situation prevails as far as alternative vocabulary is concerned.

1 Sam. 23:18

MT	ויהונתן הלך לביתו
	and Jonathan went **to his house**...
Babylonian tradition	and Jonathan went **to his house** (ויהונתן אזל לביתיה)...
t2i = t6a[PM]	and Jonathan went **on his way** (ויהונתן אזל **לאורחיה**)...
	(Sperber: t12sc, Kimhi)
Hebrew mss[65]	ויהונתן הלך **לדרכו**
	and Jonathan went **on his way**...

In this case the *prima manus* of t6a follows the reading of t2i. It has subsequently been corrected to follow the remainder of our Ashkenazi and Mixed Western witnesses (i.e. the reading of the Babylonian text). This may be the influence of idiomatic phraseology (e.g. Tg. 1 Sam. 1.18; 15.20; 20.26; 24.8; 26.25; 30.2. Cf. variants to Tg. 1 Sam. 26:25 page 209) or the reading of the text against which t6a has been corrected (see pages 98–9).

---

64 Hebr. Mss: Cambridge, St. John's College A 2 (Ashkenazi/Italian? twelfth cent. = Kennicott 96); Copenhagen, The Royal Library Cod. Hebr. 17. (1346 = Kennicott 174).

65 Hebr. Mss: Cambridge, Gonville & Caius College Library 404/625 (Ashkenazi, thirteenth/fourteenth cent. = Kennicott 93); Copenhagen, The Royal Library Cod. Hebr. 7–9 (fourteenth/fifteenth cent., 1361 according to Kennicott = Kennicott 171); Milano, Biblioteca Ambrosiana B 56 Inf. (Ashkenazi, thirteenth cent. = Kennicott 187); Parma, Biblioteca Palatina Cod. Parm. 2874 (according to Kennicott: Sephardi cursive, 1305 = Kennicott 246; (manuscript no longer extant, see Richler, *Hebrew Manuscripts in the Biblioteca Palatina in Parma* §484); Parma, Biblioteca Palatina Cod. Parm. 2874 (Sardinia, 1310 according to Kennicott = Kennicott 251); Parma, Biblioteca Palatina Cod. Parm. 1832 (Sephardi, fifteenth = de Rossi 4); Parma, Biblioteca Palatina Cod. Parm. 3104 (Ashkenazi, 1335 = de Rossi 20); Parma, Biblioteca Palatina Cod. Parm. 3290 (Ashkenazi, thirteenth–fourteenth cent. = de Rossi 716); Parma, Biblioteca Palatina Cod. Parm. 3187–3189 (Ashkenazi, fourteenth cent. = de Rossi 737); Parma, Biblioteca Palatina Cod. Parm. 3105 (Ashkenazi, twelfth/thirteenth cent. = de Rossi 211); Kennicott 224 (see note 81 below).

Chapter Five. Agreements with Ancient Versions and Hebrew Manuscripts

1 Sam. 25:1

MT	ויקם דוד וירד אל מדבר פארן
	David got up and **went down** to the desert of Paran.
Babylonian tradition	David got up and **went down** to the desert (ונחת למדברא) of Paran.
t2i = t725a	David got up and **went** to the desert (ואזל למדברא) of Paran. (cf. Sperber t12sc ונפק)
Hebrew mss (more than 20)	ויקם דוד **וילך** אל מדבר
	David got up and **went** to the desert...

This may be a case of the interchange of common translation equivalents (see chapter six §2).

1 Sam. 3:9

MT	והיה אם יקרא אליך ואמרת דבר יהוה
	...and if he should call you then you must say, 'Speak, Lord...'
Babylonian tradition	...and if he should call you (ויהי אם יקרי לך) then you must say, 'Speak, Lord...'
t7i = t701i, t705i[PM], t6a[PM], t713a, t720a	...and it will happen **that** he will call you (ויהי **ארי** יקרי לך) then you must say, 'Speak, Lord...'
Hebrew mss + Citations[66]	והיה **כי** יקרא אליך
	...and it will happen **that** he will call you...

The variant reading may have arisen due to the repetition of the expression 'because you called' (MT: כי קראת; Tg.: ארי קריתא), in the preceding narrative (1 Sam. 3:5, 6, 8), though the correspondence is not exact.

2.d. Minuses

	MT	Babylonian Tradition	Variant	Versions
1 Sam 23.9	אל אביתר הכהן	לאביתר כהנא	t713a omits כהנא	Few mss + citation[67] omit הכהן
1 Sam 25.9	ככל הדברים	ככל פיתגמיא	t3i, t701i, t705i[correct]	Ms[68] omit כל כפיתגמיא.

---

66 Hebr. Mss: Parma, Biblioteca Palatina Cod. Parm. 2292 (according to Kennicott 'scriptus Germanico', 1281 = Kennicott 145; manuscript no longer extant, see Richler, *Hebrew Manuscripts in the Biblioteca Palatina in Parma* §484); Hebrew of t713a (= Kennicott 182).

67 Hebr. Mss: 1 Sam. 23:9 Hebrew of t705i (= Kennicott 154); Hebrew of t713a (= Kennicott 182); Kennicott 224 (see note 81 below), Parma, Biblioteca Palatina Cod. Parm. 2874 (according to Kennicott: Sephardi cursive, 1305 = Kennicott 246; manuscript no longer extant, see Richler, *Hebrew Manuscripts in the Biblioteca Palatina in Parma* §484).

68 Hebr. Ms.: Copenhagen, The Royal Library Cod. Hebr. 17 (1346 = Kennicott 174).

The Transmission of Targum Jonathan in the West

3. Variants Supported by Ancient Versions but not Hebrew Manuscripts

The existence of variants in the medieval Targum manuscripts that agree with the reading of one or more of the ancient Versions but are not supported by known Hebrew manuscripts presents an apparent difficulty for the theory advanced above. But as we will see, the difficulty is indeed only apparent.

There are a few genuine cases that require our consideration:

3.a. Pluses

1 Sam. 19:10

MT	Saul sought to strike a spear through David (בדוד) and into the wall, but he escaped from before Saul (ויפטר מפני שאול) and the spear struck the wall...
Babylonian tradition	...but he departed from before Saul (t724b: אתפטר t2506b: ואיפטר מן קדם שאול)...
t2i = t7i, t232i/s^{PM}, t5a, t725a	...but **David** departed from before Saul (ואתפטר **דוד** מן קדם שאול)...
Versions	Vulgate: *et declinavit **David** a facie Saul* LXX: καὶ ἀπέστη **Δαυιδ** ἐκ προσώπου Σαουλ

1 Sam. 22:14

MT	וחתן המלך וסר אל משמעתך ...the son in law of the king and master over your bodyguard(?)...
Babylonian tradition	...the son in law of the king and master over your bodyguard(?) (ורב על משמעתך)...
t2i = t232i/s, t701i, t725a	...the son in law of the king and master over **all** your bodyguard(?) (על **כל** משמעתך) (Sperber: t12sc)
Versions	LXX: καὶ ἄρχων **παντὸς** παραγγέλματός σου

2 Sam. 10:14

MT	וינסו מפני אבישי ...and they fled from before Abishai...
Babylonian tradition	...and they fled from before Abishai (וערקו מן קדם אבישי)
t705i	...and **even they** fled from before Abishai (וערקו **אף** אינון מן קדם אבישי)

Chapter Five. Agreements with Ancient Versions and Hebrew Manuscripts

Versions	LXX mss[69]: καὶ ἔφυγαν **καὶ αὐτοὶ** (= Armenian and Ethiopic versions).
	Peshitta: ܘܥܪܩܘ ܐܦ ܗܢܘܢ ܡܢ ܩܕܡ ܐܒܝܫܝ
	Vulgate: *fugerunt **et ipsi** a facie Abisai*

3.b. Alternative Vocabulary

1 Sam. 13:5

MT	ופלשתים נאספו להלחם עם ישראל שלשים אלף רכב
	The Philistines gathered together to fight with Israel, thirty thousand chariots…
Babylonian tradition	thirty thousand (תלתין אלפין)…
t7i = t718i	**three** thousand (**תלתא** אלפין)…
Versions	Peshitta: ܬܠܬܐ ܐܠܦܝܢ
	LXX mss: **τρεῖς** χιλιάδες

The Peshitta and the Antiochene witnesses to the Septuagint,[70] probably represent an attempt to rationalise a seemingly implausible number.[71] The same explanation is applicable to manuscripts t7i and t718i (or to the variant Hebrew manuscripts towards which they were revised).

1 Sam. 25:6

MT	ואמרתם כה לחי
	You will say thus, 'For he who lives!' (or possibly: 'For my brother!' See discussion below).
Babylonian tradition	You will say thus, 'For your life…' (ותימרון כדין לחייך)
t5a[PM]	You will say thus, For **my brothers**…' (ותימרון כדין **לאחיי**)
Versions	Vulgate: *fratribus meis*

In t5a the corrector adds לחייך in the margin and a circular marker is placed above לאחיי in the text. It is unclear whether the corrector intends by this that לחייך should be read in place of לאחיי (which is vocalised) or in addition to it.

The significance of the vocalisation of the Masoretic Text (לֶחָי, i.e. in pause) is ambiguous. It may signal a contraction of לְאָחִי, the reading understood by the Vulgate (or the *alef* was present in the *Vorlage*).[72] But it may equally be the

---

69 LXX mss: Escurial, γ. ii. 5 (Brooke, McLean, Thackeray = c; Rahlfs = 376); Rome, Vat., Urbin. Gr. 1 (Brooke, McLean, Thackeray = x; Rahlfs = 247).

70 LXX manuscript variants given in Fernández Marcos and Busto Saiz (eds), *El texto antioqueno de la Biblia griega*, I, *1–2 Samuel* (mss boc₂e₂ i.e. 'Lucianic' recensions, in Brooke, McLean, Thackeray ed.).

71 Barthélemy, *Critique textuelle de l'Ancien Testament*, I, 177–8.

72 Barthélemy, *Critique textuelle de l'Ancien Testament*, I, 212. Cf. Pss 22:23; 69:9.

pausal form of לָחָי 'to the one who lives'.[73] Among the medieval commentators, Isaiah di Trani explains that the *alef* has disappeared; Rashi, Kimhi (who cites the Targum), Joseph Kara, and Joseph Caspi, on the other hand, all connect the form to חיים.[74] The Ashkenazi manuscript t5a in its *prima manus* and corrected form appears to reflect both possible readings (if both are to be read, this would be a 'conflated reading').

1 Sam. 25:15

MT	כל ימי התהלכנו אתם בהיותנו בשדה
	... all the days we were going about with them, when we were in the **field**.
Babylonian tradition	... all the days we were going about with them, when we were dwelling in the **field** (כד הוינא שרן בחקלא).
t705i	... all the days we were going about with them, when we were dwelling in the **desert** (כד הוינא שרן במדברא).
Versions	Vulgate: *in deserto*
	Peshitta: ܡܢ ܒܡܕܒܪܐ

1 Sam. 25.4 clearly states that David was in the desert (cf. 1 Sam 25.1). Manuscript t705i harmonises the two verses as the Vulgate and Peshitta (or their *Vorlage*) has evidently also done.

3.c. Variations in Person or Number (inc. Pronominal suffix)

1 Sam. 17:55

MT	אמר אל אבנר שר הצבא בן מי זה
	...he said to Abner, the head of the army, Whose son is this?
Babylonian tradition	...he said to Abner, the head of the army (רב חילא), Whose son is this?
t5a = t713a, t720a	...he said to Abner, the head of **his** army (רב חיליה), Whose son is this?
Versions	LXX ('Lucianic'): τὸν ἄρχοντα τῆς δυνάμεως **αὐτοῦ**
	Peshitta: ܕܚܝܠܗ

---

73 See S.R. Driver, *Notes on the Hebrew Text and the Topography of the Books of Samuel* (Oxford 1913), 196.

74 y.Sanh. 20b gives the Aramaic קיומא, evidently taking the Hebrew to be derived from חיים (as the standard text of Targum Jonathan). See Goshen-Gottstein, *Fragments of Lost Targumim*, Vol 2, §11.28. Cf. also Ralbag's comments (*Commentary on Samuel, ad loc*) with the reading of LXX εἰς ὥρας.

Chapter Five. Agreements with Ancient Versions and Hebrew Manuscripts

3.d. Analysis

Despite *prima facia* appearances, none of the examples given above requires us to look outside the Targum text itself for an explanation. The addition of 'all' (כל; i.e. 1 Sam. 22:14) is common throughout the Western Targum manuscripts, though usually in idiomatic expression (e.g. 1 Sam. 6:9 above; cf. variants to 2 Sam. 18:19; 2 Sam. 24:22, page 190), as is the addition of pronominal suffixes (i.e. 1 Sam. 17:55) and the specification of persons (i.e. 1 Sam. 19:10, cf. chapter seven §2.c). The emphatic 'even they' (אַף אִנוּן) is also relatively common phraseology (1 Sam. 14:15, 21–2; 19:20–1), usually replicating the Hebrew גם המה. In these cases, therefore, the possibility that the variant has arisen accidentally in the process of transmitting the Targum is strong. Equally, the variation in number in 1 Sam. 13:5 could easily be a scribal slip. The Hebrew of 1 Sam. 25:6, though not impossible to explain, is problematic; the variant reading of the *prima manus* of manuscript t5a reflects the explanation of the form adopted in the Vulgate and by Isaiah di Trani. The correction reflects the explanation of most of the medieval commentators.

Yet another explanation of the agreement is also possible. Despite the impressive labours of the likes of de Rossi, Kennicott, and Ginsburg, variant readings have been collated from only a fraction of the known extant Hebrew manuscripts — and that is not even to mention those manuscripts that have been lost to the ravages of time or remain unknown to the scholarly world. Thus, it is not impossible that our Targum manuscripts have indeed been revised towards Hebrew manuscripts the contents of which remain — at least for the time being — unknown.

Conclusions

So, to return to the question with which I began this chapter, could Targum manuscripts of the Ashkenazi and Mixed Western group preserve genuinely ancient alternative readings of the Targum, which might reflect an alternative Hebrew *Vorlage*? In short, this is unlikely in the extreme. Why?

In the previous chapter it was demonstrated that the Targum manuscripts of the Ashkenazi and Mixed Western group have been sporadically revised towards the Hebrew text, or perhaps one should say, under the influence of the Hebrew text. Most of the examples presented above reflect exactly the same phenomenon. Yet manuscripts of the Hebrew text that circulated in Europe differed in some details from the text of Codex Leningradensis, with the result that the Targum manuscripts of the Ashkenazi and Mixed Western group occasionally reflect the variant readings in these Hebrew manuscripts, rather than the standard text of Codex Leningradensis.[75] In such cases then, at best, the variant Targum manuscripts are merely secondary witnesses to a variant reading in a medieval European Hebrew manuscript, the value of which for text criticism of the Hebrew Bible is in any case extremely limited.[76] As such, they hardly deserve their own siglum in a critical edition of the Hebrew Bible (an honour accorded to t705i in *Biblia Hebraica Stuttgartensia* and several manuscripts, including t2i, in the *Biblia Hebraica Quinta*).

This conclusion is strengthened by the observation that those manuscripts that exhibit a strong tendency to revise towards a Hebrew text in line with the text of Codex Leningradensis, e.g. manuscripts t720a, t713a, t6a, t705i and t2i, also show a strong tendency to agree with variant Hebrew manuscripts (and/or one or more of the ancient Versions). This strongly suggests that the revision of the Aramaic text towards the Hebrew text took place in Europe. Such a hypothesis is further strengthened by the presence in the Targum manuscripts of variant readings supported by medieval European witnesses to the Hebrew text but not by the principal ancient Versions.

We can also conclude that these variants have entered the Targum textual tradition sporadically and over many generations of manuscripts. That at least some revisions must have been taken over from the *Vorlage* (and therefore passed down the 'generations') is supported by the appearance of the same revisions in multiple Targum manuscripts. For example, t2i and t3i contain the same variant reading (i.e. revision) at 2 Sam. 11:7 (see above); the two manuscripts are textually extremely similar (t2i may even have served as the *Vorlage* for t3i[77]); it is therefore almost a certainty that at least one of them (i.e. t3i) has copied this variant from his *Vorlage*. Likewise, one might point to several cases in which the Hebrew text of a given manuscript corresponds to

---

75 A conclusion already advanced by Smelik in respect of Ms 11 Göttweig (i.e. t725a); he writes: 'the presence of Hebrew variant readings in the manuscript apparently led to adjustment of the Aramaic text...a different Hebrew text resulted in adjustment of the Targum'. Smelik, 'Orality, Manuscript Reproduction, and the Targums', 79; also Smelik, 'Trouble in the Trees!' 261, 265.
76 Tov, *Textual Criticism of the Hebrew Bible*, 37–9.
77 van Staalduine-Sulman, 'An Electronic Edition of Targum Samuel', 32.

Chapter Five. Agreements with Ancient Versions and Hebrew Manuscripts

the reading of Codex Leningradensis, while the Targum text in the same manuscript agrees with variant Hebrew manuscripts (e.g. t705i 1 Sam. 10:14; t2i 1 Sam. 25:1; t705i 2 Sam. 5:3; t7i, t713a, t6a 1 Sam. 30:8).[78]

Each Targum manuscript therefore probably contains a mixture of revisions introduced by the scribe and variant readings taken over from its *Vorlage*.[79] If this is indeed the case, we are unlikely to be able to identify the exact Hebrew manuscript(s) against which the Targum has been revised. Indeed, no particular pattern of correspondence emerges from the comparison with the Kennicott and de Rossi manuscripts, although one or two of their manuscripts do crop up repeatedly (e.g. Kennicott 150, 187, 224, 246; de Rossi 545). As one might have expected, these four manuscripts are all European — Ashkenazi with the exception of Kennicott 246[80] — and date from the twelfth to the fourteenth century.[81] Kennicott 150 is, in fact, one of our Targum manuscripts, i.e. Or. fol. 1–4, Staatsbibliothek, Preußischer Kulturbesitz, Berlin [t5a]. The evidence is sufficient to demonstrate that corresponding variant readings were attested in European manuscripts of the Hebrew Bible in the relevant time period, so that a theory of revision towards variant Hebrew manuscripts is plausible (though not decisive in every case), particularly when one bears in mind that the manuscripts known to Kennicott and de Rossi represent only a fraction of what must once have existed.

To sum up, when Targum manuscripts of the Ashkenazi and/or Mixed

---

78 At 2 Sam. 5:1 the variant Targum reading is reflected in the Hebrew text of t705i, while the reading of MT is in fact recorded in the masorah (marked פליג).

79 Cf. Smelik, 'Trouble in the Trees!', 265, who notes that some scribes appear to have adjusted their Aramaic text to the Hebrew variant found in their bilingual exemplar (see also Smelik, *The Targum of Judges*, 643).

80 In a Sephardi hand according to Kennicott (*Dissertatio generalis in Vetus Testamentum hebraicum*, 432–3), though the manuscript is no longer extant; see Richler, *Hebrew Manuscripts in the Biblioteca Palatina in Parma* §484.

81 Kennicott 224 (*alias* Königsberg 2; Codex Regiomontanus 2) presents a puzzle. The location and fate of the manuscript are currently unknown. Kennicott, who knew the manuscript only second-hand via the labours of Lilienthal (cf. T.C. Lilienthal, *Commentatio critica sistens duorum codicum mstorum Biblia Hebraica ontinentium qui Regiomonti Borussorum asservantur praestantissimorum notitiam, cum praecipuarum variantium lectionum ex utroque codice excerptarum sylloge* [Regiomonti et Lipsiae 1770], 44–101), dates the manuscript to the beginning of the twelfth century; B. Kennicott, *Dissertatio generalis in Vetus Testamentum hebraicum Hebraicum cum Variis Lectionibus ex Codicibus Manuscriptis et Impressis* (Brunovici 1783), 424. The ordering of the prophets is consistent with this period and suggests a German origin; P. Brandt, *Endgestalten des Kanons: das Arrangement der Schriften Israels in der jüdischen und christlichen Bibel* (Bonner biblische Beiträge 131, Berlin 2001), 144 cf. 156.

Western group agree with one or more of the ancient Versions but there is no extant Hebrew manuscripts supporting the variant, we must exclude two possibilities before we can conclude that the Targum manuscript preserves a genuinely ancient reading. First, that a medieval European Hebrew manuscript containing the variant reading once existed and is either now lost or has simply never been studied. Secondly, that the variant could not have arisen independently in the ancient Versions and in the medieval Targum manuscripts, for example, because the Hebrew text was in some way problematic (e.g. a missing definite object marker), by pure accident (e.g. omission or addition of copula), or due to any of the revisionary tendencies that we find in the Targum manuscripts (which I will describe in the chapters that follow). We must be particularly sceptical when the agreement is with a version such as the 'Lucianic' recension of the Septuagint, since this recension itself exhibits a tendency to 'improve' the text.[82] I have found no cases in which these two possibilities can be satisfactorily excluded. On the one hand our knowledge of the content of medieval European Hebrew manuscripts is too limited, and on the other, the Ashkenazi and Mixed Western Targum manuscripts are marked throughout with traces of revisionary activity.

There is no evidence, then, that any of the variant readings in the European Targum manuscripts ought to be considered earlier than the reading of the Eastern textual tradition on the basis of agreement with variant readings in the ancient Versions. Their agreement with the ancient Versions does not relate to a period before the Masoretic Text had been stabilised, but to a much later period, in some cases possibly contemporary to the date of the manuscript itself.

---

82 See e.g. Brock, *The Recensions of the Septuagint Version of I Samuel*, 298.

Chapter Six

Conventional and Contextual Changes

1. Conventional Renderings

It is clear from the preceding chapters that the Hebrew text has exerted a strong influence over the shape of the Targum's text in its European transmission. An almost equally strong influence arises from within the Targum text itself. In all our manuscripts containing the continuous text we can observe a tendency to introduce, at certain points in the text, wording that is frequent or idiomatic throughout the Targum or that occurs in the immediate textual context.

1.a. Accidental Additions

In its most basic form a small addition is made to the text to 'complete' an idiom in common usage elsewhere in Targum Jonathan. In these cases the scribe has probably introduced the addition automatically on account of the frequency with which the idiom occurs. Perhaps the simplest example of this phenomenon, and one that occurs relatively frequently, concerns the formula 'the men of' (construct state, either plural אנשי, or singular אינש) plus either a personal name or a location. This formula is extremely common in Targum Jonathan where it either translates the same construction in the underlying Hebrew (e.g. Tg. 1 Sam. 11:8, 9; 13:6; 14:22, 24; 15:4; 17:2 etc), or replaces a gentilic noun (e.g. the 'Ashdodim' of the Hebrew text become 'the men of Ashdod' Tg. 1 Sam. 5:6) or a noun expressing collectivity (e.g. 'his household' ביתו, becomes 'the men of his household' Tg. 1 Sam. 1:21; 2:32; 3:12, 13, etc.). Due to the frequency with which this formula occurs in the Western manuscripts it has been introduced accidentally into the text at points where the Targum originally lacked it, in adherence to the underlying Hebrew. For example:

The Transmission of Targum Jonathan in the West

	Babylonian Tradition	**Variant**	**Hebrew**
1 Sam. 25:17	and upon all his household (ביתיה)	and upon all **the men of** his household (אנש ביתיה) t2i	ועל כל ביתו
2 Sam. 7:25	and upon his household (ביתיה)	and upon **the men of** his household (אינש ביתיה) t713a	ועל ביתו
2 Sam. 9:9	and to all his household (ביתיה)	and to **all the men of** his household (אינש ביתיה) t713a	ולכל ביתו
2 Sam. 10:11	If the Arameans (ארם) become stronger than me…	If the **men of** Aram (אינש ארם) become stronger than me… t5a	אם תחזק ארם ממני

The reverse tendency can also be observed in 2 Samuel 10. In verses 13, 14, and 16 the Hebrew reads 'the Arameans' (ארם), which in the Babylonian text is rendered '*the men of* Aram (באנשׁ ארם)'. This becomes 'the Arameans (ארם)' in t713a, t720a, t7i at verse 13, in t725a, t2i, t3i at verse 14, and in t5a, t6a, t713a, t705i at verse 16. Equally in 2 Sam. 2:3 the Babylonian tradition reads 'David brought up the men who were with him, each with *the men* of his household… (גבר ואנש ביתיה)'. t2i replaces this with '…each with his household (גבר וביתיה = MT איש וביתו)'. These cases may result from an accommodation of the text to the underlying Hebrew (see chapter four). That there is no consistency in any manuscript even though the instances are in close proximity suggests that the changes are entirely haphazard.

The language of warfare, a topic with which the books of Samuel are much concerned, also yields numerous examples of this phenomenon. Although מלחמה is often translated simply with קרבא 'battle' (e.g. Tg. 1 Sam. 14:22; 17:13, 20; 29:4 etc), the Hebrew מלחמה 'war' or חיל 'might, army' is also frequently rendered with the idiom עבדי קרבא 'those fighting (lit. making) the battle' throughout Targum Jonathan (in Tg. Sam. e.g. Tg. 1 Sam. 4:2; 14:23, 52; 16:18; 17:20, 28, 33; 18:5, 17; 19:8; 31:3; Tg. 2 Sam. 8:10; 11:7; 17:8; 18:8 cf. Tg. 2 Sam. 22:25; 22:40). In 2 Sam. 1:25, t232i/s introduces this common idiom (perhaps with the intention of indicating that the heroes of Israel were active participants in the battle, rather than passive victims).

Chapter Six. Conventional and Contextual Changes

2 Sam. 1:25

MT   איך נפלו גברים בתוך המלחמה
How the heroes have fallen in the midst of the war!

Babylonian tradition   איכדין איתברו גיבריא בגו קרבא
How the heroes have been broken in the midst of the battle!

t232i/s   אכדין איתקטלו גיבריא בגו **עבדי** קרבא
How the heroes have been killed in the midst of **those fighting** (lit. making) the battle!

A comparable case is found in 2 Sam. 1:27, where the reading of the Babylonian tradition, 'but the weapons of battle (מני קרבא) were lost', mirrors the underlying Hebrew (כלי מלחמה), whereas t720a has the more elaborate 'but the weapons of *the fighters of* the battle (מאני עבדי קרבא) were lost', and t713a 'but the weapons *of the men fighting* the battle (מני גברי עבדי קרבא) were lost'.

The combination 'to fight' גוח (in *aphel*, often the infinitive) and קרב 'battle' is also extremely common (in Tg. Sam.: Tg. 1 Sam. 4:1, 9, 10; 7:10; 8:20; 12:9 etc.), resulting in numerous fluctuations in expressions using these terms. For example, in 2 Sam. 2:28 and 2 Sam. 11:20 the Babylonian tradition reads the infinitive 'to fight (לאגחא)' for the underlying Hebrew להלחם. In both cases Western texts append the noun 'battle' (i.e. לאגחא קרבא; t3i in 2 Sam. 2:28; t2i, t232i/s in 2 Sam. 11:20). Likewise, in 2 Sam. 12:27 the Babylonian textual tradition replicates the Hebrew (נלחמתי ברבה) word for word with 'I fought against (אגחית) Rabbah', whereas all the Ashkenazi and Mixed Western texts read the fuller 'I waged war (אגחית קרבא) against Rabbah'.

One finds several cases where the reverse can be observed. In 1 Sam. 17:1, for example, the Babylonian textual tradition reads 'to wage war' (לאגחא קרבא), while manuscripts t6a, t713a, t720a and t2i offer the shorter 'to the battle' (לקרבא = MT למלחמה). The Babylonian tradition reads 'and we will wage war together (lit: like one)' (ונגיח קרבא כחדא) at 1 Sam. 17:10, while manuscripts t3i, t701i, t705i, and t718i read simply 'and we will fight together' (ונגיח כחדא = MT ונלחמה יחד). Similarly, in 1 Sam. 17:28 we find 'you came down in order to see *those fighting* the battle' (למחזי עבדי קרבא נחתתא) in the Babylonian tradition according to t707b, but the shorter 'you came down in order to see the battle' (למיחזי קרבא נחתתא) in the Babylonian manuscript t2506b and the Western manuscripts t725a and t701i; and at 2 Sam. 23:9 the Babylonian textual tradition offers the longer 'and they were gathered there to wage war (לאגחא קרבא)...' while t5a and t713a give the shorter 'and they were gathered there to fight (לאגחא)...' for the Hebrew

למלחמה. This latter group of variants may result from accommodation to the Hebrew text (see chapter four), though the frequency with which the terms involved can be found in Targum Samuel make random interchange more likely.

Vocabulary concerning God is particularly susceptible to this phenomenon since stereotypical expressions are extremely common. The simplest and most compelling example concerns the divine title:

1 Sam. 2:2

MT		ואין צור כאלהינו
	There is no rock like our God!	
Babylonian tradition		לית דתקיף אלא אלהנא
	There is none who is strong except our God!	
t5a	There is none who is strong except **the Lord** our God (אלא **יוי** אלהנא).	

This formulation 'the Lord our/your/their/etc. God' occurs hundreds of times in Targum Jonathan (54 times in Targum Samuel alone, e.g. Tg. 1 Sam. 2:30; 7:8; 10:18; 12:9, 12, 14, 19, etc.). We find several other examples of this exact formula being introduced into the text in manuscript t725a (e.g. Tg. 1 Sam. 12:10: Babylonian tradition פלחנא דיוי, t725a פולחנא דיוי אלהנא; 1 Sam. 15:26: Babylonian tradition קצתא בפתגמא דיוי 'you have rejected the word of the Lord', t725a קצתה בפתגמא דיוי אלהך; 1 Sam. 30:23 Babylonian tradition יוי, t725a יוי אלהנא).

Other frequently occurring examples concern nouns commonly found in a genitive construction, with 'the Lord' as the modifier noun:

1 Sam. 2:1

MT	[no Hebrew text]	
Babylonian tradition		לשבחא בבית מקדשא
	...to praise in the Temple.	
t232i/s = t6a[correct], t720a		לשבחא בבית מקדשא **דיוי**
	...to praise in the Temple **of the Lord**.	

The Temple is usually referred to as 'the Temple *of the Lord*' in Targum Samuel (i.e. Tg. 1 Sam. 1:7, 24; 3:3, 15; Tg. 2 Sam. 12:20 cf. Tg. 1 Sam. 2:29,[1] 32; Tg. 2 Sam. 15:25), though not always (i.e. Tg. 2 Sam. 21:19).

---

[1] But note that t232i/s reads קדמי בבית מקדשא at 1 Sam. 2:29; the Babylonian tradition reads קדמי בבית מקדשי.

Chapter Six. Conventional and Contextual Changes

1 Sam. 2:1

MT	[no Hebrew text]
Babylonian tradition (t2520b, t2527b, t1126b)	דעתידין דייתון ית ארונא בעגלתא חדתא ...who will bring the Ark on a new cart...
t2i = t232i/s, t3i, t7i, t701i, t705i, t718i, t5a, t6a, t713a, t720a, t725a (= t707b)	דעתידין דייתון ית ארונא **דיוי** בעגלתא חדתא ...who will bring the Ark **of the Lord** on a new cart...

The Ark is frequently referred to as the Ark *of the Lord* (e.g. Tg. 1 Sam. 3:3; 4:6, 13, 18, 19, 21, 22, and frequently), usually following the underlying Hebrew ארון (ה)אלהים or ארון יהוה. Where the Hebrew refers simply to 'the Ark' (הארון) in the books of Samuel, the Targum replicates this literally, i.e. without the addition דיוי (e.g. Tg. 1 Sam. 6:13; Tg. 2 Sam. 11:11). The current example, however, is part of a Targumic addition. One finds exactly the same addition ('Ark *of the Lord*' for 'Ark') in manuscript t6a at 2 Sam. 11:11, where the underlying Hebrew is הארון. As the table above shows, the Babylonian materials are divided at this point. t707b is the exception and is somewhat inferior in quality to t2520b and t2527b. Nonetheless, this disparity demonstrates that the phenomenon enumerated here is not confirmed to the European transmission, though evidently much more common in that corpus, a point to which I will return in due course.

Another common designation of the Ark in Targum Jonathan is 'the Ark of the Covenant of the Lord (ארון קימא דיוי)' (in Tg. Sam: Tg. 1 Sam. 4:3, 4, 5; Tg. 2 Sam. 15:24), a direct translation of the Hebrew ארון ברית יהוה. As in the previous example, this expression replaces the shorter 'Ark of the Lord (ארונא דיוי)' of the Babylonian tradition in several places in our European manuscripts (i.e. 1 Sam. 7:1: t6a, t713a, t720a Hebr. ארון יהוה; 2 Sam. 15:24: t725a, t2i Hebr. ארון האלהים;[2] 2 Sam. 15:25: t2i Hebr. ארון האלהים).

2 Sam. 24:16

MT	Then the angel (המלאך) stretched out his hand to Jerusalem...
Babylonian tradition	Then the angel (מלאכא) stretched out his hand to Jerusalem...
t232i/s^{PM}	Then the angel **of the Lord** (מלאכא דיוי) stretched out his hand to Jerusalem...

The expression 'angel of the Lord' is very common in Targums Onqelos

---

[2] Possibly under influence of the appearance of the expression earlier in the same verse.

and Jonathan, usually for the Hebrew מלאך יהוה or מלאך אלהים (e.g. Tg. Onq. Gen. 16:7, 9, 10, 11; 21:17; 31:11 etc.; Tg. 1 Kgs 19:7; Tg. 2 Kgs 1:3, 15; Tg. Isa. 37:36 etc.), and appears later in the verse. In this case the accidental introduction of the familiar idiom has been subsequently deleted by the corrector.

Comparable are those cases in which a reference to God is modified or qualified in some way:

1 Sam. 17:46

MT	Codex Leningradensis: כי יש אלהים לישראל.
	(Several manuscripts: בישראל).
	…that Israel has a God (or: …that there is a God in Israel)
Babylonian tradition	…and all the inhabitants of the land will know that there is a God in Israel (דאית אלה בישראל).
t720a = t7i, t232i/s, t6a, t713a, (Sperber: t12sc, t703s, t706s, t734s)	…an **everlasting** God in Israel (דאית אלהא **קיימא** בישראל).

This is a common appellation used elsewhere in Targum Jonathan where it is not warranted by the underlying Hebrew (e.g. Tg. 2 Kgs 1:3, 6, 16; 5:15; Tg. Isa. 65:16, also in Tg. Neof. and Frg. Tg.[P,V] Gen. 16:13; Tg. Ps.-J. Num. 23:19).[3] A number of further cases reflect the Hebrew (used adjectively e.g. Tg. Josh. 3:10; Tg. Hos. 2:1; Tg. Jer. 10:10; 23:26 cf. Tg. Isa. 40:8, also e.g. Tg. Ps.-J. Deut. 4:33; 5:26; used predicatively e.g. Tg. 1 Sam. 25:34; Tg. 2 Sam. 14:11; 22:47; Tg. 1 Kgs 17:1, 12; 18:10; Tg. Zeph. 2:9).

2 Sam. 24:23

MT	May the Lord your God (יהוה אלהיך) be favourable to you (ירצך)!
Babylonian tradition	May the Lord your God (יוי אלהך) accept your sacrifice with favour.
t705i	May **the Memra** of the Lord your God (**מימרא** דיוי אלהך) accept your sacrifice with favour.

The expression 'the Memra of the Lord' is extremely common in Targum Jonathan, often replacing the divine name as a means of avoiding

---

[3] Sperber records the addition אלהא חייא וקיימא under the siglum 'Fr' to 2 Sam. 22:8; 22:13. Unfortunately Sperber does not tell us to which manuscripts 'Fr' refers (see my 'The Critical Importance of Targum Fragments'). Many of the same readings, including the appellation אלהא חייא וקיימא, can also be found in Italian mahzorim, which contain an exegetically fuller version of the Targum to 2 Samuel 22 for the seventh day of Pesach, e.g. ms Parm. 3132, Biblioteca Palatina, Parma; ms Rossiana 437, Biblioteca Apostolica Vaticana; ms Sassoon 405, Sassoon Collection, Letchworth; ms Opp. Add. fol. 11, Bodleian Library, Oxford; ms Parm. 3008, Biblioteca Palatina, Parma.

Chapter Six. Conventional and Contextual Changes

anthropomorphism (e.g. Tg. 1 Sam. 28:15; Tg. 1 Kgs 1:17, 30, 37; Tg. Isa. 8:5; 10:20 etc.). Unsurprisingly then we find other examples of this formula being introduced into the text (e.g. Tg. 1 Sam. 24:16 Babylonian tradition 'may the Lord be judge…'; t5a 'may *the Memra of* the Lord be judge…'; 2 Sam. 7:1 Babylonian tradition 'the Lord caused his enemies to desist from roundabout'. t5a '…*the Memra of* the Lord…').

Another technique employed by the Targum to avoid anthropomorphism is to remove God from direct action by introducing the idiom 'from before' (e.g. 1 Sam. 3:8 MT 'that the Lord was calling to the lad'; Tg. 'that *from before* the Lord was called to the boy'. Cf. Tg. 1 Sam. 1:5, 6, 20; 2:12, 20; 3:7, 8; 9:9, etc.), with the result that this idiom is extremely common. At 1 Sam. 5:9 three Ashkenazi manuscripts (t6a[PM], t713a, t720a) introduce this expression where it is lacking in other witnesses, i.e. reading 'there was a stroke *from before* the Lord (מן קדם יוי)' in place of 'there was a stroke of the Lord (מחתא דיוי) against the city'.

The phenomenon of 'completing' idiomatic phrases can be detected in a host of other mundane expressions. For example:

1 Sam. 9:26

MT	They got up early (וישכמו) — as the dawn was breaking…
Babylonian tradition	They got up early (ואקדימו) — as the dawn was breaking…
t232i/s	They got up early **in the morning** (ואקדימו בצרפא) — as the dawn was breaking (כמסק צפרא)…

The formulation adopted in t232i/s occurs frequently (Cf. Tg. 1 Sam. 1:19; 5:4; 17:20; 29:10). The wording of the following phrase (כמסק צפרא) may have influenced the copyist.

2 Sam. 22:27

MT	[no Hebrew]
Babylonian tradition	…you separated his seed from all the dross of Pharaoh and the Egyptians who devised plans against your people…
t720a	…against your people **Israel**.

The expression 'your people Israel' occurs earlier in Targum Samuel (Tg. 2 Sam. 7:23, 24), and the formula 'people' + pronominal suffix + 'Israel' is common (Tg. 1 Sam. 9:16; Tg. 2 Sam. 3:18; 5:12; 7:7, 11).

Two cases concern the interchange of idiomatic expressions that occur in two forms, one with the word 'all (כל)', and one without.

The Transmission of Targum Jonathan in the West

2 Sam. 18:19

MT	…because the Lord vindicated [i.e. delivered] him (שפטו) from the hand of his enemies.
Babylonian tradition	…it was avenged for him [by] the Lord (אתפרע ליה יוי) from the hand of his enemies.
t5a = t713a, t720a	…from the hand of **all** (כל) his enemies.

The expression 'from the hand of *all* enemies' is common (e.g. Tg. Judg. 8:34; Tg. 2 Sam. 3:18; 22.1; Tg. 2 Kgs 17:39; etc.)

2 Sam. 24:22

MT	ויעל אדני המלך הטוב בעינו (בעיניו *Qere*:) May my master the king offer up that which seems right in his eyes.
Babylonian tradition	ויסיק רבוני מלכא דתקין בעינוהי May my master the king offer up that which seems right in his eyes.
t232i/s	ויסק ריבוני מלכא **כל** דתקין בעינוהי May my master the king offer up **all** that seems right in his eyes.

The expressions 'that which seems right in his eyes' (e.g. Tg. 1 Sam. 1:23; 14:40; 24:5 etc.) and '*all* that seems right in his eyes' (e.g. Tg. 1 Sam. 11:10; 14:36 cf. Tg. 2 Sam. 3:19) can both be found in Targum Samuel. The text of t232i/s appears to have accidentally switched the formulation.

This phenomenon even extends to typical grammatical constructions. For example, verbs in the imperative are often strengthened in Targum Jonathan with the particle כען (e.g. Tg. 1 Sam. 9:3, 18; 10:15; 14:17, 29 etc), representing the Hebrew נא. This common structure is accidentally imported into the text at 1 Sam. 12:19 in manuscripts t6a, t713a, t720a, t701i, t705i, which read 'Pray *please* on your servants' behalf (צלי כען על עבדך)!' instead of the reading of the Babylonian textual tradition, 'Pray on your servants' behalf (צלי על עבדך)', which reflects the structure of the Hebrew.

As I mentioned above, it is not only European manuscripts that have been affected by this phenomenon. In 2 Sam. 3:10, for example, t707b and t710y are the only witnesses to read 'the throne of *the kingdom of* David' (כרסי מלכותא דדוד), in place of the shorter 'the throne of David' (כורסי דוד)'. The formula 'the throne of the kingdom…' is extremely common in Targum Jonathan (e.g. Tg. 2 Sam. 7:13, 16; 14:9; Tg. 1 Kgs 1:13, 17, 20, 24, 27; Tg. Isa. 14:13; Tg. Jer. 33:17; 49:38; Tg. Jon. 3:6; etc.), so it may well have been introduced accidentally in these two manuscripts (or in a common 'ancestor').

The adjustments to the text described above have almost certainty occurred

Chapter Six. Conventional and Contextual Changes

accidentally, the copyist simply introducing automatically, subconsciously, the more familiar phraseology: no consistent pattern can be detected in any given manuscript and the adjustments add little to the sense of the text. By contrast, in the following examples the addition, though common, does seem to add a degree of clarity or exegetical embellishment to the verse, so that one questions whether their presence can be considered pure accident.

1.b. Additions of Idiomatic Expressions?

In a number of further cases we can be less certain that the addition is the result of idiomatic usage.

1 Sam. 2:8

MT
מקים מעפר דל מאשפת ירים אביון
להושיב עם נדיבים וכסא כבוד ינחלם

He raises the poor from the dust, from the ash heap He will lift up the needy; to seat them among nobles, and allotting them seats of honour.

Babylonian tradition
אתקין גיהנם לרשיעיא וצדיקיא עבדי רעותיה שכליל להון תבל

He has established Gehenna for the wicked and [as for] the righteous ones — those who do his will — he founded for them the world.

t705i = t718i, t701i, t6a, t713a (≈ t3i)
אתקין גיהנם לרשיעיא **עברי מימריה** וצדיקיא עבדי רעותיה שכליל להון תבל

He has established Gehenna for the wicked — **those who transgress his Memra** — and [as for] the righteous ones — those who do his will — he founded for them the world.

t5a, t725a, and t7i add exactly the same addition after ורשיעיא in the following verse (t7i with the misreading חברי for עברי; t5a with the erroneous עבדי על מימריה). The notion of transgressing the Word of God is widespread in Targum Jonathan (e.g. Tg. Isa. 26:19; 28:21; 31:9; 32:5; Tg. Jer. 2:20; Tg. Ezek. 1:8; Tg. Hos. 6:5; Tg. Hab. 3:2, 6), normally as a Targumic addition or an abstract rendering of the underlying Hebrew, but occasionally reflecting the Hebrew more closely (e.g. Tg. Isa. 43:2; Tg. Jer. 17:13 cf. Tg. 1 Sam. 15:24 Saul says 'I have sinned, because I have transgressed the Memra of the Lord' [עברית על מימרא דיוי]). The expression has been added in the current verse to strengthen its force and add a degree of specificity, in spite of the fact that there is no justification in the Hebrew. t3i has עבדיה מימריה 'his servant, his Memra', apparently a misreading of the addition.

The Transmission of Targum Jonathan in the West

1 Sam. 2:10

MT   עלו (ק: עליו) בשמים ירעם

                against them (*qere,* lit. him) He will thunder in the heavens

Babylonian tradition   מן שמיא בקל רם ישקיף יוי יעביד פורענות

                from the heavens with a raised voice the Lord will strike, He will perform retribution

t6a = t5a, t713a, t720a[PM]   מן שמיא בקל רם **יכלי** וישקיף יוי ויעביד פורענות

                from the heavens with a raised voice (t5a 'great voice' בקל רב) the Lord will **call** and strike and ('and' added by corrector in t5a) perform retribution (t713a omits 'retribution')

The Hebrew verb רעם is rare in the Prophets, occurring only twice again (1 Sam. 7:10; 2 Sam. 22:14). The text of the Ashkenazi manuscripts seems to have been influenced by the wording from 1 Sam. 7:10, i.e. ואכלי יוי בקל רב (cf. 2 Sam. 22:14).

1 Sam. 17:43

MT   ויקלל הפלשתי את דוד באלהיו

                ...and the Philistine cursed David by his god.

Babylonian tradition   ולטיט פלשתאה ית דוד בטעותיה

                ...and the Philistine cursed David by his idol.

t6a = t713a, t720a, t7i   ולטיט פלישתאה ית דוד **בשום** טעוותיה

                ...and the Philistine cursed David **in the name of** his idol.

The addition 'the name of' to indicate agency can be compared to similar usage elsewhere in Targums Onqelos and Jonathan, usually reflecting the underlying Hebrew, though occasionally as Targumic addition (e.g. Tg. Isa. 19:18; Tg. Jer. 2:8; 5:7; 12:16; 17:15; 23:13; Tg. Jon. 1:3, 10; Tg. Zeph. 1:5). For example, in the Lord's name one may speak (מלל e.g. Tg. Onq. Deut. 18:22; Tg. 1 Kgs 22:16), praise (שבח e.g. Tg. Isa. 24:14), bless (ברך e.g. Tg. Onq. Deut. 10:8; 21:5; Tg. 2 Sam. 6:18; Tg. Isa. 24:15), pray (צלי e.g. Tg. Onq. Gen. 12:8; 16:13; 21:33; 26:25; Tg. Onq. Deut. 32:3; Tg. 1 Kgs 18:24; Tg. 2 Kgs 5:11; Tg. Isa. 12:4), call out (קרא e.g. Tg. Onq. Exod. 33:19; 34:5), serve (שמש e.g. Tg. Onq. Deut. 18:7), or swear an oath (קום e.g. Tg. 1 Sam. 20:42; Tg. Isa. 19:18; ימי e.g. Tg. Onq. Exod. 20:7; Tg. Onq. Deut. 5:11). One recalls too that David comes out to meet Goliath 'in the name of the Lord' (Tg. 1 Sam. 17:45).

The name in which an action is conducted need not be the Lord's, e.g. to write a letter (e.g. Tg. 1 Kgs 21:8) or seek peace in someone's name (e.g. Tg. 1 Sam. 25:5). Similar actions are also carried out 'in the name of idols' (בשום

Chapter Six. Conventional and Contextual Changes

טעותא) by Israel's enemies or those gone astray (e.g. to prophesy: Tg. Jer. 2:8; 23:13, 27; to speak: Tg. Onq. Deut. 18:20; to call upon: Tg. 1 Kgs 18:24, 25; to swear an oath: Tg. Jer. 5:7; 12:16; cf. also Tg. Josh. 23:7).

The idiom 'to curse by the name of…' is found only once again in Targums Onqelos and Jonathan, in Targum Jonathan 2 Kgs 2:24, 'He went on his way and he saw them so he cursed them in the name of the Lord (ולטנון בשמא דיוי) …' where it reflects the underlying Hebrew (i.e. ויקללם בשם יהוה).[4]

2 Sam. 20:18

MT	[No Hebrew text]
Babylonian tradition	ואמרת למימר אידכר כען מא דכתיב בספר אוריתא למישאל בקרתא בקדמין
	She said, Let me remind [you] now what is written in the book of the Law: first to ask in the town.
t2i = t3i, t725a	ואמרת למימר אדכר כען מא דכתיב בספר אוריתא **דמשה** למישאל **בשלם** קרתא בקדמיתא
	She said, Let me remind [you] now what is written in the book of the Law **of Moses**: first to seek **peace** with the town.
t720a = t6a, t713a, t7i[correct]	…אוריתא **דמשה** למישאל בקרתא…
	…the Law **of Moses**: first to ask in the town…
t705i (Sperber: t702s)	…אוריתא למישאל **בשלמא** בקרתא…
	…the Law: first to seek **peace** with the town…

The first of the two additions here ('Law *of Moses*') may well be accidental, the expression 'the Law of Moses' being idiomatic in the prophets, in the Hebrew and reflected in the Targum (e.g. = Hebr. תורת משה Tg. Josh. 8:31, 32; 23:6; Tg. 1 Kgs 2:3; Tg. 2 Kgs 14:6; 23:25; Tg. Mal. 3:22). The expression has been added in the current verse, in spite of the fact that there is no justification in the Hebrew (cf. also additions to Tg. 1 Sam. 17:39 in t10r, t702s; to Tg. 1 Kgs 5:13 in t702s; and Tosefta Targum to Tg. Judg. 5:6 in t727y[margin], t720a, t10r, t734s; all recorded by Sperber *ad loc*).

The expression 'to seek peace' or 'to inquire about the well-being' (למשאל בשלם) is also prevalent, either as a direct translation (e.g. Tg. 1 Sam. 10:4; 17:22; 25:5; 30:21; Tg. 2 Sam. 8:10; 11:7) or as a typically Targumic

---

4   Cf. also Tg. Ps.-J. Exod. 21:17 'And the one that curses his father or his mother by the Ineffable Name (בשמא מפרשא) will surely die'. (cf. Tg. Ps.-J. Lev. 20:9). The variant in t7i to 1 Sam. 25:9 may also be an example of the adoption of an idiomatic reading. t7i: 'The servants of David came and spoke with Nabal according to all these words *in the name of the Lord of David* (בשמא דיוי דדוד)…' All other witnesses read simply בשמא דדוד. The variant may, however, have arisen by graphic confusion (דדוד/דיוי).

abstract rendering (e.g. Tg. 1 Sam. 10:27 = הביאו לו מנחה; 1 Sam. 13:10 לברכו), but here the addition seems to be intended to aid clarity.[5]

2 Sam. 22:30

MT	באלהי אדלג שור
	...by my God I will jump over a wall
Babylonian tradition	...and by the Memra of my God (במימר אילהי) I will conquer all strongly fortified cities.
t713a	...and with **the help of** the Memra of my God (ובסעד מימ׳ אלהי) I will conquer all strongly fortified cities.

The Memra of the Lord is frequently said to be 'at someone's aid' (בסעד, usually + pronominal suffix) in Targum Jonathan (e.g. Tg. 1 Sam. 3:19; 10:7; 16:18; 17:37; 18:12, 14, 28; 20:13; Tg. 2 Sam. 5:10; 7:3, 9; 14:17). It seems that this idiomatic expression has been recycled (and recast slightly) in the text of t713a.

2 Sam. 23:4

MT	[No Hebrew text]
Babylonian tradition	טוביכון צדיקיא עבדתון לכון עובדין טבין דאתון עתידין לאזהרא בזיהור יקרכון
	Blessed be you, righteous ones! You have done for yourselves good deeds so that you are destined to shine (i.e. flourish) in the light of your gloriousness...
t5a	טוביכון צדיקי׳ עבדתון לכון עובדין טבין דאתון עתידין **לאיתקיימא** לאזהרא בזיהור יקריה יקריכון
	...so that you are destined to be **preserved** (or: **established**) to shine in the light of your gloriousness...

The reward of the 'righteous' (צדיקיא) is something of a *Leitmotiv* in Targum Jonathan, and the promise of their future 'establishment' is found elsewhere, particularly in the Isaiah Targum (e.g. Tg. Isa. 49:8; 55:13).

In these cases, we might ask whether the copyist has been influenced by common usage, or by the desire to offer clarification of an exegetical point (in which case we should group these examples with those in chapter seven).

---

5 The limited availability of textual data led Bacher to conclude that בשלמא had been accidentally omitted in the First and Second Rabbinic Bibles, and Buxtorf's edition. In fact it is a secondary addition in the text of t705i; Bacher, 'Kritische Untersuchungen zum Prophetentargum', 39.

Chapter Six. Conventional and Contextual Changes

1.c. Summary

In the cases just discussed an addition has been introduced into the text based on idiomatic expressions found frequently in Targum Jonathan. When one examines the texts synoptically one sees a pattern emerging of common wording seeping into other locations in the text. It is impossible to say with certainty whether any individual addition has been made accidentally or deliberately, in particular where the idiom is prevalent (e.g. Temple *of the Lord*, Ark *of the Lord*). Manuscript t232i/s contains numerous examples and these are probably best understood as errors given the quality of this manuscript's transmission as a whole (see pages 91–2). On the other hand, the quality of the transmission of manuscripts t7i and t6a is relatively good (see pages 90–1, 98–9) and both show a tendency to embellish the text (see chapter seven), so that it is intrinsically more likely that the variants in t7i and t6a are the conscious work of the copyist (or the *Vorlage*). Cases like those found in t713a and t720a are more finely balanced, since both display a tendency to embellish the text, yet the quality of the transmission of the text in both manuscripts is rather poor so that the judgment could go either way. The important point, however, is that the reading is secondary and in most cases it is likely to have originated in Italy or Ashkenaz.

2. Interchange of Common Translation Equivalents

A similar phenomenon to that described above is the interchange of one common word for another.[6] In many cases this concerns an alternative translation equivalent for a single Hebrew word. By way of illustration, consider the following cases of the synonymous Aramaic nouns גבר and אנש (meaning 'man').

	Babylonian Tradition	**Variants**	**Hebrew**
1 Sam. 24:5	גברי דוד	אינשי דוד t232i/s (cf. t3i עבדי דוד probably a graphic confusion)	אנשי דוד
1 Sam. 25:2	וגברא במעון	ואנש במעון t2i	ואיש במעון

---

6   Cf. Bacher, 'Kritische Untersuchungen zum Prophetentargum', 55.

The Transmission of Targum Jonathan in the West

2 Sam. 20:7	גברי יואב	אנשי יואב t2i = t725a, t705i	אנשי יואב
2 Sam. 2:5	אינשי יביש גלעד	גברי יבש גלעד t701i	אנשי יביש גלעד

Both nouns are extremely common (the noun אנש occurring 116 times and גבר some 305 times in the Targum of Samuel), particularly in formulations of relation to a person (i.e. 'men of David') or place ('the men of Jabesh Gilead'), and both frequently translate the Hebrew איש 'man' in Targum Samuel (= אנשא x 64; = גברא x 273). On occasion a copyist has simply switched one for another.

Several other extremely common translation equivalents are accidentally switched in multiple places. A number of common, near synonymous, verbs are affected. For example:

The two common verbs for coming or entering (i.e. *coming into* a place):

	Babylonian Tradition	**Variants**	**Hebrew**
1 Sam. 18:6	והוה במיעלהון	והוה במיתיהון t713a = t720a	בבואם
1 Sam. 20:29	לא על	לא אתא t2i = t5a	לא בא
1 Sam. 23:10	למיעל	למיתי t2i למיחת t6a^{correct} = t5a	לבוא
2 Sam. 4:7	ואתו	ועלו t7i = t6a, t713a	ויבאו
2 Sam. 6:17	ואעילו	ואיתיאו t705i (Sperber: t10r, t710y)	ויבאו
2 Sam. 13:10	ואעילת	ואייתיאת t5a	ותבא
2 Sam. 13:36	אתו	עלו t725a	באו

Comparable examples can be found in other common verbs of motion, for example:

1 Sam. 15:32	ואתא	ואזל t2i = t7i, t713a, t720a, t725a	וילך
1 Sam. 23:27	ואיזיל	ואיתא t232i/s	ולכה

Chapter Six. Conventional and Contextual Changes

1 Sam. 29:10	ותיזלון	ותהלכון t5a	ולכו

Common verbs of fleeing:

1 Sam. 17:24	ואפכו	וערקו t6a^{PM} = t713a, t720a	וינסו
1 Sam. 17:51	ואפכו	וערקו t6a = t713a, t720a	וינסו
1 Sam. 19:8	ואפכו	וערקו t6a^{PM}	וינסו
2 Sam. 10:14	וערקו	ואפכו t6a^{correct} = t713a, t725a	נס

Common verbs of dying:

1 Sam. 14:45	ולא מית	ולא איתקטיל t713a = t720a	ולא מית
2 Sam. 1:4	מיתו	איתקטלו t705i	מתו
2 Sam. 11:24	ואתקטלו	ומיתו t720a	וימותו

Common Verbs of striking and killing (where the Hebrew root נכה could carry either sense):[7]

1 Sam. 6:19	וקטל בעמא שבעין (t710y: וקטל בסבי עמא שבעין)	ומחא t720a	ויך
1 Sam. 19:8	ומחא בהון מחא סגיאה	וקטל בהון קטול סגי t720a = t713a	ויך בהם מכה גדולה
1 Sam. 22:19	מחא	קטל t705i	הכה
1 Sam. 23:2	ואיקטול	ואימחי t705i	והכיתי
2 Sam. 5:25	וקטל	ומחא t2i = t705i, t713a, t725a	ויך

---

7   The use of מחי at 1 Sam. 23:2 in t705i may be a revision towards the Hebrew text (as I suggested in my earlier paper, 'The Transmission of Targum Jonathan in the West', 40), the Aramaic מחי more closely reflecting the semantic range of the Hebrew root הכה.

Common verbs of taking:[8]

1 Sam. 9:22	דבר	ונסיב t5a	ויקח
2 Sam. 10:4	ונסיב	ודבר t2i = t3i, t7i, t232i/s, t701i, t705i, t718i, t6a, t713a, t720a	ויקח
2 Sam. 14:2	ודבר	ונסיב t5a	ויקח
2 Sam. 21:8	ודבר	ונסיב A + MW	ויקח

Verbs of giving:

1 Sam. 8:14	ויתן	ויהב t2i	ונתן
1 Sam. 8:15	ויתין	ויהב t725a	ונתן

Verbs of putting or placing (where the sense is figurative):

1 Sam. 8:1	ומני	ושוי t2i = t725a	וישם
2 Sam. 8:14	מני	שוי t7i	שם

The verbal phrase for being a king:

1 Sam. 23:17	ואת תמלוך	ואת תהי מלכא t705i	ואתה תמלך
2 Sam. 2:4	למהוי מלכא	למלכא t705i = t701i	למלך (noun, cf. Vrs.)
2 Sam. 2:7	למהוי מלכא	למלכא t705i	למלך (noun)

The Targum uses the verbal clause 'to be king' (הוי + מלכא) to translate both the simple noun (מֶלֶךְ) in the Hebrew (e.g. 1 Sam. 15:1, 11, 17, 23; 2 Sam. 2:4, 7, etc) and the verb (מָלַךְ e.g. 1 Sam. 16:1; 18:7; 1 Kgs 2:15, etc).

A few common nouns are repeatedly affected; for example, the two common means of expressing the concept of descendants:

---

8 On 2 Sam. 10:4 cf. Bacher, 'Kritische Untersuchungen zum Prophetentargum', 53.

Chapter Six. Conventional and Contextual Changes

2 Sam. 4:8	ומזרעיה	ומבנוהי t705i = t5a, t713a	ומזרעו
2 Sam. 22:51	ולזרעיה	ולבנוהי t713a (also liturgical text t133a)	לזרעו

The two common nouns corresponding to the English 'word':

2 Sam. 7:21	מימרך	פיתגמך t701i	דברך
2 Sam. 16:23	בפיתגמא	במימרא t720a = t713a	בדבר

Two synonymous terms for 'enemy':

2 Sam. 4:8	בעיל דבבך	סנאך t720a	
2 Sam. 5:20	סנאי	בעלי דבבי t705i = t713a	איבי

Numerous further individual examples can be found:

	Babylonian Tradition	**Variants**	**Hebrew**
1 Sam. 1:11	ואימסריניה	ואתניניה t7i	ונתתיו
1 Sam. 9:8	למיעני	לאתבא t720a = t713a[correct]	לענות
1 Sam. 11:4	וארימו	וזקפו t725a	וישאו
1 Sam. 12:9	פולחנא דיוי	דחלתא דיוי t232i/s	יהוה
1 Sam. 20:5	ואנא אסחרא אסחר	ואנא מיתב איתב t718i	ישב אשב
1 Sam. 24:12	חטיתי	חבית t705i = t725a	חטאתי
2 Sam. 5:17	משחו	רביאו t705i = t713a	משחו
2 Sam. 10:3	שלח	שדר t713a	שלח
2 Sam. 16:23	ביומיא האינון	בעידנא ההיא t720a = t713a	בימים ההם

All the examples given above concern the interchange of translation equivalents found elsewhere in Targum Jonathan. All are relatively common.[9] It is interesting to note that verbs are more susceptible to this form of interchange than nouns.

Another commonly occurring idiom that must be added to this current category is the formula '(those) of the house of' (דבית)' preceding a proper name, expressing a collectivity. For example, Targum Samuel frequently speaks of 'the tribe of *the house of* Benjamin (שבטא דבית בנימין)' (i.e. Tg. 1 Sam. 4:12; 9:1; 10:20, 21; 22:7; Tg. 2 Sam. 19:18; 20:1), but almost as frequently we find the shorter formula 'the tribe of Benjamin (שיבט בנימין)' (i.e. Tg. 1 Sam. 9:4, 16, 21; Tg. 2 Sam. 16:11; 19:17; 21:14). The same can be observed with other common proper names (e.g. Israel, Judah, Ephraim, etc.). In our European manuscripts we find the frequent interchange of the two formulae.

In the following examples one or more manuscript(s) adds the expression '(those) of the house of' (דבית)', where it is absent in all other witnesses:

1 Sam. 2:28	...tribes of **the house of** Israel...	t713a, t720a
1 Sam. 9:4	...tribe of **the house of** Benjamin...	t232i/s
1 Sam. 15:15	from **the house of** Amalek (Babylonian text: from the Amalekites)	t713a, t720a
1 Sam. 18:16	all Israel and those of **the house of** Judah (Babylonian text: all Israel and Judah)	t2i
2 Sam. 2:4	the men of the tribe **of the house of** Judah	t232i/s, t720a
2 Sam. 2:9	and over those **of the house of** Jezreel	t701i, t705i
2 Sam. 3:10	over Israel and over those **of the house of** Judah	t3i, t7i, t232i/s, t701i, t718i, t6a, t725a
2 Sam. 15:2	from one of (t720a + the cities of) the tribes **of the house of** Israel	t7i, t720a
2 Sam. 20:2	and the men **of the house of** Judah	t713a, t720a

In the following cases one or more manuscript(s) replaces the longer formula with the shorter, omitting the clause '(those) of the house of (דבית)'.

1 Sam. 4:12	from the tribe of Benjamin	t5a, t713a, t720a
1 Sam. 10:20	the tribe of Benjamin was seized	t705i, t713a, t720a

---

9 The relevant references can be found in de Moor, *et al* (eds), *A Bilingual Concordance to the Targum of the Prophets*.

Chapter Six. Conventional and Contextual Changes

1 Sam. 10:21	He brought the tribe of Benjamin near	t713a, t720a
1 Sam. 13:15	to the hill country of Benjamin	t713a, t720a
1 Sam. 15:7	Saul smote the Amelakites	t713a, t720a
1 Sam. 15:32	the king of Amalek	t713a, t720a
1 Sam. 22:7	sons of the tribe of Benjamin	t713a, t720a
1 Sam. 28:18	and you did not carry out his fierce wrath against Amalek	t705i, t5a
1 Sam. 30.16	from the land of Judah	t705i
2 Sam. 1.1	David returned from smiting Amalek (t725a: the Amalekites)	t7i, t725a
2 Sam. 2.9	and over Ephraim	t725a
2 Sam. 2.9	and over Benjamin	t232i/s
2 Sam. 2.31	the servants of David killed from Benjamin…	t705i, t5a, t720a
2 Sam. 3.19	even Abner spoke before Benjamin…	t2i

It it clear from the above table that manuscripts t713a, t720a, and t232i/s have been particularly susceptible to this fault.

2.a Revisions towards Hebrew Text?

The category of variants being discussed here ('Interchange of common translation equivalents') is to be distinguished from the category presented in chapter four because the lexemes concerned are near-synonyms, so that the revised text of the Targum is no 'closer' to the underlying Hebrew than the original form of the Targum. In cases of revision towards the Hebrew text, the variant reading of the Targum replicates either in form or sense the underlying Hebrew more closely than the original text of the Targum had done. The reality by which these two groups of variants came about is, of course, likely to have been blurred and in some cases it is difficult to choose between the two categories.

For example, the swapping of the deferent 'before him' for the literal translation 'in his eyes' appears *prima facie* to be an attempt to reflect more closely the wording of the Hebrew:

2 Sam. 11:27

| Babylonian Tradition | Variant | Hebrew |
| and bad was the thing that David did before the Lord (קדם יוי). | …that he did in the eyes of the Lord (בעיני יוי).
t705i (NB. 'David' is omitted, perhaps by accident). | בעיני יהוה |

A further example is the following, but here the witnesses to the Babylonian textual tradition diverge:

1 Sam. 3:18

Babylonian tradition	Variant	Hebrew
He will do that which is proper before him (דתקין קדמוהי) t2521b	He will do that which is right in his eyes (דתקין בעינוהי) t707b = t2i, t705i	Qere: הטוב בעיניו בעיניו

Manuscript t2521b is of superior quality to t707b.[10]

These instances, however, must be compared to other examples of the interchange of the two terms that show the reverse trend:

	Babylonian Tradition	Variants	Hebrew
1 Sam. 1:18	בעינך	קדמך t720a = t713a, t6a[PM]	בעיניך
1 Sam. 16:22	בעיני	קדמי t6a = t713a, t720a	בעיני
1 Sam. 29:9	בעיני	קדמי t701i = t705i	בעיני
2 Sam. 13:5	לעיני	קדמי t720a	לעיני
2 Sam. 13:6	לעיני	קדמי t2i = t720a, t725a	לעיני

One might also compare the following case, in which the scribe of t709b first writes 'in his eyes' as the scribe of t725a has done (both under the influence of the Hebrew) before correcting his error interlinear with 'before him':

2 Sam. 10:12

Babylonian Tradition	Variant	Hebrew
and the Lord will do that which is proper before him (קדמוהי) t709b[correct]	and the Lord will do that which is proper in his eyes (בעינוהי) t709b[PM] = t725a	בעיניו

The same difficulty applies to the interchange of the Aramaic adjectives תקן 'proper' (or 'right, correct') and טב 'good' for the Hebrew טוב, which has a relatively broad semantic range that would permit either translation.

---

10   Martínez Borobio, *Targum Jonatan de los Profetas Primeros en tradición babilónica*, Vol. 2, *I–II Samuel*, 25–6.

Chapter Six. Conventional and Contextual Changes

	Babylonian Tradition	**Variants**	**Hebrew**
1 Sam. 29:6	לא תקין את	לא טב את t2i = t725a	לא טוב אתה
2 Sam. 15:3	פתגמך תקנין	פתגמך טבין t2i	דברך טובים (v. many mss read דבריך)
2 Sam. 17:14	מלכא דאחיתפל תקנא	מלכא דאחיתפל טבתא t2i = t701i	צת אחיתפל הטובה

In this example, the variant in 1 Sam. 29:6, which occurs only in t725a and t2i, may be an attempt to harmonise with the occurrence of the same wording earlier in the verse, which in the Ashkenazi and Mixed Western tradition is טב.

Certain prepositions are prone to the same difficulty. For example:

	Babylonian Tradition	**Variants**	**Hebrew**
1 Sam. 19:23	ואזל לתמן	ואזל תמן t2i = t3i, t232i/s, t7i, t718i, t6a, t713a, t720a, (Sperber: t12sc, t703s, t706s)	וילך שם
2 Sam 2:2	וסליק לתמן דויד	וסליק תמן דויד t2i = t705i, t5a, t720a (cf. t232i/s (וסליק תמן לתמן דויד) (Sperber: t10r, t734s, t716y)	ויעל שם דוד

The Hebrew שם 'there' is translated in Targum Jonathan with both תמן (cf. 1 Sam. 1:3, 22, 28; 2:14; 3:3; 4:4; etc) and לתמן (cf. 1 Sam. 1 Sam. 9:6; 10:5, 10; 19:23; 20:6; 22.3; 2 Sam. 2:2; 23:9). Variations in prepositions in fact occur extremely frequently throughout the European manuscripts, most apparently completely at random (see §4), making it impossible to classify cases such as these with any degree of certainty.

Although somewhat different in nature, the following example is apparently a 'correction' of the Targum text based on the expected translation equivalents:

2 Sam. 7:23

Babylonian Tradition	**Variant**	**Hebrew**
...whom you redeemed for yourself from Egypt — [from among the] nations (גוים) — and its gods.	...whom you redeemed for yourself from Egypt — [from among the] nations (עממין) — and its gods (t713a: 'and their judges' (ודייניהון). t3i = t7i, t718i, t6a, t713a	...whom you redeemed for yourself from Egypt — [from among the] nations (גוים) — and its gods.

The Transmission of Targum Jonathan in the West

The normal translation of the Hebrew גוים in Targum Jonathan is עממין (or determined: עממיא). Only here in Targum Jonathan is גוים used, so it may have originated as an accidental Hebraism. If this were the case, the Hebraism occurred earlier enough in the Targum's transmission for it now to be the reading of the majority of textual witnesses. A handful of European manuscripts (i.e. t6a, t713a, t3i, t7i t718i) 'correct' the text by introducing the expected term.

Uncertain Cases

A few additional cases probably also belong to this category, but the translation equivalents are too infrequent for the results to be incontestable:

1 Sam. 19:24

Babylonian Tradition	Variant	Hebrew
and even he **praised** (ושבח) before Samuel.	and even he **acted insanely** (ואישתטי) before Samuel. t3i	and even he **prophesied** (ויתנבא) before Samuel.

The verbal root שטי is employed only three times in Targum Jonathan as a translation of the Hebrew verbal root נבא 'to prophesy' (i.e. Tg. 1 Sam. 18:10; Tg. 1 Kgs 18:29; Tg. Ezek. 13:2). Slightly more frequently it chooses the root שבח 'to praise' (i.e. Tg. 1 Sam. 10:5, 6, 10, 11, 13; 19:20, 21, 23, 24). It is possible that the text of t3i has been affected by the similar wording in Targum 1 Sam. 18:10 or 21:16.

1 Sam. 21:12

Babylonian Tradition	Variant	Hebrew
Do they not **make themselves heard** (משמעין) about this one (לדין) with musical instruments…?	Do they not **praise** (משבחין) this one (לדין) with musical instruments…? t3i = t6a, t725a (≈ t713a, t720a הוו משבחין)	Do they not **sing** (יענו) about this one (לזה) in the dances…?

The Hebrew verbal root ענה has several meanings, but of those cases where it has the sense 'to sing', Targum Jonathan twice translates with the root שבח 'to praise' (i.e. Tg. 1 Sam. 18:7; Tg. Isa. 27:2 Cf. Tg. Onq. Num. 21:17) and twice with the root שמע 'to hear' (i.e. Tg. 1 Sam. 21:12; 29:5).

Chapter Six. Conventional and Contextual Changes

2 Sam. 4:11

Babylonian Tradition	Variant	Hebrew
על שיוייה	על משכביה	על משכבו
	t725a = t713a (under the influence of 2 Sam. 4:7?)	

The noun שויא 'bed' renders the Hebrew משכב 'bed' in 2 Sam. 4:11; 11:2, 13; 13:5; and 1 Kgs 1:47. By contrast, in Judg. 21:11–12; 2 Sam. 4:7; 2 Kgs 6:12; Isa. 57:8; and Ezek. 32:25, Targum Jonathan prefers the Aramaic cognate משכבא.

2 Sam. 6:18

Babylonian Tradition	Variant	Hebrew
David ceased (ושיצי) offering the burnt offering and sacrifice…	David ceased (ופסק) offering… t2i	ויכל

The Aramaic verb שיצי 'to finish' is the common choice for translating the Hebrew כלה (Tg. Josh. 8:24; 10:20; 19:49, 51; 24:20; Tg. Judg. 3:18; 15:17; Tg. 1 Sam. 3:12; 13:10; 15:18; 18:1; 24:17; Tg. 2 Sam. 6:18; 11:19; 13:36; 21:5; 22:39; Tg. 1 Kgs 3:1; 7:40; 8:54; 9:1; 22:11; Tg. 2 Kgs 10:25; 13:17; Tg. Isa. 1:28; 10:18; 16:4; 29:20; 31:3; 49:4; Tg. Jer. 5:3; 9:15; 10:25; 14:12; 26:8; 43:1; 44:27; 49:37; 51:63; Tg. Ezek. 5:12; 13:14; 20:13; 22:31; 42:15; 43:23; Tg. Hos. 11:6; Tg. Amos 7:2; Tg. Zech. 5:4). Nonetheless, Targum Jonathan opts to translate the Hebrew root כלה with the alternative verb, פסק 'to cease' on two occasions (Tg. 1 Sam. 10:13; Tg. Mal. 3:6). In this case, manuscript t2i appears to have accidentally replaced the more common translation equivalent with a less commonly occurring one.

2.b. Summary

Since the vast majority of the cases given above concerns the interchange of common alternative translation equivalents for a given Hebrew word one can conclude that the copyist still had the Hebrew text in mind when he copied the Aramaic (in most of our manuscripts he would have copied the verse in Hebrew immediately before copying it in Aramaic) and that this has exerted an influence on his word choice in Aramaic. In other words, the copyist reads נתן in the Hebrew and has in mind that this is translated with יהב (as it frequently is), so he writes יהב in place of the expected נתן. Since none of the manuscripts shows a clear pattern of adjustment of the text, which might suggest a deliberate process of standardisation, these interchanges of vocabulary can be considered to have occurred accidentally and haphazardly. It is simply the frequency with which the wording occurs that causes the scribe to err.

Indeed, it is not merely the Western texts that are blighted by this phenomenon. We can point to a few examples where t710y, a Yemenite text of good quality, almost certainly contains the secondary reading, whereas the Western manuscript preserves the original reading (supported by the Babylonian textual tradition):

	t710y	Variants	Hebrew
1 Sam. 25.38	ומחא יוי	ותבר יוי t707b = A + MW	ויגף יהוה
2 Sam. 2:24	אתו	מטו t707b = A + MW (t6a[PM] מטו אתו a combined reading)	באו
2 Sam. 17:19	מדעם	פיתגמא t724b, t2523b = A + MW	הדבר

Interchanged of Common Wording Unconnected to Wording of the Hebrew Text.

Although the evidence presented above suggests that the copyist had the Hebrew word in mind, we cannot be certain that this is, in fact, what has occurred in every case. Take, for example, the interchange of the two common Aramaic translation equivalents for the Hebrew איש, namely גבר and אנש, both meaning 'man' (pages 195–6). We can, in fact, find cases in sections of Targumic addition where one of these two nouns is swapped for another, for example:

	Babylonian Tradition	**Variant**
1 Sam. 15.23	אינש דבצר	גבר דבצר t725a

Since this is an addition, rather than a direct translation of the Hebrew, we can eliminate the possibility that the Hebrew wording has influenced the copyist. In this case, similar wording earlier in the verse explains the change.

Another good example of this phenomenon concerns the language of warfare to which I drew attention earlier (pages 184–6). The combination 'to fight' גוח (in *aphel,* often the infinitive) plus קרב 'battle' and 'to make' עבד (often participle: 'those making...') plus קרב 'battle' are both extremely

Chapter Six. Conventional and Contextual Changes

common (in Tg. Sam.: Tg. 1 Sam. 4:2; 14:23, 52; 16:18; 17:20 etc), with the result that the two terms are sometimes interchanged in Western manuscripts. At 1 Sam. 18:5 the Babylonian tradition reads 'and Saul appointed him over the men making battles (גברי עבדי קרבא)...' whereas manuscript t3i offers us '...the men fighting battles (גברי מגיחי קרבא)...' The underlying Hebrew is simply 'the men of war (אנשי המלחמה)'. In the same chapter (verse 17) we find the reverse: t710y[11] reads 'and fight (ואגיח) the battles of the people of the Lord!' Whereas t5a has 'and make (עבד) the battles of the people of the Lord!' (possibly under the influence of the preceding expression, עביד קרבין). The underlying Hebrew is והלחם. A final example in 2 Sam. 22:35, i.e. David's song of deliverance, may show the influence of the liturgical text form: the Babylonian textual tradition reads 'to make (למעבד) war...', whereas t6a, t720a, t7i and t232i/s have 'to wage (לאגחא) war...', the reading of several liturgical manuscripts (i.e t1601i, t1679i, t1647i, t1618i, t1621i, page 328), though the influence of conventional phraseology can hardly be ruled out.

Occasionally one finds an example in which an idiomatic expression has overridden the existing translation. For example, at 2 Sam. 9:6 the Babylonian textual tradition reads 'and he fell upon his face and worshipped (ונפל על אפוהי וסגיד)', a direct translation of the underlying Hebrew (ויפל על פניו וישתחו). Manuscript t713a, however, reads 'and he fell down upon his face *upon the ground* (על ארעא)'. The copyist allows a familiar idiom (e.g. 1 Sam. 17:49; 20:41; 2 Sam. 14:4, 22) to override the correct wording of the text.

Similarly in 2 Sam. 15:14 manuscript t720a replaces 'David said' (ואמר דויד), the direct translation of the Hebrew (ויאמר דוד), with 'the king said (ואמר מלכא)', for the simple reason that the expression 'the king said' is extremely common, particularly at the start of a verse (e.g. 1 Sam. 17:56; 22:16–18; 2 Sam. 3:38; 7:2; 9:3 etc.). Likewise, in 1 Sam. 14:48 the formula 'from the hand of...' has caused the scribe of t725a (or his *Vorlage*) to write 'and saved Israel from the hand of *their enemies* (מיד בעלי דבביהון)', where the Babylonian tradition has 'from the hand of those despoiling them (מיד בזזיהון)', a faithful rendering of the Hebrew (מיד שסהו; the pronominal suffix being accommodated to reflect the implied collective subject of the Hebrew). The Hebrew verbal root שסה is nowhere else translated with בעיל דבבא in Targum Jonathan.

---

11 The Babylonian textual tradition lacks this verse with the exception of two words preserved in t2506b.

The Transmission of Targum Jonathan in the West

3. Contextual Renderings

3.a. Interchange of Vocabulary

The phenomenon of frequently occurring wording leaching into other parts of the text also has its localised form. In some cases one suspects that the use of a particular translation equivalent has caused the scribe to employ that same translation equivalent for other occurrences of the same Hebrew word (cf. §2) in the immediate context. In these cases one might say that there is a localised harmonisation within the Targum. Consider the following examples:

1 Sam. 20.2

Babylonian Tradition	Variant	Hebrew
Why would my father **conceal** (ומדין כסי) from me this thing?	Why would my father **hide** (ומא דין יטמיר) from me this thing? t713a = t720a	Why would my father **conceal** (ומדוע יסתיר) from me this thing?

The two Aramaic verbs (כסי, טמר) are more or less synonymous ('to hide, conceal'). However, the Hebrew root סתר 'to hide, conceal' is translated with the Aramaic verb כסי only here in Targum Jonathan. By contrast, the translation of סתר with the verb טמר is common throughout Targum Jonathan, but occurs in particular three times in the same chapter as the example just given (i.e. Tg. 1 Sam. 20:5, 19, 24 cf. 23:19; 26:1).

2 Sam. 24:16

Babylonian Tradition	Variant	Hebrew
he said to the angel that was **destroying** (דימחביל) among the people...	...that was **killing** (דמקטיל)... t5a = t701i	...to the **destroying** angel (למלאך המשחית)

Although the Aramaic verbs חבל and קטל both translate the Hebrew שחת in Targum Jonathan, the wording of manuscripts t5a and t701i is in fact taken over from the following verse, where the murderous angel is mentioned again. The Babylonian tradition follows the Hebrew in distinguishing between the two references: in verse 16 the angel is 'destroying' (מחדיל), for the Hebrew למלאך המשחית; while in verse 17 it is 'killing' (מקטיל), reflecting the Hebrew המלאך המכה.

In other cases the interchange of vocabulary is unrelated to the translation equivalents employed elsewhere in Targum Jonathan: language in one verse of the Targum has simply been repeated (or rehashed) in another verse. For example:

Chapter Six. Conventional and Contextual Changes

1 Sam. 18:20

Babylonian Tradition	Variant	Hebrew
...and the matter was **fitting** in his eyes (וכשר פתגמא בעינוהי).	...and the matter was **beautiful** in his eyes (ושפר פתגמא בעינוהי). t705i	...and the matter was **correct** in his eyes (ויישר הדבר בעיניו).

The switch of wording in t705i may have occurred under the influence of 1 Sam. 18:5, where a similar expression occurs, i.e. 'and it was beautiful in the eyes of all the people (ושפר בעיני כל עמא)'. The Aramaic root שפר, whether in verbal, nominal, or adjectival form, never corresponds to the Hebrew root ישר in Targum Jonathan.

1 Sam. 25:9

Babylonian Tradition	Variant	Hebrew
David's **lads** (עולימי דוד) came and spoke with Nabal...	David's **servants** (עבדי דוד) came and spoke with Nabal... t3i	David's lads (נערי דוד) came and spoke with Nabal...

The equivalence עבד for Hebrew נער is otherwise unknown in Targum Jonathan. The wording has simply been taken over from the following verse.

1 Sam. 26:25

Babylonian Tradition	Variant	Hebrew
and Saul returned to his **place** (ושאול תב לאתריה)...	and Saul turned back to his **way** (ושאול תב לאורחיה)... t5a	and Saul returned to his **place** (ושאול שב למקומו)

This phrase is immediately preceded by the words 'and David went on his way (לאורחיה)'. The wording in t5a is simply a repetition.

1 Sam. 29:9

Babylonian Tradition	Variant	Hebrew
...but the **leaders** of the Philistines (רברבי פלשתאי) said, 'He shall not go up with us in battle.'	...but the **rulers** of the Philistines (טורני פלשתאי) said, 'He shall not go up with us in battle.' t701i	...but the **leaders** of the Philistines (שרי פלשתים) said, 'He shall not go up with us in battle.'

The Hebrew שר 'leader, official' is never translated טרון 'tyrant, ruler' in Targum Jonathan. Manuscript t701i has simply taken over the wording of 1 Sam. 29:7.

The Transmission of Targum Jonathan in the West

2 Sam. 19:25

Babylonian Tradition	Variant	Hebrew
and he did not **wash white** (חור) his garments…	and he did not **wash** (שטף) his garments… t713a = t720a	and he did not **wash** (כבס) his garments…

Although the Aramaic verb חור 'to whiten, wash' is rare (for Hebrew כבס otherwise only Tg. Mal. 3:2 and variant to Tg. Jer. 4:14), the Aramaic שטף is used for Hebrew כבס 'to wash' nowhere else in Targum Jonathan. It does, however, appear eight words earlier on in the current verse, where it is applied to the washing of the feet (for Hebrew עשה רגליו), and from where manuscripts t713a and t720a have evidently taken it over.

Although not an interchange of vocabulary, we find a contextual harmonisation in the following case. The person has been adapted (from second plural to first plural) in order to avoid an abrupt change in person mid-verse:

2 Sam. 19:11

Babylonian Tradition	Variant	Hebrew
למא אתון שתקין why are **you** keeping quiet… = MT	למא אנחנא שתקין why are **we** keeping quiet… t5a, t725a, t232i/s, t718i (Sperber: t711y i.e. base text)	למה אתם מחרשים why are **you** keeping quiet…

The text as we find it in the Masoretic Text reads 'But Absalom, whom we anointed over us, has died in battle. Now why do you sit idle instead of escorting (JPS, אתם מחרשים להשיב) the king back?' The evident incongruity (i.e. whom are the rebellious Israelites addressing?) is resolved in several of the European manuscripts.

3.b. Additions

In addition to the interchange of vocabulary, we can identify numerous examples in which a copyist has imported additional wording from the nearby context. It is clear that some cases are the result of scribal error. For example:

1 Sam. 20:24

Babylonian Tradition	Variant	Hebrew
So David hid in the field and it was the New Moon (והוה ירחא)…	So David hid in the field and it was **the intercalation** of the month (והוה עיבור ירחא)… t705i (≈ t701i והא עיבור)	So David hid in the field and it was the New Moon (ויהי החדש)…

210

Chapter Six. Conventional and Contextual Changes

The reference to the intercalation of the New Moon in 1 Sam. 20:27, 34 (the only two occurrences of the word in Samuel cf. Tg. Amos 8:5; variant to Tg. 1 Kgs 4:19) shows that this variant in t705i and t701i is an error, because in verses 27 and 34 the intercalation occurs on the day following the events being described in verse 24.

Indeed, one suspects that the majority of cases of this type are the result of scribal sloppiness, yet one cannot exclude altogether the possibility that we are dealing with a deliberate process of internal harmonisation. Some further examples:

1 Sam. 2:4

Babylonian tradition	Variant	Hebrew
...mighty deeds will be done for them (יתעבדן להון גבורן)	...**miracles and** mighty deeds will be done for them (יתעבדן להון ניסין וגבורן) t5a^{correct} (t5a^{PM}: יתעבדון)	≈ those who stumble gird on strength

This additional wording is taken over directly from Targum 1 Sam. 2:1.

1 Sam. 2:16

Babylonian tradition	Variant	Hebrew
Wait until the fat pieces have been taken up (דייתסקון תרביא) then take for yourself whatever you want.	Wait until the fat pieces have been taken up **to the altar** (דיתסקון תרביא למדבחא) then take for yourself whatever you want. t725a = t5a^{correct}, t6a, t713a, t720a	Let them first turn the fat to smoke (קטר יקטירון כיום החלב) then take for yourself whatever you want.

The additional wording is taken over from the preceding verse.

1 Sam. 2:32

Babylonian tradition	Variant	Hebrew
...you will see the trouble that will come upon the men of your house on account of sins that you have sinned in my Temple (דחבתון בבית מקדשי)...	...on account of sins that you have sinned **before me** in my Temple (דחבתון קדמי בבית מקדשי) t6a = t713a, t720a	[none]

The addition 'before me' is repeated several times in the preceding verses (e.g. 1 Sam. 2:28, 29, 30), including before the expression 'in my Temple' (בבית מקדשי; 1 Sam. 2:29).

The Transmission of Targum Jonathan in the West

1 Sam. 9:5

Babylonian Tradition	Variant	Hebrew
They came into the land in which there was a prophet (נבייא) and Saul said...	They came into the land in which there was a prophet **of the Lord** (נבייא דיוי) and Saul said... t5a	They came into the land of Zuph (צוּף) and Saul said...

The Targum exegesis is derived from צוף, either by connecting it to the Hebrew צפה or its Aramaic cognate צפי 'to look out' (perhaps even 'foresee'). The addition in manuscript t5a harmonises the reference to the prophet with that of Targum 1 Sam. 9:6, 7, 8, 10, where the prophet is referred to as 'the prophet of the Lord'. (cf. also Tg. 1 Sam. 2:27).

1 Sam. 15:7

Babylonian Tradition	Variant	Hebrew
Saul smote those of the house Amalek (ית דבית עמלק)...	Saul smote **the city of** the house of Amalek (ית קרתא דבית עמל)... t725a	Saul smote the Amalekites (את עמלק)...

This addition harmonises with the description of 1 Sam. 15:5 ('Saul came to the city of the house of Amalek...').

1 Sam. 15:14

Babylonian Tradition	Variant	Hebrew
Samuel said, If you have fulfilled [your promise] (קיימתא) then what is this sound of sheep in my ears...	Samuel said, If you have fulfilled **the word of the Lord** (קיימתא פיתגמא דיוי) then what is this sound of sheep in my ears... t713a = t720a	Samuel said, Then what is this sound of sheep in my ears...?

The additional wording in t713a and t720a is taken over directly from the end of the preceding verse ('I have fulfilled the word of the Lord!').

1 Sam. 23:2

Babylonian Tradition	Variant	Hebrew
Go and you shall kill the Philistines and you will deliver Keilah (ותפרוק ית קעילה)!	...and you will deliver **the inhabitants of** Keilah (ותיפרוק יתבי קעילה)! t705i = t5a ...and you will save **the inhabitants of** Keilah (ותשיזיב ית יתבי קעילה)! t2i	Go and you shall strike the Philistines and you will save Keilah (והושעת את קעילה)!

Chapter Six. Conventional and Contextual Changes

As the action unfolds, we are told that David delivered the inhabitants of Keilah (ופרק דוד ית יתבי קעילה Tg. 1 Sam. 23:5 cf. 23:11, 12). Three European manuscripts harmonise the words of the Divine command (1 Sam. 23:2) with the outcome (on the choice of verb, cf. below page 336).

1 Sam. 23:7

Babylonian Tradition	Variant	Hebrew
It was told to Saul that David had come to Keilah (אתא דוד לקעילה) and Saul said…	It was told to Saul that David had come to Keilah **and waged war** (אתא דוד לקעילה **ואגיח קרבא**) and Saul said… t3i	It was told to Saul that David had come to Keilah (בא דוד קעילה) and Saul said…

The additional wording in t3i is taken over from Targum 1 Sam. 23:5 ('David and his men went to Keilah and waged war…').

2 Sam. 7:7

Babylonian Tradition	Variant	Hebrew
In every place where I have gone (דהליכית) with all the sons of Israel…	In every place where I have **caused my Shekinah to dwell** (דאשריתי שכינתי) with all the sons of Israel… t713a	In every [place] where I have gone about (התהלכתי) with all the sons of Israel…

This additional wording is taken over from the preceding two verses ('Will you build before me a house in which my Shekinah may dwell? Because I have not caused my Shekinah to dwell in a house… but my Shekinah was dwelling in tents…' Tg. 2 Sam. 7:7).

2 Sam. 24:24

Babylonian Tradition	Variant	Hebrew
I will not offer up before the Lord my God free burnt offerings (עלוון מגן)…	…burnt offerings **and sacrifice** (עלוון וניכסת מגן)… t5a	I will not offer up before the Lord my God free burnt offerings (עלות חנם)…

The wording is taken over directly from the following verse ('and he offered burnt offerings and holy sacrifices' Tg. 1 Sam. 24:25).

In a few isolated cases, wording appears to have been adopted from another point removed from the immediate narrative context in which the change occurs. For example, in one case the wording adopted in manuscript t701i appears five chapters earlier on, yet the variation is otherwise difficult to explain unless we assume that the scribe has recalled wording from earlier in the Targum:

The Transmission of Targum Jonathan in the West

1 Sam. 15:26

Babylonian Tradition	Variant	Hebrew
I will not return with you because you have rejected the word of the Lord (קצתא בפיתגמא דיוי)...	I will not return with you because you have rejected the **worship** of the Lord (קצתא בפולחנא דיוי)... t701i	I will not return with you because you have rejected the word of the Lord (מאסתה את דבר יהוה)...

The idea of rejecting the worship of the Lord (i.e. קוץ + פלחן) is rare in Targum Jonathan, so this is not a conventional rendering in the normal sense. The expression appears earlier in Targum Samuel however, in Targum 1 Sam. 10:19 (then again only Tg. Zech. 11:8 cf. Tg. 1 Sam. 8:7), and the two passages are thematically linked: the people's rejection of the Lord in favour of a king (1 Sam. 10:19), and Saul's rejection of the Lord's command (1 Sam. 15:26). It seems the scribe of manuscript t701i (or his *Vorlage*) has allowed the first passage to influence the wording of the second.

Equally, in one case found in manuscripts t6a[PM], t713a, and t720a the wording may have been adopted from 12 chapters earlier in the text.

1 Sam. 24:7

Babylonian Tradition	Variant	Hebrew
Far be it from me from before the Lord (חס לי מן ק' יוי) if I should do this thing...	Far be it for me **to sin** before the Lord (חס לי מלמחטי קדם יוי) if I should do this thing... t720a = t6a[PM], t713a	Far be it for me from the Lord (חלילה לי מיהוה) if I should do this thing...

The reading in t6a[PM], t713a, and t720a is probably a small clarifying gloss, but it is difficult to escape the impression that in the wording of 1 Sam. 12:23, where the Hebrew has 'far be it for me *to sin* against the Lord (חלילה לי מחטא ליהוה)', a reading replicated in the Targum (חס לי מלמחטי קדם יוי) has been adopted to clarify the Hebrew.

4. Random Variations

Before I proceed to an analysis of the more interesting and substantive variants in the next chapter, I want to make some brief comments on the vast number of minor and irrelevant variations that are evidently the consequence of the carelessness with which the Targum has been transmitted in Europe. We do not need to dwell on these at length, but it will be useful to note some general

Chapter Six. Conventional and Contextual Changes

categories because they demonstrate the fluidity of the text in its European transmission. None of the manuscripts reveals a pattern in any of these categories, indicating the entirely random and accidental nature of such variations.

The Western manuscripts are replete with **variants in the conjugation of verbs** *via à vis* the Babylonian text tradition. Frequently the variation is a possible alternative reading of the vocalised Hebrew text, for example by treating a *waw* preceding a perfect as *conversive* instead of *conjunctive waw* (e.g. 1 Sam. 3:13 Babylonian tradition והויתי; t6a, t713a, t720a, t232i/s ואיחוי; MT וְהִגַּדְתִּי), or adopting an alternative vocalisation of the same Hebrew consonants (e.g. 1 Sam. 5:11 Babylonian tradition וכנשו = MT וַיַּאַסְפוּ *qal*, t5a ואכנישו = Hebr. וַיַּאַסְפוּ *hifil*; 1 Sam. 28:1 Babylonian tradition וכנשו = MT וַיִּקָּבְצוּ *qal*; t705i ואיתכנישו = Hebr. וַיִּקָּבְצוּ? *hifil*). Other cases concern an accommodation of the verbal conjugation to the form of the Hebrew text (e.g. 2 Sam. 15:30 Babylonian tradition וסלקין, t725a, t2i וסליקו, MT ועלו) or in order to improve the narrative flow (e.g. 1 Sam. 8:10 Babylonian tradition דשאלין = MT השאלים, t713a, t720a, t725a, t2i דשאילו; 1 Sam. 30:11 Babylonian tradition ויהבו ליה לחמא ואכל 'they gave him bread and he ate' = MT ויתנו לו לחם ויאכל; t705i למיכל 'to eat').

Equally, we find numerous examples where one or more European manuscript(s) introduces a lexeme that rarely or never translates the underlying Hebrew in places where the Babylonian textual tradition uses a commonly occurring equivalent (e.g. 1 Sam. 15:12 Babylonian tradition ונחת, t7i ונפק, MT וירד; 1 Sam. 18:2 Babylonian tradition למתב, t705i למיזל, MT לשוב; 1 Sam. 23:2 Babylonian tradition ותפרוק, t725a, t2i ותשיזיב, MT והושעת; 2 Sam. 19:27 Babylonian tradition מלכא, t713a, t720a רבוני, MT המלך cf. start of verse). Such cases are legion in the European manuscripts. The majority must be considered as the result of scribal carelessness, though some might be accounted for in other ways (e.g. as reflecting faulty Hebrew manuscripts); it is impossible to be certain.

Other minor parts of speech are extremely susceptible to random variations. **Prepositions**, for example, are particularly fluid. The prefixed -ל and the independent form לות are switched very often (e.g. 1 Sam. 2:34 Babylonian tradition לות, t725a, t232i/s, t701i ל-, MT אל; 1 Sam. 4:14 Babylonian tradition לעלי, t5a לות עלי, MT לעלי), but all prepositions are affected. Even non-synonymous prepositions are frequently interchanged (e.g. 1 Sam. 14:33 Babylonian tradition לותי, t713a, t720a קדמי, MT אלי; 2 Sam. 7:20

215

Babylonian tradition קדמך, t725a, t2i עמך, MT אליך). Such variation is found equally in sections of Targumic addition, confirming that the variations are random and accidental (e.g. 1 Sam. 5:12 Babylonian tradition לצית שמיא, t720a לשמיא; 1 Sam. 17:33 Babylonian tradition למיזל על פלשתאה, t5a, t6a, t713a, t720a, t725a, t2i, t3i, t7i, t232i/s, t701i, t718i למיזל עם פלישתאה).

Similarly, the **definite object marker** is added and omitted with great frequency. There is a slight tendency in the European manuscripts to add the direct object marker where the Babylonian textual tradition follows the Hebrew by leaving the direct object unmarked (e.g. 1 Sam. 28:3 Babylonian tradition הסיר האבות ואת הידענים MT, פלי ית בידין וית זכורו, t5a, t2i פלי בידין וזכורו; 2 Sam. 2:6 Babylonian tradition דעבדתון פיתגמא הדין, t713a, t720a, t705i דעבדתון ית פיתגמא הדין, MT עשיתם הדבר הזה)[12], representing a minor grammatical improvement. Occasionally, and quite coincidentally, the resulting form agrees with variant Hebrew manuscripts (e.g. 1 Sam. 17:36 Babylonian tradition אף דובא, t6a[PM], t720a, t725a[PM], t7i, t232i/s אף ית דובא see further chapter five). The opposite tendency, that is to say the omission of the definite object marker where it is required, is also found (e.g. 1 Sam. 2:5 Babylonian tradition ואיתינשיו ית מיסכינותהון, t720a, t701i, t718i omit ית; 1 Sam. 30:7 Babylonian tradition וקריב אביתר איפודא, t718i וקריב אביתר ית איפודא).

We have noted elsewhere that כל 'all' is often added in idiomatic formulations (see examples 2 Sam. 18:19; 24:22 pages 189–90). One finds additional cases where its addition cannot be explained (e.g. 1 Sam. 18:27 Babylonian tradition הוא וגברוהי, t725a הוא וכל גברוהי)[13].

Conclusions

From the preceding analysis it will be clear that conventions of Targum Jonathan's language have affected the wording of the text as it has been transmitted in Europe. A sort of linguistic osmosis has occurred, by which more frequently-occurring phraseology diffuses into other parts of the text. This process takes the form of small additions to the original wording in order to 'complete' an idiom, or the substitution of one (or more) lexeme(s) for

---

12 Note the Masorah Parva: יא חס את (i.e. one of 11 cases of this phrase lacking the definite object marker).

13 The conventional expression is in fact הוא וגברוהי e.g. 1 Sam. 27:3; 29:11; 30:31.

another. Generally speaking this change is caused by one of two factors: either by wording that is common throughout Targum Jonathan (and/or Onqelos) or by similar language or phraseology in the surrounding literary context.

The tendency to introduce conventional phraseology can be found in all the manuscripts but it is much more clearly evident in some than in others. Additions, whether under the influence of commonly occurring wording or the immediate context, are fairly common in t2i, t232i/s, t705i, t5a, t6a, t713a, and t720a. Manuscripts t713a and t720a were particularly prone to add or omit the phrase 'the house of...' The scribes of both manuscripts were relatively careless, so we might conclude that these variations are a product of the copyists' sloppiness. Yet both manuscripts also contain a good number of what we might call 'exegetical' variants, as we will see in the next chapter, so many of these 'conventional' variants may be taken over from their *Vorlagen*. After all, these 'conventional' variants are not erroneous forms and require a certain familiarity with Targum Jonathan, which means that the scribe who introduced them must have had at least a reasonable understanding of the text and its language. Likewise, this probably explains why we find so few examples in t718i and t3i, the scribes of which clearly had a very limited grasp of Aramaic. Equally, the interchange of very common vocabulary — clearly the variant requiring the least competence — is found throughout the manuscripts.

Very few of the variants are shared by all of the manuscripts in either of our two groups (i.e. Ashkenazi and Mixed Western).[14] Closely-related manuscripts (e.g. t713a and t720a; t705i and t701i) share many of the variant readings of course. Some readings are shared by multiple manuscripts within one group (e.g. 2 Sam. 18:19 t5a, t713a, t720a, page 190), or by manuscripts originating from a single socio-geographical area, for example the variant at 1 Sam. 17:43 is found in manuscripts t7i, t6a, t713a, and t720a (page 192), all of which are of Ashkenazi provenance, while the variant to 2 Sam. 1:25 (page 185) is found in t232i/s and several other manuscripts of Sephardi provenance (yet another reason to be suspicious of its inclusion in the Mixed Western group). Others are found across multiple textual groups (e.g. the plus 'those who disregard his Memra' 1 Sam. 2:8; page 191).

Broadly speaking there does seem to be a reflection of the socio-geographic divisions between Jewish communities in the period in which our

---

14 In line with van Staalduine-Sulman's assessment, see page 48.

manuscripts were produced. Some readings that bridge these divides (which were in any case rather porous) may go back to a very early stage in the text's transmission in the West. But, given their nature, many of these variants could well have arisen independently. I will return to the question of textual groupings in the concluding chapter.

Chapter Seven

Exegetical Variants, Clarifications, and the Influence of Liturgical Texts

1. Enriching of the Text

Although few in number, there are nonetheless several examples among the Mixed Western manuscripts in which the text has been changed in order to add a further nuance or thought to the material. This is typically achieved by addition rather than substitution. Of these, only a tiny handful can be considered genuinely interpretative. One such example is the transformation of 'Rome' into '*sinful* Rome', which can be found in diverse European manuscripts.

1 Sam. 2.5

MT	[no Hebrew text]
Babylonian tradition	כין ירושלם דהות כאיתא עקרא עתידא דתיתמלי מעם גלותהא ורמי דמליא סגי עממיא יסופן משיריתהא תיצדי ותחרוב
	Thus Jerusalem, which is like a barren woman, will be filled by the people of her Exile, and Rome, which is full of many peoples, her armies will come to an end, she will be desolate and laid waste.
t705i^{correct} = t5a, t6a^{correct}, t720a	...ורומי **חייבתא** דהות מליא סגי עממיא...
	...and **sinful** Rome, which is full of many peoples...
t3i = t725a (Sperber: t734s)	...ורומי **חייבתא** דמליא סגי עממיא...
	...and **sinful** Rome, which [is] full of many peoples...

The role of Rome as the archetypal enemy of Israel's past and their eschatological foe is widespread in rabbinic literature. Frequently concealed behind ciphers such as 'sinful kingdom' (מלכות חייבת), 'Esau',[1] or 'Edom', Rome was one of a sequence of superpowers,[2] the more recent counterpart of Babylon,[3] whose kingdom would come to an end in the eschatological age when the House of David would be restored.[4] Works such as the

---

1 The Tosefta Targum to Isa. 49:25 speaks of 'Esau' and 'Ishmael', apparently referring to the Christian West and the Islamic East; R. Kasher, 'Eschatological Ideas in the Tosefta Targums to the Prophets', *Journal of the Aramaic Bible* 2 (2000), 25–59, pp., 45–7, cf. 55, 58–9.
2 E.g. b. Pesaḥ. 119a; Tg. Hab. 3.17; cf. Rashi on Daniel, 11:21–2
3 See Esth. Rab. 4, פתח שמואל.
4 E.g. b. Pesaḥ 54b; b.Sanh. 97b–98b; Gen. Rab. 2.3.

pseudepigraphical Book of Zerubbabel, written in Palestine shortly before the rise of Islam, which describes an eschatological battle between the tyrannical powers of both Church and State personified in the figure of Armilius (a cipher for Rome) and the Messiah ben Joseph (the forerunner of the Davidic Messiah) were widely influential among medieval European Jewry.[5]

The historical wickedness and sins committed by the Roman Empire in destroying Jerusalem are found throughout the Targums — it is a particular preoccupation of Targum Lamentations as one might expect (e.g. Tg. Lam. 1:19; 4:17, 22; 5:11) — as is Rome's future role as the Messiah's opponent. Such ideas are clearly present in those Targums that were in circulation in those places and periods in which the manuscripts of the Mixed Western group were copied (i.e. twelfth–fifteenth century Italy and Ashkenaz). For example, according to the Fragment Targum to Num. 24:19 preserved in manuscript Ebr. 440 (Biblioteca Apostolica, Vatican City), a German manuscript copied around 1300 CE[6]: 'a king is destined to rise up from the House of Jacob and he will destroy all those who remain from the sinful city, which is Rome (מן כרכא חייבא דא היא רומי)'.[7] Targum Neofiti, a pre-1517 Italian manuscript in an Italian square script,[8] may originally have shared this characterisation of

---

5 J. Dan, *The Hebrew Story in the Middle Ages* (Sifrut 5, Jerusalem 1974), 35–46 (on 'Armilius' also incorporating the Church, see 42–3); Strack and Stemberger, *Introduction to the Talmud and Midrash*, 327–8; Stemberger, *Die Römische Herrschaftim Urteil der Juden* (Erträge der Forschung 195, Darmstadt 1983), 59–164 (on the Book of Zerubbabel, 138–43). For text with (French) translation, critical notes, and introduction see I. Lévi, 'L'Apocalypse de Zorobabel et le roi de Perse Siroès', *Revue des Études Juives* 68 (1914), 129–60 and 69 (1919), 108–21. See further D. Berger, 'Three Typological Themes in Early Jewish Messianism: Messiah Son of Joseph, Rabbinic Calculations, and the Figure of Armilus', *Association for Jewish Studies Review* 10:2 (1985), 141–64, pp. 143–9, 155–62, and references there. On the notion of two messiahs in the Targum to the Prophets see R.P. Gordon, 'The Targumist as Eschatologist', in J.A. Emerton, et al. (eds), *Congress volume: Göttingen 1977* (Supplements to Vetus Testamentum 29, Leiden 1978), 113–30, pp. 121–2; Gordon, 'The Ephraimite Messiah and the Targum(s) to Zechariah 12.10', in J.C. Exum and H.G. Williamson (eds), *Reading from Right to Left: Essays on the Hebrew Bible in Honour of David J. A. Clines* (Journal for the Study of the Old Testament Supplement 373, London 2003), 184–95, esp.192–4; D.C. Mitchell, 'Messiah bar Ephraim in the Targums', *Aramaic Studies* 4:2 (2006), 221–41, pp. 221–32 (though Mitchell's dating of the traditions is far from convincing, cf. Kasher, 'Eschatological Ideas in the Toseftot Targum to the Prophets', 31–2, 58–9).

6 Richler (ed.), *Hebrew Manuscripts in the Vatican Library*, 387. Siglum = Frg.Tg[V].

7 = Frg. Tg.[P], Ms Hébr. 110 of the Bibliothèque Nationale, Paris; fifteenth/sixteenth century; Sephardi square script.

8 Richler (ed.), *Hebrew Manuscripts in the Vatican Library*, 387.

Rome — here and in other verses — but subsequently lost it as a result of censorship.⁹ The Fragment Targum also contains an eschatological vision of the King Messiah coming out from the midst of Rome as does the Tosefta Targum to Obadiah 21,¹⁰ while Targum Pseudo-Jonathan, the only surviving manuscript of which was written in an Ashkenazi (or possibly Italian) hand in the sixteenth century,¹¹ describes an eschatological battle in which the King Messiah will overcome the armies of Rome and Constantinople (Tg. Ps.-J. Num. 24:24. Cf. also Tg. Ps.-J. Gen. 36:43 רומי חייבתא; Tg. Ps. 108:11 כרכא דרומי רשיעא). Such themes are equally widespread in the Tosefta Targums to the Prophets. The Tosefta Targums to Zech. 4:7 and Obadiah 21, known respectively from an eleventh/twelfth century Ashkenazi and a sixteenth century Italian manuscript for example, promise the destruction of 'sinning Rome' (רומי חייבתא) and 'the wicked Roman Kingdom (מלכות רומיתא רשיעא)' at the arrival of the Messiah.¹²

This characterisation of Rome as adversary is present in the eschatological and messianic expectations expressed in Targum Jonathan,¹³ but the wording

---

9 C.T.R. Hayward, 'A Portrait of the Wicked Esau in the Targum of Codex Neofiti 1', in D.R.G. Beattie and M.J. McNamara (eds), *The Aramaic Bible: Targums in their Historical Context* (Journal for the Study of the Old Testament Supplement 166, Sheffield 1994), 291–309, pp. 292, 306–9. But cf. R. Le Déaut, *La nuit pascale: essai sur la signification de la Pâque juive à partir du Targum d'Exode XII 42* (Analecta Biblica 22, Rome 1963), 271–2.

10 Frg. Tg.ᵛ Exod. 12:42; Frg. Tg.ᴾ Exod. 15:18.

11 London, British Library Add. 27031; Italian hand according to Levine, 'British Museum Aramaic Additional Ms 27031', 3; German according to Margoliouth, *Catalogue of the Hebrew and Samaritan Manuscripts in the British Museum*, §99.

12 Kasher, *Targumic Toseftot to the Prophets* §137ב, §144א l.72–7, cf. §144ז; Kasher, 'Eschatological Ideas in the Toseftot Targum to the Prophets', 32–6, 38, 47, 49, 55. Cf. Grelot, 'Une Tosephta Targoumique sur Zacharie, II, 14–15', *Revue Biblique* 73 (1966), 197–211, p. 197.

13 J. Ribera Florit, 'La exegesis rabinica postbiblica reflejada en la version aramea de los Profetas', *El Olivo* 4:13 (1981), 61–85, pp. 78–81; Ribera Florit, 'El Targum de Habacuc', 329–30, 332. For further discussion on eschatology in Tg. Jon. see Ribera Florit, 'La escatología en el Targum Jonatan (Tg Jon) y su relación con el Targum Palestinense (Tg Pal)', in V. Collado-Bertomeu and V. Vilar Hueso (eds), *Simposio Bíblico Español (Córdoba, 1985)* (Córdoba 1987), 487–99. Cf. Grelot, 'L'exégèse messianique d'Isaie, LXIII, 1–6', *Revue Biblique* 70 (1963), 371–80. Rome is explicitly mentioned in Tg. Isa. 34:9; 54:1; Tg. Ezek. 39:16; Tg. Mich. 7:8, 10; Tg. Hab. 3:17. See further P.V.M. Flesher and B. Chilton, *The Targums: a Critical Introduction* (Studies in the Aramaic Interpretation of Scripture 12, Leiden 2011), 169–98, who deal with the question of the dating and development through the Tannaitic and Amoraic phrases of Targum Jonathan.

'sinful Rome' is absent.[14] Nonetheless, חייב 'guilty' is a common Targumic addition and in the books of Samuel usually expresses the notion of one deserving death on account of his guilt (e.g. Tg. 1 Sam. 14:43; 20:31; 26:16; Tg. 2 Sam. 12:5; 16:7, 8; 19:29; 21:1); as such it fits perfectly within an eschatological framework in which the righteous are finally vindicated.

Taking the preceding observations into account, the reading of our Ashkenazi and Mixed Western manuscripts is to be understood as a secondary addition that intends to strengthen the image already present in the original text. The choice of vocabulary reflects the richer textual tradition found in the Palestinian Targums, Targum Pseudo-Jonathan, and the Tosefta Targums to the Prophets. Although a direct literary borrowing cannot be established, our Ashkenazi and Mixed Western manuscripts seem to reflect the contemporary intellectual milieu. It is reasonable to assume that this intellectual milieu (and therefore the origin of this variant) is to be located in medieval Italy and/or Ashkenaz, where the Palestinian Targums, Targum Pseudo-Jonathan, and the Tosefta Targums to the Prophets were clearly popular, as the extant manuscript evidence attests.

Other comparable textual emendations in European manuscripts can be found, for example, in the Targum to Isa. 11:4, a prophecy describing the coming of the Davidic Messiah and his future activities. In this text the anonymous 'wicked' (רשיעא) of the Babylonian tradition is explicitly identified as Armilius (ארמילוס cf. Tg. Ps.-J. Deut. 34:3) in some European textual traditions, namely in the First and Second Rabbinic Bibles, a marginal note in Codex Reuchlinianus No. 3 (= t705i) under the heading לישנא אחרינא (pointing to a variant manuscript, see chapter nine),[15] and the *Arukh* of R. Nathan b. Jehiel of Rome, which one can plausibly assume reflects a genuine variant manuscript at this point. A second example is found in the Targum to Zech. 4:7, where the 'foolish kingdom' (מלכותא טפשתא) is explicitly identified as Rome in the variant texts of Codex Reuchlinianus No. 3 and manuscript Montefiore 7 [H 116] (Sephardi, 1486), the latter of these two being an incorporated Tosefta Targum (see page 251).[16]

---

14 The only example of חייב applied to a land is Cushan, כושן חייבא Tg. Hab. 3:7, but this may be derived from the personal name רשעתים כושן (Judg. 3:8, 10), which becomes כושן חיבא in Tg. Jon. (via root רשע).

15 Cf. main text: ארמלגון, second marginal reading: ארמלגוה, probably corruptions.

16 Cf. also Targum of Lamentations 4:22 in its Western (i.e. Paul de Lagarde, *Hagiographa*

Chapter Seven. Exegetical Variants

A second exegetical expansion occurs in the same verse:

1 Sam. 2:5

MT	[no Hebrew text]
Babylonian tradition	...ירושלם דהות כאיתא עקרא עתידא דתיתמלי מעם גלותהא...
	...Jerusalem, which is like a barren woman, is destined to be filled by the people of her Exile...
t3i = t6a^{correct} (Cf. Sperber: t12sc דלא ילדה; t734s מעם שבי).	...ירושלם דהות כאיתא עקר׳ **דלא ילדה** עתידא דתיתמלי מעם **שבי** גלוותה...
	...Jerusalem, which is like a barren woman **who has not borne children**, is destined to be filled by the people of **the captivity of** her Exile...
t720a = t5a^{correct} ≈ t725a (שבי for תבו and גלותא for גלותאה), t713a (omits דלא ילדה, reads תבו שבי not).	...ירושלים דהוות **דמיא** כאיתתא עקרתא **דלא ילדה** עתיד׳ דתיתמלי מעם **תבו** גלוותאה...
	...Jerusalem, which **resembles** a barren woman **who has not borne children**, is destined to be filled by the people **returning from** her Exile...

The first of these two enrichments, 'like a barren woman *who has not borne children*', or the more elaborate 'which *resembles* a barren woman who has not borne children', may be influenced by phraseology elsewhere in the official Targums. In line with the Hebrew, the language of Gen. 11:30 in Targum Onqelos is similar, reading 'Sarai was barren; she had no children (והות שרי עקרא לית לה ולד)'. Comparable is Targum Jonathan to Judg. 13:3 ('his wife was barren and had no children' ואתתיה עקרא ולית לה ולד), which again follows the underlying Hebrew. The point may be to stress that the woman had *never* borne children, as opposed to her having become infertile after the birth of children. The usage is, however, too infrequent for this to be considered simply a conventional rendering.

A more compelling association is with Targum Jonathan's rendering of Isa. 54:1:[17]

שבחי ירושלם דהות כאתא דהות עקרא דלא ילדת בועי תשבחא ודוצי דהות כאיתא דלא עדיאת ארי סגיאין יהון בני ירושלם צדיתא מבני רומי יתיבתא אמר יוי

Rejoice, *O Jerusalem, which was like* a barren woman *that* had not borne children! Cry

---

chaldaice [Leipzig 1873]) and Yemenite (i.e. Albert van der Heide, *The Yemenite Tradition of the Targum of Lamentations: Critical Text and Analysis of the Variant Readings* [Studia post-biblica 32, Leiden 1981]) textual traditions. The relationship between these two traditions is a matter of debate.

17 van Staalduine-Sulman sees this plus as an 'associative translation' referring to Tg. Isa. 54:1; van Staalduine-Sulman, *The Targum of Samuel*, 211 n. 1

out in praise and rejoice *since she [Jerusalem] was like a woman who* has never become pregnant! Because the sons of deserted *Jerusalem will be* more numerous than the sons of inhabited *Rome*, says the Lord!

Tg. Isa. 54.1

This is expanded from the Hebrew text:

רני עקרה לא ילדה פצחי רנה וצהלי לא חלה

כי רבים בני שוממה מבני בעולה אמר יהוה

Rejoice, O barren woman, [who] has not borne children! Break forth in joyous shouts and cry, [who] has not writhed [in labour pains]!

Because the children of the desolate [will be] more numerous than the children of the married, says the Lord.

The particular technique exhibited by the Targum to Isa. 54:1, namely supplying concrete referents in cases where the Hebrew text has figurative and imaginative language, is a characteristic feature of Targum Jonathan, but in the case of Isa. 54:1, such an interpretation of the text runs throughout rabbinic and medieval Jewish literature.[18] A good example of the association between the barrenness of a woman and the destruction of Jerusalem is found in Pesiqta de Rab Kahana:

Rabbi Reuven: 'Sing, O barren woman!' (Isa 54.1), [means] 'Conceive, O barren woman!' Rabbi Meir, 'barren woman' (עקרה) [means], having been uprooted (עקורה), i.e. a nation that the nations of the world uprooted. This refers to what is written, 'Remember, O Lord, against the Edomites the day of Jerusalem, who said, Rase it! Rase it to its foundations!' (Ps. 137.7)

(Pesiq. Rab Kah. 20 ד"ה ב א"ר ראובן)

Yet in many places the text is read as a consolatory reference to Zion on the basis of the recurring theme in the Hebrew Bible of the Lord making barren women fertile. The text is associated in several places with a number of other Scriptural texts in which infertile women subsequently conceive; among these is 1 Sam. 2:21 (as well as Gen. 11:30, mentioned above), in which Hannah is

---

18 See b.Ber. 10a and references below. In his commentary to the verse Rashi explains the phrase 'Sing, O barren woman!' (רני עקרה) as referring to 'Jerusalem, which was like one who had not borne children (ירושלים אשר היתה כלא ילדה)' without further comment. Kimhi (*Commentary on Isaiah, ad loc*) cites the Targum by way of explanation.

Chapter Seven. Exegetical Variants

said to bear sons and daughters when the Lord 'visited' (פקד) her.[19] Such examples provide reassurance of future restoration on the logic that if the Lord acted thus for Hannah or Sarah then surely he will act thus for Jerusalem too. The logic is summed up in a saying attributed to Rabbi Levi, 'in every place [in Scripture] where it is said [that] she did not have [children], she [ended up] having [children]!'[20]

Using this same logic, the Provençal exegete Rabbi Joseph Caspi (1279–1340?) connects Isa. 54:1 with 1 Sam. 2:5 and relates this to the restoration of Jerusalem after the Babylonian exile. 'The children of the desolate (בני שוממה)', he explains, are the children of Israel, while 'the children of the married (בני בעולה)', are the children of Assyria (בני אשור). 'All the titles' he goes on 'relate to a past time, in the time of the Second Temple, and this is the sense of "Even the barren bears seven, but the one with many children has become infertile (1 Sam. 2:5)."'[21]

Although we cannot establish a direct literary borrowing between the two texts, that this Isaiah text should have exerted an influence on the transmission of the text of the Targum to Samuel is not unsurprising when one bears in mind the prominent place it occupied in the liturgy: Isa. 54:1 begins the haftarah reading for seder תולדות נח (Gen. 6:9–11:32) and again for seder כי תצא (Deut. 21:10–25:19) in the Ashkenazi tradition; the list of haftarot given in Codex Reuchlinianus No. 3 gives Isa. 54:1–10 as the reading for seder שפטים (Deut. 16:18–21:9).[22] Although we know that the Targum text was no longer publicly read on every shabbat, it did serve as a study aid and may have been consulted as such in preparation for the shabbat service.

The addition of the noun 'captivity' (שבי) is harder to place. There are a number of cases in Targum Jonathan where 'captivity' (שבי) and 'exile' (גלו) are set in poetic parallelism following the underlying Hebrew text (e.g. Tg. Isa. 20:4; Tg. Jer. 48:46; Tg. Ezek. 12:11 cf. Tg. Nah. 3:10), but the words are not linked in a grammatical construction. The addition of the noun 'captivity' (שבי) does occur in other places in some manuscripts. According to Sperber's

---

19 Pesiq. Rab. 32 דבר אחר ענייה; cf. Midr. Sam. 6:4; 'Ag. Ber. 53a.
20 Hebr. בכל מקום שנאמר אין לה הוה לה Gen. Rab. 38.14 (≈ Pesiq. Rab Kah. 20.3).
21 Rabbi Joseph Caspi, *Commentary on Isaiah*, 54.1.
22 A table of haftarot readings showing variations between communities is given in A. Dotan (ed.), *Biblia Hebraica Leningradensia: Prepared According to the Vocalization, Accents, and Masora of Aaron ben Moses ben Asher in the Leningrad Codex* (Peabody, MA 2001), Appendix E.

apparatus multiple witnesses of Targum Onqelos, including the First and Second Rabbinic Bibles and Codex Solger (Stadtbibliothek, Nürnberg), read 'the captivity of your exile' (שבי גלותך) at Deut. 30:3 in place of 'your exile' (גלותך); the Antwerp Polyglot and the Second Rabbinic Bible read 'she will be filled by the people of *the captivity* of her exile' (מעם שבי גלותהא) at Targum Jonathan to Isa. 66:8, in place of simply 'she will be filled by the people of her exile' (מעם גלותהא). In all these cases the addition obviously seeks to add a nuance to the text, but the shade of the nuance is not clear nor is its origin (the combination is unknown in rabbinic literature).[23]

1 Sam. 2:20

MT	ישם יהוה לך זרע
	May the Lord give you descendants
Babylonian tradition	יקיים יוי לך בנין כשרין
	May the Lord raise up for you **fit** offspring.
t232i/s	May the Lord raise up for you **male** offspring (בנין דיכרין).

Although the temptation to emphasise the male gender of a child can be found on a couple of other occasions in the tradition of Targum Jonathan,[24] this current variant appears to be based on Hannah's petition in 1 Sam. 1:11, to which 1 Sam. 2:20 is effectively a response. 'O Lord of Hosts!' she prays 'If you were only to look upon the lowliness of your maidservant and remember me and not forget your maidservant then you would give to your maidservant the offspring of men (זרע אנשים)' (1 Sam. 1:11). The wording 'offspring of men' (זרע אנשים) is odd. David Kimhi (c.1160–1235 CE) explains in his commentary on 1 Sam. 1:11 that it must refer to male children (פירוש: זכרים) because Hannah goes on to promise that a razor would not touch his head and this, he notes, one would not say of females (נקבות).[25] Furthermore, in his commentary to 1 Sam. 2:20 Kimhi explains that the words 'in place of the request that he requested' (תחת השאלה אשר שאל) refer to other sons, who could provide for them in their old age in place of Samuel (השאלה הוא שמואל, he

---

23 Cf. Kimhi, *Commentary on Kings*, 2 Kgs 17:26.
24 Tg. 1 Sam. 4:20 (בר דכר ילידת; Hebr. בן ילדת); and in the לי'א variant in t705i to 2 Sam. 18:18 (בר דכר; Babylonian trad. בר קיים; Hebr. בן). Cf. Tg. 1 Chron. 24:2 (בנין דכרין = Hebr. בנים). For בנין כשרין cf. Tg. Jon. 1 Sam. 16:1; Tg. 2 Sam. 18:20; Tg.Ps. 127:3.
25 He cites the Targum (בר בגו בני אינשא), which is unmistakably masculine but also singular, as confirmation of his conclusion. Kimhi, *Commentary to 1 Samuel*, 1 Sam. 1:11.

Chapter Seven. Exegetical Variants

explains) who was dedicated to the service of the Lord.[26] Whether or not the scribe who emended the text was familiar with Kimhi's commentaries is a moot point. Nonetheless Kimhi usefully articulates the logic that is clearly at play.

2 Sam. 23:4

MT	וכאור בקר יזרח שמש
	[He who rules justly...is] like the light of the morning when the sun rises...
Babylonian tradition	וכשמשא דעתיד לאזהרא בזהור יקריה על חד תלת מאה ארבעין ותלתא בניהור שבעת יומיא
	...and like the sun that will shine with the light of its glory 343 times, with the light of seven days...
t5a (Sperber: t716y cf. t10r)	...with **the light of seven stars and** the light of seven days (בניהור שבעא כוכביא וניהור שבעא יומיא)...
t713a	...with **the light of seven stars and** the seven days **that were from the beginning** (בניהור שבעת כוכביא ושבעת יומיא דמבראשית)...

Both the rendering of Targum Jonathan according to its Babylonian tradition and the tradition preserved in the glosses of our two Ashkenazi manuscripts have been dealt with at length by Smelik.[27] The reference to light shining 343-fold (here and in Tg. Judg. 5:31) is elliptical; it apparently refers to the primaeval light of the first days of creation, before the sun, moon, and stars had been set in the firmament, an association derived from Isa. 30:26 (i.e. $343 = 7 \times 7 \times 7$). This primaeval light is elsewhere identified with the Glory of God (see Tg. Hab. 3:4). The eschatological association between the righteous and this primaeval light is widespread, as Smelik has shown.

The new element in the gloss in our two Ashkenazi manuscripts is the 'stars'. The association between the righteous and stars goes back at least to the book of Daniel (12:3), i.e. 'Those who are wise will shine like the brightness of the firmament, and those who cause many to become righteous [will shine] like the stars for ever and ever',[28] itself an allusion to Isa. 53:11.[29]

---

26 He again cites the Targum (בנין כשרין) without further comment. Kimhi, *Commentary to 1 Samuel*, 1 Sam. 2:20.

27 W. Smelik, 'On the Mystical Transformation of the Righteous into Light in Judaism', *Journal for the Study of Judaism* 26:2 (1995), 122–44. esp. 131–41. Cf. also Bacher, 'Kritische Untersuchungen zum Prophetentargum', 47; van Staalduine-Sulman, *The Targum of Samuel*, 673–6.

28 Cf. for example, Pesiq. Rab. 11.5 'Even as the stars shine in the firmament, so will they [Israel] shine in the time to come'.

29 See e.g. D.D. Hannah, 'Isaiah within Judaism of the Second Temple Period', in S. Moyise and

The tradition that associates the seven 'stars', namely the sun, the moon, Mercury, Venus, Mars, Jupiter, and Saturn, is found again in Targum Pseudo-Jonathan, where the lamp-stands of the Tabernacle are said to be arranged in such a way as to correspond to the seven stars (or planets), which move in their orbits in the firmament, which are themselves 'comparable to the righteous who give light to the world by their merit' (Tg. Ps.-J. Exod. 39:37; 40:4 Cf. Tg. Esth. I 3:7). The glosses in the two Ashkenazi manuscripts fuse the two traditions, i.e. that of the primaeval light with that of the light of the celestial bodies.

2. Clarifications

As any student of the Hebrew Bible will know, the text of the Hebrew Bible is occasionally obscure, and as any student of the ancient Versions will know, translation often provided a good opportunity for such obscurities to be remedied. This is no less so in the text of the Targum, a fact acknowledged long ago in rabbinic circles: 'Were it not for the Targum of this verse, we would not know its meaning.' (b.Sanh. 94b; b.Mo'ed Qaṭ. 28b; b.Meg. 3a). However, while Targum Jonathan normally resolves lexical difficulties, its fidelity to the underlying Hebrew means that contextual ambiguities can remain. All the manuscripts of the Mixed Western group show a tendency to resolve such ambiguities. This process can be further subdivided into: a) clarifications that merely make explicit what is already implied or evident from the context; b) clarifications that deal with technical matters such as specifying the subject or object of a verb where this is missing.

It is worthwhile stating at the beginning that it is not always easy to separate a genuine addition, purposefully introduced by a scribe to aid clarity, from simple accident. The addition of 'this day' to the phrase 'the Lord has restrained you *this day* from shedding (די מנעך יוי יומא דין) innocent blood,' for example, which is to be found at 1 Sam. 25:26 in manuscript t2i, may be intended to add a degree of specificity (cf. Tg. 1 Sam. 25:10), but equally the accidental repetition of extremely widespread terminology can hardly be excluded.

M.J.J. Menken (eds), *Isaiah in the New Testament: The New Testament and the Scriptures of Israel* (London 2005), 30.

Chapter Seven. Exegetical Variants

2.a. Explication and Specification by Addition

One of the most characteristic aspects of the language of the Hebrew Bible is that it occasionally expresses things with extreme brevity. Where this terseness has been transferred into the Targum text our European scribes sometimes cannot resist the temptation to elaborate. As a result of its terseness, the text often leaves room for ambiguity. Our European manuscripts expunge the ambiguity and in so doing add their own nuance to the text. The tendency is particularly prevalent in t705i, to a lesser extent in t7i, and sporadically in the remaining manuscripts.

The following examples found in manuscripts t718i and t3i best exemplify this explication of the implied sense:

2 Sam. 13:3

MT   ויונדב איש חכם מאד
                Jonadab was a very shrewd man

Babylonian tradition   ויונדב גבר חכים לחדא
                Jonadab was a very shrewd man

t718i = t3i   ויונדב גבר חכים לבישא ופורענותא (ולפורענותא i3t) לחדא
                Jonadab was a man very shrewd [in doing] **evil and retribution**

The following narrative, in which Jonadab devises a plan by which Amnon might rape his sister, Tamar, makes clear that the underlying Hebrew חכם must be understood in a pejorative sense. The textual traditions of t718i and t3i make this clear by means of a short addition. Rashi, in his commentary on this verse, provides a similar clarification, 'a man shrewd *at [doing] wickedness*' (איש חכם לרשעה).

Let us now turn to t705i, where this tendency is most clearly evinced.

1 Sam 19:5

MT   וישם את נפשו בכפו
                (Lit.:) He put his soul in his hand

Babylonian tradition   ומסר ית נפשיה כעל גב לאתקטלא
                He risked his own life…

t705i   ומסר ית נפשיה כעל גב **ידיה** לאיתקטלא
                He handed over his life as though upon the back **of his hand** to be killed…

A similar variant is found in t705i to Tg. 1 Sam. 28:21, (ואשים נפשי בכפי) מסרית נפשי כעל גב בידיי לאיתקטלא (Hebr. נפשי בכפי), where the remainder of manuscripts read without בידיי. Elsewhere t705i renders the Hebrew כף with יד

(2 Sam. 14:16; 18:12, 14; 19:10; 22:1) and גב ידיה is not idiomatic in any of the Targums, so this is probably a deliberate alteration of the text. The formula מסר נפש כעל גב is in fact a fixed idiom in Targum Jonathan (cf. Tg. Judg. 9:17; 12:3; Tg. 1 Sam. 28:21), hence my translation of the Babylonian text. If read literally it is rather odd, i.e. 'he handed over his soul as though upon the back to be killed.' The scribe behind the change in t705i seems to have been unfamiliar with the idiom and attempts to improve the phraseology (here and Tg. 1 Sam. 28:21; Tg. Judg. 12:3) by 'completing' the expression (cf. Tg. Ps. 119:109).[30]

1 Sam. 20:18

MT		ויאמר לו יהונתן מחר חדש
	Jonathan said to him, Tomorrow [there is] a moon.	
Babylonian tradition		ואמר ליה יהונתן מחר ירחא
	Jonathan said to him, Tomorrow [there is] a moon.	
t705i		ואמר ליה יהונתן מחר **ריש** ירחא
	Jonathan said to him, Tomorrow [there is] a **new** moon.	

The idiom ריש ירחא does replace Hebrew חדש in Targum Onqelos (Tg. Onq. Num. 28:14 cf. Tg. Onq. Deut. 33:14), though rarely. In the current example our scribe has based his emendation on the context, wishing to add a degree of precision.[31] Rashi explains that it was the custom of those who ate at the king's table to come to the table on festival days,[32] stressing the particular sense of חדש as 'new moon', rather than simply 'month'.

1 Sam. 26:3

MT	ויחן שאול בגבעת החכילה אשר על פני הישימן על הדרך
	Saul camped in the hill country of Hachilah, which is in the direction of Yeshimon, on the road.
Babylonian tradition	Saul camped in the hill country of Hachilah, which is in the direction of Yeshimon (דעל אפי ישימון), on the road.
t705i	Saul camped in the hill country of Hachilah, which is in the direction of **the house of** Yeshimon (דעל אפי **בית** ישימון), on the road.

Manuscript t705i provides further specification of the place (cf. Tg. Onq. Num 21:20; 23:28; see also pages 277–8).

---

30 See further van Staalduine-Sulman, *The Targum of Samuel*, 396.
31 As van Staalduine-Sulman, *The Targum of Samuel*, 406 n. 1590.
32 Rashi, *Commentary on Samuel, ad loc*. Hebr. ודרך כל אוכלי שולחן המלך לבא ביום מועד אל השולחן. Cf. the explanation of R. Joseph Kara, *Commentary on Samuel, ad loc.*

Chapter Seven. Exegetical Variants

1 Sam. 31:12

MT	וישרפו אתם שם
	...and they burnt them there.
Babylonian tradition	וקלון עליהון כמא דקלן על מלכיא תמן
	...and they burnt over them as they used to burn over the kings there.
t705i	וקלו עליהון **בוסמיא** כמא דקלו על מלכיא תמן
	...and they burnt **spices** over them as they used to burn over the kings there.

'Spice' בסם is nowhere else in Targums Onqelos or Jonathan the object of the verb קלי 'to burn, roast,' affirming that this is a secondary addition. The Hebrew is terse but clear. The original rendering of the Targum, 'they burnt *upon them*',[33] however leaves the reader to fill in an object for the verb, since the bodies of Saul and his sons are no longer the direct object of the verb, which t705i willingly supplies.[34]

The explanation offered by the scribe responsible for the emendation that appears in t705i is reflected across the medieval commentators. Joseph Kara (before *c*.1060–70), working in northern France, explains simply that spices were burnt in order that the pleasing odour might ascend, quoting in support the Targum (according to the standard text).[35] Isaiah di Trani (the Younger), writing around two centuries after t705i was produced, explains that the episode relates to their embalming in which many spices were applied to prevent a bad smell developing, and during which many spices were also burnt.[36] Kimhi offers a number of different answers to the question of what was being burnt, including embalming spices (citing Gen. 50:2).[37] Rashi cites the Targum here according to the standard text[38] but does not mention spices. However, he adds, 'According to our custom: we burn kings and this is not

---

33 van Staalduine-Sulman explains the expression 'to burn upon someone' as idiomatic, refering to the practice of burning the royal accoutrements in honour of a deceased king; see van Staalduine-Sulman, *The Targum of Samuel*, 476.

34 The limited availability of textual data led Bacher to conclude that בוסמיא had been accidentally omitted in the First and Second Rabbinic Bibles, and Buxtorf's edition. In fact it is a secondary addition in the text of t705i; Bacher, 'Kritische Untersuchungen zum Prophetentargum', 39.

35 Hebr. ששפרו בשמים כדי לעלות הריח, ומשחו בהם עצמות שאול ועצמות בניו; ותרגום וקלו עליהון כמא דקלו על מלכיא תמן R. Joseph Kara, *Commentary on Samuel, ad loc.*

36 Hebr. והיא החנטה, שעושים עליהם הבשמים רבים שלא יסריחו, ושורפים בשמים באותה החנטה Isaiah di Trani, *Commentary on Samuel, ad loc.*

37 Kimhi, *Commentary on Samuel, ad loc.*

38 With minor variants: כמה for כמא; דקלו for דקלן. Rashi, *Commentary on Samuel, ad loc.*

because of superstitious practices'.[39] Isaiah di Trani also makes this point with a citation from Jer. 34:5 (וכמשרפות אבותיך המלכים הראשונים... כן ישרפו לך).[40]

2 Sam. 2:18

MT	ועשהאל קל ברגליו כאחד הצבים אשר בשדה
	Asahel was quick of foot like one of the gazelles in the field.
Babylonian tradition	ועשהאל קליל בריגלוהי כחד מן טביא דבחקלא
	Asahel was quick of foot like one of the gazelles in the field.
t705i = t5a	ועשהאל קליל בריגלוהי כחד מן **בני** טביא דבחקלא
	Asahel was quick of foot like one of **the sons of** the gazelles in the field.

Were it not for the foregoing examples, one might struggle to explain the current example. The point seems to be that he is compared to a youthful gazelle, rather than to one on its last legs.

A second manuscript t7i, also clearly exhibits the clarificatory tendency, as can be seen in the following examples:

1 Sam. 17:26

MT	כי חרף מערכות אלהים חיים
	...since he is putting to shame the lines of the the living God.
Babylonian tradition	ארי חסיד סידרי עמא דיוי קימא
	[David said... 'What will be done to the man that kills that Philistine'] ...since he is putting to shame the lines of the people of the everlasting God.
t7i = t5a^{correct}, t6a	ארי חסיד סידרי **קרבא ד**עמא דיוי קיימא
	(cf. t713a, t720a, t10r סדרי עבדי קרבא, a 'conflated reading') ...since he is putting to shame the **battle** lines of the people (t6a דעמיה) of the everlasting God.

The reading of the Babylonian tradition stands closer to the underlying Hebrew; the alternative offered by t7i makes explicit what is already clearly implied in the context, namely that the arrangement described was one of war (cf. 1 Sam. 17:2) and exactly the same variant is found in t7i at 1 Sam. 17:36, confirming a deliberate intervention in the text. These two instances (i.e. 1 Sam. 17:26, 36) are the only two occurrences of the rendering סדרי עמא for the Hebrew המערכה, although elsewhere one finds סדרי ישראל for Hebrew מערכות ישראל (1 Sam. 17:8, 10, 45) and סדרי פלשתאי for Hebrew מערכות פלשתים (1 Sam. 17:23

---

39 Hebr. כדתנן שורפין על המלכים ולא מדרכי האמורי. Rashi, *Commentary on Samuel, ad loc.*
40 Cf. t. Šabb. 7.18.

Chapter Seven. Exegetical Variants

[*Qere*]; 23.3), so the presence of קרב is not customary in Targum Jonathan.

The idiom סדרי קרבא or סדרא דקרבא is otherwise rare in Targum Jonathan. One finds only the following examples: Tg. 1 Sam. 4:16 (סדרא דקרבא = Hebr. המערכה); and Tg. Joel 2:5 (סדרי קרבא = Hebr. מלחמה).[41] The expression סדרי קרבא is, however, extremely common in Targum Neofiti, Targum Pseudo-Jonathan, the Fragment Targums, and the hagiographic Targums, where it is usually Targumic addition,[42] or translates מלחמה,[43] לחם (verb),[44] or other terms.[45] Since our knowledge of these Targums derives solely from manuscripts copied in Italy and Ashkenaz a possible influence cannot be excluded.

1 Sam. 17:49

MT	וישלח דוד את ידו אל הכלי ויקח משם אבן ויקלע ויך את הפלשתי אל מצחו
	David reached his hand into the bag (cf. 1 Sam. 17:40) and he took from there a stone and he swung and struck the Philistine on the forehead.
Babylonian tradition	ואושיט דויד ית ידיה למנא ונסיב מיתמן אבנא ואחזר ומחא ית פלישתאה על בית עינוהי
	David reached his hand into the bag and he took from there a stone and he swung and struck the Philistine on the forehead.
t7i = t6a, t720a (cf. t713a < ומחא) (Sperber: t10r < ואחזור ומחא)	ואושיט דוד ית ידיה למנא ונסיב מתמן אבני **ואקלעה בקילעא** ואחזור ומחא ית פלש׳ על בית עינוהי
	David reached his hand to the bag and he took a stone from there **and he slung it with a sling** and he swung and struck the Philistine on the forehead.

The lexeme חזר (here in *aphel*) has a rather general sense when one compares it to the underling Hebrew (root קלע), the semantic range of which is rather precise. The reading of t7i reflects the precision of the Hebrew root by the addition of a gloss, thereby making explicit what the action of the verb חזר, which in *aphel* has the sense literally of 'causing to turn', implies. By

---

41 Cf. also the marginal variant to Tg. 1 Sam. 4:12 in t705i (under the heading ספר אחר).
42 E.g. Tg. Neof. Gen. 11:4; Tg. Neof. Exod. 14:13, 14, 20; Tg. Neof. Num. 20:21; 24:20; 27:17(x2); 28:3; Tg. Neof. Deut. 2:5, 19; 28:7; Tg. Ps.-J. Gen. 11:4; 37:7; 49:11; Tg. Ps.-J. Exod. 14:13, 14, 20; 15:9; 17:9; 23:27; 32:18; Tg. Ps.-J. Num. 20:21; 21:35; 24:17; 24:20; 27:17(x2); Tg. Ps.-J. Deut. 2:19; Frg. Tg.[P.V.] Gen. 11:4; 14:9; 15:1; Frg.Tg.[V] Gen. 32:2, etc.
43 E.g. Tg. 1 Chron. 11:13; Tg. 2 Chron. 12:15; 13:3; 15:19; 16:19; 20:15; 27:7; 32:8; Tg. Ps. 76:4 ≈ וחרב ומלחמה; Tg. Neof. Gen. 14:8; Tg. Neof. Exod. 1:10; 13:17; Tg. Neof. Num. 21:33; 32:6; 32:27; Tg. Neof. Deut. 2:9, 24, 32; 3:1; 4:34; 20:1, 2, 3, 5, 6, 7, 12, 20; 21:10; 29:6; 33:7; Tg. Ps.-J. Gen. 14:8; Tg. Ps.-J. Exod. 1:10; Tg. Ps.-J. Num. 10:9; 31:14, 21; Tg. Ps.-J. Deut. 2:9 etc.
44 Usually with למסדרא סדרי קרבא, e.g. Tg. 2 Chron. 11:1; Tg. Neof. Exod. 17:8, 9, 10; Tg. Neof. Deut. 20:4, 10, 19; Tg. Ps.-J. Num. 22:11; Tg. Ps.-J. Deut. 1:42 etc.
45 Hebrew קרב Tg. Ps. 78:9; 144:1; צבא Tg. Neof. Num. 31:6; Tg. Ps.-J. Num. 31:3.

introducing the noun 'sling', the scribe makes more explicit the connection to the following verse, which begins: 'So David prevailed over the Philistine with sling and stone (t7i: ותקיף דו׳ מן פלש׳ בקילעא ובאבנא...).'

1 Sam. 21:3

MT	ויאמר דוד לאחימלך הכהן
	David said to Ahimelech the priest...
Babylonian tradition	ואמר דוד לאחימלך כהנא
	David said to Ahimelech the priest...
t7i	ואמ׳ דוד לאחימ׳ כהנ׳ **רבא**
	David said to Ahimelech the **High** Priest...

The expression 'High Priest' is, of course, common (e.g. Tg. Onq. Lev. 4:3; 4:5; 4:16; Tg. Onq. Num. 35:25; 35:28; Tg. Josh. 20:6; Tg. 2 Kgs 12:11; Tg. Jer. 52:24; Tg. Hag. 1:14; etc.), but it normally reflects the underlying Hebrew (e.g. הכהן המשיח, הכהן הגדול, הכהן הראש), cropping up occasionally also in some expansive sections of Targum (e.g. Tg. Isa. 61:10; Tg. Ezek. 1:1; etc.). Since Ahimelek was indeed a High Priest in Nob, the textual tradition of t7i simply adds this detail as a minor gloss, though it is odd that he does not add the same embellishment to the references to 'Ahimelech the priest' in the preceding verse.[46]

Other examples are scattered throughout the remaining manuscripts. For example:

1 Sam. 17:30

MT	ויסב מאצלו אל מול אחר ויאמר כדבר הזה וישבהו העם דבר כדבר הראשון
	He turned aside from beside him to opposite another and he said according to this word and the people answered him a word like the first word.
Babylonian tradition	He turned from towards him to opposite another (ואסתחר מלותיה לקביל אוחרן)...
t6a = t713a, t720a	He turned from towards him to opposite another **place** (ואיסתחר מלוותיה לקביל **אתר** אוחרן)...

The context clearly requires that he turned to face the assembled people and not another individual. The singular אחרן could be taken to imply either. The Ashkenazi manuscripts eliminate the ambiguity.

---

46 Cf. van Staalduine-Sulman, *The Targum of Samuel*, 412 n. 1659.

Chapter Seven. Exegetical Variants

1 Sam. 20:5

MT	הנה חדש מחר ואנכי ישב עם המלך לאכול
	See, tomorrow is a [new] moon and I will sit with the king to eat.
Babylonian tradition	See, tomorrow is a [new] moon and I will dine with the king to eat (למיכל).
t713a	See, tomorrow is a [new] moon and I will dine with the king to eat **bread** (למיכ׳ **לחמא**).

Although the expression 'to eat bread' can be found elsewhere in Targum Jonathan (i.e. Tg. 1 Sam. 2.36 פתא דלחמא; Tg. 2 Kgs 4:8; Tg. Ezek. 44:3) and Targum Onqelos (Tg. Onq. Gen. 31:54; 37:25; Tg. Onq. Exod. 18:12) it is not frequent and here it is a small clarifying gloss.

1 Sam. 21:7

MT	ויתן לו הכהן קדש כי לא שם לחם כי אם לחם הפנים המוסרים מלפני יהוה
	So the priest gave him consecrated because there was no bread there except the bread of Presence, which is removed from before the Lord.
Babylonian tradition	So the priest gave him consecrated (ויהב ליה כהנא קודשא)...
t2i	So the priest gave him consecrated **bread** (ויהב ליה כהנא לחים קודשא)...

It is clear from the context that the Hebrew קדש (here: 'consecrated thing, object') refers to consecrated bread (as opposed to 'common' bread לחם חול).[47] The textual tradition of t2i eliminates the last sliver of ambivalence.

1 Sam. 30:23

MT	לא תעשו כן אחי את אשר נתן יהוה לנו וישמר אתנו ויתן את הגדוד הבא עלינו בידנו
	Do not do thus my brothers with that which the Lord has given us. He has preserved us and given the troop that came upon us into our hand.
Babylonian tradition	...He has preserved us (ונטר יתנא) and handed over the army that came upon us into our hands.
t5a^PM	...He has preserved us **in the way in which we went** (ונטר יתנא באורחא דהליכנא בה) and handed over the army that came upon us into our hands.

The addition attempts to deal with the terse expression of the Hebrew (i.e. וישמר אתנו lit. 'he kept us'). In what sense, the text of manuscripts t5a asks, has the Lord 'kept' them? The explanation draws on common phraseology (cf. Tg. Josh. 24:17; Tg. 2 Sam. 22:22; Tg. 1 Kgs 8:25; Tg. Neof. Gen. 28:20).

---

47 Cf. Joseph Kara, *Commentary on Samuel*, ad loc.

The Transmission of Targum Jonathan in the West

2 Sam. 5:8

MT   ויאמר דוד ביום ההוא כל מכה יבסי ויגע בצנור ואת הפסחים ואת העורים שנאו (ק: שנאי) נפש דוד

David said in that day, 'Anyone who smites the Jebusites and reaches the water channel and the lame and the blind, who are hateful to David.

Babylonian tradition   ואמר דוד ביומא ההוא כל דיקטול יבוסאה ויישרי למכבש כרכא וית חטאיא וית חייביא רחיקת נפשא דדוד

David said in that day, 'Anyone that would kill the Jebusites and begin to capture the capital city! And the soul of David loathed sinners and trespassers…'

t705i   ואמר דוד ביומא ההוא כל דקטל יבושאה וישרי למיכבש **קרתא יתמני לרישא** וית חטאיא וית חייבייא רחיקת נפשא דדוד

David said in that day, 'Anyone who would kill the Jebusites and begins to capture **the town will be appointed to the head**! And the soul of David loathed sinners and trespassers…'

There is an evident obscurity in the Hebrew text, which appears to break off suddenly. The Septuagint translator resolved this by rendering the obscure Hebrew 'water channel' (צנור), with 'dirk (i.e. a small knife),' giving the reading 'Everyone who strikes the Jebusite, let him attack with a dirk…'.[48] The standard Targum text partially resolves the difficulty. An explanation for the elaboration found in t705i can be found in Rashi's commentary on the text:

'Here is a case' Rashi says, 'of a short reading (מקרא קצר) that says, "anyone who smites the Jebusites and reaches the water channel (כל מכה יבסי ויגע בצנור)", without explaining what will be done to him. 1 Chronicles 11.6 provides an explanation: "anyone who smites the Jebusites first will be chief and commander (כל מכה יבוסי בראשונה יהיה לראש ולשר).'[49]

This is not to imply that the text tradition of t705i is dependent on Rashi but, merely on the same observation, almost certainly relying on the text of 1 Chron. 11:6.[50] As an aside, it is worth noting that Rashi also cites the Targum to this verse according to the standard text (with a minor variation: למכבש ית כרכא for למכבש כרכא).

---

48 Πᾶς τύπτων Ιερουσαῖον ἁπτέσθω ἐν παραξιφίδι… LXX 2 Sam. 5:8.

49 According to the text of M. Cohen (ed.), *Mikra'ot Gedolot 'Haketer Mikra'ot Gedolot 'Haketer: A Revised and Augmented Scientific Edition of 'Mikra'ot Gedolot' based on the Aleppo Codex and early Medieval Manuscripts; Samuel I & II.* (Ramat-Gan 1993).

50 As van Staalduine-Sulman, *The Targum of Samuel*, 510 n. 229.

Chapter Seven. Exegetical Variants

2 Sam. 15:2

MT	ויאמר אי מזה עיר אתה ויאמר מאחד שבטי ישראל עבדך
	He said, 'From which town are you?' He said, 'Your servant is from one of the tribes of Israel.'
Babylonian tradition	He said, 'From which town are you?' He said, 'Your servant is from one of the tribes of Israel (מיחד שיבטיא דישראל).'
t713a = t720a	'...from one **of the towns of** the tribes of (t720a: + the house of) Israel (מחדא **קרת'** דשיבטיא דישר').'

Manuscripts t713a and t720a provide a direct answer to the question (i.e. 'From which *town*...?'), lacking in the Hebrew text and Babylonian tradition of the Targum.

2 Sam. 23:2

MT	רוח יהוה דבר בי ומלתו על לשוני
	The Lord's spirit speaks by me; his word is upon my tongue.
Babylonian tradition	David said, 'In a spirit of prophecy before the Lord I am speaking these things (אנא ממליל אילין) and the words of his holiness I am reciting with my mouth.'
t5a	David said, 'In a spirit of prophecy before the Lord I am speaking these **words of praise** (אנא מליל מילין דתושבחן) and the words of his holiness I am reciting with my mouth.'

Manuscript t5a seems to specify what the Targum text intends by אלין, 'these things'.[51]

Numerous examples belonging to this category relate to the addition of a verb, the purpose of which is simply to improve the narrative flow or to eliminate the possibility for mis-understanding. Such cases tend not to impart a new nuance to the text:

1 Sam. 23:9

MT	וידע דוד כי עליו שאול מחריש הרעה
	David knew that Saul was plotting(?) evil against him
Babylonian tradition	וידע דויד ארי עלוהי שאול כמין בישתא
	David knew that Saul was plotting(?) evil against him
t2i	וידע דוד ארי עלוהי שאול כמין **בעי** בישתא
	David knew that Saul was lying in wait **seeking** evil against him

The meaning of the Hebrew מחריש הרעה is unclear in the context, and the medieval commentators (e.g. Isaiah di Trani, Levi ben Gershon, Kimhi) all make clarifying observations. In his commentary Rashi cites the Targum

---

51 As van Stalduine-Sulman, *The Targum of Samuel*, 667 n. 1379.

237

without further comment in order to clarify, giving a variant Aramaic text that has the definite object marker (כמין ית בישתא). Yet while the Targum evidently struck Rashi as providing all the elucidation necessary this is hardly self-evident. Although כמן can take a direct object as it does in Targum 2 Sam. 15:14 (for נדח in *hifil*, following the Hebrew), in the Targums כמן is normally intransitive, with the sense 'to lie in wait, ambush.' In order to make sense of the Aramaic then one must either assume an uncommon meaning for כמן (as Rashi) or one must supply some additional wording. The latter is the solution in the textual tradition of t2i.

1 Sam. 18:22

MT	ויצו שאול את עבדו [ק: עבדיו] דברו
	Saul commanded his servants, Speak…
Babylonian tradition	ופקיד שאול ית עבדוהי מלילו
	Saul commanded his servants, Speak…
t705i	ופקיד שאול ית עבדוהי **למימר** מלילו
(Sperber: t702s, t734s)	Saul commanded his servants **saying**, Speak…

The verb פקד does not normally introduce direct speech; where it does למימר is employed (e.g. Tg. 2 Sam. 13:28; Tg. 2 Sam. 18:5, 12). The introduction of למימר is a minor clarification that aims to mark clearly the start of the contents of the command. A comparable example is found at Tg. 2 Sam. 22:26 in manuscript t701i, where a scribe has added the 'missing' verb (למיעבד; בכין אשלימתא מימר למיעבד רעותך עימיה; Babylonian tradition lacks למיעבד).

1 Sam. 17:36

MT	והיה הפלשתי הערל הזה כאחד מהם
	[David said to Saul…] and this uncircumcised Philistine will be like one of them [i.e. the wild animals]!
Babylonian tradition	[David said to Saul…] and this uncircumcised Philistine will be like one of them [wild animals] (ויהי…כחד מינהון)!
t6a = t713a, t720a	[David said to Saul…] and this uncircumcised Philistine will **be considered as** one of them [wild animals] (ויהי…**חשיב** כחד מנהון)!

Goliath will not actually be like a lion or a bear. Rather, David will approach him as an opponent in the same way that he approaches a lion or a bear when it attacks his flock. As Isaiah di Trani comments, David wished that he would be like one of the wild animals.[52] The Ashkenazi manuscripts

---

52 I.e. והיה הפלשתי הערל הזה כאחד מהם - יהי רצון שיהיה כאחד מהם Isaiah di Trani, *Commentary on Samuel, ad loc.*

Chapter Seven. Exegetical Variants

eradicate any possible ambiguity.

2.b. Explications and Specification by Substitution

There are only very few occasions where we find that one word has been substituted for another with an apparently explicatory or clarificatory aim.

2 Sam. 19:14

MT   אם לא שר צבא תהיה לפני כל הימים תחת יואב
[Say to Amasa, 'Are you my bone and my flesh? Thus God will do to me and thus he will continue to do] if you do not become chief of the army before me always in place of Joab!'

Babylonian tradition   אם לא רב חילא **תהי** קדמי כל יומיא חלף יואב
…if **you** do not **become** chief of the army before me always in place of Joab!

t705i   אם לא רב חילא **איימנינך** קדמי כל יומיא חלף יואב
…if **I** do not **appoint you** head of the army before me always in place of Joab!

The adjustment in t705i is a logical explication of the implied sense of the verse: it is not simply that Amasa will become head of the army, but that David will appoint him to this position. The scribe behind the adjustment in t705i perhaps wished to stress that this act was part of David's attempt to reconcile divided loyalties after Absalom's revolt.

2 Sam. 20:15

MT   וישפכו סללה אל העיר ותעמד בחל וכל העם אשר את יואב משחיתם להפיל החומה
…so they cast up a mound against the city and it stood against the outer wall and all the people that were with Joab were destroying [it] to make the wall fall down.

Babylonian tradition   וצברו מליתא על קרתא ואקפה משרין וכל עמא דעם יואב מתעשתין לחבלא **שורא**
…so they heaped up a mound against the city and the armies surrounded it and all the people that were with Joab were planning to destroy the **wall**.

t232i/s   וצברו מיליתא על קרתא ואקפה משירין וכל עמא דעם יואב מיתעשתין לחבלא **קרתא**
…so they heaped up a mound against the city and the armies surrounded it and all the people that were with Joab were planning to destroy the **town**.

The rendering 'they were planning[53] to damage, destroy' and the translation of the Hebrew 'rampart' (חל) earlier in the verse as 'army' (i.e. משרין = Hebrew חַיִל)[54] in the Targum makes the reference to the wall at the end of the verse difficult. Joab and company intended to destroy the whole city in which the rebel Sheba son of Bichri was sheltering, not simply the walls (though one might consider the walls a synecdoche). The scribe who adjusted the text of t232i/s may also have been seeking to harmonise with, for example, 2 Sam. 20:19, where the Targum text refers to destroying the city (לחבלא קרתא for Hebrew להמית עיר).

The adjustment in t232i/s is based upon the internal logic of the Targum text, but the commentaries of Kimhi, Joseph Kara, and Rashi are also instructive on this point. According to the commentators the 'rampart' (Hebr. חל cf. Ps. 122:7) earlier in the verse may be understood as the outer wall (cf. LXX προτείχισμα) while the more general term 'wall' (חומה) may be understood as the inner wall (cf. LXX τεῖχος), based on the interpretation of those two terms in Lam. 2:8 in b.Pesaḥ. 96a (שורא ובר שורא).[55] The relevant point is that the two Hebrew terms 'rampart' (חל) and 'wall' (חומה) are not synonymous, as the Hebrew text might imply: rather, the commentators understand the verse to convey the notion of penetrating into the city.

Although somewhat different in character — involving an adjustment in number rather than an alteration in lexeme — the following case is comparable as it seeks to provide an additional level of clarity.

1 Sam. 1:19

MT	וישבו ויבאו אל ביתם הרמתה
	Then they returned and they came to their house (*singular*), to Ramah.
Babylonian tradition	Then they returned and they came to their **house** (לביתהון),
t705i =	Then they returned and they came to their **houses** (לבתיהון), to Ramah.
t232i/s, t725a	

The Versions have struggled with the Hebrew because the verb is plural, yet the house is singular. If the subject of the plural verbs is Elkanah's

---

53 Despite the similarity to the reading of LXX (ἐνοοῦσαν) the Targum's מתעשתין (root: עשת) does not imply a variant Hebrew *Vorlage*. The *Vorlage* read משחתם as the Masoretic text does, see Tg. Jer. 5:6.

54 Cf. LXX Ps. 122:7 בחילך = ἐν τῇ δυνάμει σου.

55 See their commentaries on Samuel, *ad loc.*

immediate family, then we might expect the singular suffix, i.e. 'to his house' (e.g. Gen. 19:3). This is the solution adopted by the Septuagint (εἰς τὸν οἶκον αὐτοῦ), Vulgate, and Old Latin (both read: *in domum suam*),[56] which read the singular suffix, referring to Elkanah. The European Targum manuscripts adopt the alternative solution, which is to assume that the plural verbs apply to the entirety of Elkanah's retinue and to set the houses in plural.

2.c. Specification of Person

Whether unconsciously or deliberately, in a number of places a scribe has supplied a subject or object (direct or indirect) of a verb that he perceived to be 'missing'; in other words, where the original text contains an ambiguity or vagueness. For example:

2 Sam. 23:9

MT	...עם דוד בחרפם בפלשתים נאספו שם למלחמה ויעלו איש ישראל
	...with David when they put the Philistines to shame(?). They gathered there to wage war; and the men of Israel went up.
Babylonian tradition	...עם דוד כד חסידו פלשתאי ואתכנישו תמן לאגחא קרבא וסליקו אנש ישראל
	...with David when the Philistines jeered. They gathered there to wage war; and the men of Israel went up.
t232i/s	...עם דוד כד חסדו פלישתאי ואיתכנישו **פלישתאי** לתמן לאגחא קרבא...
	...when the Philistines jeered. The **Philistines** gathered there to wage war...

The addition offered by t232i/s is a clarifying gloss. Without this gloss it is unclear who the subject of the verb is, whether Israel or the Philistines. The ambiguity is reflected in the Hebrew but resolved in some Greek witnesses,[57] which also add the missing subject: καὶ οἱ ἀλλόφυλοι 'and the foreigners' (ἀλλόφυλος is used frequently of the Philistines in LXX e.g. Judg. 3:3, 31; 10:7, 11, etc.).

Referring to the Hebrew בחרפם,[58] 'in their taunting/reproaching', Kimhi notes Targum Jonathan's translation 'when the Philistines jeered' (כד חסידו פלשתאי), observing 'it is his [Jonathan's] opinion that "in their taunting" (בחרפם) refers to the Philistines, but if this is so then "the Philistines" (בפלשתים) would be superfluous (נוספת). According to the plain sense (פשט) "in their

---

56 Old Latin according Palimpsest Vindobonensis.
57 See Brooke, McLean, Thackeray edition *ad loc*.
58 On the difficulty presented by this form and the solution of Chronicles and the ancient Versions see Barthélemy, *Critique textuelle de l'Ancien Testament*, I, 314.

taunting" (בחרפם) refers instead to those "warriors" (הגבורים) who presented themselves to wage war against the Philistines who had gathered there to wage war, and Israel went up before them and these three warriors went down to them.'[59]

A similar ambiguity exists in the following example:

1 Sam. 28:14

MT	וידע שאול כי שמואל הוא ויקד אפים ארצה וישתחו
	Saul realised that it was Samuel and he bowed down face to the ground and worshipped.
Babylonian tradition	וידע שאול ארי שמואל הוא וכרע על אפוהי על ארעא וסגיד
	Saul realised that it was Samuel and he bowed his face down to the ground and worshipped.
t705i	וכרע **שאול** על אפוהי על ארעא וסגיד...
(Sperber: t12sc)	...and **Saul** bowed his face down to the ground and worshipped.

In the example just given the ambiguity is more theoretical than actual: one can be almost certain from the narrative context that it is Saul who falls to the ground, and is therefore the object of the verb, and not Samuel. In t705i the final sliver of doubt is eliminated.

Equally, in the following examples, the implied referent hardly needs stating so that the specification of the person seems redundant. That the subject has been repeated accidentally is, of course, a possibility in such cases.

1 Sam. 2:5

MT	שבעים בלחם נשכרו
	Those who were sated must hire themselves out for bread
Babylonian tradition	Upon the sons of Haman she prophesied and said, 'Those who were sated in bread (ואמרת דהוו סבעין בלחמא) and proud on account of riches and much money have become impoverished...
t713a	Upon the sons of Haman she prophesied and said, '**Haman and his sons** who were sated in bread (ואמרת **המן ובנוהי** דהוו שבעין בלחמא) and proud on account of riches and much money have become impoverished...

Despite the opening of the verse, the text of t713a specifies that both Haman and his sons suffer the same fate.

---

59 Kimhi, *Commentary on Samuel, ad loc.*

Chapter Seven. Exegetical Variants

1 Sam. 15.27

MT	ויסב שמואל ללכת ויחזק בכנף מעילו ויקרע
	As Samuel turned to go he grasped firmly the edge of his robe and it was torn.
Babylonian tradition	As Samuel turned to go he grasped firmly the edge of his robe (ואתקיף בכנף מעיליה ואיתבזע) and it was torn.
t232i/s	...he grasped firmly the edge of **Samuel's** robe (מעיליה **דשמואל** ואיתבזע) and it was torn.
Hebrew Mss	4Q51 + שאול
Version	LXX: καί ἐκράτησεν Σαουλ τοῦ πτερυγίου τῆς διπλοΐδος αὐτοῦ

As the Hebrew text stands it is unclear who is the subject of the verb חזק. It could be either Saul or Samuel. Either Saul grabbed Samuel's cloak or *vice versa*. Although the alternative reading of 4Q51 and the Septuagint differs from manuscript t232i/s the motivation is apparently the same.

1 Sam. 15:29

MT	And the Faithful One of Israel (נצח ישראל) will not lie...
Babylonian tradition	...it has already been decreed concerning you from before the Master of Israel's victory (מריה ניצחניה דישראל), before whom there is no falsehood...
t5a = t701i (Sperber: t734s)	...it has already been decreed concerning you from before **the Lord**, the Master of Israel's victory (**יוי** מרי נצחניה דישראל), before whom there is no falsehood...

The poetic reference to the Lord is uncommon (in Targums Onqelos and Jonathan only at Tg. Onq. Exod. 15:3). The adjustment in manuscripts t5a and t701i ensures that no ambiguity remains.

The following examples all exhibit the same tendency:

1 Sam. 17:47

MT	And the whole of this assembly shall know that it is not by the sword or by the spear that the Lord delivers, because the battle is the Lord's and he will give you into our hand (ונתן אתכם בידנו).
Babylonian tradition	...because from before the Lord is victory [in] battles and he will deliver you into our hands (וימסר יתכון בידנא).
t5a = t6a	...because from before the Lord is victory [in] battles and **the Lord** will deliver you into our hands (וימסר **יוי** יתכון בידנא).

1 Sam. 18:2

MT	Saul took him in that day and did not permit him to return (ולא נתנו לשוב) to his father's house.
Babylonian tradition	Saul took him in that day and did not permit him to return (ולא שבקיה למתב) to his father's house.

The Transmission of Targum Jonathan in the West

t725a	Saul took him in that day and **Saul** did not permit him to return (ולא שבקיה שאול לתוב) to his father's house.

1 Sam. 24:7

MT	לשלח ידי בו כי משיח יהוה הוא
	…to stretch out my hand against him, because he is the anointed of the Lord!
Babylonian tradition	לאושטא ידי ביה ארי משיחא דיוי הוא
	…to stretch out my hand against him, because he is the anointed of the Lord!
t705i	לאושטא ידי **במלכא** ארי משיחא דיוי הוא
	…to stretch out my hand **against the king**, because he is the anointed of the Lord!

2 Sam. 5:3

MT	ויבאו כל זקני ישראל אל המלך חברונה ויכרת להם המלך דוד ברית
	All the elders of Israel came to the king, to Hebron, and the king David established a covenant with them…
Babylonian tradition	ואתו כל סבי ישראל לות מלכא לחברון
	All the elders of Israel came to the king, to Hebron…
t2i = t725a	ואתו כל סבי ישראל לות **דוד** מלכא לחברון
	All the elders of Israel came to **David** the king, to Hebron…

2 Sam. 5:23

MT	וישאל דוד ביהוה ויאמר לא תעלה
	David inquired of the Lord and he said, 'You shall not go up…'
Babylonian tradition	David inquired of the Memra of the Lord and he said, 'You shall not go up (ואמר לא תיסק)…'
t5a	David inquired of the Memra of the Lord and **the Lord** said, 'You shall not go up (ואמר **יוי** לא תיסק)…'

2 Sam. 10:1

MT	וימת מלך בני עמון וימלך חנון בנו תחתיו
	…the king of the Amonites died and Hannun his son ruled in his stead.
Babylonian tradition	…the king of the Amonites died (ומית מלכא דבני עמון) and Hannun his son ruled in his stead.
t5a	…**Nahash** the king of the Amonites died (ומית נחש מלכא דבני עמון) and Hannun his son ruled in his stead.

The king is named in the following verse (2 Sam. 10:2).

Chapter Seven. Exegetical Variants

2.d. Adding Pronominal Suffixes

Not dissimilar to the preceding category, a pronoun is supplied on occasion to add an additional level of specificity. Sometimes this is simply to resolve an apparent textual discrepancy, as in the following case:

1 Sam. 2:20

MT	וברך עלי את אלקנה ואת אשתו ואמר ישם יהוה לך זרע מן האשה הזאת תחת השאלה אשר שאל ליהוה והלכו למקמו
	Eli would bless Elkanah and his wife saying, 'May the Lord give you offspring from this woman because of the request that you have asked from before the Lord.' And they would go to his place.
Babylonian tradition	וברוך עלי ית אלקנה וית איתתיה ואמר יקיים יוי לך בנין כשירין מן :t2520b איתתא הדא חלף שאילתא דישאיל מן קדם יוי ואזלו לאתריה
	(ואזלו גבר לאתריה :t707b)
	Eli would bless Elkanah and his wife saying, 'May the Lord raise up for you fit sons from this woman because of the request that you have asked from before the Lord.' And they would go to **his** place.
t232i/s = t6a, t713a, t720a (Sperber: t711y i.e. base text)	...ואזלו לאתרי**הון**
	...And they would go to **their** place.

The plural pronoun offered in t232i/s, t6a, t713a, and t720a fits the flow of the narrative better and is, in fact, the reading of some Hebrew manuscripts and the Peshitta (though the singular 'his' may be intended to specify that the pair returned to Elkanah's native city).[60]

The addition of a pronoun can also play an exegetical role, as in the following example:

1 Sam. 2:10

MT	יהוה יחתו מריבו (ק: מריביו)
	Those contending with the Lord will be broken...
Babylonian tradition	יוי יתבר בעלי דבבא דקימין לאבאשא לעמיה
	The Lord will break the enemies who are rising up to do evil to his people...
t718i	יוי יתבר בעלי דבב**נא** דקיימין לאבאשא לעמיה
	The Lord will break **our** enemies who are rising up to do evil to his people...

It is noteworthy that a number of examples of this category of variant are to be found in 2 Samuel 22, a unit in which the continuous text appears to have

---

60 Cf. 1 Sam. 2:11; Kimhi, *Commentary on Samuel, ad loc.*

been influenced in some manuscripts by alternative readings found in liturgical forms of the text (see §3 below). In the following examples the additional pronoun is also present in some of the liturgical sources. The purpose of its addition remains the same — namely to provide further specification or clarification — but the possibility arises that the copyist of the continuous text has taken over the pronoun from a liturgical form of the text (consciously or subconsciously).

2 Sam. 22:1

MT	and from the hand of Saul	ומכף שאול
Babylonian tradition	and also David from Saul's sword	ואף לדוד מחרבא דשאול
t718i = t701i (omits דשאול in error)	and also David **He saved** from Saul's sword	ואף דוד **שיזיב** מחרבא דשאול
t2i = t3i, t7i, t725a, t713a (cf. t5a שזביהא) (Sperber: t10r, t702s, t734s)	(t2i דוד) and also David **He saved** from Saul's sword	ואף לדוד **שיזביה** מחרבא דשאול

The verb 'to save' (שיזב), witnessed in many Western manuscripts but missing in the text's Eastern tradition, may have entered the text under influence of the liturgical text forms (see §3 below).

2 Sam. 22:28

MT	Poor people you will save! Your eyes are upon the exalted – you will bring low!	ואת עם עני תושיע ועיניך על רמים תשפיל
Babylonian tradition	And the people, the house of Israel, who are called in this world 'a poor people' you will redeem; and by your Memra the strong ones who are prevailing over them you will bring down.	וית עמא בית ישראל דמתקרן בעלמא הדין עם חשיך את עתיד למפרק ובמימרך תקיפיא דמתגברין עליהון תמאיך
t232i/s	And **your** people, the house of Israel…	וית עמ**ך** בית ישראל...

The additional pronoun is, however, not always to be found in liturgical sources, as is the case in the following example. Of course, this observation may need to be adjusted as liturgical sources are studied further.

Chapter Seven. Exegetical Variants

2 Sam. 22:4

MT	[no Hebrew text]	
Babylonian tradition		אמר דוד בתשבחא
	David said in a psalm…	
t701i		ואמר דוד בתושבחתיה
	And David said in **his** psalm…	

3. Agreements with Liturgical Sources

Liturgical compositions, such as mahzorim, that follow Italian rites preserve a longer text of 2 Samuel 22, the haftarah for the seventh day of Passover, and attest to its continued public recital in the synagogue in the middle ages. The pluses *vis à vis* the Babylonian text tradition can mostly be classified as 'redundant' (no pejorative sense is intended), that is to say that when omitted a complete text more or less corresponding to Targum Jonathan remains, although the text has become somewhat jumbled in the process of transmission and the text varies to some extent from one mahzor to the next (see chapter ten).[61] The text of those sources (mostly haftarot collections) that reflect Ashkenazi rites, by contrast, varies only as much as do the Ashkenazi manuscripts containing the continuous text of Targum Jonathan.

When one compares all the manuscripts containing the continuous text that are included in this study with these liturgical sources one notes a striking number of shared readings, in particular with the embellished text form of the Italian mahzorim. Excluding those cases where coincidence seems likely, sufficient cases remain that a literary dependence of some sort is a possibility.

The relation between liturgical and continuous text forms can be detected in a number of additions or alternative word choices, mostly relating to single words. In at least one case a larger expansion may betray a genetic relationship:

2 Sam. 22:47

MT	[no Hebrew text]	
Babylonian tradition		בכין על ניסא ופורקנא דעבדתא לעמך אודיאו
	Therefore, because of the miracle and the redemption that you performed for your people, they gave thanks…	

---

61 See Kasher, *Targumic Toseftot to the Prophets*, 22 (on 'redundant' expansion); 28–9 (oral transmission).

The Transmission of Targum Jonathan in the West

t232i/s	בכין על ניסא ופורקנא דעבדת **למישיחך ולשיארא** דעמך **ישראל** אודיאו Therefore, because of the miracle and the redemption that you performed **for your Anointed One and for the remnant of** your people **Israel** they gave thanks…
t7i = t713a, t720a (Sperber: t10r, t716y)	בכין על ניסא ופורקנא דעבדתא לעמך **בית ישר׳** אודיאו Therefore, because of the miracle and the redemption that you performed for your people, **the House of Israel**, they gave thanks…

The first addition in t232i/s, 'for your Anointed One and for the remnant of (your people)', which gives the verse a messianic interpretation (cf. esp. Tg. Hab. 3:17–18)[62], is certainly a 'conventional' rendering in the sense that the phraseology is standard, but its arrival in the text preserved in t232i/s may be explained in one of two ways. The words may have been imported into the current verse based on the wording of Tg. 2 Sam. 22:32 (ופורקנא דעבדת למישיחך ולשיארא דעמך) or perhaps Tg. Hab. 3:17–18. An alternative explanation is that the addition reveals the influence of a liturgical source, since all the Italian mahzorim examined in this study (the verse is omitted in the Ashkenazi mahzorim), as well as the example included by Kasher in his *Targumic Toseftot to the Prophets*,[63] offer this reading. The further addition of 'Israel' (or 'House of Israel') may be based on conventional usage elsewhere,[64] or may likewise also be related to a liturgical tradition, the reading being known in liturgical sources belonging to the Sephardi tradition.[65]

Other smaller embellishments also agree with liturgical forms of the text, e.g.:

2 Sam. 22:3

MT	[no Hebrew text]
Babylonian tradition	מיד כל חטופין שיזיב יתי
	From the hand of all robbers He saved me.

---

62 On these two verses see J. Shunary, 'תוספת משיחא בתרגום יונתן לנביאים', *Tarbiz* 42 (1973) 259–65, p 265.

63 Also a mahzor according to the Italian rite (fifteenth cent.), Kasher, *Targumic Toseftot to the Prophets* §70, l.11–13. The reading also appears in Sperber's 'Fr' source, which was probably also (fragments?) of a mahzor; on which see my, 'The critical importance of Targum Fragments'.

64 For 'people' + 'Israel' see e.g. Tg. Josh. 8:33; Tg. Judg. 11:23; Tg. 1 Sam. 9:16; 15:1; 27:12; Tg. 2 Sam. 3:18; 5:12; 7:7, 8, 10, 11, 23, 24; 18:7 etc. For 'people' + 'House of Israel' see e.g. Tg. Josh. 10:13; Tg. 2 Sam. 1:2; 22:28; Tg. Isa. 1:2; 9:1, 2; Tg. Jer. 31:14, 22; Tg. Ezek. 36:38; Tg. Joel 2:26, 27; Tg. Amos 9:1.

65 'House': Ms Sassoon 1017 (Sassoon Collection; Siddur; Sephardi; fifteenth cent.); 'House of Israel': Ms Valmadonna 89 (Richler 130).

Chapter Seven. Exegetical Variants

t718i = t2i, t5a, t725a (שיזבתיה)	מיד כל חטופין **ואניסין** שיזיב יתי From the hand of all robbers **and thieves** He saved me.

This addition 'thieves' is found in all the Ashkenazi mahzorim examined in this study (i.e. t159a, t99a, t133a, t63a) though it is absent from the Italian tradition. Kimhi cites this variant form in his *Commentary on Samuel* (*ad loc*).

2 Sam. 22:9

MT		עלה עשן באפו
	Smoke rose from his nose…	
Babylonian tradition	The insolence of Pharaoh (זדוניה דפרעה) went up like smoke before him…	
t5a = t6a^{correct}, t713a, t720a, t725a, t2i, t3i, t7i, t718i (Sperber: t716y, t10r, t702s, t734s)	The insolence of **wicked** Pharaoh (זדוניה דפרעה **רשיעא**) went up like smoke before him…	

The same plus ('wicked') is found in all the liturgical sources examined in this study.[66]

2 Sam. 22:27

MT	[no Hebrew text]
Babylonian tradition	דחשיבו מחשבן על עמך בלבילתנון כמחשבתהון [Jacob, who walked in purity before you, you chose his sons from all the peoples, you set apart his seed from every blemish of Pharaoh and the Egyptians] who thought thoughts against your people, you confused them according to their plans.
t7i = t2i, t3i, t718i, t232i/s, t5a, t6a^{correct}, t713a, t720a, t725a (Sperber: t702s, t734s, t12sc)	דחשיבו מחשבן **בישן** על עמך בלבלתינון במחשבתהון …who thought **evil** thoughts against your people, you confused them according to their plans.

This reading is also found in the liturgical version of the text in t1647i, t1618i, and t1621i (the verse is omitted in the Ashkenazi liturgies). The expression 'evil thoughts' is not found in Targum Onqelos and appears in Targum Jonathan only in Ezekiel 38.10, where it reflects the Hebrew; it is more frequent in later Palestinian Targums (e.g. Tg.Ps. 21:12; Tg. Prov. 6:18; Tg. Esth. II 3:8; Tg. Ps.-J. Gen. 50:20; Tg. Ps.-J. Deut. 32:32), including the parallel verse in Tg. Ps. 18:27 (see pages 251–2), but nonetheless there is no compelling case for assuming that the variant has arisen due to conventional usage.

---

66 A paraphrastic addition according to Bacher, 'Kritische Untersuchungen zum Prophetentargum', 50.

The Transmission of Targum Jonathan in the West

2 Sam. 22:40

MT	תכריע קמי תחתני
	You made those rising up against me bow down beneath me!
Babylonian tradition	You broke the people who were rising up (עממיא דקיימין) to do evil to me beneath me!
t713a	You broke **strong** peoples who were rising up (עממין **תקיפין** דקיימין) to do evil to me beneath me!

The liturgical manuscripts t1601i, t1679i, t1647i, t1618i and t1621i have a similar plus (i.e. 'the people who are becoming strong and rising up…' עממיא דתקיפין וקיימין). This language is formulaic in the Latter Prophets (e.g. Tg. Isa. 2:13; 9:4; 43:2; 47:14; Tg. Jer. 5:6; 11:16; Tg. Ezek. 15:7; 19:12, 14; 21:37; etc) so we cannot rule out the possibility that we here have a case of conventional rendering (see chapter six).

An alternative word choice occasionally matches the reading of liturgical texts too, for example:

2 Sam. 22:6

MT	חבלי שאול סבני קדמני מקשי מות
	The cords of Sheol encircle me, the snares of death confronted me.
Babylonian tradition	משרית רשיעין אקפוני **קדמוני** דמזינין במני קטול
	Camps of wicked ones encircled me, those armed with deadly weapons **approach** me.
t7i = t718i, t232i/s, t6a, t720a	Camps of wicked ones encircled me, those armed with deadly weapons **meet** me (ערעוני t718i: ארעוני)…

Both Ashkenazi and Italian liturgical texts employ the root ערע at this point (or with the alternative spelling ארע)[67] in place of קדם, which reflects the underlying Hebrew (cf. Tg. 2 Kgs 19:32; Tg. Isa. 37:33). Where the verse is preserved, the liturgical texts also adopt the root ערע in 2 Sam. 22:19 for the underlying Hebrew יקדמני, although the majority of them actually reads both verbs (i.e. ערעוני וקדמוני).[68]

Other very minor variants may also be attributable to the influence of liturgical forms of the text. Some variant features, such as the use of an alternative verb (e.g. t2i שיזיב יתי דבבי מבעלי in place of פריק יתי דבבי מבעלי at 2 Sam. 22:3; t7i, t232i/s לאגחא קרבא for למעבד קרבא at 2 Sam. 22:35), or an alternative conjugation of the verb (t718i, t3i וקביל מהיכליה — t3i omits *waw* —

---

67 *Italian*: t1601i; t1679i; t1647i; t1618i; t1621i; Ashkenazi: t159a; t99a; t133a; t63a.
68 t1601i; t1639i; t1679i; t1618i; t1621i. Reading only ערע : t1647i; t159a.

Chapter Seven. Exegetical Variants

for ומקביל at 2 Sam. 22:7; t701i, t2i מקביל צלותהון for מיתקבלא at 2 Sam. 22:42; t3i אתייהב for מתיהיב at 2 Sam. 22:3), find parallels in the liturgical sources. Of course these minor variants also permit a number of other possible explanations (e.g. error, conventional renderings, etc).

Evaluating the evidence presented here is far from straightforward. The occasional agreement in individual readings hardly amounts to an unequivocal case for the influence of liturgical forms on the continuous text of Targum Jonathan in its European transmission or for a common source underlying both text types. The cases are relatively few and no single manuscript exhibits a complete correspondence (though manuscripts t7i and t718i are more clearly marked by this phenomenon than others). Equally, some (but not all) of the variations could easily be accounted for by the other tendencies that we have observed in the European continuous text, so the level of agreement might, in fact, be less than the examples presented above suggest.

The situation is further complicated by the fact that many of the agreements appear in continuous texts of Ashkenazi origin, but only in Italian liturgical texts, so the possibility that the scribes of our Ashkenazi manuscripts have been influenced by formulae unconsciously imprinted in the memory by the synagogue liturgy is problematic at best. A plausible channel of influence is not apparent, but these expansions to 2 Samuel 22 in the continuous text may have had their origin in material that originated in the liturgy[69] but that no longer had any liturgical function in medieval Europe at the time the expansions entered the continuous text tradition. Such material may have been preserved in the margins or integrated into the text (either with or without the designation 'tosefta').[70] In any case the sporadic nature of the variants suggests we are not dealing with a process of deliberate revision.

For the sake of completeness, we must also mention at this point Targum Psalms, since David's song of thanksgiving in 2 Samuel 22 has its parallel in Psalm 18. Although the extant manuscripts and citations of Targum Psalms demonstrate that it circulated in Italy and Ashkenaz in the period with which

---

69 On the link between Tosefta Targums and the liturgy see chapters ten and eleven.
70 E.g. At Zech. 4:7 (fl. 251v), for example, the longer readings of manuscript Montefiore 7 [H116] (Montefiore Endowment; Sephardi, 1486), show unmistakably the traces of Tosefta Targum material, but the unit is not marked as 'tosefta' in the margin as other Tosefta Targums in the manuscript are (e.g. fl.11r, 1 Sam. 17:42; fl. 14v, 1 Sam. 18:19; etc); Kasher, *Targumic Toseftot to the Prophets* §144(ז). The same phenomenon is noted in several of our European manuscripts, see chapter eleven.

we are concerned,[71] it does not appear to have influenced the transmission of the text of Targum Samuel. The variants to 2 Samuel 22 described above are not reflected in Targum Psalms (the longer addition to 2 Sam. 22:47 is in any case part of a Targumic addition not found in Tg.Ps.), with the exception of the variant reading to 2 Sam. 22:27 (מחשבן בישן; Tg.Ps. 18:27).

4. Some Problematic Cases

The generally poor state of the textual transmission among the European manuscript often makes it difficult to distinguish an intentional variant from a simple misreading by a scribe, for example:

1 Sam. 2:1

MT	[no Hebrew text]
Babylonian tradition	בכין תימר כנישתא דישראל
	then the assembly of Israel will say…
t232i/s	בכין תימר כנישתא **דייי**
	then the assembly **of the Lord** will say…

The expression 'assembly *of the Lord*' is unknown in Targum Jonathan but appears occasionally in Onqelos (cf Tg. Onq. Num. 27:17; 31:16), whereas the form 'congregation of Israel' (or 'the congregation of the sons of Israel') is widespread (e.g. Tg. Josh. 22:18; 22:20; Tg. 1 Sam. 2:1; Tg. 1 Kgs 8:5; Tg. Isa. 27:2; 51:9, 10; Tg. Jer. 2:24; 5:7; etc), so this is probably not a conventional rendering.

This last example highlights the difficulty faced in analysing such variants in cases where a manuscript's transmission is poor. We cannot exclude the possibility of error, but equally we must weigh t232i/s's tendency to err against the relative frequency of deliberate changes in the manuscript. This problem is acute in t718i, where deliberate variation becomes difficult to separate from

---

71 See D.M. Stec, *The Targum of Psalms: Translated, with a Critical Introduction, Apparatus, and Notes* (The Aramaic Bible 16, Collegeville, MI 2004), 2, 21–2. Although the underlying Hebrew of Tg. Jon. and Tg. Ps. differs slightly 'the two targumim are virtually identical' (Stec, *The Targum of Psalms*, 49 n.1); that Tg. Ps. used the text of Tg. Jon. as its base explains this fact, see M. Smelik and W. Smelik, 'Twin Targums: Psalm 18 and II Samuel 22', in A. Rapoport-Albert and G. Greenberg (eds), *Biblical Hebrews, Biblical Texts: Essays in Memory of Michael P. Weitzman* (Journal for the Study of the Old Testament Supplement Series 333, Sheffield 2001), 244–81, p. 247.

error. For example, 'the pestilence will be lifted from upon the *land* (מעל ארעא)' (2 Sam. 24:21), in place of 'from upon the *people* (מעל עמא)'; or 'Arwan said to the *king* (למלכא)' (2 Sam. 24:22), instead of 'to *David* (לדוד)'. These are not graphic errors, but equally it is hard to detect any purpose behind them. In a similar example, 1 Sam. 1:25, t718i reads 'so *they slaughtered* and sacrificed (ודבחו ונכסו) the bull…', in place of simply 'sacrificed' (ונכסו). The reading of t718i may have arisen as an error, but since the underlying Hebrew שחט is rendered in Targum Jonathan with נכס very frequently, but with דבח only once (Tg. Hos. 5:2; and never in Onqelos), there is a case for assuming that this is a deliberate alteration. Perhaps a scribe wished to sharpen a distinction between the act of slaughter, which after all is all that the Hebrew שחט implies, and an act of offering. Kimhi refines the sense of שחט in a similar way, explaining that Hannah and Elkanah brought Samuel to the Temple, where he was to learn the law and the commandments at the feet of Eli, after they had slaughtered the bullock *as a sacrifice* (אחר ששחטו את הפר לקרבן).[72]

Conclusion

In this chapter I have attempted to bring together all those variants in our European manuscripts that alter the text in apparently deliberate and significant ways. Some such alterations of the text appear to reflect the influence of fuller text forms (sometimes referred to as Tosefta Targums), which are now known to us in mahzorim, but which may have circulated in the margins of manuscripts or in separate collections. I will examine these in more detail in chapters ten and eleven. The evidence is far from decisive, however.

The vast majority of the variants in this chapter proved, on closer examination, to be cases of clarification where the text admitted more than one possible explanation, or of explication where what is clearly implied in the text is stated explicitly. Clarifications and explications were achieved by small additions or substitutions of vocabulary. These textual emendations often provide us with an explanation similar to that offered by one or more of the great medieval commentators (a point to which I will return shortly).

We found only a handful of variants in the entire corpus that enrich the text by means of additions that could be considered genuinely exegetical. Their

---

72 Kimhi, *Commentary on Samuel, ad loc.*

character makes it difficult to pin down the origin of these embellishments: they echo traditions attested in a diffuse range of sources, often including the wider corpus of Targumic literature. We can nonetheless say that they would fit comfortably within the melée of medieval European Jewish thought, and this, in my view, is the context in which they entered the text of Targum Samuel. At the same time the paucity of these variants is striking. Whereas in other chapters I have included only a selection of the more convincing cases, in section 1 of this chapter I have included as many cases as I could find, a total of five cases. It is clear that, despite the many minor tweaks and accidental modifications to the Targum text, in general the copyists did not feel at liberty to adjust, rewrite, or embellish the text. Truly creative engagement with the text was limited.[73] In terms of its status Targum Jonathan was clearly not of a kind with, for example, Targum Pseudo-Jonathan, whose text continued to evolve well into the medieval period. Rather, its text enjoyed a (semi-) canonical status and so retained *grosso modo* its basic shape.

---

73 Cf. the somewhat overstated conclusion of Chilton on the basis of Codex Reuchlinianus No. 3 and his study of one Sephardi manuscript (Hébreu 75, Bibliothèque Nationale, Paris): 'during the thirteenth and later centuries (as well as during the twelfth), the work of the meturgemanin was creative, and hardly a simple matter of preservation. As they handed on the Targumic tradition, they attempted to make sense of it, so that their texts are structurally ambivalent, and would remain so, until the fifteenth century saw an attempt to distinguish Targum Jonathan as such from the attempts to perpetuate its interpretative ingenuity in new idioms. The manuscript reminds us that, while definite versions of the Targumim were received in given places, no such version was truly final'. Chilton, 'HEBR. 75 in the Bibliothèque Nationale', 148.

Chapter Eight

Linguistic Features

Our European manuscripts contain a vast number of extremely minor variants. Many of these reflect orthographic tendencies in late Western manuscripts. In general the Western manuscripts favour a fuller orthography. For example, all exhibit a strong inclination towards *plene* spellings, though this is introduced inconsistently. The orthography of personal and gentilic nouns is particularly fluid.[1] Likewise, the Western manuscripts (especially manuscripts t2i, t3i, and t720a) tend to favour the independent form of the relative pronoun (i.e. די) over the prefixed form (i.e. -ד). The manuscripts are, however, far from consistent.[2] The independent form of the preposition מן sometimes replaces the prefixed form (e.g. 1 Sam. 1:3 t6a מן קרתיה, 1 Sam. 2:10 t705i מן גוג, 1 Sam. 9:3 t713a, t720a, t705i מן עולימיא), yet the reverse also occurs, although less frequently (e.g 1 Sam. 4:16 t6a, t713a, t720a, t232i/s מסדרא דקרבא). Full forms are usually preferred to contracted forms (e.g. 1 Sam. 3:4, 11 etc. t710y האנא, A + MW הא אנא; 1 Sam. 9:14 t710y האנון, t6a, t713a, t720a, t725a, t2i, t232i/s הא אינון; 1 Sam. 20:2 t710y ומדין, t5a, t725a, t232i/s ומה דין, t6a, t713a, t720a, t2i, t3i, t7i, t701i, t718i מא דין). In many cases, accommodation to the available line space accounts for the inconsistencies given above.

Among these minor variants we also detect features that reflect the linguistic setting in which the manuscripts were transmitted and although historical philology is not the focus of this study it will be worth noting briefly a few such features. In short, the European manuscripts contain some variants that show features characteristic of Western Aramaic dialects. Tempting as it may be to imagine that such features provide a link between our texts and the Palestine of Antiquity, such an explanation is fallacious. There is no reason to

---

1   To give just one example from many: t718i 2 Sam. 21:1 גבעונאי but 2 Sam. 21:2 לגיבעונאי. The general state of inconsistency is nicely exhibited in t701i, in which the orthography differs between two occurrences of a word that has been accidentally repeated on the following page (e.g. 1 Sam. 17.13 תלתא ¶ תלתה; 1 Sam. 17:48 ואזיל ¶ ואזל). Cf. Smelik, 'How to Grow a Tree', 505; Smelik, *Targum of Judges*, 131.

2   For example, 1 Sam. 1:17 manuscripts t6a, t713a, t720a, t2i and t3i introduce the independent form (i.e. די בעית; t710y דבעית); yet the prefixed form is retained in these manuscripts for the occurrences in 1 Sam. 1:23.

imagine that such variation has arisen outside Europe. Aramaic texts of distinct dialects circulated widely in medieval Europe (see chapter two); it is not hard to imagine that a scribe, lacking proficiency in Aramaic — as was certainly the case with some of our copyists (see chapter three §3) — or in a moment of carelessness, mingled distinct dialectic elements. We might also point to Targum Pseudo-Jonathan, a late text (post-seventh/eighth century) that mixes Palestinian and Babylonian dialect features and which may well have reached its current form at the hands of European Jewry;[3] or to the Targums of the Writings.[4]

The presence of Western Aramaic features is most evident in the pronominal suffixes. In masculine plural nouns the suffix is appended to the termination *ai*. This termination is usually retained in the orthography of Palestinian Aramaic with the first singular suffix (‏י- 'my'), e.g. פתגמיי, but omitted in the Babylonian Aramaic of Targums Jonathan and Onqelos where the form would be פתגמי.[5] The Western forms crop up in the European manuscripts, although no manuscript adopts them consistently (e.g. 1 Sam. 2:1 t725a, t2i, t3i בעלי דבביי; 1 Sam. 2:24 t2i, t3i בניי; 1 Sam. 20:42 t5a, t720a, t725a, t2i, t232i/s, t705i בניי; 1 Sam. 2:30 t720a, t2i, t3i, t705i דיניי cf. t713a דינאיי, ta5, ta6, t725a דינאי; 1 Sam. 4:10 t713a, t720a רגליי; 1 Sam. 15:11 t713a, t720a פיתגמיי; 1 Sam. 30:23 t2i, t3i אחיי; 2 Sam. 2:22 t5a, t713a, t2i, t705i אפיי, etc.).[6] In Galilean Aramaic the *yod* is also retained in the second singular feminine suffix on masculine plural nouns; isolated examples of this are found in our manuscripts (e.g. 1 Sam. 25:35 t705i אפייך).[7] Finally, the third masculine

---

3   Maher, *Targum Pseudo-Jonathan: Genesis*, 8–14; E. Cook, 'Rewriting the Bible: the Text and Language of the Pseudo-Jonathan Targum', unpublished Ph.D. dissertation (University of California 1986), 36; cf. G. Dalman, *Grammatik des Jüdisch-Palästinischen Aramäisch: nach den Idiomen des Palästinischen Talmud des Onkelostargum und Prophetentargum und der Jerusalemischen Targume: Aramäische Dialektproben* (Darmstadt 1978 [1927]), 27–8, 32–3.

4   For a brief overview and further bibliography see Flesher and Chilton, *The Targums*, 233–5.

5   Dalman, *Grammatik des Jüdisch-Palästinischen Aramäisch*, 204; D.M. Golomb, *A Grammar of Targum Neofiti* (Harvard Semitic Monographs 34, Chico, CA 1985), 51; S.E. Fassberg, *A Grammar of the Palestinian Targum Fragments from the Cairo Genizah Genizah* (Harvard Semitic Studies 38, Atlanta, GA 1990), 114–15.

6   The orthographic inconsistency it demonstrated by the presence of typically Babylonian orthographic features: 1 Sam 2:1 t713a דבבאי; 1 Sam. 20:42 t3i, t701i בנאי; 1 Sam. 2:30 t5a, t6a, t725a דינאי; 1 Sam. 4:10 t6a, t2i, t232i/s רגלאי. Cf. the preposition קדם, e.g. 1 Sam. 2:29 t3i קדמיי, t5a קדמאי; 1 Sam. 9:16 t705i קדמיי; etc. Targum Pseudo-Jonathan uses both קדמי and קדמיי (e.g. Tg. Ps.-J. Lev. 20:26). Cf. also Smelik, 'How to Grow a Tree', 505.

7   Dalman, *Grammatik des Jüdisch-Palästinischen Aramäisch*, 90, 204.

Chapter Eight. Linguistic Features

singular suffix attached to a verb in imperative is typically -יִהי in Babylonian texts. The Palestinian form -יֵה is found sporadically in our Western manuscripts (e.g. 1 Sam. 16:12 A + MW מְשִׁחְיֵה; 1 Sam. 20:40 t6a^PM, t701i, t705i אוֹבְלִיֵה),[8] though again none is consistent (e.g. 2 Sam. 11:25 t5a, t6a^PM, t725a, t2i, t3i, t7i, t701i, t705i וְתִקִיפֵּהּ, t720a, t232i/s, t718i וְתִקְפֵּהּ, t6a^correct, t713a וְתִקִיפֵּהּ).[9]

Certain orthographic features also suggest the influence of Western Aramaic. The denotation of final $\bar{a}$ with the termination -ה predominates in the West, and is typical of good manuscripts of Galilean Aramaic, whereas the termination -א predominates in the East.[10] Scattered examples of this orthography are found in our European manuscripts (e.g. 1 Sam. 2:23 t6a, t713a, t720a, t725a, t232i/s, t705i לְמָה; 1 Sam. 3:17 t5a, t720a, t725a, t7i, t232i/s, t705i מָה; 1 Sam. 20:21 t705i, t6a^PM וְלְכָה; 1 Sam. 25:33 t7i וּבְרִיכָה; etc.),[11] including in verbal conjugations (e.g. 1 Sam. 8:5 t713a, t720a סָבְתָה; 1 Sam. 13:14 t232i/s, t701i נְטַרְתָה; 1 Sam. 30:8 t3i אַדְבְּקָה תַדְבִּיק; 2 Sam. 1:14 t6a לְאוֹשָׁטָה; 2 Sam. 1:5 t725a יְדַעְתָה; 2 Sam. 7:23 t720a דִיהַבְתָה), and for the definite article, a typically Palestinian feature[12] (2 Sam. 3:8 t701i דְכַלְבָה; 2 Sam. 11:24 t720a שׁוּרָה). Similarly, the use of א as a vowel letter to denote $\bar{a}$, is a common feature of Targum Pseudo-Jonathan and other late Aramaic texts,[13] and is also found in our European manuscripts (e.g. 1 Sam. 20:29; 21:1; 24:4; 2 Sam. 16:22 t232i/s עָאל; 1 Sam. 25:2 t713a, t725a, t2i, t232i/s, t701i, t705i עָאן; 1

---

8   Dalman, *Grammatik des Jüdisch-Palästinischen Aramäisch*, 374–5.
9   To this category we might add the use of the suffix *-hwm* instead of *-hwn* in t2i noted by Levine, who adds 'this is not quite an error, though, insofar as it is a suffix found in Palestinian texts'; Levine, *The Aramaic version of Lamentations*, 22. This feature may, however, result from the influence of Biblical Aramaic (e.g. Ezra 5:3–5, 8–10; 6:9; 7:24). This feature is not found in Targum Samuel in this manuscript.
10 Cook, 'Rewriting the Bible', 111, 113; F.Y. Kutscher, *Studies in Galilean Aramaic* (trans. M. Sokoloff, Ramat Gan 1976), 349. The orthography of the Palestinian Targum manuscripts is fluid; see Fassberg, *A Grammar of the Palestinian Targum Fragments from the Cairo Genizah*, 61, 64.
11 Levine notes the mixing of ultima א and ה, with א most prevalent, in t2i; Levine, *The Aramaic Version of Jonah*, 26.
12 K. Beyer, *The Aramaic Language, its Distribution and Subdivisions* (trans. J.F. Healey; Göttingen 1986), 21.
13 Cook, 'Rewriting the Bible', 111. Cf. also Golomb, *A Grammar of Targum Neofiti*, 18; Fassberg, *A Grammar of the Palestinian Targum Fragments from the Cairo Genizah*, 61–2; Klein, *Genizah Manuscripts of Palestinian Targum to the Pentateuch*, Vol. 1 (Cincinnati, OH 1986), xxxvi.

Sam. 2:9 t5a, t6a, t713a, t720a, t725a, t2i, t3i מאן; 1 Sam. 2:25 t6a, t725a, t2i, t3i מאן; and frequently).

The very frequent designation of consonantal *waw* (ו) and *yod* (י) with וו and יי (e.g. 1 Sam. 1:5 t705i וולד; 1 Sam. 1:6 t6a וולד; 1 Sam. 4:5 t5a, t6a, t720a, t725a, t2i, t3i, t7i, t232i/s, t701i, t705i, t718i קיימא; 1 Sam. 4:7 t6a, t725a, t2i, t3i, t232i/s, t705i, t718i ווי) is also characteristic of the orthography of Targum Pseudo-Jonathan and other late manuscripts, but is also found, for example, in the Genizah manuscripts of Palestinian Targum to the Pentateuch.[14]

Several variations in spelling may also reflect a late Western context: the spelling ערע of the verb 'to meet' is common across dialects, while the spelling ארע, which is more typical of Late Jewish Literary Aramaic,[15] appears in t718i (e.g. 1 Sam. 9:18; 2 Sam. 22:6 for t710y קדמוני, 2 Sam. 22:19 for t710y יקדמוני). The consonantal shift from *kaph* to *qoph,* found in a few cases in our manuscripts (e.g. 1 Sam. 13:20/21 t710y כולביה, t713a, t720a קולביה; 1 Sam. 26:5 t710y כרקומא, t720a קרקומא also 1 Sam. 26:7; 2 Sam. 6:14 t710y כרדוט, t701i קרדוט), is also a feature of Targum Pseudo-Jonathan's orthography.[16] The Babylonian textual tradition of both Jonathan and Onqelos uses the form אתו 'wifehood, matrimony'. This is sporadically substituted for the form אנתו (or אינתו) in the European manuscripts (e.g. 1 Sam. 18:17: t5a, t2i, t7i; 1 Sam. 18:19: t5a, t725a, t2i, t7i; 1 Sam. 18:27: t725a, t2i, t7i; 1 Sam. 25:39: t5a, t713a, t720a, t725a, t7i[correct], t718i; 1 Sam. 25:40: t5a, t720a, t725a, t718i; 1 Sam. 25:42: t5a, t720a, t232i/s, t718i; 2 Sam. 11:27: t5a, t720a, t232i/s; 2 Sam. 12:9: t725a, t7i; 2 Sam. 12:10: t5a, t720a, t725a). None of the manuscripts is consistent, though manuscript t5a adopts אנתו on all but one occasion in the two books of Samuel.[17] To these examples, we might add the spelling ברת 'daughter', as opposed to בת for the singular construct form (e.g. 1 Sam. 18:20: t713a, t720a; 1 Sam. 18:28: t713a, t720a; 2 Sam. 3:7: t713a; 2 Sam. 6:20: t7i; 2 Sam. 6:23: t713a). The Eastern text of Targums Onqelos and Jonathan always employs the latter form (בת); the former form (ברת) is typical in Late Jewish Literary Aramaic, but it is

---

14 Cook, 'Rewriting the Bible', 113–16; Klein, *Genizah Manuscripts of Palestinian Targum to the Pentateuch,* Vol. 1, xxxvi.
15 Cook, 'Rewriting the Bible', 123; Dalman, *Grammatik des Jüdisch-Palästinischen Aramäisch,* 99.
16 Cook, 'Rewriting the Bible', 124.
17 Incidentally, the First Rabbinic Bible has consistently adjusted the form in both Targums Onqelos and Jonathan.

Chapter Eight. Linguistic Features

also found at Qumran and in Targum Neofiti.[18]

Although the vocalisation of the European manuscripts is not studied in this volume (see pages xix–xx) the tendency towards *plene* spelling allows us to observe a vocalic change that occurs sporadically in Galilean Aramaic in certain words, namely the transition from *a* to *e* or *i* in closed syllables (e.g. 1 Sam. 1:24 t710y דקמחא, t5a, t6a, t713a, t720a, t725a, t3i, t705i, t718i דקימחא).[19]

Conclusions

While not all the examples given above carry equal weight for determining the linguistic setting in which our European manuscripts were transmitted, taken together they point clearly to the influence of Western Aramaic. The result is a dialectically mixed text. Nonetheless, while some manuscripts (in particular, t2i, t3i, t705i, t720a) exhibit these features more strongly than others, none shows a level of consistency that might suggest a deliberate attempt to accommodate the language to a particular dialect. On this point they are to be distinguished from Targum Pseudo-Jonathan, which is written in 'an artificially unified dialect of literary Aramaic'.[20] Indeed in some respects, such as their tendency to introduce the proleptic suffix pronoun into genitive constructions employing the particle -ד,[21] they show themselves to be linguistically distinct from Targum Pseudo-Jonathan, which has a marked preference for the construct state.[22] Rather, the linguistic variations have arisen haphazardly.

In other words, it is the extent of individual scribes' (or multiple generations of scribes?) familiarity with other dialects of Aramaic that accounts for the variations in our Targum manuscripts rather than any

---

18 S.E. Fassberg, 'The Forms of "Son" and "Daughter" in Aramaic', in H. Gzella and M.L. Folmer (eds), *Aramaic in its Historical and Linguistic Setting* (Veröffentlichungen der Orientalischen Kommission 50, Wiesbaden 2008), 41–53, pp. 45–6. Also Beyer, *The Aramaic Language*, 22.

19 Fassberg, 'The Forms of 'Son' and 'Daughter' in Aramaic', 45–6. Also Beyer, *The Aramaic Language*, 22.

20 Cook, 'Rewriting the Bible', 281.

21 1 Sam. 16:15 t232i/s עבדוהי דשאול; 1 Sam. 16:18 t725a, t2i ומימריה דיוי; 1 Sam. 18:28 t5a, t6a, t725a, t2i, t3i, t7i, t232i/s, t705i, t718i בסעדיה דדוד; 2 Sam. 3:27 t6a בדמיה דעשהאל; 2 Sam. 6:20 t7i ברתיה דשא[ול]; 2 Sam. 7:27 t6a, t713a בליביה דעבדך; 2 Sam. 24:1 t6a, t701i רוגזיה דיוי; 2 Sam. 24:25 t7i, t718i צלותהון דדיירי ארעא.

22 Cook, 'Rewriting the Bible', 212–15.

particular 'Western' or 'Eastern' origin. Texts from a wide spectrum of Aramaic dialects were in circulation in Europe in the period during which our Targum manuscripts were copied. The scribes who copied our Targum manuscripts were influenced by the Aramaic of these texts. Palestinian forms of Aramaic have exerted a stronger influence over our Targum manuscripts than, say, that of the Babylonian Talmud, though there is no consistent pattern. This picture fits well with the hypothesis that the majority of variants found in our European manuscripts arose late in the process of transmission, probably in the medieval period, and probably within Europe.[23]

---

23 Cf. Smelik, 'How to Grow a Tree', 505, who concludes that all variations in spelling and contractions are due to the copyist and not his exemplar. Also, S.A. Kaufman, 'Dating the Language of the Palestinian Targums and their Use in the Study of First Century CE Texts', in D.R.G. Beattie and M.J.McNamara (eds), *The Aramaic Bible: Targums in their Historical Context* (Journal for the Study of the Old Testament Supplement 166, Sheffield 1994), 118–41.

Chapter Nine

Marginal Notes in Codex Reuchlinianus No. 3

Codex Reuchlinianus No. 3 (i.e. Badische Hof- und Landesbibliothek, Karlsruhe, Germany; siglum: t705i), known by the name of the famous German Hebraist, Johannes Reuchlin, who acquired it in 1498, was written in 1105/1106 CE or 1108 CE by a certain Serach bar Jehuda (זרח בר יהודה).[1] It contains the Hebrew text of the Prophets with Targum Jonathan alternating with the Hebrew verse and is of exceptionally high quality, being lauded by Kennicott with the words *codex hic antiquissimis et præstantissimis merito accensendus est.*[2]

This codex is of particular interest to students of Targum Jonathan because of the great quantity of marginal readings to the Targum text. Although one occasionally finds marginal notes in other manuscripts of Targum Jonathan,[3] I know of no manuscript comparable to Codex Reuchlinianus No. 3 in terms of the extent of its marginal notations.

These marginal notes are from a different though similar hand to that of the main text;[4] they are therefore later than the consonantal text, but may have been added during a second stage of production along with the vocalisation.[5] They appear under various designations, some of which are familiar from manuscripts of other Targums,[6] which are usually rendered as follows:

---

1   See von Abel and Leicht. *Verzeichnis der Hebraica in der Bibliothek Johannes Reuchlins*, 100 n. 16.
2   'This codex deserves to be reckoned among the most ancient and most excellent', Kennicott, *Vetus Testamentum hebraicum*, II. *Prophetae et Hagiographia*, 84 (Cod. 154). One cannot resist adding here an account of the codex's history recorded by Sperber: 'It [Codex Reuchlinianus No. 3] is in excellent condition, a fact which is even the more noteworthy if we consider that it had seen good and bad times. It was buried in a grave during the 30 years war so as to escape being taken away by the invading Swedish Armies, and this is not exactly a healthy repository for a manuscript'. Sperber, *The Bible in Aramaic*, IVB, 140
3   Ms Hébreu 75, Bibliothèque Nationale, Paris, headed נ"א i.e. נוסח אחר (e.g. f211v to Isaiah); Codex Solger, Stadtbibliothek, Nürnberg, headed ל' א' and ס' א' (e.g. Judg. 4:7).
4   Sirat *et al.*, *Codices hebraicis*, III, *de 1085 à 1140*, 51.
5   Bacher, 'Kritische Untersuchungen zum Prophetentargum', 34.
6   E.g. the designation לשון אחר is commonly used in manuscripts of the Targum of Job to introduce alternative words and phrases (see C. Mangan, J.F. Healey and P.S. Knobel, *The Targum of Job, Proverbs, Qohelet* [The Aramaic Bible 15, Edinburgh 1991], 10–11) and some of the variant

The Transmission of Targum Jonathan in the West

ס' א', ספ' אח'	ספרא אחרינא or ספר אחר	Another Book
תרג' ירוש', ירוש'	תרגום ירושלמי, ירושלמי	Targum Yerushalmi or Palestinian Targum
תר' אח'	תרגום אחר	Another Targum
ל' א',ליש' אח'	לישנא אחרינא	Another Version
ו' ד', וא' דא'	אית דאמרי	There are some who say(?)
Not abbreviated	פליג	Disagreement
פי'	פירוש	Explanation

The marginalia, however, present the student of Targum Jonathan's textual history with two problems: (1) Codex Reuchlinianus No. 3 contains no information concerning what the various designations indicate, nor the purpose that the marginalia were intended to serve; and (2) Codex Reuchlinianus No. 3 is the oldest extant near complete manuscript of Targum Jonathan known to us. Consequently, those sources that may have been employed in compiling the marginalia are no longer available.

1. Past Research

Of all the marginalia in Codex Reuchlinianus No. 3, those designated 'Targum Yerushalmi' and 'Another Targum' have been the object of sustained scholarly attention since Zunz first proposed that they may be remnants of a once-complete Palestinian Targum to the Prophets, a theory that he otherwise based on citations in medieval works of a Targum to the Prophets at variance to Targum Jonathan.[7] Zunz's view is still maintained by some scholars,[8] and the notes do indeed display some Palestinian language features,[9] but if these traits

---

marginal readings in Neofiti (Díez Macho, *Neophyti 1: Targum Palestinense Ms de la Biblioteca Vaticana*, I, *Génesis*, 24–8). Alternative readings to Targum Canticles and Proverbs are designated תרגום אחר in Ms Barberini Or. 161–164, Biblioteca Apostolica, Vatican City.

7   Zunz, *Die gottesdienstlichen Vorträge der Juden historisch entwickelt*, 77–9.
8   E.g. 'These [marginal notes under rubric "Targum Yerushalmi" or "Another Targum"] are probably remnants of a recension, or recensions of a complete Palestinian Targum of the Prophets';. Alexander, 'Jewish Aramaic Translations of Hebrew Scriptures', 224. Also Díez Merino, 'La triple recensión del Targum a los Profetas (babilónica, yemení y palestina) con sus tres tradiciones (babilónica, yemení y tiberiense)', 298. Cf. his 'Targum Manuscripts and Critical Editions'.
9   Kasher, *Targumic Toseftot to the Prophets*, 15. Cf. for example the marginal note to Judg. 8:31 (ופלקתיה : ירו' for ולחינתיה) the lexeme פלקתא is found within the Targumic corpus only in Tg. Neof. (Gen. 22:24); Tg. Ps.-J. (Gen. 22:24; 25:6; 29:24, 29; 35:22; 36:12), the Frg. Tgs (Gen.

Chapter Nine. Marginal Notes in Codex Reuchlinianus No. 3

are the residue of an original Palestinian form, the language has since been adapted to the language of Targum Jonathan in many cases, as Kahle pointed out, so that their pristine Palestinian form has been lost.[10]

Grelot, in particular, accepted the view that the Targum Yerushalmi marginalia represented *morceaux* of an ancient Palestinian Targum (mooting the possibility that it contained only the haftarot),[11] which had been stripped of much of its haggadic content and reduced in order to bring the text closer to the Masoretic Text, resulting in the text of Targum Jonathan.[12] Grelot published two papers in which he compared two of the Targum Yerushalmi marginalia (Isa. 10:32; 66:1) to Tosefta Targums found in manuscript Urbinati 1 (Biblioteca Apostolica, Vatican City; t2i). In both cases he believed the text of Codex Reuchlinianus No. 3 to be the earlier, while manuscript Urbinati Ebr. 1 showed traces of later development. In the case of Isa. 10:32 he concluded that the version of manuscript Urbinati Ebr. 1 (also preserved in Add 26,879 British Library, London; i.e. t720a) represented an abridgement of the Targum Yerushalmi text in Codex Reuchlinianus No. 3, while a separate and further abridged recension was to be found in the Second Rabbinic Bible (1525), and manuscripts Or 2211 and Or. 1474 of the British Library.[13]

In a response to Grelot's 1966 paper 'Une Tosephta Targoumique sur Zacharie, II, 14–15', Kasher quite rightly rejected Grelot's basic conclusion, namely that the Tosefta Targums preserved an earlier form of the text than Targum Jonathan. First, he criticised Grelot (and Sperber, who Grelot followed) for failing to pay attention to the manuscript traditions, which showed that the Tosefta Targums were not consistent, even within a single

---

22:24), and Tg. Chr. (1 Chron. 1:32; 2:46; 2:48; 3:9; 7:14; 2 Chron. 11:21); see Smelik, *The Targum of Judges*, 518.

10 Kahle, *Masoreten des Westens*, II, 10. Kahle treated the Codex Reuchlinianus No. 3 notes along with the materials headed תוספתא דארעא דישראל in Ms. Montefiore 7 [H 116] (Montefiore Endowment), those printed in the Leiria edition (1494), and those cited by Kimhi.

11 P. Grelot, 'Le Targoum d'Isaie X, 32–34 dans ses diverses recensions', *Revue Biblique* 90 (1983), 202–28, p. 227. A view that Zunz had rejected, Zunz, *Die gottesdienstlichen Vorträge der Juden historisch entwickelt,* 77–8.

12 Grelot, 'Le Targoum d'Isaie X, 32–34 dans ses diverses recensions', 212; Grelot, 'L'exégèse messianique d'Isaie, LXIII, 1–6', 379.

13 Grelot, 'Le Targoum d'Isaie X, 32–34 dans ses diverses recensions'; Grelot, 'Deux Toseftas targoumiques inédites sur Isaïe LXVI' (also Grelot, 'A propos d'une Tosephta Targoumique', *Revue Biblique* 80 (1973), 363). Smelik observed a similar process of reduction in the case of Judg. 5:5 (without sharing Grelot's conclusion that Targum Jonathan was a shortened version of the same text), Smelik, *The Targum of Judges*, 165, 414–19.

tradition (not all the Ashkenazi manuscripts contain the same Tosefta Targums, for example).[14] He then pointed out that if, as Grelot himself had argued, the Tosefta Targums contained material borrowed from Targum Jonathan to Zephaniah, this would undermine Gerlot's argument for the priority of the Tosefta version. Equally, if Grelot were right that Targum Jonathan is a stripped down version of the Tosefta Targum, then we should find Targum Jonathan integrated into the Tosefta Targums, yet this is not always the case. Finally, Kasher pointed out that the exegetical tradition in the Tosefot sometimes differs from that of Targum Jonathan.[15] I will return to Kasher below.

The importance of these discussions is evident. However, they do not address the marginalia of Codex Reuchlinianus No. 3 as a whole. In fact, Bacher's article of 1874 still remains the last sustained and comprehensive attempt to explain the system of the marginalia of Codex Reuchlinianus No. 3 in its entirety.[16] Bacher held the codex in high regard, calling it 'the document which, above all others, forms the groundwork of all criticism of the text of the Targum of the Prophets.'[17] He placed particular weight on the value of 'its numerous and important marginal glosses,'[18] the significance of which he understood in terms of the contribution he believed they could make to text-criticism of the Targum and to an understanding of the history of its development.[19]

In Bacher's view, each of the five headings[20] under which the marginalia are arranged points towards a particular physical source that lay before the

---

14 R. Kasher, 'התוספתות התרגומיות להפטרת שבת־חנוכה', *Tarbiz* 45 (1975/76), 27–45, p. 29. Kasher's own study was based on six manuscripts of Ashkenazi and Sephardi origins (27–8).
15 Kasher, 'התוספתות התרגומיות להפטרת שבת־חנוכה', 29–32.
16 Bacher, 'Kritische Untersuchungen zum Prophetentargum', 1–72. Bacher also discusses the main text of the Codex (including its peculiar vocalisation, 35–8) and the Bomberg and Buxtorf editions (38–42). He compares these editions and identifies a number of places where Codex Reuchlinianus No. 3 preserves the earlier reading (42–55).
17 Bacher, 'Notes on the Critique of the Text of the Targum of the Prophets', 651–5.
18 Bacher, 'Notes on the Critique of the Text of the Targum of the Prophets', 651.
19 Bacher, 'Kritische Untersuchungen zum Prophetentargum', 3.
20 Bacher treated תרגום אחר and תרגום ירושלמי as a single category. He examined the category פירוש, which contains only comments on the text in Hebrew, separately concluding: 'Vielleicht kann man diese Fragmente als Ueberreste eines ganzen Targumcommentars ansehen'. Bacher, 'Kritische Untersuchungen zum Prophetentargum', 38.

Chapter Nine. Marginal Notes in Codex Reuchlinianus No. 3

copyist as he was preparing the codex.[21] That individual variants occasionally appeared with more than one heading confirmed his conclusion that the headings referred to specific physical sources,[22] so that in Bacher's view the compiler of the marginalia consulted five manuscript sources, giving to each a separate heading.[23] Bacher's position concerning the relationship of the individual *sigla* to particular sources was adopted by Sperber in his editions of Targum Jonathan.[24]

Bacher divided the marginalia into two major groups: a 'predominantly haggadic group' ('vorwiegend agadische Gruppe'), to which he assigned the notes headed תרגום ירושלמי, ספר אחר and תרגום אחר; and a second group of a non-haggadic character, to which the ואי דא, לישנא אחרינא and פליג marginalia belonged. According to Bacher, this latter group consisted of variants within one and the same Targum, whilst the materials stemming from the predominantly haggadic group represented distinct versions, which, on the basis of similar traditions in the midrashim and Babylonian Talmud, he dated from a period when Babylonian Targum traditions had entered Palestinian circles.[25]

Churgin examined — in a somewhat cursory fashion — the haggadic marginalia (i.e. those under the headings ספר אחר, תרגום אחר and תרגום ירושלמי) in his classic *Targum Jonathan to the Prophets* of 1927. In a very brief analysis of only a few examples Churgin found that the notes under these three headings had 'many characteristic points in common' suggesting that 'they may have a common source'. The similarity between these marginalia led him to dismiss Bacher's identification of each of the headings with individual

---

21 '…jede der fünf Ueberschriften bezieht sich auf ein besonderes dem Abschreiber vorgelegenes Targumexemplar.' Bacher, 'Kritische Untersuchungen zum Prophetentargum', 34. Cf. also 'Diese bestehen nämlich in abweichenden Uebersetzungen zu einzelnen Versen, oder Wörtern, wie sie nach verschiedenen Targumexemplaren…zu den betreffenden Stellen zugeschrieben wurden.' Bacher, 'Kritische Untersuchungen zum Prophetentargum', 2.

22 Bacher, 'Kritische Untersuchungen zum Prophetentargum', 34–5.

23 Bacher identified only 5 sources because he treated the ירושלמי, תרגום ירושלמי and תרגום אחר marginalia as a single source (see note 20)

24 'the vast majority of marginal notes here do offer an indication of their source, for they quote the respective manuscripts under various individual *sigla*. And whenever a given variant is found in two such manuscripts, then the *sigla* of both of them are preceding the note… judging by the *sigla* used, there were 6 such individually identified manuscripts consulted by the annotator of Codex Reuchlinianus (or his *Vorlage*)', Sperber, *The Bible in Aramaic*, II, ix, §8. Sperber believed some of the marginal notes to stand closer to the *Ur-Targum* than the main text of the codex, see Sperber, *The Bible in Aramaic*, IVB, 140–1, where he cites Bacher.

25 Bacher, 'Kritische Untersuchungen zum Prophetentargum', 35, 57–8.

sources. He concluded that the marginalia explained or complemented the rendering of Targum Jonathan and therefore post-dated the official Targums. Although he conceded that the marginalia may preserve in some cases a reading earlier than that which now stands in Targum Jonathan, he believed some of the material to be as late as the Islamic period.[26]

A more recent engagement with the marginalia as a complete system was offered by Smelik in his *The Targum of Judges* (1995), including the comparison of the variants with other known textual witnesses. Smelik rejected entirely Bacher's conclusion that each of the sigla referred to an individual physical source. In his view, לישנא אחרינא, וא׳ דא׳ and פליג 'do not represent manuscripts'.[27] Rather Smelik judged them to be glosses and substitutions to the text. Concerning the remaining materials, Smelik heavily criticised Bacher's approach of dating material based on haggadic parallels, and rejected his identification of the sources on these grounds. In Smelik's view the copyist had only one other manuscript of 'virtually the same text' (identified by ספר אחר), another manuscript containing a 'different Targum,' which the compiler considered to be of Palestinian origin (תרגום ירושלמי), and a 'collection of alternative translations' (תרגום אחר), somewhat similar to the Fragment Targums.[28]

In 1996 Kasher published his study of the Tosefta Targums to the Prophets; more than half of the Tosefta Targums included in this volume are in fact marginal notes of Codex Reuchlinianus No. 3 bearing the designations Yerushalmi, Targum Yerushalmi, Another Targum, Another Book, Another Version, and a few with no heading. The particular importance of Kasher's study for understanding the marginalia in Codex Reuchlinianus No. 3 lies in his classification of these notes according to their dialect.[29] As Kasher had already pointed out in his earlier response to Grelot (see above), one could not simply take on trust the Palestinian provenance of the notes headed 'Targum Yerushalmi' or simply 'Yerushalmi.' Indeed, his study of their linguistic

---

26 P. Churgin, 'Targum Jonathan to the Prophets', in L. Smolar and M. Aberbach, *Studies in Targum Jonathan to the Prophets* (New York 1983 [1927]), 229–380, pp. 379–80 (151–2).
27 Smelik, *The Targum of Judges*, 173.
28 Smelik, *The Targum of Judges*, 173–4.
29 He was not able to classify dialectically the following notes: Another Version 144d, 148; Targum Yerushalmi 134; Another Targum 123b; Another Book 123b. The numbers refer to the sections in Kasher, *Targumic Toseftot to the Prophets*.

Chapter Nine. Marginal Notes in Codex Reuchlinianus No. 3

character suggested a much more complicated picture.[30] His linguistic analysis revealed that while some of the Yerushalmi, Targum Yerushalmi, Another Targum, and Another Book marginalia are cast in a Palestinian dialect,[31] the language of the majority of notes under each of these headings is in fact close to that of Targum Jonathan itself (a small majority in the case of Targum Yerushalmi and Another Targum, a large majority for the remainder),[32] with a small number reflecting a mixed dialect (i.e. Eastern and Western features).[33] None of the marginalia under the heading Another Version is in a Palestinian dialect; rather the language is close to that of Targum Jonathan or, in one case, mixed.[34]

Kasher also analysed the connection of Tosefta Targums, including these marginal notes, to the liturgy. He was able to establish a link with known haftarot for about half of the marginalia that he included, the proportions being roughly the same for each of the headings.[35] That many of the Tosefta Targums could not be connected to the liturgy did not in Kasher's view invalidate the possibility that the phenomenon originated in the liturgy, since our knowledge of ancient liturgical cycles is still far from complete. Indeed, Kasher believed

---

30 Kasher, 'התוספתות התרגומיות להפטרת שבת־חנוכה', 37. See also Kasher, *Targumic Toseftot to the Prophets*, 15, 19.
31 Targum Yerushalmi: 3, 51, 74a, 87, 99, 100a, 101, 103, 104, 111; Yerushalmi: 5a, 7, 17, 49, 78, Another Targum: 32, 109; Another Book: 32, 38, 60, 92. The numbers refer to the sections in Kasher, *Targumic Toseftot to the Prophets*.
32 Targum Yerushalmi: 24a, 46, 76, 77, 83, 105, 106, 108, 110, 118, 124, 138; Yerushalmi: 6, 11, 13, 14, 15, 18, 19, 20, 34, 36, 43, 53a, 54, 55; Another Targum: 4a, 113, 146; Another Book: 33, 37, 39, 42, 44, 61, 66, 67, 68, 90a, 91, 97, 117, 127a, 143, 146. The numbers refer to the sections in Kasher, *Targumic Toseftot to the Prophets*.
33 Targum Yerushalmi: 45, 52, 96, 102, 115a, 135, 147; Yerushalmi: 9, 12, 23, 35, 88; Another Targum: 40, 130; Another Book: 130. The numbers refer to the sections in Kasher, *Targumic Toseftot to the Prophets*.
34 Mixed 16; close to Targum Jonathan 47, 48, 50. The seven notes studied by Kasher that have no heading are close to Targum Jonathan in their language: 4c, 24e, 41, 73, 107a, 149, 150. The numbers refer to the sections in Kasher, *Targumic Toseftot to the Prophets*.
35 With a connection to a known liturgical cycle — Targum Yerushalmi: 3, 24a, 51, 52, 74a, 83, 87, 100a, 103, 104, 106, 108, 111, 115a, 118, 124, 138; Yerushalmi: 5a, 9?, 10, 11, 23, 49, 53a, 54, 55, 78, 88; Another Targum: 4a, 109, 123a, 130; Another Book: 42, 61, 66, 67, 68, 123a, 127a, 130; Another Version: 48, 50; No heading: 4c, 24e, 41, 73, 107a, 144d, 149. With no connection — Targum Yerushalmi: 45, 46, 76, 77, 96, 99, 101, 102, 105, 110, 134, 135, 147; Yerushalmi: 6, 7, 8, 12, 13, 14, 15, 17, 18, 19, 20, 34, 35, 36, 43; Another Targum: 32, 40, 113, 146; Another Book: 32, 33, 37, 38, 39, 44, 60, 90a, 91, 92, 97, 117, 143, 146; Another Version: 16, 47; No heading: 148, 150. The numbers refer to the sections in Kasher, *Targumic Toseftot to the Prophets*.

the connection to the liturgy to be sufficiently strong to conclude that the Tosefta Targums as a phenomenon originated in the liturgy. The liturgical setting gave the meturgeman the freedom to create more midrashic forms with the result that some of the Tosefta Targums are midrashic expansions of Targum Jonathan, while others represented a distinct tradition. On the basis of his analysis of their language he suggested that the phenomenon originated in Palestine, although many of the Tosefta Targums had undergone a metamorphosis with the result that only traces of their original Palestinian character remained; in some cases this had resulted in multiple recensions of the same Tosefta Targum. They were not, however, the remnants of a once-complete Palestinian Targum to the Prophets.[36]

More recently the topic of Tosefta Targums, and in particular those marginal notes from Codex Reuchlinianus No. 3 classified as such, has been addressed by Houtman.[37] Houtman studied notes under the headings Another Book, Another Version, Yerushalmi, and Targum Yerushalmi, including many that Kasher had not included in his edition of the Tosefta Targums. Houtman found that only five of the nineteen variants headed Another Book that she examined could be characterised as haggadic. The remainder either gave an explanation of a word or phrase or, in four cases, kept closer to the Hebrew text than the main text of Targum Jonathan. Of the notes headed Another Version Houtman studied three of the larger notes used by Kasher, considering the smaller notes to be irrelevant for the study of Tosefta Targums. She found these to be subsitutions for the main text of Targum Jonathan, which aimed to make sense of an enigmatic Hebrew text or resolve apparent incongruities. Since these notes can be characterised as substitutions rather than additions, Houtman concluded that the title 'Tosefta Targum' was not strictly applicable. In Houtman's view the marginalia headed Another Book were taken from 'one of the manuscripts of Targum Jonathan that he [the scribe of Codex Reuchlinianus No. 3] had at his disposal', while those headed Another Version refers to 'a specific source that the copyist used in addition to his base text'.[38]

Her analysis of eleven Yerushalmi and Targum Yerushalmi notes confirmed

---

36 Kasher, *Targumic Toseftot to the Prophets*, 16–18; Kasher, 'התוספתות התרגומיות להפטרת שבת־חנוכה', 30–1, 33–6, 38.
37 Houtman and Sysling, *Alternative Targum Traditions*, 61–97, 131–3.
38 Houtman and Sysling, *Alternative Targum Traditions*, 132.

many of Kasher's conclusions, namely, that they exhibited a closer relation to Palestinian Aramaic than those notes under other headings (except 'Another Targum'), and that they showed a partial correspondence to liturgical traditions. Houtman tentatively suggested that there may be a difference between the Yerushalmi and the Targum Yerushalmi notes, implying a distinct source: the Yerushalmi marginalia were generally explanatory while the Targum Yerushalmi were 'substitute Targum'. Nonetheless, she concedes that 'the difference is, however, not always clear'.[39] She makes no proposal concerning the sources from which the scribe of Codex Reuchlinianus No. 3's marginalia may have derived these materials.

Finally, brief mention must be made of Damsma's recent study, *The Targumic Toseftot to Ezekiel*, in which she examines two of the marginal notes in Ezekiel (1:8 headed ספר אחר and 28:13 headed both ספר אחר and תרגום אחר). Damsma noted the parallels between the note to Ezek. 28:13 and rabbinic literature,[40] accepting (*contra* Bacher) that this did not demonstrate dependence of the former on the latter since both could have drawn from a common pool of exegetical tradition. The exegetical content showed an affinity to Palestinian exegetical tradition and Damsma identified some linguistic features that hinted at a Palestinian provenance. On the basis of their linguistic profile (at least for 28:13: the note to Ezek. 1:8 being too short to yield significant clues), she tentatively dated the material to the Geonic period.[41]

2. Aims

It will be apparent from the preceding survey that much has changed since Bacher's day. I hope to be able to take the discussion forward by offering a new proposal for understanding the system of marginalia as a whole. Put simply, the following question will be addressed:

What was the likely format and content of the sources from which the marginalia were drawn?

I hope to bring a new clarity to the discussion by separating the question of the ultimate origins of the content of the marginalia from the question of the likely

---

39 Houtman and Sysling, *Alternative Targum Traditions*, 97.
40 For rabbinic parallels see also my *Adam, Satan, and the King of Tyre*, 112.
41 A. Damsma, *The Targumic Toseftot to Ezekiel* (Studies in Aramaic Interpretation of Scripture 13, Leiden 2012), 113–17; 129–42; 180–2.

sources from which the compiler might have drawn as he put together the marginalia in this particular codex. What sort of sources could the compiler have consulted? And, what was their likely format and content?

First, I will begin by describing the general character of the material appearing under each of the headings, considering its form, linguistic features, relation to the main text, and so forth. Secondly, I will describe a number of physical characteristics impinging on the marginal notes, such as their layout. Finally, I will make some tentative suggestions as to the sources of the marginal materials and the meaning of the differing headings.

I have used the marginalia to 1 Samuel as a sample study, so many of the examples are drawn from there. Notes appearing under the heading פירוש 'explanation' are not considered in this analysis because they are simply 'commentirenden Glossen' in Hebrew, as Bacher observed.[42]

3. Characterisation of the Marginalia's Content

3.a. 'Another Version' לישנא אחרינא

This is the most frequent type of variant. According to Bacher they are of 'exegestischer oder paraphrastischer Art' and contain hardly any haggadah.[43] Bacher further divided the group into variants of an exegetical nature (from 1 Samuel: Tg. 1 Sam. 19:13, 16; 20:29; 30:16); those evincing a freer relation to the Hebrew text than the main text (from 1 Samuel: Tg. 1 Sam. 8:2; 17:49; 22:14, 15; 23:22; 25:8, 39; 26:2; 30:23); variant words without major distinction between the לישנא אחרינא and the main text (from 1 Samuel: Tg. 1 Sam. 11:7; 18:12; 24:6, 8; 25:8; 25:39); and the rest that had the purpose of correcting the main text.[44] It is my view that Bacher's characterisation of the

---

42 Though they are too few in number to bear out Bacher's suggestion that 'vielleicht kann mann diese Fragmente als Ueberreste eines ganzen Targumcommentars ansehen'; Bacher, 'Kritische Untersuchungen zum Prophetentargum', 38. To give just one example: Tg. Isa. 7:25, the main text reads ארבעת ארבעה (in multiple manuscripts); the פירוש marginal note reads: כמ׳ רביע לש׳ מרבץ (according to the codex; Bacher incorrectly gives רִיבַע לש׳ מרבץ) meaning that the root רביע is the Aramaic equivalent of Hebrew רבץ. That is to say that the verb 'to lie down' is to be understood, not the cardinal number 'four'. The notes may be drawn from collections of Targumic expositions on various passages that served as study material for synagogal preaching; Smelik, *The Targum of Judges*, 77.
43 Bacher, 'Kritische Untersuchungen zum Prophetentargum', 28–9.
44 I.e. '...hat eine ziemlich grosse Anzahl anderer den Zweck, orthographische, grammatische

Chapter Nine. Marginal Notes in Codex Reuchlinianus No. 3

לישנא אחרינא variants requires refinement.

Of the forty-three לישנא אחרינא notes that occur in 1 Samuel,[45] eleven of these concern small orthographic variants or variants in vocalisation. Some preserve a correct form where the main text is probably at fault, but others are simply alternative forms,[46] and in some cases the reading of the main text is preferable,[47] so that Bacher's view that these minor variants had the purpose of correcting the main text cannot be sustained.

The remaining לישנא אחרינא notes from 1 Samuel fall into one of the following groups:

(1) *Alternative form of the same lexeme*: e.g. 1 Sam. 2:24 main text דרנניןד;[48] there are two marginal notes under the siglum לישנא אחרינא at this point:[49] דרנניןד מרנין, sense unclear, perhaps 'those who were complaining were complaining'(?);[50] and מרנניןד, the *pael* participle.[51]

(2) *Alternative lexeme* to that which stands in the main text but with a more or less *synonymous meaning*: e.g. 1 Sam. 11:7 main text זייעא/margin רתיתא, both 'shaking'; 1 Sam. 8:2 גגודיןד/דינין, 'judges'; 1 Sam. 25:8 יום טב/יומא דשירותא 'the feast/festival day'; or 1 Sam. 30:16 רטישין 'scattered'/פריסין 'spread'.[52]

---

und andere Fehler des Cod[ex] R[euchlin] zu berichtigen.' Bacher, 'Kritische Untersuchungen zum Prophetentargum', 32.

45 Sperber fails to record 13 of these 1 Sam. 1:6 margin וּמִצְהָבָא | main text וּמִצְהֲבָא ; 1 Sam. 2:24 וְאִית[וּ]כָח | 1 Sam. 12:7 וּגְעָין | וּגְעָין; 1 Sam. 6:12 וְאַכְוְיָא | וְאַכְנָא; 1 Sam. 6:12 דרנניןד | דרנניןד מרנין; 1 Sam. 21:8 חֲמִים | חָמִים; 1 Sam. 21:7 וִית בדן | ית שמשון [דאתי מן] שיבט דן 1 Sam. 12:11 | וְאֶתְוְנַכָח ; 1 לְחַיָּיךָ | לְחַיָּךָ; 1 Sam. 25:6 גְרֵמִית | גְרֵמִית; 1 Sam. 22:22 אדומאה רב רעיא | רבן תלמידיא דלשאול Sam. 25:18 מאנן דְבִלְתָא | מַאנָן דְבִילתא; 1 Sam. 26:1 בֵּית יְשִׁים' | יִשִׁימוֹן; 1 Sam. 28:3 פְּלֵי | פְּלֵי). NB. The vocalisation is barely legible in the marginalia at many points, so the vocalisation offered here should be accepted only as provisional.

46 E.g. in spelling, 1 Sam. 17:26 חִיסְדָּא, margin חִסוּדָא (= t713a, t720a, t725a); 1 Sam. 25:18 main text מאנן דבילתא, margin מאן דבלתא 'vessels of pressed-figs'; 1 Sam. 22:22, main text גְרֵמִית; marginal גְרַמִית.

47 E.g. 1 Sam. 6:12, main text: וּגְעָין peal participle feminine plural to match the preceding אָזְלָן; against marginal reading וְגָעָן.

48 Codex Reuchlinianus No. 3 preserves the correct reading (from root רגן) where t2520b has an erroneous reading (רדנין) as does t707b (רכנין).

49 Sperber notes only the second of the two.

50 Reading מרנניןד for מרנין (a scribal error?).

51 Many discrepancies are found among the textual witnesses with respect to this lexeme. See van Staalduine-Sulman, *The Targum of Samuel*, 224.

52 The marginal note to 1 Sam. 21:14 margin main text וְאִשְׁתַּעֲמַם | main text וְאִישְׁתַּמַם 'to be confounded' formally belongs to this category, but the roots are clearly related.

(3) *Alternative lexeme* to that which stands in the main text with a *different meaning*. In the majority of cases the marginal variant further specifies what is meant by the word in the main text, perhaps best exemplified by 1 Sam. 19:13, 16 where the marginal note reads גונכא דמעזי 'a blanket that [is made] from goat', replacing the more general reading of the main text, נודא דעיזיא 'the skin of goats'. Similar refinements are offered by Kimhi who suggests the text refers to a pillow (כר) made from the hair of a goat and Rashi, who explains that the Hebrew refers to a skin that has been skinned whole, giving a technical term for this (חמת; cf. Joseph Kara). Some are more overtly interpretative, for example, 1 Sam. 22:14 where משמעתך 'your following' (van Staalduine-Sulman: 'bodyguard') becomes שימושך 'your service', the same wording as Rashi. In most cases they offer a more refined reading than that of the main text, and are freer in the relationship to the Hebrew text as Bacher noted.[53] One might call all such variants minor exegetical clarifications.

(4) *Additions*. These vary in length, but are generally shorter than those that appear under the siglum ספר אחר. In character they sometimes appear simply to add emphasis or clarity, but in other cases they are clearly exegetical. The former type can be seen in the following examples:[54]

1 Sam. 12:11

t705i main text: וית בדן

and Bedan

t705i margin: וית שמשון דאתי מן שיבט דן

and Samson who is from the tribe of Dan

The marginal note could almost be a translation of Rashi, who explains the Hebrew thus: 'This is Samson, who comes from the tribe of Dan (זה שמשון שבא משבט דן)'.[55]

1 Sam. 18:12

t705i main text: בסעדיה וית שאול רחיק

[because the Memra of the Lord had come] to his (i.e. David's) aid and had withdrawn from Saul

t705i margin: ומעילוי שאול איסתלק

but was departed from upon Saul

---

53 Bacher, 'Kritische Untersuchungen zum Prophetentargum', 29.

54 1 Sam. 26:1 שימון margin: בית ישימ׳ should probably also belong to this category (but cf. pages 277–8).

55 Cf. also b.Roš Haš. 25a.

Chapter Nine. Marginal Notes in Codex Reuchlinianus No. 3

The marginal material does not replace the reading of the main text, as is suggested by Bacher.[56] The placement marker stands between the two words, rather than above the word as is customary, indicating that this reading is in addition to the words in the main text.

1 Sam. 25:39

t705i main text: ושלח דוד ושאיל באביגיל

    and David sent and asked for Abigail

t705i margin: ושדר דוד ומליל על עיסק אביגיל

    and David sent and spoke of the matter concerning Abigail

Bacher records only the first word of this marginal note (ושדר) of this variant in error, and then as 1 Sam. 25:29.[57]

1 Sam. 26:2

t705i main text: בחורי ישראל

    the chosen ones of Israel

t705i margin: עולימי גיברי ישראל

    the young men of the heroes of Israel

The placement marker usually found in the main text to indicate the word to which the marginal note refers is either absent in Codex Reuchlinianus No. 3 or is illegible. Our choice is dictated by the context (with Sperber). Bacher records the marginal note incorrectly as עולימי י', categorizing it on that basis under the 'nicht bedeutsamen Varianten' (insignificant variants), presumably because this lexeme could simply replace בחירי י'.[58] The Ashkenazi manuscripts t6a[correct], t713a, and t720a read here עולימי ישראל, a partial correspondence to the marginal note in Codex Reuchlinianus No. 3.

Bacher classified the following three examples as 'exceptions' (Ausnahmen) to his general characterisation of the לישנא אחרינא variants as non-haggadic:[59]

---

56 Bacher, 'Kritische Untersuchungen zum Prophetentargum', 31, also Sperber, *ad loc*, followed by van Staalduine-Sulman, *The Targum of Samuel*, 389 n. 1457.
57 Bacher, 'Kritische Untersuchungen zum Prophetentargum', 30.
58 Bacher, 'Kritische Untersuchungen zum Prophetentargum', 30.
59 Bacher, 'Kritische Untersuchungen zum Prophetentargum', 28 n. 2.

The Transmission of Targum Jonathan in the West

1 Sam. 11:11

t705i main text: מיחם יומא

from the heat of the day

t705i margin: עד ארבע שעי יומא ומן אסקות עלת תדירא דצפרא

until the fourth hour of the day and from the offering up of the burnt offering of the daily morning offering

1 Sam. 12:2

t705i main text: ואנא קשית וסיבית ובני הא אינון עימכון

I have become old and grey, and my sons, behold, they are with you

t705i margin: קשישית [ו]סיבית ובני הא אוטיבו אורחתהון והא אינון באולפן עימכון

I have become old and grey, and my sons, behold, they mended their ways. And behold, they are with you in instruction

1 Sam. 21:8

t705i main text: רב רעיא דלשאול

[and his name was Doeg the Edomite], Saul's chief shepherd

t705i margin: רבן תלמידיא דלשאול

the teacher of Saul's disciples

Rashi (*Commentary on Samuel, ad loc*) identified Doeg as the president of the Great Sanhedrin (אב בית דין; cf. Kimhi) and explains the perplexing word choice of the Hebrew (נעצר לפני יהוה) as: 'he keeps himself before the Tent of Meeting to occupy himself with the Law'.

I find Bacher's characterisation of these as 'haggadic' oversimplified. Rather, they are exegetical.[60]

3.b. 'Disagreement' פליג

In terms of their character the marginalia under the siglum פליג are very similar to the Masoretic פליג notes to the Hebrew text in the codex. They appear to catalogue acceptable alternative Targumic renderings, sometimes based on variants in the Hebrew text itself. This designation normally stands after the variant, commenting on the variant reading rather than introducing it.

Many examples concern matters of alternative vocalisation in the Hebrew text. For example, the Hebrew text of Josh. 9:24 reads וּנַעֲשֶׂה, vocalised in Codex Leningradensis[61] (i.e. the Tiberian tradition) as וַנַּעֲשֶׂה (in t705i: וַנֲעֲשֶׂה),[62]

---

60 Cf. Houtman and Sysling, *Alternative Targum Traditions*, 78–80.

61 According to the edition: Dotan (ed.), *Biblia Hebraica Leningradensia*.

62 A Masorah note is attached to this word in the Hebrew of Codex Reuchlinianus No. 3. It reads ל׳ קמץ בליש׳, indicating that the *qamets* occurs only once in this form. This is particularly

i.e. 1st plural imperfect consecutive *qal*. However, the text might also be vocalised וְנַעֲשֶׂה, in which case the *waw* no longer has an inversive force (i.e. the sense of the imperfect remains). The first of these two alternative vocalisations is reflected in the פליג reading (i.e. ועבדנא), the other in the main text of the codex (i.e. ונעביד).[63]

The example to Judg. 10:1 does not concern alternative vocalisation, but alternative readings of a lexeme where two homonyms exist. The Hebrew דודו is translated in the base text as a personal name; the marginal note reads אחבוהי 'his uncle', translating the word דודו according to its meaning (in both cases the vocalisation is דּוֹדוֹ). Kimhi knew both traditions from variant versions of the Targum.[64]

Another example (1 Sam. 2:16) relates to the *Ketiv-Qere* readings of the Hebrew. The base text of Codex Reuchlinianus No. 3 translates the *Ketiv* (ליה = MT לו), while the marginal reading translates the *Qere* (לא = MT לֹא).[65] Manuscript t701i also follows the *Ketiv* here and scattered examples of variants connected to the *Ketiv-Qere* can be found throughout the Asheknazi and Mixed Western manuscripts (see chapter four §7).

These examples confirm that the variation arose due to an issue in the Hebrew text itself. This is not, however, always the case. Some examples concern alternative choices of lexemes, confirming Smelik's tentative proposal that they 'represented another Hebrew-Aramaic equation elsewhere in the corpus, along the lines of the Masorah to Targum Onqelos which also contains alternative Hebrew-Aramaic equations'.[66] For example, the main text of Codex Reuchlinianus No. 3 at 1 Sam. 4:19 uses the cognate כרע 'to bend down' to translate the Hebrew root כרע, the translation equivalent found frequently elsewhere in Targum Jonathan (e.g. Judg. 5:27; 7:5, etc.). The פליג at this point

---

interesting because it relates to the form as vocalised in Codex Reuchlinianus No. 3, rather than the tradition represented in the Codex Leningradensis.

63 According to Bacher the example at Isa. 7:25 would be similar: MT יעדרון, main text יתפלחון, margin יפלחון to which Bacher adds '(activ)'; Bacher, 'Kritische Untersuchungen zum Prophetentargum', 34, but unfortunately Bacher has read by metathesis, thereby reversing the metathesis יתחלפון, which is what the marginal note actually reads (correctly recorded by de Lagarde and Sperber).

64 Cited with comment by Smelik, *The Targum of Judges*, 534. Cf. Lxx and Vulgate, which also translate as a kinship term.

65 These two examples (i.e. Judg. 10:1; 1 Sam. 2:16) are taken from Houtman, 'Is There a System to the Variant Targumic Readings in Codex Reuchlin?' (see acknowledgements).

66 Smelik, *The Targum of Judges*, 173.

reads וחמטת. The root חמט 'to kneel down' is used once again (Isa. 46:1) to translate the root כרע. This view fits with the notion of the פליג representing an acceptable alternative Targumic rendering of the Hebrew text.

3.c. *'There are some who say'(?)* ואית דאמרי

The exact meaning of the abbreviation ו' ד' and וא' דא' is unclear. The form וא' דא' may abbreviate ואית דאמרי or ואית דאמרין 'there are some who say,' the form found in the Masorah to Onqelos,[67] or ואיכא דאמרי with the same meaning.[68] The presence of the form וא' דא' makes Bacher's suggestion that the abbreviation stands for ואית דמתרגמי unlikely,[69] although the form ו' ד' could of course have such a meaning.

Bacher subdivided the marginal notes under this designation into 'exegetical variants' (1 Sam. 7:2; 23:26; 2 Sam. 1:10; 4.2^{bis}; Ezek. 40:19; 43:22), variant readings where the main text stands closer to the Hebrew text (1 Sam. 23:19; 2 Sam. 3:27; 6:21; Isa. 1:5; 58:6; Jer. 15:26; 36:22; 49:13; Ezek. 27:10; 33:10; 34:24; Hos. 11:8), and 'other variants' (i.e. the remainder), a category for which he gives no elaboration.[70] According to Bacher, notes under this heading could be explained along the same lines as those appearing under the other headings, namely that they referred to physical sources that lay before the compiler.[71] Bacher rightly placed the וא' דא' notes into the non-haggadic group but went on to conclude that 'these designations likewise indicate that we are dealing with variants within one and the same Targum'.[72]

---

67 E.g. Exod. 4:26, see M.L. Klein, *The Masorah to Targum Onqelos: as Preserved in MSS Vatican Ebreo 448, Rome Angelica Or. 7, Fragments from the Cairo Genizah and in Earlier Editions by A. Berliner and S. Landauer* (Targum Studies, New Series 1, Binghamton, NY 2000) and adopted by Sperber, *The Bible in Aramaic*, IVB, 19; Sperber, *The Bible in Aramaic*, II, ix.

68 As G. Klein, 'Bemerkungen zu Herr Dr. Bacher's Kritische Untersuchungen zum Prophetentargum', *Zeitschrift der Deutschen Morgenländischen Gesellschaft* 29 (1875), 157–61, p. 157.

69 Bacher, 'Kritische Untersuchungen zum Prophetentargum', 3, 32.

70 Bacher, 'Kritische Untersuchungen zum Prophetentargum', 32–3. Sperber places the long variant to 1 Sam. 6:19 (61r) under the siglum ואיכא דאמרי in his critical edition, though it is clearly headed ירוש' in Codex Reuchlinianus No. 3 and carries the decoration typical of that siglum (i.e. a vertical line of 3–5 dots, extending above the *shin*). The variant is correctly classified by de Lagarde.

71 Bacher, 'Kritische Untersuchungen zum Prophetentargum', 32, 34.

72 Bacher, 'Kritische Untersuchungen zum Prophetentargum', 35.

Chapter Nine. Marginal Notes in Codex Reuchlinianus No. 3

The notes designated ואֿ דאֿ (all the notes in 1 Samuel carry this longer form of the abbreviation) are similar in many respects to those designated לֿ אֿ. However, they can be distinguished from the לֿ אֿ notes by the fact that in the majority of the examples that I considered there appeared to be an ambiguity or obscurity in the underlying Hebrew that permits more than one possible explanation. The possible alternatives are reflected in the main text and in the marginal note.

3.c.i. Obscure Vocabulary in the Hebrew Text

A striking number of the instances with the designation ואֿ דאֿ carry a Masorah marking in the Hebrew text in multiple manuscripts, though not necessarily in Codex Reuchlinianus No. 3 itself.[73] Where this phenomenon is found among the notes in the two books of Samuel, the marginal note attached to the Targum text, appears to deal with some difficulty or obscurity that arises in the Hebrew text itself rather than from within the Targum. Let us consider some examples:

1 Sam. 23:19

וסליקו אינש זיף לות שאול לגבעתא למימר הלא דוד מיטמר עימנא במצדתא בחרשא בגבעת חכילה
דמדרום **לִישִׁימוֹן**

The men of Ziph went to Saul, to the hill country, to say, Is not David hiding himself with us in the fortress in the forest in the hill country of Hachilah, to the south of <u>Yeshimon</u>?

Marginal variant: למדברא

Corresponding Hebrew: הישימון

The Masorah to the Hebrew text provides us with an explanation for the marginal note to the Aramaic. The Masorah note indicates that the noun ישימון is only spelt *plene* on two occasions, here and 1 Sam. 23:24,[74] where the same note occurs to the Targum text. The ensuing difficulty with the Hebrew text is, therefore, whether the form ought to be taken as a proper noun,[75] as the main text of Targum Jonathan has done (= בית ישימון Tg. Onq. Num. 21:20; 23:28; Tg. Neof. Deut. 32:10; Frg. Tg.[V] Deut. 32:10; Tg. 1 Sam. 26:1; 26:3), or as a

---

[73] The Masorah has been established based on C.D. Ginsburg, *The Massorah Compiled from Manuscripts Manuscripts* (The Library of Biblical Studies, New York 1975 [1880–1905]), 4 Vols.; and *Biblia Hebraica Stuttgartensia* with G.E. Weil, *Massorah Gedolah: Manuscrit B. 19a de Léningrad* (Rome 1971), 2 Vols. Of the examples given, 1 Sam. 2.14; 23.19; 2 Sam. 1:10 carry Masoretic notes in other manuscripts, but not in Codex Reuchlinianus No. 3.

[74] When taking the definite article, cf. Pss 68:8; 78:40; 106:14; 107:4.

[75] Which could take the article, see Joüon and Muraoka, *A Grammar of Biblical Hebrew* §137b.

common noun, the reading assumed by the marginal variant (= צדיותא Tg. Isa. 43:19, 20). The marginal note therefore reflects an ambiguity in the Hebrew text rather than a difficulty in the Aramaic. This note is similar in character to the פליג note attached to Judg. 10:1 (page 275).

In two further examples of this type, the marginal note provides additional clarification to a rare word in the Hebrew text:

1 Sam. 2:14

וקבע ליה באיורא או בדודא או בקידרא או **במילסא** כל דמסיק משליא נסיב כהנא לנפשיה כדין עבדין לכל ישראל דאתן לדבחא תמן בשילו

And he stuck it into the pan or into the cauldron or into the cooking pot or into <u>the cooking vessel</u>. Everything that the fork brought up the priest took for himself. Thus they were doing to all Israel, whoever came to sacrifice there in Shiloh.

Marginal variant: באילפיסא

Corresponding Hebrew: בפרור

In this episode the servant of the priest takes a three pronged fork (משיליא דליה תלת שנין), sets it in various different containers, and what is drawn out is then given to the priest. The Hebrew word carries a Masoretic note, indicating that בפרור occurs on only three occasions (i.e. Judg. 6:19; 1 Sam. 2:14; Num 11:8). The main text translates מליסא, simply 'a pot', using a noun that occurs only here in the Targumic corpus. The two other instances of בפרור (i.e. Judg. 6:19; Num. 11:8) translate with the lexeme קדרא (as does Tg. Neof. to Num. 11:8; also in the commentary attributed to Joseph Kara, *ad loc*), so the possibility that we are dealing with alternative translation equivalents in this case can be eliminated. In 1 Sam. 2:14 the lexeme קדרא has in fact been used to translate the preceding Hebrew word (i.e. קלחת).

The marginal note reads באילפיסא 'in the stew-pot'. The lexeme אילפיס is also unknown in the Targumic corpus (with the exception of the marginal note to Judg. 6:19, which will be discussed below, pages 293–4). It appears, however, in the Talmudim in halachic discussions where it indicates a specific type of cooking pot. The discussion in b.Pesaḥ. 37a is of particular relevance. Here a debate is recorded that concerns whether food cooked in an אילפס is liable to חַלָּה, i.e. the share set aside for the priest. The purpose of the וא' דא' note here is therefore to identify the type of pot under discussion; in so doing it also provides a rabbinical explanation for the episode.

Chapter Nine. Marginal Notes in Codex Reuchlinianus No. 3

Comparable is the following example:

2 Sam. 1:10

וקמית עלוהי וקטלתיה ארי ידענא ארי לא יחי בתר דנפל ונסבית כלילא דעל רישיה **וטוטפתא** דעל דרעיה ואיתיתינון לות ריבוני הלכא

I stood over him and I killed him because I knew that he would not live after he had fallen. Then I took the crown that was upon his head and the bracelets that were upon his arms and I brought them here to my master.

Marginal variant: ותפילין 'phylacteries'

Corresponding Hebrew: ואצעדה

The Hebrew lexeme occurs once more in the Hebrew Bible (i.e. Num. 31:50), but the combination with conjunctive *waw* is unique, as the Masorah Parva records. In neither case is the exact sense of the Hebrew lexeme clear, though its general sense is apparent. The marginal note in this instance disagrees with the main text's exegesis, rather than its translation. Saul was not simply wearing decorative items, as the main text of Targum Jonathan implies, but items with a religious function (cf. e.g. Tg. Onq. Deut. 6:8; b.Ber. 6a). The purpose of the note is therefore comparable to that of 1 Sam. 2:14. Again, the marginal note concerns an obscurity in the Hebrew text.[76]

3.c.ii. Further Explanation of the Underlying Hebrew

In a number of instances the main text of Targum Jonathan reflects the underlying Hebrew closely, but in so doing it replicates an obscurity in the

---

76 The note attached to 1 Sam. 23:26 is perhaps also to be grouped with the examples just given:
והוה דוד מיתבעית למיזל מן קדם שאול ושאול וגברוהי **כמנין על דוד** וגברוהי למיחדהון
David was afraid to go out in the presence of Saul and Saul and his men were ready to ambush David and his men in order to seize them.
Marginal variant: מקפין לדוד 'were encircling David' | Corresponding Hebrew: עטרים אל דוד.
There is no Masorah to the Hebrew. The root כמן is used freely to translate a number of roots in Targum Jonathan (e.g., כמן = Targumic addition Ezek. 21:21; ארב Josh. 8:4; Judg. 9:32, 34, 43; 16:2; 21:20v; Mic. 7:2; Hos. 7:6; בקש 1 Sam. 24:10; חרש 1 Sam. 23:9; נדח 2 Sam. 15:14; עטר 1 Sam. 23:26; עין 1 Sam. 18:9; עקב Jer. 9:3 (x2); צדה 1 Sam. 24:12; שור Hos. 13:7; שים 1 Sam. 15:2; 2 Sam. 13:32; 1 Kgs 20:12; שמר Jer. 20:10; שקד Jer. 5:6.). The marginal note may be an attempt to clarify the Hebrew root עטר (as van Staalduine-Sulman, *The Targum of Samuel*, 428, n. 1799). Although its meaning 'to surround' is well established, the verb is generally not applied to the action of people. The occurrence in Isa. 23:8, the only other example of the verb עטר in the corpus covered by the 'official' Targums (i.e. Onqelos and Jonathan), may be an exception, but the Hebrew is obscure and the Targum translates figuratively.

The Transmission of Targum Jonathan in the West

Hebrew rather than explaining it. In these instances the marginal note provides an explanation for the underlying Hebrew where the main text of Targum Jonathan has failed to do this.

The clearest example of this is found in the following example:

2 Sam. 4:2

ותרין גברין רבני תרתין משיריין **הוו בר שאול** שום חד בענה ושום תיניינא רכב בני רמון דמבארות מבני בנימן ארי אף בארות מתחשבא על דבית בנימן

Two men, the chiefs of the two camps, <u>were a son of Saul</u>. The name of one Baanah, the name of the second Rekab, the sons of Rimmon, who was from Beerot, from the sons of Benjamin, because even Beerot is considered to be of the house of Benjamin.

Marginal variant 1: עם בר שאול 'with Saul's son'
Marginal variant 2: מגניסת שאול 'from the family of Saul'
Corresponding Hebrew: היו בן שאול

The main text of Codex Reuchlinianus No. 3 faithfully represents the underlying Hebrew. The Hebrew contains a difficulty that the main Targum text therefore fails to resolve (cf. 2 Sam. 3:27). The two marginal notes provide alternative explanations of this difficulty in the Hebrew. The medieval commentators (Rashi, Ralbag, Isaiah di Trani, Joseph Caspi) assume that a *lamed* is missing (i.e. היו לבן שאול cf. LXX δύο ἄνδρες ἡγούμενοι συστρεμμάτων τῷ Μεμφιβόσθε υἱῷ Σαούλ). Kimhi offers this as a possibility along with two others, including the reading עם בר שאול, to which he adds כתרגומו, indicating that this reading was known from the manuscript of Targum available to him.

A further example:

1 Sam. 7:2

והוה מיומא דשרא ארונא בקירית יערים וסגיאו יומיא והוו עשרין שנין **וְאִיתְנָהִיאוּ** כל בית ישר' בתר פולחנא דייי

And it came to pass from the day that the Ark resided in the town of Jearim. The days increased and twenty years passed. And all the house of Israel <u>yearned</u> after the service of the Lord.

Marginal variant: וְאִיתְוַוכָחוּ 'and they were admonished'
Corresponding Hebrew: וינהו

The Masoretic note attached to the Hebrew indicates that its form is otherwise unattested. The Hebrew root itself (i.e. נהה) is only used on two other occasions (Mic. 2:4; Ezek. 32:18). In neither case is this translated by the Aramaic root יכח, so we are not faced with an alternative translation equivalent.[77] As with other notes under this heading, the purpose of the note is to explain the underlying Hebrew, which is obscure, where the main text has failed to do so.[78] In the two other occurrences of the root (i.e. Mic. 2:4; Ezek. 32:18) the sense is clearly that of distraught lamentation. But such a meaning is difficult to apply in the current verse, which reads וינהו כל בית ישראל אחרי יהוה (the preposition אחרי, in particular, causing the difficulty).

The main text of Targum Jonathan uses the cognate root, i.e. נהי,[79] which carries the sense of 'to yearn' (normally followed by -ל + noun or infinitive, see Jer. 3:17, cf. 15:19; 30:21; 32:22; 33:13), so there is no problem with the Aramaic. The marginal note, however, provides a different Aramaic explanation of the contextually obscure Hebrew.

A comparison is to be made with 1 Sam. 12:7, where the root יכח is again employed in a comparable literary context: in both places Samuel calls upon the people to return to the service of the Lord to avert an evil that has come upon them (cf. e.g. 1 Sam. 7:3 with 1 Sam. 12:20–1). That the marginal note is an attempt to express the contextual force of the Hebrew, rather than provide an alternative lexeme to replace the main text of Targum Jonathan, is confirmed by the fact that the root יכח is never otherwise followed by בתר.[80]

---

77 Within Targum Jonathan the root יכח translates the following: יכח Isa. 2:4; 11:3, 4; 29:21; Ezek. 3:26; Mic. 4:3; Hos. 4:4; Amos 5:10; שפט Isa. 6:5; מול Josh. 5:2 [Tosefta Targum], 3 [Tosefta Targum], 4 [Tosefta Targum], 5 [Tosefta Targum] (x2); מלל Josh. 5:7 [Tosefta Targum]; ידע Ezek. 16:2; שפט 1 Sam. 12:7; Ezek. 20:4 (x2); 22:2 (x2); 23:26; קשש Zeph. 2:1 [variant]; ריב Hos. 2.4; Mic. 6:1 [variant]; דין 2 Sam. 19:10; נהה 1 Sam. 7:2 [variant]. It appears in Targumic addition at Josh. 10:41 [variant]; Isa. 66:1 [variant]; Jer 8:19.

78 The obscurity of the Hebrew probably accounts for the reading of the principal Greek witnesses (i.e. ἐπέβλεψε/αν, ἐπέστρεψεν), better than the assumption of an alternative *Vorlage* (i.e. ויפן / ויפנו). See further Barthélemy, *Critique textuelle de l'Ancien Testament*, I, 157–8.

79 Ezek. 32:18 translates with root נבי; Mic. 2:4 translates figuratively אילא 'lamentation'. In both cases the Targum is expansive and the sense 'to yearn' inappropriate.

80 2 Sam. 3:27 may also belong to this group: ומית בדם עשאל אחוהי '*and [Abner] died on account of the blood of Asahel his brother*'; Marginal variant: חלף דקטל עשאל אחוהי ; Corresponding Hebrew: בדם עשהאל אחיו. The main text of Targum Jonathan stands close to the underlying Hebrew text. The marginal note makes the intended sense explicit where the main text of Targum Jonathan maintains the reading of the Hebrew text (the intended meaning can be established based on 2 Sam. 3:30).

The Transmission of Targum Jonathan in the West

3.c.iii. Alternative Vocalisation of the Hebrew Text

The above examples make clear that the וא׳ /דא׳ notes deal with a difficulty in the Hebrew. It is possible to explain other notes under this heading by considering the vocalisation of the Hebrew. Although there does not appear to be a difficulty in the Hebrew vocalisation as it is now found in the major codices and in Codex Reuchlinianus No. 3 itself, the Aramaic note can be explained by assuming an alternative vocalisation of the underlying Hebrew.

1 Sam. 30:17

ומחנון דוד מקיבלא ועד עידן רמשא ביומא דבתרוהי ולא אישתיזב מינהון איניש אלהין ארבע מאה גבר עולים דרכיבו על **ינקייא** ואפכו

David struck them from dark until evening time on the following day. And not a single man from among them was spared except 400 young men who mounted <u>young animals</u> and fled.

Marginal variant: גמלייא

Corresponding Hebrew: הגמלים

There is no Masoretic notation associated with the Hebrew, and the Hebrew is seemingly straightforward. The main text of the Targum, which reads ינקייא, connects the form with the verbal sense of the Hebrew root גמל, i.e. 'to wean', a reading that would be possible in an unvocalised text (i.e. גְּמֻלִים).[81] Elsewhere ינקא translates a number of different forms, including ברכה 'a young camel' (Jer. 2:23).[82] The marginal note gives the sense of the Hebrew according to its current vocalisation (הַגְּמַלִּים), namely 'the camels', which is the normal translation equivalent in Targum Jonathan for the Hebrew noun (e.g. 1 Sam. 15:3; 1 Kgs 10:2; 2 Kgs 8:9; Isa. 23:7; 30:6; etc.).[83] This variant is also found

---

81 Contra van Staalduine-Sulman, *The Targum of Samuel*, 470 n. 2117, there is no reason therefore to ascribe to ינק a meaning that differs from its common meaning 'young child, suckling' as Klein proposed in his 'Bemerkungen zu Herr Dr. Bacher's 'Kritische Untersuchungen zum Prophetentargum', 161.

82 For sense of the Hebrew cf. Isa. 60:6. Elsewhere יונק = ינקא 1 Sam. 15:3; 22:19; Isa. 11:8; Jer. 44:7; ילד 1 Kgs 12:8, 10, 14; 2 Kgs 2:24; Isa. 57:5; נער 2 Kgs 2:23; Jer. 51:22; Isa. 3:4; 11:6; עול Isa. 65:20; עולל 2 Kgs 8:12; Isa. 13:16v, Jer. 6:11; 9:20; רך Ezek. 17:22.

83 The example in 1 Sam. 22:18 may perhaps belong to this category: ואמר מלכא לדואג איסתחר את וּשְׁלָט בכהניא *The king said to Doeg, Return and <u>he overpowered</u> the priests! [So Doeg the Edomite returned and he overpowered the priests.]* Marginal variant: וּשְׁלוֹט | Corresponding Hebrew: וּפְגַע. The marginal note gives the imperative (cf. Tg. Judg. 8:21), whereas the main text reads the perfect. As it stands the Hebrew text reads the imperative (וּפְגַע), but an unvocalised text might also be read as a perfect (וּפָגַע). Contextually, however, the perfect is clearly erroneous. The marginal note may perhaps relate to a Hebrew text in which the ופגע had

in a number of extant manuscripts.[84] Manuscript t6a is an interesting case. The text originally read גמליא but was then corrected to ינקיא!

3.d. *'Another Book'* ספר אחר

As Bacher observed,[85] about a quarter of the ספר אחר variants is haggadic, of which about half can be traced back to the Babylonian Talmud, a view confirmed by more recent analysis.[86] However, this category of variants is similar in many respects to the לישנא אחרינא class discussed above, being distinguished only by the extent, frequency, and haggadic nature of its additional exegetical material.

As is the case with the לישנא אחרינא, we find among the ספר אחר minor textual variants (e.g. Tg. 1 Sam. 31:4 ויתלעבון also the reading of the Babylonian textual tradition, instead of the near synonym ויתעלבון of the main text and a few other manuscripts from the Mixed Western group, i.e. t2i, t3i, t718i); or the correct reading where the main text preserves an error, e.g. Tg. 1 Sam. 5:11 reading קטול instead of קרתא (an error) of the main text.

Furthermore, one finds among the marginalia under the siglum ספר אחר a significant number of short additions that are explanatory, but not haggadic, and as such are comparable to many of the additions found under the siglum לישנא אחרינא. Consider the following examples taken from 1 Samuel:

1 Sam. 17:18, reading לרב דממנא על אלפא גובריא 'to the commander who is appointed over a thousand men' in place of the simpler לרב אלפא of the main text.[87]

1 Sam. 26:20, which reads כמא דרדיף בר ניצצא ית קוראה בטוריא 'as a young hawk pursues partridge in the hills' in place of the main text's כמא דמתרדיף קוראה בטוריא 'as partridge is pursued in the hills'.[88]

These examples are explanatory, but not haggadic. One does find among the

---

been incorrectly vocalised. One cannot however exclude the possibility that the abbreviation וא׳ דא׳ stands for ואינו דוקא or ואינו דאיק ('but it is not accurate') in this instance. See the list of see Masoretic abbreviations in Klein, *The Masorah to Targum Onqelos*, 26.

84 t6a[PM], t713a, t720a, t725a[correct], t2i, t7i. Plus, according to Sperber's critical apparatus: ms Or. 1471, British Library (t727y); ms Or. 2371, British Library (t716y) Rabbinic Bible (1515/17); Ms. Montefiore 7 [H 116] (Montefiore Endowment) (t702s); Leiria edition (1494) (t734s).

85 Bacher, 'Kritische Untersuchungen zum Prophetentargum', 22.

86 See Houtman and Sysling, *Alternative Targum Traditions*, 61–78.

87 See Houtman and Sysling, *Alternative Targum Traditions*, 67.

88 See Houtman and Sysling, *Alternative Targum Traditions*, 69.

ספר אחר notes genuine haggadah.[89] However, in order to characterise the ספר אחר source as a whole one must conclude that, where it expands the main text, it aims to explain the perceived sense of the text. Often this explanation is dependent on known haggadic traditions. Consequently, I would say that Bacher's categorization of the ספר אחר marginalia as fitting into 'the predominantly haggadic group' is somewhat misleading. Rather, the ספר אחר marginalia might best be characterised as similar in character to the לישנא אחרינא marginalia, but with some fuller and sometimes haggadic expansions.

3.e. Another Targum, Palestinian Targum ירושלמי, ירושלמי תרגום, and תרגום אחר.

In terms of their content and language the תרגום ירושלמי, ירושלמי and תרגום אחר marginalia are difficult to distinguish; indeed Bacher included תרגום אחר variants among the תרגום ירושלמי marginalia. However, given that the compiler seemed to have worked systematically it is unlikely that he simply mixed up his vocabulary. Rather, it is more plausible to suggest that we are dealing with two (or possibly three)[90] distinct though similar sources each indicated by its own siglum.

All three concern sizeable variants that give mostly haggadic explanations for obscurities or ambiguities in the text,[91] sometimes in the form of an addition to the main text, and sometimes in the form of text intended to substitute the main text. Let us give some brief examples:

1) The main text of 1 Sam. 3:14 reads:
> the sin of the house of Eli will never be forgiven by means of sacrifices or by offerings.

In the margin under the heading ירושלמי, one finds the addition 'rather, by being occupied in the Law and by good deeds.' This addition is related to

---

89 See Houtman and Sysling, *Alternative Targum Traditions*, 62–7.
90 Some marginalia receive the shorter designation ירוש'. In terms of content these are indistinguishable from those headed תרגום ירושלמי. They may represent an alternative source, or the scribe may simply fluctuate between ירוש' and ירוש' תרג' in his abbreviating תרגום ירושלמי. See page 269.
91 For a recent discussion of the תרגום ירושלמי marginalia, see Houtman and Sysling, *Alternative Targum Traditions*, 82–97. The two examples of תרגום אחר to Tg. Judg. are discussed by Smelik, *The Targum of Judges*, 559–60, 599–600. The later example, to Tg. Judg. 18:3–4, is haggadic. Further examples of תרגום אחר have been collected by Kasher, *Targumic Toseftot to the Prophets*, §§4a, 32, 40, 109, 113, 123b, 130, 146.

Chapter Nine. Marginal Notes in Codex Reuchlinianus No. 3

rabbinic haggadah.[92]

2) The main text of 1 Sam. 10:22 reads:

> And once again they inquired of the Memra of the Lord, 'Is there another man here?' And the Lord said, 'Yes! He is hiding among the things (מניא)'.

The marginal note under the heading תרגום ירושלמי reads:

> And once again they inquired of the Memra of the Lord, 'Is there another man here for whom the kingdom is appropriate?' And the Lord said, 'Yes! He is hiding in the house of study, praying and reading in the desirable things (במאני) of the Law.'[93]

3) The main text of Judg. 18:3–4 reads:

> They were at the house of Micah and they recognised the voice of the Levite boy and they turned to there and they said to him, 'Who brought you here? What are you doing here? What do you want?' And he said to them, 'Micah did like this and like that to me. He hired me and I became a priest for him.'

In the bottom margin under the heading תרגום אחר stands the following long variant:

> They arrived at the house of Micah and they recognised the kindness of the voice of the boy and they turned towards him there and they said to him, 'What has brought you here? To perform foreign worship? Did you not come from Moses, the righteous one, of whom it was said "you shall not draw near" (Exod. 3:5)? And what are you doing here? A sacrifice for foreign worship? Did you not come from Moses the pious one, about whom it was said, "Because of this Moses, the man" (Exod. 32:1)? And what do you want? To be a priest for an idol? Did you not come from Moses, the humble one, to whom it was said, "But you, stand at my side!" (Deut. 5:31)?' And he said to them thus: 'I had become poor and we possess a tradition that it is proper for a man to rent himself for foreign service rather than be dependent on others. And thus Micah did, so he hired me and I become a priest for him.'

The marginal material is related to Talmudic tradition.[94]

As can be seen in the preceding examples, the material arranged under these headings (ירושלמי, תרגום ירושלמי and תרגום אחר) cannot easily be distinguished on the basis of their content. Generally, they offer an exegetically fuller version, often of a haggadic nature. There are, however, a few examples

---

92 van Staalduine-Sulman, *The Targum of Samuel*, 6 and references there.
93 On both these examples see Houtman and Sysling, *Alternative Targum Traditions*, 82, 90–1.
94 b. B. Bat. 110a; Yal. Judg.§73; see Smelik, *The Targum of Judges*, 600.

The Transmission of Targum Jonathan in the West

that relate to individual words.[95] These short variants relate to alternative wording or minor clarifications rather than to errors or variant vocalisation as one finds under ספר אחר and לישנא אחרינא.

4. The Layout

Thus far I have considered the content of the marginalia, in particular their nature and their relation to the main text. We must now turn our attention to their layout and distribution.

4.a Multiple Notes to the Same Point in the Main Text

There are a few instances in the codex where more than one marginal note is associated with a single word or phrase in the main text, with each of the marginal notes having its own siglum. In some cases the two sigla are different. For example, at Tg. Jer. 6:4, the main text reads טולי רמשא 'the shadows of the evening [grew long]'. In the margin under the siglum וא' דא' appears the reading טולי שימשא 'shadows of the sun'. To the same point in the text one finds the marginal note טולי מישרא 'shadows of the valley',[96] marked with the siglum פליג.

There are a few cases in the codex where two or more marginal notes are associated with a single word or phrase in the main text, each bearing their own siglum, yet the siglum for each of the marginal notes is the same. For

---

95 Josh. 5:3 marginal note (headed תרג' ירוש') reads איזמיליין טיזרין 'flint knives', main text איזמלוון חריפין 'sharp knives'; Josh. 13:3 the marginal note (headed ירוש') reads מן נילוס 'from the Nile', instead of the place name 'Shihor' (= MT); Josh. 19:47 (headed ירוש') reads לפמיאס 'to Pamias' in place of the main text's ללשם 'to Leshem' (= MT); Judg. 8:31 (headed ירו') reads ופלקתיה 'and his concubine' for the synonymous ולחינתיה. In Judg. 1:13 the main text reads עתניאל בר קנז אחוהי דכלב דזעיר מיניה 'Atniel son of Kenaz, the brother of Caleb, who was smaller than him'. Two notes both under the heading ירוש' are added here. The first is placed between the words דכלב דזעיר and reads מן אימיה 'from his mother'; the second is attached to the word מיניה and reads דילידת אימיה לקנז 'whom his mother bore to Kenaz'. Judg. 4:21 main text reads נסיבת יעל אישת חבר ית סיכת משכנא 'Jael, the wife of Heber took the tent peg'. The marginal note headed ירוש' (attached to סיכת) reads ית דשר (not ית דשרא as Sperber), 'the reed (of)'.
96 The פליג note may derive from a Hebrew text that had a variant reading in its Hebrew text, i.e. a text that read עֲרָבָה 'plain, steppe' (or עֶרֶב? cf. Isa. 21:13) in place of עֶרֶב (=MT). מישרא frequently translates עֲרָבָה (e.g. Jer. 2:6; 17:6; 39:4, 5; 52:7, 8 and frequently). If this is the case, the פליג note offers an alternative translation equivalent, as it does in other instances (see above, §3.b).

Chapter Nine. Marginal Notes in Codex Reuchlinianus No. 3

example, at 1 Sam. 2:24 there are two marginal notes that relate to the lexeme דרנין of the main text. Each note gives a variant reading (דרנגין מרנין and מרנגין) and both are headed individually with the siglum לישנא אחרינא (see page 271). A similar case is found at 1 Sam. 25:18 where two marginal notes are attached to מנן דבילתא 'vessels of pressed-figs'. Each gives a variant reading (מאנן דבלתא 'vessels of pressed-figs' and עיגולי דבלתא 'portions of pressed-figs') and both are headed individually with the siglum לישנא אחרינא. On one occasion (2 Sam. 12:8) there are no less than four separate variant readings,[97] each separately bearing the siglum לישנא אחרינא. This phenomenon is found only with notes bearing the siglum לישנא אחרינא and on one occasion with וא' דא'.

4.b. Multiple Designations to a Single Marginal Note

A single marginal note is sometimes given more than one siglum. The following combinations occur as two clearly marked separate headings to the same marginal note: תרגום אחר + ספר אחר (Judg. 12:6; 18:3, Ezek. 28:13, Amos 8:10; Zech. 3:2)[98] and ספר אחר + פליג (Josh. 4:19). Bacher lists several further examples.[99]

In a few places one also finds triple designations (ס' א' + ל' א' + ו' ד'), which occur to Jer. 17:7; 29:12; 31:28; 33:13; 35:14; 46:6; 48:38; Ezek. 16:39; and twice to Hos. 2:21. The variants are such that they might conceivably fall into any of these three categories: they concern alternative lexemes[100] or, in one case, an alternative pronominal suffix.[101] In some cases the main text reflects more closely the Hebrew text (i.e. Jer. 33:13; 35:14; 48:38; Hos. 2:21), in other cases the marginal note is closer (i.e. Jer. 31:28; 46:6; Ezek. 16:39?). In the

---

97 The facsimile is unclear, though there are discernibly four separate words in the margin, recorded by de Lagarde, *ad loc.* Sperber records only the three that concern consonantal variants, ignoring the fourth altogether.

98 In the case of Judg. 18:3 the heading ספר אחר stands immediately to the side of the main text, to indicate the point to which the variant is related. The variant is written in the bottom margin and headed תרג' אח'. Both headings are written above the marginal note, or in the case of Zech 3.2 ספ' אח' is written above the note while תר' אח' is written below.

99 Bacher, 'Kritische Untersuchungen zum Prophetentargum', 34–5.

100 I.e. Jer. 17:7 בסעדיה, margin רוחצניה; Jer. 29:12 ואיקבל, margin ואעביד; Jer. 31:28 דחדי מימרי, margin: דחשבית; Jer. 33:13 על יד משיחא, margin לפיתגמי משיחא; Jer. 35:14 לותי, margin: למימרי; Jer. 46:6 איתקטילו, margin: איתקילו; Jer. 48:38 אגריהון (i.e. אֲגַר), margin: איגוריהון (i.e. אִיגוֹר); Ezek. 16:39 שורך, margin איגורך.

101 I.e. Hos. 2:21 ואיקיימינך, margin ואיקיימינכון. The lexeme is ואיקיימינך repeated in the verse (the second occurence is spelled ואיקימינך); the same variant is attached to it on both occurrences.

majority of cases the marginal note is supported by one or more of the Yemenite manuscripts employed by Sperber.[102] In three cases the reading of t705i's main text is otherwise unknown,[103] and may in two of the instances be a revision towards the Hebrew text.[104] It is not impossible that the same variant was known to the compiler of t705i's marginalia through three separate sources (i.e. 'ס 'א + 'א 'ל + 'ו 'ד'), however in all of these cases several aspects of the physical layout of the materials raise suspicions as to whether or not they ought to be considered as part of the system employed elsewhere in the codex.

First of all, notes carrying this triple designation appear only in Jeremiah, Ezekiel, and Hosea, which are consecutive in the codex, and where there are generally very few notes. It is possible, of course, that the same variant appeared in three different sources *only* in these three books and nowhere else, but on the balance of probability this seems unlikely. Secondly, although the size of their lettering makes these notes difficult to assess palaeographically, the formation of some of the letters, in particular the *aleph*, points to a second hand. Finally, in some instances notes carrying the triple designation, which concern only a single word, stand in the upper margin (Jer. 17:7; 29:12; Hos. 2:21). Variants under the heading תרגום ירושלמי, תרגום אחר and ספר אחר often stand in the upper margin due to their length. Occasionally variants headed ספר אחר consisting of only a few words also appear there (e.g. 2 Sam. 21:12; 2 Kgs 16:25). But with one exception (Isa. 58:5, where a single-word note marked לישנא אחרינא appears in the top margin), short variants normally stand to the side of the text when they relate to a word in the first line of a column.[105]

The correspondence between those notes bearing the triple designation and the Yemenite manuscripts recorded by Sperber may also be taken to imply that they derive from a different source from the remainder of the notes, where no such correspondence is discernible.

If the notes carrying the triple designation are indeed from a second hand, one may conclude that a second scribe has added to the original marginalia without understanding fully the system of headings in use.[106] Perhaps the

---

102 Namely, ms Or. 2211, ms Or. 1474, ms Or. 1473 all of the British Library.
103 I.e. Jer. 35:14; Jer. 46:6; Hos. 2:21.
104 I.e. Jer. 35:14; Hos. 2:21.
105 Josh. 7:23 ('ירוש); 1 Sam. 2:14 (ואי דא'); 1 Sam. 7:2 (ואי דא'); 1 Sam. 23:22 ('ליש' אח); 1 Kgs 1:34 ('ספ' אח).
106 The same may also be true for the notes headed ו ס ד א (Ezek. 9:10), and ד ו א ל (Jer. 49:19).

compiler observed that the variants he recorded most closely resembled the notes under the three headings ספר אחר, לישנא אחרינא, and וא׳ דא׳, so placed these three headings above each variant arranging the headings one above the other to form a triangle and placing a decorative mark above them.[107]

4.c. Distribution

The marginalia are not spread equally throughout the codex. 1 Samuel, which has formed the basis of our sample study, contains approximately seventeen per cent of the total number of the marginalia while accounting for only around eight per cent of the text. By contrast Jeremiah contains approximately twelve per cent of all the marginalia, yet constitutes around fifteen per cent of the total text.[108] When one examines the individual sigla the picture is more interesting still. 1 Samuel, for example, contains forty-three readings under the siglum לי׳ א׳ / ליש׳ אח׳, which constitutes around twenty-three per cent of the total number of notes bearing this siglum in the whole codex; Jeremiah by contrast contains only twenty-one such notes, around eleven per cent. The density in 1 Samuel is therefore high. One also observes that some of the sigla do not appear in certain books. For example, while 1 Samuel contains nine occurrences of וא׳ דא׳, the book of 1 Kings, a book of comparable length, contains not a single one.

5. Relationship to other Textual Witnesses

In preparing the marginalia the compiler may have consulted other written sources, among them other copies of Targum Jonathan. Thus, one might assume that although these manuscripts are no longer known to us — t705i being the oldest extant continuous text of Targum Jonathan — copies of these manuscripts or later 'descendants' may still be extant. The marginalia were therefore compared to all the manuscripts of the Mixed Western group (to which Codex Reuchlinianus No. 3 belongs), as well as to the Ashkenazi group and those sources collated by Sperber in his critical edition. In only ten cases was there a

---

107 The ordering of the headings is inconsistent i.e. sometimes the order — from bottom to top — is ד׳ ו׳ + לי׳ א׳ + ס׳; on another occasion ל׳ א׳ + ס׳ א׳ + ו׳ ד׳; etc.
108 These figures are based on Bacher, 'Kritische Untersuchungen zum Prophetentargum', 3 and the critical apparatus in Sperber, *The Bible in Aramaic*, II–III. Consequently, they can only be considered indicative rather than authoritative.

correspondence (sometimes only partial) between the marginal reading and extant manuscripts. This concerned the sigla לישנא אחרינא (i.e. 1 Sam. 2:1; 9:4; 17:26; 20:18; 26:2; 30:23), ספר אחר (i.e. 1 Sam. 5:11 – the correction of an error); פליג (i.e. 1 Sam. 2:16); and וא׳ דא׳ (i.e. 1 Sam. 30:17). It is clear that no significant correlation exists between the marginalia and any of the extant manuscripts containing the continuous text examined.[109] Similarly, comparison with those variant Targum traditions found in quotations in rabbinic and medieval Jewish literature (as far as Goshen-Gottstein was able to collate these in his *Fragments of Lost Targumim*) and the Tosefta Targums collated by Kasher reveals no pattern of correspondence. It is worth reiterating before we jump to any conclusions on the basis of this observation that our extant materials probably represent only a fraction of what once must have existed.

Conclusions

Let me return to the question with which I began, namely:

What was the likely format and content of the sources from which the marginalia were drawn?

The available material does not allow a definitive answer to this question: The codex gives us no explanation of the system and questions remain about many points of detail. Nonetheless, it seems worthwhile to recapitulate our findings and attempt to sketch a plausible picture of the sources employed by the marginalia's compiler and the purpose of the various headings, even if this must remain tentative. It is clear from our characterisation of the notes that each category is in some respects distinct in terms of its content, yet there is also some commonality between some of the categories.

לישנא אחרינא

In particular, under the headings ספר אחר and לישנא אחרינא one finds synonyms, correct forms where the main text is at fault, and short additions that aim to provide additional clarification. Yet the לישנא אחרינא notes also contain variants

---

109 Smelik reached a similar result based on a comparative study of extant manuscripts of Targum Judges; Smelik, *The Targum of Judges*, 172–3. Cf. also A. Damsma, 'An Analysis of Targum Ezekiel and its Relationship to the Targumic Toseftot', Ph.D. dissertation (University College London 2008), Appendix G (NB. This material is not included in the published version of the thesis, i.e. Damsma, *The Targumic Toseftot to Ezekiel*).

that relate to orthography or vocalisation or which offer a variant conjugation of the verb, which are uncommon under the siglum ספר אחר; under the siglum ספר אחר one also finds larger additions of a haggadic nature, missing from the לישנא אחרינא notes. The presence of very similar types of notes under the sigla ספר אחר and לישנא אחרינא would suggest that these two sigla refer to distinct physical sources rather than providing a classification of the variants according to their type. If the latter had indeed been the case, one would expect all the notes of a similar character to appear under a single siglum.

Furthermore, the presence of multiple variants to a single point in the text marked with the same siglum (see §3.a and §3.c), would seem to preclude the notion that the designation לישנא אחרינא refers to a single manuscript since a single manuscript could not offer multiple readings of a single lexeme in the main text, though, of course, a manuscript that contained marginalia could. It is plausible to assume that the siglum לישנא אחרינא refers to the work — in this case, the standard text of Targum Jonathan —but does not distinguish between individual manuscript copies. In other words, I suggest that the compiler of the marginalia consulted multiple copies of the text of Targum Jonathan, which he designated with the siglum לישנא אחרינא; he found variant readings in the manuscripts he consulted and he recorded these in the margin, marking each with the same heading regardless of the manuscript in which they appeared. In this context then לישנא אחרינא would have the sense, 'another copy'.

In terms of their character, the לישנא אחרינא notes reflect the sort of variants found in extant manuscripts of the main text of Targum Jonathan, namely variants in orthography and vocalisation, the interchange of individual lexemes, alternative verbal conjugation, and some short explanatory glosses (a phenomenon attested particularly in Western manuscripts). It is therefore plausible to assume that the siglum לישנא אחרינא refers to manuscript copies of the standard text of Targum Jonathan into which variants had crept in the process of transmission. The scribe consulted multiple manuscripts containing the standard text-tradition of Targum Jonathan and recorded those variants that he found and that he considered to be of significance (he does not appear to have recorded scribal errors, for example).

ספר אחר

The phenomenon of multiple variants to a single point in the text being marked with the same siglum is not observed for ספר אחר notes, which may imply that the scribe had only one copy of this source at his disposal.¹¹⁰ Although variants relating to orthography, the conjugation of verbs, and vocalisation are uncommon among the ספר אחר notes, one does find single alternative lexemes (e.g. near-synonyms) and the correct reading where the main text of Codex Reuchlinianus No. 3 preserves an error. This suggests that at certain points the text designated ספר אחר followed the text of Targum Jonathan closely. Yet this version is also characterised by the presence of longer readings of an exegetical and often haggadic nature. It is plausible to suggest therefore that the scribe had at his disposal an exegetically fuller version of a Targum to the Prophets. This brings to mind the relationship between Targum Pseudo-Jonathan and the Onqelos Targum, which share many close verbal contacts but differ in the quantity and content of the haggadah that they contain, Pseudo-Jonathan offering a much fuller tradition than Onqelos.¹¹¹ If the tentative suggestion that the ספר אחר notes reflect a version of the Targum to the Prophets comparable to Targum Pseudo-Jonathan for the Torah could be substantiated by additional external evidence, this would be of great significance for the field of Targum studies.

וא׳ ד א׳

The notes under the headings וא׳ דא׳ and פליג provide variant readings in Aramaic, yet both seem to relate to matters arising from within the Hebrew text itself. Among the examples in 1 Samuel two cases are found where a reading headed וא׳ דא׳ or פליג is found in the main text of extant manuscripts (i.e. פליג 1 Sam. 2:16 לא | לי; וא׳ דא׳ 1 Sam. 30:17 גמלייא | ינקייא).

Let us begin with the וא׳ דא׳ notes. The analysis above suggests that these notes relate to instances where the underlying Hebrew text is problematic in some way. They deal with features in the Hebrew text that the main text of Targum Jonathan has failed to clarify or which permits an alternative explanation to that given by the main text. That the notes are of a fundamentally explanatory nature is suggested in some cases by their

---

110 Although other explanations cannot be excluded altogether: the copies he consulted may have exhibited remarkable consistency; he may have been selective in the variants he recorded; he may have had multiple copies that covered only parts of the text and therefore did not overlap; etc.

111 Exactly how this relationship is to be explained remains a matter of some dispute; for a brief overview and further bibliography see Maher, *Targum Pseudo-Jonathan: Genesis*, 1 n. 5.

Chapter Nine. Marginal Notes in Codex Reuchlinianus No. 3

vocabulary, which reflects other corpora of rabbinic literature, rather than being drawn from within the Targumic corpus. For example, תפילין (Tg. 2 Sam. 1:10) and אילפיס (Tg. 1 Sam. 2:14) are otherwise unknown in Targum Jonathan, but are widespread in rabbinic literature.[112] These notes may have arisen in oral tradition, as the heading וא׳ דא׳ would imply if understood as an abbreviation of ואית דאמרי or ואית דאמרין. One possibility is that this category of notes had been transmitted in the form of marginal notations alongside the main text of Targum Jonathan. If this were so, the notes might have originated in discussions at an early stage in the establishment of the official text of Targum Jonathan. This would imply that the compiler of the marginalia in Codex Reuchlinianus No. 3 copied these notes from another manuscript(s) containing marginal notations.

However, one must also take into account the fact that the reading of the marginal note attached to 1 Sam. 30:17 (main text: ינקייא | marginal וא׳ דא׳: גמלייא) appears in the main text of a number of other manuscripts (as I noted above). The question then arises: if the scribe found the reading גמלייא in other manuscript copies of Targum Jonathan that he consulted why is this variant not recorded under the heading לישנא אחרינא? One possibility, of course, is simply that none of the manuscripts consulted by our scribe contained this variant reading, so that the heading לישנא אחרינא was not appropriate. The reading גמלייא would be the more obvious translation equivalent for the underlying Hebrew (i.e. הגמלים), so it is plausible to suggest that the text could have been 'corrected' in other manuscripts (perhaps by the incorporation of marginal notations?). This theory may explain the case of the וא׳ דא׳ note to 1 Sam. 2:14, where the lexeme אילפיס appears under the heading וא׳ דא׳. This lexeme is otherwise unknown in the Targumic corpus with the exception of Tg. Judg. 6:19, where it is found as a marginal note under the siglum לישנא אחרינא. There a different lexeme stands in the main text of Targum Jonathan (i.e. בורמא), but the underlying Hebrew is the same (i.e. פרור). If our assumption concerning לישנא אחרינא is correct (i.e. that it refers to copies of the standard text of Targum Jonathan) then one must assume that the lexeme אילפיס stood in the main text of at least one manuscript. As the Masorah notes, there are only three

---

112 Although in this case the lexeme מליסא (i.e. reading of the main text) is also not found elsewhere in Targum Jonathan. Also, for example, גניסת (Tg. 2 Sam. 4:2), never found in the main text, though appears in a few cases in marginal material. i.e. תרג׳ ירוש׳ 1 Sam. 17:4; תרג׳ ירוש׳ Josh. 15:6; ל׳ א׳ Josh. 18:7.

verses in the Hebrew Bible where the form בפרור is employed. So it is again plausible to assume that the main text of one of the manuscripts had been 'corrected', not only because the underlying Hebrew is uncommon, but also because the Aramaic בורמא of Tg. Judg. 6:19 is obscure, being unknown in the corpora of mainstream rabbinic literature.

A second possibility is that the scribe did indeed find the variant in one or more of the manuscripts he consulted but nonetheless wanted to indicate that in his view the variant had arisen as a result of a difficulty in the Hebrew itself (or that it belonged correctly to a traditional system of marginal notation?). וא' דא', if understood as an abbreviation of ואית דאמרי or ואית דאמרין, would then indicate a division of opinion concerning how the underlying Hebrew was correctly to be read. The former of these two possibilities seems more likely, but it is acknowledged that a significant degree of uncertainty remains.

פליג

The פליג notes seem simpler to explain. Those notes gathered under the siglum פליג offer an acceptable alternative Targumic rendering of the Hebrew text (i.e. homonyms, vocalisation, or alternative translation equivalents found elsewhere in Targum Jonathan or Targum Onqelos). In some cases, the reading of the main text of the Targum may reflect the reading of the main text of an authoritative Hebrew manuscript against which it was compared, while the notes marked פליג record an alternative translation based on the Masorah of that Hebrew manuscript. That marginal readings marked with the notation פליג appear in the main text of other manuscripts (i.e. 1 Sam. 2:16 main text ליה | margin לא) can be accounted for in the same way as those notes carrying the designation וא' דא', namely, the compiler of the marginalia in Codex Reuchlinianus No. 3 either did not find the reading in the manuscripts he checked or he wished to indicate that the alternative reading was acceptable *vis à vis* the Hebrew.

תרגום אחר, *and* תרגום ירושלמי, ירושלמי

The distribution and content of the marginalia under the three headings תרגום ירושלמי, ירושלמי and תרגום אחר, suggest that we are not dealing with a continuous text, since such a text would doubtless also have preserved many more minor textual variants. Rather, they suggest that the materials are drawn from sources that preserved a collection of short units of Targum of an exegetically fuller nature. The presence of some short variants, however,

Chapter Nine. Marginal Notes in Codex Reuchlinianus No. 3

would seem to suggest that at certain points the text followed the main text of Targum Jonathan with only these minor exceptions, while at other points it contained large expansions; where the source-text differed from that of Codex Reuchlinianus No. 3, the compiler of the marginalia recorded this.

From what sort of source might such notes be drawn? The compiler of the marginalia may have found these materials either in liturgical texts — a number of the Tosefta Targums known to us, for example, are preserved in liturgical works[113] — or in a format similar to the Fragment Targums to the Pentateuch, which are related to the liturgy.[114] A comparison between the marginalia under these three headings and liturgical traditions indicates a partial correspondence. Of the sixty-eight marginal readings under the headings תרגום ירושלמי or simply ירושלמי sixteen correspond to known haftarot of the Palestinian triennial cycle,[115] twenty-three to variations of the Babylonian annual cycle.[116] Of the ten תרגום אחר marginalia, seven may be connected to the Palestinian cycle,[117] and four to the Babylonian cycle.[118] To this observation I would add that sixteen of the marginalia under the heading(s) תרגום ירושלמי or ירושלמי relate to either the first or last verse of either a *parashah petuhah* or *setumah* (that is, an open or closed paragraph),[119] as do four examples under the heading תרגום אחר.[120] This

---

113 See Kasher, *Targumic Toseftot to the Prophets* (a list of manuscripts consulted is given on pages 303–6). See also chapter ten.

114 Klein, *The Fragment-Targums of the Pentateuch*, 19–23; B.Z. Wacholder 'Prolegomenon', in J. Mann, *The Bible as Read and Preached in the Old Synagogue, I. The Palestinian Triennial Cycle: Genesis and Exodus* (New York 1971 [1940]), xxxvii.

115 Namely, Josh. 5:3, 15; 6:27; 14:15; 24:19 (?); Judg. 5:4, 5; 1 Kgs 2:9 (?); 8:9; 2 Kgs 13:21; Isa. 1:21; 11:3; 33:7; 49:24; 54:10; 66:1. Josh. 24:19 is preserved only in the Romanian rite. On the relation between Romanian and Palestinian rites, see C. Perrot, *La lecture de la Bible dans la synagogue: les anciennes lectures palestiniennes du shabbat et des fêtes* (Collection Massorah, série 1, Études classique et textes, 1, Hildesheim 1973), 49–50.

116 Namely, Josh. 5:3, 15; Judg. 4:21; 5:4, 5; 1 Sam. 12:5; 1 Kgs 2:9; 3:27; 8:9; 2 Kgs 5:19; Isa. 1:21; 11:3; 49:24; 54:10; 66:1; Jer. 46:17. In addition, according to the haftarot marked in Codex Reuchlinianus No. 3 itself, Josh. 13:19 served as the haftarah to מטות (i.e. Num. 30:2–32:42).

117 I.e. Josh. 6:1; Judg. 18:3 (x2); Isa. 11:11; Ezek. 28:13; Amos 8:10(?); Zech. 3:2.

118 I.e. Josh. 6:1; Isa. 11:11; Jer. 9:22; Zech. 3:2.

119 I.e. Josh. 22:20; 24:15, 19; Judg. 2:1; 12:8; 1 Sam. 10:22; 12:5; 1 Kgs 16:34; 2 Kgs 5:19; 13:21; Isa. 1:21; 21:5; 33:7; 49:24; 54:10; 66:1. According to the Aleppo Codex, which preserves a more ancient tradition of division that conforms more closely to the Palestinian lectionary cycle, see F. Langlamet, 'Les divisions massorétiques du livre de Samuel', *Revue Biblique* 91 (1984), 492, 494. In other traditions 1 Kgs 17:13 is the last verse of a paragraph.

120 Josh. 6:1; Isa. 11:11; 45:7; Jer. 9:22.

traditional division of the text is ancient[121] — although customs differed before they became fixed in the halachah[122] — and corresponds to lectionary custom.[123] In addition there is a correspondence between five of the marginalia under the headings תרגום ירושלמי or ירושלמי and the sedarim of the Prophets,[124] being either the first or final verse;[125] a further two are the penultimate verse of a seder.[126] Two of the ten notes under the תרגום אחר heading also correspond to the sedarim. Although still a matter of scholarly debate, the sedarim of the Prophets may correspond to the Palestinian liturgical cycle[127] (NB. it is a well-established fact that the sedarim of the Torah mark the weekly readings according to the Palestinian liturgical cycle).[128] The correspondence between the תרגום ירושלמי or ירושלמי notes and

---

121 E.g. b.Šabb. 103b; Sifra Lev. 1:1; 1:9.

122 In particular following Maimonides, e.g. *Hilkhot Sefer Torah* VIII.4; see A. Dotan, 'Masorah', in M. Berenbaum and F. Skolnik (eds), *Encyclopaedia Judaica²*, Vol. XIII. (Detroit 2007), 603–56, p. 607.

123 However, the division of the text into parashiyyot probably does not originate in the lectionary cycle. On the contrary, the selection of the haftarot readings probably took account of existing text divisions, as Oesch has argued; J.M. Oesch, *Petucha und Setuma: Untersuchungen zu einer überlieferten Gliederung im hebräischen Text des Alten Testaments* (Orbis Biblicus et Orientalis 27, Freiburg 1979), 34–6. Contra C. Perrot, 'Petuhot et Setumot: étude sur les alinéas du Pentateuque', *Revue Biblique* 76 (1969), 50–91, pp. 74–6; cf. also Langlamet, 'Les divisions massorétiques du livre de Samuel', 481–519, pp. 492, 494.

124 According to the sedarim of Codex Aleppo (which can be viewed at http://www.aleppocodex.org/) and those of Codex Leningradensis according to Dotan (ed.), *Biblia Hebraica Leningradensia*, see note on xviii of his introduction. These manuscripts are in agreement as far as the cited verses are concerned. The sedarim are not marked in Codex Reuchlinianus No. 3. The tradition of the sedarim is a stable one, not differing significantly between manuscripts, see J. Offer, 'The Masoretic Divisions (Sedarim) in the Books of Prophets and Hagiographa', [in Hebrew], *Tarbiz* 58:2 (1989), 155–89, pp. 156–9.

125 I.e. Josh. 6:27; 10:42; 14:15; 18:28; Judg. 3:31.

126 I.e. 1 Kgs 8:9; Isa. 49:24.

127 A number of scholars have argued in favour of a correspondence; for references see Perrot, *La Lecture de la Bible dans la Synagogue,* 47; also A. Büchler, 'The Reading of the Law and Prophets in a Triennial Cycle. II', *Jewish Quarterly Review* 6:1 (1893), 1–73, see 32–4. Offer attempted to refute this hypothesis. He observed that the sedarim correspond with the beginning of haftarot (so far as they are known) in 9.4% of cases, or the end of haftarot in 31.6% cases. In Offer's view this indicated that there was no compelling agreement; Offer, 'The Masoretic Divisions (Sedarim) in the Books of Prophets and Hagiographa', 170–1. However, when one considers that our knowledge of the Palestinian cycle is far from complete and that significant variations existed within it (Perrot, *La Lecture de la Bible dans la Synagogue*, 47, 53), an agreement between the sedarim and haftarot of 40% can hardly be dismissed as pure coincidence.

128 Perrot, *La Lecture de la Bible dans la Synagogue*, 37.

Chapter Nine. Marginal Notes in Codex Reuchlinianus No. 3

the liturgical system, though not complete, is nonetheless significant.

In my view the hypothesis that the ירושלמי, תרגום ירושלמי, and תרגום אחר marginalia had their origins in liturgical practice is plausible, though the case is far from decisively settled. In particular, one must bear in mind that our knowledge of the Palestinian cycle remains rather incomplete.[129] The six variants to 1 Samuel 17, for example, can be connected to the Italian liturgical tradition (falling within the haftarah to parashat *Ki Tetze*),[130] but in the case of this haftarah the Italian custom probably preserves a Palestinian tradition.[131] This hypothesis can be further strengthened by the observation that, in six cases of תרגום ירושלמי and ירושלמי and two cases of תרגום אחר, Tosefta Targums differing in terms of their content from marginalia in Codex Reuchlinianus No. 3 can be found to the same point in the Masoretic Text.[132] The Tosefta Targums exhibit a strong connection to the lectionary.[133] With one exception, Jer. 9:22, which so far as is known is only connected to the annual cycle (being read on the morning of the 9th of Av), these relate to portions of the text that were probably read in the Palestinian cycle.[134]

The exact format in which the compiler of Codex Reuchlinianus No. 3's marginalia found his material cannot be known, whether in liturgical works (e.g. mahzorim), in the margins of other manuscripts, or in collections appearing in other codices (i.e. formats in which the Fragment Targums to the Pentateuch are found). Incidentally, if one pursues the analogy with the

---

129 See Wacholder 'Prolegomenon'; Perrot, *La Lecture de la Bible dans la Synagogue*, 24–36, 53. Cf. also the discussion in Houtman and Sysling, *Alternative Targum Traditions*, 134–5.
130 Houtman and Sysling, *Alternative Targum Traditions*, 82–97.
131 The reading of 1 Samuel 17 as a haftarah to parashah *Ki Tetze*, for example, can be found in two haftarot fragments from the Cambridge Genizah collection, namely T-S K26.36 and West. Coll. Misc.70 (Both: Oriental square script; Tiberian vocalisation), which were not recorded in the standard works on the subject: Perrot, *La Lecture de la Bible dans la Synagogue*, or Wacholder 'Prolegomenon'; but see van Staalduine-Sulman, *The Targum of Samuel*, 60 n. 46 and references there. A striking number of tiny fragments also preserve sections of Tg. 1 Samuel 17, e.g. T-S B7.2 (1 Sam. 17:13–18); T-S NS 161.137 (1 Sam. 17:3–4); T-S NS 161.286 (1 Sam. 17:4–39); T-S AS 21.248 (1 Sam. 17:32–8); T-S AS 62.541 = T-S AS 62.543-547 (1 Sam. 17:42–3; 18:6–10); T-S AS 70.102 (1 Sam. 17:9–26). It is impossible to determine their original context due to their size. On individual fragments see M.L. Klein, *Targumic Manuscripts in the Cambridge Genizah Collections* (Cambridge 1992).
132 Kasher, *Targumic Toseftot to the Prophets*, §§4, 5, 24, 53, 74, 100, 115, 123.
133 Smelik, 'Orality, Manuscript Reproduction, and the Targums', 66–7; see also in Houtman and Sysling, *Alternative Targum Traditions*, 134–5.
134 I.e. Josh. 6:1, 27; Judg. 5:5; 1 Sam. 17:8; 1 Kgs 2:9; 2 Kgs 13:21; Isa. 49:24.

Fragment Targums to the Pentateuch, the differing headings used in the Codex Reuchlinianus No. 3 marginalia (i.e. תרגום ירושלמי, ירושלמי, תרגום אחר) may point to separate collections, five recensions of the Fragment Targum being known; incidentally, similar headings are used for the Fragment Targums in their manuscripts.[135] If they were found in compilations intended for study, this could account for the presence of material unrelated to the liturgy, while explaining why there is an apparent emphasis on units connected to liturgical cycles, which would naturally have been the focus of frequent study.

Concluding Remarks

In summary, I have suggested the following as a plausible hypothesis for explaining the marginalia of Codex Reuchlinianus No. 3. The compiler consulted a number of copies of the standard text of Targum Jonathan (לישנא אחרינא). He also consulted another continuous text of a Targum to the Prophets, which contained a text largely parallel to that of Targum Jonathan, yet containing many longer exegetical and haggadic readings (ספר אחר). In addition to these sources the scribe recorded the variants that he found in short units of (an) exegetically fuller version(s), probably preserved in liturgical texts or in the margins of other codices (תרגום ירושלמי, ירושלמי, תרגום אחר). It remains unclear whether the compiler of Codex Reuchlinianus No. 3's marginalia found the variants designated וא׳ דא׳ and פל׳יג in written sources. Perhaps they belonged to a traditional system of critical marginal notes, which the scribe copied from his *Vorlage*. In either case, the פל׳יג notes record acceptable alternative Targumic renderings of the Hebrew text or its Masorah; the וא׳ דא׳ notes deal with instances where the underlying Hebrew is problematic.

This proposed explanation can account for the individual notes that carry multiple headings (see above, §4.b), i.e., in a number of cases the compiler

---

135 Of which we have a number of extant editions dating from a similar period to Codex Reuchlinianus No. 3, e.g. Ebr. 440, fols 198–227, Vatican Library, thirteenth century; Solger, 2.2°, fols 119–47, Stadtbibliothek, Nürenberg, 1291 CE; Or. 10794 Gaster Collection, fol 8, British Library, London, twelfth/thirteenth century; T-S AS 72.75,76,77, University Library, Cambridge, ninth/tenth–mid eleventh century. See Klein, *The Fragment-Targums of the Pentateuch*, 26–33. This analogy was already made by Bacher, 'Kritische Untersuchungen zum Prophetentargum', 58; followed (tentatively) by Smelik, *The Targum of Judges*, 174; and has been developed in Houtman and Sysling, *Alternative Targum Traditions*, 132–3.

Chapter Nine. Marginal Notes in Codex Reuchlinianus No. 3

found the same variant reading in two of the exegetically fuller versions (i.e. תרגום אחר and ספר אחר); and in one case (Josh 4:19) the reading preserved in the main text of the ספר אחר source provides an acceptable alternative of the Hebrew (i.e. פליג).[136]

We cannot know, however, the exact process by which the system of marginalia was compiled, nor the location of its composition, since the scribe who added the marginalia to Codex Reuchlinianus No. 3 may simply have copied the entire system from his *Vorlage*. Such a work may have been undertaken in one of Italy's famous academies, perhaps in the flourishing centres at Rome, Bari, or Lucca.[137] But equally if the scribe took the marginalia over from his *Vorlage* one's mind turns to the Palestinian academies, with which Italian Jews maintained strong links,[138] particularly since the system of vocalisation of the main text is connected to Palestine.[139]

The scribe's access to sources may have been limited and this may account for the distribution of the material throughout the codex (see above §4.c). He may, for example, have had access to multiple manuscripts containing Targum Jonathan (i.e. לישנא אחרינא) for the books of Samuel, but only one for the book of Jeremiah. Of course, the manuscripts may not have been complete — perhaps just loose leaves or quires — or may have been partially illegible due to wear or damage. Equally, the variations in the distribution of the notes may result from any number of external factors that resulted in the interruption or curtailment of work or may simply reflect the scribe's personal interest.

The multiple-source hypothesis outlined above is also able to account for the fact that only some of the marginalia are vocalised and others not: one can easily imagine that some of the sources were themselves vocalised, while others were either unvocalised or the vocalisation may have been illegible.[140]

---

136 MT לחדש הראשון; Tg. לירחא קדמאה, translating *ad verbum* | Marginal note (פליג, ספר אחר): לירחא דניסן translating *ad sensum*, Nissan being the first month of the Jewish year.

137 C. Roth, *The History of the Jews of Italy* (Philadelphia, PA 1946), 90–2; A. Milano, 'Italy', in M. Berenbaum and F. Skolnik (eds), *Encyclopaedia Judaica*², Vol. X. (Detroit 2007), 795–816, p. 798.

138 A. Milano, *Storia degli ebrei in Italia* (Torino 1963) for references in the relevant period see 62, 65, 87.

139 Morag, 'The Vocalization of Codex Reuchlinianus: Is the "Pre-Masoretic" Bible Pre-Masoretic?', 216–37.

140 Though there may be several contributing factors, for example, whether or not the vocalisation is relevant, which it often is with the single-word variants, but less so with the longer variants.

The Transmission of Targum Jonathan in the West

The possibility that the source materials use differing vocalisation systems must also be borne in mind.[141]

In this chapter I have attempted to formulate a plausible hypothesis to explain the perplexing marginalia of Codex Reuchlinianus No. 3. Further work is now required to strengthen (or refute) this theory. In particular, a technical analysis (including of the ink) of all the marginalia in order to determine whether or not they all stem from the same hand and date is now an urgent desideratum. Further collation of other extant sources of the Targum to the Prophets would also increase the base of material available for comparative analysis.

The conclusions reached in this chapter remain provisional, but if they are correct then the value of Codex Reuchlinianus No. 3's marginalia for the study of the textual history of Targum Jonathan (particularly the לישנא אחרינא notes), the study of other (Palestinian?) Targum traditions, and for our understanding of the role, function, and status of Targum within Western medieval Jewish culture, would be difficult to underestimate.

---

141 Of the three major systems of vocalisation (Palestinian, Babylonian, and Tiberian), the unusual vocalisation of Codex Reuchlinianus No. 3 is a subset of the Tiberian system. Sperber, in his introduction to the facsimile edition of Codex Reuchlinianus No. 3, argued that the vocalisation system of Codex Reuchlinianus No. 3 was pre-Masoretic. This conclusion has been thoroughly refuted by Morag, who renamed it a 'fuller Palestinian' system from the post-Masoretic period (Morag, 'The Vocalization of Codex Reuchlinianus', 216–37). Vocalisation systems began to be committed to writing in the seventh/eighth century CE, based on earlier oral traditions. The hegemony of the Tiberian system began around 1000 CE. See I. Yeivin, *Introduction to the Tiberian Masorah* (trans. and ed. E.J. Revell; Masoretic Studies 5, Missoula, MT 1980), 10.

Chapter Ten

The Targum Text in Liturgical Manuscripts

During the period with which we are concerned specific sections of the Targum were read aloud in the synagogue in Italy and Ashkenaz during certain festivals, as was outlined in chapter two. As a result, a version of the Targum has been preserved in liturgies for the festal rituals (mahzorim) in Italy, and in haftarot collections in Ashkenaz. In this section previous research on liturgical Targum texts will be surveyed,[1] the manuscripts examined will be described, a translation of the texts will be provided, and their content discussed.

1. Previous Research

The function of the Targum in medieval European liturgical customs is a topic that has received scant scholarly attention and would reward a fuller and more comprehensive study than can be offered here. In some cases the Targum text that one encounters in Ashkenazi and Italian liturgical sources is longer and exegetically richer than that which we find in the continuous text; as a result, these units have often been classified as Tosefta Targums and dealt with in the scholarly literature as part of the wider body of Tosefta Targums, which incorporates a wide range of materials drawn from diverse sources, differing from one another in length, dialect, and relationship to the standard text of Targum Jonathan (see chapter eleven).

A survey of previous research on the Tosefta Targums has recently been published by Houtman and Sysling[2] and need not be repeated here. Rather, attention will be drawn briefly to those works that have concerned themselves in particular with the Targum as found in liturgical manuscripts.

In 1877 de Lagarde published an article cataloguing manuscripts then in the possession of the Protestant administration in Erfurt.[3] Among the collection

---

1 The term 'liturgical manuscripts' is employed here broadly to include not only liturgies *sensu stricto*, for example mahzorim, which reflect a usage of Targum during the synagogue liturgy, but also collections of haftarot whose purpose was study.
2 Houtman and Sysling, *Alternative Targum Traditions*, 42–6.
3 De Lagarde, 'Hebräische Handschriften in Erfurt', in his *Symmicta*, pp. 129–64.

de Lagarde records a thirteenth century Ashkenazi manuscript (now Or. fol. 1214, Staatsbibliothek, Preußischer Kulturbesitz, Berlin [t63a]) containing the Pentateuch with Onqelos, the Five Scrolls, and the Haftarot. After each of the haftarot for the five festal days of Pesach and the two days of Shavuot, the Targum was given. The reading for the seventh day of Passover followed the custom typical in Ashkenazi sources of giving the Targum only for the first fourteen and last two verses of 2 Samuel 22 (in contrast to the Italian custom where the whole chapter is given). De Lagarde noted the differences from the running text of Codex Reuchlinianus No. 3 (t705i) according to his edition without giving any further analysis; the variant readings noted by de Lagarde are typical of Ashkenazi liturgical sources (see below).

In his *Das Buch des Propheten Ezechiel* (1886) Cornill considered the value of the haftarot readings to Ezekiel that de Lagarde had published for reconstructing the Targum's *Urtext*. According to Cornill each exhibited its own peculiarities, showing no agreement with the three recensions that he had identified (see pages 9–11) and this, as well as their length, persuaded Cornill that they were essentially a later development. As such he judged their value for reconstructing the putative *Urtext* to be limited, so decided to exclude them from his study.[4]

The study of European liturgical manuscripts remained dormant until Díez Macho breathed new life into it.[5] During his study of the manuscripts of the Jewish Theological Seminary in New York, Díez Macho encountered a large fragment (Ms ENA 2576, f.5), the remnant of a fourteenth century Sephardi mahzor, containing a version of the Targum to Jos. 5:5–6:1 that differed totally from Targum Jonathan. The text was in Babylonian Aramaic, similar to that of Targum Jonathan, yet Díez Macho observed that the same text was preserved in the Cairo Genizah fragments collected in Cambridge (T-S B13.2) in Palestinian Aramaic. This demonstrated in Díez Macho's view how the Palestinian Targum has been converted into Babylonian Aramaic, especially

---

4 Cornill, *Das Buch des Propheten Ezechiel*, 120.
5 To this a caveat must be added: the source to which Sperber assigns the siglum 'Fr', signifying 'various Biblical fragments with Targum, of the Taylor Schechter Collection of the University Library in Cambridge', resembles extremely closely the Italian liturgical texts examined below. The identity of the fragments that he consulted, however, remains a mystery: none of the fragments in Klein's catalogue (Klein, *Targumic Manuscripts in the Cambridge Genizah Collections*) contains the readings recorded by Sperber. Perhaps he consulted a mahzor?

Chapter Ten. The Targum Text in Liturgical Manuscripts

under the influence of Targum Jonathan,[6] and therefore the Palestinian origin of the text.[7]

Díez Macho later published a second unit of 'Palestinian' Targum (containing Ezek. 37:1–14), which had been preserved in a section of the Salonica Pentateuch containing the haftarot readings for Pesach. He noted that its distinct haggadah was also to be found in Mahzor Vitry, though the placement and extent of the haggadah differed in the two sources. The remainder of the text otherwise corresponded to the text of Targum Jonathan. Such an observation was applicable to other haftarot readings in Mahzor Vitry. Although the mahzor did not distinguish these expansions from the remainder of the text, the additional material was known from (what he regarded as) Palestinian sources, either from Targum Chronicles (in the case of the unit from Ezek. 37:1–14) or from the margins of other manuscripts under the heading 'Targum Yerushalmi'. This suggested to Díez Macho that Palestinian Targum material had been incorporated into the text of Targum Jonathan.[8]

At the beginning of his career, in 1956, Díez Macho had published a Targum text from the Cambridge Genizah collection (T-S B12.1) containing the unpointed text of a Targum to 1 Kgs 2:3–8 with Hebrew lemmata in an oriental square script,[9] the text of which differed from that of the received text of Targum Jonathan. Díez Macho says of this text: 'it is a new variant recension of the same text, characterised by being more paraphrastic, by some explanatory additions to the literal translation of the Hebrew text that are lacking in the *textus receptus* of Jonathan'.[10] The additional material in this fragment (of which Díez Macho reproduced only 1 Kgs 2:3–5) belongs clearly

---

6 Díez Macho, *El Targum*, 94, n. 202; Díez Macho, 'The Recently Discovered Palestinian Targum', 238. Cf. Díez Macho, 'Nueva fuente para el Targum Palestino del día séptimo de Pascua y primero de Pentecostés', 235. Cf. Grelot, 'Une Tosephta Targoumique sur Zacharie, II, 14–15', 201.

7 A. Díez Macho, 'Un nuevo Targum a los Profetas', *Estudios Biblicos* 15 (1956), 287–95, pp. 290–2. Cf. Díez Macho, 'Un segundo fragmento del Targum Palestinense a los Profetas', *Biblica* 39 (1958), 198–205, 229–36, pp. 199–200; Díez Macho, 'Nuevos manuscritos importantes, biblicos o liturgicos, en Hebreo o Arameo', 3–22, §47; Díez Macho, 'Importants manuscrits hébreux et araméens aux États Unis', §9.

8 Díez Macho, 'Un segundo fragmento del Targum Palestinense a los Profetas', 198–205. Cf. Houtman and Sysling, *Alternative Targum Traditions*, 240–7.

9 Klein, *Targumic Manuscripts in the Cambridge Genizah Collections*, §326.

10 A. Díez Macho, 'Fragmento de una nueva recension del Targum Jonatan ben 'Uzziel a los Profetas (=T.-S. B 121)', *Sefarad* 16 (1956), 405–6, p. 406.

to Kasher's 'redundant integrated expansion' category. We have only a single leaf, so it is impossible to be certain of the context in which the text was originally set; but given its character and *mise en page* a liturgical collection is certainly plausible.

In 1994 Díez Merino presented a paper to the Fifth Congress of Jewish Studies in Copenhagen (published in 1998) in which he compared the longer text form of the Targum of the prayer of Habakkuk (Hab. 2:20; 3:1–10, 18–19) preserved in the Mahzor Vitry (according to the Hurwitz edition) — strictly speaking a prescriptive halachic compilation for the old French rite, rather than a liturgy *per se*[11] — to the text found in Codex Reuchlinianus No. 3. He concluded that once one had excluded variations in *matres lectionis*, cases of homoioteleuthon and other errors, which are numerous in the Mahzor Vitry text, and the addition or omission of formulaic expressions (such as בלבב שלים), which is a common feature in the Tosefta Targums and fuller liturgical text forms,[12] there remained 'very few variant readings among the two Aramaic texts', so that he could conclude that 'it is essentially the same Western tradition read by Codex Reuchlinianus [No. 3] and Mahzor Vitry'.[13]

While Díez Merino's basic conclusion that the two texts are broadly similar can be upheld, the conclusions he draws from this observation are rather foggy. According to Díez Merino the Mahzor Vitry text followed 'the Western tradition of the Targum to the Prophets, namely the Palestinian tradition' while Sperber's base text follows 'the Eastern tradition'.[14] This is to confuse two quite distinct text types: Sperber's base text does indeed adhere to the Eastern textual tradition. But there is also a Western textual tradition found in manuscripts containing the continuous text of Targum Jonathan that is close to the Eastern continuous text tradition though distinct from it; this Western textual tradition is quite different from the Western Tosefta Targum tradition and must be distinguished from it.

---

11 Reif, *Judaism and Hebrew Prayer*, 169–70. The French rite had an existence of its own that was of significance until the thirteenth century when the distinction from other Ashkenazi rites breaks down. Díez Merino records that Mahzor Vitry contains the following Targum to the haftarot: Josh. 3:5–7; 5:2–6:27 (Pesach); 2 Kgs 21:1–2; 22:1–13, 15, 50–1 (second day); Ezek. 37:1–14 (Sabbath); 2 Sam. 21:20–2; 22:1–13, 15, 50–1 (seventh day); Isa. 10:32–4; 11:1–11; 12:4–6 (last day); Ezek. 1:1–12; 3:12 (Shavuot); Hab. 2:20–3:11, 18–19; Díez Merino, 'Mahzor Vitry and the Palestinian Targum to the Prophets', 201.
12 Díez Merino, 'Mahzor Vitry and the Palestinian Targum to the Prophets', 210.
13 Díez Merino, 'Mahzor Vitry and the Palestinian Targum to the Prophets', 204.
14 Díez Merino, 'Mahzor Vitry and the Palestinian Targum to the Prophets', 202.

Chapter Ten. The Targum Text in Liturgical Manuscripts

The Western tradition of the Targum to the Prophets is not universally Palestinian in its current form. Furthermore, Díez Merino is over-hasty in defining both texts as Palestinian: his analysis proceeds from the presupposition that the marginalia of Codex Reuchlinianus No. 3 are Palestinian, but such an assumption is open to question (see the discussion of past research on Codex Reuchlinianus No. 3's marginalia, chapter nine §1). Moreover, he notes that the text contains some Eastern Aramaic features (such as ארי not ארום), a fact he does not satisfactorily explain.[15]

A more refined approach to the study of the fuller text of the Targum to the Prophets found in liturgical manuscripts appeared around the same time, in the form of Kasher's *Targumic Toseftot to the Prophets* (1996). In this volume Kasher collated a number of versions of Targum readings to the Prophets which were to be found in European liturgical texts. Of those sources originating from Ashkenaz or Italy the Tosefta Targums appeared in two types of sources: mahzorim and collections of haftarot, which are normally found in manuscripts containing the Torah and Megillot. From the mahzorim following Western Ashkenazi rites, Kasher records Tosefta Targums to Josh. 6:1, the haftarah for the 1st day of Pesach, Ezek. 37:1 for the shabbat of the intermediate days of Pesach, Isa. 10:32–3 for the eighth day of Pesach, Ezek. 1:12 for the first day of Shavuot, and Hab. 3:1–2, 11 for the second day of Shavuot.[16] From Italian mahzorim he records: 2 Samuel 22 for the seventh day of Pesach, and Isa. 10:32–3 for the eighth day of Pesach.[17] In addition Kasher

---

15 Díez Merino, 'Mahzor Vitry and the Palestinian Targum to the Prophets', 204.
16 Laud. Or. 321 (Bodleian Library, Oxford; thirteenth cent.) [Siglum ל], Western rite; Mahzor Vitry, Add. 27200–27201 (British Library, London; thirteent cent.) [siglum ט]; Mahzor Worms, Heb. 4° 781 (National Library, Jerusalem; 1272 CE) [siglum י]; Parma 3000 (Biblioteca Palentina, Parma; fourteenth cent.) [siglum ק], French rite. See Kasher, *Targumic Toseftot to the Prophets*, §4a, §107b, §131b, §142a. The Mahzor Worms probably reflects the rite of Würzburg, see Beit-Arié, 'The Worms Mahzor', 19–20. It shows many connections to the French rite (e.g. in its *piyyutim*), see Fleischer, 'Prayer and Piyyut in the Worms Mahzor'.
17 Add. 17058 (British Library, London; sixteenth cent.); Add. 27070 (British Library, London; sixteenth cent.) [siglum ה³]; Sassoon 1028 (Sassoon Collection, Letchworth; 1397 CE). See Kasher, *Targumic Toseftot to the Prophets*, §70, §107b. Kasher lists several further mahzorim that are not used in the critical apparatuses, i.e. Add. 19944/19945 (British Library, London; Italian rite, 1441 CE); Parma 3136 (Biblioteca Palantina, Parma; French rite, fourteenth cent.); Parma 3003 (Biblioteca Palantina, Parma; Italian rite, sixteenth cent.); Parma 2887 (Biblioteca Palantina, Parma; Ashkenazi rite, fourteenth cent.); Hébreu 640 (Bibliothèque Nationale, Paris; Ashkenazi Rite, fourteenth cent.); Sasson 1017 (Sassoon Collection, Letchworth; Sephardi rite, sixteenth cent.). Kasher, *Targumic Toseftot to the Prophets*, 306.

The Transmission of Targum Jonathan in the West

recorded several Tosefta Targums appearing in volumes containing — with a few exceptions — the Torah, haftarot, and the Five Scrolls (i.e. Megillot). He records no Italian manuscripts of this sort, but several of the Ashkenazi manuscripts contain Tosefta Targums to Isa. 10:32–3 for the eighth day of Pesach, and Hab. 3:1–2, 11 for the second day of Shavuot;[18] many include an additional Tosefta Targum to Josh. 6:1 for the first day of Pesach,[19] and one also contains Tosefta Targums to Isa. 66:1–2, 23 for Rosh Hodesh and Zech. 2:14–4:7 for the shabbat of Hanukkah.[20] According to Kasher's analysis these Tosefta Targums consisted principally of 'integrated expansions' (ההרחבה המשולבת) — in other words additional wording added to the basic text of Targum Jonathan,[21] and their language is close to that of Targum Jonathan itself.[22]

As one might expect given the overall direction of Targum research, which I outlined in chapter one, Eastern liturgical sources have attracted more interest than their Western counterparts. Sperber consulted two collections of haftarot for his edition of Targum Jonathan to the Former Prophets and one for the

---

18 Add. 11639 (British Library, London; Torah + haftarot for festivals and special shabbats; thirteenth cent.) [siglum ס]; Nicholson 33 (University Library, Sydney; + Job 14–15th Cent.) [צ]; Or. Qu. 9 (Staatsbibliothek, Preußischer Kulturbesitz, Berlin; 1233 CE) [סא]; Ebr. 480 (Biblioteca Apostolica, Vatican City; start of fourteenth cent.) [סז]; Hebr. 28 (Oesterreichische Nationalbibliothek, Vienna; fourteenth cent.) [סח]. Kasher, *Targumic Toseftot to the Prophets*, §107b, §142a.

19 Opp. 14 (Bodleian Library, Oxford; 1340 CE) [siglum א]; Kennicott 3 (Bodleian Library, Oxford; 1293 CE) [ג]; Add. 9403 (British Library, London; twelfth-fourteenth cent.) [ב]; Harley 1861 (British Library, London; + Job, thirteenth-fourteenth cent.) [ל]; Levy 19 (Staats- und Universtaetsbibliothek, Hamburg; 1309 CE) [גל]; Ms Cent. V App. 2 (Stadtbibliothek, Nürnberg; 1297 CE) [ע]; Sassoon 282 (Sassoon Collection, Letchworth; 1189 CE) [ף]. See Kasher, *Targumic Toseftot to the Prophets*, §4a.

20 Parma 1854 (Biblioteca Palantina, Parma; c.1200 CE; Torah + haftarot for Leviticus and Numbers + festivals) [siglum ר]; Kasher, *Targumic Toseftot to the Prophets*, §120, §144a. Kasher includes Parma 2520 (Biblioteca Palantina, Parma; Torah, Former Prophets, Megillot + haftarot for festivals), which contains a Tosefta Targum to Jeremiah 9.22 (9th Av), among the Ashkenazi sources, but according to the National Library of Israel catalogue the manuscript is Sephardi. See Kasher, *Targumic Toseftot to the Prophets*, §123a, p303. See also the earlier discussion in Kasher, 'התוספתות התרגומיות להפטרת שבת־חנוכה'.

21 Kasher, *Targumic Toseftot to the Prophets*, 22–3.

22 Houtman and Sysling discussed several of the Tosefta Targums from Kasher's collection. Of the liturgical sources they treated the Tosefta Targum to 2 Samuel 22, proposing that it may be defined as *Targumic darashah*; Houtman and Sysling, *Alternative Targum Traditions*, 128–30, 133–4.

Chapter Ten. The Targum Text in Liturgical Manuscripts

Latter Prophets.[23] One suspects that the choice of manuscripts was a practical one — they were all in London. By searching through Sperber's critical apparatus, one can quickly get an impression of the relationship between these liturgical texts and the continuous texts recorded by Sperber. The haftarot preserve a consonantal text that is more or less the same as the continuous text of the Yemenite tradition. There are some minor variations — sometimes shared with other manuscripts containing a continuous text — but nothing more than one might expect from any text transmitted manually.[24] The vocalisation, on the other hand, varies from that of Sperber's main text (Or. 2210 and Or. 2211 British Library, London) frequently, but this is hardly unexpected since it continued to be used in the synagogue and so would more naturally reflect developments in pronunciation and dialect than a text used only for study. In short, there is nothing in the haftarot to obfuscate their basic textual affinity — at least as far as the consonants are concerned — to the continuous text in the Yemenite tradition.

Van Staalduine-Sulman reached a similar conclusion concerning the texts from Yemenite liturgical sources in her stemmatological analysis of the books of Samuel. Based on an analysis of four randomly selected Yemenite haftarot collections, van Staalduine-Sulman concluded that 'there is no textual division between continuous and liturgical texts'. The liturgical texts did not reveal a tendency 'to add liturgical phrases or homiletical expansions to the text in haftarot collections', but formed an integral part of the textual tradition to which they belong, be that Yemenite or Babylonian — the two being in any case closely related.[25]

---

23 Former Prophets: Sassoon 332 (Sassoon Collection, Letchworth), fourteenth century, Yemenite, haftarot collection; Or. 2364 (British Library, London), a fifteenth century, Yemenite, Torah with haftarot. Latter Prophets: Or. 1470 (British Library, London), 1484 CE, haftarot collection for the whole year according to the Yemeni rite.

24 To pick a couple of examples almost at random: Or. 2364 (British Library, London) reads רב for רם at 1 Sam. 2:10, and יומא for יחדא at 1 Sam. 20:19, in both cases agreeing with Or. 2371 (British Library, London), a manuscript containing the continuous text. There are a few larger variants, e.g. Or. 2364 reads 'and the word of the Lord...' in place of 'and a word of prophecy from before the Lord...' at 1 Kgs 18:1, more closely reflecting the Hebrew. Cf. 2 Kgs 4:31.

25 van Staalduine-Sulman, 'An Electronic Edition of Targum Samuel', 7. The manuscripts concerned were: Ms. C 91 (Institute of Oriental Studies, St. Petersburg; siglum t1169y), Yemen, eighteenth century; Ms. Add. 3452 (University Library, Cambridge; siglum t1269y), Yemen, eighteenth century CE; Ms. Heb. 38vo, 6919 (Allony Collection, Jerusalem; siglum t1270y), Yemen, eighteenth–nineteenth century CE; Ms. fol. 18 (Temple of Solomon, Jerusalem; siglum t1272y), Yemen, eighteenth century CE.

In conclusion, van Staalduine-Sulman advances the possibility that the haftarot manuscript had been created by taking the various liturgical readings from continuous manuscripts: 'There was no separate haftarot tradition in which haftarot manuscripts were copied from haftarot manuscripts only', she writes.[26] This last point is rather injudicious. There is no reason *a priori* why liturgical manuscripts copied from other liturgical manuscripts would be more likely to alter the form of the text than those copied from continuous texts. Perhaps to the contrary, since the texts continued to be read in front of an audience many of whom would have known the texts more or less by heart and who evidently placed a high value on the transmission of the text unaltered.[27] Furthermore, the frequent variation in vocalisation between the haftarot and the continuous text noted by Sperber in his critical apparatus may point, on the contrary, to an independent tradition of copying. Nonetheless, van Staalduine-Sulman's analysis affirms the basic textual affinity between the continuous and liturgical texts in the Yemenite tradition.[28]

In addition to Yemenite liturgical sources, van Staalduine-Sulman also subjected a number of oriental fragments (mostly from the Cairo Genizah) to stemmatological analysis. In several cases the fragment in question is too small for us to be certain of its original context, but in other cases it is clear that the fragment originally belonged to a haftarot collection. However, the fragmentary nature of the materials meant that in most cases they were too small to be placed within the stemma. The most that could be said was that one or two minor variant readings pointed 'more to the Eastern side' of the stemma for some of the fragments, and 'more to the Western side' for others.[29] One

---

26 van Staalduine-Sulman, 'An Electronic Edition of Targum Samuel', 43.
27 A. Shinan, 'Live Translation: on the Nature of the Aramaic Targums to the Pentateuch', *Prooftexts* 3:11 (1983), 41–9, pp. 42–3; Smelik, *The Targum of Judges*, 37.
28 This conclusion makes her recommendation that Yemenite haftarot be excluded from a future critical edition perplexing. If they are 'an integral part of the entire Yemenite tradition', (van Staalduine-Sulman, 'An Electronic Edition of Targum Samuel', 45) and the Yemenite tradition is second in importance only to the Babylonian tradition, then surely their use in a critical edition would be highly desirable — even if a selection among the extant materials must be made for practical reasons.
29 van Staalduine-Sulman, 'An Electronic Edition of Targum Samuel', 42. Eastern: Ms. Or. 5556 F/12 (British Library, London; siglum F1200); Ms. Heb. d. 64, fols. 19–24 (Bodleian Library, Oxford; siglum F1262) — Possibly connected to Yemenite tradition [van Staalduine-Sulman, 'An Electronic Edition of Targum Samuel', 28]; Ms. T-S B 15.3 (University Library, Cambridge; siglum F3002); Ms. T-S B 17.9 (University Library, Cambridge; siglum F3005); Ms. T-S NS

Chapter Ten. The Targum Text in Liturgical Manuscripts

fragment from a fourteenth century haftarot collection written in an oriental semi-cursive script with Babylonian supra-linear vocalisation could be placed with the Babylonian text family, though exhibiting some closeness to the Yemenite family (the two families being, in any case, extremely close).[30] In the case of manuscript T-S B 15.5 of Cambridge University Library, a haftarot collection in a Yemenite square script, with Babylonian vocalisation and Tiberian accents,[31] the degree of certainty with which it can be placed in the stemma is unclear. In one place van Staalduine-Sulman writes: 'Most Cairo Genizah fragments are too small to be given a well-argued place in a family. Three fragments are large enough: F3003 [i.e. T-S B 15.5 Cambridge University Library] and F3004 [i.e. T-S B 16.20 Cambridge University Library] seem to be related to the roots of Codex Solger, F3001 [i.e. T-S B 12.6 Cambridge University Library] has kinship to the Babylonian tradition'. Yet a few pages earlier she writes: 'Two variant readings [within the group "Codex Solger and the Rabbinic Bibles"] point to a distant kinship with two Cairo Genizah fragments, which are too small to justify a definite place in the stemma: F3003 (T-S B 15.5) and F3004 (T-S B 16.20)'.[32]

In sum, it is clear from this previous research that the Eastern textual tradition preserved a text more or less identical with the continuous text form, while liturgical manuscripts in the West vary in terms of their relationship to the continuous text tradition. Some Ashkenazi manuscripts with a liturgical structure, such as the manuscript studied by de Lagarde, are comparable to the continuous text as we find it in Ashkenazi manuscripts. Other Ashkenazi sources and all the Italian sources examined in the studies discussed above

---

32.98 (University Library, Cambridge; siglum F3006). Western: Ms. T-S K 26.2 (University Library, Cambridge; siglum F3012); Ms. T-S NS 128.14 (University Library, Cambridge; siglum F3013); Ms. T-S AS 69.200 (University Library, Cambridge; siglum F3014).

30 I.e. Ms B 133 (Saltykov-Shchedrin State Public Library, St. Petersburg; siglum t1126b) van Staalduine-Sulman, 'An Electronic Edition of Targum Samuel', 24.

31 Klein, *Targumic Manuscripts in the Cambridge Genizah Collections*, 31.

32 van Staalduine-Sulman, 'An Electronic Edition of Targum Samuel', 41, 38. Van Staalduine-Sulman did study, in addition, one fourteenth–fifteenth century Franco-German manuscript containing the haftarot, some of which (parashat Tzav, Pesach, and Shavuot) have the Targum (Ms. Add. 9403/1, British Library, London; siglum t2190i). In addition Targum 1 Sam. 2:1–5, 10 stands in the margin on fol. 227v. The text belonged to the so-called 'Italian Tradition' (see my comments on pages 69–70), but proved to be replete with errors (to the extent that van Staalduine-Sulman recommended that it not be included in a new edition), van Staalduine-Sulman, 'An Electronic Edition of Targum Samuel', 30–2, 46, 58, 79.

offer a text quite distinct from the continuous text tradition, being more similar to other Tosefta Targums.

2. Aims

Kasher's collection of Tosefta Targums made available a wealth of new material enabling one to get an impression of the nature of the liturgical forms of the text as it circulated in Europe. It is clear from the texts gathered by Kasher that the text preserved in liturgical manuscripts in the Western tradition differs significantly from the continuous text (to the extent that they are categorised as Tosefta Targums) and that the copying tradition of the liturgical and continuous manuscripts was therefore separate.[33]

Yet Kasher's collection covers only a tiny amount of the available data (a simple statement of fact, rather than a criticism). The description of liturgical texts in many catalogues is insufficient to establish whether or not the Targum is present in many manuscripts, but even counting only those manuscripts known to preserve the Targum, the number is vast. A full and exhaustive study of this material is still to be done. For now, we must content ourselves with a sample study of a small selection of such texts.

In the present study I hope to add to the body of available material and edge the discussion forward by examining the same text (namely, the Targum to 2 Samuel 22) in multiple liturgical manuscripts. A comparative study of this nature will allow us to say something of the relationship between the various manuscripts, the character of the text, and its relation to the continuous text of Targum Jonathan.

3. Description of Manuscripts

The number of known liturgical manuscripts is vast and the cataloguing often insufficiently detailed to establish whether or not the Targum is present. For practical reasons, then, a selection had to be made from among these manuscripts to provide a sample study. In order to be able to draw historical

---

33 So that it is not necessary to create a stemma of these texts in order to 'show whether haftarot collections and mahzorim in Western traditions have a copying tradition that is separate from the continuous manuscripts', as van Staalduine-Sulman recommended ('An Electronic Edition of Targum Samuel', 43).

Chapter Ten. The Targum Text in Liturgical Manuscripts

conclusions from the comparison, where possible manuscripts were selected whose date and provenance could be established and that were roughly contemporary to the manuscripts containing the continuous text included in this study. Such a selection of material can, of course, only provide us with preliminary results; it is to be hoped that an exhaustive study of the liturgical texts can be realised in the future.

Italian sources:

The following are all mahzorim adhering to the Roman rite (with some minor variations). They include the Targum to the haftarot for Pesach and Shavuot.

> [t1601i] Parm. 3008 (de Rossi 959), Biblioteca Palatina, Parma (Italy): written in Perugia 1400 CE.
>
> [t1639i] Opp. Add. fol. 11 (Neubauer 1057), Bodleian Library, Oxford (United Kingdom): San Severino, 1424 CE.
>
> [t1679i] Sassoon 405, Sassoon Collection, Letchworth (United Kingdom): Perugia, 1415 CE.
>
> [t1647i] Rossiana 437, Biblioteca Apostolica, Vatican (Vatican City): Lucca, 1447 CE.
>
> [t1618i] Parm. 3132, (de Rossi 61), Biblioteca Palatina, Parma (Italy): Macerata, 1403 CE.
>
> [t1621i] Vaticani Ebr. 545, Biblioteca Apostolica, Vatican (Vatican City): Ortona, 1419/20 CE.

Ashkenazi sources:

The following manuscripts contain the Torah, Haftarot, and the Five Scrolls (i.e. Megillot). The Targum is preserved for Pesach and Shavuot.

> [t159a] Levy 19 (Kennicott 380), Staats- und Universitaetsbibliothek, Hamburg (Germany): Oxford? 1309 CE. Includes Job.
>
> [t99a] Hébreu 44, Bibliothèque Nationale, Paris (France): Paris, 1303 CE.
>
> [t133a] Valmadonna 1 (Sassoon 282; Richler 1), Valmadonna Trust Library, London (United Kingdom): England or Normandy, 1189 CE.[34]
>
> [t63a] Or fol. 1214 (Kennicott 603; Erfurt 4), Staatsbibliothek, Preußischer Kulturbesitz, Berlin (Germany): thirteenth century.

Five mahzorim and one siddur following the French rite were checked, of which the following two were found to contain the Targum to 2 Samuel 22:

> [t1631a] Abt. 701, Nr. 759, 5, 6 Landeshauptarchiv, Koblenz (Germany): *c.* thirteenth/fourteenth century.
>
> [t1614a] Parm. 2894 (de Rossi 1198) Biblioteca Palatina, Parma (Italy): thirteenth century.

---

34 On this manuscript see Attia, 'Targum Layout in Ashkenazic Hebrew Manuscripts', 101.

The format of the materials in each group (i.e. whether mahzorim or collections of haftarot, etc.) was largely dictated by the materials themselves. With few exceptions, the only liturgical sources of Italian provenance containing the relevant section of Targum were mahzorim. Among the Ashkenazi sources, on the other hand, the Targum text is found only in haftarot collections, often appearing at the end of a codex containing Torah and Megillot, with the exception of a few (though not all) mahzorim following the French rite. This suggests that the text of Targum 2 Samuel 22 was read customarily in Italy[35] (as it was in parts of the Sephardic region).[36] In Ashkenaz, however, this was not the custom except among some French communities; elsewhere in Ashkenaz the Targum to the haftarot served only as a study aid in order to prepare for the liturgy,[37] rather than featuring during the liturgy itself.[38]

This general distinction is supported by the introductory formulae that precede the Aramaic text. We find the following in the Italian mahzorim:

t1601i

> Day one (of the festival days): [the section] 'So [the Lord] saved...' (i.e. beginning Exod. 14.30).[The reader] concludes with Samuel, [beginning] 'David spoke...' (i.e. beginning 2 Sam 22.1), then [the haftarah is] translated. Proclaim: 'That which was spoken by Samuel the prophet.'

t1639i

The text follows that of the corresponding *parashah* (i.e. Exod. 13:17–15:26). This is followed by (191v):

---

35 See S.C. Reif, 'Codicological Aspects of Jewish Liturgical History', *Bulletin of the John Rylands University Library of Manchester* 75:3 (1993), 117–31, pp. 126–7; Lehnardt, 'The Role of Targum Samuel in European Jewish Liturgy', 56–7. The expense of commissioning a codex written on vellum makes it likely they were owned by communities; the hazzan may have used them for leading the communal prayers. Reif, *Judaism and Hebrew Prayer*, 179.

36 See H.M. Patmore and J.M. Tanja, 'Initial Observations Concerning the Text of Targum 2 Samuel 22 as Preserved in European Liturgical Manuscripts', in A. Houtman, H.-M. Kirn and E. van Staalduine-Sulman (eds), *A Jewish Targum in a Christian World* (Jewish and Christian Perspectives 27, Leiden 2014), 63–80, p. 66.

37 This accounts for the presence of cantilation marks in the Targum text of some manuscripts (e.g. t232i/s; see Smelik, 'Orality, Manuscript Reproduction, and the Targums', 72) and the markings of the haftarot (e.g. t718i).

38 See chapter two and Lehnardt, 'The Role of Targum Samuel in European Jewish Liturgy', 44–7, 57–8; cf. also Attia, 'Targum Layout in Ashkenazic Hebrew Manuscripts', 118–20; Houtman, 'The Role of the Targum in Jewish Education in Medieval Europe', 81, 88–90.

Chapter Ten. The Targum Text in Liturgical Manuscripts

A semi-kaddish is recited then another Torah scroll is taken out then the last person called up to the Torah (המפטיר) reads in it from parashah Phinehas (Num 25.10–30.1) [the section] 'You shall offer' (i.e. beginning Num 28.19), and this is written above in the order for the first day of the intermediate days of the festival, and concludes with Samuel and [the haftarah] is translated. Proclaim: 'That which was spoken by Samuel the prophet.'

t1679i

The haftarah appears first in Hebrew, where it is headed:

And the last person called up to the Torah (מפטיר) reads [the section] 'You shall offer' (i.e. beginning Num 28.19) until the end of the section. Then [the reader] concludes with Samuel.

The Targum follows and is separately headed:

[The haftarah] is translated. Proclaim: 'That which was spoken by Samuel the prophet.'

t1647i

Haftarah from the first day of the last days of Pesach. Proclaim: 'That which was spoken by David the leader.'

t1618i

The reading of the Hebrew is introduced as follows:

Another book is taken out then the last person called up to the Torah (המפטיר) reads in it from parashah Phinehas [the section] 'You shall offer' (i.e. beginning Num 28.19), until the end of the section, then concludes with [the section in] Samuel [beginning] 'And David spoke to the Lord' (i.e. 2 Sam 22.1).

The Targum text is headed simply:

Proclaim: 'That which was spoken by Samuel the prophet.'

t1621i

The Hebrew text is headed:

After this another Torah scroll is taken out and the last person called up to the Torah (המפטיר) reads in it: [the section] 'You shall offer' (i.e. beginning Num 28.19), as on the preceding day, then concludes with Samuel.

The Transmission of Targum Jonathan in the West

The Aramaic text is headed:

The Targum of the haftarah begins.

The two French mahzorim are comparable.

t1631a

The Hebrew text is headed simply:

For the seventh (day) of Pesach.

The Aramaic text is headed

Proclaim: '[The word] that was spoken by David the King as Jonathan ben Uzziel explained (it).'

The headings are in Hebrew, with the exception of the various formulae with which the reader is instructed to introduce the text (e.g. *'That which has been preserved by Samuel the prophet,' 'That which was spoken by Samuel the prophet,' 'That which was spoken by David the leader.'*). It seems clear from these detailed instructions that the Targum was indeed intended to be read as part of the liturgy. The headings in the Ashkenazi collections of haftarot are of a different character, being altogether much more reticent:

t159a

On the first festival day (יום טוב) of the final days of Pesach [the lectionary] is concluded with Samuel.

t99a

Is headed simply:

For the seventh day [of Pesach].

Followed by the Hebrew lemma (וידבר).

t133a

Seventh day of Pesach. [The lectionary] is concluded with Kings (sic).

The text that follows is that of 2 Samuel. The scribe has perhaps confused the reading with that for the second day of Pesach (i.e. 2 Kgs 23:1–10, 21–5).

No special heading is given in manuscript t63a.

The instructions as to how the text ought to be read correctly during the

Chapter Ten. The Targum Text in Liturgical Manuscripts

service and the various introductory formulae, which are present in the mahzorim with a greater or lesser degree of detail, are irrelevant in the Ashkenazi context in which the Targum plays no liturgical role and are therefore left out.

The same contrast between the Italian and Ashkenazi sources can be noted in the closing blessing, which is to be found in the Italian mahzorim[39] but not the Ashkenazi haftarot collections. All the Italian texts contain the same blessing, with which the reading of the Targum is to be concluded:

> 'May the name of the great and holy God be blessed and praised for this for all eternity'

A further notable contrast between the Italian and Ashkenazi sources is the extent of the text they contain. The Italian mahzorim preserve the complete text of 2 Samuel 22. The Ashkenazi sources by contrast contain only the start of the chapter (the shortest containing the first fourteen verses, the longest the first twenty-five)[40] and the last two verses, leaving out the intervening text:

t99a and t63a = 2 Sam. 22:1–14, 50–1

t159a and t1614a = 2 Sam. 22:1–19, 50–1

t133a = 2 Sam. 22:1–25, 50–1

The reason for this is unclear. Since this phenomenon is noted in both a mahzor (t1614a) and in haftarot collections that were intended to aid in the preparation for the liturgy even if they were not themselves used in the liturgy, it is possible that the preserved units of Targum reflect local liturgical customs, since it is permissible to skip in the prophetic reading (m.Meg 4.4).

The layout of the text also differs to some extent between the manuscripts. In the Italian sources and the French mahzor t1614a the Hebrew and Aramaic texts are presented apart, either with the Hebrew text preceding the Aramaic (t1679i, t1618i, t1621i), appearing in the inside column next to the Hebrew text (t1639i, with Hebrew lemmata), or standing in the centre of the page, surrounded by the Hebrew text in the margins (t1647i). Of the Ashkenazi sources the Aramaic is preceded by the Hebrew text in t63a. In manuscripts t159a, t1631a, and t133a the Hebrew and Aramaic texts alternate by three

---

39 The ending of the text is missing in t1631a.

40 The extent of the text in t1631a is unknown. Only two folios are preserved (Róth, *Hebräische Handschriften*, Vol. 2, 171–2). The Targum to 2 Sam. 22:1–21 is preserved on folio 2, but the text originally continued onto another page, which is now lost.

verses for the first three verses, then verse by verse, as described in the Tosafot to Megillah 24a.[41] The Hebrew and Aramaic then alternate, until verses 19 and 26 respectively, where the Aramaic stops. The Hebrew continues until the end and the Aramaic resumes at verse 50. The Hebrew text is not given in manuscript t99a, though Hebrew lemmata are given in the Aramaic text.

4. Text and Translation

Below a translation of a representative Italian and Ashkenazi manuscript is offered. Manuscript Parm. 3008 of the Biblioteca Palatina Parma [t1601i] was selected to represent the Italian tradition on account of its overall quality; Valmadonna 1 of the Valmadonna Trust Library London [t133a] was selected because its text covers more verses than any of the other Ashkenazi manuscripts, though the manuscript is far from perfect — scribal errors are evident at several points as they are in all Ashkenazi manuscripts — and no priority is implied by its selection. Many insignificant variants (e.g. scribal errors, variations in verb conjugation etc.) are not noted. Omissions and additions of the conjunctive *waw* are commonplace, and are to be considered insignificant. A synopsis of the Aramaic texts can be found in Appendix 3. Variations from the Babylonian tradition are shown in bold font. Omissions are indicated with [<].

2 Sam. 22:1

Babylonian tradition: David praised in prophecy before the Lord the words of this song concerning all the days that the Lord saved Israel from the hand of all their enemies and also David from Saul's sword.

t1601i: David praised in prophecy before the Lord the words of this song concerning all the days that the Lord saved Israel from the hand of all their enemies and also David **he saved him** from Saul's sword.

t133a: David praised in prophecy before the Lord **all**[42] the words of this song concerning all the days that the Lord saved **him and**[43] Israel from the hand of

---

41 Cf. Smelik, 'Orality, Manuscript Reproduction, and the Targums', 58.
42 t159a, t63a, t1614a, t1631a < 'all'.
43 t159a '[the Lord saved] me and Israel'; t99a, t63a, t1614a, t1631a '[the Lord saved] Israel'.

Chapter Ten. The Targum Text in Liturgical Manuscripts

all their enemies[44] and also David[45] **he saved** from Saul's sword.

2 Sam. 22:2

Babylonian tradition: And he said, The Lord is my strength and my security and he saves me.

t1601i: And he said, The Lord is my strength and my security and he saves me.

t133a: And he said, The Lord is my strength and my security. [<][46] He saves me.

2 Sam. 22:3

Babylonian tradition: My God who has favoured me draws me to his fear; my strength, because from before him is given to me strength and redemption to overcome my enemies; my security, that upon his Memra I trust in times of distress, protecting me from my enemies. And he promises to raise my horn [i.e. 'strength'] by his redemption. My support whose Memra was a support for me when I was fleeing from before my pursuers; my redemption from my enemies and also from the hand of all robbers he saved me.

t1601i: [<] God, who has favoured me, draws me to his fear; my strength, because from before him is given to me strength and redemption to overcome my enemies;[47] my security,[48] that upon his Memra I trust in times of distress, protecting me from[49] my enemies. And he promises to raise my horn by his redemption.[50] My support whose Memra was a support for me when I was fleeing from before my pursuers; **he saved me from those who hated me;**[51] and also from the hand of all robbers **he saved me, and from the hand of Saul, the king, he redeemed me**.

t133a: [<] God, who has favoured me, draws me to his fear; my strength, because from before him[52] is given to me strength and redemption to overcome

---

44 t1614a adds here ויתיר 'and more'(?). Probably an error. Cf. Tg. 2 Sam. 23:4, 5.
45 t1614a 'the hand of David' (error?).
46 t159a, t99a, t63a, t1614a, t1631a + 'and [he saves me]'.
47 t1647i + 'all [my enemies]' Cf. 2 Sam. 22:1.
48 t1621i 'my security my security' (dittography).
49 t1601i: מבעלי דבבי. t1639i 'against my enemies' (על בעלי דבבי).
50 t1639i, t1647i, t1618i 'by my redemption'.
51 'he saved me from those who hated me' : t1639i 'he saved me from those who hate me; he redeemed me from my enemies'.
52 t159a 'before you (sg)'. Possibly a graphic error?

my enemies; my security, that upon his Memra I trust [in times of distress, protecting me from my enemies. And he promises to raise my horn by his redemption.[53] My support whose Memra was a support for me][54] when I was fleeing from before my pursuers; **he protected**[55] **me from my enemies**; and also from the hand of all robbers **and thieves** he saved me.[56]

2 Sam. 22:4

Babylonian tradition: David said in a song, I pray before the Lord since he always [lit. in every time] redeems me from my enemies.

t1601i: David said in a song, **I open my mouth and** pray before the Lord since he redeems me in every time **of distress**[57] from the hand of my enemies.

t133a: David said in a song, I pray before the Lord[58] since he always redeems me[59] from my enemies

2 Sam. 22:5

Babylonian tradition: Because distress — like a woman who sits upon a birthing stool and she does not have [enough] strength to give birth and she is in danger of dying — surrounded me; a group of sinners frightened me.

t1601i: Because distress — like a woman who sits upon a birthing stool and there is no strength **in her**[60] to give birth and she is in danger of dying[61] — surrounded me; a group of **liars**[62] frightened me.

t133a: Because distress, — like a woman who sits upon a birthing stool and she does not have [enough] strength to give birth and she is in danger of dying — surrounded me **and**[63] a group of sinners[64] frightened me.

---

53 t99a 'by my redemption'.
54 This entire phrase is omitted in t133a, but present in the remaining Ashkenazi witnesses. The omission in t133a is probably by parablepsis between two occurrences of מימריה.
55 t1614a, t1631a 'he redeemed me'.
56 t63a, t1614a 'he redeemed me'.
57 t1639i, t1647i, t1618i < 'of distress'.
58 t1614a + 'and before my God I am pleading for favour' cf. Tg. 2 Sam. 22:7.
59 t1631a 'he saves me'.
60 Babylonian trad. וחיל לה למילד; t1601i וחיל לית בה למילד; t1647i לה.
61 t1639i < 'of dying' (למטת).
62 t1639i 'sinners'.
63 t99a, t1614a, t1631a < 'and'.
64 t1614a, t1631a + '[a group of sinners] by her (בה)'.

Chapter Ten. The Targum Text in Liturgical Manuscripts

2 Sam. 22:6

Babylonian tradition: Camps of wicked ones surrounded me; those armed with deadly weapons came before me.

t1601i: Camps of wicked ones surrounded me; those armed[65] with deadly weapons **met** me.[66]

t133a: **Many wicked camps**[67] surrounded me; those armed with deadly weapons **met** me.[68]

2 Sam. 22:7

Babylonian tradition: David said, When I am distressed, I pray before the Lord and before my God I entreat [mercy], and from his Temple my prayer is received and my request is fulfilled before him.

t1601i: David said, When I am distressed, I **open my mouth**[69] **and** pray before the Lord; before my God I **pray and** entreat [mercy], and from his Temple my prayer is received and my request is fulfilled before him **in the time of my prayer**.

t133a: David said, When I am distressed,[70] I pray before the Lord and before my God I am pleading for favour, and from his Temple my prayer is received and my request **that is from**[71] before him is fulfilled.

2 Sam. 22:8

Babylonian tradition: The earth was shaken up, and shuddered; the foundations of the heavens trembled and were bent down because of the strength of his wrath.

t1601i: The earth was shaken up, and shuddered, **and made to tremble**, and the foundations of the heavens trembled, **the mountains were made to**

---

65 Root זין *pael* ptc pass.
66 t1639i 'came before me'.
67 'Many wicked camps': t159a 'Wicked camps'; t99a, t63a, t1614a, t1631a 'Camps of wicked ones'.
68 t1614a, t1631a 'came before me'.
69 'I open my mouth and [pray]': t1639i <; t1621i 'I call and [pray]'.
70 'When I am distressed' (כד עקא לי). t1614a, t1631a 'When (there is) distress, trouble' (כד עקא).
71 'that is from (דמן)': t159a <; t99a, t63a, t1614a, t1631a 'from' (מן).

319

tremble, and the depths of the sea rolled around because the wrath **of our**[72] **living and enduring God** was **strong.**[73]

t133a: The earth was shaken up, and shuddered; the foundations[74] of the heavens trembled and were bent down because his wrath was **strong.**[75]

2 Sam. 22:9

Babylonian tradition: The insolence of Pharaoh went up like smoke before him, therefore he sent forth his anger like burning fire that was from before him destroying; his wrath like coals of burning fire from his Memra.

t1601i: The insolence of **wicked** Pharaoh went up like smoke **in his presence [lit. face]**, therefore he sent forth his anger like burning fire [<] from[76] before him destroying,[77] **and** his wrath like **burning coals of fire**[78] from his Memra.

t133a: The insolence of **wicked** Pharaoh went up like the smoke **of the furnace** before him [<] destroying;[79] his wrath like coals of burning fire from his Memra.

2 Sam. 22:10

Babylonian tradition: He caused the heavens to bend down and his glory was revealed and dark cloud (forming) a path before him.

t1601i: He caused the heavens to bend down and his glory was revealed **in his majesty**[80] and dark cloud (forming) a path before him.

t133a: He caused the heavens to bend down and his glory was revealed and dark cloud (forming) a path before him.

---

72 t1639i, t1647i, t1618i, t1621i 'the [living and enduring God]'.
73 t1601i, t1679i 'strong (תְּקוֹף)'; t1639i, t1647i, t1618i, t1621i 'strength' (תקוף).
74 t99a 'and [the foundations]'.
75 t159a, t99a, t63a 'strength' (תקוף) i.e. because of the strength of his wrath.
76 'from': t1639i, t1621i 'that was from'.
77 Read משיציא for משצין.
78 t1639i 'like coals of burning fire'.
79 'like the smoke of the furnace before him, destroying': t159a, t99a, t63a, t1614a, t1631a 'like smoke (t159a+ 'that was from') before him, therefore he (t1631a: 'the king') sent forth his anger like burning (t1614a < 'burning') fire that was from before him, destroying.' This phrase (בכין שלח רגזיה כאישא בערא דמן קדמוהי) is probably omitted in t133a by parablepsis between the two occurrences of קדמוהי.
80 But read בגבורתיה 'in his might' as other liturgical texts.

Chapter Ten. The Targum Text in Liturgical Manuscripts

2 Sam. 22:11

Babylonian tradition: He was revealed in his majesty upon quick angels and led in power upon the wings of the wind.

t1601i: **He caused his Presence to rest upon** quick angels and **he was revealed in glory** and led in power upon the **face**[81] of the wind.

t133a: He was revealed in his majesty upon quick angels and led in power upon the wings of the wind.

2 Sam. 22:12

Babylonian tradition: He caused his Presence to dwell in the darkness, a dense cloud all around him pouring down forceful water from the mass of light clouds in the height of the world.

t1601i: **So** he caused his Presence to dwell in the darkness **and** a dense cloud all around him pouring down forceful water from the **mass**[82] of light clouds in the height of the world.

t133a: **So** he caused his Presence to dwell in the darkness **and** a dense cloud all around him pouring down forceful **clouds** [but read: water][83] from the mass[84] of light clouds in the height of the world.

2 Sam. 22:13

Babylonian tradition: From the splendour of his glory the heavens of the heavens are shining; his wrath like coals of fire burning from his Memra.

t1601i: From[85] the splendour of the glory **of the living and enduring God the heavens and**[86] the heavens of the heavens are shining **and**[87] from his wrath **like burning coals of fire** from his Word.

---

81 *Sic* t1601i פני. Probably read כנפי רוחא 'the wings of the wind' with t1639i, t1647i, t1618i, t1621i. Cf. t1679i אפי.
82 All the Italian mahzorim employ the noun רגפה, a synonym of רכפה the noun employed in the Babylonian tradition (as well as t159a, t99a, t133a, t63a). See note 84.
83 Another case of parablepsis in t133a (note ענניו קלילין later in the verse). All other Ashkenazi manuscripts read 'water' (מיין).
84 t1614a, t1631a employ the synonym רגפה (for רכפה). See note 82.
85 t1639i, t1647i read 'And from…'.
86 t1679i omits 'the heavens and the heavens of'.
87 t1639i omits 'and'.

321

t133a: From the splendour of his glory the heavens of the heavens are shining; his wrath like coals of fire burning from his Memra.

2 Sam. 22:14

Babylonian tradition: From the heavens the Lord shouted and the Most High lifted up his Memra.

t1601i: From the heavens the Lord shouted and the Most High lifted up his **voice**.

t133a: From the heavens the Lord shouted[88] and the Most High lifted up **by** his Memra.[89]

[t99a, t63a stop here; resume at 2 Sam. 22.50]

2 Sam. 22:15

Babylonian tradition: He sent his stroke like arrows and he scattered them (with) lightening and he confounded them.

t1601i: He sent[90] his stroke **against them**[91] and he scattered them **with** lightening and he confounded them.

t133a: He sent his stroke like arrows and he scattered them (with) lightening and he confounded them.

2 Sam. 22:16

Babylonian tradition: And the depths of the sea were seen; the foundations of the world were revealed by the rebuke (that was) from before the Lord, from the Memra of the strength of his wrath.

t1601i: And the depths of the sea were seen **and** the foundations of the world were revealed by **a rebuking wind** (במזופית רוח) from before the Lord, from the

---

88 t1631a reads אכלינון with pronominal suffix, for אכלי '[the Lord] shouted'. The object is ambiguous so the meaning of the verb is uncertain. Either '[the Lord] restrained them' or '[the Lord] called them'. The two verbs (כלי) are homonymic.

89 t159a^correct reads 'Most High from his Memra'. Verb omitted in error. t99a reads 'Most High lifted up a voice'. t1631a reads (correctly) with the Italian tradition: 'the Most High lifted up his voice'. t1614a omits the entire verse in error.

90 t1639i, t1679i, t1618i, t1621i read 'he will send' (i.e. ישלח for ושלח).

91 'against them': t1639i 'like arrows'; t1647i, t1618i, t1621i 'against them like arrows'.

Memra of the strength of his wrath.[92]

t133a: And the depths of the sea were seen **and** the foundations of the world[93] were revealed [<] — his rebuke[94] from before the Lord, [<] the Memra of the strength of his wrath.

2 Sam. 22:17

Babylonian tradition: A strong king who dwells in strength on high sent his prophets: he led me, he saved me from many peoples.

t1601i: A strong king who dwells **in his Presence in the** highest **heavens**[95] **will send** his prophets. He led me, he saved me from many peoples.

t133a: A strong king who dwells in strength on high sent[96] his prophets: he led me, he saved me from many peoples.

2 Sam. 22:18

Babylonian tradition: He saved me from those who hate me because they seized me; from my enemies because they overcame me.

t1601i: He saved me from those who hate me because they seized me,[97] **and** from my enemies because they overcame me.

t133a: He saved me[98] from those who hate me because they **surrounded** me;[99] from my enemies because they overcame me.

2 Sam. 22:19

Babylonian tradition: They will go before me in the day of my wandering, but the Memra of the Lord supports me.

---

92 t1618i 'the strength of the wind of his wrath'.
93 t159a reads 'the foundations of the heavens earth' (i.e. שכלולי שמיא תבל) in error cf. 2 Sam. 22:8.
94 The text of t133a is problematic (probably corrupt). t159a reads with Babylonian trad.: 'by the rebuke (that was) from before the Lord'.
95 t1639i 'A strong king who dwells in strength on high' (= Babylonian trad.); t1647i, t1618i omit 'who dwells'.
96 t1631a 'will send'.
97 t1647i, t1618i 'they surrounded me' (i.e. אקפוני for תקפוני) cf. 2 Sam. 22:6.
98 'from many peoples. He saved me' (22:17–18): t1614a < by parablepsis between occurrences of שזבני.
99 t159a 'they seized me' (cf. note 97). t1614a 'he brought me out' (אפקני by metathesis).

The Transmission of Targum Jonathan in the West

t1601i: **They met me**, they will go before me[100] in the day of my wandering, but the Memra of the Lord supports me.

t133a: They **went** before me[101] in the day of my wandering, but the Memra of the Lord supports me.

[t159a, t1614a stop here; resume at 2 Sam. 22:50]

2 Sam. 22:20

Babylonian tradition: He brought me out to the open space and he saved me because he has favoured me.

t1601i: He brought me out to the open space and he saved me because he has favoured me.

t133a: He brought me out to the open space and he saved me because he has favoured me.

2 Sam. 22:21

Babylonian tradition: David said, The Lord will recompense me according to my merit, according to the purity of my hands he will repay me.

t1601i: David said, The Lord will **repay** me[102] according to my merit, according to the purity of my hands he will repay me.

t133a: [<] The Lord will recompense me[103] according to my merit, according to **my** purity [<][104] he will repay me.

[t1631a stops here]

2 Sam. 22:22

Babylonian tradition: Because I kept ways that are proper before the Lord and I did not walk in evil before my God,

t1601i: Because I kept ways that are proper before the Lord and I did not walk in evil before my God,

---

100 t1639i, t1679i, t1618i 'They met me and they went before me' (i.e. וקדמוני for יקדמוני); t1647i omits 'they will go before me' (i.e. יקדמוני).
101 t159a 'They met me'; t1631a 'They will go before me'.
102 t1639i 'The Lord will recompense me' (ישלמינני = Babylonian trad.; t1601i יגמלני).
103 t1631a 'The Lord will repay me' (יגמליני), with Italian witnesses.
104 t1631a 'according to the purity of my hands'.

t133a: Because I kept the way (*sic*) that are proper before the Lord and I did not walk in evil before my God,

2 Sam. 22:23

Babylonian tradition: because all his judgements are revealed to me in order to do them; and his statutes: I did not cease from them.

t1601i: because all **the** judgements **of his will** are revealed[105] to me in order to do them; and his statutes: I did not cease from them.

t133a: because all his judgements are revealed to me in order to do them; [<] his statutes: I did not cease from them.

2 Sam. 22:24

Babylonian tradition: I was perfect in his fear and I was guarding my soul from sins.

t1601i: I was perfect **in respect of**[106] his fear and I was guarding my soul from sins.

t133a: I was perfect in **the** fear **of the Lord** and I was[107] guarding my soul from sins.

2 Sam. 22:25

Babylonian tradition: The Lord has given back to me according to my merit; according to my purity before his Memra.

t1601i: The Lord has given back to me according to my merit **and** according to my purity before his Memra.

t133a: The Lord has given back to me according to my merit **and** according to my purity before **his eyes**.

[t133a stops here; resumes at 2 Sam. 22:50]

2 Sam. 22:26

Babylonian tradition: [As for] Abraham, since he was found to be pious before

---

105 The form גלן can be m.pl. (here: passive), see Dalman, *Grammatik des Jüdisch-Palästinischen Aramäisch*, 350.
106 Preposition –ל. Babylonian trad. reads ב.
107 t133a reads הוה נטר, probably in error (for והויתי נטר).

The Transmission of Targum Jonathan in the West

you, so you continued to deal kindly[108] with his seed; [as for] Isaac, since he was perfect in your fear, so you fulfilled the Memra [109] of your will with him.

t1601i: [As for] Abraham, since he was found to be pious before you, so you continued to deal kindly with his seed, **and** Isaac, since he was perfect **in respect of** your fear, so **you did** your will with him **completely**.[110]

2 Sam. 22:27

Babylonian tradition: [As for] Jacob, who walked in purity before you, you chose his sons from all the peoples, you separated his seed from every idol; [as for] Pharaoh and the Egyptians who devised plans against your people, you disturbed them in their thoughts.[111]

t1601i: [As for] Jacob, who walked in purity before you, you choose his sons from all the peoples **and** you separated his seed from every idol;[112] [as for] Pharaoh and **his camps**[113] who devised plans[114] against your people, you disturbed them in their thoughts.

2 Sam. 22:28

Babylonian tradition: The people, the house of Israel, who are called in this world 'a poor people' you will redeem; and by your Memra the strong who are overpowering them, you will bring down.

t1601i: **Your** people,[115] the house of Israel, who are called in this world 'a poor people' you will redeem **them and call them 'a beloved people,' since your focus always remains on the humble in spirit**;[116] and by your Memra the strong[117] who are overpowering them, you will bring down.

---

108 t1639i omits 'to deal' resulting in the sense 'therefore You increased kindness (i.e. אסגיתא חסדא) with his seed'.
109 t1618i omits 'the Memra of'.
110 Lit. 'You finished/fulfilled/completed to do Your will with him'.
111 Read במחשבתהון (manuscript: כמחשבתהון).
112 t1618i 'from all idols'; t1639i 'from the idol of Pharaoh'.
113 t1618i 'and the Egyptians' (= Babylonian tradition).
114 t1647i, t1618i, t1621i 'evil plans'.
115 t1639i, t1647i, t1618i, t1621i 'the people'.
116 t1601i (+ t1679i) reads דבכל עינך במכיכי רוח מיתיתא[ב]א. Probable homoioarcton. Read דבכל עידן עינך with t1639i, t1647i, t1618i, t1621i.
117 Read תקיפיא (manuscript: תקיפא).

Chapter Ten. The Targum Text in Liturgical Manuscripts

2 Sam. 22:29

Babylonian tradition: Because you are the Master, the light of Israel, O Lord! And the Lord will bring me out from darkness to light, and he will show me the world that is destined to come to (-ל) the righteous.

t1601i: Because you are the Master,[118] the light of Israel [<]! And the Lord will bring me out[119] from darkness to light, and He will show me[120] the world that is destined to come to (על) the righteous.

2 Sam. 22:30

Babylonian tradition: Because by your Memra I will enlarge armies; by the Memra of my God I will subdue all strongly fortified cities.

t1601i: Because by your Memra I will **gather together**[121] armies; [<][122] I will subdue **and I will break**[123] all strongly fortified cities.

2 Sam. 22:31

Babylonian tradition: God, whose way is upright – the Law of the Lord is precious! He is strength (תְקוּף) for all who put their trust in his Memra.

t1601i: God, whose way is upright — the Law of the Lord is precious! He is **strong** (תקיף) for all who put their trust in his Memra.[124]

2 Sam. 22:32

Babylonian tradition: Therefore on account of the miracle and the redemption that you will do for your anointed one and for the remnant of your people who will be left, all peoples, nations, and tongues will confess and say 'There is no god except the Lord!' because there is none except you; and your people will say 'There is none that is strong except our God!'

t1601i: Therefore by the miracle and by the redemption that **was done**[125] for

---

118 t1639i 'Memra of' (i.e. מימריה for מריה), an error.
119 t1621i 'has brought me out' (i.e. אפקני for יפקיני).
120 t1621i 'He caused me to dwell (perhaps "assigned me a dwelling")' (ואשריאני for ויחזיבני).
121 Manuscript: אכנש. Possibly originally dittography of אכבש 'I will subdue' later in verse. t1621i has אכבש in both places. t1639i 'I will enlarge' (אסגי = Babylonian tradition).
122 t1639i reads 'by the Memra of my God'.
123 t1639i omits 'and I will break'.
124 t1639i 'in him' (עלוהי for על מימריה).
125 I.e. דאתעבד. t1639i 'that you will do' (i.e. דתעביד = Babylonian tradition).

your anointed and for the remnant of your people who will be left, all peoples, nations, and tongues will confess and say 'There is no god except the Lord!'[126] because there is none except you; and your people will say 'There is no **god** except our God!'[127]

2 Sam. 22:33

Babylonian tradition: The God who helps me with power and makes perfect my way.

t1601i: The God who helps me with power and makes perfect my way.

2 Sam. 22:34

Babylonian tradition: Making my feet quick like the roe-deer and he will establish me over the house of my strength.

t1601i: Making my feet quick like the roe-deer and he will establish me over the house of my strength.

2 Sam. 22:35

Babylonian tradition: Teaching my hands to make war and making my arms strong like a bronze bow.

t1601i: Teaching (my hands)[128] **to wage** war and **he broke the peoples that were strong**[129] like a bronze bow my arms (*sic*).

2 Sam. 22:36

Babylonian tradition: You gave to me strength; you redeemed me and by your Memra you made me great.

t1601i: You gave to me **help**[130] **and** you redeemed me **by your strength** and by your Memra you made me great.

---

126 t1621i 'except our God the Lord'.
127 t1639i 'There is none that is strong except our God!' (= Babylonian tradition).
128 Read with t1639i, t1679i, t1647i, t1618i, t1621i 'my hands' (ידי). t1601i omits, probably in error.
129 'he broke the peoples that were strong': t1639i 'making (my arms) strong' (ומתקף = Babylonian tradition).
130 t1639i 'strength' (= Babylonian tradition).

Chapter Ten. The Targum Text in Liturgical Manuscripts

2 Sam. 22:37

Babylonian tradition: You enlarged my stride before me but my knee did not shake.

t1601i: You enlarged my stride before me[131] but my knee did not shake.

2 Sam. 22:38

Babylonian tradition: I pursued those who hated me and I exterminated them and I did not relent until I had finished them off.

t1601i: I pursued **after** those who hated me and I exterminated them and I did not relent **from them** until I had finished them off.

2 Sam. 22:39

Babylonian tradition: And I exterminated them and finished them off and they were not able to stand so they fell down dead under the soles of my feet.

t1601i: And **I trampled them**[132] and finished them off and they were not able to stand so they fell down dead under the soles of my feet.

2 Sam. 22:40

Babylonian tradition: You helped me with force to make war; you broke the peoples who were rising up to do evil against me under me.

t1601i: You helped me with force to make war; you broke the peoples[133] who were **strong and** rising up[134] to do evil against me under me.[135]

2 Sam. 22:41

Babylonian tradition: And those who hated me you broke before me, those who turn the neck, my enemies, and I exterminated them.

t1601i: And those who hated me **you handed over**[136] before me, those who turn the neck **and** my enemies, and I exterminated them.

---

131 t1639i 'beneath me'.
132 I.e. דששתינון. t1639i, t1621i 'I exterminated them' (i.e. שיציתינון).
133 t1621i 'to make war with the peoples'.
134 t1639i 'the peoples who were rising up'.
135 t1621i 'you broke under me' (evidently transposed from earlier in the verse).
136 t1639i 'you broke'.

The Transmission of Targum Jonathan in the West

2 Sam. 22:42

Babylonian tradition: They seek help but there is no redemption for them, and pray before the Lord, but their prayer is not received.

t1601i: They seek help but there is no redemption for them; [<] praying before the Lord, but their prayer is not received.[137]

2 Sam. 22:43

Babylonian tradition: And I trampled them like the dust of the earth, like the mud of the markets I trod upon them, I stamped upon them.

t1601i: And I trampled them like the dust of the earth, like the mud of the markets I trod upon them, I stamped upon them.

2 Sam. 22:44

Babylonian tradition: You will save me from the dissension of the people, you will appoint me the head for the peoples; a people that I have not known will serve me.

t1601i: You saved me from the dissension of peoples, you will appoint me **to** the head of the peoples; **the** people that I have not known will serve me.

2 Sam. 22:45

Babylonian tradition: The sons of the peoples will be subjugated to me; at the report of the ear they will obey me.

t1601i: The sons of the peoples will be subjugated to me; at the **hearing** of the ear they will obey me.

2 Sam. 22:46

Babylonian tradition: The sons of the peoples will come to an end and they will move from their fortresses.

t1601i: The sons of the peoples will come to an end and **they will be laid waste** and move from their fortresses.

2 Sam. 22:47

Babylonian tradition: Therefore because of the miracle and the redemption that

---

137 t1639i 'but He does not receive their prayer'.

Chapter Ten. The Targum Text in Liturgical Manuscripts

you have done for your people, they give thanks, and say, 'He is enduring, the Lord! Blessed is the strong one! From before whom is given to us strength and redemption! And the God of the strength of our redemption is exulted!

t1601i: Therefore because of the miracle and the redemption **that will be done for your anointed one and** for **the remnant of** your people, **who will remain, they will rejoice and give thanks, and say,** 'He is enduring,[138] the living,[139] strong and fearful God! Blessed! Strong![140] From before whom is given **to me** strength and redemption! And God, the strength of our redemption, is exulted!

2 Sam. 22:48

Babylonian tradition: God who has carried out retribution for me and has broken under me the peoples who are rising up to do evil to me;

t1601i: God who has carried out retribution for me and has broken under me the peoples **who are strong**[141] **like the bow of bronze;**[142]

2 Sam. 22:49

Babylonian tradition: he redeemed me from those who hate me; and over all those who are rising up to do evil to me you will enable me to prevail; from Gog and the armies of violent peoples who are with him you will save me.

t1601i: **saving me**[143] from those who hate me; and **also**[144] on account of (על)[145] those who are rising up to do evil to me **you will save me;**[146] from Gog and from the armies, violent peoples, who **are come to wage war** with **me** you will save me.

2 Sam. 22:50

[Text resumes in Ashkenazi manuscripts]

Babylonian tradition: Therefore I will give thanks before you, O Lord, among

---

138 t1647i reads 'before' (i.e. קדם) for 'He is enduring' (i.e. קיים הוא). Probably in error.
139 t1621i adds 'great'.
140 t1647i 'Blessed and strong!'
141 t1647i omits 'who are strong'.
142 'who are strong like a bow of copper': t1639i 'who are rising up to do evil to me' (= Babylonian tradition).
143 t1639i 'he redeemed me' (= Babylonian tradition).
144 t1639i omits 'also' (= Babylonian tradition).
145 t1647i 'because of all' (בכל).
146 t1639i 'you will enable me to prevail' (= Babylonian tradition).

the peoples and to your name I will sing a song.

t1601i: Therefore I will give thanks before you, O Lord, [<] and to your name I will sing a song.[147]

t133a: Therefore I will give thanks before you, O Lord, among the peoples and to your name I will sing song**s**.

2 Sam. 22:51

Babylonian tradition: Continuing to do redemption with his king and doing goodness to his anointed one, to David, and to his seed for ever.

t1601i: Continuing to do redemption with his king[148] and doing goodness to his anointed one, to David, and to his seed for ever.

t133a: Continuing to do redemption with his king and doing goodness to his anointed one, to David, and to his sons[149] for ever.

5. Quality of the Texts

The liturgical texts clearly reflect a very fluid process of transmission in which the text has been augmented and adjusted. Some changes are deliberate, in particular in the Italian liturgies, but such fluidity has also left the text badly corrupted in most of our witnesses: cases of omission by parablepsis,[150] confusions between graphically similar forms and metathesis,[151] meaningless or erroneous additions (including dittography),[152] and Hebraisms[153] are all frequent and at points the text teeters precariously on the edge of incomprehensibility and it is difficult to imagine the text being successfully read aloud.[154]

---

147 t1639i: 'songs' (i.e. plural).
148 t1621i: 'with kings'.
149 t159a, t99a, t63a, t1614a: 'his seed'.
150 E.g. t133a 2 Sam. 22:3; t1601i, t1679i 2 Sam. 22:28; t1614a 2 Sam. 22:18.
151 E.g. t1601i 2 Sam. 22:10 (בגבורתיה for בקבורתיה); t1601i, t1679i 2 Sam. 22:11 (פני, אפי for כנפי); t1639i 2 Sam. 22:29 (מריה for מימריה); t1647i 2 Sam. 22:47 (קדם for קיים הוא); t133a 2 Sam. 22:24 (הוה נטר for והויתי נטר); t1614a 2 Sam. 22:17 (אפקני for אקפוני).
152 E.g. t1614a 2 Sam. 22:1 (ויתיר); t159a 2 Sam. 22:16 (שכלולי שמיא תבל).
153 E.g. t1647i 2 Sam. 22:15 בברקים; t1647i 2 Sam. 22:43 כטיט; t1621i 2 Sam. 22:43 שוקים.
154 Although the vocalisation is not treated in this study, it displays numerous difficulties. Not all the texts are vocalised (t1618i, for example, is unvocalised). t1621i is a vocalised text but

Chapter Ten. The Targum Text in Liturgical Manuscripts

6. Linguistic Features

Some of the Italian liturgical texts exhibit features characteristic of Palestinian forms of Aramaic. t1601i, for example, uses ‑יי for the first person singular suffix on a plural masculine noun (e.g. דבביי 2 Sam. 22:3 cf. 2 Sam. 22:35 דרעיי t1601i, t1639i, t1679i, t1618i) and reads הוינא, the first singular perfect form of the verb 'to be' (2 Sam. 22:3), in place of the pronoun אנא.[155] t1679i and t1601i uses ‑יי for the 3rd singular masculine suffix on masculine plural nouns (באפוי 2 Sam. 22:9; בנוי 2 Sam. 22:27).[156] The picture is, however, inconsistent across the manuscripts. t1647i and t1621i have הוינא (t1647i הווינא), but read דבבי; whereas t1639i and t1618i read דבביי and אנא. In the two Ashkenazi mahzorim one finds דבביי (e.g. t1631a; 2 Sam. 22:3), but no other markings of Palestinian Aramaic. The transition from *a* to *e* or *i* in closed syllables, a vocalic change that occurs sporadically in Galilean Aramaic in certain words, is also found in a number of liturgical witnesses (e.g. קירבני 2 Sam. 22:3 t1601i, t1639i, t1679i, t1621i, t133a).[157]

The use of ‑ל to mark the direct object (i.e. accusative particle; 2 Sam. 22:2, 4), rather than ית, is another distinctive feature of the Italian liturgical texts. Both Jewish Palestinian and Babylonian Aramaic texts display this trait — so it is not decisive from a dialectic point of view — but it is nonetheless a common feature in the Midrashic portions of the Palestinian Targum.[158]

---

some words are left unvocalised (e.g. רמפתי 2 Sam. 22:37; כסוון 2 Sam. 22:43). The vocalisation and consonants do not always correspond (e.g. פָּירְקָנִי t1639i 2 Sam. 22:3). Lehnardt has studied the vocalisation of of Tg. 2 Samuel 22 in several Italian mahzorim and arrived at similar conclusions. Lehnardt concluded that the problematic vocalisation represented attempts to enable a reader with limited knowledge of Aramaic and no familiarity with a performative aural tradition to carry out his task of performing the Targum in a liturgical setting; Lehnardt, 'The Role of Targum Samuel in European Jewish liturgy', 51–8.

155 J.A. Lund, 'The First Person Singular Past Tense of the Verb *hwh* in Jewish Palestinian Aramaic', *Maarav* 4 (1987), 191–9.

156 Cook writes: 'The form והי- appears throughout Aramaic (including Biblical Aramaic) until the Late period, when in Western Aramaic, the ה syncopates and yields וי-, although the older orthography still sometimes appears as a historical spelling. *Targum Onqelos* uniformly uses והי- and the Palestinian Targums normally have וי-'. E. Cook, 'The "Kaufman Effect" in the Pseudo-Jonathan Targum', *Aramaic Studies* 4:2 (2006), 123–32, p. 127. Cf. Cook, 'Rewriting the Bible', 132; Fassberg, *A Grammar of the Palestinian Targum Fragments from the Cairo Genizah*, 114–15.

157 See page 259.

158 E. Martínez Borobio, 'YT and L – Before the Direct Object in the Aramaic of the Palestinian Targum', *Sefarad* 47:1 (1987), 159–62 also Sokoloff, *A Dictionary of Jewish Babylonian*

The two Ashkenazi mahzorim also show a few distinguishing linguistic traits. For example, at 2 Sam. 22:8 both prefer the verbal root רעש 'to be in commotion' to the near-synonymous (at least in the context) root רגש, favoured by all the other Western textual witnesses. Similarly, in 2 Sam. 22:11 t1614a reads על גדפי רוחא 'upon the wings of the wind', the noun גדף replacing its synonym כנף, preferred by the remaining witnesses. Neither lexeme is dialectically distinct, though both are found in Late Jewish Literary Aramaic, so it would be plausible to assume a degree of adaptation of the text towards prevailing linguistic preferences at a late stage in its transmission.[159] Other trends that may reflect a late setting are the spelling ארע 'to meet' in place of ערע (in t159a, t63a at 2 Sam. 22:6), the use of א as a vowel letter (e.g. 2 Sam. 22:6 במאני קטול in all Italian witnesses and t159a, t133a, t63a),[160] and the sufformative -יא for the masculine plural nouns in the determined state (e.g. יומייא t1618i 2 Sam. 22:1; שמייא t1639i, t1679i, t1618i, t1621i; t1631a 2 Sam. 22:10), an orthography typical of Targum Pseudo-Jonathan.

7. The Character of the Italian Texts

The text of the Italian mahzorim is distinct from the remainder of the witnesses and forms a clearly unified text family. As will be clear from the preceding presentation of the text, the Italian liturgical text is marked by a number of long pluses *vis à vis* the standard text of Targum Jonathan, which can be found in all the mahzorim studied. For example (pluses underlined):

2 Sam. 22:3 '...and also from the hand of all robbers he saved me, and from the hand of Saul, the king, he redeemed me.'

2 Sam. 22:8 'The earth was shaken up, and shuddered, and made to tremble, and the foundations of the heavens trembled, the mountains were made to

---

 Aramaic, 611–12 and M. Sokoloff, *A Dictionary of Jewish Palestinian Aramaic of the Byzantine Period* (Ramat-Gan 1990), 274, for further references and bibliography. Cf. Fassberg, *A Grammar of the Palestinian Targum Fragments from the Cairo Genizah*, 252–3.

159 Cf. Damsma, *The Targumic Toseftot to Ezekiel*, 180–2, who concludes that the Tosefta Targums to Ezekiel that she studied date to the geonic period.

160 See chapter 'YT and L – Before the Direct Object in the Aramaic of the Palestinian Targum', *Sefarad* 47:1 (1987), 159–62.

tremble, and the depths of the sea rolled around because the wrath <u>of our living and enduring God</u> was strong.'

2 Sam. 22.28 '…you will redeem <u>them and call them 'a beloved people,' since your focus always remains on the humble in spirit.</u>'

2 Sam. 22.47 'and the redemption <u>that will be done for your anointed one and for the remnant of</u> your people, <u>who will remain, they will rejoice</u> and give thanks…'

In terms of their content, one is struck by the formulaic nature of the pluses, which draw either on the immediate literary context, as is the case with the plus in 2 Sam. 22:3 (cf. MT / Tg. 2 Sam. 22:1) and the expression 'depth of the sea' in 2 Sam. 22:8 (= Tg. 2 Sam. 22:16 cf. Tg. Isa. 51:10; Tg. Mic. 7:19), or they echo expressions found elsewhere in Targums Onqelos or Jonathan. The reference to the 'beloved people' in 2 Sam. 22:28, for example, echoes Targum Onqelos to Deuteronomy (e.g. 7:6; 14:2; 26:18),[161] and the 'the humble in spirit', Targum Isaiah (e.g. 57:15).[162] Similarly the trembling (root זוע) of the earth (see Tg. Joel 4:16; Tg. Isa. 13:13; Tg. Jer. 10:10; Tg. Hag. 2:21 cf. Tg. 1 Sam. 14:15) and the mountains (see Tg. Isa. 5:25 cf. Tg. Isa. 28:21) as a result of God's wrath in the plus of 2 Sam. 22:8. The clause '<u>that will be done for your anointed one and</u> for <u>the remnant of</u> your people' in the expanded text of 2 Sam. 22:47 is almost a direct citation from Targum 2 Sam. 22:32 (or Targum Habakuk 3:18).[163]

The immediate literary context and Targums Onqelos and Jonathan as a whole provide the source material for the overwhelming majority of the remaining smaller pluses and substitutions. Many simply recycle wording found elsewhere in 2 Samuel 22 itself. The plus 'his glory was revealed <u>in his majesty</u>' (2 Sam. 22:10) imports the wording of the following verse (2 Sam. 22:11), while the plus and substitution in 2 Sam. 22:11, i.e. '<u>He caused his Presence to rest</u> upon quick angels and <u>he was revealed in glory</u>', re-hashes the 'his glory was revealed' from the preceding verse and the wording at the start of the following verse, i.e. 'So he caused his Presence to dwell in the darkness'. Likewise, the substitution of the verb 'I exterminated them

---

161 Cf. Goshen-Gottstein, *Fragments of Lost Targumim*, Vol 1, §7.23.
162 Cf. Tg. Ps. 34:19; Tg. Esth. II 6.11 'the Holy One raised the poor from the dust, and those low in spirit [מכיכי רוחא] from the rubbish heap', a citation of Ps. 113:7.
163 See page 248.

(ושיציתינון)', with 'I trampled them (דששתינון)' (2 Sam. 22:39), found in manuscripts t1601i, t1679i, t1647i, and t1618i, is taken over from verse 43; the plus 'in every time <u>of distress</u>' (דבכל עידן עקא 2 Sam. 22:4 t1601i, t1679i, and t1621i) is taken over from the preceding verse (2 Sam. 22:3); and the interchange of the verbs of פרק and שיזב in 2 Sam. 22:3 (in t1601i t1679i, t1647i, t1618i, t1621i) and 2 Sam. 22:49 (t1601i, t1679i, t1647i, t1618i, t1621i) can be accounted for by their recurrence in the passage.[164]

Others among the smaller pluses or substitutions adopt stock phraseology from elsewhere in Targum Jonathan. For example, the variant text in 2 Sam. 22:38, i.e. 'I pursued <u>after</u> those who hated me... I did not relent <u>from them</u> until I had finished them off', simply reflects the normal syntax (e.g. 'pursue *after*' 1 Sam. 17:53; 23:25, 28; 24:15; 26:18; 30:8; 2 Sam. 2:19, 28; 17:1; etc.; 'turn *from*' 1 Sam. 15:11, 29; 16:18; 17:15, 57; 18:6; 23:28; 24:2; 2 Sam. 1:1; 2:26; etc.). The idea of opening the mouth found in the plus '<u>I open my mouth</u> (פתח פומי ומצלי) <u>and</u> pray' (2 Sam. 22:4; 2 Sam. 22:7 except t1621i; t1639i) is, similarly, idiomatic (e.g. Tg. 1 Sam. 2:1; 2 Sam. 12:14 etc). Comparable is 'the peoples will come to an end <u>and they will be laid waste</u>' in 2 Sam. 22:46 — the pairing of the verbs סוף and צדי being stock phraseology in Targum Jonathan (e.g. Tg. Isa. 3:26; 32:19; 42:14; Tg. Ezek. 24:11 cf. Tg. 1 Sam. 2:5). A further example is the readings 'a band of <u>liars</u>' (סיעת שקרין 2 Sam. 22:5) in t1601i, t1679i, t1647i, and t1621i (= Tg. Jer. 9:1; Tg. Hos. 7:5).

In other cases, common phraseology reflecting the characteristic ideology of Targum Jonathan is introduced: for example, 2 Sam. 22:17 '<u>in his Presence in the</u> highest <u>heavens</u>' (= Tg. Isa. 32:15; 33:5; 38:14; Tg. Mic. 6:6 cf. 2 Sam. 22:11,12), and the appellation 'strong and fearful God' in 2 Sam. 22:47 (= Tg. Onq. Deut. 10:17 cf. Tg. Isa. 9:5; 10:21; Tg. Jer. 32:18).[165] The similar divine qualification '<u>the living and enduring God</u>' (i.e 2 Sam. 22:8, 13, 47), combines a divine title conventional in Targum Jonathan (i.e. 'enduring Lord' יוי קיימא)[166] with a literal translation of the Hebrew that this term normally translates in Targums Onqelos and Jonathan. In other words the Aramaic אלהא חייא would

---

164 At 2 Sam. 22:3 manuscript t1639i combines the two readings (שיזבני מן סנאי פרקני), perhaps a 'combined reading' showing the secondary influence of the continuous text tradition.
165 2 Sam. 22:23 'the judgements of his will' ≈ Tg. Ezek. 44:24; Tg. Zeph. 2:3 (cf. also 2 Sam. 22:26); 2 Sam. 22:16 'a rebuking wind (במזופית רוח)' (cf. Tg. Isa. 32:15 also Tg. 1 Sam. 16:14–16; Tg. 1 Kgs 18:12; Tg. Isa. 40:7).
166 Cf. page 188.

Chapter Ten. The Targum Text in Liturgical Manuscripts

be a literal translation of the Hebrew אלהים חיים; in Targums Onqelos and Jonathan the Hebrew אלהים חיים is normally translated יוי קיימא (Tg. Onq. Deut. 5:26; Tg. 1 Sam. 17:26, 36; Tg. 2 Kgs 19:4, 16; Tg. Isa. 37:4, 17; Tg. Jer. 10:10; 23:36).[167]

The more elaborate plus to 2 Sam. 22:35, i.e. 'he broke the peoples that were strong like a bronze bow', found in manuscripts t1601i, t1679i, t1647i, t1618i, and t1621i, is inspired by the presence of the comparative 'like a bow' and developed from the verb מתקיף ('making strong') of the standard textual tradition, but it is nonetheless simply importing a simile (i.e. 'the people who are strong like...') widespread in Targum Jonathan (e.g. Isa. 9:4; 43:2; 47:14; Jer. 11:16; Ezek. 15:7 etc 'like fire' cf. Jer. 5:6 'like nocturnal wolves'; Ezek. 17:24 'like moist wood'; Amos 9:3 'like a serpent'). One notes the same elaboration in 2 Sam. 22:40 in these manuscripts and, indeed, the same manuscripts replace 'the peoples who are rising up to do evil to me' in 2 Sam. 22:48 with this entire clause from verse 35 (i.e. 'the peoples who are strong like the bow of bronze').

In the example from 2 Sam. 22:14, the alternative reading found in the Italian liturgical texts, namely 'the Most High lifted up his voice (קליה)', more closely reflects the underlying Hebrew (קולו), whereas all the Eastern witnesses and the majority of the remaining Western witnesses read 'the Most High lifted up his Memra' (see also below). The reading of t1639i 'You enlarged my stride beneath me (תחותיי = MT תחתני)', for 'before me' (2 Sam. 22:37), may also be influenced by the Hebrew text.

In one case the text of the Italian mahzor may reveal the influence of the Targum to the seder for 7th Day of Passover (Exod. 13:17–15:26), for which 2 Samuel 22 serves as the haftarah, namely the reading 'Pharaoh and his camps' in place of 'Pharaoh and the Egyptians' at 2 Sam. 22:27 in manuscripts t1601i, t1679i, t1647i, t1618i, t1621i (= Exod. 15:4 but cf. also Tg. Isa. 51:9; Tg. Ezek. 32:31).

At two points it is possible that the text has been influenced by the wording of the Targum of the parallel text in Psalm 18. Specifically, the substitution '[The Lord] will repay me' (יגמלני) 2 Sam. 22:21 t1601i, t1679i, t1647i, t1618i,

---

[167] The title 'living God' is employed in Targums Neofiti (i.e. Deut. 4:33; 5:26), Pseudo-Jonathan (e.g. Num. 24:4), the Fragment Targums (e.g. Frg. Tg.P Exod. 12:2; Num. 23:19; Frg. Tg.V Num. 23:19). The full appellation 'the living and enduring God' crops up in Tg. Ps. 42:3. On this point see Houtman and Sysling, *Alternative Targum Traditions*, 129–30.

t1621i) for '[The Lord] will recompense me' (ישמלינני) and the plus 'evil plans' (2 Sam. 22:27 t1647i, t1618i, t1621i), match the wording of the parallel verses in Targum Psalms (יגמלנני Tg. Ps. 18:21; מחשבן ביש Tg. Ps. 18:27 also Tg. Ps. 21:12; Tg. Ezek. 38:10 cf. Tg. Ps.-J. Gen. 50:20; Tg. Ps.-J. Deut. 32:32). In neither case is the association overwhelmingly strong, so the resemblance may well be coincidental.

It will be clear from the foregoing analysis that, despite some variations that have evidently arisen as the text was circulated,[168] the texts preserved in the Italian mahzorim form a clear unity, although t1639i occasionally adheres to the standard text where the remainder has a plus or substitution. The language of the pluses and substitutions (and they are indeed substitutions) is formulaic or idiomatic; in the main it recycles phraseology from within Targum Jonathan itself. As such the longer form of the text merits the designation 'Tosefta' ('addition'): It is certainly a secondary expansion to the shorter standard text form.[169]

In terms of its content, the theological tenor of the Italian liturgical text form is readily apparent: it heightens the status of God, emphasises his special relationship with Israel, and stresses his power over their worldly oppressors. This leads to a clearly stated promise of future redemption, evident not only in the long plus of 2 Sam. 22:47, but also elsewhere in the switch from the perfect to the imperfect tense (e.g. 2 Sam. 22:17).

8. The Character of the Ashkenazi Texts

In contrast to the Italian liturgies, the Ashkenazi sources — both mahzorim and haftarot collections — contain a text that is basically the same as the continuous text tradition. There are only a few possible exceptions that may represent readings peculiar to the liturgical text-form. In one case, namely 2 Sam. 22:14, an Ashkenazi mahzor (i.e. t1631a) shares the reading of the Italian mahzorim noted above, namely 'his voice' instead of 'his Memra'. One Ashkenazi haftarot collection, t99a, may combine the two readings at this point:[170] t99a reads 'the Most High exalted the voice of his Memra (קל

---

168 Cf. Smelik, 'Orality, Manuscript Reproduction, and the Targums', 66–71.
169 See the discussion of Tosefta Targums in chapter eleven.
170 On 'combined readings' see Smelik 'Trouble in the Trees!', 262–6; Smelik 'Orality,

Chapter Ten. The Targum Text in Liturgical Manuscripts

מימריה)'. It is quite possible, however, that the underlying Hebrew has influenced the text here.[171] If that is the case then the resemblance between the Targum texts may be coincidental.

A second such case might be 2 Sam. 22:1, where all the continuous texts read 'David praised in prophecy before the Lord the words of this hymn [...]' Two of the Ashkenazi haftarot collections (i.e. t99a, t133a) read '*all* the words of this hymn [...]'. This reading does not appear in the continuous text tradition so far as this has been preserved, but the same reading is offered by one eighteenth century Sephardi haftarot collection (Or. 9916, British Library, London; siglum: t1188s) and a few other liturgical manuscripts of diverse origins,[172] so this may point to a distinct liturgical text tradition, though not one that is confined to the Ashkenazi zone. The phrase 'all the words' is, however, far from uncommon in Targum Samuel (e.g. 1 Sam. 3:18; 8:10, 21; 19:7; 25:9, 12; 2 Sam. 7:17; 13:21; 14:19; 15:35 etc) so this conclusion remains highly speculative.

The Ashkenazi haftarot collections are otherwise marked by the fairly frequent occurrence of readings unique to one manuscript, a feature that one equally finds in Ashkenazi continuous texts. These variants are mostly of little significance. For example, in 2 Sam. 22:1 t133a reads מידא דכל ('from the hand of all…'), while all other witnesses read מיד כל (except t99a and t713a, which read מידא כל, an error); and at 2 Sam. 22:6 t133a reads משיריין רשיען סגיאן 'many wicked camps', while the remainder lack סגיאן. Only in the mahzor t1631a do we find a variant with a hint of an exegetical character: the text reads 'Therefore *the King* sent forth his anger like burning fire' (בכין שלח מלכא רוגזיה כאישא בערא 2 Sam. 22:9), where all other texts read simply '*he* sent…'. The appellation of God as king is common in the Prophets (Isa. 6:5; 33:22; Jer. 10:7 etc), though the current example may be inspired by Targum 2 Sam. 22:17.

A single variant in t133a may show the influence of the Targum to the corresponding seder portion (i.e. Exod. 13:17–15:26): at 2 Sam. 22:9 t133a reads 'the insolence of wicked Pharaoh went up like the smoke of the furnace before him…' The expression 'smoke of the furnace' occurs in Targum Onqelos as well as Targum Neofiti to the seder portion (i.e. Exod. 19:18). The

---

Manuscript Reproduction, and the Targums', 77.
171 See Patmore 'The Transmission of Targum Jonathan in the West', 37–51 and chapter four.
172 See Patmore and Tanja, 'Initial Observations Concerning the Text of Targum 2 Samuel 22 as Preserved in European Liturgical Manuscripts', 70–1.

wording is, however, not confined to this seder portion (e.g. also Tg. Onq. and Tg. Neof. Gen. 19:28 cf. Tg. Judg. 5:5; Tg. Ps. 68:9), nor can some sort of textual corruption be definitely excluded (t133a omits seven words here by parablepsis between two instances of קדמוהי), so the influence of the seder portion remains speculative.

The Ashkenazi mahzor t1631a shares with the Italian mahzorim the reading '[The Lord] will repay me' (יגמליני 2 Sam. 22:21) for '[The Lord] will recompense me' (ישמליני), which is shared with the parallel verse in Targum Psalms (יגמלני Tg. Ps. 18:21).

Several of these unique readings ostensibly originated in scribal error. For example, at 2 Sam. 22:3 t159a reads קדמך instead of the expected קדמוהי; at 2 Sam. 22:3 t133a omits the clause בעדן עקא...סמך לי 'in the time of distress...[his Memra] was a support for me' (the phrase מגן עלי 'he protects me' is transposed to later in the verse where it replaces פרקני 'my redemption') and the text between the two occurrences of קדמוהי 'before him' in 2 Sam. 22:9, evidently by parablepsis; 2 Sam. 22:9, where t159a reads כתננא דמן קדמוהי 'like smoke that was from before him', the remaining manuscripts reading without דמן (the expression דמן קדמוהי is taken over in error from later in the verse); and t99a reads ענגים for עננין 'clouds' at 2 Sam. 22:12, clearly a Hebraism.

The text of mahzor t1614a, in particular, has become quite corrupted in transmission. For example, 'burning' (בערא) is omitted after 'like fire' (כאישא) in 2 Sam. 22:9; verse 2 Sam. 22:14 is omitted altogether; and the phrase 'and before my God I am pleading for favour' (וקדם אלהי אנא מתחנן) is inserted into 2 Sam. 22:4 after 'I pray before the Lord' (אנא מצלי קדם יוי), evidently as the result of the use of this formulation (i.e. 'I pray before the Lord and before my God I am pleading for favour') in 2 Sam. 22:7. Similarly, at the end of 2 Sam. 22:1, t1614a reads מיד כל בעלי דבביהון ויתיר ואף יד דוד שיזב מחרבא דשאול 'from the hand of all their enemies and more(?) and also the hand of David he saved from Saul's sword'. The form ויתיר is left unvocalised, indicating a correction, but even excluding ויתיר, the reference to David's hand here is nonsensical.

To reiterate what was said earlier, the Ashkenazi liturgical sources contain a text that is basically the same as the continuous text tradition, though the text is now in a bad state in the Ashkenazi liturgical sources. The mahzor t1631a stands out from the group, however. It shares a scattering of readings with the Italian mahzorim, though none of the long pluses characteristic of that group of manuscripts, and contains one possible exegetical plus (2 Sam. 22:9). This may

Chapter Ten. The Targum Text in Liturgical Manuscripts

indicate that the text remained (or in any case, had been) in liturgical use, but we cannot be certain on the basis of so little.

9. Relationship between Liturgical and Continuous Texts

As will be evident from the preceding analysis the Italian liturgies preserve a text that is quite distinct from the continuous text tradition, while the text preserved in the Ashkenazi liturgies is essentially that of the continuous text tradition, with a few variants that belong only to liturgical texts (though we cannot exclude the possibility of coincidence, given the relative paucity of manuscripts). The liturgical texts, however, all reflect to a greater or lesser extent their transmission in the West. That is to say, we find a significant number of examples in which the same reading appears in Western liturgical texts and Western continuous texts, but not in the Eastern texts.[173]

For example, when compared to the Eastern textual tradition all the Italian and Ashkenazi liturgical manuscripts read an additional verb at the end of in 2 Sam. 22:1, i.e. '…and also David <u>he saved</u> from Saul's sword', as do most of the continuous texts from these two text families (only t6a, t720a, t232i/s and t705i follow the Eastern text in reading without this verb, see page 246). The form of the verb differs somewhat between the Western witnesses (e.g. lacking object pronoun t99a, t63a, t1614a, t701i, t718i; participle t1631a, t159a), but such slight variations are quite common among the Western manuscripts so that the basic textual affinity between the Western textual witnesses is not obfuscated.

A further clear example is found in 2 Sam. 22:9. In this verse all the liturgical texts in the Italian and Ashkenazi traditions read '<u>wicked</u> Pharaoh (פרעה רשיעא)'. This is the common reading shared by many of the Western textual witnesses examined in this study (e.g. of the continuous texts in the Ashkenazi and Mixed Western families: t5a, t6a^{correct}, t713a, t720a, t725a, t2i, t3i, t7i, t718i, see page 249).

In one instance common readings of this type are confined to a single culturally contiguous zone. In 2 Sam. 22:3 the Babylonian tradition reads 'and

---

[173] In addition to the examples given below, see Patmore and Tanja, 'Initial Observations Concerning the Text of Targum 2 Samuel 22 as Preserved in European Liturgical Manuscripts', 72–4.

also from the hand of all robbers (חטופין) he saved me'. Manuscripts t159a, t99a, t133a, t63a, t1614a, and t1631a all read: 'and also from the hand of all robbers (חטופין) <u>and thieves</u> (אניסין) he saved me' (t63a 'redeemed me'). The reading is shared with the continuous text of t5a, t725a, t2i, t718i, see pages 248–9). These four manuscripts belong to two different textual families within the stemma (Ashkenazi and Mixed Western), but they were all written in Ashkenaz. Evidently these sources incorporate some variant readings that were in circulation in Ashkenaz but unknown in other areas.

While we might be tempted to explain these variants as being the influence of liturgical usage on the copying of the continuous text tradition, such a possibility is only really conceivable in the case of the Italian mahzorim and even then unlikely since most of the readings distinct to the Italian mahzorim are not found in the continuous texts. It is more plausible to accept that in these cases we are dealing with local, rather than distinctly liturgical, readings.

Conclusions

The decisive point arising out of the above survey is that the liturgical texts show clear affinities to the Western continuous text tradition. These liturgical texts clearly belong in the Western textual tradition. Although some of the variant readings found throughout the Western manuscripts may preserve variants attested in the texts from which the Western manuscripts ultimately derive, the relatively high degree of variation between the separate textual traditions, as well as between manuscripts within a single textual tradition, make the existence of a single Western *Urtext* extremely unlikely. Although the European Jewish communities were separated from one another by geographical, political, and cultural boundaries, there was nonetheless significant mobility between the communities as a result of commercial networks or forced migration due to persecution, especially during the fourteenth and fifteenth centuries, the period in which most of the liturgical manuscripts used in this study were produced. These links between otherwise distinct European Jewish communities may account for the degree of commonality between all Western textual witnesses: variant readings characteristic of Western manuscripts but not found in Eastern manuscripts may have originated in Europe, perhaps independently in more than one

Chapter Ten. The Targum Text in Liturgical Manuscripts

location, and subsequently been diffused among the different textual traditions of European Jewry.

Equally, some distinctly Western readings may reflect the influence of alternative Pentateuchal Targum traditions that were circulating in Europe at the same time. Targum Neofiti (Palestinian origin, but known only from an Italian manuscript),[174] Targum Pseudo-Jonathan (probably reached its current form in Europe; the only known manuscript, Add. 27031 British Library, London is sixteenth century Ashkenazi or Italian),[175] and the Fragment Targums according to Ebr. 440 Biblioteca Apostolica, Vatican City (German manuscript, *c.* 1300),[176] for example, all employ the term 'wicked Pharaoh' in the seder for the 7th day of Pesach, for which 2 Samuel 22 is the haftarah (e.g. Tg. Neof. Exod. 15:9; Tg. Ps.-J Exod. 15:1, 9, 21, Frg. Tg.^{V} Exod. 15:9). That this reading crops up in many of the Western manuscripts of the Targum to the Prophets (2 Sam. 22:9) may reveal the influence of the alternative Targum traditions of the seder — an influence that could easily have exerted itself within Europe.

The liturgical texts clearly belong to the Western textual tradition, but the Western textual tradition itself is the result of a haphazard blend of the factors just described. While the Italian liturgical texts diverge in significant ways from the continuous text, the Ashkenazi sources, both mahzorim and haftarot collections, preserve a text that differs from that found in manuscripts containing the continuous texts no more than the manuscripts containing the continuous text differ among themselves.

Concerning the Italian liturgical sources, the text largely follows that of the standard text of Targum Jonathan but with some significant pluses and substitutions. Unfortunately history has bequeathed us only two Italian manuscripts of the continuous text of Targum Samuel, but if these two manuscripts are representative of the continuous text tradition in Italy then it is clear that in Italy the liturgical text had a textual form and transmission history distinct from that of the continuous text. The preservation of this richer textual form may plausibly be connected to its continued use in the liturgy; indeed,

---

174 Richler, *Hebrew Manuscripts in the Vatican Library*, 528–9.
175 Italian hand according to Levine, 'British Museum Aramaic Additional Ms 27031', 3; German according to Margoliouth, *Catalogue of the Hebrew and Samaritan Manuscripts in the British Museum*, §99.
176 Richler, *Hebrew Manuscripts in the Vatican Library*, 387.

other sections of Targum, including to the Pentateuch, occurring in European liturgies are also distinguished by their fuller exegetical character.[177]

Some of the Italian liturgical manuscripts show Palestinian dialect features. Díez Macho noted this phenomenon in a number of other texts, concluding that it indicated that the text in question was of Palestinian origin[178] (but possibly in various centres that stood under the influence of Palestinian traditions, rather than in Palestine itself)[179] but had been altered under the influence of Targum Jonathan[180] (in its Western transmission in the case of the Italian mahzorim). In my view this remains a plausible explanation and this raises the possibility that the textual embellishments characteristic of the Italian liturgical manuscripts may ultimately stem from Palestinian traditions. Certainly in terms of their liturgy, the Italian community can be characterised as 'the spiritual heir of the homeland [i.e. Palestine]'.[181]

---

[177] See e.g. Kaufman and Maori, 'The Targumim to Exodus 20', 16–23; Díez Macho, 'Nueva fuente para el Targum Palestino del día séptimo de Pascua y primero de Pentecostés'; also Gleßmer, *Einleitung in die Targume zum Pentateuch*, 154–64. On Mahzor Vitry see Díez Macho, 'Valiosos manuscritos bíblicos en la Biblioteca Nacional y Universitaria de Estrasburgo', §1; A. Díez Macho, 'Nuevos fragmentos de Tosefta Targumica', *Sefarad* 16 (1956), 313–24, pp. 313–15. See also pages 63–4.

[178] Díez Macho, 'Un nuevo Targum a los Profetas', 290–2; Díez Macho, 'Nuevos manuscritos importantes, biblicos o liturgicos, en Hebreo o Arameo', §47; Díez Macho, 'Importants manuscrits hébreux et araméens aux États Unis', §9; Díez Macho, 'Un segundo fragmento del Targum Palestinense a los Profetas', 199–200.

[179] Cf. comments below and Smelik, 'Orality, Manuscript Reproduction, and the Targums', 66–71.

[180] Díez Macho, *El Targum*, 94 n. 202; Díez Macho, 'Nueva fuente para el Targum Palestino del día séptimo de Pascua y primero de Pentecostés', 235.

[181] Reif, *Judaism and Hebrew Prayer*, 164–5.

Chapter Eleven

Tosefta Targums

When applied to the Targum to the Prophets, the term *tosefta* (plural: *toseftot*), meaning literally 'an addition', refers to a wide range of materials drawn from diverse sources, which differ from one another in terms of their length, dialect, connection to known liturgical cycles, and relationship to the standard text of Targum Jonathan. They are not cut from the same cloth but are the fruit of the work of different Targumists, from different times, locations, and traditions.[1] It is simply a handy catch-all term that usefully refers to a group of texts that are distinguished from the standard text of Targum Jonathan by their fuller exegetical character and typically also by their format; nonetheless, it is clear that they are to be located within a broadly Palestinian tradition and that they circulated independently from Targum Jonathan.

Tosefta Targums are commonly found either in the margins of manuscripts, normally one containing a version of the standard text of Targum Jonathan (as we saw in chapter nine), incorporated into the running text of Targum Jonathan,[2] or they are presented as the haftarah reading in a liturgical setting such as prayer books or collections of haftarot in which Targum Jonathan is not present (as we noted in the previous chapter). They are sometimes marked with a heading, either 'Tosefta' or one of a number of other titles (e.g. 'Palestinian Tosefta', 'Another Book', 'Targum Yerushalmi'), but on other occasions they are incorporated into the running text of Targum Jonathan without any indication. We find all three of these formats in the manuscripts studied in this book. We have dealt already with some of the marginal texts and with liturgical sources (chapters nine and ten respectively).

---

1 A good overview of the situation is provided by Kasher, *Targumic Toseftot to the Prophets*, 13–64. See also Houtman and Sysling, *Alternative Targum Traditions*, 41–136 (a survey of previous research is given on pp. 42–6); Smelik, 'Orality, Manuscript Reproduction, and the Targums', 66–71.
2 Cf. Smelik, *The Targum of Judges*, 163ff, 643ff.

The Transmission of Targum Jonathan in the West

1. Tosefta Targums Incorporated into the Running Text

Several of our manuscripts contain Tosefta Targums that have been incorporated into the text of Targum Jonathan. Although, as we have seen, the text preserved in these manuscripts has been subject to changes in the course of its transmission, the additions that we discuss below are distinguished clearly from other emendations of the text by their length and character, and as such can be confidently identified as Tosefta Targums that have become incorporated into the running text, although no indication of this is given in the manuscripts themselves.[3] In the Mixed Western group of manuscripts we find the following incorporated Tosefta Targums:

1 Sam. 2:6

Hebrew Text

The Lord causes death and makes alive, sends down to Sheol and raises up.

Babylonian Tradition

All these are the mighty work of the Lord, who is ruler in the world: he causes death but has promised to make alive; sends down to Sheol but will also raise to eternal life.

t705i

All these are the mighty work of the Lord, who is ruler in the world: he causes death but has promised to make alive; sends down to Sheol but will also raise to eternal life. But Korah son of Izhar son of Kohath sons of Levi from whom Samuel my son came forth, was brought down to Sheol because he stood up and was divided against Moses and Aaron, the righteous ones. They will come up from the place into which they have been swallowed and they will confess that there is no God except Him!

In Codex Reuchlinianus No. 3 (t705) longer additions of a similar character to this example are normally collected in the margin under headings such as 'Targum Yerushalmi' or 'Another Targum' (see chapter nine), so its inclusion in the running text of the manuscript is unexpected. To date we know of no other manuscript containing this Tosefta Targum; it therefore seems likely that the Tosefta Targum had already been incorporated into the running text of Targum Jonathan before the system of marginalia that Codex Reuchlinianus

---

3   See in addition to the examples given here, Smelik's comments in his *The Targum of Judges*, 163–4 (also 166–70).

Chapter Eleven. Tosefta Targums

No. 3 preserves was composed.

This Tosefta Targum was first published by de Lagarde and subsequently discussed by Bacher, who categorised it as a 'haggadic amplification'.[4] The text was reprinted by Sperber in his critical apparatus and by Kasher in his collection of Tosefta Targums. Kasher identified the language of the Tosefta Targum as being close to that of Targum Jonathan itself and classified the text as a 'concluding expansion'. Tosefta Targums of this type are tagged on to the end of the standard Targum text: if one removes the expansion, the standard text remains unchanged. In Kasher's view such expansions are generally intended to encourage the congregation and to arouse in it faith in future justice and redemption (the kingdom of the Lord, the Messiah, the rebuilding of Jerusalem and the Temple, and the ingathering of the Exiles are common themes in such passages). Such a liturgical connection is apt, since 1 Sam. 1:1–2:10 served as the haftarah for the first day of the New Year (*Rosh haShanah*) in all lectionary traditions.[5] The text appears to reflect a dispute recorded in the Mishnah centred on the question whether or not Korah and his followers would rise to eternal life, in which R. Eliezer cites 1 Sam. 2:6 ('the Lord causes death and makes alive; brings down to Sheol and raises up') to support his view that they would.[6]

The remaining example concerns an incorporated Tosefta Targum in 1 Sam. 17:8, which records Goliath challenging the assembled armies of Israel. This particular Tosefta Targum evidently circulated widely since it is recorded in a number of sources (some of which head the text 'Tosefta').[7] Although all clearly stem from the same basic textual tradition, the six European manuscripts that preserve this Tosefta Targum exhibit a degree of textual variation in vocabulary, word order, and small pluses or minuses. There is sufficient coherence between some of the manuscripts that we can arrange them into three rough groupings. A representative text from each group is given below; the full text of all the manuscripts can be found in appendix 4 (for t705i see appendix 2).

---

4   Bacher, 'Kritische Untersuchungen zum Prophetentargum', 49.
5   Kasher, *Targumic Toseftot to the Prophets*, §41, 21–2.
6   m.Sanh. 10.3. The text is cited and discussed by Kasher, *Targumic Toseftot to the Prophets*, §41. Also Houtman and Sysling, *Alternative Targum Traditions*, 108–9; van Staalduine-Sulman, *The Targum of Samuel*, 213–14.
7   See Sperber, *The Bible in Aramaic*, II, *ad loc*; Kasher, *Targumic Toseftot to the Prophets*, §53b, §53g; van Staalduine-Sulman, *The Targum of Samuel*, 352.

The Transmission of Targum Jonathan in the West

1 Sam. 17:8

Hebrew Text

He stood and called to the battle lines of Israel and said to them, 'Why are you coming out to set [yourselves] in order [for] battle?! Am I not the Philistine and you the servants of Saul? Choose for yourselves a man and let him come down to me'.

Babylonian tradition

He stood up and called to the ranks of Israel and said to them, 'Why have you come out to the battle line?! Am I not the Philistine and you the servants of Saul? Choose for yourself a man and let him come down to me'.

Group 1 (t720a = t6a, t713a)

He stood up and proclaimed against the battle lines[8] of Israel and said to them, 'Why are you coming out to the battle line (t6a + 'with the Philistines')?! Am I not (t6a + 'he') Goliath, the Philistine who is from Gath, who killed the two sons of Eli the priest (t6a omits 'priest'), Hofneh and Pinhas, and captured the Ark of the covenant of the Lord and brought it to the house of Dagon my idol and was it not there in the towns of the Philistines seven months? Also every battle — even the battle that was against them — for the Philistines I went out at the head of the army and we were victorious in battle and we threw down those who had been killed like the dust of the earth. Yet until now the Philistines have not declared me fit[9] to be even (t6a omits 'even') chief of the thousand over them. But you, who are of the house of Israel, what mighty deed (t6a omits 'mighty deed') has Saul, the son of Kish who was from the hill country, done for you that you appointed him king over you? If he were a heroic man he would come down and fight with me, but if he is a weak man [then] choose for yourselves someone [else] and he shall come down to me.'

Group 2 (t718i = t725a)[10]

He stood up and proclaimed **to** the battle lines of Israel and said to them, 'Why are you coming out to the battle line **with the Philistines**?![11] Am I not Goliath the Philistine

---

8 t720a reads erroneously בסידרא קרבא דישר׳. The reading of t6a[PM] and t713a is to be preferred: בסידרי קרביא דישר׳. t6a has subsequently been corrected in line with Group 1: ואכריז *בסידרי*#על# סידרי# קרביא דישראל.

9 t6a reads אקשה. A error for אכשרו?

10 For ease of comparison significant variations from the Group 1 text are set in bold (e.g. alternative lexeme, construction, suffix, etc). A minus is indicated by [<]. Corrections are given between ##; the text of the *prima manus* between **.

11 'with the Philistines' (עם פלשתאי) is left unvocalised in t725a. A correction?

who is from Gath, who killed the two sons of Eli, **the priests** Hofneh and Pinhas, and took away (t725a: 'captured') [< def. obj. marker] the Ark of the covenant of the Lord and brought it to the house of Dagon my idol and was it not there in the towns of the Philistines **six** months? **And** also every battle – even the battle **that was against you – from** the Philistines **we** went out[12] **at the call of a voice**(?)[13] [<] and threw down those who had been killed like the dust of the earth. **Yet still** the Philistines have not declared me fit to be [<] chief of the thousand over them. But you, **O sons of** Israel, what [<] has Saul, the son of Kish [<] done for you that you appointed him king over you? If he were a heroic man he would come down and fight with me, but if he is a weak man, choose for yourselves someone [else] and he shall come down to me.'

Group 3 (t232i/s)

He stood up and **called to** the ranks of Israel[14] and he said to them, 'Why **have you come out** to the battle line?! Am I not [<] the Philistine that is from Gath, who killed the two sons of Eli, the **priests** Hofneh and Pinhas, and captured [< def. obj. marker] the Ark of the covenant of the Lord and brought it to the house of Dagon my idol and was it not there in the towns of the Philistines **three** months? **And** also every battle – even the battle **that was against you – from** the Philistines we went out **at the call of a voice(?)** [<] and threw those who had been killed like the dust of the earth. Yet until now **they** have not declared me fit to be [<] chief of the thousand over them. But you, **O sons of Israel**, what is [<] Saul, the son of Kish [<] to you that you appointed him king over you? If he were a heroic man he would **come** and fight with me, but if he is a weak man, choose for yourselves someone [else] and he shall come down to me.'

Codex Reuchlinianus No. 3 (t705i) Marginalia ('ירוש')

Am I not, Goliath, the Philistine who fought with you in Aphek and defeated you and took from you the Ark of the Lord? You are Saul's servants but if you say, 'We trust in the Memra of the Lord, the Master of victory in battle,' then call him and let him come down to me.

Once again the Tosefta Targum is connected to the liturgical cycle, in this case as the haftarah reading for the seder Deut. 21:10–25:19 (כי תצא) according to Maimonides and to some variations of the Italian rite.[15] The language is close

---

12 = t725a; t718i נפקא.
13 Cf. 2 Sam. 23:8
14 The manuscript reads סידריה ישראל, an erroneous form. Read סידרי ישראל?
15 See Kasher, *Targumic Toseftot to the Prophets*, §53a. The list of haftarot recorded in Codex Reuchlinianus No. 3 (t705i), however, which generally follows the Italian rite, does not record

to that of Targum Jonathan and this Tosefta Targum belongs to Kasher's 'integrated expansion' (ההרחבה המשולבת) category, in which the Tosefta Targum is absorbed into the standard text in such a way that the standard text would no longer remain if the Tosefta Targum were removed.[16] As Kasher has already noted, several of the traditions preserved in this Tosefta Targum are known from earlier sources: the tradition that Goliath killed the sons of Eli, Hofneh and Pinhas, is recorded in Pseudo-Philo's *Biblical Antiquities* (late first century CE); and Goliath is connected with the capture of the Ark in a haggadic discussion associated with third century Palestinian *amoraim* in Midrash Samuel (11:1).[17]

Many of the details are simply drawn from elsewhere in the books of Samuel (e.g. 1 Sam. 4:3–5; 5:2). The expression 'the call of a voice' (? לפום קלא), shared by groups 2 and 3 is also found in Targum Jonathan 2 Sam. 23:8 in all textual traditions.[18] Likewise, the seven month duration of the Ark's stay in the towns of the Philistines is based on 1 Sam. 6:1. The three month séjour of t232i/s is apparently (mistakenly) derived from 2 Sam. 6:11, where the Ark is said to have rested three months in the household of Obed-edom the Gittite after David diverted it there following the Lord's smiting of Uzzah for having touched it. The basis of the tradition that this stay lasted only six months recorded in t718i (and Sperber t702s, t734s) is unclear. It may be connected to the six months that are said to have elapsed between the death of Samuel and the anointing of David as king in Hebron.[19]

Leaving aside for the moment the marginal note in t705i, the European manuscripts exhibit significant commonality: they clearly belong to the same basic textual tradition with some variation. Some readings are shared by two of the three groups: groups 1 and 2 read 'the battle lines of Israel' (t713a: בסידרי קרביא דישר׳; t720a, t718i, t725a have singular קרבא) whereas group 3 reads 'the ranks of Israel' (t232i/s סידריה ישראל, read: סידרי); and employ the pronoun plus participle in the phrase '[Why] are you coming out...?' (אתון נפקין), rather than the imperfect (תיפקון), as in group 3. Groups 1 and 3 agree against group 2 in reading 'yet until now' (ועד כען), rather than 'yet still' (ועדיין). Groups 2 and 3

---

this haftarah (also t7i).

16 Kasher, *Targumic Toseftot to the Prophets*, 22–3.
17 Kasher, *Targumic Toseftot to the Prophets*, §53a; van Staalduine-Sulman, *The Targum of Samuel*, 349.
18 See further van Staalduine-Sulman, *The Targum of Samuel*, 352.
19 Tosafot Ta'an. מאימתי 5b.

Chapter Eleven. Tosefta Targums

share the common 'from the Philistines we went out at the call of a voice(?)' in the place of 'for the Philistines I went out at the head of the army and we were victorious in battle'; '*to* the battle lines' (על סידרי קרבא), in place of '*against* the battle lines' (בסידרא קרבא); the address 'you, O sons of Israel', where group 1 has 'you, who are of the house of Israel'; and the omission of any reference to Saul's 'mighty deed' and to his being 'from the hill country'. Other readings, in particular the three possible durations for the Ark's stay in the cities of the Philistines (three, six, or seven months), mark the three groups as distinct.

Within group 1 it is clear that manuscript t6a stands somewhat apart (the significant variations are noted in the text above). As we noted above, the opening phrase in t6a has been corrected from ואכריז בסידרי קרביא דישראל 'and proclaimed *against* the battle lines of Israel', the reading of group 1, to ואכריז על סידרי קרביא דישראל 'proclaimed *to* the battle lines of Israel', the reading of group 2. This is another example of the correction of the manuscript against another textual tradition, a phenomenon strongly evident in manuscript t6a (see pages 98–9). Nonetheless, the text of the *prima manus* contains readings distinct to group 1, e.g. 'you, who are of the house of Israel', as well as others unique to group 2, e.g. 'with the Philistines'. This may imply that the text contained in manuscript t6a is a composite or mixed tradition, though our data remain too limited to be decisive.[20]

The text preserved in the marginal note in t705i clearly belongs to none of the groups presented above. It represents a distinct tradition. The additional material is a composite: the reference to Aphek is derived from 1 Sam. 4:1, while the expression 'We trust in the Memra of the Lord, the Master of victory in battle' is derived from the exchange between the Assyrian general and Hezekiah in 2 Kgs 1:22.[21]

What might account for this state of textual fluidity, which is characteristic of many of the Tosefta Targums? It has been argued that such fluctuation reflects an oral transmission,[22] but our study of the continuous text tradition in European manuscripts requires that this conclusion be refined. Some variations clearly reflect trends that have been identified in the continuous text tradition. For example, manuscript t718i employs the verb 'I took away [the Ark]' (ואייתיתי), where the remainder read 'I captured' (ושביתי); this can be connected

---

20 See here also van Staalduine-Sulman, *The Targum of Samuel*, 348–54.
21 van Staalduine-Sulman, *The Targum of Samuel*, 348–9.
22 Kasher, *Targumic Toseftot to the Prophets*, 28–34.

to the accidental interchange of common vocabulary, a phenomenon widely attested in the continuous text of the European manuscripts (see chapter six §2). Equally, as was pointed out above, there is a degree of recycling of material found elsewhere in the Targum, a tendency that is also widespread in the continuous text tradition in the European manuscripts (see chapter six §1). So textual fluidity does not necessarily indicate oral transmission. That being said, there is a great deal more variation in this Tosefta Targum than we would expect to find in a unit of similar size in the continuous text tradition. If the Tosefta Targum circulated independently of the continuous text tradition, as seems likely, it would have been regarded as less 'canonical' than the continuous text, with the result that each copyist would have felt a greater degree of liberty to adapt the text according to his own insights, either exegetical or poetic.[23] Of course, the historical reality may well be a mixture of both factors (i.e. oral transmission and 'free' written transmission).

Conclusions

The Tosefta Targums examined above and the liturgical text forms examined in the previous chapter have much in common. For a start, all are connected to the liturgy. Yet while such a connection can be established for many of the Tosefta Targums, it is not applicable to all, so it remains a matter of debate whether or not the Tosefta Targums ought to be considered to have been originally simply Targum to the haftarot.[24] Regardless of their ultimate origins, we can be certain that during the period with which we are concerned certain sections of the Targum were read aloud in the synagogue in Italy and Ashkenaz during certain festivals, as we saw in chapter ten.

The language of both the Tosefta Targums and the liturgical texts examined in this study also share similar characteristics: their language is essentially that of Targum Jonathan, with pluses and some substitutions.[25] These variations

---

23 Cf. Smelik, *The Targum of Judges*, 165.
24 Kasher, *Targumic Toseftot to the Prophets*, 16–18, argues for the origins of Tosefta Targum in the haftarot. His conclusions have been questioned by Houtman and Sysling, *Alternative Targum Traditions*, 134–5. See further Patmore, 'The Marginal Notes to the Targum Text of Codex Reuchlinianus No. 3', 80–3; Smelik, 'Orality, Manuscript Reproduction, and the Targums', 66–7; Houtman, 'The Role of Abraham in Targum Isaiah', 5.
25 The same is true of all those Tosefta Targums taken from liturgical sources that Kasher

Chapter Eleven. Tosefta Targums

from the standard text of Targum Jonathan often recycle material found elsewhere in Targum Jonathan (or Onqelos) or drawn from the Hebrew Bible itself. Some variations are simply the result of common forces that also affect the transmission of the standard text of Targum Jonathan in Italy and Ashkenaz (e.g. the interchange of common vocabulary). Finally, where we have multiple textual witnesses to a given Tosefta Targum, there is a significant degree of variation among these witnesses, as there is among the liturgical texts.

What, if anything, might this tell us about the phenomenon of Tosefta Targums (under which heading is here subsumed the liturgical text form)? The first thing that must be said is that any generalisation about Tosefta Targums is impossible: their character, date, and provenance vary too much for that.[26] The conclusions that follow must, therefore, remain limited in their validity to the texts studied in this chapter.

Zunz's suggestion that there once existed a complete Palestinian Targum to the Prophets has cast a long shadow over the study of the Tosefta Targums.[27] One might propose that the pluses in the Tosefta Targums are, in fact, minuses in the standard text of Targum Jonathan, intended to bring the text closer to the underlying Hebrew.[28] This is possible in principle, but the substitutions cannot be explained in this way: in some cases the standard text of Targum Jonathan is less like the Hebrew text than the liturgical text form or Tosefta Targum. A second problem with such an explanation is the diversity among the textual witnesses of the Tosefta Targums.[29] Nor should we get carried away by 'Palestinian' linguistic features.[30] Such features do not *ipso facto* place a text physically in Palestine. Rather, they show that the text has been transmitted in a setting influenced by the great Palestinian schools.[31] One such setting would be Italy. Equally, the presence of material from the very early rabbinic period could only indicate an early date for the Tosefta Targums if those sources from

---

included in his *Targumic Toseftot to the Prophets*, see chapter eleven.

26 See Houtman and Sysling, *Alternative Targum Traditions*, 41–6.
27 Zunz, *Die gottesdienstlichen Vorträge der Juden historisch entwickelt*, 77–9.
28 As, e.g., Grelot, 'Une Tosephta targoumique sur Zacharie, II, 14–15'. Note Kasher's critique of Grelot (and Sperber, on whose edition his analysis was based) for failing to note additional Tosefta Targums to Zech. 3:1–4:7 in the manuscript (London, British Library, Add. 26879), Kasher, 'התוספתות התרגומיות להפטרת שבת־חנוכה', 27. Also Grelot, 'Deux Toseftas targoumiques inédites sur Isaïe LXVI' (note his correction, Grelot, 'A propos d'une Tosephta targoumique').
29 See discussion of Kasher on Grelot, pages 263–4.
30 As Grelot, 'Le Targum d'Isaïe X, 32–34 dans ses diverses recensions'.
31 Smelik, 'Orality, Manuscript Reproduction, and the Targums', 66–71.

which these traditions are known (e.g. in the case of the Tosefta Targum to 1 Sam. 2:6, the Mishnah) were not also in circulation in much later periods.[32] This is not the case.

The Tosefta Targums do not suggest the existence of a once-complete Palestinian Targum to the Prophets (or even to the haftarot). To my mind, the hypothesis that the Tosefta Targums are secondary, developed from Targum Jonathan itself, accounts more plausibly for the data.[33] The recycling of imagery and expressions from elsewhere in Targum Jonathan in particular indicates that the longer forms of the Tosefta Targum are derivative not original.[34] The variations between textual witnesses suggest that the text circulated widely and was adapted freely in the process of transmission.

---

32 See Kasher, *Targumic Toseftot to the Prophets*, 63–4
33 As Houtman and Sysling concluded in their *Alternative Targum Traditions*, 240–7.
34 Ironically, in his article 'Une Tosephta targoumique sur Zacharie, II, 14–15' Grelot argues that Tg. Tos. Zech. 2:14–15 drew on Tg. Zeph. 3:5, thereby undermining his own argument for the priority of the Tosefta Targum, as Kasher pointed out, see pages 263–4.

Chapter Twelve

Conclusion

1. Summary of Results

The aim of this book has been to identify textual variants in the manuscripts of Targum Jonathan belonging to two textual families (according to the stemmatological analysis) consisting primarily of Italian and Ashkenazi manuscripts and to identify patterns in these variants that might help us understand how and why the text changed in the course of its European transmission.

We began by demonstrating that the text of Targum Samuel has been frequently adapted towards the Hebrew text by replacing, omitting, or adding words that correspond to the Hebrew but that are not represented, or are represented only abstractly, in the Babylonian text tradition (chapter four).

It seems likely that these revisions took place in medieval Europe, with the result that the modified Targum text sometimes reflects variants in the manuscripts of the Hebrew text that circulated in Europe. This phenomenon has resulted in some apparent agreements between medieval European Targum manuscripts and the ancient Versions (chapter five). Although we do not have Hebrew manuscript evidence to support all the variants of this type, it is plausible to assume that at least some further cases might reflect variant Hebrew manuscripts that are now lost or remain unstudied. Equally, many such cases could easily have arisen independently since the Hebrew is in some way perplexing or problematic. In short, there is no real reason to assume that such agreements reflect genuine ancient readings of the Targum.

Given the close link between the Targum and the Hebrew text — not only their textual affinity but also often in terms of their *mise en page* — it is not surprising that the Hebrew text should have influenced the wording of the Targum as it was transmitted. Likewise, since Targum Jonathan forms a coherent textual whole (with Onqelos to some extent), we should also not be surprised to find that commonly-occurring wording in the Targum has seeped through the text over the course of time replacing less commonly-occurring phraseology — a process I describe as 'linguistic osmosis'. Likewise, we saw that the wording is sometimes altered under the influence of language in the immediate literary context (chapter six).

Genuine exegetical modifications of the text proved to be few in number. These were examined in chapter seven, where it was shown that they often reflect traditions that can be found elsewhere in the corpus of Targumic literature and that are reflected in a wide range of sources. These variants could easily have arisen in medieval Europe. A much larger number of those variants that alter the text in deliberate and significant ways simply aim to clarify an obscurity in the text or make explicit what is implied but open to misunderstanding. This is achieved by small additions or the substitution of vocabulary. A few of the apparently deliberate and significant variants seem to reflect the influence of the wording of longer and exegetically richer versions of the text known, for example, from mahzorim (chapter seven).

Finally, we turned our attention from the continuous text of Targum Samuel to materials in different formats that preserve isolated units of the text or units of a text of significantly different character from the standard textual traditions; namely, the marginalia in Codex Reuchlinianus No. 3, Tosefta Targums, and liturgical manuscripts.

Among the marginal notes in Codex Reuchlinianus No. 3 (chapter nine) were found material containing the same sorts of variants that we found in the Italian and Ashkenazi manuscripts of the continuous text, so we proposed that the compiler had consulted a number of locally-available copies of the standard text of Targum Jonathan and had noted any interesting variants under the heading 'Another Version.' He consulted another source that was very similar in character, but contained some longer exegetical and haggadic expansions; he noted the interesting variants and marked them 'Another Book'. In addition, he knew of material of a much richer exegetical character from liturgical texts or in the margins of other codices, which he designated 'Another Targum' or 'Palestinian Targum'. We cannot be sure where or when exactly the full system of marginalia was compiled: it is certainly plausible to assume that this took place in the famous and influential Italian academies, possibly in multiple stages. Nor can we pin down the sources used: there is no clear correspondence to the textual witnesses now known to us and evidence from the codex itself suggests that the compiler's access to sources (or perhaps his use of the sources) was limited.

Chapter Twelve. Conclusion

The longer and exegetically richer materials in the margins of Codex Reuchlinianus No. 3 headed 'Another Targum' or 'Palestinian Targum' share many characteristics with the versions of the text of Targum Samuel of the so-called Tosefta Targums, which are found incorporated into the running text of several of our manuscripts, and with the text found in some liturgies, which preserve a closely-related textual tradition (chapter ten, eleven). There is a great deal of variation among the witnesses to these longer and exegetically richer text forms, but we can nonetheless say that their text is basically that of the standard text of Targum Jonathan with a significant quantity of additional material, as well as many minor variations typical of European Targum manuscripts. Much of the additional material simply 'recycles' wording and ideas prevalent elsewhere in the Targum. In a handful of cases it may be drawn from Pentateuchal Targum traditions that were circulating in Europe. Taken together, one is left with the impression that these longer and exegetically fuller text forms are derived from Targum Jonathan and not *vice versa*.

2. Reflections on Stemma

As I described in chapters one and three, this study has examined a series of manuscripts that form two textual families (Mixed Western and Ashkenazi) as defined by the *stemma codicum* produced on the basis of sample verses. At the end of this study, it is appropriate to offer some reflections on these groupings.

At the time our manuscripts were produced Western Jewry was divided into three principal socio-geographic blocks: Sepharad, Ashkenaz, and — closely related to Ashkenaz — Italy. While far from being homogenous, the communities in each of these zones enjoyed a degree of cultural uniformity. Consequently, we might expect manuscripts copied in each of these zones to reflect local variations. In general terms this is the pattern that emerges from the stemmatological analysis. As I explained in chapter three, the *stemma codicum* produced by van Staalduine-Sulman was based solely on variants in the text, rather than on any external factors such as the script, codicology, provenance, etc. That the resulting stemma agrees to a large extent with a grouping of the manuscripts based on such external factors suggests that the stemmatological analysis is broadly accurate. The Mixed Western group, however, presents something of an anomaly. It contains mostly Ashkenazi manuscripts, plus two Italian manuscripts and one Sephardi manuscript. What are we to make of this?

First, as I pointed out earlier (pages 69–70), the relationship between the Ashkenazi manuscripts and the Italian manuscripts is not unexpected: the two communities were extremely closely linked. The presence of a Sephardi manuscript (t232i/s) is much more problematic. The Sephardi world was not entirely cut off from the Ashkenazi and Italian worlds of course, so contamination across these cultural boundaries is possible. This, however, is not what has happened in the case of t232i/s. The presence of this manuscript in the Mixed Western group is the result of inherent weaknesses in the production of a stemma of the Western texts. Why?

Both the groups that have been examined in this book lack internal coherence. There are almost no readings that are shared exclusively by all the textual witnesses of either of the two groups. Some manuscripts within each group are very closely related (in particular t2i to t3i; t701i to t705i; t720a to t713a),[1] but there is also a significant number of agreements between manuscripts belonging to different groups: t725a, for example, shares a number of distinct readings with t2i.[2] It is possible, therefore, that these manuscripts adhere together more because they differ from the other groups than because of their mutual likeness.[3]

A further difficulty arises from the patterns of change that have been identified within the manuscript in these two groups. The influence of the Hebrew text, commonly occurring wording, and the surrounding literary context — even many of the clarifying glosses we observed in chapter seven — could easily have arisen independently in more than one manuscript, so their significance for establishing the genealogical relationship between texts is seriously diminished (perhaps even to the point of zero). Among all the significant variants that we identified, these types of changes constitute the overwhelming majority. Equally, features such as the presence or absence of the copula or the addition or omission of idiomatic phrases such as 'the house

---

[1] Confirming the analysis of van Staalduine-Sulman, 'An Electronic Edition of Targum Samuel', 30–2.

[2] To give just a few examples: chapter 5: 1 Sam 25:1; 2 Sam. 4:7; 11:7; chapter 6: 1 Sam. 8:1; 29:6; 2 Sam. 13:6; chapter 7: 2 Sam. 5:3; etc.

[3] As Houtman suggested for the 'Ashkenazi' group of manuscripts of the Targum of Isaiah; Houtman, 'Textual Tradition of Targum Jonathan to Isaiah', 152.

Chapter Twelve. Conclusion

of [Israel/Judah/Benjamin/etc]' — features noted alongside many others by van Staalduine-Sulman as distinguishing the Ashkenazi text-family from the other text families[4] — are meaningless for the purposes of forming the stemma. They fluctuate far too frequently.

Two further phenomena found in the Ashkenazi manuscripts raise important questions for the use in forming the *stemma codicum*: 1) some manuscripts have been copied from one *Vorlage*, but corrected against another; and, 2) some manuscripts combine the readings of more than one *Vorlage* into a single text. These two phenomena have been dealt with in chapter three. The former is unmistakably present in manuscript t6a, and probably in t5a too; the latter is more common in manuscripts t713a, t6a, t5a, and t2i.

On this basis, one might characterise the transmission of the Targum in the West as exhibiting a limited degree of consistency within socio-geographic entities and over time, but lacking homogeneity generally as a result of repeated modification of the text and through continual cross-contamination of traditions.

In her analysis of the stemma van Staalduine-Sulman concludes:

> Taking into account the diversity of the other manuscripts (Italian, Sephardic, Ashkenazic, Rabbinic Bibles), we must assume that the text of Targum Samuel made its entrance into North Africa and Europe in at least four different stages. One led to the Italian tradition, a second one to the Solger Codex and the other two to the richer Sephardic and Ashkenazic traditions. Contamination led to more similarities between these Western traditions.[5]

It should by now be clear that the textual situation is more complicated than this and that this model now requires some rethinking. The lack of consistency between the Italian and Ashkenazi manuscripts and the evidence of cross-contamination (at least in some manuscripts) makes an 'Italian' (read 'Mixed Western') and a separate 'Ashkenazi' *Urtext* (as van Staalduine-Sulman implies) unlikely. Copies of Targum Jonathan in a form more or less resembling the Babylonian textual tradition (at least in its consonants) could equally have arrived in Italy and Ashkenaz from the East (possibly via Palestine) in several stages. As these manuscripts were copied through

---

4 I.e. 'typical variant readings of the Ashkenazic tradition, not occurring in other traditions'; van Staalduine-Sulman, 'An Electronic Edition of Targum Samuel', 34–5.
5 van Staalduine-Sulman, 'An Electronic Edition of Targum Samuel', 24–5.

successive generations, and as they circulated around Italy and in the Ashkenazi zone, the text was modified, sometimes deliberately, sometimes accidentally, and alternative readings known from other manuscripts (or perhaps from citations, or even memory) were absorbed into the text so that eventually the text degraded to the point that its Eastern character was lost.

3. Implications

The point arising from what has just been said that needs to be stressed is that the analysis suggests that the textual variants in the Italian and Ashkenazi manuscripts (we leave out t232i/s for the time being) arose sporadically and haphazardly over many generations as the text was transmitted in Europe. In other words, the bulk of the variants entered the text in Europe in the Middle Ages. Some of the material that became incorporated into the continuous text, such as the Tosefta Targums, may have had its origins in Palestine, but there is no real reason to doubt that it was incorporated into the continuous text in Europe, where the bulk of the revisionary activity took place, during the Middle Ages. Its presence in the continuous text cannot, therefore, justify a generalisation, such as that of Martin: 'Targum Jonathan in its Tiberian form probably arose from a conflation of the old Palestinian form and the Babylonian form'.[6] This is misleading.

This fits well with the picture of Targum Jonathan's function and status in medieval Italy and Ashkenaz that emerged in chapter two. It is clear that Targum Jonathan enjoyed a respected — 'semi-canonical' if you like — status. The text has changed in its European transmission, but it has not changed in dramatic ways. It is of quite a different order from, for example, the Hekhalot literature, many of the midrashim, or Targum Pseudo-Jonathan, whose transmission was extremely fluid. The text retained its basic shape. Yet at the same time its status remained somewhat ambiguous and there were no formal strictures to ensure unaltered transmission. So we find some embellishments and alterations, but the creative input is extremely limited. Comments such as those of Harrington and Saldarini (who liken Targum Jonathan's transmission

---

6 Martin, 'The Babylonian Tradition and Targum', 434. Cf. also my comments on Ho's view that some readings in Western texts reflected the Palestinian version that had survived the Babylonian redaction, pages 49–52.

to that of the Hekhalot literature) are wild exaggerations, quite detached from the textual reality; they write: 'The individual manuscripts of what we call *Targum Jonathan* tend almost to constitute separate works. The process by which these works were shaped was so varied and fluid that the search for 'one' text or the 'original' text may be illusionary'.[7]

If it is correct to conclude that the majority of the textual variants in Italian and Ashkenazi manuscripts arose in Italy and the Ashkenazi zone in the Middle Ages then the value of these variants for reconstructing the earliest recoverable form of Targum Jonathan is extremely limited — I might even dare to say nil. This has significant implications for their use in text-criticism of the Hebrew Bible. At best, variants in Ashkenazi and Italian Targum manuscripts may act as a secondary witness to a variant medieval Hebrew manuscript circulating in those areas. The value of variant medieval Hebrew manuscripts is open to discussion: I judge them to be of limited value, but others will disagree. In any case, if Hebrew manuscript support is lacking, variant readings in European Targum manuscripts should be used in text-criticism of the Hebrew Bible with extreme caution, if at all. If they are to be used, the critic must ask whether the variant could have arisen independently as a result of the revisionary pressures this study has identified.

Another important implication from this study is that we evidently only have in our possession a tiny fraction of the materials containing Targum Jonathan (or a variant version thereof) that must once have existed. Despite their similarity in terms of their character, the marginal notes under the heading 'Another Version' in Codex Reuchlinianus No. 3 show no significant correspondence to any of our known manuscripts. In fact most of the marginalia in this codex are unknown from any other source. Equally, I have checked all the examples that I have discussed against the 'lost Targums' collected by Goshen Gottstein. Again there is no correspondence.[8] All of this suggests that further archival research could well prove rewarding (particularly if the continuous alternative Targum version behind the notes entitled 'Another Book' in Codex Reuchlinianus No. 3 could be found).

---

7 Harrington and Saldarini, *Targum Jonathan of the Former Prophets*, 2.
8 At least some of these variant readings reflect an Ashkenazi origin; Goshen-Gottstein, *Fragments of Lost Targumim*, Intro xx.

4. A Future Edition of Targum Jonathan

The need for a new critical edition will be recognised by all who work with Targum Jonathan. In 2004 the International Organisation for Targumic Studies adopted a proposal establishing the International Targum Text Edition Project, which, it is hoped, will in time turn this ambition into a reality. Before work on the planned new editions could begin some preliminary analytical work on the extant witnesses was necessary. This study aims to address that necessity. So what sort of a role might the manuscripts we have studied play in any future critical edition of Targum Jonathan? If they are of little or no value for recovering the Targum's original form, why include them at all?

Any edition deserving the name *critical* must aim to be as comprehensive as possible. This is axiomatic. But the inclusion of Western manuscripts is also justified because readers may well reach different conclusions about their text-critical value than that which has been proposed in this book. Furthermore, text-critical value is not the only sort of value that a manuscript may have. The Western Targum manuscripts are of great interest from a text-historical point of view. These, after all, were the versions of the text that medieval European Jews read, heard, and cited in their own literature. Access to the variant readings in European manuscripts will aid scholars of medieval European Jewish literature and culture.

When it comes to grouping the manuscripts for the purpose of a critical edition I would suggest that it is adequate to group the manuscripts based on their provenance — at least for the Western manuscripts — rather than undertaking the costly and time-consuming process of forming a *stemma codicum* on the basis of variants in the texts themselves, though I accept that this is a pragmatic, rather than a strictly scientific position. The work involved in evaluating each individual variant to decide whether or not it could be used to establish a genetic relationship is both prohibitive and unlikely to achieve incontestable results, as we have seen. Furthermore, the stemmatological analysis that has been undertaken for various books has led, with only a few questionable exceptions (such as t232i/s), to groupings that broadly reflect the socio-geographical divisions by which a manuscript's provenance is usually defined. The lack of strong coherence between the Italian and Ashkenazi manuscripts means that a grouping based on provenance is at least as likely to prove an adequate point of departure as a *stemma codicum*.

Chapter Twelve. Conclusion

Among these groupings, texts belonging to the Babylonian group ought to serve as the base text for any new edition. Sperber's base text (i.e. t711y) has been influenced by the Western text in both its vocalisation and its consonants, as we have seen throughout this book. A better base text is required. Thankfully the work of preparing such a text has already been completed for many of the books of Targum Jonathan, as was outlined in chapter one. The Western manuscripts have their rightful place in the *apparatus criticus*. In presenting the Western manuscripts the editor will need to select carefully among the myriad of available variants. Most are mere errors, which can safely be ignored. The same is true of the vocalisation, except where it preserves some particularly noteworthy characteristic. The non-erroneous readings on the other hand should be presented exhaustively. Furthermore, we must treat each manuscript individually. The lack of homogeneity among Western manuscripts suggests they do not go back to a Western prototype. Rather they reflect a situation in which the text has been subject to years of development and cross-fertilisation between textual traditions, a situation that endured over a long period of time in different regions with no sense that the text should be transmitted in exact replica. Any attempt to reconstruct the 'Ashkenazi' prototype (*Urtext*) is likely to be chasing after wind. Nor can we justifiably adopt a single manuscript as the best representative of a tradition. The Western traditions are too diverse for that.[9]

What of the liturgical texts and Tosefta Targums? The Ashkenazi mahzorim and haftarot collections preserve a text that differs from the Babylonian textual tradition no more than the Ashkenazi manuscripts containing the continuous text do. These can be treated alongside the witnesses of the continuous text. The Italian mahzorim by contrast contain a longer text that is essentially indistinguishable in character from the Tosefta Targums that have been incorporated into the running text in our manuscripts, and for which the term Tosefta Targum is wholly appropriate. These sources do not take us back to a form of the Targum that pre-dates the Babylonian redaction. Rather they are derived from that redacted form. Their value for reconstructing the original form of the Targum is therefore virtually zero, but they are nonetheless a wonderfully rich source for understanding the ongoing exegetical engagement with the text. No edition would be complete without them, but they present a

---

9   Cf. Houtman's comments in her 'Textual Tradition of Targum Jonathan to Isaiah', 153.

real challenge as to how one might best present them. The number of manuscripts is vast and the textual transmission extremely fluid, so a practical selection will need to be made. This will be determined by the text in question. Some (for example many of those found in Codex Reuchlinianus No. 3) are known from only one source, while others are preserved in multiple manuscripts with a great deal of variation, as we saw in chapter ten.

Chapter Thirteen

Bibliography

Primary Sources (Editions)

Caspi, J., *Commentary on Samuel* — according to the edition of M. Cohen (ed.), *Mikra'ot Gedolot 'Haketer* (Ramat-Gan 1993).

Cohen, M. (ed.), *Mikra'ot Gedolot 'Haketer: A Revised and Augmented Scientific Edition of 'Mikra'ot Gedolot' based on the Aleppo Codex and early Medieval Manuscripts; Samuel I & II.* (Ramat-Gan 1993).

de Lagarde, P., *Hagiographa chaldaice* (Leipzig 1873).

—— *Prophetae chaldice e fide Codicis Reuchliniani* (Leipzig 1872).

Fernández Marcos, N. and J. Ramón Busto Saiz (eds), *El texto antioqueno de la Biblia griega,* I, *1–2 Samuel* (Textos y Estudios 'Cardenal Cisneros' 50, Madrid 1989).

Hebrew Text — Elliger, K. and W. Rudolph et al., *Biblia Hebraica Stuttgartensia* (Deutsche Bibelgesellschaft, 5th ed, Stuttgart 1997). Occassionally reference is made to Dotan, A. (ed.), *Biblia Hebraica Leningradensia: Prepared According to the Vocalization, Accents, and Masora of Aaron ben Moses ben Asher in the Leningrad Codex* (Peabody, MA 2001).

Isaac ben Moses of Vienna, ספר אור זרוע (Zhitomir 1862).

Isaiah di Trani, *Commentary on Samuel,* – according to the edition of M. Cohen (ed.), *Mikra'ot Gedolot 'Haketer.*

Isaiah the Elder of Terrani, *Piskei HaRid: the Rulings of Rabbi Isaiah the Elder* [in Hebrew] (Jerusalem 1966).

—— *Teshuvot HaRid: the Responsa of Rabbi Isaiah the Elder* [in Hebrew], ed. A.J. Wertheimer (Jerusalem 1967).

Jacob b. Moses Moellin (מהרי"ל), *Responsa of Rabbi Yaacov Molin - Maharil,* ed. Yitzchok Satz [in Hebrew] (Jerusalem 1979).

—— *New Responsa of Rabbi Yaacov Molin – Maharil,* ed. Y. Satz [in Hebrew] (Jerusalem 1977).

Jacob of Marvège, שאלות ותשובות מן השמיים, ed. R. Margaliot (Jerusalem 1957).

Kara, J., *Commentary on Samuel* – according to the edition of M. Cohen (ed.), *Mikra'ot Gedolot 'Haketer* (Ramat-Gan 1993).

Kimhi, D., *Commentary on Samuel* – according to the edition of M. Cohen (ed.), *Mikra'ot Gedolot 'Haketer* (Ramat-Gan 1993).

Lucifer of Cagliari, *De Athanasio*: Diercks, G.F. (ed.), *Luciferi calaritani opera quae supersunt* (Corpus Christianorum Series Latina 8. Turnhout 1978).

Mahzor Vitry: Hurwitz, S. (ed.), מחזור ויטרי לרבינו שמחה (Jerusalem 1963).

Meir ben Baruch of Rothenburg, שאלות ותשובות מהר"ם מרוטנבורג (Sudilkov 1835).

Nathan ben Yehiel, *Aruch completum,* ed. A. Kohut (New York 1955).

Old Latin — Morano Rodríguez, Ciriaca, *Glosas marginales de Vetus Latina en las Biblias Vulgatas españolas: 1–2 Samuel* (Textos y Estudios 'Cardenal Cisneros' de la Biblia Políglota Matritense 48, Madrid 1989); F. Marcos, and B. Saiz (eds), *El texto antioqueno de la Biblia griega* (see separate entry); Lucifer of Cagliari (see separate entry); Fischer, 'Palimpsestus Vindobonensis (see separate entry).

Peshitta — The Peshitta Institute Leiden (ed), *The Old Testament in Syriac According to the*

Peshitta Version, II.2, *Judges–Samuel* (Leiden 1978).
Rashi, *Commentary on Samuel* – according to the edition of M. Cohen (ed.), *Mikra'ot Gedolot 'Haketer.*
Septuagint — Brooke, A. England, N. McLean and H. St.J. Thackeray (eds), *The Old Testament in Greek: According to the Text of Codex Vaticanus, Supplemented from Other Uncial Manuscripts, with a Critical Apparatus Containing the Variants of the Chief Ancient Authorities for the Text of the Septuagint, Vol. 2, Part 1, I and II Samuel* (Cambridge 1927). In some cases (indicated in the text): A. Rahlfs (ed.), *Septuaginta, I, Leges et Historiae* (Stuttgart 1962).
Targum (Babylonian tradition) — Martínez Borobio, E. (ed.), *Targum Jonatan de los Profetas Primeros en tradición babilónica*, Vol. 3, *I–II Reyes* (Textos y Estudios 'Cardenal Cisneros' 63, Madrid 1998).
—— (ed.), *Targum Jonatan de los Profetas Primeros en tradición babilónica*, Vol. 1, *Josué – Jueces* (Textos y Estudios 'Cardenal Cisneros' 46, Madrid 1989).
—— (ed.), *Targum Jonatan de los Profetas Primeros en tradición babilónica*, Vol. 2, *I–II Samuel* (Textos y Estudios 'Cardenal Cisneros' 38, Madrid 1987).
Targum (Sperber) — Sperber, A. (ed.), *The Bible in Aramaic Based on Old Manuscripts and Printed Texts, Vol. II, The Former Prophets According to Targum Jonathan* (Leiden 1959).
Targum Esther II — B. Grossfeld, *The Targum Sheni to the Book of Esther: a Critical Edition Based on MS. Sassoon 282 with Critical Apparatus* (New York 1994).
Tosafot — Steinsalz, A., תלמוד בבלי (Jerusalem 2012).
Vulgate — Gryson, R. (ed.), *Biblia Sacra Iuxta Vulgatam Versionem* (Stuttgart 1994).
References in rabbinic and medieval Jewish literature were located using: Bar-Ilan University, *The Global Jewish Database: The Responsa Project* (online).

Secondary Literature

Adler, M., 'A Specimen of a Commentary and Collated Text of the Targum to the Prophets. Nahum', *Jewish Quarterly Review* 7:4 (1895), 630–57.
Alexander, P.S., 'Jewish Aramaic Translations of Hebrew Scriptures', in M.J. Mulder (ed.) *Mikra: Text, Translation, Reading and Interpretation of the Hebrew Bible in Ancient Judaism and Early Christianity* (Peabody, MA 2004 [1988]), 217–53.
—— *The Targum of Lamentations: Translated, with a Critical Introduction, Apparatus, and Notes* (The Aramaic Bible 17B. Collegeville, MI 2008).
Aptowitzer, V., *Das Schriftwort in der rabbinischen Literatur*, Parts I–III (Sitzungsberichte Akademie der Wissenschaften in Wien. Philosophisch-Historische Klasse Bd. 153, Nr. 6, Bd. 160, Nr. 7, Vienna 1906–11).
Assemanus, S.E. and .S. Assemanus, *Bibliothecæ apostolicæ vaticanæ, Codicum manuscriptorum, Catalogus*, I, *Codices Ebraicos et Samaritanos* (Paris 1926 [1761]).
Attia, E., 'Targum Layout in Ashkenazic Hebrew Manuscripts: Preliminary Methodological Observations, in A. Houtman, H.-M. Kirn and E. van Staalduine-Sulman (eds), *A Jewish Targum in a Christian World* (Jewish and Christian Perspectives 27, Leiden 2014), 99–122.
Bacher, W., 'Targum', in C. Adler and I. Singer (eds), *The Jewish Encyclopedia* (New York/ London 1906), Vol. 12, 57–63.
—— 'Isaie, liv, 7', *Revue des Études Juives* 44 (1902), 283–5.
——'Notes on the Critique of the Text of the Targum of the Prophets', *Jewish Quarterly Review* 11 (1899), 651–5.
—— 'Gegenbemerkungen und Nachträge das Prophetentargum betreffend', *Zeitschriften der Deutschen Morgenländischen Gesellschaft* 29 (1875), 319–21.

Chapter Thirteen. Bibliography

—— 'Kritische Untersuchungen zum Prophetentargum nebst einem Anhange über das gegenseitige Verhältniss der pentateuchischen Targumim', *Zeitschriften der Deutschen Morgenländischen Gesellschaft* 28 (1874), 1–72.

—— 'Alte aramäische Poesien zum Vortrage des Haphtara-Targum', *Monatsschrift für die Geschichte und Wissenschaft des Judenthums* 22:5 (1873), 220–8.

Barnes, W.E., 'The Targum on the Later Prophets', *Journal of Theological Studies* 28 (1927), 283–5.

Barol, M, 'Menachem ben Simon aus Posquieres und sein Kommentar zu Jeremia und Ezechiel', *Monatsschrift für Geschichte und Wissenschaft des Judentums* 51:2 (1907), 183–204.

Barthélemy, D., *Critique textuelle de l'Ancien Testament*, I, *Josué, Juges, Ruth, Samuel, Rois, Chroniques, Esdras, Néhémie, Esther* (Orbis Biblicus et Orientalis 50/1, Fribourg and Göttingen 1982).

—— *Critique textuelle de l'Ancien Testament*, II, 2: *Isaïe, Jérémie, Lamentations* (Orbis Biblicus et Orientalis 50/2. Fribourg and Göttingen 1986).

—— *Critique textuelle de l'Ancien Testament*, III, *Ézéchiel, Daniel et les 12 Prophètes* (Orbis Biblicus et Orientalis 50/3. Fribourg and Göttingen 1992).

Baskin, J.R., 'Rabbinic-Patristic Exegetical Contacts in Late Antiquity: A Bibliographical Reappraisal', in W. Scott Green (ed.), *Approaches to Ancient Judaism*, Vol. 5, *Studies in Judaism and its Greco-Roman Context* (Brown Judaic Studies 32, Atlanta, GA 1985), 53–80.

Beit-Arié, M., 'The Script and Book Craft in the Hebrew Medieval Codex', in P. van Boxel and S. Arndt (eds), *Crossing Borders: Hebrew Manuscripts as a Meeting-place of Cultures* (Oxford 2009), 21–34.

—— and E. Engel, *Specimens of Medieval Hebrew Scripts*, Vol. II, *Sefardic Script* (Jerusalem 2002).

—— *Hebrew Manuscripts of East and West: Towards a Comparative Codicology. The Panizzi Lectures 1992* (London 1993).

—— 'The Worms Mahzor: its History and its Paleography and Codicological Characteristics', in M. Beit-Arié (ed.), *Worms Mahzor: MS. Jewish National and University Library Heb 4⁰781/1. Introductory Volume* (Jerusalem 1985), 13–35.

—— *The Makings of the Medieval Hebrew Book: Studies in Palaeography and Codicology* (Jerusalem 1993).

—— *Hebrew Codicology: Tentative Typology of Technical Practices Employed in Hebrew Dated Medieval Manuscripts* (Jerusalem 1981 [1976]).

Berger, D., 'Three Typological Themes in Early Jewish Messianism: Messiah Son of Joseph, Rabbinic Calculations, and the Figure of Armilus', *Association for Jewish Studies Review* 10:2 (1985), 141–64.

Berger, M., 'Rabbi Samuel Ben Meir's attitude toward Midrash', in H. Blumberg et al. (eds), *"Open Thou Mine Eyes..." Essays on Aggadah and Judaica Presented to Rabbi William G. Braude on his Eightieth Birthday and Dedicated to his Memory* (Hoboken, NJ 1992), 21–40.

Berliner, A., *Beiträge zur Geschichte der Raschi-Commentare* (Berlin 1903).

—— *Targum Onkelos*, Vol 1 (Berlin 1884).

—— *Targum Onkelos*, Vol 2, *Noten, Einleitung und Register* (Berlin 1884).

Bernheimer, C., *Codices hebraici bybliothecae Ambrosianae* (Florence 1933).

—— *Paleografia ebraica* (Firenze 1924).

Beyer, K., *The Aramaic Language, its Distribution and Subdivisions* (trans. J.F. Healey; Göttingen 1986).

Blenkinsopp, J., *Isaiah 1–39* (Anchor Bible 19, London 2000).

Bonfil, R., *Jewish Life in Renaissance Italy* (trans. Anthony Oldcorn; Berkeley, CA 1994).

Bons, E., J. Joosten and S. Kessler (eds), *La Bible d'Alexandrie*, Vol. 23:1, *Les Douze Prophètes; Osée* (Paris 2002).

The Transmission of Targum Jonathan in the West

Brambach, W., *Die Handschriften der Badischen Landesbibliothek in Karlsruhe, II, Orientalische Handschriften: Neudruck mit bibliographischen Nachträgen* (Wiesbaden 1970 [1892]).

Brandt, P., *Endgestalten des Kanons: das Arrangement der Schriften Israels in der jüdischen und christlichen Bibel* (Bonner biblische Beiträge 131, Berlin 2001).

Brock, S., *The Recensions of the Septuagint Version of I Samuel* (Torino 1996).

Brockington, L.H., 'Septuagint and Targum', *Zeitschrift für die alttestamentliche Wissenschaft* 66 (1954), 80–6.

—— Review of 'J.F. Stenning, The Targum of Isaiah (Oxford: Clarendon Press, 1949)', *The Journal of Theological Studies* (New Series) 1:1 (1950), 88–9.

Bromberg, A.Y., 'האם ראה רש"י תרגום יונתן בן עוזיאל' *Sinai* 57:1–2 (Year 29: 1965), 91.

Brown, J.P., 'The Septuagint as a Source of the Greek Loan-words in the Targums', *Biblica* 70:2 (1989), 194–216.

Büchler, A., 'The Reading of the Law and Prophets in a Triennial Cycle. II', *Jewish Quarterly Review* 6:1 (1893), 1–73.

Chilton, B., 'HEBR. 75 in the Bibliothèque Nationale', in Paul V.M. Flesher (ed.), *Targum and Scripture: Studies in Aramaic Translations and Interpretation in Memory of Ernest G. Clarke* (Studies in the Aramaic Interpretation of Scripture 2, Leiden 2002), 141–8.

—— *The Isaiah Targum: Introduction, Translation, Apparatus and Notes* (The Aramaic Bible 11, Edinburgh 1987).

Churgin, P., 'The Targum and the Septuagint', *The American Journal of Semitic Languages and Literatures* 50:1 (1933), 41–65.

—— 'Targum Jonathan to the Prophets', in L. Smolar and M. Aberbach, *Studies in Targum Jonathan to the Prophets* (New York 1983 [1927]), 229–380.

Clarke, E.G., 'The Neofiti I Marginal Glosses and the Fragmentary Targum Witnesses to Gen. VI–IX', *Vetus Testamentum* 22 (1972), 257–65.

Cohen, J., *The Friars and the Jews: The Evolution of Medieval Anti-Judaism* (Ithaca, NY 1982).

Cook, E., 'The "Kaufman Effect" in the Pseudo-Jonathan Targum', *Aramaic Studies* 4:2 (2006), 123–32.

—— 'Rewriting the Bible: the Text and Language of the Pseudo-Jonathan Targum', unpublished Ph.D. dissertation (University of California 1986).

Cornill, C.H., *Das Buch des Propheten Ezechiel* (Leipzig 1886).

—— 'Das Targum zu den Propheten', *Zeitschrift für die alttestamentliche Wissenschaft* 7 (1887), 177–202.

Coxe, Henry Octavius, *Catalogus codicum mss. qui in collegiis aulisque Oxoniensibus hodie adservantur*, Vol. 2 (Oxford 1852).

Dalman, G., *Grammatik des Jüdisch-Palästinischen Aramäisch: nach den Idiomen des Palästinischen Talmud des Onkelostargum und Prophetentargum und der Jerusalemischen Targume: Aramäische Dialektproben* (Darmstadt 1978 [1927]).

Damsma, A., *The Targumic Toseftot to Ezekiel* (Studies in Aramaic Interpretation of Scripture 13, Leiden 2012).

—— 'An Analysis of Targum Ezekiel and its Relationship to the Targumic Toseftot', Ph.D. dissertation (University College London 2008).

Dan, J., The Hebrew Story in the Middle Ages [in Hebrew] (Siffrut 5, Jerusalem 1974).

de Boer, P.A.H., review of 'M.H. Goshen-Gottstein, *The Book of Isaiah, Sample Edition with Introduction* (Jerusalem: The Hebrew University Bible Project, 1965)', *Vetus Testamentum* 16:2 (1966), 247–52.

—— *Research into the Text of I Samuel I–XVI: a Contribution to the Study of the Books of Samuel* (Amsterdam 1938).

Chapter Thirteen. Bibliography

de Lagarde, P., *Prophetae chaldaice e fide codicis Reuchliniani* (Leipzig 1872).

—— *Symmicta*, 2 Vols (Göttingen 1877).

de Moor, J.C., et al. (eds), *A Bilingual Concordance to the Targum of the Prophets*, 21 Vols (Leiden 1995–2005).

—— and F. Sepmeijer, 'The Peshitta and the Targum of Joshua', in P.B.Dirksen and A.van der Kooij (eds), *The Peshitta as a Translation: Papers Read at the II Peshitta Symposium held at Leiden 19–21 August 1993* (Monographs of the Peshitta Institute Leiden 8, Leiden 1995), 129–76.

Delekat, L., 'Ein Septuagintatargum', *Vetus Testamentum* 8 (1958), 225–52.

Delitzsch, F., *Liber Jeremiae* (ed. S. Baer; Leipzig 1890).

de Rossi, A., *The Light of the Eyes* (trans. Joanna Weinberg; New Haven 2001).

de Rossi, J.B., *Variae lectiones veteris testamenti ex immensa Mss. editorumq. codicum congerie haustae et ad samar. textum, ad vetustiss. versiones, ad accuratiores sacrae criticae fontes ac leges examinatae*, Vols 1–2 (Parma 1785).

—— *Scholia critica in V. T. libros sue supplementa ad varias sacri textus lectiones* (Parma 1798).

Deutsch, E., *Literary Remains of the Late Emanuel Deutsch, with a Brief Memoir* (London 1874).

Diamond, C.B., 'The Dependence of Rashi and Kimhi on Targum in their Commentaries on Amos', unpublished MA thesis (Hebrew Union College 1963).

di Capua, A., 'Catalogo dei codici ebraici della bibliotheca Angelica', in *Cataloghi dei codici orientali di alcune biblioteche d'Italia* (Firenze 1878), 85–103

Díez Macho, A., 'Nueva fuente para el Targum Palestino del día séptimo de Pascua y primero de Pentecostés', *Salmanticensis* 28 (1981) 235–57.

—— Review of 'Alexander Sperber, *The Bible in Aramaic*, IV B, *The Targum and the Hebrew Bible* (Leiden: Brill, 1973)', *Journal for the Study of Judaism* 6:2 (1975), 217–36.

—— 'Un nuevo manuscrito del Targum Fragmentario', in L. Álvarez Verdes and E.J. Alonso Hernández (eds), *Homenaje a Juan Prado: miscelánea de estudios bíblicos y hebraicos* (Madrid 1975).

—— *Targum to the Former Prophets: Codex New York 229 from the Library of the Jewish Theological Seminary of America* [in Hebrew] (Jerusalem 1974).

—— *El Targum: introducción a las traducciones aramaicas de la Biblia* (Barcelona 1972).

—— *Manuscritos hebreos y arameos de la Biblia: contribución al estudio de las diversas tradiciones del texto del Antiguo Testamento* (Studia Ephemeridis 'Augustinianum' 5, Rome 1971).

—— 'Manuscritos babilónicos de la Biblia procedentes del Yemen, II (Textos Arameos)', *Augustinianum* 9 (1969), 427–545.

—— *Neophyti 1: Targum Palestinense; Ms de la biblioteca Vaticana*, Vol. 1, *Génesis* (Madrid and Barcelona 1968).

—— 'A New List of the So-called 'Ben Naftali' Manuscripts, Preceded by an Inquiry into the True Character of these Manuscripts', in G. Rolles Driver, D. Winton Thomas and W. Duff McHardy (eds), *Hebrew and Semitic Studies: Presented to Godfrey Rolles Driver, in Celebration of his Seventieth Birthday 20 August 1962* (London 1963), 16–52.

—— with J.A.G. Larraya, 'El Ms. 4083 f. 9 de la biblioteca nacional y universitaria de Estrasburgo: Fragmento de Amós 1.8–3.7, en Hebreo y Targum babilónicos', *Estudios Biblicos* 19 (1960), 91–5.

—— with J.A.G. Larraya, 'El Ms. 4084 ff. I–II de la biblioteca nacional y universitaria de Estrasburgo: un largo fragmento del Targum de Jonathan ben 'Uzziel en texto babilonico', *Estudios Biblicos* 19 (1960), 75–90, 361–8.

—— 'A New Fragment of Isaiah with Babylonian Pointing', *Textus* 1 (1960), 132–43.

—— 'The Recently Discovered Palestinian Targum: its Antiquity and Relationship with the Other

Targums', in *Congress Volume, Oxford, 1959* (Supplements to Vetus Testamentum 7, Leiden 1960), 222–45.

—— 'Onqelos Manuscript with Babylonian Transliterated Vocalization in the Vatican library (Ms. Eb. 448)', *Vetus Testamentum* 8 (1958), 113–33.

—— 'Un segundo fragmento del Targum Palestinense a los Profetas', *Biblica* 39 (1958), 198–205, 229–36.

—— 'Importants manuscrits hébreux et araméens aux États Unis', International Organization of Old Testament Scholars, *Volume du Congrès, Strasbourg 1956* (Supplements to Vetus Testamentum 4, Leiden 1957).

—— 'Valiosos manuscritos bíblicos en la biblioteca nacional y universitaria de Estrasburgo', *Estudios Biblicos* 16 (1957), 83–8.

—— 'Nuevos manuscritos bíblicos babilónicos', *Estudios Biblicos* 16 (1957), 235–77.

—— 'Un manuscrito yemeni de la Biblia babilonica: el Ms. 299 (Emc.105) del Seminario Teologico Judio de Nueva York', *Sefarad* 17 (1957), 237–79.

—— 'Nuevos manuscritos importantes, biblicos o liturgicos, en Hebreo o Arameo', *Sefarad* 16 (1956), 3–22.

—— 'Un nuevo Targum a los Profetas', *Estudios Biblicos* 15 (1956), 287–95.

—— 'Fragmentos de una nueva recension del Targum Jonatan ben 'Uzziel a los Profetas (=T.-S. B 12_1)', *Sefarad* 16 (1956), 405–6.

—— 'Nuevos fragmentos de Tosefta Targumica', *Sefarad* 16 (1956), 313–24.

—— 'Importante hallazgo bíblico.' *Estudios Bíblicos* 13 (1954), 207–10.

Díez Merino, L., 'La Biblia aramea completa de la Universidad de Salamanca', *Helmantica* (2001), 173–227.

—— 'Targum del profeta Zacarías en la tradición sefardí', *Aula Orientalis* 17–18 (1999–2000), 269–85.

—— 'Mahzor Vitry and the Palestinian Targum to the Prophets', in U. Hoxen, H. Trautner-Kromann and K.L. Goldschmidt Salamon (eds), *Jewish Studies in a New Europe: Proceedings of the Fifth Congress of Jewish Studies in Copenhagen 1994* (Copenhagen 1998), 199–211.

—— 'Targum Manuscripts and Critical Editions', in D.R.G. Beattie and M.J. McNamara (eds), *The Aramaic Bible: Targums in their Historical Context* (Journal for the Study of the Old Testament Supplement Series 166, Sheffield 1994), 51–91.

—— 'La triple recensión del Targum a los Profetas (babilónica, yemení y palestina) con sus tres tradiciones (babilónica, yemení y tiberiense)', in H. Merklein, K. Müller and G. Stemberger (eds), *Bibel in jüdischer und christlicher Tradition: Festschrift für Johann Maier zum 60 Geburtstag* (Bonner biblische Beiträge 88, Frankfurt am Main 1993), 275–98.

—— 'Fidelity and Editorial Work in the Complutensian Targum Tradition', in J.A. Emerton (ed.), *Congress Volume - Leuven 1989* (Supplements to Vetus Testamentum 43, Leiden 1991), 360–82.

—— 'Los discípulos de la escuela targúmica de la Universidad de Barcelona', *Henoch* 13 (1991), 65–92.

—— 'Los fundadores de la escuela targúmica de la Universidad de Barcelona', *Henoch* 12 (1990), 77–97.

—— 'El profesor Alejandro Díez Macho y los estudios aramaico-targúmicos (12-V-1916 a 6-X-1984)', *Estudios Bíblicos* 43 (1985), 5–56.

—— 'Los manuscritos targúmicos españoles', in R. Aguirre and F. García López (eds), *Escritos de Biblia y oriente: miscelánea conmemorativa del 25.o aniversario del Instituto Español Bíblico y Arqueológico* (Casa de Santiago) de Jerusalén (Bibliotheca Salmanticensis. Estudios 38, Salamanca 1981), 359–86.

Chapter Thirteen. Bibliography

───── 'Targum al Cantar de los Cantares (texto arameo del Códice Urbinati 1 y su traducción)', *Anuario de Filología* 7 (1981), 237–84.

───── 'La Biblia aramea de Alfonso de Zamora', *Cuadernos bíblicos* 7 (1981), 63–98.

Dirksen, P.B., 'The Old Testament Peshitta', in M.J. Mulder (ed.) *Mikra: Text, Translation, Reading and Interpretation of the Hebrew Bible in Ancient Judaism and Early Christianity* (Peabody, MA 2004 [1988]), 255–97.

───── 'Targum and Peshitta: Some Basic Questions', in P.V.M. Flesher (ed.), *Targum Studies*, Vol. 2, *Targum and Peshitta* (South Florida Studies in the History of Judaism 165, Atlanta, GA 1998), 3–13.

Dogniez, C., 'Some similarities between the Septuagint and the Targum of Zechariah', in H. Ausloos et al. (eds), *Translating a Translation: The LXX and its Modern Translations in the Context of Early Judaism* (Leuven 2008), 89–102.

Dorival, G., *La Bible d'Alexandrie*, Vol. 4, *Les Nombres* (Paris 1994).

Dotan, A., 'Masorah', in M. Berenbaum and F. Skolnik (eds), *Encyclopaedia Judaica*^{2}, Vol. XIII. (Detroit 2007), 603–56.

───── (ed.), *Biblia Hebraica Leningradensia: Prepared According to the Vocalization, Accents, and Masora of Aaron ben Moses ben Asher in the Leningrad Codex* (Peabody, MA 2001).

Driver, S.R., *Notes on the Hebrew Text and the Topography of the Books of Samuel* (Oxford 1913).

Elbogen, I., *Jewish Liturgy: a Comprehensive History* (trans. R.P. Scheindlin; Philadelphia 1993 [1913 German ed.; 1972 Hebrew ed.]).

Fassberg, S.E., 'The Forms of "Son" and "Daughter" in Aramaic', in H. Gzella and M.L. Folmer (eds), *Aramaic in its Historical and Linguistic Setting* (Veröffentlichungen der Orientalischen Kommission 50, Wiesbaden 2008), 41–53.

───── *A Grammar of the Palestinian Targum Fragments from the Cairo Genizah* (Harvard Semitic Studies 38, Atlanta, GA 1990).

Fernández Marcos, N., 'Der Barberini-Text von Hab 3 – eine neue Untersuchung', in Heinz-Josef Fabry and Dieter Böhler (eds), *Im Brennpunkt: Die Septuaginta*, Vol. 3, *Studien zur Theologie, Anthropologie, Ekklesiologie, Eschatologie und Liturgie der Griechischen Bibel*, Beiträge zur Wissenschaft vom Alten und Neuen Testament 174 (Stuttgart 2007), 151–80.

───── *The Septuagint in Context: Introduction to the Greek Version of the Bible*, (trans. Wilfred G.E. Watson; Leiden 2000).

Ferrer Costa, J., 'El Targum d'Osees. Traducció crítica catalana del text arameu', *Anuari de Filologia*, Secció E, *Estudis Hebreus i Arameus*, 15:2 (1992), 61–92.

───── 'El Targum d'Osees en tradició Iemenita', unpublished Ph.D. dissertation (Universitat de Barcelona 1989).

Fischer, B., 'Palimpsestus Vindobonensis, II, Manuscript 115 of the Books of Kingdoms, 1 Rg 1,14 – 4 Rg 17,19', in his *Beiträge zur Geschichte der lateinischen Bibeltexte* (Vetus Latina: Die Reste der altlateinischen Bibel 12, Freiburg 1986), 315–81.

Fleisher, E., 'Prayer and Piyyut in the Worms Mahzor', in M. Beit-Arié (ed.), *Worms Mahzor: MS. Jewish National and University Library Heb 4°781/1. Introductory Volume* (Jerusalem 1985), 36–78.

Flesher, P.V.M., and B. Chilton, *The Targums: a Critical Introduction* (Studies in the Aramaic Interpretation of Scripture 12, Leiden 2011).

Flesher, P.V.M., 'The History of Aramaic in Judaism', in J. Neusner, A.J. Avery-Peck and W.S. Green (eds), *The Encyclopedia of Judaism*, Vol. 1 (Leiden 2003), 85–96.

Fontela, C.A., 'El Targum al Cantar de los Cantares (edicion critica)', unpublished Ph.D. dissertation (la Universidad Complutense de Madrid 1987).

Fraade, S.D., 'Scripture, Targum, and Talmud as Instruction: a Complex Textual Story from the

Sifra', in J. Magness and S. Gitin (eds), *Hesed ve-emet: Studies in Honor of Ernest S. Frerichs* (Brown Judaic Studies 320, Atlanta, GA).

—— 'Rabbinic Views on the Practice of Targum, and Multilingualism in the Jewish Galilee of the Third-sixth Centuries', in L.I. Levine, *The Galilee in Late Antiquity* (New York and Jerusalem 1992).

Frankel, Z., 'Nachtrag zu der diesjährigen Programmarbeit: *Zu dem Targum der Propheten*', *Monatsschrift für Geschichte und Wissenschaft des Judentums* 21:4 (1872), 192.

—— *Zu dem Targum der Propheten* (Jahresbericht des jüdisch-theologischen Seminars 'Fraenkel'scher Stiftung', Breslau 1872).

—— *Ueber den Einfluss der palästinischen Exegese auf die alexandrinische Hermeneutik* (Leipzig 1851).

Garel, M., *D'une main forte: manuscrits hebreux des collections françaises* (Paris 1991).

Geiger, A., 'Umschau. Das Thargum zu den Propheten', *Jüdische Zeitschrift für Wissenschaft und Leben* 10 (1872), 198–201.

Gelston, A., 'The Twelve Prophets: Peshitta and Targum', in P.V.M. Flesher (ed.), *Targum Studies, Vol 2, Targum and Peshitta* (South Florida Studies in the History of Judaism 165, Atlanta, GA 1998), 119–39.

Ginsburg, C.D., *The Massorah Compiled from Manuscripts* (The Library of Biblical Studies, New York 1975 [1880–1905]), 4 Vols.

—— *The Earlier Prophets. Diligently Revised According to the Massorah and the Early Editions with the Various Readings from mss. and the Ancient Versions* (London 1926 [1894]).

—— 'The Dagheshed Alephs in the Karlsruhe-MS., being an Explanation of a Difficult Massorah', in *Verhandlungen des Fünften Internationalen Orientalisten-Congresses* II:1 (Berlin 1882), 136–41.

Ginsburger, M., 'Les introductions araméennes à la lecture du Targoum', *Revue des Études Juives* 73 (1921), 14–26, 186–94.

—— *Pseudo-Jonathan: Thargum Jonathan ben Usiël zum Pentateuch nach der Londoner Handschrift Brit. Mus. add. 27031* (Berlin 1903).

—— 'Aramäische Introduktionen zum Thargumvortrag an Festtagen', *Zeitschrift der Deutschen Morgenländischen Gesellschaft* 44 (1900), 113–24.

—— *Das Fragmententhargum: Thargum jeruschalmi zum Pentateuch* (Berlin 1899).

Gleßmer, U., *Einleitung in die Targume zum Pentateuch* (Texte und Studien zum Antiken Judentum 48, Tübingen 1995).

Golomb, David M., *A Grammar of Targum Neofiti* (Harvard Semitic Monographs 34, Chico, CA 1985).

Gordon, R.P., 'The Ephraimite Messiah and the Targum(s) to Zechariah 12.10', in J.C. Exum and H.G. Williamson (eds), *Reading from Right to Left: Essays on the Hebrew Bible in Honour of David J. A. Clines* (Journal for the Study of the Old Testament Supplement 373, London 2003), 184–95.

—— *Studies in the Targum to the Twelve Prophets: from Nahum to Malachi* (Supplements to Vetus Testamentum 51, Leiden 1994).

—— 'Alexander Sperber and the Study of the Targums', in D.R.G. Beattie, M.J. McNamara (eds), *The Aramaic Bible: Targums in their Historical Context* (Journal for the Study of the Old Testament Supplement Series 166, Sheffield 1994), 92–102.

—— 'Foreword to the Reprinted Edition', in A. Sperber (ed.), *The Bible in Aramaic*, Vols 1–4 (Leiden 1992).

—— 'The Targumist as Eschatologist', in J.A. Emerton, et al. (eds), *Congress volume: Göttingen 1977* (Supplements to Vetus Testamentum 29, Leiden 1978), 113–30.

Chapter Thirteen. Bibliography

―― 'Sperber's Edition of the Targum to the Prophets: a Critique', *Jewish Quarterly Review (New Series)* 64 (1973–4), 314–21.

―― 'An Inner-Targum Corruption (Zech. I.8)', *Vetus Testamentum* 25:2 (1975), 216–19.

―― 'Targum Variant Agrees with Wellhausen!', *Zeitschrift für die alttestamentliche Wissenschaft* 87:2 (1975), 218–19.

Goshen-Gottstein, M., with the assistance of R. Kasher, *Fragments of Lost Targumim*, 2 Vols [in Hebrew] (Bar-Ilan Institute for the History of Jewish Bible Research: Sources and Studies 1:3; Ramat-Gan 1983, 1989).

―― 'Biblical Manuscripts in the United States', *Textus* 2 (1962), 28–59.

Gottlieb, L., 'Composition of Targums after the Decline of Aramaic as a Spoken Language', *Aramaic Studies* 12 (2014), 1–8.

Grelot, P., 'Le Targoum d'Isaie X, 32–34 dans ses diverses recensions', *Revue Biblique* 90 (1983), 202–28.

―― 'A propos d'une Tosephta Targoumique', *Revue Biblique* 80 (1973), 363.

―― 'Deux Toseftas targoumiques inédites sur Isaïe LXVI', *Revue Biblique* 79 (1972), 511–43.

―― 'Une Tosephta targoumique sur Zacharie, II, 14–15', *Revue Biblique* 73 (1966), 197–211.

―― 'L'exégèse messianique d'Isaie, LXIII, 1–6', *Revue Biblique* 70 (1963), 371–80.

Griño, R., 'El Meturgeman de Elias Levita y el 'Aruk de Natan Ben Yehiel como fuentes de la lexicografia targumica', *Biblica* 60 (1979), 110–17.

Grossman, A., 'The School of Literal Jewish Exegesis in Northern France', in M. Sæbo (ed.), *Hebrew Bible / Old Testament: The History of its Interpretation*, Vol. 1, Part 2, *The Middle Ages* (Göttingen 2000).

―― *The Early Sages of Ashkenaz: Their Lives, Leadership and Works (900–1096)* [in Hebrew] (Jerusalem 1981).

Hahn, O., T. Wolff, H.-O. Feistel, I. Rabin and M. Beit-Arié, 'The Erfurt Hebrew Giant Bible and the Experimental XRF Analysis of Ink and Plummet Composition', *Gazette du livre médiéval* 51 (2007), 16–29.

Halevy, M., 'האם ראה רש"י את תרגום יונתן בן עוזיאל', *Sinai* 60:3–4 (Year 31: 1966), 191.

Hannah, D.D., 'Isaiah Within Judaism of the Second Temple Period', in S. Moyise and M.J.J. Menken (eds), *Isaiah in the New Testament: The New Testament and the Scriptures of Israel* (London 2005).

Harl, M., et al., *La Bible d'Alexandrie*, Vol. 23:4–9, *Les Douze Prophètes* (Paris 1999).

Harrington, D.J. and A.J. Saldarini, *Targum Jonathan of the Former Prophets* (The Aramaic Bible 10, Edinburgh 1987).

Hayward, C.T.R., *Saint Jerome's Hebrew Questions on Genesis: Translated with Introduction and Commentary* (Oxford Early Christian Studies, Oxford 1995).

―― 'A Portrait of the Wicked Esau in the Targum of Codex Neofiti 1', in D.R.G. Beattie and M.J. McNamara (eds), *The Aramaic Bible: Targums in their Historical Context* (Journal for the Study of the Old Testament Supplement 166, Sheffield 1994), 291–309.

―― 'Saint Jerome and the Aramaic Targumim', *Journal of Semitic Studies* 32:1 (1987), 105–23.

―― 'Jewish Traditions in Jerome's Commentary on Jeremiah and the Targum of Jeremiah', *Proceedings of the Irish Biblical Association* 9 (1985), 100–14.

Heller, C., 'A Critical Essay on the Palestinian Targum to the Pentateuch' [in Hebrew] *Haibri* (New York 1921).

Ho, A., *The Targum of Zephaniah: Manuscripts and Commentary* (Studies in the Aramaic Interpretation of Scripture 7, Leiden 2009).

Hoffman, J., '*Akdamut*: History, Folklore, and Meaning', *Jewish Quarterly Review* 99:2 (2009), 161–83.

Houtman, A. and H. Sysling, *Alternative Targum Traditions: The Use of Variant Readings for the Study in Origin and History of Targum Jonathan* (Studies in the Aramaic Interpretation of Scripture 9, Leiden 2009).

Houtman, A., 'The Role of the Targum in Jewish Education in Medieval Europe', in A. Houtman, H.-M. Kirn and E. van Staalduine-Sulman (eds), *A Jewish Targum in a Christian World* (Jewish and Christian Perspectives 27, Leiden 2014), 81–98.

—— 'The Role of Abraham in Targum Isaiah', *Aramaic Studies* 3:1 (2005), 3–14.

—— 'Wat is er met de lijdende knecht gebeurd? De lezing van Jesaja 52:13–53:12 volgens Targoem Jonathan', *Nederlands Theologisch Tijdschrift* 59:3 (2005), 235–51.

—— 'Different Kinds of Tradition in Targum Jonathan to Isaiah', in P. van Reenen et al. (eds), *Studies in Stemmatology II* (Amsterdam and Philadelphia 2004), 269–83.

—— review of 'Paul V.M. Flesher (ed.), *Targum and Scripture: Studies in Aramaic Translations and Interpretation in Memory of Ernest G. Clarke* (Studies in the Aramaic Interpretation of Scripture 2, Leiden 2002)', *Journal for the Study of Judaism in the Persian, Hellenistic and Roman Period*, 35:1 (2004), 77–9.

—— 'Planning a New Targum Edition: Look Before you Leap', *Journal for the Aramaic Bible* 2:2 (2000), 213–31.

—— 'Textual Tradition of Targum Jonathan to Isaiah', in J. Targarona Borrás (ed.), *Jewish Studies at the Turn of the Twentieth Century: Proceedings of the 6th EAJS congress, Toledo, July 1998*, Vol. 2 (Leiden 1999), 145–53.

—— 'Targum Isaiah According to Felix Pratensis.' *Journal for the Aramaic Bible* 1 (1999), 191–202

Joüon, P. and T. Muraoka, *A Grammar of Biblical Hebrew* (Subsidia Biblica 27, Rome 2006), § 137b.

Kahle, P., *Masoreten des Ostens: Die ältesten punktierten Handschriften des Alten Testaments und der Targum* (Leipzig 1913).

—— *Masoreten des Westens*, II, *Das palästinische Pentateuchtargum, die palästinische Punktation, der Bibeltext des Ben Naftali* (Text und Untersuchungen zur vormasoretischen Grammatik des Hebräischen 4; Beiträge zur Wissenschaft vom Alten und Neuen Testament 50, Stuttgart 1930).

—— *The Cairo Geniza: the Schweich Lectures of the British Academy 1941* (London 1947).

—— 'Die Aussprache des Hebräischen in Palästina vor der Zeit der Tiberischen Masoreten' *Vetus Testamentum* 10 (1960), 375–85.

Kasher, A., 'האם ראה רש"י תרגום יונתן בן עוזיאל', *Sinai* 58–1–2 (Year 30: 1965), 90–3.

Kasher, M.M., *Torah Shelema*, Vol. 24, *Aramaic Versions of the Bible* [in Hebrew] (Jerusalem 1974).

Kasher, R., 'Eschatological Ideas in the Toseftot Targum to the Prophets', *Journal of the Aramaic Bible* 2 (2000), 25–59.

—— *Targumic Toseftot to the Prophets* [in Hebrew] (Sources for the Study of Jewish Culture 2, Jerusalem 1996).

—— 'התוספתות התרגומיות להפטרת שבת־חנוכה', *Tarbiz* 45 (1975/76), 27–45.

Kaufman, S.A. and Y. Maori, 'The Targumim to Exodus 20: Reconstructing the Palestinian Targum', *Textus* 16 (1991), 13–78.

Kaufman, S.A., 'Dating the Language of the Palestinian Targums and their Use in the Study of First Century CE Texts', in D.R.G. Beattie and M.J.McNamara (eds), *The Aramaic Bible: Targums in their Historical Context* (Journal for the Study of the Old Testament Supplement 166, Sheffield 1994), 118–41.

Kedar, B., 'The Latin Translations', in M.J. Mulder (ed.) *Mikra: Text, Translation, Reading and Interpretation of the Hebrew Bible in Ancient Judaism and Early Christianity* (Peabody, MA 2004 [1988]), 299–338.

Chapter Thirteen. Bibliography

Kennicott, B., *Vetus Testamentum hebraicum cum variis lectionibus*, Vol. 1 (Oxford 1776).

—— *Dissertatio Generalis in Vetus Testamentum Hebraicum cum Variis Lectionibus ex Codicibus Manuscriptis et Impressis* (Brunovici 1783).

Klein, G. 'Bemerkungen zu Herr Dr. Bacher's Kritische Untersuchungen zum Prophetentargum', *Zeitschrift der Deutschen Morgenländischen Gesellschaft* 29 (1875), 157–61.

Klein, M.L., *The Masorah to Targum Onqelos: as Preserved in MSS Vatican Ebreo 448, Rome Angelica Or. 7, Fragments from the Cairo Genizah and in Earlier Editions by A. Berliner and S. Landauer* (Targum Studies, New Series 1, Binghamton, NY 2000).

—— 'Cairo Genizah Targum Texts: Old and New', in D.R.G. Beattie and M.J.McNamara (eds), *The Aramaic Bible: Targums in their Historical Context* (Journal for the Study of the Old Testament Supplement 166, Sheffield 1994), 18–29.

—— 'Introductory Poems (*R'shuyot*) to the Targum of the *hafṭarah* in Praise of Jonathan Ben Uzziel', in S.F. Chyet and D.H. Ellenson (eds), *Bits of Honey: Essays for Samson H. Levey* (Atlanta, GA 1993), 43–56.

—— *Targumic Manuscripts in the Cambridge Genizah Collections* (Cambridge 1992).

—— '*Serugin* (Shorthand) of Onqelos from the Cairo Genizah', in R.Ratner, et al. (eds), *Let your Colleagues Praise you: Studies in Memory of Stanley Gevirtz*, Part 2. *Maarav* 8 (1992), 275–87.

—— *Genizah Manuscripts of Palestinian Targum to the Pentateuch*, Vol. 1 (Cincinnati, OH 1986).

—— *The Fragment-Targums of the Pentateuch: According to their Extant Sources* (Analecta Biblica 76, Rome 1980).

Klein, S., 'Targumische Elemente in der Deutung biblischer Ortsnamen bei Hieronymus', *Monatsschrift für Geschichte und Wissenschaft des Judentums* 83:1 (1939), 132–41.

Klostermann, A., review of 'P. de Lagarde, Prophetae Chaldaice e fide codicis reuchliniani (Leipzig: Teubneri, 1872)', *Theologische Studien und Kritiken* 46:4 (1873), 731–67.

Knobel, P.S., 'Targum Qoheleth: a Linguistic and Exegetical Inquiry', unpublished Ph.D. dissertation (Yale University 1976).

Korpel, M.C.A., J.C. de Moor, and F. Sepmeijer, 'Consistency with Regard to Tenses: Targum and Peshitta in Two Samples from Deutero-Isaiah', in Association Internationale Bible et Informatique (AIBI); la Faculté des Lettres de l'Université de Provence, *Bible et informatique: traduction et transmission: actes du cinquième colloque international, Aix-en-Provence, 1–4 September 1997* (Travaux de Linguistique Quantitative 65, Paris 1998), 195–220.

Kroeze, D.J.D and E. van Staalduine-Sulman, 'A Giant Among Bibles: "Erfurt 1" or Cod. Or. fol. 1210–1211 at the Staatsbibliothek zu Berlin', *Aramaic Studies* 4 (2006), 193–205.

Kutscher, F.Y., *Studies in Galilean Aramaic* (trans. M. Sokoloff; Ramat-Gan 1976).

Lambert, M., 'Note additionnelle', *Revue des Études Juives* 44 (1902), 285.

Landauer, S., '"Studien zu Merx" *Chrestomathia targumica*', *Zeitschrift für Assyriologie und Vorderasiatische Archäologie* 3:1 (1888), 263–92.

Langlamet, F., 'Les divisions massorétiques du livre de Samuel', *Revue Biblique* 91 (1984), 481–519.

Le Déaut, R., 'La Septante, un Targum?', in R. Kuntzmann and J. Schlosser (eds), *Études sur le Judaïsme hellénistique: congrès de Strasbourg (1983)* (Paris 1984), 147–95.

—— and J. Robert, *Targum des Chroniques (Cod. Vat. Urb. Ebr. 1)*, Vol. 1, *Introduction et traduction* (Analecta Biblica 51, Rome 1971).

—— *La nuit pascale: essai sur la signification de la Pâque juive à partir du Targum d'Exode XII 42* (Analecta Biblica 22, Rome 1963).

Lehnardt, A., *Qaddish: Untersuchungen zur Entstehung und Rezeption eines rabbinischen Gebetes* (Texts and Studies in Ancient Judaism 87, Tübingen 2002).

—— '"Therefore they Ordained to Say it in Aramaic." Some Remarks on Language and Style of the Kaddish', in J. Targarona Borrás and Á. Sáenz-Badillos (eds), *Jewish Studies at the Turn of the*

Twentieth Century: Proceedings of the 6th EAJS congress, Toledo, July 1998, Vol. 1, *Biblical, Rabbinical, and Medieval Studies* (Leiden 1999), 303–10.

Lehnardt, P.Sh., 'The Role of Targum Samuel in European Jewish Liturgy', in A. Houtman, H.M. Kirn, and E. van Staalduine-Sulman (eds), *A Jewish Targum in a Christian World* (Jewish and Christian Perspectives 27, Leiden 2014), 32–62.

Levine, É., 'The Targums', in M. Sæbø (ed.), *Hebrew Bible / Old Testament, The History of its Interpretation*, Vol. I, *From the Beginnings to the Middle Ages (Until 1300)*, Part 1, *Antiquity* (Göttingen 1996), 323–31.

—— 'Codex Urbinates Ebr. 1; A "Targum" Text', *Biblische Zeitschrift* 24 (1980), 95–100.

—— *The Aramaic Version of Qohelet* (New York 1978).

—— *The Aramaic Version of Lamentations* (New York 1976).

—— *The Aramaic Version of Jonah* (Jerusalem 1975).

—— *The Aramaic Version of Ruth* (Analecta Biblica 58, Rome 1973).

—— 'British Museum Aramaic Additional MS 27031', *Manuscripta* 16:1 (1972), 3–13.

Lévi, I., 'L'Apocalypse de Zorobabel et le roi de Perse Siroès. (Suite)', *Revue des Études Juives* 69 (1919), 108–21.

—— 'L'Apocalypse de Zorobabel et le roi de Perse Siroès.' *Revue des Études Juives* 68 (1914), 129–60.

Levy, J., *Chaldäisches Wörterbuch über die Targumim und einen grossen Theil des Rabbinischen Schriftthums* (Leipzig 1867–8).

Lilienthal, T.C., *Commentatio critica sistens duorum codicum mstorum Biblia Hebraica continentium qui Regiomonti Borussorum asservantur praestantissimorum notitiam, cum praecipuarum variantium lectionum ex utroque codice excerptarum sylloge* (Regiomonti et Lipsiae 1770).

Lund, J.A., 'The First Person Singular Past Tense of the Verb *hwh* in Jewish Palestinian Aramaic', *Maarav* 4 (1987), 191–9.

Luzzatto, A., 'La Bibbia ebraica della biblioteca "Berio" di Genova', *Miscellanea di Storia Ligure* 4 (1966), 41–65.

Madan, M., 'עוד לשאלה האם ראה רש"י את תרגום יונתן בן עוזיאל', *Sinai* 60:1–2 (Year 31: 1966), 95.

Maher, M., *Targum Pseudo-Jonathan: Genesis. Translated, with Introduction and Notes* (The Aramaic Bible 1B, Collegeville, MN 1992).

Mangan, C., J.F. Healey and P.S. Knobel, *The Targum of Job, Proverbs, Qohelet* (The Aramaic Bible 15, Edinburgh 1991).

Margoliouth, G., *Catalogue of the Hebrew and Samaritan Manuscripts in the British Museum*, Part 1 (London 1899).

Martelli, V.A. and L. Mortara Ottolenghi, *Manoscritti biblici ebraici decorati: provenienti da Biblioteche italiane pubbliche e private* (Milan 1966).

Martin, M., 'The Babylonian Tradition and Targum', in R. de Langhe (ed.), *Le Psautier. Ses origines. Ses problèmes littéraires. Son influence: études présentées aux XIIe journées bibliques (29–31 août 1960)* (Leuven 1962), 425–51.

Martínez Borobio, E., 'YT and L – Before the Direct Object in the Aramaic of the Palestinian Targum', *Sefarad* 47:1 (1987), 159–62.

May, R.A. (ed.), compiled under the direction of M. Beit-Arié, *Catalogue of the Hebrew Manuscripts in the Bodleian library: Supplement of Addenda and Corrigenda to Vol. I* (A. Neubauer's Catalogue) (Oxford 1994).

McHardy, W.D., review of 'J.F. Stenning, *The Targum of Isaiah* (Oxford: Clarendon Press, 1949)', *The Hibbert Journal* 48 (1950), 190–2.

McIvor, J.S., *The Targum of Chronicles. Translated, with Introduction, Apparatus, and Notes* (The Aramaic Bible 19, Edinburgh 1994).

Chapter Thirteen. Bibliography

McNamara, M., *The New Testament and the Palestinian Targum to the Pentateuch* (Analecta Biblica 27, Rome 1966).

Meiser, M., 'Samuelseptuaginta und Targum Jonathan als Zeugen frühjüdischer Geistigkeit', in M. Karrer and W. Kraus, with M. Meiser (eds), *Die Septuaginta: Texte, Kontexte, Lebenswelten*, Wissenschaftliche Untersuchungen zum Neuen Testament 219 (Tübingen 2008), 323–35.

Melamed, E.Z., *Bible Commentators*^{2}, 2 Vols [in Hebrew] (Jerusalem 1978).

Merx, A., 'Bemerkungen über die Vocalisation der Targume' in *Verhandlungen des fünften internationalen Orientalisten-Congresses gehalten zu Berlin im September 1881, II, Abhandlungen und Vorträge des fünften internationalen Orientalisten-Congresses gehalten zu Berlin 1881, Section 1, Abhandlungen und Vorträge der semitischen und afrikanischen Section*. (Berlin 1882), 142–188.

—— *Chrestomathia Targumica quam collatis libris manu scriptis antiquissimis Tiberiensibus editionibusque impressis celeberrimis ad codices vocalibus Babylonicis instructos* (Porta linguarum orientalium 8, Berlin 1888).

Metzger, T. and M. Metzger, *Jewish Life in the Middle Ages: Illuminated Hebrew Manuscripts of the Thirteenth to the Sixteenth Centuries* (New York 1982), 310 no. 240.

Meyer, R. review of *Corpus Codicum Hebraicorum Medii Aevi, II, The Pre-Masoretic Bible. Codex Reuchlinianus, No. 3 of the Badische Landesbibliothek in Karlsruhe (formerly Durlach No. 55), with a General Introduction: Masoretic Hebrew*, by A. Sperber (Copenhagen 1956) – *Codices Palatini, I, The Parma Pentateuch (Ms. Parma No. 1849, formerly de Rossi No. 2)*, Vol. 1–3, by A. Sperber. Ebenda: 1959 – *A Grammar of Masoretic Hebrew, a General Introduction to the Pre-Masoretic Bible*, by A. Sperber (Copenhagen 1959. *Vetus Testamentum* 11 (1961), 474–86.

Milano, A., 'Italy', in M. Berenbaum and F. Skolnik (eds), *Encyclopaedia Judaica*^{2}, Vol. X. (Detroit 2007), 795–816.

—— *Storia degli ebrei in Italia* (Torino 1963).

Millgram, A.E., *Jewish Worship* (Philadelphia, PA 1975 [1971]).

Mitchell, D.C., 'Messiah bar Ephraim in the Targums', *Aramaic Studies* 4:2 (2006), 221–41.

Morag, S., 'The Vocalization of Codex Reuchlinianus: is the "Pre-Masoretic" Bible Pre-Masoretic?' *Journal of Semitic Studies* 4:3 (July 1959), 216–37.

Moreschini, C., and E. Norelli, *Early Christian Greek and Latin Literature: a Literary History, II, From the Council of Nicea to the Beginning of the Medieval Period* (trans. M.J.O'Connell, Peabody, MA 2005 [1996]).

Morrison, C.E., *The Character of the Syriac Version of the First Book of Samuel* (Monographs of the Peshitta Institute Leiden 11, Leiden 2001).

Mortara Ottolenghi, L., 'La decorazione del codice biblico ebraico della biblioteca "Berio" di Genova', *Miscellanea di Storia Ligure* 4 (1966), 68–84.

Narkiss, B., 'Maḥzor', in M. Berenbaum and F. Skolnik (eds), *Encyclopaedia Judaica*^{2} Vol. XIII (Detroit 2007), 363–6.

—— 'The Relation Between the Author, Scribe, Masorator, and Illuminator in Medieval Manuscripts', in J. Glénisson and C. Sirat (eds), *La paléographie hébraïque médiévale: colloque international sur la paléographie hébraïque médiévale (1972: Paris)* (Colloques internationaux 547, Paris 1974), 79–86.

Neubauer, A.D., *Catalogue of the Hebrew Manuscripts in the Bodleian Library and in the College Libraries of Oxford* (Oxford 1994 [1886]).

Oesch, J.M., *Petucha und Setuma: Untersuchungen zu einer überlieferten Gliederung im hebräischen Text des Alten Testaments* (Orbis Biblicus et Orientalis 27, Freiburg 1979).

Offer, J., 'The Masoretic Divisions (sedarim) in the Books of Prophets and Hagiographa' [in Hebrew], *Tarbiz* 58:2 (1989), 155–89.

Patmore, H.M. and J.M. Tanja, 'Initial Observations Concerning the Text of Targum 2 Samuel 22 as Preserved in European Liturgical Manuscripts', in A. Houtman, H.-M. Kirn and E. van Staalduine-Sulman (eds), *A Jewish Targum in a Christian World* (Jewish and Christian Perspectives 27, Leiden 2014), 63–80.

Patmore, H.M., 'The Transmission of Targum Jonathan in the West: Initial Results from the Mixed Western Textual Group', *Aramaic Studies* 10 (2012), 23–52.

—— 'The Marginal Notes to the Targum Text of Codex Reuchlinianus No. 3', *Aramaic Studies* 10 (2012), 53–85.

—— *Adam, Satan, and the King of Tyre: The Interpretation of Ezekiel 28:11–19 in Late Antiquity* (Jewish and Christian Perspectives 20, Leiden 2012).

—— 'The Critical Importance of Targum Fragments', *Genizah Fragments* 59 (April 2010).

Pauli, C.W.H., *The Chaldee Paraphrase on the Prophet Isaiah* (London 1871).

Perrot, C., *La lecture de la Bible dans la synagogue: les anciennes lectures palestiniennes du shabbat et des fêtes* (Collection Massorah, série 1, Études classique et textes, 1, Hildesheim 1973).

—— 'Petuhot et Setumot: étude sur les alinéas du Pentateuque', *Revue Biblique* 76 (1969), 50–91.

Peters, C., 'Zur Herkunft der Pešitta des ersten Samuel-Buches', *Biblica* 22 (1941), 25–34.

—— 'Peschittha und Targumim des Pentateuchs: ihre Beziehungen untersucht im Rahmen ihrer Abweichungen vom Masoretischen Text', *Muséon* 48 (1935), 1–54.

Praetorius, F., *Das Targum zu Josua in jemenische Überlieferung* (Berlin 1899).

—— *Das Targum zum Buch der Richter in jemenischer Überlieferung* (Berlin 1899).

Prijs, J., 'Über Ben Naftali-Bibelhandschriften und ihre paläographischen Besonderheiten', *Zeitschrift für die Alttestamentliche Wissenschaft* 69 (1957), 171–84.

Reif, S.C., 'The Cairo Genizah and its Treasures with Special Reference to Biblical Studies', in D.R.G. Beattie and M.J.McNamara (eds), *The Aramaic Bible: Targums in their Historical Context* (Journal for the Study of the Old Testament Supplement 166, Sheffield 1994), 30–50.

—— *Judaism and Hebrew Prayer: New Perspectives on Jewish Liturgical History* (Cambridge 1993).

—— 'Codicological Aspects of Jewish Liturgical History', *Bulletin of the John Rylands University Library of Manchester* 75:3 (1993), 117–31.

Ribera Florit, J., 'El Targum de Abdías', in A. Hilhorst, E. Puech and E. Tigchelaar (eds), *Flores Florentino: Dead Sea Scrolls and other Early Jewish Studies in Honour of Florentino Garcia Martinez* (Supplements to the Journal for the Study of Judaism 122, Leiden 2007), 713–27.

—— 'Le Targum', in A. Schenker and P. Hugo (eds), *L'enfance de la Bible hébraïque: L'histoire du texte de l'Ancien Testament à la lumière des recherches récentes* (Le Monde de la Bible 52, Geneva 2005), 220–37.

—— 'Targum de Joel', *Miscelanea de Estudios Arabes y Hebraicos, Seccion de Hebreo* 53 (2004), 271–86.

—— *Targum de Ezequiel: introducción, traducción crítica y notas* (Biblioteca midrásica 27, Estella 2004).

—— 'El Targum de Habacuc', *Anuari de Filologia* E, 11 (2002–3), 319–32.

—— 'Las investigaciones Targúmicas en España a partir de la obra de A. Díez Macho (1984–2001)', *Miscelanea de Estudios Arabes y Hebraicos, Seccion de Hebreo* 50 (2001), 849–58.

—— *Targum Jonatán de los Profetas Posteriores en tradición babilónica: Ezequiel* (Textos y Estudios 'Cardenal Cisneros' 62, Madrid 1997).

—— 'Relación entre el Targum y las versiones antiguas: los Targumes de Jeremías y Ezequiel comparados con LXX, Peshitta y Vulgata', *Estudios Biblicos* 52 (1994), 317–28.

—— 'Relationship between Semantics and Vocalization: Some Examples from Yemenite Manuscripts of Targum Jeremiah', in E. Fernández Tejero and M.T. Ortega Monasterio (eds),

Estudios Masoréticos (Madrid 1993), 111–17.
—— *Targum Jonatán de los Profetas Posteriores en tradición babilónica: Jeremías* (Textos y Estudios 'Cardenal Cisneros' 52, Madrid 1992).
—— 'La puntuación babilónica del Targum de Jeremías en relación con la del texto hebreo.' *Sefarad* 52 (1992), 201–8.
—— 'The Babylonian Tradition of the Targum Jeremiah', in A. Dotan (ed.), *Proceedings of the Ninth Congress of the International Organization for Masoretic Studies 1989* (Masoretic Studies 7, Atlanta 1992), 101–9.
—— *Traducción del Targum de Jeremías* (Biblioteca Midrásica 12, Estella 1992).
—— 'Puncualizaciones sobre las diversas recensiones y tradiciones del Targum de los Profetas', *Anuari de Filologia*, E, *Estudis hebreus i arameus* 15 (1993), 149–53.
—— 'El Targum de Malaquias', *Estudios Biblicos* 48 (1990), 171–97.
—— 'The Babylonian Masoretic Tradition Reflected in the mss of the Targum to the Latter Prophets', in E.J. Revell (ed.), *Proceding of the Eigth Congress of the International Organization for Masoretic Studies 1988* (Masoretic Studies 6, Atlanta 1990), 103–8.
—— *Targum Jonatán de los Profetas Posteriores en tradición babilónica: Isaías* (Textos y Estudios 'Cardenal Cisneros' 43, Madrid 1988).
—— *El Targum de Isaías: versión crítica, introducción y notas* (Biblioteca Midrásica 6, Valencia 1988).
—— 'La escatología en el Targum Jonatan (Tg Jon) y su relación con el Targum Palestinense (Tg Pal)', in V. Collado-Bertomeu and V. Vilar Hueso (eds), *Simposio Bíblico Español (Córdoba, 1985)* (Córdoba 1987), 487–99.
—— 'Elementos comunes del Targum a los Profetas y del Targum Palestinense', in N. Fernández Marcos, F. Trebolle Barrera and F. Fernández Vallina (eds), *Simposio bíblico Español (Salamanca 1982)* (Madrid 1984), 477–93.
—— 'La versión aramaica del Profeta Sofonías', *Estudios Bíblicos* 40 (1982), 127–58.
—— 'La exegesis rabinica postbiblica reflejada en la version aramea de los Profetas.' *El Olivo* 4:13 (1981), 61–85.
—— 'La versión aramaica del profeta Nahum', *Anuario de Filología* 6 (1981), 291–322.
—— 'La versión aramaica del profeta Ageo', *Anuario de Filología* 4 (1978), 290–1.
—— *Biblia babilonica: Profetas Posteriores (Targum)* (Salamanca 1977).
—— 'Fragmento babilónico hebreo-arameo del profeta Jeremías (Ms. 238b del JThS – ENA St. 20; Jer 31, 22a–32, 1h)', *Anuario de Filología* 2 (1976), 253–70.
—— 'Fragmento babilonico-yemeni sobre los Profetas', in L. Álvarez Verdes and E.J. Alonso Hernández (eds), *Homenaje a Juan Prado: miscelánea de estudios bíblicos y hebraicos* (Madrid 1975).
Richler, B. (ed.), with M. Beit-Arié in collaboration with N. Pasternak, *Hebrew Manuscripts in the Vatican Library: Catalogue* (Studi e Testi 438, Vatican City 2008).
—— (ed.), with palaeographical and codicological descriptions by M. Beit-Arié, *Hebrew Manuscripts in the Biblioteca Palatina in Parma: Catalogue* (Jerusalem 2001).
Rieder, D., 'האם ראה רש"י את תרגום יונתן בן עוזיאל', *Sinai* 30 58:1–2 (Year 30: 1965), 93–4.
Roth, C., *The History of the Jews of Italy* (Philadelphia, PA 1946).
Róth, E., *Hebräische Handschriften*, Vol. 2, ed. H. Striedl with L. Tetzner (Verzeichnis der Orientalischen Handschriften in Deutschland VI, 2, Wiesbaden 1965).
Rowlands, E.R., 'Targum and the Peshitta Version of the Book of Isaiah', *Vetus Testamentum* 9:2 (1959), 178–91.
Rowley, H.H, review of 'J.F. Stenning, *The Targum of Isaiah* (Oxford: Clarendon Press, 1949)', *Bibliotheca Orientalis* 6:5 (1949), 159–60.

The Transmission of Targum Jonathan in the West

Running, L.G., 'A Study of the Relationship of the Syriac Version to the Massoretic Hebrew, Targum Jonathan, and Septuagint Texts in Jeremiah 18', in A. Kort and S. Morschauser (eds), *Biblical and Related Studies Presented to Samuel Iwry* (Winona Lake, IN 1985), 227–35.

Sabbathier, P., *Bibliorum sacrorum latinæ versiones antiquæ, seu Vetus Italica, et Cæteræ quæcunque in codicibus Mss. & antiquorum libris reperiri potuerunt: quæ cum Vulgata latina, & cum textu græco comparantur: accedunt præfationes, observationes, ac notæ, indexque novus ad Vulgatam è regione editam, idemque locupletissimus* (Turnhout 1976 [1743]).

Schiller-Szinessy, S.M., *Catalogue of the Hebrew Manuscripts Preserved in the University Library, Cambridge, Vol. 1* (Cambridge 1876).

Schilling, K. (ed.), *Monumenta Judaica: 2000 Jahre Geschichte und Kultur der Juden am Rhein, I, Katalog: Eine Ausstellung in Kölnischen Stadtmuseum 15. Oktober 1963 – 15 März 1964.* (Köln 1963).

Schwarz, A.Z., *Die hebräischen Handschriften in Österreich* (außerhalb der Nationalbibliothek in Wien), Vol I, *Bibel — Kabbala* (Leipzig 1931).

Sed-Rajna, G., *Les manuscrits hébreux enluminés des bibliothèques de France* (Corpus of Illuminated Manuscripts 7, Oriental Series 3, Leuven 1994).

Segert, S., review of 'Alexander Sperber (ed.), *The Bible in Aramaic, Vol. 1, The Pentateuch according to Targum Onkelos* (Leiden: Brill, 1959); Alexander Sperber (ed.), *The Bible in Aramaic, Vol. 2, The Former Prophets according to Targum Jonathan* (Leiden: Brill, 1959)', *Archiv Orientální* 28:4 (1960), 701–4.

Shinan, A., 'Live Translation: on the Nature of the Aramaic Targums to the Pentateuch', *Prooftexts* 3:11 (1983), 41–9.

Shunary, J., 'תוספת משיחא בתרגום יונתן לנביאים', *Tarbiz* 42 (1973) 259–65.

Silbermann, S., *Das Targum zu Ezechiel nach einer südarabischen Handschrift* (Leipzig 1902).

Sirat, C., *Hebrew Manuscripts of the Middle Ages* (ed. and trans. N. de Lange, Cambridge 2002).

—— et al., *Codices hebraicis litteris exarati quo tempore scripti fuerint exhibentes*, III, *de 1085 à 1140*, (Monumenta Palaeographica Medii Aevi: Series Hebraica, Turnhout 2002).

Smelik, M. and W. Smelik, 'Twin Targums: Psalm 18 and 2 Samuel 22', in A. Rapoport-Albert and G. Greenberg (eds), *Biblical Hebrews, Biblical Texts: Essays in Memory of Michael P. Weitzman* (Journal for the Study of the Old Testament Supplement Series 333, Sheffield 2001), 244–81.

Smelik, W.F., 'Code-switching: The Public Reading of the Bible in Hebrew, Aramaic and Greek', in L. Morenz and S. Schorch (eds), *Was ist ein Text?: alttestamentliche, ägyptologische und altorientalistische Perspektiven* (Beihefte zur Zeitschrift für die alttestamentliche Wissenschaft 362, Berlin 2007), 123–51.

—— 'Trouble in the Trees! Variant Selection and Tree Construction Illustrated by the Texts of Targum Judges', *Aramaic Studies* 1:2 (2003), 247–87; reprinted in P. van Reenen, A. den Hollander and M. van Mulken (eds), *Studies in Stemmatology* II (Amsterdam 2004), 167–206.

—— 'Orality, Manuscript Reproduction, and the Targums', in A. den Hollander, U. Schmid and W. Smelik (eds), *Paratext and Megatext as Channels of Jewish and Christian Traditions: The Textual Markers of Contextualization* (Jewish and Christian Perspectives 6, Leiden 2003), 49–81.

—— 'How to Grow a Tree: Computerised Stemmatology and Variant Selection in Targum Studies', in J. Cook (ed.), *Bible and Computer: the Stellenbosch AIBI-6 Conference: Proceedings of the Association Internationale Bible et Informatique, 'From alpha to byte'*, University of Stellenbosch, 17–21 July, 2000 (Leiden 2002).

—— 'Language, Locus, and Translation Between the Talmudim', *Journal of the Aramaic Bible* 3 (2001), 199–224.

Chapter Thirteen. Bibliography

—— 'The Rabbinic Reception of Early Bible Translations as Holy Writings and Oral Torah', *Journal of the Aramaic Bible* 1 (1999), 249–72.

—— 'Translation and Commentary in One: The Interplay of Pluses and Substitutions in the Targum of the Prophets.' *Journal for the Study of Judaism* 29:3 (1998), 245–60.

—— 'Concordance and Consistency: Translation Studies and Targum Jonathan', *Journal of Jewish Studies* 49:2 (1998), 286–305.

—— *The Targum of Judges* (Oudtestamentische Studiën 36, Leiden 1995).

—— 'On the Mystical Transformation of the Righteous into Light in *Judaism*', *Journal for the Study of Judaism* 26:2 (1995), 122–44.

Sokoloff, M. and J. Yahalom, 'Aramaic Piyyutim from the Byzantine Period', *Jewish Quarterly Review* 75:3 (1985), 309–21.

Sokoloff, M., *A Dictionary of Jewish Palestinian Aramaic of the Byzantine Period* (Ramat-Gan 1990).

—— *A Dictionary of Jewish Babylonian Aramaic* (Ramat-Gan 2002).

Speier, S., 'The Relationship Between the "Arukh" and "Targum Neofiti I"' [in Hebrew] *Leshonenu* 31:1 (1966), 23–32; 31:3 (1967), 189–98; 34–3 (1970), 172–9.

—— 'תרגום יונתן ופירוש רש"י לישעיה יד, לא: ואין בודד במועדו', *Tarbiz* 34:2 (1965), 194–5.

Sperber, A., *The Bible in Aramaic*, IVB, *The Targum and the Hebrew Bible* (Leiden 1973).

—— *The Bible in Aramaic*, IVA, *The Targum and the Hebrew Bible* (Leiden 1968).

—— *The Pre-Masoretic Bible, I. The Codex Reuchlinianus No. 3 of the Badische Landesbibliothek in Karlsruhe* (Copenhagen 1965).

—— 'Specimen of a Targum Edition', in S. Lieberman et al. (eds), *Louis Ginsberg Jubilee Volume: on the Occasion of his Seventieth Birthday*, Vol. 1 (New York 1945), 293–303.

—— 'The Targum Onkelos in its Relation to the Masoretic Hebrew Text', *Proceedings of the American Academy for Jewish Research* 6 (1934 / 35), 309–51.

—— 'Zur Sprache des Prophetentargums', *Zeitschrift für die Alttestamentliche Wissenschaft* 45 (1927), 267–87.

—— 'Zur Textgestalt des Prophetentargums', *Zeitschrift für die Alttestamentliche Wissenschaft* 44 (1926), 175–6.

Stec, D.M., *The Targum of Psalms: Translated, with a Critical Introduction, Apparatus, and Notes* (The Aramaic Bible 16, Collegeville, MI 2004).

Steinberg, T.L., *Jews and Judaism in the Middle Ages* (Westport, CT 2008).

Steinschneider, M., *Die hebræischen Handschriften der K. Hof- und Staatsbibliothek in Muenchen* (München 1875).

—— *Die Handschriften-Verzeichnisse der Königlichen Bibliothek zu Berlin*, Vol. 2 (Berlin 1878)

Stemberger, G., *Die Römische Herrschaft im Urteil der Juden* (Erträge der Forschung 195, Darmstadt 1983).

Stenning, J.F., *The Targum of Isaiah* (Oxford 1949).

Stoebe, H.J., *Das zweite Buch Samuelis* (Kommentar zum Alten Testament 8:2, Gütersloh 1994).

Strack, H.L. and G. Stemberger, *Introduction to the Talmud and Midrash*[2] (trans. and ed. M. Bockmuehl, Edinburgh 1996).

Stroll, M., *The Jewish Pope: The Ideology and Politics in the Papal Schism of 1130* (Studies in Intellectual History 8, Leiden 1987).

Stummer, F. 'Beiträge zu dem Problem "Hieronymus und die Targumim"' *Biblica* 18 (1937), 174–81

—— 'Einige Beobachtungen über die Arbeitsweise des Hieronymus bei der Übersetzung des Alten Testaments aus der Hebraica Veritas', *Biblica* 10 (1929), 3–30.

Tal, A., 'The Role of Targum Onqelos in Literary Activity During the Middle Ages', in H. Gzella and M.L. Folmer (eds), *Aramaic in its Historical and Linguistic Setting* (Veröffentlichungen der Orientalischen Kommission 50, Wiesbaden 2008), 159–71.

Ta-Shma, I.M., *Creativity and Tradition: Studies in Medieval Rabbinic Scholarship, Literature and Thought* (Harvard, MA 2006).

—— *Talmudic Commentary in Europe and North Africa: Literary History, I, 1000–1200* [in Hebrew] (Jerusalem 1999).

ter Haar Romeny, B., 'A Reply to "Points of Agreement Between the Targum and Peshitta Versions of Kings against the MT: a Sounding" by Percy S.F. van Keulen', in P.S.F. van Keulen and W.Th. van Peursen (eds), *Corpus Linguistics and Textual History: a Computer-assisted Interdisciplinary Approach to the Peshitta* (Studia Semitica Neerlandica 48, Assen 2006), 237–43.

Tov, E., *Textual Criticism of the Hebrew Bible*[3], 2 Vols (Minneapolis, MN 2011).

van der Heide, A., *The Yemenite Tradition of the Targum of Lamentations: Critical Text and Analysis of the Variant Readings* (Studia post-biblica 32, Leiden 1981).

van der Kooij, A., *Die Alten Textzeugen des Jesajabuches: Ein Beitrag zur Textgeschichte des Alten Testaments* (Orbis Biblicus et Orientalis 35, Freiburg and Göttingen 1981).

van Keulen, P.S.F., 'Points of Agreement Between the Targum and Peshitta Versions of Kings Against the MT: a Sounding', in P.S.F. van Keulen and W.Th. van Peursen (eds), *Corpus Linguistics and Textual History: a Computer-assisted Interdisciplinary Approach to the Peshitta* (Studia Semitica Neerlandica 48, Assen 2006), 205–35.

van Staalduine-Sulman, E., 'A Variety of Targum Texts', in A. Houtman, H.-M. Kirn, and E. van Staalduine-Sulman (eds), *A Jewish Targum in a Christian World* (Jewish and Christian Perspectives 27, Leiden 2014), 9–31.

—— 'Standard List of Sigla for Targum Manuscripts.' (Amsterdam 2012; http://www.targum.nl/pdf/2012%20Standard%20list%20of%20sigla.pdf, retrieved 9 June 2013).

—— 'An Electronic Edition of Targum Samuel.' (Kampen 2009; http://www.targum.nl/pdf/An%20Electronic%20Edition%20of%20Targum%20Samuel.pdf, retrieved 19 October 2010).

—— 'Vowels in the Trees: the Role of Vocalisation in Stemmatology.' *Aramaic Studies* 3:2 (2005), 215–40.

—— *The Targum of Samuel* (Studies in the Aramaic Interpretation of Scripture 1, Leiden 2002).

van Zijl, J., 'Errata in Sperber's Edition of the Targum Isaiah', *Annual of the Swedish Theological Institute in Jerusalem* 4 (1965), 189–91.

—— 'A Second List of Errata in Sperber's Edition of Targum Isaiah', *Annual of the Swedish Theological Institute in Jerusalem* 7 (1968–9), 132–4.

—— 'Is. XLVIII 7 According to the Targum Br. Mus. Or. MS 2211', *Vetus Testamentum* 18:4 (1968), 560–1.

Viezel, E., 'Targum Onkelos in Rashi's Exegetical Consciousness', *The Review of Rabbinic Judaism* 15 (2012), 1–19.

von Abel, W. and R. Leicht. *Verzeichnis der Hebraica in der Bibliothek Johannes Reuchlins* (Pforzheimer Reuchlinschriften 9, Ostfildern 2005).

Wacholder, B.Z. 'Prolegomenon', in J. Mann, *The Bible as Read and Preached in the Old Synagogue, I. The Palestinian Triennial Cycle: Genesis and Exodus* (New York 1971 [1940]).

Weil, M., 'האם ראה רש"י את תרגום יונתן בן עוזיאל', *Sinai* 30 59:1–2 (Year 30: 1966), 96.

Weil G.E., *Massorah Gedolah: Manuscrit B. 19a de Léningrad* (Rome 1971), 2 Vols.

Weiss, R., *The Aramaic Targum of Job* [in Hebrew] (Tel-Aviv 1979).

Weitzman, M.P., *The Syriac Version of the Old Testament: an Introduction* (University of Cambridge Oriental Publications 56, Cambridge 1999).

—— 'Peshitta, Septuagint and Targum', in René Lavenant (ed.), *VI Symposium Syriacum 1992:*

Chapter Thirteen. Bibliography

University of Cambridge, Faculty of Divinity 30 August – 2 September 1992 (Orientalia Christiana Analecta 247, Rome 1994), 51–84.

Werner, P. (ed.), *Jüdische Handschriften. Restaurieren. Bewahren. Präsentieren. Vol. 1, Jüdische Kultur im Spiegel der Berliner Sammlung* (Berlin 2002).

White, E., 'A Critical Edition of the Targum of Psalms', unpublished Ph.D. dissertation (McGill University 1988).

Winton Thomas, D., review of 'Alexander Sperber (ed.), *The Bible in Aramaic,* Vol. 1, *The Pentateuch According to Targum Onkelos* (Leiden: Brill, 1959)', *Journal of Semitic Studies* 5 (1960), 286–8.

—— review of 'Alexander Sperber (ed.), The Bible in Aramaic, Vol. 2, *The Former Prophets According to Targum Jonathan* (Leiden: Brill, 1959).', *Journal of Semitic Studies* 5 (1960), 430–1.

Wolfsohn, L., *Das Targum zum Propheten Jeremias in jemenischer Überlieferung* (Halle 1902).

Yeivin, I., *Introduction to the Tiberian Masorah* (trans. and ed. E.J. Revell; Masoretic Studies 5, Missoula, MT 1980).

—— *Genizah Bible Fragments with Babylonian Massorah and Vocalization*, Vols 1–5 (Jerusalem 1973).

Zotenberg, H., *Manuscrits orientaux. Catalogues des manuscrits hébreux et samaritains de la bibliothèque Impériale* (Paris 1866).

Zunz, L., *Die gottesdienstlichen Vorträge der Juden historisch entwickelt: Ein Beitrag zur Alterthumskunde und biblischen Kritik, zur Literatur- und Religionsgeschichte* (Hildesheim 1966 [1832]).

Chapter Fourteen

Appendices

1. Colopha (Chapter Three)

t2i

אני יצחק ברבי שמעון הלוי מסרתי

חצי הספר להנדיב ר' אליעזר בר

שמואל השם יזכהו להגות בו בניו

ובני בניו עד סוף כל הדורות

אמן סלה: וסיימתי

לשנת חמשת אלפים

בחמשים וחמשה לפרט בחמשה עשר בכסליו

The opening words are completely illegible on the microfilm. According to Assemanus ברבי reads ברביש a name, i.e. 'Barabis'. According to Weiss, *The Aramaic Targum of Job,* ברבי.

t3i

אני יחיאל הסופר כתבתי הספר הזה מתורגם מר"ח כסליו שנת נ"ו לפרט עד ר"ח ואדר שנת נ"ז לפרט לר' יעקב בר יצחק

Blessing:

הצור יזכהו להגות בו וזרעו אחריו ככתוב. לא ימוש ספר התורה הזה מפיך והגית בו יומם ולילה למען תשמר לעשות ככל הכתוב בו כי אז תצליח את דרכיך ואז תשכיל: וכ' תורה צוה לנו משה מרשה קהלת יעקב: וכ' ואתם הדבקים ביהוה אלהיכם חיים כלכם היום: חזק ואמץ כי אתה תנחיל אתו:

t7i

תם ונשלם חמשה

חומשי תורה ת[הלה] ל[אל]

אשר לכל העולם

מאיר אורה

חזק ונתחזק מאיר י[שמרהו] צ[ורו]

Then:

תם ונשלם ספר ואלה הדברים

שבח לאל שהוא גבור על כל גבורים

ומלך על כל מלכים ושרים

ואדיר על כל אדירים

The Transmission of Targum Jonathan in the West

וסיימתי אותו יום א' פרש[ת] לא יהי[ה] לך אחרי[ם]
שנת מלך ביפיו עיניך תחזינה משרים
וישלח לנו גואל לגאול כל ישראל חברים
בשנת צחק יעשה לנו אלהים בפאר והידורים
ויפ[דה] אותנו מבין הגוים הצוררים
וישיב אותנו לאדמתינו שמחים ונאדרים
ו[ישא] אותנו על כנפי נשרים
המאיר לארץ ולדרים ומאיר על כל מאורים

Benediction:

הכותב לא יזק אמן אמן סלה

Note:

לעולם אדם שמו על ספרו יכתבנו
פן יבא אדם מן השוק ויקחנו
לכן שמי פה ואת א[בי] כתבתי
כדי להראות לעמים זכותי
אני הוא מאיר ......וצ[ריך] א[תה] ל[דעת]
ישמריני וייחייני מי אשר לישראל
מאיר

Additional note:

תמו דברי הנביאים ותרי עשר
שבח לא[ל] א[ל]הי הרוחות לכל בשר
אלו כתובים וחמש מגילות בערכה
אשר כתבתי אלו הסימנים בשנת טובה
וברכה

t232i/s

זה הספר בכל החכמות שחבר אנקילוס
ישמו אמר זה יסוד העולם ויש בו חכמת
הלמוד בכל החכמות שבעולם ובניאן
כל המדינות ועמודה שבעה שבעה
נשלם בזמן באחרית [...]
משלושה אל[פים] קתעז בימי
[...]

t701i

נשלם פירוש מלכים על ידי מנחם צמח ב"ר אברהם יעקב ב"ר בנימן ז"ל ב"ר יחיאל ע"ה לר'
דוד בן יוסף בן קמחי ז"ל והשלמתי אותו יום ב' י"ד בכסלו שנת פ"ז הנה בפרסקטי היושבת על
נהר מראנה ושלום

Chapter Fourteen. Appendices

t705i

נשתלם זה ספר נביאים תרגומא וקרא'
על ידי זרח בר יהודה זוטר ספרא'
בשנת דא תתסו ליצירה'
ובתתרלח לחורבן בית הבחירה'
שייבנה בימינו במהרה'
ויזכינו ללמוד בהם וללמד בלי פגע וצרה'
ויתקיים בי הכתוב לא ימוש ספר התורה
הזה מפיך והגית בו יומם ולילה למען
תשמור לעשות ככל הכתוב בו כי
אז תצליח את דרכיך
ואז תשכיל:

N.B. The transcription of von Abel and Leicht, *Verzeichnis der Hebraica in der Bibliothek Johannes Reuchlins*, p. 99, contains a printing error (ככל appears before ובתתרלח).

t5a

חזק ונתחזק הסופר ברוך בר אברהם לא יוזק אמן סלה

2. t705i Marginalia (Chapter Nine)

The point in the text to which the marginal note(s) correspond is indicated by bold type or *. The vocalisation of the marginalia is often barely legible and is omitted in the following list. Readers should consult the manuscript itself or Sperber's facsimile edition (*The Pre-Masoretic Bible*, Vol. 1, *The Codex Reuchlinianus No 3*) for the vocalisation.

1 Sam. 1:6 (55r)

ומצהבא לה צרתה...
ל' א' ומצהבא

1 Sam. 2:1 (56r)

...בכין רמת קרני במתנתא **דיהב** לי יוי...
ל' א' דמני

1 Sam. 2:14 (57r)

וקבע ליה באיורא או בדודא או בקידרא או **במילסא** כל דמסיק משליא נסיב כהנא לנפשיה...
וא' דאמ' באילפיסא

The Transmission of Targum Jonathan in the West

1 Sam. 2:16 (57r)

ואמר ליה גברא אוריך עד דיתסקון תרביא וסב לך כמא דרעיא נפשך ואמר **ליה** ארי כען תתן ואם לא יסבון מינך בעל כורחך

לא **פליג**

1 Sam. 2:22 (57r)

ועלי סיב לחדא ושמע ית כל דעבדין בנוהי לכל ישראל **וית דשכבין ית נשיא דאתן לצלאה** בתרע משכן זימנא

ספ׳ אח׳ וית דמשהן ית קרבני נשיא דמדכיין דאתן לצלאה

1 Sam. 2:24 (57r)

לא בני ארי לא תקנא שמועתא דאנא שמע **דרבנין** עמא דיוי

ל׳ א׳ דרבנין מרנין

ל׳ א׳ מרנין

1 Sam. 3:3 (58r)

ובוצין בית מקדשא דיוי עד לא טפא ושמואל **#**[**שכיב**]#** **בעזרת** ליואי וקלא אישתמע בהיכלא דיוי דתמן ארונא דיוי

בעזרת **פליג**

1 Sam. 3:14 (58v)

ובכין קיימית לבית עלי אם ישתבקון חובי בית עלי **בניכסת קודשין ובקורבנין עד עלמא**

ירוש׳ אלהין במעסק באוריתא ובעובדין טבין

1 Sam. 4:12 (59r)

ורהט גברא משיבטא דבית בנימן מסידרא ואתא *לישילו*#לשילו# ביומא ההוא ולבושוהי מבוזעין ועפרא רמי ברישיה

ספ׳ אח׳ ורהט שאול בר קיש גברא דמן שיבט בנימן מסידרי קרבא ואתא לשילו ביומא ההוא על יד מלאכא דארהטיה] מת[מן

1 Sam. 4:19 (59v)

וכלתיה איתת פינחס מעדיא למילד ושמעת ית שמועתא דאישתבי ארונא דיוי ודמית חמוהא ודאיתקטיל בעלה **וכרעת** וילידת ארי בעתוה חיבלהא

וחממט **פליג**

1 Sam. 5:6 (60r)

ותקיפת מחתא דיוי על אינש אשדוד ואצדינון ואלקי יתהון **בטחוריא** ית אשדוד וית תחומהא

בטחרייא **פליג**

1 Sam. 5:11 (60r)

ושלחו וכנשו ית כל טורני פלשתאי ואמרו שלחו ית ארון אלהא דישראל ויתוב לאתריה ולא יקטל יתי וית עמי ארי הוה שיגוש **קרתא** בכל קרתא תקיפת לחדא מחתא דיוי תמן

ס׳ א׳ קטול

388

Chapter Fourteen. Appendices

1 Sam. 6:7 (60v)

וכען סבו ועיבידו עגלתא חדתא ותרתין תורן חדא ותרתין תורן **מיניקן** דלא נגדא בניר ותיסרון ית תורן בעגלתא ותתיבון בניהון מבתריהון לגאו

ל' א' מניקן

1 Sam. 6:12 (60v)

ואכוינא תורתא באורחא על אורח בית שמש בכבישא חד אזלין מיזל **וגעין** ולא סטאה לימינא ולשמאלא וטורני פלישתאי אזלין בתריהון עד תחום בית שמש

ל' א' ואכו[ונ]א

ל' א' וגעין

1 Sam. 6:19 (61r)

וקטל בגברי בית שמש **על דחדיאו ארונא דייי כד גלו** וקטל בסבי עמא שבעין גברא ובקהלא חמשין אלפין גברא ואתאבלו עמא ארי מחא יוי בעמא מחא סגיאה

ירוש' על דחדיאו בתבריהון דיש -ובזו ית ארונא דייי כד גלא

1 Sam. 7:2 (61v)

והוה מיומא דשרא ארונא בקירית יערים וסגיאו יומיא והוו עשרין שנין **ואיתנהיאו** כל בית ישר' בתר פולחנא דיוי

וא' דא' ואיתווכחו

1 Sam. 8:2 (62r)

והוה שום בריה בוכרא יואל ושום תינייה אביה **דינין** בבאר שבע

ל' א' נגודין

1 Sam. 9:4 (63r)

ועבר בטורא דבית אפרים ועבר בארע דלמא ולא אשכחו ועברו בארע **מתברא** ולית ועבר בארע שיבט בנימן ולא אשכחו

ל' א' מדברא

1 Sam. 10:22 (65r)

ושאילו עוד במימרא דייי האית עוד הכא גברא ואמר יוי הא הוא טמיר במניא

תרג' ירוש' ושאילו עוד במימרא דיוי האית עוד הכא גברא דחזיא ליה מלכותא ואמר יוי הא הוא בבית אולפנא טמיר ומצלי וקרי במאני ריגוג אוריתא

1 Sam. 11:2 (65r)

ואמר להון נחש מלכא דבני עמון אם תעבדון כהדא איגזר לכון קים **במיקר** לכון כל עיינא דימינא ואישוינה חיסודא על כל ישראל

תרג' ירוש' במחקותי מן אוריתא דילכון תפקדתא דכתיבא בג[ו]ה דלא ידכון עמונאי ומואבאי למיעל בקהלא דיוי ואשוי[נה] חיסודא על כל ישראל

389

The Transmission of Targum Jonathan in the West

1 Sam. 11:7 (65v)

ונסיב פדן תוריא והדמיה ושלח בכל תחום ישראל ביד איזגדיא למימר דליתוהי נפיק בתר שאול
ובתר שמואל כדין יתעביד לתוריה ונפל **זייעא** מן קדם יוי על עמא ונפקו כגברא חד
ל׳ א׳ רתיתא

1 Sam. 11:11 (65v)

והוה ביומא דבתרוהי ומני שאול ית עמא תלתין משיריין ועלו בגו משריתא במטרת צפרא ומחו
ית בני עמון **עד מיחם יומא** והוה דאישתארו ואיתבדרו ולא אישתארו בהון תרין דערקין כחדא
ל׳ א׳ עד ארבע שעי יומא ומן אסקות עלת תדירא דצפרא

1 Sam. 12:2 (66r)

וכען הא מלכא מדבר ברישכון ואנא **קשית וסיבית ובני הא אינון עימכון ואנא הליכית**
קדמיכון מזעורי עד יומא הדין
ל׳ א׳ קשישית וסיבית ובני הא אוטיבו אורחתהון והא אינון באולפן עימכון

1 Sam. 12:3 (66r)

הא עד דאנא קיים אסהידו בי קדם יוי וקדם משיחיה תורא דמן דברית וחמרא דמן **שחרית** וית מן
עשקית וית מן אנסית ומיד מן קבילית ממון דשקר וכבשית מיניה עיני בדינא ואתיב לכון
שחרית **פליג**

1 Sam. 12:5 (66r)

ואמר להון סהיד מימרא דיוי בכון וסהיד משיחיה יומא דין דלא אשכחתון בידי מידעם **ואמר סהיד**
ירוש׳ ונפלת ב[...] מן שמיא [...]סהיד

1 Sam. 12:7 (66r)

וכען איתעתדו **ואיתיכח** עימכון קדם יוי ית כל זכוותא דיוי דעבד עימכון ועם אבהתכון
ל׳ א׳ ואתווכח

1 Sam. 12:11 (66v)

ושלח יוי ית גדעון **וית בדן** וית יפתח וית שמואל ושיזיב יתכון מיד בעלי דבביכון מסחור סחור
ויתיבתון לרוחצן
ל׳ א׳ ית שמשון [דאתי מן] שיבט דן

1 Sam. 12:25 (folio missing)

main text missing
וא׳ דאמ׳ עובדיכון

1 Sam. 17:4 (67r)

ונפק **גברא מביניהון ממשירירית פלישתאי גלית שמיה** מגת רומיה שית אמין וזרתא
תרג׳ ירוש׳ גברא פולומרכא דאיתיליד מביני תרתי גניסן מן שמשון דהוה מן שיבט דן ומן ערפה
דהות מן בני מואב גלית שמיה

1 Sam. 17:5 (67r)

וקולס דנחש על רישיה **ושיריין גלבין הוא לביש ומתקל** שיריינא חמשא אלפין תיקלין נחשא
תרג׳ יר׳ ושיריין דגלד נוני ימא רבא הוא לביש ועלוהי שיריין דנחשא ומתקל

Chapter Fourteen. Appendices

1 Sam. 17:8 (67r)

וקם ואכלי על סידרי ישראל ואמר להון למא תיפקון לסדרא קרבא **הלא אנא פלישתאה ואתון עבדין לשאול בחרו לכון גברא וייחות לוותי**

ירוש׳ הלא אנא גלית פלישתאה דעבדית עימכון קרבא באפק ונצחית יתכון ונסבית מן ידיכון ית ארונא דיוי ואתון עבדין לשאול ואם אתון אמרין על מימרא דיוי מרי נצחן קרביא אנחנא מתרחצין קרו ליה ויחות לותי

1 Sam. 17:10 (67r)

ואמר פלישתאה אנא חסידית ית סידרי ישראל יומא הדין * איתו לי גברא ונגיח כחדא

ירוש׳ דבעיתי מנכון קרבא ולא תגיחון קריבן קדמיי

1 Sam. 17:16 (67v)

וקריב פלישתאה **מקדים ומחשיך ואיתעתד ארבעין יומין**

ירו׳ מקדים ומחשיך בעידן קרבן תדירא דצפרא ודרמשא וחסיד ארבעין יומין

1 Sam. 17:18 (67v)

וית עשר גובנין דחלבה האילין תובל **לרב אלפא** וית אחך תסער לשלם **וית טיבהון תיתי**

ספ׳ אח׳ לרב דממנא על אלפא גיבריא

ירוש׳ יות גט פיטורי בשיהון תיסב ותיתי

1 Sam. 17:26 (67v)

ואמר דוד לגבריא דקיימין עימיה למימר מא יתעביד לגברא דיקטול ית פלישתאה דיכי ויעדי **חיסדא** מעל ישראל ארי מן פלישתאה עריליאה הדין ארי חסיד סידרי עמא דיוי קיימא

ל׳ א׳ חיסודא

1 Sam. 17:49 (69r)

ואושיט דוד ית ידיה למנא ונסיב מתמן אבנא ואחזר ומחא ית פלישתאה על בית עינוהי **וטבעת** אבנא בבית עינוהי ונפל על אפוהי על ארעא

ל׳ א׳ וטמעת אבנא בפ[י]חתיה

1 Sam. 18:12 (69v)

ודחיל שאול מן קד׳ דוד ארי הוה מימרא דיוי בסעדיה* וית שאול רחיק

ל׳ א׳ ומעילוי שאול איסתלק

1 Sam. 19:13 (71r)

ונסיבת מיכל ית **צילמניא** ושויאת על ערסא וית **ברדא** דעיזיא שויאת איסדוהי וכסיאת בלבושא

ל׳ א׳ עביטא

ל׳ א׳ גונכא דמעזי

1 Sam. 19:16 (71r)

ואתו איזגדיא והא **צילמניא** על ערסא **ובודא** דעיזיא איסדוהי

ל׳ א׳ עביטא

ל׳ א׳ וגונכא דמעזי

The Transmission of Targum Jonathan in the West

1 Sam. 20:18 (72r)

ואמר ליה יהונתן מחר ריש ירחא ותיתבעי ארי יהי **מרווח בית אסחרותא**
ל' א' מרווח בית אסחרותך

1 Sam. 20:25 (72v)

ואסחר מלכא על **שיוויה** כזמן בזמן על שיוויא דמתקן ליה בסטר כותלא וקם יהונתן ואסרן אבנר
מסיטרא דשאול והוה אתרא דדוד מרווח
וא' דא' שיוויה

1 Sam. 20:29 (72v)

ואמר שלחני כען ארי שירו ניכסת קודשיא לנא בקרתא והוא **פקיד** לי אחי וכען אם אשכחית
רחמין בעינך אישתיזב כען ואיחזי ית אחי על כן לא על לפתורא דמלכא
ל' א' בעא

1 Sam. 20:42 (73r)

ואמר יהונתן לדוד איזיל לשלם דקיימנא **תרוונא** אנחנא בשמא דיוי למימר מימרא דיוי יהי סהיד
בינא ובינך ובין בניי ובין בנך עד עלמא
תרווינבא **פליג**

1 Sam. 21:7 (73v)

ויהב ליה כהנא קודשא ארי לא הוה תמן לחם חולין לחם אילהין לחם אפיא דמעדן מן קדם יוי
לשוויותיה לחם **חמים** ביום איתנסבותיה
ל' א' חמים

1 Sam. 21:8 (73v)

ותמן גברא מעבדי שאול ביומא ההוא כניש קד' יוי ושמיה דואג **אדומאה רב רעיא** דלשאול
ליש' אח' רבן תלמידיא דלשאול

1 Sam. 21:14 (74r)

ושני ית מדעיה בעיניהון **ואישתמם** בידהון ומסרט על דשי תרעא ומחית ריריה על דיקניה
ליש' אח' ואישתעמם

1 Sam. 21:16 (74r)

חסר שטיא אנא ארי *אתיתון*#*איתיתון# ית דין *לאשתתא*#לאשטתאה# עלי **הדין ייעולללבייתי**
ספ' אח' הדין כשר למיעל לביתי

1 Sam. 22:14 (74v)

ואתיב אחימלך ית מלכא ואמר ומן בכל עבדך כדוד מהימן וחתנא דמלכא ורב על **משמעתך** ויקיר
בביתך
ל' א' שימושך

1 Sam. 22:15 (74v)

יומא דין דשריתי למישאל ליה במימרא דיוי חס לי לא ישוי מלכא בעבדיה **פיתגמא** בכל
#**# בית# אבא ארי לא ידע עבדך בכל דא פיתגם זעיר או רב
ל' א' עילתא

Chapter Fourteen. Appendices

1 Sam. 22:18 (74v)

ואמר מלכא לדואג איסתחר את **ושלט** בכהניא ואיסתחר דואג אדומאה ושלט **#הוא**# בכהניא
וקטל ביומא ההוא תמנן וחמשה גברא דכשרין למלבש אפוד דבוץ

וא׳ דא׳ ושלוט

1 Sam. 22:22 (75r)

ואמר דוד לאביתר ידענא ביומא ההוא ארי תמן דואג אדומאה ארי חואה יחוי לשאול אנא
גרימית *איסתקפה*#לאיסתקפה# בכל נפש בית אבוך

ל׳ א׳ גרמית

1 Sam. 23:19 (75v)

וסליקו אינש זיף לות שאול לגבעתא למימר הלא דוד מיטמר עימנא במצדתא בחרשא בגבעת
חכילה דמדרום **לישימון**

וא׳ דא׳ למדברא

1 Sam. 23:22 (76r)

איזילו כען **ואתקינו** עוד ודעו וחזו ית אתריה דשרי ביה מן חזהי תמן ארי אמרין לי דערים ונפיק
הוא

ליש׳ אח׳ ואיתבררו

1 Sam. 23:24 (76r)

וקמו ואזלו לזיף קדם שאול ודוד וגברוהי במדברא דמעון במישרא דמדרום **לישימון**

וא׳ דא׳ למדברא

1 Sam. 23:26 (76r)

ואזל שאול מסטר טורא מיכא ודוד וגברוהי מסטר טורא מיכא והוה דוד מיתבעית למיזל מן קדם
שאול ושאול וגברוהי **כמנין** על דוד וגברוהי למיחדהון

וא׳ דא׳ מקפין לדוד

1 Sam. 24:6 (76v)

והוה בתר כן **וחש** דוד בליביה על דפסק ית כנפא דלשאול

ל׳ א׳ ותהא

1 Sam. 24:8 (76v)

ופייס דוד ית גברוהי בפיתגמיא ולא שבקינון למקם לות שאול ושאול קם ממערתא ואזל בארחא

ל׳ א׳ ושדל

1 Sam. 24:16 (76v)

ויהי יוי לדיין ועביד דין בינא ובינך וגלי קדמוהי וידין דיני ויתפרע **עולבני** מינך

וא׳ דא׳ עלבוני

1 Sam. 25:6 (77r)

ותימרון כדין **לחייך** ואת שלם וביתך שלם וכל דלך שלם

ל׳ א׳ לחייך

The Transmission of Targum Jonathan in the West

1 Sam. 25:8 (77r)

שאל ית עולימך ויחוון לך וישכחון עולימיא רחמין בעינך ארי על **יום טב** אתינא הב כען ית דתשכח ידך לעבדך ולברך לדוד

ל׳ א׳ יומא דשירותא

1 Sam. 25:18 (77v)

ואוחיאת אביגיל ונסיבת מאתן גריצן דלחים ותרין גרבין דחמר וחמש עאן תכברא וחמש סוון קליא ומאה איתכלין דעינבין יבישין ומאתן **מנן דבילתא** ושויאת על חמריא

ל׳ א׳ מאנן דבלתא

ל׳ א׳ עיגולי דבלתא

1 Sam. 25:39 (78v)

ושמע דוד ארי מית נבל ואמר בריך יוי דין דדן ית דין חסדאי מידא דנבל וית עבדיה מנע מלמיעבד בישא וית בישת נבל אתיב יוי ברישיה **ושלח דוד** ושאיל באביגיל למיסבה ליה לאיתו

ל׳ א׳ ושדר דוד ומליל על עיסק אביגיל

1 Sam. 26:1 (79r)

ואתו אינש זיף לות ש[או]ל לגיבעתא למימר הלא דוד מיטמר בגבעת חכילה דעל אפי **ישימון**

ל׳ א׳ בית ישימ׳

1 Sam. 26:2 (79r)

וקם שאול ונחת למדבר זיף ועימיה תלתא אלפין גברא **בחורי ישראל** למיבעי ית דוד במדבר זיף

ל׳ א׳ עולימי גיברי ישראל

1 Sam. 26:9 (79r)

ואמר דוד לאבישי לא תחבלניה ארי מן אושיט ידיה *במשיח**#*במשיחא*#* דיוי וזכא*

ספ׳ אח׳ בדינא

1 Sam. 26:20 (80r)

וכען לא יתשד דמי על ארעא מן קדם מימרא דיוי ארי נפק מלכא דישראל למיבעי ית חלש חד **כמא דמתרדיף קוראה בטוריא**

ספ׳ אח׳ כמא דרדיף בר ניצצא ית קוראה בטוריא

1 Sam. 28:3 (80v)

ושמואל מית וספדו עלוהי כל ישראל וקברוהי ברמתא וספדו עלוהי אינש קרתיה ושאול פלי ית בידין וזכורו מן ארעא

ל׳ א׳ פלי

1 Sam. 28:19 (81v)

וימסר יוי אף ית ישראל עמך בידא דפלשתאי **ומחר** את ובנך עימי לחוד ית משריתא דישראל ימסר יוי בידא דפלשתאי

ספ׳ אח׳ ומחר את ובנך גבאי בגנז חיי עלמא

Chapter Fourteen. Appendices

1 Sam. 30:16 (83r)

ואחתיה והא **רטישין** על אפי כל ארעא אכלין ושתן **וחגגין** בכל עדאה סגיאה דשבו מארע פלשתאי ומארע יהודה

ל׳ א׳ פריסין

ספ׳ אח׳ ועבדין שירותא

1 Sam. 30:17 (83r)

ומחנון דוד מקיבלא ועד עידן רמשא ביומא דבתרוהי ולא אישתיזב מינהון איניש אלהין ארבע מאה גבר עולים דרכיבו על **ינקייא** ואפכו

וא׳ דא׳ גמלייא

1 Sam. 30:23 (83r)

ואמר דוד לא תעבדון כן אחי ית דיהב יוי לנא ונטר יתנא **ויהב** ית משריתא דאתת עלנא בידנא

ל׳ א׳ ומסר

1 Sam. 31:4 (83v)

ואמר שאול לנטיל זייניה שלוף חרבך וקטולני בה דילמא ייתון עריליא האילין ויקטלונני **ויתעלבון** בי ולא אבה נטיל זייניה ארי דחיל לחדא ונסיב שאול ית חרבא ונפל עלה

ספ׳ אח׳ ויתלעבון

2 Sam. 1:6 (84r)

ואמר עולימא דמחוי ליה **איתערעא איתערעית** בטורא דגלבע והא שאול סמיך על מורניתיה והא רתיכיא ומשירייית פרשייא אדבקוהי

ספ׳ אח׳ איזדמנא איזדמניא

2 Sam. 1:9 (84v)

ואמר לי קום כען עלי וקטולני ארי אחדני רתיתא ארי **כל עוד נפשי בי**

ל׳ א׳ ארי שלי[מ]ת כען נפשי מיני

2 Sam. 1:10 (84v)

וקמית עלוהי וקטלתיה ארי ידענא ארי לא יחי בתר דנפל ונסבית כלילא דעל רישיה **וטוטפתא** דעל דרעיה ואיתיתינון לות ריבוני הלכא

וא׳ דא׳ תפילין

2 Sam. 1:18 (84v)

ואמר לאלפא ית בני יהודה מיגד* בקשתא הא היא *היא*## כתיבא על סיפרא דאוריתא

No siglum

והיכן כתיב יהודה אתה יודוך אחיך ידך בערף איביך אי זו היא מלחמה כנגד הערף הוי אומר זה החץ

The Transmission of Targum Jonathan in the West

2 Sam. 1:21 (84v)

טורי בגלבע לא יחות עליכון טלא ומטרא לא *יהי*#תהי# בכון עללא כמיסת דיעבדון* מינה

חלתא ארי תמן איתברו תריסי גיבריא תריסא דשאול דמשיח כיד במישחא

ל' א' טורי גלבע

ספ' אח' וחקל טורייא

2 Sam. 2:29 (86r)

ואבנר וגברוהי הליכו במישרא כל ליליא ההוא ועברו ית ירדנא ואזלו כל **בתרון** ואתו למחנים

ספ' אח' פסגוותא

2 Sam. 3:5 (86v)

ושתיתאה יתר' לעג' **איתת דוד** אילין איתילידו לדוד בחברון

ספ' אח' למיכל איתת דוד

2 Sam. 3:14 (87r)

ושלח דוד איזגדין לות אישבשת בר שאול למימר הב ית איתתי ית מיכל **דארסית** לי במאה עורלי פלישתאי

ל' א' דקדשית

2 Sam. 3:27 (87v)

ותב אבנר לחברון ואפנייה יואב לגו תרעא למללא עימיה **בשיליא** ומחהי תמן בסטר ירכיה ומית בדם **עשאל אחוהי**

ספ' אח' ברז על מה דאישתלי

וא' דא' חלף דקטל עשאל אחוהי

2 Sam. 3:33 (87v)

ואלא מלכא על אבנר ואמר הכממת **רשיעין** ימות אבנר

ל' א' גבר הדיוט

2 Sam. 4:2 (88r)

ותרין גברין רבני תרתין משיריין הוו **בר שאול** שום חד בענה ושום תיניינא רכב בני רמון דמבארות מבני בנימן ארי אף בארות מתחשבא על דבית בנימן

וא' דא' מגניסת שאול

וא' דא' עם בר שאול

2 Sam. 4:4 (88r)

וליהונתן בר שאול בר לקי בתרתין ריגלוהי בר חמש שנין הוה כד אתת בסורת שאול ויהונתן מיזרעאל ונטלתיה **תורבנותיה** ואפכת והוה באיתבעותה למיערק ונפל וחגר ושמיה מפיבשת

ל' א' תורבייניתיה

2 Sam. 4:6 (88r)

והא * אתו עד גו ביתא כזבני חיטין ומחוהי בסטר ירכיה ורכב ובענה אחוהי אישתיזבו

ל'א' ואינון

Chapter Fourteen. Appendices

2 Sam. 5:7 (88v)

וכבש דוד ית חקרא דציון היא קרתא דדוד

ל׳ א׳ ואחד

2 Sam. 6:19 (90r)

ופליג לכל עמא לכל המונא דישראל למיגבר ועד איתא לגבר גריצתא דלחים חד ופלוג **חד ומנתא** חדא ואזל כל עמא גבר לביתיה

ספ׳ אח׳ חד מן שיתא בתורא וחד מן שיתא בהינא דחמרא

2 Sam. 6:21 (90v)

ואמר דוד למיכל קד׳ יוי דאיתרעי בי מאבוך ומכל ביתיה **לפקדא** יתי למיהוי מלכא על עמא דיוי על ישראל ושבחית קד׳ יוי

וא׳ דא׳ למנאה

2 Sam. 7:18 (91r)

ואתא מלכא דוד ויתיב קד׳ יוי ואמר לית אנא כמיסת יוי אלהים ומן ביתי ארי אמטיתני **עד הלכא**

ל׳ א׳ ארי אמטיתני עד מלכותא

2 Sam. 7:22 (91r)

על כן רב את יוי אלהים ארי לית כוותך ולית אלה בר מינך ככל דשמענא **אמרו** קדמאנא

דאמרו פליג

2 Sam. 11:21 (94v)

מן קטל ית אבימלך בר ירובשת הלא איתתא רמת עלוהי פלגות רכב **רחיווהי** מן שורא ומית בתבץ ולמה איתקרבתון לשורא ותימר אף עבדך אוריה חתאה מית

ל׳ א׳ רחי

2 Sam. 12:8 (95r)

ויהבית לך ית בית ריבונך וית נשי ריבונך **בחנך** ויהבית לך ית בית ישראל ויהודה ואם זעיר ואוסיף לך כאילין וכאילין

ל׳ א׳ בחונך

ל׳ א׳ בעובך

ל׳ א׳ בעטפך

ל׳ א׳ בחנך

2 Sam. 13:26 (97r)

ואמר אבשלום **ולא** ייזיל כען עימנא אמנון אחי ואמר ליה מלכא למא ייזיל עימך

ל׳ א׳ בבעו

2 Sam. 14:14 (98r)

ארי מיתא דמאית הא כמיא דמתשדין לארעא דלא איפשר להון **דיסתפון** כין לית איפשר לדיינא דקושטא לקבלא ממון דשקר ודמחשב מחשבן בדיל דלא לבדרא מיניה בידור

ל׳ א׳ דיתאספון

The Transmission of Targum Jonathan in the West

2 Sam. 15:4 (99v)

ואמר אבש' מן ימניני דיינא בארעא וקדמי ייתי כל גבר דיהי ליה דין ומצו ***ואידיניה**

ספ' אח' ואיזכיניה בדיניה

2 Sam. 15:11 (99v)

ועם אבשלום אזלו מאתן גברא מירושלם **זמינין** ואזלין לתומהון ולא ידעין כל מידעם

ספ' אח' מקצתהון זמינין ומקצתהון אזלין מן תומהון

2 Sam. 17:10 (102r)

והוא אף גבר גיבר דלביה כליביה דאריא **ממסא** מסי ארי ידע כל ישראל ארי גיבר אבוך וגברין גיברין דעימיה

ל' א' איפשר דממסא ימסי

2 Sam. 18:14 (104r)

ואמר יואב הלא מבכין אנא אישרי קדמך ונסיב תלתא **גיססין** בידיה וקבעינון בליבא דאבשלום ועד כען קיים בגו בוטמא

ל' א' לונכיין

2 Sam. 18:17 (104r)

ונסיבו ית אבשל' ורמו יתיה בחורשא לגו **קומצא** רבא ואקימו עלוהי דגור אבנין רב לחדא וכל ישראל אפכו גבר לקירווהי

ל' א' גומצא

2 Sam. 18:18 (104r)

ואבשלום נסיב ואקים ליה בחייוהי ית קמתא דבמישר מלכא ארי אמר לית לי **ברא** בדיל לאדכרא שמי וקרא לקמתא על שמיה וקרא לה אתרא דאבשלום עד יומא הדין

ל' א' בר דכר

2 Sam. 21:1 (108r)

והוה כפנא ביומי דוד תלת שנין שתא בתר שתא ובעא דוד רחמין מן קדם יוי ואמר יוי על שאול ועל בית חייבי קטול על דקטל **ית גבעונאי**

ספ' אח' על דקטל ית כהניא דהוו מספקין מזון לגבעונאי

2 Sam. 21:3 (108r)

ואמר דוד לגיבעו– מא אעביד לכון ובמה איכפר **ובריכו ית אחסנת עמא דיוי**

ספ' אח' ובעו רחמין דתעדי כפנא מאחסנת עמא דיוי

2 Sam. 21:5 (108r)

ואמרו למלכא גברא דשיצינא **ודחשב לנא אישתיצנא מלמידר בכל תחום ישראל**

ספ' אח' ודחשב למפסק חיויתנא יתחשב ליה כאילו אישתצנא מלמדר וגומ'

2 Sam. 21:12 (108v)

ואזל דוד ונסיב ית גרמי שאול וית גרמי יהונתן בריה מלות יתבי יבש גלעד דיגנבו יתהון **משורא דבית שאן** דצלבונון תמן פלישתאי ביומא דקטלו פלישתאי ית שאול בגלבע

ספ' אח' מרחוב בית שאן

Chapter Fourteen. Appendices

2 Sam. 22:26 (110r)

אברהם דאישתכח חסיד קדמך בכין אסגיתא למיעבד חסדא עם זרעיה יצחק דהוה שלים בדחלתך בכין אשלימתך מימר רעותך עימיה

לי אי [עם אברהם]

2 Sam. 23:33 (112r)

שמה דמן חרוד אחיאם בר שרר **דמהר גבוה**

לי אי דמטור גביה

3. Liturgical Sources (Chapter Ten)

Introductions

t1601i

יום ראשון לויושע

מפטירין בשמואל וידבר דוד

ומתרגמינן

אמיר דאיתאמר על ידי

שמאול

נבייא

t1639i

ואומר קדיש עד לעילא ומוציאין ס״ת אחר וקורא בו המפטיר בפרש׳ פנחס והקרבתם

והוא כתוב למעלה בסדר יום ראשון של חול המועד

ומפטירין בשמואל ומתרגמינן

הפטרה אמיר דאיתאמר על ידי שמואל נבייא

t1679i

Heading of Hebrew:

ומפטיר קורא והתקרבתם עד סוף פיסקא. ומפטיר בשמואל.

Heading of Targum:

ומתרגמינן

אמיר דאיתמר על ידי שמואל נבייא

t1647i

הפטרה מיום ראשון מימים אחרונים שלפסח

אמיר דאיתאמר על ידי דוד נגידא

t1618i

Heading of Hebrew:

ומוציאין ספר אחר וקורא בו המפטיר בפרש פינחס ו[ה]תקרבתם עד סוף פיסקא ומפטיר בשמואל וידבר דוד ליהוה

N.B. ו[ה]תקרבתם is an error. Read והקרבתם.

Heading of Targum:

אמיר דאיתמר על ידי שמואל נבייא

t1621i

Heading of Hebrew:

ואחר כך מוצאין ספר תורה אחר וקורא בו המפטיר והקרבתם כאתמול ומפטירין בשמואל

Heading of Targum:

ומתחילין ההפטרה תרגום

t159a

ביום טוב ראשון מן האחרונים של פסח מפטיר בשמואל

t99a

ליום שביעי

t133a

יום שביעי של פסח

מפטיר שמלכים [sic]

t1631a

Heading of Hebrew:

לשביעי של פסח

Heading of Targum:

אמיר דאיתאמר [פתגמאה] על ידיה דוד מלכא כמה דפרש יהונתן בר עוזיאל

Closing Formula

t1601i

על דא יתברך וישתבח שמא דאלהא רבא וקדישא לעלם ולעלמי עלמיא

t1639i

על דא יתברך וישתבח שמא דאלהא רבא וקדישא לעלם ולעלמי עלמייא

t1679i

על דא יתברך וישתבח שמא דאלהא רבא וקדישא לעלם ולעלמי עלמייא

t1647i

על דא יתברך וישתבח שמא דאלהא רבא וקדישא לעלם ולעלמי עלמייא

t1618i

על דא יתברך וישתבח שמא דאלהא רבא וקדישא לעלם ולעלמי עלמייא

t1621i

על דא יתברך וישתבח שמא דאלהא רבא וקדישא לעלם ולעלמי עלמיא

Synopsis

Babylonian Tradition Compared to t1601i and t133a

KEY:

Illegible text [...]

מי[מרי]ה Unclear characters

מממריה Original wording

#מממריה# Corrected wording

Minus compared to the Babylonian tradition [>]

Variants from the Babylonian tradition in bold font (excluding orthography, spelling, minor errors etc.)

2 Sam. 22:1

t2520b

ושבח דוד בנבואה ק׳ יוי ית פתגמי תשבחתא הדא על כל יומיא דשיזיב יוי ית ישר׳ מיד כל בעלי דבביהון ואף לדוד מחרבא דשאול

t1601i

ושבח דוד בנבואה קדם יוי ית פיתגמי תושבחתא הדא על כל יומיא דשיזיב יוי ית ישראל מיד כל בעלי דבביהון ואף לדוד **שיזביה** מחרבא דשאול

t133a

ושבח דוד בנבואה קדם יוי ית **כל** פיתגמי תושבחת׳ הדא על כל יומיא דשיזיב יוי **יתיה וית** ישר׳ מידא דכל בעלי דבביהון ואף לדוד **משיזבא** מחרבא דשאול

2 Sam. 22:2

t2520b

ואמר יוי תוקפי ורחצני ומשיזיב יתי

t1601i

ואמר יוי תוקפי ורוחצני ומשיזיב **לי**

t133a

ואמר יוי [תוקפי] ורוחצני [>] משזיב [ית]י

The Transmission of Targum Jonathan in the West

2 Sam. 22:3

t709b

אלהי דאתרעי בי קרבני לדחלתיה תקפי דמן קדמוהי מתיהיב לי תקוף ופורקן לאתגברא על בעלי דבבי רחצני דעל מימריה אנא רחיץ בעידן עקא מגין עלי מיבעלי דבבי ואמר לארמא קרני בפרקניה סומכני דהוה מימריה סמך לי כד הויתי עריק מן קדם רדפי פרקני מבעלי דבבי ואף מיד כל חטופין שיזיב יתי

t1601i

אלה**א** דאיתרעי בי קירבני לדחלתיה תוקף דמן קדמוהי מתיהיב לי תקוף ופורקן לאיתגברא על בעלי דבבי **הוינא** רחיץ בעידן עקא מגן עלי מבעלי דבביי ואמר לארמא קרני בפורקניה סומכני דהוה מימריה סמיך לי כד הויתי עריק מן קדם רדפיי **שיזבני** מן **שנאיי** ואף מיד כל חטופין שיזיב יתי **ומידא דשאול מלכא הוה פריק לי**

t133a

אלה**א** דאיתרעי בי קירבני לדחלתיה תוקף דמן קדמוהי **איתיהיב** לי תקוף ופורקן לאיתגברא על בעלי דבבי רוחצני דעל מימריה אנא רחיץ [>] כד הויתי עריק מן קדם רודפי **מגן עלי** מבעלי דבבי ואף מיד כל חטופין **ואניסין** שיזיב יתי

2 Sam. 22:4

t2520b

אמר דוד בת[וש]בחא אנא מצלי ק׳ יוי דבכל עידן מבעלי דבבי פריק יתי

t1601i

אמר דוד בתישבחתא אנא **פתח פומי** ומצלי קדם יוי דבכל עידן **עקא** מבעלי דבביי **הוה** פריק **לי**

t133a

אמר דוד בתושבחת׳ אנא מצלי קדם יוי דבכל עידן מבעלי דבבי פריק יתי

2 Sam. 22:5

t2520b

ארי אקיפתני עקא כאיתא דיתבא על מתברא וחיל לית לה למילד והיא מסכנא לממת סיעת חייבין בעיתת יתי

t1601i

ארי אקפתני עקא כאיתא דיתבא על מתברא וחיל לית **בה** למילד והיא מסכנא לממת סיעת **שקרין** ביעתת יתי

t133a

ארי אקפתני עקא כאיתה דיתבה על מתברא וחיל לית לה למילד והיא מסכנא לממת **וסיעת** חייבין בעיתת יתי

Chapter Fourteen. Appendices

2 Sam. 22:6

t2520b

משרית רשיעין אקפוני קדמוני דמזינין במני קטול

t1601i

משיריית **רשיען** אקפוני **ערעוני** דמזיינין במאני קטול

t133a

משייריין רשיען סגיאן אקפוני **ערעוני** דמזיינין במאני קטול

2 Sam. 22:7

t2520a

אמר דוד כד עיקא לי אנא מצלי ק׳ יוי וקדם אילהי אנא מתחנן ומקביל מיהיכליה צלותי ובעותי קדמוהי מתעבדא

t1601i

אמר דוד כד עייקא לי אנא **פתח פומי** ומצלי קדם יוי וקדם אלהי אנא **מצלי** ומתחנן ומקבל מהיכליה צלותי ובעותי קדמוהי מתעבדא **בעידן צלותי**

t133a

אמר דוד כד עקא לי אנא מצלי קדם יוי וקדם אלהי אנא מחנן ומקבל מהיכליה צלותי ובעותי **דמן** קדמוהי מתעבדא

2 Sam. 22:8

t2520b

ואתרגיפת ואתרגישת ארעא שכלולי שמיא זעו ואתרכינו ארי תקוף רוגזיה

t1601i

ואתרגיפת ואתרגישת **ואזדעזעת** ארעא ושכלולי שמיא זעו **ואזדעזעו טוריא ואתהפיכו עמקי ימא** ארי תקוף רוגזא **דאלהנא חייא וקיימא**

t133a

ואיתרגיפת ואיתרגישת ארעא שכלולי שמיא זעו ואיתרכינו ארי תקוף רוגזיה

2 Sam. 22:9

t709b

סליק זדוניה דפרעה כתננא קדמוהי בכין שלח רוגזיה כאישא בערא דמן קדמוהי משיציא מזופיתיה כגומרין דנור דלקא ממימריה

t1601i

סליק זדוניה דפרעה **רשיעא** כתננא **באפ[ו]י** בכן שלח רוגזיה כאשא בערא [>] מן קדמוהי **משיציין** ומזופיתיה כגומרין דנור **דלקן** מן מימריה

t133a

סליק זדוניה דפרעה **רשיעא** כתננא **דאתונא** קדמוהי [>] משיציא מזופיתיה כגומר[ין] דנור דלקא ממימריה

The Transmission of Targum Jonathan in the West

2 Sam. 22:10

t709b

וארכין שמיא ואתגלי יקריה וענן אמיטתא כיבש קדמוהי

t1601i

וארכין שמיא ואיתגלי יקריה **בקברתיה** (read: בגבורתיה) וענן אמיטתא כיבש קדמוהי

t133a

וארכין שמיא ואיתגלי יקריה וענן אמיטתא כיבש קדמוהי

2 Sam. 22:11

t709b

ואתגלי בגבורתיה על כרובין קלילין ודבר בתקוף על כנפי רוחא

t1601i

ואשרי שכינתיה על כרובין קלילין **ואיתגלי ביקר** ודבר בתקוף על **פני** רוחא

t133a

ואיתגלי בגבורתי׳ על כרובין קלילין ודבר בתקוף על כנפי רוחא

2 Sam. 22:12

t709b

אשרי שכינתיה בערפילא ענן יקר סח׳ סח׳ ליה מחית מין תקיפין מריכפת עננין קלילין ברום עלמא

t1601i

ואשרי שכינתיה בערפילא וענן יקר סחור ליה מחית מיין ת[ק]יפין **מריגפת** עננין קלילין ברום עלמא

t133a

ואשרי שכינתיה בערפילא וענן יקר סחור ליה מחית **עננין** תקיפין **מרוכסת** [read: מריכפת] עננין קלילין ברום עלמא

2 Sam. 22:13

t709b

מזיו יקריה מבהקין שמי שמיא מזופיתיה כגומרין דנור דלקא ממימריה

t1601i

מ[ז]יו יקריה **דאלהא חייא וקיימא** מבהיקין **שמיא** ושמי שמיא ומזופיתיה כגומרין ד[נו]ר **דלק[ו]ן** ממימריה

t133a

מזיו יקריה מבהיקין שמי שמיא מזופיתיה כגומרין דנור דלקא ממימריה

2 Sam. 22:14

t709b

אכלי מן שמיא יוי ועילאה אריס מימריה

Chapter Fourteen. Appendices

t1601i

אכלי מן שמיא יוי ועילאה ארים **קליה**

t133a

אכלי מן שמיא יוי ועילאה ארים **במימריה**

2 Sam. 22:15

t709b

ושלח מחתיה כגירין ובדרינון ברקין ושגישינון

t1601i

ושלח מחתיה **בהון** ובדרינון ברקין וש[גי]שינון

t133a

ושלח מחתיה כגירין ובדרינון ברקין ושגישינון

2 Sam. 22:16

t709b

ואיתחזיאו עמקי ימא אתגליאו שכלולי תבל במזופיתא מן ק' יוי ממימר תקוף רוגזיה

t1601i

ואיתחזיאו עמקי ימא **ואתגליאו** שכלולי תבל במזופית **רוח** מן קדם יוי ממימר תקוף רוגזיה

t133a

ואיתחזיאו עומקי ימא **ואיתגליאו** שכלולי תבל [>]מזופיתיה מן קדם יוי מימר תקוף רוגזיה

2 Sam. 22:17

t709b

שלח נביוהי מלך תקיף דיתיב בתקוף רומא דברני שיזבני מעממין סגיאין

t1601i

ישלח נביאוהי מלך תקיף דיתיב **בשכינתיה בשמי מרומא** דברני שיזבני מעממין סגיאין

t133a

שלח נביוהי מלך תקיף דיתיב בתקוף רומא דברני שיזבני מעממין סגיאין

2 Sam. 22:18

t709b

שיזבני מסנאי ארי תקפני מיבעלי דבבי ארי אתגברו עלי

t1601i

שיזבני מן שנאי ארי תקפוני **ומ**בעלי דבבי ארי איתגברו עלי

t133a

שזבני משנאי ארי **אקפוני** מבעלי דבבי ארי איתגברו עלי

2 Sam. 22:19

t709b

יקדמני ביום טלטולי והוה מימרא דיוי סמך לי

t1601i

ערעוני יקדמוני ביום טילטולי והוה מימרי**ה** דיוי סמיך לי

t133a

קידמוני ביום טילטולי והוה מימרא דיוי סמך לי

2 Sam. 22:20

t2520b

ואפיק לרווחא יתי שיזבני ארי איתרעי בי

t1601i

ואפיק לרווחא יתי שיזבני ארי איתרעי בי

t133a

ואפיק לרווחא יתי שיזבני ארי איתרעי בי

2 Sam. 22:21

t709b

אמר דוד ישלמנני יוי כזכותי כברירות ידי יתיב לי

t1601i

אמר דוד **יגמלני** יוי כזכותי כברירות ידיי יתיב לי

t133a

ישלמינני יוי כזכותי וכברותי [>] יתיב לי [>]

2 Sam. 22:22

t709b

ארי נטרית אורחן דתקנן ק׳ יוי ולא הליכית ברשע קדם אלהי

t1601i

ארי נטרית אורחן דתקנן קדם יוי ולא הליכית ברשע קדם אלהי

t133a

ארי נטרית **אורחא** דתקנן קדם יוי ולא הלכית ברשע קדם אלהי

2 Sam. 22:23

t709b

ארי כל דינוהי גלן לקבלי למעבדהון וקימוהי לא עדית מינהון

t1601i

ארי כל **דיני רעותיה** גלן לקיבלי למעבדהון וקיימוהי לא עדית מנהון

Chapter Fourteen. Appendices

t133a

ארי כל דינוהי גלו לקיבלי למיעבדהון [>|קייימוהי לא עדית מנהון

2 Sam. 22:24

t709b

והוית שלים בדחלתיה והוית נטר נפשי מחובין

t1601i

והויתי שלים ל[דחל]תיה והויתי נטר נפשי מחובין

t133a

והויתי שלים ב**דחלתא** דיוי **והוה** נטר נפשי מחובין

2 Sam. 22:25

t709b

ואתיב יוי לי כזכותי כברירותי קדם מימריה

t1601i

ואתיב יוי לי כזכותי וכברירותי קדם מימריה

t133a

ואתיב יוי לי כזכותי וכברותי קדם **עינוהי**

2 Sam. 22:26

t709b

אברהם דאשתכח חסיד קדמך בכין אסגיתא למעבד חסדא עם זרעיה יצחק דהוה שלים בדחלתך בכין אשלימתא מימר רעותך עמיה

t1601i

אברהם דאשתכח חסיד קדמך בכן אסגיתא למיעבד חסדא עם זרעיה **ויצחק** דהוה שלים **לדחלתך** בכן אשלימתא **למעבד** רעותך עמיה

2 Sam. 22:27

t709b

יעקב דהליך בברירותא קדמך בחרתא בנוהי מכל עממיא אפרישתא זרעיה מכל פסולא פרעה ומצראי דחשיבו מחשבן על עמך בלבילתנון כמחשבתהון

t1601i

יעקב דהליך בברירותא קדמך בחרת בנוי מכל עממיא **ואפרישתא** זרעיה מכל פסילא פרעה **ומשיריתיה** דחשיבו מחשבן על עמך בלבלתינון **במחשבתהון**

2 Sam. 22:28

t709b

וית עמא בית ישר' דמתקרן בעלמא הדין עם חשיך את עתיד למפרק ובמימרך תקיפיא דמתגברין עליהון תמאיך

407

The Transmission of Targum Jonathan in the West

t1601i

ויהון עמך בית ישראל דמתקרן בעלמא הדין עם חשיך את עתיד למיפרק **יתהון ולמקרי להון עם חביב דבכל עינך במכיכי רוח מיתיית]ב[א** ובמימרך תקיפא דמתגברין עליהון תמאיך

2 Sam. 22:29

t709b

ארי את הוא מריה נהוריה דישר' יוי ויוי יפקנני מחשוכא לנהורא ויחזינני בעלמא דעתיד למיתי לצדיקיא

t1601i

ארי את הוא מרי נהוריה דישראל [>] ויוי יפקינני מחשוכא לנהורא ויחזינני בעלמא דעתיד למיתי **על** צדיקיא

2 Sam. 22:30

t707b

ארי במימרך אסגי משירין במימר אילהי איכבוש כל כרכין תקיפין

t1601b

ארי במימרך **אכנש** משיריין [>] אכבש **ואתבר** כל כרכין תקיפין

2 Sam. 22:31

t707b

אילהא דכיונא אוריתא אוריתא דיוי בחירא היא תקוף הוא לכול דמיתרחצין על מימריה

t1601i

אלהא דכיוונא אוריתא אוריתא דיוי בחירא היא תקיף הוא לכל דמתרחצין על מימריה

2 Sam. 22:32

t707b

בכין על ניסא ופורקנא דתעביד למשיחך ולישארא דעמך דישתארון יודון כל עממיא אומיא ולישניא ויימרון לית אילה אילא יוי ארי לית בר מינך ועמך יימרון לית דתקיף אילא אילהנא

t1601i

בכן על ניסא ופורקנא **דאתעבד** למשיחך ולשארא דעמך דישתארון יודון כל עממיא אומיא ולישניא ויימרון לית אלה אלא יוי ארי לית בר מינך ועמך יימרון לית **אלה** אלא אלהנא

2 Sam. 22:33

t707b

אילהא דסעיד לי בחילא ומתקין שלים אורחי

t1601i

אלהא דסעיד לי בחילא ומתקין שלמ**א** אורחי

Chapter Fourteen. Appendices

2 Sam. 22:34
t707b
משוי ריגלי קלילין כאילתא ועל בית תוקפי יקימינני
t1601i
משוי רגליי קלילין כאיילתא ועל בית תוקפי יקיימינני

2 Sam. 22:35
t707b
מליף ידי למעבד קרבא ומתקיף כקשת נחשא דרעי
t1601i
מליף [>] **לאגחא** קרבא **ותבר עממיא דתקיפין** כקשתא דנחשא דרעיי

2 Sam. 22:36
t707b
ויהבת לי תקוף פרקתני ובמימרך אסגיתני
t1601i
ויהבת לי **סעיד** ופרקתני **בתוקפך** ובמימרך אסגיתני

2 Sam. 22:37
t707b
אסגיתא פיסעתי קדמי ולא איזדעזעא רכובתי
t1601i
אסגיתא פסיעתי קדמיי ולא אזדעזעא רכובתי

2 Sam. 22:38
t707b
רדפית סנאי ושיציתינון ולא תבית עד דגמרתינון
t1601i
רדפית **בתר** שנאיי ושיציתינון ולא תבית **מנהון** עד דגמרתינון

2 Sam. 22:39
t707b
ושיציתינון וגמרתינון ולא יכילו לימקם ונפלו קטילין תחות פרסת רגלי
t1601i
ודשישתינון וגמרתינון ולא יכילו למיקם ונפלו קטילין תחות פרסת רגליי

2 Sam. 22:40
t707b
וסעדתני בחילא למעבד קרבא תברתא עממיא דקיימין לאבאשא לי תחותי

t1601i

וסעדתני בחילא למעבד קרבא [ת]ברתא עממיא **דתקיפין** וקיימין לאבשא לי תחותיי

2 Sam. 22:41

t707b

וסנאי תברתא קדמי מחזרי קדל בעלי דבבי ושיציתינון

t1601i

ושנאיי **מסרתא** קדמיי מחזרי קדל ובעלי דבביי ושיציתינון

2 Sam. 22:42

t707b

בען סעיד ולית להון פריק ומצלן ק' יוי ולא מיתקבלא צלותהון

t1601i

בען סעיד ולית להון פריק [>]מצלן קדם יוי ולא מתקבלא צלותהון

2 Sam. 22:43

t707b

ודושישתינון כעפרא דאר' כסין שוקין בעטית בהון רפסתינון

t1601i

ודשישתינון כעפרא [ד]ארעא כסוון שווקין בעטית בהון רפסתינון

2 Sam. 22:44

t707b

ותשיזבינני מיפלוגת עמא תמניני רישא לעממיא עם דלא ידעית יפילחונני

t1601i

ושזבתני מפלוגת **עממין** תמניניי לריש [>]עממייא עמא דלא ידעית יפלחונני

2 Sam. 22:45

t707b

בני עממיא יתכדבון לי לשימע אודן ישתמעון לי

t1601i

בני עממיא יתכדבון לי **למשמע** אודן ישתמעון לי

2 Sam. 22:46

t707b

בני עממיא יסופון ויזועון מיבירניתהון

t1601i

בני עממיא י[ס]ופון **ויצדון** ויזועון מבירניתהון

Chapter Fourteen. Appendices

2 Sam. 22:47

t707b

בכין על ניסא ופורקנא דעבדתא לעמך אודיאו ואמרו קים הוא יוי ובריך תקיפא דמין קדמוהי
מיתיהיב לנא תקוף ופורקנא ומרמם איליה תקוף פורקננא

t1601i

בכן על ניסא ופורקנא **דיתעבד למשיחך ולשארא** דעמך **דישתארון ישבחון וי[ר]דון וייımרון**
קים הוא **אלהא חייא [גי]ברא ודחילא** ובריך תקיף [ד]מן קדמוהי מתיהב לי תקוף ופורקן
ומרומא אלהא תקוף פורקננא

2 Sam. 22:48

t707b

אילהא דעביד פורענותא לי ותבר עממיא דקיימין לבאבשא לי תחותי

t1601i

אלהא דעביד פורענותא לי ותבר עממיא **דתקיפין כקשתא דנחשא** תחותיי

2 Sam. 22:49

t707b

ופרקי מסנאי ועל דקימין לבאבשא לי תגברינני מגוג ומשירית עממין חטופין דעימיה תשיזיבנני

t1601i

ומשיזבי מן שנאיי **ואף** על דקיימין לבאבשא לי **תשיזיבנני** מן גוג ומן משיריין עממין חטופין
דאתו לאגחא קרבא עימי תשיזיבנני

2 Sam. 22:50

t707b

על כין אודי קדמך יוי בעממיא ולישמך אימר תושבחא

t1601i

על כן אודה קדמך יוי [>] ולשמך אימר תושבחא

t133a

על כן אודה קדמך יוי בעממיא ולשמך אימר **תושבחן**

2 Sam. 22:51

t707b

מסגי למעבד פורקן עים מלכיה ועביד טיבו למשיחיה לדוד ולזרעיה עד עלמא

t1601i

מסגי למעבד פורק[ן] עם מלכיה ועביד טיבו למשיחיה לדוד ולזרעיה עד עלמא

t133a

מסגי למעבד פורקן עם מלכיה ועביד טיבו למשיחיה לדוד **ולבנוהי** עד עלמא

The Transmission of Targum Jonathan in the West

Synopsis

Ashkenazi Sources Compared to t133a

KEY:

Illegible text [...]

מי[מרי]ה Unclear characters

מממריה Original wording

#מימריה# Corrected wording

Minus compared to t133a [>]

Variants from t133a in bold font (excluding orthography, spelling, minor errors etc.)

2 Sam. 22:1

ושבח דוד בנבואה קדם יוי ית כל פיתגמי תושבחתא׳ הדא על כל יומיא דשיזיב יוי יתיה וית ישר׳ מידא דכל בעלי דבביהון ואף לדוד משיזבא מחרבא דשאול

t63a

ושבח דוד בנבואה ק׳ יוי ית [>] פיתגמי תושבחתא הדא על כל יומיא דשיזיב יוי [>] ית ישר׳ **מיד כל** בעלי [>] ואף **דוד שזיב** מחרבא דשאול

t99a

ושבח דוד בנבואה קדם יוי ית כל פתגמי תושבחתא הדא על כל יומיא דשיזיב יוי [>] ית ישר׳ מידא **כל** בעלי *דבביהו*#דבביהון# ואף לדוד **שיזיב** מחרבא דשאול

t159a

ושבח דוד בנבואה קדם יוי ית [>] פתגמי תושבחתא הדא על כל יומיא דשיזיב יוי **יתי** וית ישר׳ **מיד כל** בעלי דבביהון ואף **דוד משיזיב** מחרבא דשאול

t1631a

ושבח דוד בנבואה קדם יוי ית [>] פיתגמ**יה** תושבחתא הדא על כל יומיא דשיזיב יוי [>] ית ישר׳ **מיד כל** בעלי דבביהון ואף לדוד משיזבא מחרבא דשואל

t1614a

ושבח דוד בנבואה קדם יוי ית [>] פיתגמי תושבחתא הדא על כל יומיא דשיזיב יוי [>] ית ישר׳ **מיד כל** בעלי דבביהון **ויתיר** ואף **יד דוד שיזב** מחרבא דשאול

2 Sam. 22:2

ואמר יוי [תוקפי] ורוחצני משזיב [ית]י

t63a

ואמר יוי תוקפי ורוחצני ומשזיב יתי

t99a

ואמר יוי תוקפי ורוחצני ומשזיב יתי

t159a

ואמר יוי תוקפי ורוחצני ומשזיב יתי

Chapter Fourteen. Appendices

t1631a

ואמר יוי תוקפי ורוחצני ו**שמזיב** יתי

t1614

אואמר יוי תוקפי ורוחצני ו**משזיב** יתי

2 Sam. 22:3

אלהא דאיתרעי בי קירבני לדחלתיה תוקפי דמן קדמוהי איתיהיב לי תקוף ופורקן לאיתגברא על בעלי דבבי רוחצני דעל מימריה אנא רחיץ כד הויתי עריק מן קדם רודפי מגן עלי מבעלי דבבי ואף מיד כל חטופין ואניסין שיזיב יתי

t63a

אלהא דאיתרעי בי קרבני לדחלתיה תוקפי דמן קדמוהי **מתיהיב** לי תקוף ופורקן לאיתגברא על בעלי דבבי רוחצני דעל מימריה אנא רחיץ **בעידן עקא מגן עלי מבעלי דבבי ואמר לארמא קרני בפורקניה סומכני דהוה מימריה סמך לי** כד הויתי עריק מן קדם רדפי **פרקני** מבעלי דבבי ואף מיד כל חטופין ואניסין **פריק** יתי

t99a

אלהא דאיתרעי בי קרבני לדחלתיה תוקפי דמן קדמוהי **מיתיהיב** לי תקוף ופורקן לאיתגברא על בעלי דבבי רוחצני דעל מימריה אנא רחיץ **בעידן עקא מגן עלי מבעלי דבבי ואמר *לארמי* #לארמא# קרני בפורקני סומכני דהוה מימריה סמך לי** כד הויתי עריק מן קודם רודפי **פרקני** מבעלי דבבי ואף מיד כל *חוטפין*#חטופין# ואניסין **משזיב** יתי

t159a

אלהא דאתרעי בי קרבני לדחלתיה תוקפי דמן **קדמך** אתיהיב לי תקוף ופורקן לאתגברא על בעלי דבבי רוחצני דעל מימריה אנא רחיץ **בעדן עקא מגן עלי מבעלי דבבי ואמר לארמא קרני בפורקניה סמכני דהוה מימריה סמך לי** כד הויתי עריק מן קדם רדפי **פרקני** מבעלי דבבי ואף מיד כל חטופין ואניסין שיזיב יתי

t1631a

אלהא דאיתרעי בי קרבני לדחלתיה תוקפי דמן קדמוהי **מתיהב** לי תקוף ופורקן לאיתגברא על בעלי דבביי רוחצני דעל מימריה אנא רחיץ **בעידן עקא מגן עלי מבעלי דבביי ואמר לארמא קרני בפורקני סומכני דהוה מימריה סמיך לי** כד הויתי עריק מן קדם רודפי **פורקני** מבעלי דבביי ואף מיד כל חטופין ואנסין **משזיב** יתי

t1614a

אלהא דאיתרעת בי קרבני לדחלתיה תוקפי דמן קדמוהי **מתיהיב** לי תקוף ופורקן לאיתגברא על בעלי דבבא רוחצני דעל מימריה אנא רחיץ **בעדן עקא מגין עלי מבעלי דבבי ואמר לארמא קרני בפורקני סומכני דהוה מימריה סמך לי** כד הויתי עריק מן קדם רודפי **פרקני** מבעלי דבבי ואף מיד כל חטופין ואנסין **פריק** יתי

2 Sam. 22:4

אמר דוד בתושבחת' אנא מצלי קדם יוי דבכל עידן מבעלי דבבי פריק יתי

t63a
אמ' דוד בתושבחתא אנא מצלי ק' יוי דבכל עדן מבעלי דבבי פריק יתי
t99a
אמר דוד בתושבחתא אנא מצלי קדם יוי [>| בכל עידן מבעלי דבבי פריק יתי
t159a
אמר דוד בתושבחתא אנא מצלי קדם יוי די בכל עידן מבעלי דבבי פריק יתי
t1631a
אמר דוד בתושבחתא אנא מצלי קדם יוי דבכל עידן מבעלי דבבי **משזיב** יתי
t1614a
אמר דוד בתושבחתא אנא מצלי קדם יוי **וקדם אלהי אנא מתחנן** דבכל עידן מבעלי דבבי פריק יתי

2 Sam. 22:5

ארי אקפתני עקא כאיתתא דיתבה על מתברא וחיל לית לה למילד והיא מסכנא לממת וסיעת חייבין בעיתת יתי
t63a
ארי אקיפתני עקא כאיתתא דיתבא על מתברא וחיל לית לה למילד והיא מסכנא ליממת וסיעת חייבין **בעתן** יתי
t99a
ארי אקיפתני עקא כאיתתא דיתבא על מתברא וחיל לית לה למילד והיא מסכנא לממת [>| סיעת *חייבא*#חייביא# בעיתת יתי
t159a
ארי אקיפתני עקא כאיתתא דיתבא על מתברא וחיל לית לה למילד והיא מסכנא לממת וסיעת חייבין בעיתת יתי
t1631a
ארי אקיפתני עקא כאיתתא דיתבא על מתברא וחיל לית לה למילד והיא מסכנא לממת [>| סיעת חייבין **בה** ביעתת יתי
t1614a
ארי אקיפתני עקא כאיתתא דיתבא על מתברא וחיל לית לה למילד והיא מסכנא לממת [>| סיעת חייבין **בה** ביעתת יתי

2 Sam. 22:6

משיריין רשיען סגיאן אקפוני ערעוני דמזיינין במאני קטול
t63a
משירית רשיען [>| אקפוני ארעוני דמזיינין במאני קטול
t99a
משרייית רשיעין [>| אקפוני ערעוני דמזיינין במני קטול
t159a

Chapter Fourteen. Appendices

משריין רשיען [>|] אקפוני ארעוני דמזיינין במאני קטול
t1631a

משרייית רשיען [>|] אקפוני **קדמוני** דמזיינין במני קטול
t1614a

משרייית רשיען [>|] אקפוני **קדמוני** דמזיינין במני קטול

2 Sam. 22:7

אמר דוד כד עקא לי אנא מצלי קדם יוי וקדם אלהי אנא מחנן ומקבל מהיכליה צלותי ובעותי דמן קדמוהי מתעבדא
t63a

אמר דוד כד עקא לי אנא מצלי ק' יוי וקדם אלהי אנא **מתחנן וקביל** מהיכליה צלותי ובעותי [>|] מן קדמוהי מתעבדא
t99a

אמר דוד כד עקא לי אנא מצלי קדם יוי וקדם אלהי אנא **מתחנן וקבל** מהיכליה צלותי ובעותי [>|] מן קדמוהי מתעבדא
t159a

אמר דוד כד עקא לי אנא מצלי קדם יוי וקדם אלהי אנא **מתחנן וקביל** מהיכליה צלותי ובעותי [>|] קדמוהי מתעבדא
t1631a

אמר דוד כד עקא [>|] אנא ומצלי קדם יוי וקדם אלהי אנא **מתחנן** ומקבל מהיכליה צלותי ובעותי [>|] מן קדמוהי מתעבדא
t1614a

אמר דוד כד עקא [>|] אנא ומצלי קדם יוי וקדם אלהי אנא **מתחנן וקבל** מהיכליה צלותי ובעותי [>|] מן קדמוהי מתעבדא

2 Sam. 22:8

ואיתרגיפת ואיתרגישת ארעא שכלולי שמיא זעו ואיתרכינו ארי תקיף רוגזיה
t63a

ואיתרגיפת ואיתרגישת ארעא שכלולי שמיא זעו ואיתרכינו ארי **תקוף** רוגזיה
t99a

ואיתרגפת#*ואיתרגיפת*# *ואיתרגשת*#*ואיתרגישת*# ארעא *ושכללי*#*ושכלולי*# שמיא זעו ואיתרכינו ארי **תקוף** רוגזיה
t159a

ואתרגיפת ואתרגישת ארעא שכלולי שמיא זעו ואתרכינו ארי **תקוף** רוגזיה
t1631a

ואיתרגיפת **ואיתרעישת** ארעא **ושכלולי** שמיא זעו ואיתרכינו ארי **תקוף** רוגזיה

t1614a

ואיתרגיפת **ואיתרעישת** ארעא **ו**שכלולי שמיא זעו ואיתרכינו ארי **תקוף** רוגזיה

2 Sam. 22:9

סליק זדוניה דפרעה רשיעא כתנבא דאתונא קדמוהי משיציא מזופיתיה כגומר[ין] דנור דלקא ממימריה

t63a

סליק זדוניה דפרעה רשיעא כתנבא [>|] קדמוהי **בכן שלח רוגזיה כאשא בעדא דמקדמוהי** משציא מזופיתיה כגומרין דנור דלקא ממימריה

t99a

סליק זדוניה דפרעה רשיעא כתנבא [>|] קדמוהי **בכן שלח רוגזיה כאישא בערא דמן קדמוהי** משציא מזופיתיה כגומרין דנור דלקא [>|]מימריה

t159a

סליק זדוניה דפרעה רשיעא כתנבא [>|] **דמן** קדמוהי **בכן שלח רוגזיה כאשא בערא דמן קדמוהי** משציא מזופיתיה כגומרין דנור דלקא מן מימריה

t1631a

סליק זדוניה דפרעה רשיעא כתנבא [>|] קדומוהי **בכין שלח מלכא רוגזיא כאישא בערא דמן קדמוהי** משייציא ומזופייתיה כגומרין דנור דלקא ממימריה

t1614a

סליק זדוניה דפרעה רשיעא כתנבא [>|] קדומוהי **בכין שלח רוגזיה כאישא דמן קדמוהי** משציא מזפיתיה כגומרין דנור דלקא מימריה

2 Sam. 22:10

וארכין שמיא ואיתגלי יקריה וענן אמיטתא כיבש קדמוהי

t63a

וארכין שמיא ואיתגלי יקריה וענן אמיטתא כיבש קדמוהי

t99a

וארכין שמיא ואיתגלי יקרי**א** וענן אמיטתא כיבש קדמוהי

t159a

וארכין שמיא ואתגלי יקריה וענן אמיטתא כבש קדמוהי

t1631a

וארכין שמייא ואתגלי יקריה וענן אמיטתא כבש קדמוהי

t1614a

וארכין שמיא ואיתגלי יקריה וענן אמיטתא כיבש קדמוהי

2 Sam. 22:11

ואיתגלי בגבורתי' על כרובין קלילין ודבר בתקוף על כנפי רוחא

t63a

ואיתגלי בגבורתיה על כרובין קלילין ודבר בתקוף על כנפי רוחא

Chapter Fourteen. Appendices

t99a

ואתגלי#ואיתגלי# בגבורתיה על כרובין קלילין ודבר בתקוף על כנפי רוחא

t159a

ואתגלי [בגבורתיה] על כרובין קלילין ודבר בתקוף על כנפי רוחא

t1631a

ואיתגלי בגבורתיה על כרובין קלילין ודבר בתקוף על כנפי רוחא

t1614a

ואיתגלי בגבורתיה על כרובין קלילין ודבר בתקוף על **גדפי** רוחא

2 Sam. 22:12

ואשרי שכינתיה בערפילא וענן יקר סחור ליה מחית ענניו תקיפין מרוכסת ענניו קלילין ברום עלמא

t63a

ואשרי שכינתיה בערפלא וענן יקר סחור ליה מחית **מיין קלילין מריכפת** ענניו קלילין ברום עלמא

t99a

ואשרי שכינתיה בערפילא וענן [>] סחור ליה מחית **מיין מריכפת ענניים** קלילין ברום עלמא

t159a

ואשרי שכינתיה בערפלא וענן יקר סחור ליה מחית **מיין** תקיפין **מרכפת** ענניו קלילין ברום עלמא

t1631a

ואשרי שכינתיה בערפלא [>]ענן יקר סחור ליה מחית **מיין מריגפת** תקיפין ענניו קלילין ברום עלמא

t1614a

ואשריי שכינתיה בערפלא [>]ענן יקר סחור ליה מחית **מיין מריגפת** תקיפין ענניו קלילין ברום עלמא

2 Sam. 22:13

מזיו יקריה מבהיקין שמי שמיא מזופיתיה כגומרין דנור דלקא ממימריה

t63a

מזיו יקריה מבהקין שמי שמיא מזופיתיה כגומרין דנור דלקא ממימריה

t99a

מזיו יקריה מבהקין שמי שמיא מזופיתיה *כגום*#כגומרין# דנור דלקא *ממריה*#מימריה#

t159a

מזיו יקריה מבהקין שמי שמיא ומזופיתיה כגומרין דנור דלקא מן מימריה

t1631a

ומזיו יקריה מבהיקין **ושמי** שמיא **ומזוופיתיה** כגומרין דנור דלקא מימריה

t1614a

מזיו יקריה מבהיקין שמי שמיא ומזופיתיה כגומרין דנור דלקא מימריה

2 Sam. 22:14

אכלי מן שמיא יוי ועילאה ארים במימריה

t63a

אכלי מן שמיא **#יוי# ועילאה ארים [>]מימריה

t99a

אכלי מן שמיא יוי ועילאה ארים **קל** מימריה

t159a

אכלי מן *שמים*#שמיא# יוי *ועיללאה*#ועילאה# **מן** מימריה

t1631a

אכלינון מן שמיא יוי ועילאה ארים **קליה**

2 Sam. 22:15

ושלח מחתיה כגירין ובדרינון ברקין ושגישינון

t159a

ושלח מחתיה כגירין ובדרינון ברקין ושגישינון

t1631a

ושלח מחתיה [כגר]ין ובדרינון ב[רק]ין ושגישינון

t1614a

ושלח מחתיה כגירין ובדרינון ברקין ושגישינון

2 Sam. 22:16

ואיתחזיאו עומקי ימא ואיתגליאו שכלולי תבל מזופיתיה מן קדם יוי מימר תקוף רוגזיה

t159a

ואתחזיאו עמקי ימא [>]איתגליאו **שמיא** תבל **במזופיתא** מן קדם יוי **מן** מימר תקוף רוגזיה

t1631a

ואיתחזיאו עומקי ימא ואיתגליאו שכלולי תבל **במזוופייתא** מן ק' יוי **ממימר** תקוף רוגזיה

t1614a

ואיתחזיאו עומקי ימא [>]אתגליאו שכלולי תבל מזופיתיה מן קדם יוי **ממימר** תקוף רוגזיה

2 Sam. 22:17

שלח נבויהי מלך תקוף דיתיב בתקוף רומא דברני שזבני מעממין סגיאין

Chapter Fourteen. Appendices

t159a

שלח נביאוהי מלך תקיף ויתיב בתקוף רומא דברני שיזבני מעממין סגיאין

t1631a

ישלח נביאוהי מלך תקיף דיתיב בתקוף רומא דברני שיזבני מעממין סגיאין

t1614a

שלח נביאוהי מלך תקיף דיתיב בתקוף רומא דברני שיזבני |[>

2 Sam. 22:18

שיזבני משנאי ארי אקפוני מבעלי דבבי ארי איתגברו עלי

t159a

שיזבני משנאי ארי **תקפוני** ומבעלי דבבי ארי איתגברו עלי

t1631a

שיזבני מ[סנ[א]י] ארי **תקפני** מבעלי דבבי ארי איתגברו עלי

t1614a

[>| משנאי ארי **אפקני** מבעלי דבבי ארי איתגברו עלי

2 Sam. 22:19

קידמוני ביום טילטולי והוה מימרא דיוי סמך לי

t159a

ערעוני ביום טילטולי והוה מימרא דיוי סמך לי

t1631a

יקדמוני ביום טלטולי והוה מימרא דיוי סמך לי

t1614a

קדמוני ביום טילטולי והוה מימרא דיוי סמך לי

2 Sam. 22:20

ואפיק לרווחא יתי שיזבני ארי איתרעי בי

t1631a

ואפיק לרווחא יתי שזבני ארי איתרעי בי

2 Sam. 22:21

ישלמינני יוי כזכותי וכברותי יתיב לי

t1631a

יגמלינני יוי כזכותי |[>**כברירות ידי** יתיב לי

2 Sam. 22:50

על כן אודה קדמך יוי בעממיא ולשמך אימר תושבחן

t63a

על כין אודה קדמך יוי בעממיא ולשמך אימר תושבחן

t99a

על כן אודי קדמך יוי בעממייא ולשמך אימר תושבחן

t159a

על כן אודי **#קדמך# **יהוה** בעממיא ולשמך אימר תושבחן

t1614a

על **דין** אודה קדמך יוי בעממיא ולשמך אימר תשבחן

2 Sam. 22:51

מסגי למיעבד פורקן עם מלכיה ועביד טיבו למשיחיה לדוד ולבנוהי עד עלמא

t63a

מסגי למעבד פורקן עם מלכיה ועביד טיבו למשיחיה לדוד **ולזרעיה** עד עלמא

t99a

מגי למיעבד פורקן עם מלכיה ועיבד טיבו למשיחיה לדוד **ולזרעיה** עד עלמא

t159a

מסגי למעבד פורקן עם מלכיה ועביד טיבו למשיחיה לדוד **ולזרעיה** עד עלמא

t1614a

מסגי למעבד פורקן עם מלכיה ועבד ט[יבה] למשיחיה לדוד **ולזרעיה** עד עלמא

Synopsis

Italian Sources Compared to t1601i

KEY:

Illegible text […]

מי]מרי[ה Unclear characters

מממריה Original wording

#מימריה# Corrected wording

Minus compared to t1601i [<]

Variants from t1601i in bold font (excluding orthography, spelling, minor errors etc.)

2 Sam. 22:1

ושבח דוד בנבואה קדם יוי ית פיתגמי תושבחתא הדא על כל יומיא דשיזיב יוי ית ישראל מיד כל בעלי דבביהון ואף לדוד שיזביה מחרבא דשאול

t1618i

ושבח דוד בנבוא[ה] קדם יוי ית פתגמי תושבחתא הדא על כל יומיא דשיזיב יוי ית ישראל מיד כל בעלי דבביהון ואף לדוד שיזביה מחרבא דשאול

Chapter Fourteen. Appendices

t1621i

ושבח דוד בנבואה קדם יוי ית פתגמי תושבחתא הדא על כל יומיא דשזיב יוי ית ישראל מיד כל בעלי דבביהון ואף לדוד שיזביה מחרבא דשאול

t1639i

ושבח דוד בנבואה קדם יוי ית פיתגמי תושבחתא הדא על כל יומיא דשזיב יוי ית ישראל מיד כל בעלי דבביהון ואף לדוד שיזביה מחרבא דשאול

t1647i

ושבח דוד בנבואה קדם יוי ית פתגמי תושבחתא הדא על כל יומיא דשזיב יוי ית ישראל מיד כל בעלי דבביהון ואף לדוד שיזביה מחרבא דשאול

t1679i

ושבח דוד בנבואה קדם יוי ית פיתגמי תושבחתא הדא על כל יומיא דשזיב יוי ית ישראל מיד כל בעלי דבביהון ואף לדוד שיזביה מחרבא דשאול

2 Sam. 22:2

ואמר יוי תוקפי ורוחצני ומשיזיב לי

t1618i

ואמר יוי תוקפי ורחצני ומשיזיב לי

t1621i

ואמר יוי תוקפי ורוחצני ומשיזיב לי

t1639i

ואמר יוי תוקפי ורוחצני ומשיזיב לי

t1647i

ואמר יוי תוקפי ורוחצני ומשזב לי

t1679i

ואמר יוי תוקפי ורוחצני *והוה לי לפרוק*## ומשיזיב לי

2 Sam. 22:3

אלהא דאיתרעי בי קירבני לדחלתיה תוקפי דמן קדמוהי מתיהב לי תקוף ופורקן לאיתגברא על בעלי דבבי רוחצני דעל מימריה הוינא רחיץ בעידן עקא עלי מבעלי דבבי ואמר לארמא קרני בפורקניה סומכני דהוה מימריה סמיך לי כד הויתי עריק מן קדם רדפיי שיזבני מן שנאיי ואף מיד כל חטופין שיזיב יתי ומידא דשאול מלכא הוה פריק לי

t1618i

אלהא דאיתרעי בי ק[י]רבני לדחלתיה תוקפי דמן קדמוהי מתיהב לי תקוף ופורקן לאי[תגב]רא על בעלי דבבי רוחצני דעל מימריה [אנא ... ע]קא מג[י]ן עלי מבעלי דבבי ואמר לארמא קרני בפורקנ**י** [...] כד הויתי עריק מן קדם רדפי שיזבני מן שנאי ואף מיד כל חטופין שיזיב יתי ומידא דשאול מלכא הוה פריק לי

The Transmission of Targum Jonathan in the West

t1621i

אלהא דאיתרעי בי קירבני לדחלתיה תוקפי דמן קדמוהי מתיהיב לי תקוף ופורקן לאיתגברא על
בעלי דבבי רוחצני **רוחצי** דעל מימריה הוינא רחיץ בעידן עקא מגן עלי מבעלי דבבי ואמר
לארמא קרני בפורקניה סומכני דהוה מימריה סמיך לי כד הויתי עריק מן קדם רודפי שיזבני מן
שנאי ואף מיד כל חטופין שזיב יתי ומידא דשאול מלכא הוה פריק לי

t1639i

אלהא דאיתרעי בי קירבני לדחלתיה תוקפי דמן קדמוהי מתיהב לי תקוף ופורקן לאיתגברא על
בעלי דבבי רוחצני דעל מימריה **אנא** רחיץ בעידן עקא מגין עלי **על** בעלי דבבי ואמר לארמא
קרנ**י** בפורקני סומכני דהוה מימריה סמיך לי כד הויתי עריק מן קדם רדפי שיזבני מן סנאי
פירקני מבעלי דבביי ואף מיד כל חטופין שזיב יתי ומידא דשאול מלכא הוה פריק לי

t1647i

אלהא דאיתרעי בי קרבני לדחלתיה תוקפי דמן קדמוהי מתיהב לי תקוף ופורקן לאיתגברא על **כל**
בעלי דבבי רוחצני דעל מימריה הווינא רחיץ בעידן עקא מגין עלי מבעלי דבבי ואמר לארמא
קרנ**י** בפורקני סומכני דהוה מימריה סמיך לי כד הוויתי עריק מן קדם רודפי שיזבני מן שנאי ואף
מיד כל חטופין שזיב יתי ומידא דשאול מלכא הוה פריק לי

t1679i

אלהא דאיתרעי בי קירבני לדחלתיה תוקפי דמן קדמוהי מתייהב לי תקוף ופורקן לאיתגברא על
בעלי דבבי [>] ואמר לארמא קרני בפורקניה סומכני דהוה מימריה סמיך לי כד הויתי עריק מן
קדם רדפי שיזבני מן שנאי ואף מיד כל חטופין שזיב יתי ומידא דשאול מלכא הוה פריק לי

2 Sam. 22:4

אמר דוד בתישבחתא אנא פתח פומי ומצלי קדם יוי דבכל עידן עקא מבעלי דבביי הוה פריק לי

t1618i

אמר דוד בתושבחתא אנא פתח פומי ומצלי קדם יוי דבכל עידן [>] מבעלי דבבי הוה **מפרק** לי

t1621i

אמר דוד בתושבחתא אנא פתח פומי ומצלי קדם יוי דבכל עידן עקא מבעלי דבבי הוה פריק לי

t1639i

אמר דוד בתושבחא אנא פתח פומי ומצלי קדם יוי דבכל עידן [>] מבעלי דבבי הוה פריק לי

t1647i

אמר דוד בתושבחתא אנא פתח פומי ומיצלי קדם יוי **דבכל** עידן [>] מבעלי דבביי הוה פריק לי

t1679i

אמר דוד בתושבחתא אנא פתח פומי ומצלי קדם יוי דבכל עידן עקא מבעלי דבביי הוה פריק לי

2 Sam. 22:5

ארי אקפתני עקא כאיתתא דיתבא על מתברא וחיל לית בה למילד והיא מסכנא לממת סיעת
שקרין ביעתת יתי

Chapter Fourteen. Appendices

t1618i

ארי אקפתני עקא כאיתתא דיתבא על מתברא [...] ל*[>] *#לית# בה למילד והיא ניסכנא לממת סיעת שקרין ביעתת יתי

t1621i

ארי **אקפני** עקא כאיתתא דיתבא על מתברא וחיל לית בה למילד והיא מסכנא לממת סיעת שקרין בעתת יתי

t1639i

ארי אקפתני עקא כאיתתא דיתבא על מתברא וחיל לית בה למילד והיא מסכנא [>] סיען **חייבין** בעתת יתי

t1647i

ארי אקפתני עקא כאיתתא דיתבא על מתברא וחיל **לה** [>] למילד והיא מסכנא ליממת סיעת שקרין ביעתת יתי

t1679i

ארי אקפתני עקא כאתתא דיתבא על מתברא וחיל לית בה למילד והיא מסכנא לממת סיעת שקרין ביעתת יתי

2 Sam. 22:6

משיריית רשיען אקפוני ערעוני דמזיינין במאני קטול

t1618i

משיריית רשיען אקפוני ערעוני דמזיינין במאני קטול

t1621i

משיריית רשיען אקפוני ערעוני דמריי[.]ם במאני קטול

t1639i

משיריית רשיען אקפוני **קדמובי** דמזיינין **כ**מאני קטול

t1647i

משיריית רשיען אקפוני ערעוני דמזיינין במאני קטול

t1679i

משיריית רשיען אקפוני ערעוני דמזיינין במאני קטול

2 Sam. 22:7

אמר דוד כד עייקא לי אנא פתח פומי ומצלי קדם יוי וקדם אלהי אנא מצלי ומתחנן ומקבל מהיכליה צלותי ובעותי קדמוהי מתעבדא בעידן צלותי

t1618i

אמר דוד כד עייקא לי אנא פתח פומי ומצלי קדם יוי וקדם אלהי אנא מצלי ומתחנן ומקביל מהיכליה צלותי ובעותי קדמוהי מתעבדא בעידן צלותי

t1621i

אמר דוד כד עקא לי אנא ק|ר|י ומצלי קדם יוי וקדם אלהי אנא מצלי ומקבל מהיכליה צלותי ובעותי קדמוהי מתעבדא בעידן צלותי

t1639i

אמר דוד כד עקא לי אנא [>] מצלי קדם **יהוה** וקדם אלהי אנא מצלי ומתחנן ומקבל מהיכליה צלותי ובעותי קדמוהי מיתעבדא בעידן צלותי

t1647i

אמר דוד כד עייקא לי אנא פתח פומי ומצלי קדם יוי וקדם אלהי **אלהי** אנא מצלי ומתחנן ומקבל מהיכליה צלותי ובעותי קדמוהי מתעבדה בעידן צלותי

t1679i

אמר דוד כד עייקא לי אנא פתח פומי ומצלי קדם יוי וקדם אלהי אנא מצלי ומתחנן ומקבל מהיכליה צלותי ובעותי קדמוהי מתעבדא בעידן צלותי

2 Sam. 22:8

ואתרגיפת ואתרגישת ואזדעזעת ארעא ושכלולי שמיא זעו ואזדעזעו טוריא ואתהפיכו עמקי ימא ארי תקיף רוגזא דאלהנא חייא וקיימא

t1618i

ואיתרגיפת ואיתרגישת ואיזדעזעת ארעא ושיכלולי שמייא זעו ואיזדעזעו טורייא ואיתהפיכו עמקי ימא ארי **תקוף** רוגזיה ד**אלהא** חייא וקיימא

t1621i

ואיתרגיפת ואיתרגישת ואיזדעזעת ארעא ושכלולי שמייא זעו ואיזדעזעו טורייא ואיתהפיכו עמקי ימא ארי **תקוף** רוגזיה ד**אלהא** חייא וקיימא

t1639i

ואיתרגיפת ואיתרגישת ואיזדעזעת ארעא ושכלולי שמייא זעו ואיזדעזעו טורייא ואיתהפיכו עמקי ימא ארי **תקוף** רוגזיה **אלהא** חייא וקיימא

t1647i

ואיתרגיפת ואתרגישת ואיזדעזעת ארעא ושיכלולי שמייא זעו ואיזדעזעו טוריא ואיתהפיכו עמקי ימא ארי **תקוף** רוגזיה ד**אלהא** חייא וקיימא

t1679i

ואתרגפת ואתרגשת ואזדעזעת ארעא ושכלולי שמייא זעו ואיזדעזעו טוריא ואיתהפיכו עימקי ימא ארי תקיף רוגזא דאלהנא חייא וקיימא

2 Sam. 22:9

סליק זדוניה דפרעה רשיעא כתננא באפ[ו]י בכן שלח רוגזיה כאשא בערא מן קדמוהי משציין ומזופיתיה כגומרין דנור דלקן מן מימריה

t1618i

סליק זדוניה דפרעה רשיעא כתננא באפוהי בכן שלח רוגזיה כאישא בערא מן קדמוהי **משיציא** ומזופיתיה כגומרין דינור דלקן [>]מימריה

t1621i

סליק זדוניה דפרעה רשיעא כתננא באפוהי בכן שלח רוגזיה כאשא בערא **דמן** קדמוהי **משצייא** ומזופיתיה כגומרין דנור דלקן ממימריה

Chapter Fourteen. Appendices

t1639i

סליק זדו**ני** דפרעה רשיעא כתנבא **קדמוהי** בכן שלח רוגזיה כאשא בערא ד**מן** קדמוהי **משיציאה** *ומאפיתיה*#ומזופיתיה# כגומרין דנור דלק**א** [>] מימריה

t1647i

סליק זדוניה דפרעה רשיעא כתנבא באפוהי בכן שלח רוגזיה כאשא מן קדמוהי משציין ומזופיתיה כגומרין דנור דלקן ממימריה

t1679i

סליק זדוניה דפרעה רשיעא כיתנבא באפוי בכן שלח רוגזיה כאישא מן קדמוהי משציין ומזופיתיה כגומרין דנור דלקן מן מימריה

2 Sam. 22:10

וארכין שמיא ואיתגלי יקריה ב**ק**בורתיה וענן אמיתתא כיבש קדמוהי

t1618i

וארכין שמייא ואיתגלי יקריה בגבורתיה וענן *אמיתתא*#אמיתתא כיבש קדמוהי

t1621i

וארכין שמייא ואיתגלי יקריה בגבורתיה וענן אמיתתא כבש קדמוהי

t1639i

וארכין שמייא ואיתגלי יקריה [ב]גבורתיה וענן אמיתתא כיבש קדמוהי

t1647i

וארכין שמייא ואיתגלי יקריה בגבורתיה וענן אמיטתא כבש קדמוהי

t1679i

וארכין שמייא ואיתגלי יקריה בגבורתיה וענן אמיטתא כיבש קדמוהי

2 Sam. 22:11

ואשרי שכינתיה על כרובין קלילין ואיתגלי ביקר ודבר בתקוף על פני רוחא

t1618i

ואשרי שכינתיה על כרובין קלילין ואיתגלי ביקר ודבר בתקוף על **כנפי** רוחא

t1621i

ואשרי שכינתיה על כרובין קלילין ואיתגלי ביקר ודבר בתקוף על **כנפי** רוחא

t1639i

ואשרי שכינתיה על כרובין קלילין ואיתגלי ביקר ודבר בתקוף על **כנפי** רוחא

t1647i

ואשרי שכינתיה על כרובין קלילין ואיתגלי ביקר ודבר בתקוף על **כנפי** רוחא

t1679i

ואשרי שכינתיה על כרובין קלילין ואיתגלי ביקר ודבר בתקוף על **אפי** רוחא

2 Sam. 22:12

ואשרי שכינתיה בערפילא וענן יקר סחור סחור ליה מחית מיין ת[ק]יפין מריגפת עננין קלילין ברום עלמא

t1618i

ואשרי שכינתיה בערפילא וענן יקר סחור ליה מחית מיין תקיפין מריגפת ענגין קלילין ברום עלמא

t1621i

ואשרי שכינתיה בערפילא וענן יקר סחור ליה מחית מיין תקיפין מרגפת ענגין קלילין ברום עלמא

t1639i

ואשרי שכינתיה בערפיל**ייא** וענן יקר סחור ליה מחית מיין תקיפין מריגפת ענגין קלילין ברום עלמא

t1647i

ואשרי שכינתיה בערפלא וענן יקר סחור ליה מחית מיין תקיפין מריגפת ענגין קלילין ברום עלמא

t1679i

ואשרי שכינתיה בערפלא וענן יקר סחור ליה מחית מיין תקיפין מריגפת ענגין קלילין ברום עלמא

2 Sam. 22:13

מ[ז]יו יקריה דאלהא חייא וקיימא מבהיקין שמיא ושמי שמיא ומזופיתיה כגומרין ד[נו]ר דלק[ן] ממימריה

t1618i

מזיו יקריה דאלהא חייא וקיימא מבהיקין שמיא ושמי שמיא ומזופיתיה כגומרין דנור דלקן ממימריה

t1621i

מזיו יקריה דאלהא חייא וקיימא מבהיקין שמיא ושמי שמיא ומזופיתיה כגומרין **כ**נור דלקן [>]מימריה

t1639i

ומזיו יקריה דאלהא חייא וקיימא מבהקין [>] ושמי שמיא [>] [>]מזופיתיה כגומרין דנור דלק**א** [>]מימר[י]ה

t1647i

ומזיו יקריה דאלהא חייא וקיימא מבהיקין שמיא ושמי שמיא ומזופיתיה כגומרין דנור דלקן ממימריה

t1679i

מזיו **יקרא** דאלהא חייא וקיימא מבהיקין שמיא [>] ומזופיתיה כגומרין דנור דלקן ממימריה

2 Sam. 22:14

אכלי מן שמיא יוי ועילאה ארים קליה

t1618i

אכלי מן שמיא יוי ועילאה ארים קליה

Chapter Fourteen. Appendices

t1621i
אכלי מן שמייא יוי ועילאה ארים קליה
t1639i
אכלי מן שמייא יוי ועילאה ארים קליה
t1647i
אכליה מן שמיא יוי ועילאה ארים קליה
t1679i
אכלי מן שמייא יוי ועילאה ארים קליה

2 Sam. 22:15

ושלח מחתיה בהון ובדרינון בברקין וש[גי]שינון
t1618i
ישלח מחתיה בהון **כגירין** ובדרינון בברקין ושגישינון
t1621i
ישלח מחתיה בהון **כגירין כ**ברקין ושגישינון
t1639i
ישלח מחתיה [>] **כגירין** ובדרינון בברקין ושגישינון
t1647i
ושלח מחתיה בהון **כגירין** ובדרינון בברק**ים** ושגישינון
t1679i
ישלח מחתיה בהון ובדרינון בברקין ושגישינון

2 Sam. 22:16

ואיתחזיאו עמקי ימא ואתגליאו שכלולי תבל במזופית רוח מן קדם יוי ממימר תקוף רוגזיה
t1618i
ואיתחזיאו עמקי ימא ואיתגליאו שכלולי תבל במזופית רוח מן קדם יוי ממימר תקוף **רוח** רוגזיה
t1621i
ואיתחזיאו עמקי ימא ואיתגליאו שכלולי תבל במזופית רוח מן קדם יוי ממימר תקוף רוגזיה
t1639i
ואיתחזיאו עמקי ימא ואיתגליאו שכלולי תבל במזופית רוח מן קדם יוי ממימר תקוף רוגזיה
t1647i
ואיתחזיאו עמקי ימא ואיתגליאו שכלולי תבל במזופית רוח מן קדם יוי ממימר תקוף רגזיה
t1679i
ואיתחזיאו עמקי ימא ואיתגליאו שכלולי תבל במזופית רוח מן קדם יוי ממימר תקוף רוגזיה

2 Sam. 22:17

ישלח נביאוהי מלך תקיף דיתיב בשכינתיה בשמי מרומא דברני שיזבני מעממין סגיאין
t1618i
ישלח נביאוהי מלך תקיף [>] **ד**שכינתיה בשמי מרומא דברני שיזבני מעממין סגיאין

t1621i

ישלח נביאוהי מלך תקיף דיתיב בשכינתיה בשמי מרומא דברני שיזבני מעממין סגיאין

t1639i

ישלח נביאוהי מלך תקיף דיתיב **בתקוף רומא** דברני שיזבני מעממין סגיאין

t1647i

ישלח נביאוהי מלך תקיף [>] בשכינתיה בשמי מרומא דברני שיזבני מעממין סגיאין

t1679i

ישלח נביאוהי מלך תקיף דיתיב בשכינתיה בשמי מרומא דברני שיזבני מעממין סגיאין

2 Sam. 22:18

שיזבני מן שנאי ארי תקפוני ומבעלי דבבי ארי איתגברו עלי

t1618i

שיזבני מן שנאי ארי **אקפוני** ומבעלי דבביי ארי איתגברו עלי

t1621i

שיזבני מן שנאי ארי תקפוני ומבעלי דבביי ארי **יתגרו** עלי

t1639i

שיזבני מן שנאי ארי תקפוני ומבעלי דבבי ארי איתגברו עלי

t1647i

שיזבני מן שנאי ארי **אקפוני** ומבעלי דבביי ארי אתגברו עלי

t1679i

שיזבני מן שנאי ארי תקפוני ומבעלי דבביי ארי איתגברו עלי

2 Sam. 22:19

ערעוני יקדמוני ביום טילטולי והוה מימריה דיוי סמיך לי

t1618i

ארעוני וקדמוני ביום טילטולי והוה מימר**א** דיוי סמיך לי

t1621i

ערעוני יקדמוני ביום טילטולי והוה מימר**א** דיוי סמיך לי

t1639i

ערעוני וקדמוני ביום טילטולי והוה מימר**א** דיוי סמיך לי

t1647i

ערעוני [>] ביום טלטולי והוה מימר**א** דיוי סמיך לי

t1679i

ערעוני וקדמוני ביום טילטולי והוה מימר**א** דיוי סמיך לי

2 Sam. 22:20

ואפיק לרווחא יתי שיזבני ארי איתרעי בי

t1618i

ואפיק לרווחא יתי שיזבני ארי איתרעי בי

Chapter Fourteen. Appendices

t1621i
ואפיק לרווחא יתי שיזבני ארי איתרעי בי
t1639i
ואפיק לרווחא יתי שיזבני ארי איתרעי בי
t1647i
ואפיק לרווחא יתי שיזבני ארי אתרעי בי
t1679i
ואפיק לרווחא יתי שיזבני ארי איתרעי בי

2 Sam. 22:21
אמר דוד יגמלני יוי כזכותי כברירות ידיי יתיב לי
t1618i
אמר דוד יגמלני יוי כזכותי כברירות ידיי יתיב לי
t1621i
אמר דוד יגמלני יוי כזכותי כברירות ידיי יתיב לי
t1639i
אמר דוד **ישלמינני** יוי כזכותי כברירות ידי יתיב לי
t1647i
אמר דוד יגמלני יוי כזכותי כברירות ידיי יתיב לי
t1679i
אמר דוד יגמלני יוי כזכותי כברירות ידיי יתיב לי

2 Sam. 22:22
ארי נטרית אורחית דתקנן קדם יוי ולא הליכית ברשע קדם אלהי
t1618i
ארי נטרית ארחן דתקנן קדם יוי ולא הליכית ברשע קדם אלהי
t1621i
ארי נטרית אורח**א** דתקנן קדם יוי ול**א** הליכית ברשע קדם אלהי
t1639i
ארי נטרית אורחן דתקנן קדם יוי ולא הליכית ברשע קדם אלהי
t1647i
ארי נטרית אורחן דתקנן קדם יוי ולא הליכית ברשע קדם אלהי
t1679i
ארי נטרית אורחן דתקנן קדם יוי ולא הליכית ברשע קדם אלהי

2 Sam. 22:23
ארי כל דיני רעותיה גלן לקיבלי למעבדהון וקיימוהי לא עדית מנהון
t1618i
ארי כל דיני רעותיה גלן לקבלי למיעבדהון וקימוהי לא עדית מינהון

t1621i

ארי כל דיניה רעותיה גלן לקבלי למיעבדהון וקיימוהי לא עדת מנהון

t1639i

ארי כל דינוהי רעותיה גלן לקבלי למעבדהון וקימוהי לא עדית מנהון

t1647i

ארי כל דיני רעותיה גלן לקבלי למעבדהון וקיימוהי לא **אעדה** מנהון

t1679i

ארי כל דיניה רעותיה גלן לקיבלי למיעבדהון וקיימוהי לא עדית מינהון

2 Sam. 22:24

והויתי שלים ל[דחל]תיה והויתי נטר נפשי מחובין

t1618i

והויתי שלים לדחלתיה והויתי נטר נפשי מחובין

t1621i

והויתי שלים לדחלתיה והויתי נטר נפשי מחובין

t1639i

והויתי שלים לדחלתיה והויתי נטר נפשי מחובין

t1647i

והויתי שלים לדחלתיה והויתי נטר נפשי מחובין

t1679i

והויתי שלים לדחלתיה והויתי נטר נפשי מחובין

2 Sam. 22:25

ואתיב יוי לי כזכותי וכברירותי קדם מימריה

t1618i

ואתיב יוי לי כזכותי וכברירותי [>] מימריה

t1621i

ואתיב יוי לי כזכותי וכברירותי קדם **מ**מימריה

t1639i

ואתיב יוי לי כזכותי וכברירותי קדם מימריה

t1647i

ואתיב יוי לי כזכותי וכברירותי קדם מימריה

t1679i

ואתיב יוי לי כזכותי וכברירותי קדם מימריה

2 Sam. 22:26

אברהם דאשתכח חסיד קדמך בכן אסגיתא למיעבד חסדא עם זרעיה ויצחק דהוה שלים לדחלתך בכן אשלימתא למעבד רעותך עימיה

Chapter Fourteen. Appendices

t1618i

אברהם *ח*## דאישתכח חסיד קדמך בכין אסגיתא למיעבד חסדא עם זרעיה ויצחק דהוה שלים לדחלתך בכין אשלימתא למיעבד רעותך עימיה

t1621i

אברהם **דישתכח** חסיד קדמך בכן אסגיתא למיעבד חסדא עם זרעיה ויצחק דהוה שלים לדחלתך בכן אשלימתא למיעבד רעותך עמיה

t1639i

אברהם דאישתכח חסיד קדמך בכן אסגיתא [>] חסדא עם זרעיה ויצחק דהוה שלים לדחלתך בכן אשלמתא למעבד רעותך **בהדיה**

t1647i

אברהם דאישתכח חסיד קדמך בכן אסגיתא למיעבד חסדא עם זרעיה ויצחק שלים לדחלתך בכן אשלימתא למיעבד רעותך עמיה

t1679i

אברהם דאישתכח חסיד קדמך בכן אסגיתא למיעבד חסדא עם זרעיה ויצחק דהוה שלים לדחלתך בכן אשלימתא למיעבד רעותך עמיה

2 Sam. 22:27

יעקב דהליך בברירותא קדמך בחרת בנוי מכל עממיא ואפרישתא זרעיה מכל פסילא פרעה ומשיריתיה דחשיבו מחשבן על עמך בלבלתינון במחשבתהון

t1618i

יעקב דהליך בברירותא קדמך [ב]חרת בנוהי מכל עממייא ואפרישתא זרעיה מכל פסילא פרעה ומשירייתיה דחשיבו מחשבן **בישן** על עמך בלבלתנון במחשבתהון

t1621i

יעקב דהליך בברירותא קדמך בחרת בנוהי מכל עממייא ואפרישתא זרעיה מכל פסילה פרעה ומשירייתיה דחשיבו מחשבן **בישן** על עמך בילבלנון במחשבתיהון

t1639i

יעקב דהלך בברירותא קדמך בחרת בנוהי מכל עממייא ואפרישתא זרעיה מכל פסולה **דפרעה ומצראי** דחשיבו מחשבן על עמך בלבלתינון במחשבתהון

t1647i

יעקב דהליך בברירותא קדמך בחרת בנוהי מכל עממייא ואפרישתא [זר]עיה מכל פסילייא פרעה ומשירייתיה דחשיבו מחשבן **בישן** [>] עימך בלבלתינון במחשבתהון

t1679i

יעקב דהליך בברירותא קדמך בחרת בנוי מכל עממייא ואפרישתא זרעיה מכל פסילא פרעה ומשיריתיה דחשיבו מחשבן על עמך בלבילתהון במחשבתהון

2 Sam. 22:28

ויהון עמך בית ישראל דמתקרן בעלמא הדין עם חשיך את עתיד למיפרק יתהון ולמקרי להון עם חביב דבכל עינך במכיכי רוח מיתיית[ב]א ובמימרך תקיפא דמתגברין עליהון תמאיך

The Transmission of Targum Jonathan in the West

t1618i

ויהון עמ**א** בית ישראל דמתקרן בעלמא הדין עם חשיך את עתיד למי[פ]רק יתהון ולמיקרי להון עם
חביב דבכל **עיד**[**ן**] עינך במכיכי רוח**א** מתייתבא ובמימ[רך] תקיפ[.] דמתגברין **על** עליהון תמאיך

t1621i

ויהון עמ**א** בית ישראל דמיתקרין בעלמא הדין עם חשיך את עתיד למיפרק יתהון ולמיקרי להון
עם חביב דבכל **עידן** עיינך במכיכי רוח**א** מתיבתא ובמימרך תקיפא דמתגברין עליהון תמאיך

t1639i

ו**ית** עמ**א** בית ישראל דמתקרן בעלמא הדין עם חשיך את עתיד למיפרק יתהון ולמיקרי להון עם
חביב דבכל **עידן** עינך במכיכי רוח**א** מתייתבא ובמימרך תקיפא דמתגברין עליהון תמאיך

t1647i

ויהון עמ**א** בית ישראל דמתקרן בעלמא הדין עם חשיך את עתיד למפרק יתהון ולמיקרי להון עם
חביב דבכל **עידן** עיינך במכיכי רוח**א** מתי**בתא** ובמימרך תק[י]פא דמתגברין עליהון תמאיך

t1679i

ויהון עמך בית ישראל דמיתקרן בעלמא הדין עם חשיך את עתיד למיפרק יתהון ולמיקרי להון עם
חביב דבכל עינך *במכיכי*#במכיכי# **רוחא** מתייתבא ובמימרך תקיפא דמתגברין עליהון תמאיך

2 Sam. 22:29

ארי את הוא מרי נהוריה דישראל ויוי יפקינני מחשוכא לנהורא ויחזינני בעלמא דעתיד למיתי על
צדיקיא

t1618i

ארי את הוא מ[...] נהוריה דיש[ראל |>]יוי יפקינני מחשוכא לנהורא ויחז[יננ]י ב]עלמא דעתיד
למיתי על צדיקייא

t1621i

ארי את הוא מריה נהורי דישראל ויוי **אפקני** מחשוכא לנהורא **ואשריאני** בעלמא דעתיד למיתיה
על צדיקיא

t1639i

ארי את הוא **מימריה** נהוריה דישראל |>]יוי יפקינני מחשוכא לנהורא ויחזינני בעלמא דעתיד
למיתי על צדיקייא

t1647i

ארי את הוא מרי נהוריה דישראל ויוי יפקינני מחשוכא לנהורא ויחזינני בעלמא דעתיד למיתי על
צדיקיא

t1679i

ארי את הוא מריה נהוריה דישראל ויוי יפקינני מחשוכא לנהורא ויחזינני בעלמא דעתיד למיתיה
על צדיקיא

2 Sam. 22:30

ארי במימרך אכנש משיריין אכבש ואתבר כל כרכין תקיפין

Chapter Fourteen. Appendices

t1618i

ארי במימרך אכניש משיריין אכביש [ואיתב]ר כל כרכין תקיפין

t1621i

ארי במימרך אכבש אכבש משיריין ואתבר כל כרכין תקיפין

t1639i

ארי במימרך **אסגי** משיריין **ובמימר אלהי אכבש** כל כרכין תקיפין

t1647i

ארי במימרך אכניש משיריין אכבש ואתבר כל כרכין תקיפין

t1679i

ארי במימרך אכנש משיריין אכבש ואתבר כל כרכין תקיפין

2 Sam. 22:31

אלהא דכיוונא אורחיה אורייתא דיוי בחירא היא תקיף הוא לכל דמתרחצין על מימריה

t1618i

אלהא דכיוונא אורחיה אורייתא דיוי בחירא **הוא** תקיף הוא לכל דמת[רחצי]ן על מימריה

t1621i

אלהא דכיוונא אורחיה אורייתא דיוי בחירא היא תקיף הוא לכל דמתרחצין על מימריה

t1639i

אלהא דכיוונא אורחיה אורייתא דיוי בחירא היא תקיף הוא לכל דמתרחצין **עלוהי**

t1647i

אלהא דכיוונא אורחיה *אריתא#*אוריתא# דיוי בחירה היא תקיף הוא לכל דמתרחצין על מימריה

t1679i

אלהא דכיוונא אורחיה אורייתא דיוי בחירא היא תקיף הוא לכל דמתרחצין על מימריה

2 Sam. 22:32

בכן על ניסא ופורקנא דאתעבד למשיחך ולשארא דעמך דישתארון יודון כל עממיא אומיא ולישניא ויימרון לית אלה אלא יוי ארי לית בר מינך ועמך יימרון לית אלה אלא אלהנא

t1618i

בכן על ניסא ופורקנא דאיתעביד למשיחך ולש[ארא ד]עמך *ישתארון*#דישתארון# יודון כל עממיא אומייא ולישנייא ויימרון לית אלהא אלא יוי ארי לית [בר] מינך ועמך יימרון לית אלהא אלא אלהנא

t1621i

בכן על ניסא ופורקנא דאיתעביד למשיחך ולשארה דעמך די ישתארון יודון כל עממיא אומייא ולישנייא ויימרון לית אלהא אלא **אלהנא** יוי ארי לית בר מינך ועמך יימרון לית אלהא אלא אלהנא

t1639i

בכן על ניסא ופורקנא **דתעביד** למשיחך דישתארון דעמך יודון כל עממיא אומייא ולישנייא ויימרון לית אלהא אלא יוי ארי לית בר מינך ועמך יימרון לית **דתקיף** אלא אלהנא

433

The Transmission of Targum Jonathan in the West

t1647i
בכן על ניסא ופורקנא דאיתעביד למשיחך ולישאראה דעמך דישתארון יודון כל עממייא אומייא
ולישנייא ויימרון לית אלהא אלא יוי ארי לית בר מינך ועמך יימרון לית אלהא אלא אלהנא

t1679i
בכין על ניסא ופורקנא דאיתעביד למשיחך ולאשרא דעמך דישתארון יודון כל עממייא אומייא
ולישנייא ויימרון לית אלה אלא יוי ארי לית בר מינך ועמך יימרון לית אלה אלא אלהנא

2 Sam. 22:33
אלהא דסעיד לי בחילא ומתקין שלמא ארחי

t1618i
אלהא דסעיד לי בחילא ומתקין שלמא ארחי

t1621i
אלהא דסעיד לי בחילא ומתקן שלמא אחריה

t1639i
אלהא דסעיד לי בחילא ומתקין **שלים** ארחי

t1647i
אלהא דסעיד לי בחילא ומתק**ן** שלמא ארחי

t1679i
אלהא דסעיד לי בחילא ומתקין שלמא אורחי

2 Sam. 22:34
משוי רגליי קלילין כאיילתא ועל בית תוקפי יקיימינני

t1618i
משו[ה] רגלי קלילין [כ]א[יי]לתא ועל בית תוקפי יקיימינני

t1621i
משווה ריגלי קלילין כאיילתא ועל בית תוקפי יקיימינני

t1639i
משוי ריגלי קלילין כאיילתא ועל בית תוקפי יקיימינני

t1647i
משוי ריגליי קלילין כאיילתא ועל בית תוקפי יקיימינני

t1679i
משוי ריגליי קלילין כאיילתא ועל בית תוקפי יקיימינני

2 Sam. 22:35
מליף לאגחא קרבא ותבר עממיא דתקיפין כקשתא דנחשא דרעיי

t1618i
מליף **ידיי** לאגחא קרבא ותבר [ע]ממייא דתקיפין כקשתא דנחשא דרעיי

t1621i
מאלף **ידיי** לאגחא קרבא ותבר עממייא דתקיפין כקשתא דנחשא דרועיי

Chapter Fourteen. Appendices

t1639i

מלוֹף **ידיי למעבד** קרבא [<] **ומתקף** כקשת נחשת דרעיי

t1647i

מליף **ידיי** לאגחא קרבא ותבר עממיא דתקיפין כקשתא דנחשא דרעאי

t1679i

מליף **ידיי** לאגחא קרבא ותבר עממייא דתקיפין כקשתא דנחשא דרעיי

2 Sam. 22:36

ויהבת לי סעיד ופרקתני בתוקפך ובמימרך אסגיתני

t1618i

ויהבת לי סעיד ופרקתני בתוקפך ובמימרך אסגיתני

t1621i

ויהבת לי סעיד ופרקתני בתוקפך ובמימרך אסגיתני

t1639i

ויהבת לי **תקוֹף** ופרקתני בתוקפך ובמימרך אסגיתני

t1647i

ויהבת לי סעיד ופרקתני בתוקפך ובמימרך אסגיתני

t1679i

ויהבת לי סעיד ופרקתני בתוקפך ובמימרך אסגיתני

2 Sam. 22:37

אסגיתא פסיעתי קדמיי ולא אזדעזעא רכובתי

t1618i

אסגיתא פסיעתי קדמי ולא איזדעזעא רכובתי

t1621i

אסגיתא פסיעתי קדמיי ולא איזדעזעא **רמפתי**

t1639i

אסגית פסיעתי **תחותיי** ולא איזדעזעא רכובתי

t1647i

אסגיתא פסיעתי קדמיי ולא איזדעזעא ריכובתי

t1679i

אסגיתא פסיעתי קדמי ולא איזדעזעא רכובתי

2 Sam. 22:38

רדפית בתר שנאיי ושיציתינון ולא תבית מנהון עד דגמרתינון

t1618i

רדפית בתר שנא[י] ושיציתינון ולא תבית מינהון עד דגמרתינון

t1621i

רדפית בתר שנאיי ושיציתינון ולא תבית מנהון עד דגמרתינון

t1639i
רדפית בתר שנאיי ושיציתינון ולא תבית מנהון עד דגמרתינון
t1647i
רדפית בתר שנאי ושיציתינון ולא תבית מינהון עד דגמרתינון
t1679i
רדפית בתר שנאיי ושיציתינון ולא תבית מינהון עד דגמרתינון

2 Sam. 22:39
ודששתינון וגמרתינון ולא יכילו למיקם ונפלו קטילין תחות פרסת רגליי
t1618i
ודששתינון וגמרתינון ולא יכילו למיקם ונפלו קטילין תחות [פ]רסת ריגליי
t1621i
ושיציתינון וגמרתינון ולא יכילו למיקם ונפלו קטילין תחות פרסת ריגליי
t1639i
ושיציתינון וגמרתינון ולא יכילו *ממיקם*#למיקם# ונפלו קטילין תחות פרסת רגליי
t1647i
ודששיתינון וגמרתינון ולא יכילו למיקם ונפלו קטילין תחות פרסת ריגליי
t1679i
ודששתינון וגמרתינון ולא יכילו למיקם ונפלו קטילין תחות פרסת ריגליי

2 Sam. 22:40
וסעדתני בחילא למעבד קרבא [ת]ברתא עממיא דתקיפין וקיימין לאבשא לי תחותי
t1618i
וסעדתני בחילא למעבד קרבא תברתא עממייא דתקיפין וקיימין לאבשא לי תחותי
t1621i
וסיעדתני בחילא למיעבד קרבא **עם** עממיא דתקיפין וקיימין לאבשא לי **תברת** תחותי
t1639i
וסעדתני בחילא למעבד קרבא תברת עממייא [>] **ד**קיימין לאבאשא לי תחותי
t1647i
וסעדתני בחילא למעבד קרבא תברת עממייא דתקיפין וקיימין לאבאשא לי תחותי
t1679i
וסעדתני בחילא למעבד קרבא תברת עממייא דתקיפין וקיימין לאבאשא לי תחותי

2 Sam. 22:41
ושנאיי מסרתא קדמיי מחזרי קדל ובעלי דבביי ושיציתינון
t1618i
וסנאי מסרת קדמי מחזרי קדל ובעלי דבב[י ו]שיציתינון
t1621i
וסנאיי מסרתא קדמיי מחזרי קדל ובעלי דבביי ושיציתינון

Chapter Fourteen. Appendices

t1639i

ושנאי **תברת** קדמיי מחזרי קדל ובעלי דבביי ושיציתינון

t1647i

ושנאיי מסרת קדמיי מחזרי קדל ובעלי דבביי ושיציתינון

t1679i

וסנאיי מסרתא קדמיי מחזרי קדל ובעלי דבביי ושיציתינון

2 Sam. 22:42

בען סעיד ולית להון פריק מצלן קדם יוי ולא מתקבלא צלותהון

t1618i

בען סעיד ולית להון פריק מצלן קדם יוי ולא מתקבלא צלותהון

t1621i

בען סעיד ולית להון פריק מצלן קדם יוי ולא מתקבלא צלותהון

t1639i

בען סעיד ולית להון פריק מצלן קדם יוי ולא **מקבל** צלותהון

t1647i

בען סעיד ו**ד**לית להון פריק מצלן קדם יוי ולא **מקבלא** צלותהון

t1679i

בען סעיד ולית להון פריק מצלן קדם יוי ולא מתקבלא צלותהון

2 Sam. 22:43

ודשישתינון כעפרא [ד]ארעא כסוון שווקין בעטית בהון רפסתינון

t1618i

ודששתינון כעפרא ד[ארעא] כסוון שווקין בעטית **יתהון** רפסתינון

t1621i

ודששתינון כעפרא דארעא כסוון שו**קים** בעטית בהון רפסתינון

t1639i

ודששתינון כעפרא דארעא כסוון שוקין בעטית בהון רפסתינון

t1647i

ודששתינון כעפרא דארעא **כטיט** שקין בעטית **יתהון** רפשתינון

t1679i

ודשיצתינון כעפרא דארעא כסוון שווקין בעטית בהון רפסתינון

2 Sam. 22:44

ושזבתני מפלוגת עממין תמניניי לריש עממייא עמא דלא ידעית יפלחונני

t1618i

ושיזבתני מפלוגת עממין תמניני לריש עממיא עמא דלא ידעית יפלחונני

t1621i

ושיזבתני מפלוגת עממין תמניני לריש עממיא עמא דלא ידעית יפלחונני

437

t1639i

ו**תשיזבנני** מפלוגת עממין תמנינני [>]רישא ל**עממייא עם** דלא ידעית יפלחונני

t1647i

**#ושיזבתני# מפלגות עממין תמנינני לריש עממייא עמא דלא ידעית יפלחונני

t1679i

ושיזבתני מפלגות עממין תמנינני לריש עממייא עמא דלא ידעית יפלחונני

2 Sam. 22:45

בני עממיא יתכדבון לי למשמע אודן ישתמעון לי

t1618i

בני עממיא *יסופון*## יתכדבון לי למשמע אודן ישתמעון לי

t1621i

בני עממיא יתכדבון לי למישמע אודן ישתמעון לי

t1639i

בני עממייא יתכדבון לי למשמע אודן **ישמעון** לי

t1647i

בני עממיא **יתדבדבון** לי למשמע אודן ישתמעון לי

t1679i

בני עממיא יתכדבון לי למשמע אודן ישתמעון לי

2 Sam. 22:46

בני עממיא י[ס]ופון ויצדון ויזועון מבירניתהון

t1618i

בני עממיא יסופון ויצדון ויז[ו]עון מבירניתהון

t1621i

בני עממיא יסופון ויצודון ויזעון מבירניתהון

t1639i

בני עממיא יסופון ויצדון ויזעון מבירניתהון

t1647i

בני עממיא יסופון ויצדון ויזעון מברנייתהון

t1679i

בני עממייא יסופון ויצדון ויזעון מבירניתהון

2 Sam. 22:47

בכן על ניסא ופורקנא דיתעבד למשיחך ולשארא דעמך דישתארון ישבחון וי[ו]דון ויימרון קיים הוא אלהא חייא [גי]ברא ודחילא ובריך תקיף [ד]מן קדמוהי מתיהב לי תקוף ופורקן ומרומא אלהא תקוף פורקננא

Chapter Fourteen. Appendices

t1618i

בכן על ניסא [ו]**פו**|**ר**]**קנא דאיתעביד** למשיחך ולישארא דעמך דישתארון ישבחון ויודון ויימרון קיים הוא אלהא חייא גיברא ודחילא ובריך תקיף דמין קדמוהי מתיהב לי תקוף ופורקן ומרומם אלהא תקוף פורקננא

t1621i

בכן על ניסא ופורקנא דיתעבד למשיחך ולשארה דעמך דישתארון ישבחון ויודון ויימרון קיים הוא אלהא חייא **רבא** גיברה ודחילא ובריך תקיף דמין קדמוהי מתיהב לי תקוף ופורקן ומרומא אלהא תקוף פורקננא

t1639i

בכן על ניסא ופורקנא דיתעבד למשיחך ולשארא דעמך דישתארון ויודון ויימרון קיים הוא אלהא חייא גיברא ודחילא ובריך תקיף דמין קדמוהי מתיהב לי תקוף ופורקן ומרומא **אלא** תקוף פורקננא

t1647i

בכן על ניסא ופורקנא **דאיתעביד** למשיחך ולישארא דעמך דישתארון ויודון ויימרון **קדם**[>] אלהא חייא גיברא ודחילא ובריך **ותקיף** דמן קדמוהי מתיהב לי תקוף ופורקן ומרומא אלהא תקוף פורקנא

t1679i

בכן על ניסא ופורקנא דיתעביד למשיחך ולשארא דעמך דישתארון ישבחון ויודון ויימרון קיים הוא אלהא חייא גיברא ודחילא ובריך תקיף דמן קדמוהי מתיהב לי תקוף ופורקן ומרומא אלהא תקוף פורקננא

2 Sam. 22:48

אלהא דעביד פורענותא לי ותבר עממיא דתקיפין כקשתא דנחשא תחותיי

t1618i

אלהא דעביד פורענותא לי [ו]**תבר** עממיא דתקיפין כקשתא דנחשא תחותי

t1621i

אלהא דעביד פורענותא לי ותבר עממיא דתקיפין כקשתא דנחשא תחותיי

t1639i

אלהא דעביד פורענותא לי ותבר עממיא **דקיימין לאבאשא לי** תחותיי

t1647i

אלהא דעביד פורענותא לי ותבר עממיא [>] כקשתא דנחשא תחותיי

t1679i

אלהא דעביד פורענותא לי ותבר עממיא דתקיפין כקשתא דנחשא תחותיי

2 Sam. 22:49

ומשיזבי מן שנאי ואף על דקיימין לאבשא לי תשיזבינני מן גוג ומן משיריין עממין חטופין דאתו לאגחא קרבא עימי תשיזבינני

The Transmission of Targum Jonathan in the West

t1618i

ומשיזבית#ומשיזבי# [מן] שנאי ואף על דקיימין לאבאשא לי תשיזביננ‎י מן גוג ומן משיריין עממין חטופין ד[את]ו ל[אגח]א קרבא עמי תשיזיבנני

t1621i

ומעיזבי מן שנאיי ואף על דקיימין לאבאשא לי תשיזבינני מן גוג ומן משיריין עממין חטופין דאתו לאגחא קרבא עמי תשזיבנני

t1639i

ופרקי משנאי [>] **ועל** דקיימין לאבאשא לי **תגברינני** מגוג וממשיריית עממין חטופין דאתו לאגחא קרבא **דעמיה** תשיזבינני

t1647i

ומשזבי מן שנאיי ואף **בכל** דקיימין לאבאשא לי תשיזבני מן גוג ומן משיריין עמימין חטופין דאתו לאגחא קרבא עימי תשיזבינני

t1679i

ומשיזבי מן שנאיי ואף על דקיימין לאבאשא לי תשיזבינני מן גוג ומן משיריין עממין חטופין דאתו לאגחא קרבא **קרבא** עמי תשיזבינני

2 Sam. 22:50

על כן אודה קדמך יוי ולשמך אימר תושבחא

t1618i

על כן אודה קדמך יוי ולשמך אימר תושבח[א]

t1621i

על כן אודה קדמך יוי ולשמך **אזמר** תושבחתא

t1639i

על כן אודה קודמך יוי ולשמך אימר **תושבחן**

t1647i

על כן אודה קדמך יוי ולשמך אימר תושבחתא

t1679i

על כן אודה קדמך יוי ולשמך אימר תושבחא

2 Sam. 22:51

מסגי למעבד פורק[ן] עם מלכיה ועביד טיבו למשיחיה לדוד ולזרעיה עד עלמא

t1618i

למ[יעב]ד פורקן עם מלכיה ועביד טיבו *למשיחה*#למשיחיה# לדוד ולזרעיה עד [מסגי] עלמא

t1621i

מסגי למיעבד פורקן עם מל**כייא** ועביד טיבו למשיחיה לדוד ולזרעיה עד עלמא

t1639i

מסגי למעבד פורקן עם מלכיה ועביד *טבו*#טיבו* למשיחיה לדוד ולזרעיה עד עלמא

440

Chapter Fourteen. Appendices

t1647i

מסגי למעבד פורקן עם מלכיה ועביד טיבו למשיחיה לדוד ולזרעיה עד עלמא

t1679i

מסגי למעבד פורקן עם *עבדיה*#מלכיה# ועיבד טיבו למשיחיה לדוד ולזרעיה עד עלמא

4. Tosefta Targums (Chapter Eleven)

1 Sam. 2:6

Hebrew Text

יהוה ממית ומחיה מוריד שאול ויעל

Babylonian tradition (t2520b)

כל אלין גבורתא דיוי דהוא שליט בעלמא ממית ואמר לאחאה מחית לשאול ואף עתיד לאסקא בחיי עלמא

t705i

כל אילין גבורתא דיוי דהוא שליט בעלמא ממית ואמר לאחאה מחית לשאול ואף עתיד לאסקא בחיי עלמא ברם קרח בר יצהר בר קהת בר לוי דמיניה נפק שמואל ברי איתחת לשאול על עיסק דקם ואיתפלג על משה ואהרן צדיקיא יסקון מבית בליעתהון ויודון דלית אלה בר מיניה

1 Sam. 17:8

Hebrew Text

ויעמד ויקרא אל מערכת ישראל ויאמר להם למה תצאו לערך מלחמה הלוא אנכי הפלשתי ואתם עבדים לשאול ברו לכם איש וירד אלי

Babylonian Tradition (t707b)

וקם ואכלי על סידרי ישראל ואמר להון למא תיפקון לסדרא קרבא הלא אנא פלישתאה ואתון עבדין לשא[ול] בחרו לכון גברא וייחות לותי

Group 1

t720a

וקם ואכריז בסידרא קרבא דישר' ואמר להון למה אתון נפקין לסדרא קרבא הלא אנא גלית פלשתאה דמן גת דקטלית תרין בני עלי כהנא חפני ופינח' ושביתי ית ארון קיימא דיוי ואוביליתי יתיה לבית דגון טעותי והוה תמן בקירוי פלישת' שבעא ירחין אף כל קרב וקרב דהוו להון לפלשתאי אנא נפיק בריש חילא ונצחנא בקרב' ורמינא קטילין כעפרא דארע ועד כען לא אכשרו ית פלשתאי למיהו[י] אפילו רב אלפא עילויהון ואתון דבית ישראל מה גבורא עביד לכון שאו[ל] בר קיש דמגבעתא דמניתון יתיה מלכא עלויכון אם גבר גיבר הוא יחות ויעביד קרבא עמי ואם גבר חלש הוא בחרו לכון גברא וייחות לוותי

t713a

וקם ואכריז בסידרי קרביא דישר' ואמר להון למה אתון נפקין לסדרא קרבא הלא אנא גלית

The Transmission of Targum Jonathan in the West

פלשתאה דמן גת דקטלית תרין בני עלי כהנא חפני ופנחס ושביתי ית ארון קימא דיוי ואובילית
יתיה לבית דגון טעותי והו' תמן בקירוי פלשתאי שבעא ירחין אף כל קרב וקרב דהוו להון
לפלשתאי אנא נפיק בריש חילא ונצחנא בקרבא ורמינא קטילין כעפרא *דארעי*#דארעא# ועד
כען לא אכשרו יתי פלשתאי למיהוי אפילו רב אלפא עילויהון ואתון דבית ישר' מה גבורא עבד
לכון שאול בר קיש דמגבעתא דמניתון יתיה מלכא עילויכון אם גבר גיבר הוא יחות ויעביד קרבא
עמי ואם גבר חלש הוא בחרו לכון גברא וייחות לוותי

t6a

וקם ואכריז *בסידרי*#על סידרי# קרביא דישראל ואמר להון למא אתון נפקין לסדרא קרבא **עם**
פלישתאי הלא אנא **הוא** גלית פלישתאה דמן גת דקטלית תרין בני עלי [>] חפני ופנחס ושביתי ית
ארון קיימא **#**[דיוי]# ואובילית יתיה לבית דגון טעותי והוא תמן בקירוי פלישת' שבעא ירחין אף
כל קרב וקרב דהוו להון לפלישת' אנא נפיק בריש חילא ונצחנא בקרבא ורמינא קטילין בעפרא
דארעא ועד כען לא אקשה (read: אכשרו) יתי פלישתאי למיהוי [>] רב אלפא עילוויהון ואתון
דבית ישראל מא [>] עבד לכון שאול בר קיש דמן גבעתא דמניתון יתיה מלכא עילויכון אם גבר
גיבר הוא ייחות ויעבד קרבא עימי ואם גבר חלש הוא בחרו לכון גברא וייחות לותי

Group 2
t718i

וקם **וכריז על** סידרי קרבא דישראל ואמר להון למא אתון נפקין לסדרא קרבא **עים פלישתא**
הלא אנא גלית פלישתאה דמן גת דקטילית תרין בני עלי **כהניא** חפני ופנחס **ואייתיתי** [>] ארון
קיימא דיוי ואובילית יתיה לבית דגון טעותי והוה תמן בקירוי פלישתאי **שיתא** ירחי ואף כל קרב
וקרב **דהות לכון מן** פלישתאי [>] נפקא (נפקנא read:) **לפום קלא** [>] ורמינא קטיליא כעפרא
דארעא **ועדיין** לא אכ[ש]רו יתי פלישתאי למיהוי [>] רב אלפא עילויהון ואתון **בני** ישראל מא
[>] עבד לכון שאול בר קיש [>] דמניתון יתיה מלכא עילויכון אם גבר גיבר הוא יחות ויעביד
עימי קרב ואם גרב חלש הוא בחרו לכון גברא וייחות לוותי

t725a

וקם **וכריז על** סידרי קרבא [>] ישר' ואמר להון למ' אתון נפקין לסדרא קרבא **עם פלשתאי** הלא
אנא גלית פלש' דמן גת די קטלית תרין בני עלי **כהניא** חפני ופנחס ושביתי [>] ארון קיימא דיוי
ואובילית יתיה לבית דגון טעותי והוה תמן בקרוי פלשתאי **שתא** ירהי ואף כל קרב וקרב **דהות**
לכון מן פלשתאי [>] **נפקנא לפום קלא** [>] ורמינא קטיליא כעפרא *וארעא*#דארעא# **ועדיין**
לא אכשרו יתי פלשתאי למיהוי [>] רב אלפא עילויהון ואתון **בני** ישר' מה [>] עבד לכון שאול
בר קיש [>] דמניתון יתיה מלכא עילויכון אם גבר גיבר הוא יחות ויעבי' **עמי קרב** ואם גבר חלש
הוא בחרו לכון גברא ויחות לוותי

Group 3
t232i

וקם **ואכלי על** סידרי**ה** [>] ישראל ואמר להון למה **תיפקון** לסדרא קרבא הלא אנא [>]
פלישתאה דמן גת דקטלית תרין בני עלי **כהניא** חפני ופינחס ושביתי [>] ארון קיימא דיוי

Chapter Fourteen. Appendices

ואובילתיה [>] לבית דגון טעוותי והוה תמן בקירוי פלישתאי **תלתא** ירחין **ואף** כל קרב וקרב
דהות לכון מן פלישתאי **נפקנא לפום קל[א]** [>] ורמינא קטיליא כעפרא דארעא ועד [כע]ן לא
אכש[רו]ן יתי למיהוי [>] רב אלפא עילויהון ואתון **בני** ישראל מה [>] לכון שאול בר קיש [>]
דמניתון יתיה מלכא עילויכון אם גבר גיבר הוא **ייתי** ויעביד **עימי קרב** ואם גבר חלש הוא בחרו
לכון גברא וייחות לותי

Indices

Primary Sources

HEBREW BIBLE

Genesis
- 3:1 : 159
- 6:9–11:32 : 225
- 7:2–3 : 79
- 11:30 : 224
- 19:3 : 241
- 21:6 : 77
- 24:66 : 161
- 27:24 : 159
- 50:2 : 231

Exodus
- 3:5 : 285
- 4:30 : 161
- 13:17–15:26 : 63, 312, 337, 339
- 14:30 : 312
- 15:4 : 337
- 18:1–20:26 : 77
- 19–20 : 63
- 32:1 : 285

Leviticus
- 8:36 : 161

Numbers
- 11:8 : 278
- 25:10–30:1 : 313
- 30:2–32:42 : 295
- 31:50 : 279

Deuteronomy
- 1:18 : 161
- 4:4 : 76
- 5:31 : 285
- 12:20 : 111
- 14:26 : 111
- 16:18–21:9 : 225
- 18:6 : 111
- 21:10–25:19 : 225, 349
- 33:4 : 76

Joshua
- 1:6 : 76
- 1:8 : 76, 83
- 9:24 : 274
- 24:25 : 106

Judges
- 3:8 : 222
- 3:10 : 222
- 5:3 : 110
- 5:12 : 110
- 5:27 : 275
- 6:19 : 278
- 6:32 : 116
- 7:5 : 275
- 7:22 : 118
- 10:1 : 275
- 11:33 : 118
- 21:11–12 : 205

1 Samuel
- 1:1–2:10 : 347
- 1:1 : 115, 157
- 1:11 : 109, 199, 226
- 1:18 : 202
- 1:19 : 240
- 2:1 : 186–7, 252
- 2:2 : 186
- 2:4 : 211
- 2:5 : 225, 242
- 2:6 : 346–7, 441
- 2:8 : 191
- 2:10 : 192, 245
- 2:11 : 245
- 2:14 : 278
- 2:16 : 111, 133, 211, 275
- 2:20 : 226, 245
- 2:21 : 224
- 2:27 : 108
- 2:32 : 211
- 2:34 : 215
- 3:5 : 175
- 3:6 : 175
- 3:8 : 175, 189
- 3:9 : 175
- 3:13 : 215
- 3:16 : 128
- 3:17 : 158
- 3:18 : 158, 160, 202
- 3:19 : 158
- 4:1 : 351
- 4:3 : 136, 187
- 4:3–5 : 350

4:4 : 187
4:5 : 187
4:6 : 169
4:14 : 215
4:16 : 233
4:17 : 126
4:19 : 275
5:2 : 350
5:4 : 136
5:10 : 131
5:11 : 215
5:12 : 215
6:1 : 112, 350
6:4 : 131
6:8 : 124
6:13 : 187
6:14 : 118
6:15 : 118
6:18 : 118, 136
6:19 : 197
7:1 : 161, 187
7:2 : 280
7:3 : 281
7:10 : 192
8:10 : 158, 215
8:14 : 198
8:15 : 198
8:21 : 158
9:1 : 157
9:5 : 136, 212
9:7 : 109, 113
9:8 : 131, 199
9:11 : 166
9:21 : 119
9:22 : 198
9:26 : 189
10:7 : 113
10:11 : 132
10:14 : 166
10:27 : 194
11:3 : 146
11:4 : 199
11:7 : 147, 157
11:11 : 144, 145
12:9 : 199
12:10 : 119
12:11 : 115–16
12:12 : 169

12:18 : 120
12:20–1 : 281
12:23 : 214
12:25 : 137
13:2 : 113
13:10 : 194
13:13 : 137
14:7 : 110
14:12 : 119
14:13 : 137
14:18 : 144–5
14:33 : 215
14:37 : 159
14:44 : 154
14:45 : 197
14:49 : 121
15:1 : 198
15:6 : 133
15:7 : 198, 212
15:11 : 198
15:12 : 215
15:14 : 212
15:16 : 137
15:23 : 198
15:24 : 119
15:26 : 214
15:27 : 243
15:29 : 243
15:32 : 106, 196
16:1 : 198
16:21 : 114
16:22 : 202
17:1 : 185
17:2 : 232
17:8 : 232, 348, 441
17:10 : 185, 232
17:23 : 232
17:24 : 197
17:26 : 232
17:29 : 138
17:30 : 234
17:31 : 130
17:33 : 216
17:36 : 216, 238
17:39 :130
17:43 : 192
17:44 : 126
17:45 : 232

17:46 : 188
17:47 : 243
17:49 : 233
17:51 : 197
17:55 : 178
17:56 : 207
18:2 : 215, 243
18:5 : 207
18:6 : 110
18:7 : 198
18:10 : 168
18:16 : 196
18:17 : 207
18:19 : 143
18:20 : 209
18:22 : 238
19:4 : 157
19:5 : 229
19:7 : 158
19:8 : 197
19:9 : 111, 168
19:10 : 176
19:23 : 203
19:24 : 204
20:2 : 208
20:4 : 111
20:5 : 199, 235
20:16 : 138
20:18 : 230
20:24 : 210
20:27 : 173
20:28 : 157
20:29 : 196
20:30 : 173
20:31 : 114
20:32 : 157
21:3 : 234
21:7 : 235
21:12 : 204
22:1 : 163
22:3 : 163
22:5 : 163
22:14 : 176
22:16–18 : 207
22:18 : 282
22:19 : 197
23:2 : 197, 212, 215
23:3 : 233

23:5 : 163
23:7 : 213
23:9 : 175, 237–8
23:10 : 196
23:11 : 138, 159
23:17 : 198
23:18 : 174
23:19 : 277
23:24 : 277
23:26 : 279
23:27 : 196
24:5 : 195
24:7 : 214, 244
24:12 : 123, 199
25:1 : 175, 178
25:2 : 195
25:4 : 178
25:6 : 179
25:9 : 158, 175, 209
25:12 : 158
25:13 : 124–5
25:15 : 178
25:17 : 184
25:23 : 121
25:25 : 122
25:29 : 107
25:36 : 128
25:37 : 121, 158
25:38 : 206
25:39 : 124
26:1 : 162
26:3 : 230
26:7 : 121
26:10 : 129
26:23 : 166
26:25 : 163, 209
27:1 : 147
27:3 : 216
27:8 : 133–4
27:11 : 155
28:1 : 215
28:3 : 138, 216
28:14 : 242
28:15 : 111
28:17 : 113
28:20 : 161
28:21 : 229
29:3 : 139

29:6 : 203
29:9 : 202, 209
29:10 : 197
29:11 : 216
30:8 : 159
30:9 : 163
30:11 : 215
30:17 : 282
30:20 : 114
30:23 : 235
30:24 : 124
30:25 : 106
30:31 : 216
31:12 : 231

2 Samuel
1:2 : 139
1:4 : 197
1:10 : 133, 279
1:25 : 185
1:27 : 185
2:2 : 203
2:3 : 184
2:4 : 173, 198
2:5 : 196
2:6 : 216
2:7 : 198
2:16 : 111
2:18 : 232
2:24 : 206
2:26 : 112
2:28 : 185
3:1 : 122
3:8 : 106
3:21 : 111
3:22 : 130, 132
3:27 : 280–1
3:30 : 281
3:38 : 207
4:2 : 139, 280
4:7 : 169, 196, 205
4:8 : 199
4:10 : 140
4:11 : 205
5:1 : 164, 181
5:3 : 173, 244
5:6 : 163
5:8 : 236
5:10 : 115, 163

5:17 : 199
5:20 : 174, 199
5:23 : 244
5:24 : 132
5:25 : 197
6:1 : 140
6:2 : 163
6:4 : 141
6:6 : 144–5
6:8 : 173
6:11 : 350
6:12 : 163
6:17 : 196
6:18 : 205
7:2 : 158, 207
7:4 : 158
7:7 : 213
7:19 : 169
7:20 : 215
7:21 : 199
7:23 : 167, 203
7:25 : 184
8:6 : 141
9:3 : 207
9:6 : 164, 207
9:9 : 184
10:1 : 244
10:2 : 244
10:3 : 122, 199
10:4 : 198
10:11 : 184
10:12 : 202
10:13 : 184
10:14 : 176, 184, 197
10:16 : 184
11:2 : 205
11:7 : 155, 180
11:11 : 187
11:13 : 205
11:15 : 112
11:17 : 112
11:20 : 185
11:24 : 197
11:27 : 201
12:9 : 134
12:19 : 109
12:26 : 117
12:27 : 117, 185

13:3 : 229
13:5 : 202, 205
13:6 : 202
13:10 : 196
13:11 : 141
13:16 : 141
13:30 : 162
13:31 : 163
13:36 : 196
14:2 : 198
14:4 : 164
14:22 : 134
15:2 : 237
15:3 : 203
15:6 : 119
15:14 : 207
15:15 : 125
15:20 : 142
15:23 : 107
15:24 : 187
15:25 : 187
15:30 : 215
16:8 : 108
16:13 : 163
16:23 : 199
17:3 : 107
17:11 : 171
17:12 : 165
17:13 : 107
17:14 : 203
17:19 : 206
17:21 : 125
18:10 : 157
18:11 : 142
18:12 : 135
18:19 : 190
18:20 : 142
18:29 : 159
18:32 : 159–60
19:11 : 210
19:14 : 239
19:25 : 210
19:27 : 215
19:36 : 109
20:2 : 142
20:7 : 196
20:8 : 123
20:11 : 143

20:14 : 118
20:15 : 239–40
20:18 : 193
20:19 : 240
21:5 : 147
21:8 : 143, 198
21:12 : 163
21:19 : 108
22 : 247, 343
22:1 : 110, 246, 312–13, 335
22:3 : 248
22:4 : 247
22:9 : 249
22:14 : 192
22:27 : 189, 249
22:28 : 246
22:30 : 194
22:40 : 250
22:41 : 168
22:44 : 126, 167
22:45 : 168
22:46 : 168
22:52 : 199
23:2 : 237
23:4 : 194, 227
23:9 : 186, 241–2
23:11 : 116
23:16 : 156
23:17 : 156
23:20 : 107
24:7 : 117
24:16 : 187, 208
24:22 : 190
24:23 : 188
24:24 : 213

1 Kings
1:47 : 205
2:15 : 198
4:12 : 118
11:37 : 111
19:16 : 118

2 Kings
1:22 : 351
2:24 : 193
6:12 : 205
23:1–10 : 314
23:21–5 : 314

Isaiah
  5:1 : 110
  6:5 : 339
  21:13 : 286
  26:1 : 110
  30:26 : 227
  30:29 : 110
  33:15 : 77
  33:17 : 77
  33:22 : 339
  42:10 : 110
  46:1 : 276
  53:11 : 227
  54:1–10 : 225
  54:1 : 224–5
  57:8 : 205
  60:6 : 282
Jeremiah
  10:7 : 339
  26:2 : 161
  26:12 : 161
  30:2 : 161
  34:5 : 232
  36:2 : 161
  36:13 : 161
  36:20 : 161
  36:28 : 161
Ezekiel
  28:11–19 : 41
  32:18 : 281
  32:25 : 205
  45:18–25 : 26
Joel
  2:5 : 233
Micah
  2:4 : 281
Psalms
  18:44 : 127, 167
  22:23 : 177
  68:8 : 277
  69:9 : 177
  78:40 : 277
  106:14 : 277
  107:4 : 277
  113:7 : 335
  122:7 : 240
  137:7 : 224

Lamentations
  2:8 : 240
Daniel
  12:3 : 227
Ezra
  5:3–5 : 257
  5:8–10 : 257
  6:9 : 257
  7:24 : 257
Nehemiah
  13:7 : 118
1 Chronicles
  11:6 : 236
  11:34–5 : 116
  17:21 : 167

TARGUM JONATHAN
Joshua
  3:5–7 : 304
  3:10 : 188
  4:19 : 287, 299
  5:2–6:27 : 304
  5:3 : 286, 295
  5:5–6:1 : 302
  5:15 : 295
  6:1 : 295, 297
  6:27 : 295–7
  7:23 : 288
  8:4 : 279
  8:24 : 205
  8:31 : 193
  8:32 : 193
  8:33 : 248
  9:24 : 274
  10:13 : 248
  10:20 : 205
  10:41 : 281
  10:42 : 296
  11:4 : 172
  13:3 : 286
  13:19 : 295
  14:15 : 295–6
  15:5 : 172
  15:6 : 293
  18:7 : 293
  18:19 : 172
  18:28 : 296

450

19:47 : 286
19:49 : 205
19:51 : 205
20:6 : 234
22:18 : 252
22:20 : 252, 295
23:5 : 126
23:6 : 193
23:7 : 193
23:13 : 126
24:15 : 295
24:17 : 235
24:19 : 295
24:20 : 205

Judges : 71
1:13 : 286
2:1 : 295
3:18 : 205
3:31 : 296
4:7 : 261
4:21 : 286, 295
5:3 : 110
5:4 : 295
5:5 : 263, 295, 297, 340
5:12 : 110
5:18 : 127
5:31 : 227
6:19 : 293–4
7:3 : 122
7:12 : 172
7:22 : 118
8:21 : 282
8:31 : 262, 286
8:34 : 190
9:17 : 230
9:32 : 279
9:34 : 279
9:43 : 279
9:57 : 173
10:1 : 275
11:23 : 248
11:33 : 118
12:3 : 230
12:6 : 287
12:8 : 295
13:3 : 223
14:7 : 124
15:17 : 205

16:2 : 279
16:17–end : 24
18:3 : 284–5, 287, 295
18:4 : 284–5
20:6 : 126
21:11–12 : 205
21:20 : 279

1 Samuel : 24
1–2 : 40
1:1 : 73, 91, 98–9, 115, 157
1:3 : 96, 203, 255
1:5 : 98–100, 189, 258
1:6 : 89, 95, 98, 100, 189, 258, 271, 387
1:7 : 93, 186
1:8 : 92, 99–100
1:9 : 95, 98
1:10 : 94
1:11 : 90, 96, 98–100, 109, 145, 199
1:12 : 92, 98
1:13 : 90–2, 96, 98–9
1:14 : 93, 98
1:15 : 92, 99
1:16 : 89–90, 96
1:17 : 90, 255
1:18 : 91, 99, 174, 202
1:19 : 189, 240
1:20 : 94, 125, 189
1:21 : 183
1:22 : 102, 203
1:23 : 92, 98, 101, 190, 255
1:24 : 91–2, 97–100, 186, 259
1:25 : 100, 253
1:26 : 99, 102
1:27 : 92–3
1:28 : 97, 101, 203
2:1 : 73, 90, 92, 94, 96–7, 99, 102, 186–7, 211, 252, 256, 290, 336, 387
2:1–5 : 309
2:2 : 89–90, 92, 94–98, 102, 186
2:3 : 98
2:4 : 211
2:5 : 90, 92, 94, 96, 98, 101, 216, 219–26, 242, 336
2:6 : 90, 92, 93, 346, 441
2:8 : 89, 96, 191
2:9 : 258
2:10 : 88, 95, 192, 245, 255, 307, 309
2:12 : 91, 114, 119–20, 123, 189

2:13 : 102, 113
2:14 : 96–7, 203, 277–9, 288, 293, 387
2:15 : 90, 97–8
2:16 : 96, 133, 211, 275, 290, 292, 294, 388
2:17 : 94
2:19 : 90, 99
2:20 : 90, 189, 226, 245
2:21 : 91, 100–1
2:22 : 121, 388
2:23 : 97, 100–1, 257
2:24 : 256, 271, 287, 388
2:25 : 113, 258
2:26 : 91
2:27 : 108, 113, 212
2:28 : 94, 125, 200, 211
2:29 : 93, 186, 211, 256
2:30 : 90, 93–6, 100, 186, 211, 256
2:31 : 89–90, 95, 100
2:32 : 183, 186, 211
2:34 : 215
2:35 : 101
2:36 : 95–6, 235
3:1 : 96, 102
3:3 : 100, 186–7, 203, 388
3:4 : 91, 94, 255
3:5 : 96, 121, 175
3:6 : 89, 175
3:7 : 94, 98, 189
3:8 : 93, 102, 175, 189
3:9 : 95, 121, 175
3:10 : 93, 96
3:11 : 95, 255
3:12 : 183, 205
3:13 : 93, 183, 215
3:14 : 284, 388
3:15 : 119, 186
3:16 : 95, 127–8
3:17 : 91, 120, 158, 257
3:18 : 102, 158, 160, 170, 202, 339
3:19 : 95, 115, 158, 194
3:20 : 96, 120
4–6 : 40
4:1 : 185
4:2 : 92, 94, 184, 206
4:3 : 93, 135, 187
4:4 : 95, 187, 203
4:5 : 95, 187, 258

4:6 : 99, 101–2, 169, 187
4:7 : 91, 102, 258
4:8 : 88, 99–100, 102
4:9 : 88, 100, 185
4:10 : 95, 113–14, 185, 256
4:11 : 91, 98, 114
4:12 : 139, 200, 233, 388
4:13 : 102, 187
4:14 : 215
4:16 : 96–7, 233, 255
4:17 : 114, 126–7
4:18 : 101, 187
4:19 : 92, 101, 114, 187, 275, 388
4:20 : 89, 97–8, 226
4:21 : 95, 100, 114, 187
4:22 : 95, 114, 187
5:1 : 114
5:2 : 90
5:3 : 91–2, 95–6, 101–2
5:4 : 92, 95, 105, 136, 189
5:6 : 94, 183, 388
5:7 : 93, 100
5:8 : 91
5:9 : 89, 91, 96, 189
5:10 : 89, 101, 130
5:11 : 215, 283, 290, 388
5:12 : 96, 100, 216
6:1 : 105, 112, 148
6:3 : 95
6:4 : 90–1, 131
6:5 : 96
6:6 : 73, 94, 99–101
6:7 : 96, 389
6:8 : 105, 124
6:9 : 94, 96, 123, 179
6:11 : 102
6:12 : 271, 389
6:13 : 94, 187
6:14 : 118
6:15 : 96, 102
6:18 : 105, 118, 136
6:19 : 96, 113, 197, 276, 389
6:20 : 91
7:1 : 161, 170, 187
7:2 : 276, 280–1, 288, 389
7:3 : 94, 102
7:6 : 91, 95–6
7:7 : 94, 96, 100–1, 119

7:8 : 91, 186
7:9 : 89, 96
7:10 : 90, 185, 192
7:11 : 96
7:12 : 96
7:13 : 91
8:1 : 93, 198, 358
8:2 : 94, 270–1, 389
8:5 : 90, 257
8:6 : 95
8:7 : 101, 214
8:9 : 91, 95
8:10 : 158, 215, 339
8:14 : 90, 198
8:15 : 198
8:16 : 95
8:18 : 95, 100, 125–6
8:20 : 101, 185
8:21 : 158, 339
8:22 : 113
9 : 40
9:1 : 94, 102, 157, 170, 200
9:2 : 93
9:3 : 102, 190, 255
9:4 : 94, 96, 200, 290, 389
9:5 : 90, 105, 136, 212
9:6 : 99, 113, 203, 212
9:7 : 88, 98, 105, 109, 113, 212
9:8 : 94, 113, 131, 199, 212
9:9 : 102, 189
9:10 : 113, 212
9:11 : 166
9:13 : 94
9:14 : 89, 255
9:16 : 94, 189, 200, 248, 256
9:18 : 93, 190, 258
9:19 : 93
9:21 : 90, 119, 200
9:22 : 198
9:25 : 93
9:26 : 189
9:27 : 99–100
10:3 : 95
10:4 : 99–100, 193
10:5 : 90, 203–4
10:6 : 204
10:7 : 105, 113, 115, 194
10:10 : 91, 100, 203–4

10:11 : 93–4, 96, 113, 132, 204
10:12 : 93
10:13 : 204–5
10:14 : 101, 166, 181
10:16 : 93, 101
10:18 : 90, 186
10:19 : 99, 123, 173, 214
10:20 : 95, 200
10:21 : 94, 200–1
10:22 : 285, 295, 389
10:24 : 125
10:25 : 94, 113, 190
10:26 : 99–100
10:27 : 114, 194
11–12 : 40
11:2 : 389
11:3 : 105, 146
11:4 : 199
11:5 : 93
11:7 : 147, 157, 270–1, 390
11:8 : 101, 183
11:9 : 183
11:10 : 190
11:11 : 105, 144, 170, 274, 390
11:12 : 90
12:2 : 274, 390
12:3 : 89, 94, 390
12:4 : 101
12:5 : 295, 390
12:6 : 96
12:7 : 271, 281, 390
12:9 : 185–6, 199
12:10 : 119, 186
12:11 : 96, 105, 115–16, 271–2, 390
12:12 : 169, 186
12:13 : 125
12:14 : 73, 90, 119–20, 186
12:15 : 93
12:17 : 88, 123
12:18 : 105, 120
12:19 : 123, 186, 190
12:20 : 123, 173
12:24 : 120
12:25 : 82, 105, 136, 390
13:2 : 113
13:3 : 91, 94, 99
13:5 : 172, 179
13:6 : 101, 183

13:7 : 90
13:10 : 194, 205
13:12 : 105
13:13 : 137
13:14 : 257
13:15 : 201
13:16 : 90
13:17 : 97
13:20 : 258
13:21 : 73, 90, 258
14:1 : 96
14:3 : 101
14:4 : 91, 95–6
14:6 : 91
14:7 : 105, 110, 115
14:12 : 119
14:13 : 137
14:15 : 111, 179, 335
14:17 : 190
14:18 : 144–5
14:21 : 179
14:22 : 179, 183–4
14:23 : 184, 206
14:24 : 183
14:29 : 190
14:33 : 215
14:36 : 190
14:38 : 91
14:39 : 101
14:40 : 190
14:42 : 95
14:43 : 90, 222
14:44 : 154, 170
14:45 : 92, 98–9, 197
14:48 : 207
14:49 : 121
14:50 : 89
14:52 : 114, 122, 184, 206
15–17 : 40
15:1 : 198, 248
15:2 : 96, 279
15:3 : 282
15:4 : 183
15:5 : 212
15:6 : 133
15:7 : 201, 212
15:11 : 198, 256, 336
15:12 : 215

15:14 : 212
15:15 : 200
15:16 : 137
15:17 : 73, 97, 99–100, 140, 198
15:18 : 205
15:20 : 174
15:22 : 101
15:23 : 198, 206
15:24 : 119, 191
15:26 : 186, 214
15:27 : 243
15:29 : 243, 336
15:32 : 106, 196, 201
15:35 : 99–100
16:1 : 198, 226
16:8 : 89, 125
16:9 : 125
16:10 : 125
16:12 : 257
16:14–16 : 336
16:15 : 259
16:18 : 115, 184, 194, 206, 259, 336
16:21 : 114
16:22 : 202
17 : 297
17:1 : 185
17:2 : 183
17:4 : 293, 390
17:5 : 92, 390
17:7 : 89, 91, 102
17:8 : 232, 297, 348, 391, 441
17:10 : 185, 232, 391
17:13 : 73, 94, 184, 255
17:15 : 336
17:16 : 391
17:18 : 283, 391
17:20 : 184, 189, 206
17:22 : 193
17:23 : 232
17:24 : 197
17:26 : 232, 271, 290, 337, 391
17:28 : 73, 184–5
17:29 : 137
17:30 : 234
17:31 : 129
17:33 : 184, 216
17:36 : 232, 238, 337
17:37 : 115, 194

17:39 : 130, 193
17:43 : 192, 217
17:44 : 126–7
17:45 : 192, 232
17:46 : 99, 188
17:47 : 243
17:48 : 94, 255
17:49 : 91, 99–100, 207, 233, 270, 391
17:50 : 234
17:51 : 197
17:53 : 336
17:55 : 178–9
17:56 : 207
17:57 : 91, 336
18:1 : 91, 205
18:2 : 215, 243
18:5 : 184, 207, 209
18:6 : 110, 196, 336
18:7 : 198, 204
18:9 : 279
18:10 : 168, 204
18:11 : 77
18:12 : 115, 126, 194, 270, 272, 391
18:14 : 115, 194
18:16 : 200
18:17 : 114, 184, 207, 258
18:19 : 190, 258
18:20 : 209, 258
18:21 : 91
18:22 : 238
18:27 : 216, 258
18:28 : 115, 194, 258–9
19:3 : 120
19:4 : 90, 120, 157
19:5 : 229
19:7 : 158, 339
19:8 : 184, 197
19:9 : 105, 111, 115, 168
19:10 : 176, 179
19:13 : 270, 272, 391
19:16 : 270, 272, 391
19:20 : 179, 204
19:21 : 179, 204
19:23 : 203–4
19:24 : 204
20–21 : 40
20:1 : 108
20:2 : 91, 208, 255

20:4 : 105, 111, 115
20:5 : 199, 208, 235
20:6 : 203
20:7 : 123
20:9 : 123
20:10 : 120
20:12 : 120
20:13 : 115, 123, 194
20:16 : 105, 138
20:18 : 230, 290, 392
20:19 : 208, 307
20:21 : 257
20:22 : 92
20:24 : 208, 210
20:25 : 392
20:26 : 174
20:27 : 88, 211
20:28 : 97, 157, 170
20:29 : 73, 88, 101, 196, 257, 270, 392
20:30 : 93, 125, 173
20:31 : 114, 222
20:32 : 157
20:40 : 257
20:41 : 207
20:42 : 89, 192, 256, 392
21:1 : 257
21:2 : 234
21:3 : 88, 234
21:6 : 88
21:7 : 126, 235, 271, 392
21:8 : 271, 274, 392
21:12 : 204
21:14 : 271, 392
21:16 : 204, 392
22:3 : 203
22:7 : 200–1
22:8 : 96, 99–100
22:14 : 176, 179, 270, 272, 392
22:15 : 129, 270, 392
22:16 : 207
22:17 : 207
22:18 : 79, 91, 207, 282, 393
22:19 : 89, 197, 282
22:22 : 103, 271, 393
22:23 : 108
23:2 : 197, 212–13, 215
23:3 : 233
23:5 : 213

23:7 : 213
23:9 : 123, 175, 237–8, 279
23:10 : 91, 196
23:11 : 138, 213
23:12 : 213
23:15 : 108
23:17 : 198
23:18 : 174
23:19 : 208, 276—7, 393
23:22 : 270, 288, 393
23:24 : 277, 393
23:25 : 95, 98, 336
23:26 : 91, 276, 279, 279, 393
23:27 : 196
23:28 : 336
24:2 : 336
24:4 : 257
24:5 : 101, 190, 195
24:6 : 101, 270, 393
24:7 : 214, 244
24:8 : 174, 270, 393
24:10 : 123, 279
24:12 : 123–4, 199, 279
24:15 : 336
24:16 : 189, 393
24:17 : 205
24:18 : 123
24:19 : 77
25:1 : 175, 181, 358
25:2 : 195, 257
25:5 : 192–3
25:6 : 179, 271, 393
25:8 : 270–1, 394
25:9 : 77, 158, 175, 193, 209, 339
25:10 : 228
25:11 : 92
25:12 : 158, 339
25:13 : 91, 93, 105, 124–5
25:15 : 170, 178
25:17 : 114, 123, 184
25:18 : 271, 287, 394
25:21 : 90, 123
25:22 : 77
25:23 : 105, 121
25:24 : 92
25:25 : 122–3
25:26 : 123, 228
25:28 : 123

25:29 : 105, 108, 273
25:31 : 93
25:33 : 257
25:34 : 188
25:35 : 256
25:36 : 128
25:37 : 121, 158, 170
25:38 : 206
25:39 : 123–4, 258, 270, 273, 394
25:40 : 258
25:42 : 258
26:1 : 162, 171, 208, 271–2, 277, 394
26:2 : 270, 273, 290, 394
26:3 : 230, 277
26:5 : 121, 258
26:7 : 121, 258
26:9 : 394
26:10 : 129
26:16 : 114, 222
26:18 : 123, 336
26:20 : 283, 394
26:23 : 166, 171
26:25 : 174, 209
27:1 : 94, 105, 146
27:7 : 112–13
27:8 : 133–4
27:9 : 114
27:11 : 88, 112–13, 155, 170
27:12 : 248
28:1 : 215
28:3 : 138, 216, 271, 394
28:14 : 99, 242
28:15 : 111, 115, 189
28:17 : 113
28:18 : 201
28:19 : 93, 394
28:20 : 161, 170
28:21 : 229–30
28:22 : 73
29:3 : 139
29:4 : 184
29:5 : 204
29:6 : 203, 358
29:7 : 209
29:8 : 90
29:9 : 202, 209
29:10 : 189, 196
30:2 : 170, 174

30:7 : 216
30:8 : 93, 98, 100, 159, 181, 257, 336
30:11 : 215
30:12 : 99
30:16 : 114, 201, 270–1, 395
30:17 : 99, 282, 290, 292–3, 395
30:18 : 114
30:19 : 115
30:20 : 114
30:21 : 193
30:22 : 123
30:23 : 186, 235, 256, 270, 290, 395
30:24 : 124
30:25 : 106
30:27–31 : 79
31:3 : 184
31:4 : 283, 395
31:11 : 90
31:12 : 231
2 Samuel : 24, 188
1:1 : 201, 336
1:2 : 105, 248
1:4 : 197
1:5 : 257
1:6 : 395
1:9 : 395
1:10 : 105, 133, 276–7, 279, 293, 395
1:14 : 257
1:18 : 395
1:19 : 92
1:21 : 396
1:25 : 93, 184–5
1:27 : 185
2:2 : 203
2:3 : 184
2:4 : 198, 200
2:5 : 196
2:6 : 216
2:7 : 114, 198
2:9 : 200–1
2:16 : 105, 111, 115, 148
2:17 : 122
2:18 : 232
2:19 : 336
2:22 : 256
2:24 : 206
2:26 : 112, 115, 336
2:28 : 185, 336

2:29 : 396
2:31 : 201
3:1 : 105, 122
3:5 : 396
3:7 : 258
3:8 : 106, 257
3:10 : 190, 200
3:14 : 396
3:18 : 189–90, 248
3:19 : 190, 201
3:22 : 88, 130
3:27 : 259, 276, 281, 396
3:33 : 396
3:34 : 114
3:38 : 207
4:2 : 105, 139, 276, 280, 293, 396
4:4 : 396
4:6 : 396
4:7 : 169, 196, 205, 358
4:8 : 108, 199
4:10 : 105, 140
4:11 : 205
5:1 : 164, 171, 181
5:2 : 90
5:3 : 100, 173, 181, 244, 358
5:5 : 94
5:6 : 89, 163, 170
5:7 : 397
5:8 : 236
5:10 : 105, 115, 194
5:11–7:29 : 40
5:12 : 189, 248
5:17 : 199
5:20 : 199
5:23 : 244
5:24 : 132
5:25 : 197
6:1 : 105, 140
6:2 : 90
6:4 : 105, 140
6:5 : 73
6:6 : 105, 144–5
6:8 : 173
6:9 : 120
6:14 : 258
6:17 : 196
6:18 : 192, 205
6:19 : 397

6:20 : 258–9
6:21 : 90, 125, 276, 397
6:22 : 140
6:23 : 258
7:1 : 189
7:2 : 158, 207
7:3 : 115, 194
7:4 : 158
7:7 : 189, 213, 248
7:8 : 248
7:9 : 115, 194
7:10 : 111, 248
7:11 : 189, 248
7:13 : 190
7:16 : 190
7:17 : 339
7:18 : 397
7:19 : 169
7:20 : 215
7:21 : 199
7:22 : 397
7:23 : 167, 189, 203, 248, 257
7:24 : 189, 248
7:25 : 184
7:27 : 259
7:28 : 95
8:2 : 97
8:3 : 79
8:6 : 141
8:10 : 184, 193
8:14 : 198
9:3 : 97, 207
9:6 : 207
9:9 : 184
10:1 : 244
10:3 : 105, 122, 199
10:4 : 198
10:11 : 184
10:12 : 202
10:13 : 184
10:14 : 176, 184, 197
10:16 : 184
11:2 : 205
11:7 : 155, 170, 184, 193, 358
11:11 : 187
11:13 : 205
11:14 : 112
11:15 : 105, 112, 115, 122

11:17 : 112
11:19 : 205
11:20 : 185
11:21 : 397
11:24 : 197, 257
11:25 : 112, 257
11:27 : 201, 258
12:3 : 73
12:5 : 114, 222
12:8 : 73, 287, 397
12:9 : 134, 258
12:10 : 258
12:14 : 336
12:16 : 120
12:19 : 105, 109, 125
12:20 : 186
12:25 : 158
12:26 : 117
12:27 : 117, 125, 185
13:3 : 229
13:5 : 202, 205
13:6 : 88, 202, 358
13:10 : 73, 196
13:11 : 105, 141
13:16 : 105, 141
13:21 : 339
13:26 : 397
13:28 : 114, 238
13:30 : 162, 171
13:31 : 163, 171
13:32 : 279
13:36 : 196, 205
13:37 : 79
13:32 : 73
14:2 : 198
14:4 : 164, 170, 207
14:9 : 190
14:11 : 188
14:14 : 397
14:16 : 230
14:17 : 115, 194
14:19 : 339
14:21 : 128
14:22 : 134, 207
15:2 : 200, 237
15:3 : 203
15:4 : 398
15:6 : 119

15:11 : 398
15:14 : 207, 238, 279
15:15 : 105, 125
15:19 : 96
15:20 : 142
15:23 : 106, 125
15:24 : 187
15:25 : 186–7
15:26 : 98
15:30 : 215
15:32 : 139
15:35 : 339
16:5 : 95, 123
16:7 : 123, 222
16:8 : 108, 222
16:11 : 108, 200
16:18 : 125
16:22 : 257
16:23 : 199
17:1 : 336
17:3 : 107
17:8 : 184
17:10 : 114, 398
17:11 : 171
17:12 : 165, 171
17:13 : 105, 107
17:14 : 203
17:19 : 206
17:21 : 125
17:29 : 89
17:36 : 216
18:3 : 169
18:5 : 238
18:7 : 248
18:8 : 112, 184
18:10 : 157
18:11 : 142
18:12 : 79, 135, 230, 238
18:14 : 73, 230, 398
18:17 : 114, 398
18:18 : 226, 398
18:19 : 179, 217
18:20 : 142, 226
18:29 : 159, 170
19:8 : 173
19:9 : 73
19:10 : 230, 281
19:11 : 210

19:14 : 239
19:17 : 200
19:18 : 200
19:25 : 210
19:27 : 215
19:29 : 222
19:36 : 109
19:38 : 97
20:1 : 123, 200
20:2 : 105, 142, 200
20:7 : 196
20:8 : 123
20:11 : 143
20:15 : 73
20:14 : 118
20:15 : 239–40
20:18 : 193
20:19 : 240
21:1–23:8 : 40
21:1 : 222, 255, 398
21:2 : 255
21:3 : 398
21:5 : 105, 147, 205, 398
21:8 : 143, 198
21:12 : 288, 398
21:14 : 200
21:19 : 105, 108, 186
21:20–2 : 304
22 : 65, 79, 84, 86, 168, 245, 247, 251–2, 302, 310–44
22:1 : 110, 190, 230, 246, 334–5, 339–41
22:1–13 : 304
22:2 : 333
22:3 : 248, 250–1, 333–6, 340–1
22:4 : 247, 333, 336, 340
22:5 : 73, 336
22:6 : 250, 258, 334, 339
22:7 : 251, 318, 336, 340
22:8 : 111, 188, 334–6
22:9 : 249, 333, 339–41, 343
22:10 : 334–5
22:11 : 334–6
22:12 : 336, 340
22:13 : 188, 336
22:14 : 192, 337–8, 340
22:15 : 304
22:16 : 335–6
22:17 : 336, 338–9

22:19 : 250, 258
22:21 : 337, 340
22:22 : 235
22:23 : 336
22:25 : 184
22:26 : 238, 336, 399
22:27 : 189, 249, 252, 333, 337–8
22:28 : 246, 248, 335
22:30 : 194
22:32 : 248, 335
22:35 : 207, 250, 333, 337
22:37 : 337
22:38 : 336
22:39 : 205, 336
22:40 : 184, 250, 337
22:42 : 251
22:43 : 336
22:44 : 105, 126, 167
22:46 : 336
22:47 : 188, 247–8, 252, 335–6, 338
22:48 : 337
22:49 : 336
22:50–1 : 304
22:51 : 199
23:2 : 237
23:4 : 194, 227, 317
23:5 : 73, 317
23:6 : 123
23:8 : 349–50
23:9 : 79, 185, 203, 241–2
23:11 : 116
23:16 : 156, 170
23:17 : 156
23:20 : 105, 107
23:33 : 116, 399
23:37 : 89
24 : 40
24:1 : 95, 259
24:7 : 105, 117
24:9 : 73
24:12 : 88
24:16 : 187, 208
24:17 : 208
24:21 : 253
24:22 : 179, 190, 253
24:23 : 188
24:24 : 213
24:25 : 213, 259

27:11 : 73
1 Kings : 24
1:13 : 190
1:17 : 189–90
1:20 : 190
1:24 : 190
1:27 : 190
1:30 : 189
1:34 : 288
1:37 : 189
1:47 : 205
2:3–8 : 303
2:3 : 193
2:9 : 295, 297
2:15 : 198
2:44 : 173
3:1 : 205
3:27 : 295
4:12 : 118
4:19 : 211
5:9 : 172
5:13 : 193
7:40 : 205
8:5 : 252
8:9 : 295–6
8:25 : 235
8:54 : 205
8:59 : 126
9:1 : 205
9:3 : 126
9:9 : 173
9:26 : 172
10:2 : 282
12:8 : 282
12:10 : 282
12:14 : 282
16:7 : 173
16:34 : 295
17:1 : 188
17:12 : 188
17:13 : 295
18:1 : 307
18:10 : 188
18:12 : 336
18:24 : 192–3
18:25 : 193
18:29 : 204
19:7 : 188

19:16 : 118
20:12 : 279
21:8 : 112, 192
21:9 : 112
21:11 : 112
22:11 : 205
22:16 : 192

2 Kings
1:1–5:24 : 24
1:3 : 188
1:6 : 188
1:8 : 158
1:10 : 158
1:15 : 188
1:16 : 188
1:22 : 158
1:23 : 158
1:32 : 158
1:34 : 158
1:38 : 158
1:44 : 158
1:45 : 158
2:23 : 282
2:24 : 193, 282
2:26 : 112
4:8 : 235
4:31 : 307
5:5 : 112
5:6 : 112
5:7 : 112
5:11 : 192
5:15 : 188
5:19 : 295
5:26 : 122
6:12 : 205
8:9 : 282
8:12 : 282
10:1 : 112
10:25 : 205
12:11 : 234
13:17 : 205
13:21 : 295, 297
14:6 : 193
16:25 : 288
17:39 : 190
19:4 : 337
19:14 : 112
19:16 : 337

19:32 : 250
21:1–2 : 304
22:1–13 : 304
22:15 : 304
22:20 : 173
22:50–1 : 304
23:25 : 193
25:18 : 126

Isaiah : 26, 71, 358
1:2 : 248
1:5 : 276
1:21 : 295
1:28 : 205
2:4 : 281
2:13 : 250
3:4 : 282
3:26 : 336
5:1 : 110
5:21 : 140
5:25 : 335
6:3 : 66
6:5 : 281
7:25 : 270, 275
8:5 : 189
9:1 : 248
9:2 : 248
9:4 : 250, 337
9:5 : 336
10:18 : 205
10:20 : 189
10:21 : 336
10:32 : 263
10:32–4 : 304
11:1–11 : 304
11:3 : 281, 295
11:4 : 3, 6, 222, 281
11:6 : 282
11:8 : 282
11:11 : 295
12:4 : 192
12:4–6 : 304
13:13 : 335
13:16 : 282
14:13 : 190
16:4 : 205
17:7 : 6
17:13 : 126
19:18 : 192

20:4 : 225
21:5 : 295
21:13 : 286
23:7 : 282
23:8 : 279
24:14 : 192
24:15 : 192
26:1 : 110
26:19 : 191
27:2 : 204, 252
28:21 : 191, 335
29:20 : 205
29:21 : 281
30:6 : 282
30:29 : 110
31:3 : 205
31:9 : 191
32:5 : 191
32:15 : 336
32:19 : 336
33:5 : 336
33:7 : 295
34:9 : 221
35:9 : 25
37:4 : 337
37:17 : 337
37:33 : 250
37:36 : 188
38:14 : 336
40:7 : 336
40:8 : 188
40:20–7 : 25
42:10 : 110
42:14 : 336
42:21 : 25
43:2 : 191, 250, 337
43:3–12 : 25
43:19 : 278
43:20 : 278
45:7 : 295
46:1 : 276
47:14 : 250, 337
49:4 : 205
49:8 : 194
49:24 : 6, 295–7
49:25 : 6
51:6 : 56
51:9 : 252, 337

51:10 : 252, 335
54:1 : 221, 223–5
54:7 : 8
54:10 : 295
55:13 : 194
57:5 : 282
57:8 : 205
57:15 : 335
58:5 : 288
58:6 : 276
61:10 : 234
65:16 : 188
65:17 : 56
65:20 : 282
66:1 : 263, 281, 295
66:8 : 226
Jeremiah : 26
1:16 : 173
2:6 : 286
2:8 : 192–3
2:20 : 191
2:23 : 282
2:24 : 252
2:30 : 112
3:17 : 281
4:14 : 210
5:3 : 205
5:6 : 240, 250, 279, 337
5:7 : 192–3, 252
5:24 : 124
6:4 : 286
6:11 : 282
8:19 : 281
9:1 : 336
9:3 : 279
9:15 : 205
9:20 : 282
9:22 : 295, 297
10:10 : 188, 335, 337
10:25 : 205
11:16 : 250, 337
11:17 : 123
12:1 : 124
12:4 : 123, 129
12:16 : 192–3
14:12 : 205
15:19 : 281
15:26 : 276

16:10 : 173
17:5, 7 : 56
17:6 : 286
17:7 : 287–8
17:13 : 191
17:15 : 192
19:15 : 173
20:10 : 279
22:22 : 173
23:13 : 192–3
23:26 : 188
23:27 : 193
23:36 : 337
26:8 : 205
29:12 : 287–8
30:21 : 281
31:14 : 248
31:22 : 248
31:28 : 287
32:18 : 336
32:22 : 281
32:23 : 173
32:32 : 173
32:42 : 173
33:5 : 173
33:13 : 281, 287
33:17 : 190
35:14 : 287–8
35:17 : 173
36:3 : 173
36:22 : 276
36:31 : 173
39:4 : 286
39:5 : 286
41:11 : 173
43:1 : 205
44:2 : 173
44:7 : 282
44:27 : 205
46:6 : 287–8
46:10 : 112
46:14 : 112
46:17 : 295
48:38 : 287
48:46 : 225
49:13 : 276
49:19 : 288
49:37 : 205
49:38 : 190
51:22 : 282
51:24 : 173
51:60 : 173
51:63 : 205
52:7 : 286
52:8 : 286
52:24 : 234
Ezekiel : 26
1:1 : 234
1:1–12 : 304
1:8 : 191, 269
3:12 : 304
3:26 : 281
5:12 : 205
9:10 : 288
12:11 : 225
13:2 : 204
13:14 : 205
15:7 : 250, 337
16:2 : 281
16:23 : 173
16:39 : 287
17:22 : 282
17:24 : 337
19:12 : 250
19:14 : 250
20:4 : 281
20:13 : 205
20:43 : 173
21:12 : 62
21:21 : 279
21:37 : 250
22:2 : 281
22:31 : 205
23:26 : 281
24:11 : 336
27:10 : 276
28:11–19 : 41
28:13 : 269, 287, 295
31:4 : 126
32:25 : 205
32:31 : 337
33:10 : 276
34:24 : 276
36:38 : 248
37:1–14 : 303–4
38:10 : 249, 338

39:16 : 221
40:19 : 276
42:15 : 205
43:22 : 276
43:23 : 205
44:3 : 235
44:24 : 336
45:17–24 : 26
Hosea : 27
2:1 : 188
2:4 : 281
2:20 : 121
2:21 : 287–8
4:4 : 281
5:2 : 253
6:5 : 191
7:2 : 173
7:5 : 336
7:6 : 279
9:15 : 173
10:15 : 123
11:6 : 205
11:8 : 276
13:7 : 279
Joel : 31
2:5 : 233
2:26 : 248
2:27 : 248
4:16 : 335
Amos
4:10 : 281
7:2 : 205
8:5 : 211
8:10 : 287, 295
9:1 : 248
9:3 : 337
Obadiah
19 : 112
Jonah : 30
1:3 : 192
1:10 : 192
3:5–4:11 : 30
3:6 : 190
Micah
4:3 : 281
6:1 : 281
6:6 : 336
7:2 : 279

7:8 : 221
7:10 : 221
7:19 : 335
Nahum : 31
2:1 : 123
2:14 : 112
3:10 : 225
Habakkuk
2:20–3:11 : 304
3:2 : 191
3:4 : 227
3:5 : 126
3:6 : 191
3:7 : 222
3:17 : 219, 248, 221
3:18 : 248, 304, 335
3:19 : 304
Zephaniah : 26, 31
1:5 : 192
1:6 : 52
1:10 : 52
2:1 : 281
2:3 : 336
2:9 : 188
2:15 : 52
3:5 : 354
Haggai : 26
1:14 : 234
2:21 : 335
Zechariah
3:2 : 287, 295
4:7 : 222
5:4 : 205
11:8 : 214
Malachi : 26, 49–52
3:2 : 210
3:6 : 205
3:22 : 193

TARGUM ONQELOS
xvii, 6–7, 11, 13, 17–18, 20, 22–3, 36, 54–5, 59–61, 64–5, 78–9, 217, 292
Genesis
11:30 : 223
12:8 : 192
16:7 : 188
16:9 : 188
16:10 : 188

16:11 : 188
16:13 : 192
19:28 : 340
19:31 : 121
19:33–4 : 121
19:37 : 121
21:17 : 188
21:33 : 192
22:17 : 172
26:25 : 192
29:26 : 121
31:11 : 188
31:54 : 235
37:25 : 235

Exodus
4:26 : 276
14:30 : 172
15:3 : 243
15:4 : 337
15:25 : 106
18:12 : 235
19–20 : 65
19:18 : 339
20:7 : 192
33:19 : 192
34:5 : 192

Leviticus
2:5 : 61
4:3 : 234
4:5 : 234
4:16 : 234
13:6 : 62
13:56 : 62

Numbers
13:33 : 140
21:17 : 204
21:20 : 230, 277
23:28 : 230, 277
27:17 : 252
28:14 : 230
31:16 : 252
35:25 : 234
35:28 : 234

Deuteronomy
5:11 : 192
5:26 : 337
6:8 : 279
7:6 : 335

8:9 : 90
10:8 : 192
10:17 : 336
14:2 : 335
18:7 : 192
18:20 : 193
18:22 : 192
21:5 : 192
26:18 : 335
30:3 : 226
32:3 : 192
32:10 : 277
33:14 : 230

TARGUMS TO THE WRITINGS (KETUVIM)
61, 256

Psalms : 57
18 : 251, 337–8
18:21 : 338, 340
18:27 : 249, 252, 338
21:12 : 249, 338
34:19 : 335
42:3 : 337
68:9 : 340
76:4 : 233
78:9 : 233
108:11 : 221
119:109 : 230
127:3 : 226
144:1 : 233

Job : 57, 261
Proverbs : 57, 262
6:18 : 249
Megillot : 57
Canticles : 262
Lamentations
1:19 : 220
4:17 : 220
4:22 : 220, 222
5:11 : 220

Esther I
3:7 : 228
Esther II : 62
3:8 : 249
6:11 : 335
Chronicles : 57, 74, 303
1 Chronicles
1:32 : 263

2:46 : 263
2:48 : 263
7:14 : 263
11:13 : 233
11:34–5 : 116
24:2 : 226

2 Chronicles
11:1 : 233
11:21 : 263
12:15 : 233
13:3 : 233
15:19 : 233
16:19 : 233
20:15 : 233
27:7 : 233
32:8 : 233
3:9 : 263

TARGUM NEOFITI
xx, 55–7, 259, 343

Genesis
11:4 : 233
14:8 : 233
16:13 : 188
19:28 : 340
22:24 : 262
28:20 : 235
40:23 : 56

Exodus
1:10 : 233
13:17 : 233
14:13 : 233
14:14 : 233
14:20 : 233
15:9 : 343
17:8 : 233
17:9 : 233
17:10 : 233
19:18 : 339

Numbers
11:8 : 278
20:21 : 233
21:33 : 233
24:20 : 233
24:29 : 220–1
27:17 : 233
28:3 : 233

Deuteronomy
2:5 : 233
2:9 : 233
2:19 : 233
2:24 : 233
2:32 : 233
3:1 : 233
4:33 : 337
4:34 : 233
5:26 : 337
20:1 : 233
20:2 : 233
20:3 : 233
20:4 : 233
20:5 : 233
20:6 : 233
20:7 : 233
20:10 : 233
20:12 : 233
20:19 : 233
20:20 : 233
21:10 : 233
28:7 : 233
29:6 : 233
32:1 : 56
33:7 : 23

FRAGMENT TARGUMS
56–7, 295, 298, 343

Genesis
11:4 : 233
14:9 : 233
15:1 : 233
16:13 : 188
22:24 : 263
32:2 : 233
40:23 : 56

Exodus
12:2 : 337
12:42 : 221
15:9 : 343
15:18 : 221

Numbers
23:19 : 337
24:19 : 220–1

Deuteronomy
32:10 : 277

TARGUM PSEUDO-JONATHAN
  56–7, 59, 61, 256, 292, 343
Genesis
  11:4 : 233
  14:8 : 233
  22:24 : 262
  25:6 : 262
  29:24 : 262
  29:29 : 262
  35:22 : 262
  36:12 : 262
  36:43 : 221
  37:7 : 233
  49:11 : 233
  50:20 : 249, 338
Exodus
  1:10 : 233
  14:13 : 233
  14:14 : 233
  14:20 : 233
  15:1 : 343
  15:9 : 233, 343
  15:21 : 343
  17:9 : 233
  16:1 : 59
  21:17 : 193
  23:27 : 233
  32:18 : 233
  39:37 : 228
  40:4 : 228
Leviticus
  20:9 : 193
  20:26 : 256
Numbers
  1:1 : 59
  1:18 : 59
  6:11 : 60
  9:11 : 59
  10:9 : 233
  10:11 : 59
  20:21 : 233
  21:35 : 233
  22:11 : 233
  23:19 : 188
  24:4 : 337
  24:17 : 233
  24:20 : 233
  24:24 : 221
  27:17 : 233
  31:14 : 233
  31:21 : 233
Deuteronomy
  1:42 : 233
  2:9 : 233
  2:19 : 233
  4:33 : 188
  5:26 : 188
  22:5 : 59
  32:32 : 249, 338
  34:3 : 222

TOSEFTA TARGUMS
  57, 253, 266–9, 290, 295, 297, 301–54, 356–7, 360, 363
Joshua
  3:5–7 : 304
  5:1 : 78
  5:2–6:27 : 304
  5:2 : 281
  5:3 : 78, 281
  5:4 : 281
  5:5–6:1 : 302
  5:5 : 281
  5:7 : 281
  5:8 : 78
  5:14 : 78
  5:16 : 78
  5:26 : 78
  6:1 : 75, 305–6
Judges
  5 : 23
  5:1 : 87
  5:3 : 76, 86
  5:5 : 76, 85–7
  5:6 : 193
  5:8 : 76, 87
  5:11 : 87
  5:15 : 87
  5:26 : 87
1 Samuel
  2:6 : 346–7, 354
  17:8 : 78, 83, 85–7, 347–52
  17:42 : 251
  18:19 : 251

2 Samuel
- 22 : 302, 305–6, 310–44
- 21:20–2 : 304
- 22:1–13 : 304
- 22:1 : 334, 341
- 22:2 : 333
- 22:3 : 333–6
- 22:4 : 333, 336
- 22:5 : 336
- 22:6 : 334
- 22:7 : 336
- 22:8 : 334–6
- 22:9 : 333, 341, 343
- 22:10 : 334–5
- 22:11 : 335
- 22:13 : 336
- 22:14 : 337
- 22:15 : 304
- 22:16 : 335–6
- 22:17 : 336, 338
- 22:21 : 337
- 22:23 : 336
- 22:27 : 333, 337–8
- 22:28 : 335
- 22:32 : 335
- 22:35 : 333, 337
- 22:37 : 337
- 22:38 : 336
- 22:39 : 336
- 22:40 : 337
- 22:43 : 336
- 22:46 : 336
- 22:47 : 335–6, 338
- 22:48 : 337
- 22:49 : 336
- 22:50–1 : 304

1 Kings
- 2:3–8 : 303

2 Kings
- 21:1–2 : 304
- 22:1–13 : 304
- 22:15 : 304
- 22:50–1 : 304

Isaiah
- 6:1 : 78
- 10:32 : 5, 23, 87, 263
- 10:32–3 : 74, 75, 84, 305–6
- 10:32–4 : 304
- 11:1–11 : 304
- 12:4–6 : 304
- 49:25 : 219
- 66:1 : 74, 263, 306
- 66:2 : 74, 306
- 66:23 : 74, 306

Jeremiah
- 9:22 : 306

Ezekiel
- 1:1–12 : 304
- 1:12 : 305
- 1:8 : 269
- 3:12 : 304
- 28:13 : 269
- 37:1 : 305
- 37:1–14 : 303–4

Obadiah
- 1 : 75
- 21 : 221

Habakkuk
- 2:11 : 84
- 2:20–3:11 : 304
- 2:20 : 304
- 3:1 : 75
- 3:1–2 : 84, 87, 305–6
- 3:1–10 : 304
- 3:11 : 87, 305–6
- 3:18–19 : 304

Zechariah
- 2:14–15 : 354
- 2:14–16 : 84
- 2:14—4:1 : 78
- 2:14—4:7 : 76, 87, 306
- 3:1—4:7 : 84, 353
- 4:2 : 85
- 4:3 : 85
- 4:7 : 85, 221–2, 251

PALESTINIAN TARGUMS
56, 58, 64

Genesis
- 38:25 : 78
- 44:18 : 75, 78

Numbers
- 32:3 : 78

Ancient Versions

ARMENIAN

1 Samuel
   5:4 : 136

2 Samuel
   13:31 : 163

ETHIOPIC

1 Samuel
   5:4 : 136

2 Samuel
   7:4 : 158
   18:3 : 169

OLD LATIN

153–4

1 Samuel
   1:19 : 241
   6:18 : 118
   11:11 : 146
   14:18 : 144
   19:9 : 168
   26:23 : 167
   30:8 : 159

2 Samuel
   3:1 : 122
   7:19 : 169
   11:7 : 156
   13:30 : 163
   20:11 : 143

PESHITTA

149–51, 153, 170

1 Samuel
   2:20 : 245
   2:27 : 108
   4:6 : 169
   4:17 : 126
   6:4 : 131
   7:1 : 161
   9:1 : 157
   9:8 : 131
   9:11 : 166
   10:11 : 132
   10:14 : 166
   11:11 : 146
   12:12 : 169
   13:5 : 177
   14:18 : 144
   14:44 : 154
   14:49 : 121
   15:32 : 106
   17:55 : 178
   20:28 : 157, 162
   25:15 : 178
   26:23 : 167
   27:11 : 155

2 Samuel
   3:22 : 130
   4:7 : 169
   5:1 : 165
   5:6 : 163
   5:24 : 132
   6:6 : 144
   7:4 : 158
   7:19 : 169
   7:23 : 167
   10:14 : 177
   11:7 : 156
   12:19 : 109
   14:4 : 164
   15:23 : 107
   18:3 : 169
   22:44 : 127
   23:20 : 107

QUMRAN

259

1QS : 140

4Q51 : 144, 165, 243

SEPTUAGINT

152–3, 170, 182

Judges
   3:3 : 241
   3:31 : 241
   10:1 : 275
   10:7 : 241
   10:11 : 241

1 Samuel
   1:19 : 241
   2:27 : 108
   3:16 : 128
   3:18 : 161
   4:17 : 126

5:10 : 131
6:1 : 112
6:4 : 131
6:18 : 118
7:1 : 161
9:8 : 131
10:11 : 132
10:14 : 166
11:11 : 144, 146
12:12 : 169
12:25 : 137
13:2 : 114
13:5 : 177
14:18 : 144
14:44 : 154
14:49 : 121
15:6 : 133
15:27 : 243
15:32 : 106
17:31 : 130
17:39 : 130
17:44 : 126
17:55 : 178
19:9 : 168
19:10 : 176
20:4 : 111
20:30 : 173
22:14 : 176
25:6 : 178
25:36 : 128
25:37 : 158
26:1 : 162
26:23 : 167
27:11 : 155
28:20 : 162
30:8 : 159

2 Samuel
3:22 : 130
4:2 : 280
5:1 : 165
5:6 : 163
5:8 : 236
6:6 : 144
7:4 : 158
7:19 : 169
10:14 : 177
13:30 : 163
13:31 : 163

14:4 : 164
15:15 : 125
17:3 : 107
17:12 : 165
18:3 : 169
20:15 : 240
21:8 : 143
22:44 : 127, 168
23:9 : 241
23:11 : 116
23:16 : 156
24:7 : 117

Psalms
122:7 : 240

VULGATE
79, 153, 170, 179

Judges
10:1 : 275

1 Samuel
1:19 : 241
5:10 : 131
6:4 : 131
6:18 : 118
9:7 : 109
9:8 : 131
10:11 : 132
10:14 : 166
14:7 : 110
14:18 : 144
14:44 : 154
17:39 : 130
17:44 : 126
19:9 : 168
19:10 : 176
25:6 : 177
25:15 : 178
25:36 : 128
26:23 : 167
28:20 : 162

2 Samuel
3:22 : 130
4:7 : 169
5:24 : 132
6:6 : 144
7:23 : 167
10:14 : 177
11:7 : 156

13:30 : 163
13:31 : 163
14:4 : 164
17:12 : 165
18:29 : 160

RABBINIC LITERATURE

Aggadat Bereshit
   53a : 225
Babylonian Talmud : 54
— Bava Batra
   110a
— Berakhot
   6a : 279
   10a : 224
— Eruvin
   26a : 134
— Megillah
   3a : 63, 228
   23b : 63
— Mo'ed Qatan
   28b : 228
— Pesahim
   37a : 278
   54b : 219
   96a : 240
   119a : 219
— Rosh HaShanah
   25a : 116, 272
— Sanhedrin
   20b : 81
   94b : 228
   97b–98b : 219
— Shabbat
   103b : 296
— Sotah
   35a : 144
— Sukkah
   44b : 55
Deuteronomy Rabbah
   5:11 : 126
Esther Rabbah
   4 : 219
Genesis Rabbah : 54
   2:3 : 219
   38:14 : 225
Leviticus Rabbah : 54
Midrash Psalms : 54

7 : 166
18:31 : 159
62.4 : 158
79:1 : 159
Midrash Samuel : 54
   6:4 : 225
   11:1 : 350
Midrash Tanhuma : 54
   Deut. 20:9 : 126
Mishnah
— Avot
   5:22 : 122
— Megillah
   4:4 : 315
— Sanhedrin
   10:3 : 347
Palestinian Talmud : 54–5
— Sanhedrin
   20b : 178
— Sotah
   8:10 : 126
Pesiqta de Rav Kahana : 54
   20 : 224–5
Pesiqta Rabbati : 54
   8 : 159
   11 : 227
   32 : 225
Sifra Leviticus
   1:1 : 296
   1:9 : 296
Sifre Deuteronomy
   198:9 : 126
Soferim
   8:1 : 127
Tosefta
— Shabbat
   7:18 : 232
Yalqut
— Judges
   73 : 285

OTHER ANCIENT AND MEDIEVAL AUTHORS AND TEXTS

Akdamut : 65
Benjamin ben Jehuda of Rome : 80
Book of Zerubbabel : 220
David Kimhi : 3–5, 14, 57, 67, 263, 275
— *Commentary on Samuel*

1 Sam. 1:11 : 226–7
1:25 : 253
2:20 : 226–7, 245
14:18 : 144
19:13, 16 : 272
21:8 : 274
23:9 : 237
25:6 : 178
30:8 : 159
31:12 : 231
2 Sam. 4:2 : 280
13:9 : 61
20:15 : 240
22:3 : 249
23:9 : 241–2
24:7 : 117
— *Commentary on Kings*
2 Kgs 17:26 : 226
— *Commentary on Isaiah*
54:1 : 224
— Targum variants recorded by Sperber
1 Sam. 9:7 : 113
23:18 : 174
2 Sam. 14:4 : 164
17:3 : 107
21:19 : 108
23:11 : 116
Dream of Mordecai : 74, 76, 84–5
Elia Levita
— *Meturgeman* : 3
Gershom ben Judah Me'or Ha-Golah : 63
Gersonides (see Ralbag)
Hezekiah ben Manoah
— *Perush ha-Torah* : 59
Isaac ben Moses of Vienna
— ספר אור זרוע
§1.11 : 63
Isaiah di Trani the Elder
— *Piskei HaRid*
Vol 2, 548 : 55
— *Teshuvot HaRid*
§8 : 60
Isaiah di Trani the Younger : 80, 179
— *Commentary on Samuel*
1 Sam. 6:18 : 118
17:36 : 238
23:9 : 237

25:6 : 178
31:12 : 231–2
2 Sam. 4:2 : 280
Jacob b. Moses Moellin
— *Responsa*
§27 : 59
§189 : 59
Jacob of Marvège
— *Responsa*
§36 : 60
Joseph Caspi
— *Commentary on Samuel*
1 Sam. 30:8 : 159
2 Sam. 4:2 : 280
— *Commentary on Isaiah*
54:1 : 225
Joseph Kara
— *Commentary on Samuel*
1 Sam. 2:14 : 278
19:13, 16 : 272
21:7 : 235
25:6 : 178
31:12 : 231
2 Sam. 20:15 : 240
Kaddish : 66
Kedushah de-Sidra : 66
Levi ben Gershon (see Ralbag)
Lucifer of Cagliari
— *De Athanasio*
I, xiii, l.60 : 168
I, xv, l.68 : 167
Mahzor Vitry : 59, 63, 303–4
Maimonides (see Moshe ben Maimon)
Megillat Antiochus (see Scroll of Antiochus)
Meir ben Baruch of Rothenburg
— שאלות ותשובות
Part 4 No. 59 : 65
Meir ben Isaac Nehorai (see *Akdamut*)
Menahem ben Elakim
— *Arukh Goren* : 58
Menahem ben Solomon : 61
— *Sekhel Tov* : 58
— *Even Bohan* : 58
Menahem Recanate (or Recanati) : 56
Moshe ben Maimon : 349
— *Hilkhot Sefer Torah*
VIII.4 : 296

Moses de Leon (see Zohar)
Nathan ben Yehiel : 61
— *Arukh* : 3, 5, 58, 112, 222
Piyyutim : 55, 64
Pseudo-Philo
— *Biblical Antiquities* : 350
Ralbag
— *Commentary on Samuel*
   1 Sam. 23:9 : 237
              25:6 : 178
   2 Sam. 4:2 : 280
Rambam (see Moshe ben Maimon)
Rashbam : 60, 62
Rashi : 3–5, 14, 59–62, 66–7, 74, 76, 86–7
— *Commentary on Deuteronomy*
   3:4 : 62
— *Commentary on Joshua*
   1:1–4:17 : 87
— *Commentary on Samuel*
   1 Sam. 6:18 : 118
              12:11 : 272
              19:13, 16 : 272
              20:18 : 230
              21:8 : 274
              22:14 : 272
              23:9 : 237–8
              25:6 : 178
              31:12 : 231–2
   2 Sam. 4:2 : 280
              5:8 : 236
              13:3 : 229
              13:9 : 61
              20:15 : 240
— *Commentary on Kings*
   1 Kgs 10:19 : 62
— *Commentary on Isaiah*
   54:1 : 224
— *Commentary to Ezekiel*
   27:17 : 59
— *Commentary to Zephaniah*
   2:2 : 62
— *Commentary on Lamentations*
   4:1 : 62
— *Commentary on Daniel*
   11:21–2 : 219
— *Commentary on tractate Qiddushin*
   49a : 60

— *Commentary on tractate Megillah*
   3a : 60
   21b : 60, 62
   24a : 60
— Targum variants recorded by Sperber
   2 Sam. 1:10 : 133
Samson ben Abraham of Sens
— *Commentary on the Mishnah* : 59
Samuel ben Meir (see Rashbam)
Scroll of Antiochus : 54, 78–9
Sefer Zerubbabel (see Book of Zerubbabel)
Simhah ben Samuel (see Mahzor Vitry)
Solomon ben Samson
— *Siddur Haside Ashkenaz* : 59
Testament Naphtali : 78
Tosafot : 59
— *Megillah*
   3 : 62
   23b : 63
   24a : 316
— *Ta'anit*
   5b : 350
Yalkut Shimoni : 58
Zedekiah b. Abraham Anav
— *Shibbolei ha-Leket*
   29a §78 : 63
Zohar : 55

MANUSCRIPTS

Berlin, Staatsbibliothek
(Preußischer Kulturbesitz)
   Or. fol. 1–4 : xix, 29, 39–40, 43, 84–5,
      97–9, 103, 106, 108–9, 111, 113, 116,
      121–2, 124, 126, 128–9, 131–2, 135,
      139, 141, 144, 146–7, 154, 157, 159,
      162, 164, 166, 168, 172–3, 176–9, 181,
      184–7, 189–92, 194, 196–201, 203,
      206–13, 215–17, 219, 223, 227, 232,
      235, 237, 243–4, 246, 249, 255–9, 289,
      341–2, 359, 387
   Or. fol. 1210–11 : 37, 57, 71–2, 74
   Or. fol. 1214 : 6, 249–50, 302, 311,
      314–21, 332, 334, 341–2, 412–20
   Or. qu. 9 : 306
   Or. qu. 578 : 13, 28
   Or. qu. 680 : 18
Boston, Countway Library of Medicine
   Med. Ms. Heb. 5 : 70

Budapest, Hungarian Academy of Science
    Kaufmann A13 : 43
Cambridge, Gonville & Caius College
    404/625 : 135, 161–2, 172, 174
Cambridge, St. John's College
    A 2 : 126, 129, 158, 160, 162, 172, 174
Cambridge, University Library
    Add. 3452 : 307
    Ee. 5.9 : 57, 74
    Mm. 5.27 : 126, 155, 173
    T-S 2.7 (= Eb 54) : 27
    T-S 12.1 : 303
    T-S 15.1 (= Kb 7) : 27
    T-S 15.5 : 309
    T-S AS 21.248 : 297
    T-S AS 62.193, 367 (= Eb 16) : 27
    T-S AS 62.541 = T-S AS 62.543–7 : 297
    T-S AS 69.200 : 309
    T-S AS 70.102 : 297
    T-S AS 72.75, 76, 77 : 298
    T-S B 4.36; AS 62, 112, 122, 219, 269, 371, 465, 466, 476, 477, 479, 481, 541, 543–7, 620, 714, 814, 852, 865, 877, 910, 919 (= Eb 4) : 111, 137, 168, 176, 185, 207
    T-S B 7.2 : 297
    T-S B 12.6 : 309
    T-S B 13.2 : 302
    T-S B 15.3 : 308
    T-S B 16.20 : 309
    T-S B 17.9 : 308
    T-S K 26.2 : 309
    T-S K 26.36 : 297
    T-S NS 32.98 : 309
    T-S NS 128.14 : 309
    T-S NS 161.137 : 297
    T-S NS 161.286 : 297
    West. Coll. Misc. 70 : 297
Copenhagen, The Royal Library
    Cod. Hebr. 1 : 126, 155, 161
    Cod. Hebr. 6 : 109, 161
    Cod. Hebr. 7–9 : 174
    Cod. Hebr. 17 : 130, 163, 166, 174–5
Dresden, Sachsische Landesbibliothek
    Ms A.46 : 37
Ferrara, Biblioteca Comunale
    Gr. 188 I : 131

Firenze, Biblioteca Medicea Laurenziana
    Plut.I.30 : 159
    Plut.I.45 : 159
Genoa, Biblioteca Civica Berio
    B. H. I–VII : xix, 37, 39–40, 43, 69, 74, 76–8, 88, 90–1, 97–9, 103–4, 106–9, 114, 117, 122, 124, 126, 128, 131–3, 138, 141–2, 144–5, 147, 154, 159, 161, 166, 168, 172, 175–7, 181, 184, 187–8, 191–3, 195–6, 198–201, 203–4, 206–7, 216, 229, 232–4, 246, 248–51, 256–9, 283, 289, 341, 350, 385–6
Göttweig, Stiftsbibliothek
    Ms 11 : 39, 43, 87, 97–9, 101–4, 106–7, 109, 112–17, 121–8, 131–3, 136, 38, 140–3, 147, 154–5, 157, 160–2, 164, 166–7, 169, 172, 175–6, 180–1, 184–7, 191, 193, 196–207, 210–12, 215–16, 219, 223, 240, 244, 246, 249, 55–9, 271, 283, 289, 341–2, 348–52, 358, 442
Hamburg, Staats- und
Universitaetsbibliothek
    Hebr. 9 : 155
    Hebr. 45 : 54
    Levy 19 (Kennicott 380) : 249–50, 306, 311, 314–17, 319–24, 332, 334, 340–2, 400, 412–20
Holon, Judah Levi Nahum Collection
    59–67, 70–5, 78–80, 342, 365,
    347–8 (= Eb 91) : 128, 202
    496 (= Eb 124) : 206
    301, 302, 333, 335 (= Eb 87) : 187
Jena, Thueringer Universitaets- und
Landesbibliothek
    El. f.6 : 39–40, 43, 72, 86, 97–100, 103–4, 106–17, 119, 122, 124–6, 128, 130, 132–5, 140–3, 146–8, 154, 157–9, 161–2, 164, 166–7, 172, 174–5, 178, 180–1, 184–5, 187–208, 210–17, 223, 227, 232–5, 237–8, 242, 245–6, 248–50, 255–9, 271, 273, 283, 289, 339, 341, 348, 350–2, 358–9, 441–2
Jerusalem, Allony Collection
    Heb. 38vo, 6919 : 307
Jerusalem, Ben-Zvi Institute
    Jer Ben Zvi 1 ('Aleppo Codex') : 295

Jerusalem, National Library of Israel
  Heb. 4° 781 ('Mahzor Worms') : 305
Jerusalem, Rav Yosef Kapach Collection
  Ms 2 : 27, 122–3, 168, 176, 206
  Ms 5 : 43
Jerusalem, Temple of Solomon
  Ms. fol. 18 : 307
Karlsruhe, Badische Hof- und Landesbibliothek
  Reuchlinianus No. 3 : xxii, 1, 6–9, 10–15, 27–8, 31–2, 34–5, 43, 46, 49–52, 56, 65, 69–70, 74, 76, 81–3, 88, 94–5, 97–9, 102–4, 107–9, 111, 114, 116–17, 119–26, 128, 130–6, 138–40, 142, 144, 146–8, 156–9, 161, 164–7, 173, 175–6, 178, 180–1, 184–5, 187–8, 190–1, 193, 196–203, 206, 209–12, 215–17, 219, 222, 225–6, 229–33, 236, 238–40, 242, 244, 254–9, 261–300, 302, 304–5, 346–7, 349–52, 356–8, 361, 364, 387–99, 441
Koblenz, Landeshauptarchiv
  Abt. 701, Nr. 759, 5, 6 : 311, 314–24, 333–4, 338–42, 400, 412–20
Leiden, Universiteitsbibliotheek
  Or. 4720 : 55
Leipzig, Universitätsbibliothek
  B. H. fol. 1 : 57
Leningrad, Firkowitsch Collection (see St. Petersburg)
Letchworth, Sassoon Collection
  Sassoon 282 : 306
  Sassoon 332 : 29, 307
  Sassoon 405 : 188, 207, 250, 311, 313, 315, 320–2, 324, 326, 328, 332–4, 336–7, 341, 399–400, 421–41
  Sassoon 1017 : 248, 305
  Sassoon 1028 : 305
London, British Library
  Add. 9398 : 160
  Add. 9403 : 71, 306, 309
  Add. 11639 : 306, 311
  Add. 14760 : 160, 168
  Add. 15252 : 126, 168
  Add. 17058 : 305
  Add. 19943 : 70
  Add. 19944/19945 : 305
  Add. 21161 : 155, 160
  Add. 26879 : 28, 31, 43, 67, 86–7, 97–101, 103–4, 106–115, 117–19, 122, 124–8, 130–5, 140–8, 154, 157–8, 161–4, 166–7, 173, 175, 178, 180–1, 184–90, 192–3, 195–204, 206–8, 210–12, 214–17, 219, 223, 232–4, 237–8, 245, 248–50, 255–9, 263, 271, 273, 283, 289, 341, 348, 350–3, 358, 441
  Add. 27031 : 56, 221, 343
  Add. 27070 : 305
  Add. 27200–27201 ('Mahzor Vitry') : 305
  Arundel Or. 16 : 172
  Gaster Or. 10794 : 298
  Harley 1861 : 54, 306
  Harley 5709 : 157
  Harley 5719 : 70
  Harley 5722 : 135
  Harley 5774–5 : 155–6
  Kings 1 : 126
  Loan 1 : 126
  Or. 1467 : 12, 17
  Or. 1470 : 12, 29, 307
  Or. 1471 : 27, 107, 122–3, 128, 131–6, 138–9, 141, 145, 147, 164, 172, 193, 283
  Or. 1472 : xxi, 27, 88, 97, 99, 102–3, 113, 122–3, 128, 131–2, 134, 138, 145–6, 169, 190, 196–7, 206–7, 255, 258–9
  Or. 1473 : 15, 26–8, 288
  Or. 1474 : 15–16, 21, 25–8, 31, 43, 263, 288
  Or. 1476 : 12
  Or. 2091 : 172
  Or. 2201 : 126
  Or. 2210 : 12, 16, 21–2, 38, 122–3, 126, 128, 131–5, 138, 146, 211, 245, 307, 363
  Or. 2211 : 12, 14–16, 21, 26–7, 31, 42–3, 49–52, 263, 288, 307
  Or. 2228 : 12
  Or. 2348 : 126
  Or. 2363 : 12, 17
  Or. 2364 : 29, 144, 307
  Or. 2371 : 106, 108–9, 111, 116, 119, 122–3, 128, 131–6, 138–9, 141, 145–8, 203, 227, 249, 283, 307
  Or. 2626–8 : 126
  Or. 4227 : 168, 172
  Or. 5556 : 308
  Or. 9916 : 339
  Sloane 3265 : 71

London, Montefiore Endowment
    7 [H 116] : xviii, 27–8, 31, 43, 109,
        116–17, 122–4, 128, 132, 134–5,
        141, 154, 164, 166, 173, 193, 222,
        238, 246, 249, 251, 263, 283, 350
London, Valmadonna Trust Library
    Valmadonna 1 (Sassoon 282; Richler
        1) : 199, 249–50, 311, 314–16, 316–
        25, 333–4, 339–42, 400–7, 411–20
    Valmadonna 89 : 248
Madrid, Biblioteca Complutense
    Ms. 7542 : 31, 38, 44
    Villa-Amil 4 : 27, 36, 43
Madrid, Real Biblioteca del Monasterio de
San Lorenzo de El Escorial
    γ. ii. 5 : 177
Manchester, John Rylands Library
    Gaster 673 : 43
Milan, Biblioteca Ambrosiana
    13 : 130
    B 56 Inf. : 155, 160, 172, 174, 181
    E 52 Inf. : 157
Munich, Bayerische Staatsbibliothek
    Cod. Hebr. 77 : 70
    Cod. Hebr. 244 : 71
    Cod. Hebr. 302 : 70
Naples, Biblioteca Nazionale
    Lat. 1 ('Palimpsests Vindobonensis') :
        146, 156, 163
New York, Jewish Theological Seminary
    2514 : 70
    ENA 2576 : 302
    L 229 : 24, 27, 111, 113, 128, 131–2,
        134, 137–8, 146, 154, 185, 187, 190,
        202, 206, 271, 408–11, 441
    L 230 : 27, 132, 169, 202, 402–8
    L 239 : 43
    L 240 : 24
Nürnberg, Stadtbibliothek
    Cent. V App. 2 : 306
    Solger : 2, 14, 31, 39, 42–4, 48, 69, 165,
        261, 298, 309, 359
Oxford, Bodleian Library
    Can Or. 81 : 70
    Digby Or. 32–3 : 130, 157, 166
    Heb. d. 26 : 29
    Heb. d. 64 : 308
    Hunt. 11–12 : 126, 128, 135, 146, 172

'Kennicott 3' : 306
'Kennicott 5' : 38, 40, 109, 126, 165
'Kennicott 6': 135, 165
'Kennicott 10' : 163
Laud Or. 321 : 305
Laud Or. 326 : xix, 39, 67, 70, 83–4, 88,
    95–9, 103–4, 107–9, 122, 124, 126,
    128, 131–2, 134, 137, 141, 147–8, 154,
    157, 163, 166, 169, 177, 181, 185, 187,
    191, 198–200, 203–4, 206, 210, 216–
    17, 229, 245–6, 249–53, 255, 257–9,
    283, 289, 312, 341–2, 348–52, 442
Marshall Or. 3 : 157
Opp. 14 : 306
Opp. Add. 4°, 75, 76 : 38, 43, 188, 203
Opp. Add. 4°, 177 : 70
Opp. Add. 76 : 31
Opp. Add. fol. 11 (Neubauer 1057) :
    188, 250, 312, 315, 317–24, 326–34,
    336–8, 341, 399–400, 421–40
Poc. 347–8 : 126, 135
Tanner 173 : 126, 157, 159–60, 162–3, 169
Paris, Bibliothèque Nationale
    Hébreu 1–3 : 156, 160
    Hébreu 9 : 160
    Hébreu 18 : 39, 85–6, 97–9, 103, 106–9,
        111–12, 114–17, 119, 121–2, 124, 128,
        130–5, 141, 143, 146–7, 154, 157, 159,
        161, 166–7, 172, 175, 180–1, 184–7,
        189–93, 195–8, 200, 202–4, 206–7, 211,
        214–17, 219, 223, 232–4, 238, 243, 245,
        249–50, 255–9, 273, 283, 289, 341, 348,
        350–2, 359, 442
    Hébreu 29 : 173
    Hébreu 44 : 249–50, 311, 314–22, 332,
        338–42, 400, 412–20
    Hébreu 75 : 37, 43, 49, 67, 70–1, 78–80,
        88, 91–2, 97–9, 103–4, 106, 109–10,
        114, 116, 122–5, 128, 131–2, 135–6,
        138, 140–2, 147, 155, 158, 161, 166,
        172, 176, 181, 184–90, 195–6, 198–
        201, 203, 206–7, 210, 215–17, 226,
        239–40, 243, 245–6, 248–50, 252,
        254–9, 261, 289, 312, 349–52, 358,
        360, 362, 386, 442–3
    Hébreu 96 : 43, 50
    Hébreu 110 : 220
    Hébreu 637 : 70

Hébreu 640 : 305
Hébreu 1325 : 9, 29, 43
Parma, Bibliotheca Palatina
Parm. 1832 : 126, 174
Parm. 1833 : 172
Parm. 1854 : 306
Parm. 1885 : 168
Parm. 1898–9 : 64
Parm. 1996–7 : 126
Parm. 2003–4 : xvii, 18
Parm. 2009–10 : 54
Parm. 2046 : xvii
Parm. 2069 : 64
Parm. 2155 : 161
Parm. 2168 : 127
Parm. 2174 :   126, 161, 167–8
Parm. 2175 : 156
Parm. 2179 : 70
Parm. 2221 : 64
Parm. 2292 : 175
Parm. 2403 : 64
Parm. 2514–15 : 156
Parm. 2520 : 126, 306
Parm. 2577 : 64
Parm. 2750 : 70
Parm. 2808 : 126, 160, 162
Parm. 2854 : 155, 160, 165, 172
Parm. 2874 : 126, 135, 155, 160–1, 165, 169, 172, 174–5, 181
Parm. 2884 : 64
Parm. 2887 : 305
Parm. 2894 : 311, 315–23, 332, 334, 340–2, 412–20
Parm. 2938 : 172
Parm. 2939–41 : 172
Parm. 3000 : 305
Parm. 3003 : 305
Parm. 3008 : 188, 207, 250, 311–12, 316–34, 336–7, 341, 399–412, 420–40
Parm. 3053 : 70
Parm. 3073 : 161
Parm. 3091 : 155, 165
Parm. 3104 : 167, 172, 174
Parm. 3105 : 160, 172, 174
Parm. 3106 : 126, 156, 158, 172
Parm. 3109 : 167–8
Parm. 3132 : 188, 207, 249–50, 311, 313, 315, 317–18, 320–4, 326, 328, 332–4, 336–8, 341, 400–1, 420–40
Parm. 3135 : 64
Parm. 3136 : 305
Parm. 3184–86 : 172
Parm. 3187–89 : 37, 40, 43, 69, 71, 129, 158, 174
Parm. 3200 : 165, 172, 181
Parm. 3212–13 : 172
Parm. 3218 : 18
Parm. 3244 : 165
Parm. 3286–87 : 155, 160, 165
Parm. 3290 : 161, 165, 172, 174
Parm. 3293 : 129, 161
Rome, Biblioteca Angelica
Or. 72 : xix, 37, 39–40, 57, 67, 69–70, 80–1, 88–9, 92–4, 97–9, 103–4, 106, 114, 116–17, 122, 124, 126, 128, 130–4, 141, 147–8, 154, 156, 161, 163, 165–6, 175–6, 181, 185, 187, 190–1, 196, 198–200, 202–3, 206, 208–11, 213–14, 216–17, 238, 243, 246–7, 251, 256–9, 289, 341, 358, 386
Rome, Biblioteca Chigiana
R. vi. 38 : 161
St. Petersburg, Institute of Oriental Studies
C 91 : 307
St. Petersburg, National Library of Russia
Firkovich I,132 (= Kb 54,82a–84b) : 27
Firkovich B 19 A ('Leningradensis') : 119, 125, 127–9, 133–4, 145, 164–5, 170–1, 180–1, 274–5, 296
St. Petersburg, Saltykov-Shchedrin State
Public Library
Ebr. B 133 (including Ebr. B 16) : 187, 309
Salamanca, Biblioteca de la Universitaria
M1-M3 : 27—28, 31, 35–6, 38, 44, 188, 203
Strasbourg, Bibliothèque Nationale et
Universitaire
4084/1 : 187, 271, 401–3, 406, 441
Sydney, University Library
Nicholson 33 : 306
Vatican City, Biblioteca Apostolica
Ebr. 440 : 57, 220, 298, 343
Ebr. 480 : 306
Barberini Or. 161-4 : 67, 69, 75–6, 88–

90, 97–9, 103–4, 109, 115, 119, 122, 124, 126, 128, 131–3, 135–7, 141, 143, 147, 154–6,161, 166, 169, 173, 175, 180–1, 184–5, 187, 191, 193, 195, 198, 200, 203–4, 206–7, 209, 213, 216–17, 219, 223, 229, 246, 249–51, 255–6, 258–9, 262, 283, 289, 341, 358, 385

    Rossiana 436 : 64

    Rossiana 437 : 64, 188, 207, 249–50, 311, 313, 315, 317–18, 320–4, 326, 328, 331–4, 336–8, 341, 399, 401, 421–41

    Urbinati Ebr. 1 : 3, 27, 29–30, 35, 39, 43, 57, 67, 69, 72–5, 77, 88–9, 97–9, 102–4, 107, 109, 112–17, 119, 122, 124–6, 128, 130–2, 134–4, 146–7, 154–6, 159, 161–2, 165–7, 169, 172–3, 175–6, 180–1, 184–5, 187, 193, 195–8, 200–3, 205–6, 212, 215–17, 228, 235, 237–8, 244, 246, 249–51, 255–9, 263, 283, 289, 341–2, 358–9, 385

    Urbinati Ebr. 2 : 81, 132

    Urbinati Gr. 1 : 177

    Vaticani Ebr. 545 : 64, 207, 249–50, 11, 313, 315, 317, 319–22, 326–9, 331–4, 336–8, 341, 400–1, 421–40

Vienna, Oesterreichische Nationalbibliothek

    Hebr. 28 : 306

Zurich, Zentralbibliothek

    Or. 158 : 135

Current location uncertain

    Kennicott 70 : 155, 157

    Kennicott 224 : 126, 155, 165, 168, 173–5, 181

    Kennicott 294 : 157

    Kennicott 428 : 158

    Kennicott 471 : 37

PRINTED EDITIONS

First Rabbinic Bible (1517) : 2–4, 6–8, 10–11, 14, 27–9, 31, 41, 43–4, 48–9, 69, 105–6, 108–9, 111, 116, 119, 122–4, 126, 128, 130–5, 139, 141,146, 148, 154, 161, 166, 193, 196, 203, 222,226–7, 231–3, 246, 249, 258, 264, 283

Second Rabbinic Bible (1525) : 7–8, 27–9, 31, 35, 41, 43–4, 48–9, 69, 222, 226, 231, 263

Amsterdam (1720) : 4

Amsterdam (1724) : 5

Amsterdam (1726) : 8

Antwerp Polyglot (1568–72) : 3, 5, 10, 14, 27–9, 31, 106–7, 109, 116–17, 119, 124, 126, 128, 131–5, 141, 143, 145, 147, 154, 161, 166, 172, 175–6, 188, 203, 223, 226, 242, 249

Buxtorf (1618–19) : 3–5, 7–8, 10, 14–15, 48, 231, 264

Leiria edition : 13, 29, 106–7, 109, 111, 117, 122–4, 126, 128, 131–2, 134–5, 141–4, 146, 154, 157, 166, 188, 193, 203, 219, 223, 238, 243, 246, 249, 263, 283, 350

Lemberg (1808) : 8

Paris Polyglot (1645) : 10

Sabbioneta (1557) : 18

Venice (1547) : 8

Walton (1654–7) : 3–5, 10–11, 14, 29, 31, 48

Warsaw (1860–6) : 29, 31

MODERN AUTHORS

Adler : 7, 13, 31

Alexander : 62, 66, 262

Aptowitzer : 160

Assemanus : 3, 75, 385

Attia : 87, 311–12

Bacher : 7–9, 11, 13, 58, 65, 102, 105–6, 111, 114, 116, 139, 194–5, 198, 227, 231, 249, 261, 264–6, 269–76, 283–4, 287, 289, 298, 347

Barnes : 15

Barthélemy : 19, 21–2, 29, 106–7, 116, 118, 168, 177, 241, 281,

Beit-Arié : xix, 56, 67, 70–1, 74, 76, 79–84, 86–7, 305,

Berger, D : 220

Berger, M : 60

Berliner : 13, 18, 61

Bernheimer : 80, 130

Beyer : 257, 259

Bons : 152

Brambach : 81–2

Brandt : 181

Brock : 127, 156, 182

Brockington : 15, 152

Bromberg : 61
Brown : 152
Büchler : 269
Chilton : 49, 79, 105, 221, 254, 256,
Churgin : 152, 265–6
Clarke : 56
Cook : x, 256–9, 333
Cornill : 9–11, 302
Coxe : 155
Dalman : 10, 256–8, 325
Damsma : 269, 290, 334
de Boer : 20, 150
de Lagarde : 6–10, 14–15, 31, 50, 222,
   275–6, 287, 301–2, 309, 347
de Moor : xxi, 151, 200
Delekat : 152–3
Delitzsch : 81
de Rossi, A : 56
de Rossi, J.B : 127–8, 149, 170, 179, 181
Deutsch : 62
Diamond : 62
di Capua : 80
Díez Macho : xvii, 16, 18–27, 32–4, 56,
   63–4, 73, 261, 302–3, 344
Díez Merino : 16, 20, 22–3, 30, 34–6,
   64, 73, 75, 89, 262, 304–5
Dirksen : 149–50
Dogniez : 152
Dorival : 152
Dotan : 225, 274, 296
Driver : 178
Elbogen : 63
Fassberg : x, 256–9, 333–4
Fernández Marcos : 146, 152–3, 168, 177
Ferrer Costa : 21, 27–8
Fischer : 146, 153
Flesher : 55, 221, 256
Fontela : 74–5, 89
Fraade : 60
Frankel : 3–6, 152
Garel : 9, 85
Geiger : 4
Gelston : 150
Ginsburg : 82, 149, 179, 277
Ginsburger : 56–8, 65
Gleßmer : 64, 344
Golomb : 256–7
Gordon : 19–20, 22, 30, 151, 220

Goshen-Gottstein : 23, 58, 178, 290, 335, 361
Grelot : 74, 221, 263–6, 303, 353–4
Griño : 58
Grossman : 60, 70
Hahn : 72
Halevy : 62
Hannah : 227
Harl : 152
Harrington : 360–1
Hayward : 153, 221
Healey : 261
Heller : 57
Ho : 49–52, 62, 101
Hoffman : 65
Houtman : xx, 1–2, 15, 21, 30, 41–7, 49, 52,
   54, 58–60, 63, 67, 71, 87, 268–9, 274,
   275, 283–5, 297–8, 301, 303, 306, 312,
   337, 345, 347, 352–4, 358, 363
Joosten : 152
Joüon : 109, 277
Kahle : xvii, 16–19, 22–6, 82, 263
Kasher, A : 61
Kasher, M.M : 57
Kasher, R : 40, 84–5, 87, 219–21, 247–8,
   251, 262–9, 284, 290, 295, 297, 304–6,
   310, 345, 347, 349–54
Kaufman : 64, 260, 344
Kedar : 153
Kennicott : 37–8, 40, 109, 126–30, 132, 135, 146,
   149, 155–70, 172–5, 179, 181, 261, 306, 311
Kessler : 152
Klein, G : 282
Klein, M.L : 57, 65, 257–8, 276, 283, 295,
   297–8, 302–3, 309
Klein, S : 153
Klostermann : 7
Knobel : 74, 261
Korpel : 151
Kroeze : 72
Lambert : 9
Landauer : 13–14
Langlamet : 295–6
Le Déaut : 57, 74–5, 89, 152, 221
Lehnardt, A : 66
Lehnardt, P.Sh. : 63–5, 312, 333
Leicht : 81–3, 261, 387
Levine : xviii, 30, 33–4, 53, 56, 60, 73,
   86, 88–9, 221, 257, 343

Lévi : 220
Levy : 31
Lilienthal : 181
Lund : 333
Luzzatto S.D : 7
Luzzatto, A : 76–8
Madan : 62
Maher : 56, 256, 292
Mangan : 261
Maori : 64, 344
Margoliouth : 56, 86, 221, 343
Martelli : 76, 80, 93
Martin : 16, 18, 21, 360
Martínez Borobio : xviii, xxi, 21–2, 24, 27, 37, 40, 123, 128, 138, 202, 333
May : 83–4
McHardy : 15, 73
McIvor : 74
McNamara : 56
Meiser : 152
Melamed : 60–2
Merx : 11–17, 28, 36, 82
Metzger : 75
Meyer : 82
Milano : 55, 299
Mitchell : 220
Morag : 82, 299–300
Moreschini : 169
Morrison : 150–1
Mortara Ottolenghi : 74, 76, 80, 93
Muraoka : 109, 277
Narkiss : 65
Neubauer : 84
Norelli : 169
Oesch : 296
Offer : 296
Patmore : 41, 312, 339, 341, 352
Pauli : 4–6
Perrot : 295–7
Peters : 150
Praetorius : 13–16
Prijs : 82
Reif : 53, 66, 304, 312, 344
Ribera Florit : xvi, xviii–xx, 16, 18, 21–7, 30–1, 34, 41, 56, 73, 152, 221
Richler : xvii, 56, 74–5, 81, 135, 155, 161, 172, 174–5, 181, 220, 343
Rieder : 61

Robert : 57, 74–5, 89
Roth : 299
Róth : 86, 315
Rowley : 14, 20
Running : 151
Saldarini : 360–1
Schiller-Szinessy : 57
Schilling : 81
Schwarz : 87
Sed-Rajna : 85
Segert : 22
Sepmeijer : 151
Shinan : 308
Shunary : 248
Silbermann : 7, 14
Sirat : 53, 67, 74, 76, 79, 81, 83, 85, 261
Smelik : xx, 2–3, 21, 33, 36–40, 44–7, 52, 61, 63, 67, 70–1, 73, 84–5, 87–9, 93–4, 97, 101–2, 105, 150–1, 153, 180–1, 227, 252, 255–6, 260, 263, 266, 270, 275, 284–5, 290, 297–8, 308, 312, 316, 338, 344–6, 352–3
Sokoloff : 333–4
Speier : 58, 62
Sperber : 3, 6–7, 14–33, 40, 42, 49–52, 57, 82, 105–47, 154, 157, 161, 164, 166, 171–6, 188, 193, 196, 203, 210, 219, 223, 225–7, 233, 238, 242–3, 245–6, 248–9, 261, 263, 265, 271, 273, 275–6, 283, 286–9, 300, 302, 304, 306–8, 347, 350, 353, 363, 387
Stec : 252
Steinschneider : 84, 157
Stemberger : 54, 159, 220
Stenning : 7, 13–16, 20–1, 25, 29
Stoebe : 167
Strack : 54, 159, 220
Stummer : 153
Sysling : 54, 58, 268–9, 274, 283–5, 297–8, 301, 303, 306, 337, 345, 347, 352–4
Tanja : xix, 312, 339, 341
Ta-Shma : 58, 70
Tov : 134, 180
van der Heide : 223
van der Kooij : 150–1, 153
van Keulen : 150–1
van Staalduine-Sulman : v, xv, xix–xxi, 21–2, 40–1, 44, 47–9, 52, 67, 69, 71–2, 79, 82,

89, 97–100, 102, 105, 107–8, 118, 122–3, 127, 138–9, 143, 147, 156, 160, 164, 173, 180, 217,223, 227, 230–1, 234, 236–7, 271–3, 279, 282, 285, 297, 307–10, 347, 350–1, 357–9
van Zijl : 15, 21–2
Viezel : 60
von Abel : 81–3, 261, 387
Wacholder : 295, 297
Weil, M : 62

Weil G.E : 133, 277
Weiss : 75, 89, 385
Weitzman : 150–1, 153
Werner : 84–5
White : 89
Winton Thomas : 20–1, 73
Wolfsohn : 13, 16
Yeivin : 29, 300
Zotenberg : 85
Zunz : 2–3, 6, 57–8, 262–3, 353